PUBLIC RELATIONS: FROM
THEORY TO PRACTICE

Dear Mark Heckler —
From one rhetorician
to another — enjoy
public relations
from a rhetorical
perspective.

Bonita Neff

PUBLIC RELATIONS: FROM THEORY TO PRACTICE

TRICIA L. HANSEN-HORN

University of Central Missouri

BONITA DOSTAL NEFF

Valparaiso University

PEARSON

Boston   New York   San Francisco
Mexico City   Montreal   Toronto   London   Madrid   Munich   Paris
Hong Kong   Singapore   Tokyo   Cape Town   Sydney

Editor-in-Chief: Karon Bowers
Series Editorial Assistant: Saunders Robinson
Marketing Manager: Suzan Czajkowski
Production Supervisor: Beth Houston
Editorial Production Service: NK Graphics/Jenny Cooke
Composition Buyer: Linda Cox
Manufacturing Buyer: JoAnne Sweeney
Electronic Composition: NK Graphics
Cover Administrator: Linda Knowles

For related titles and support materials, visit our online catalog at www.ablongman.com.

Between the time website information is gathered and then published, it is not unusual for some sites to have closed. Also, the transcription of URLs can result in typographical errors. The publisher would appreciate notification where these errors occur so that they may be corrected in subsequent editions.

Library of Congress Cataloging-in-Publication Data

Public relations: from theory to practice / [edited by] Tricia L. Hansen-Horn,
    Bonita Dostal Neff.
        p. cm.
    Includes bibliographical references and index.
    ISBN 0-205-39355-1
        1. Public relations—Philosophy—Textbooks.   I. Hansen-Horn, Tricia L.
    II. Neff, Bonita Dostal.
    HM1221.P784 2007
    659.201—dc22

                                                                    2006051532

Printed in the United States of America

10   9   8   7   6   5   4   3   2   1   11   10   09   08   07

CONTENTS

CHAPTER THREE

Strategic Issues Management: Theoretical Underpinnings for Strategic Planning and Operations in the Public Policy Arena   31

Robert L. Heath – University of Houston

CHAPTER FOUR

Organizational-Public Relationships in Cyberspace   46

Kirk Hallahan – Colorado State University, Fort Collins

SECTION II   FUNDAMENTAL PERSPECTIVES: CREATING ACTION AND MEANING THROUGH MESSAGING   75

CHAPTER FIVE

Working with Innovators and Laggards: The Diffusion of Innovation Theory and Public Relations   76

Ann R. Carden – State University of New York College, Fredonia

CHAPTER SIX

Speech Act Theory: An Approach to Public Relations Leadership   89

Bonita Dostal Neff – Valparaiso University, Indiana

CHAPTER SEVEN

Social Constructionism and Public Relations   104

Joye Gordon – Kansas State University; Peter Pellegrin – Cloud County Community College, Kansas

CHAPTER EIGHT

Social Drama for Public Relations Practice   122

Thomas Mickey – Bridgewater State College, Massachusetts

CHAPTER ELEVEN

Following Communication Rules: A Communication-Centered Theory for Public Relations   181

María E. Len-Ríos – University of Missouri, Columbia

CHAPTER TWELVE

Integrating Social Norms Theory in Public Relations Campaign Development   195

Terry L. Rentner – Bowling Green State University, Ohio

SECTION V CRISIS COMMUNICATION—GIVING VOICE IN THE PROCESS   243

SECTION VI   CONTEXTUAL PARAMETERS—UNDERSTANDING AND CREATING THE BIG PICTURE   279

CHAPTER TWENTY

From Aardvark to Zebra Redux: An Analysis of Theory Development in Public Relations Academic Journals into the Twenty-First Century   343

Lynne M. Sallot – University of Georgia; Lisa J. Lyon; Carolina Acosta-Alzuru, University of Georgia; Karyn Ogata Jones – Clemson University, South Carolina

FOREWORD

When authors and editors begin the design and preparation of a book such as this they often ask the question, "What purpose will the finished product serve?" Readers know that a book focusing on theories related to public relations is crucial to the development of the discipline. Similarly, Robert Heath, as editor of the *Encyclopedia of Public Relations* (2005), posed in his preface an affirmative statement of such support. He addressed the topic, "Why public relations is a deserving topic for the extensive analysis it receives in this encyclopedia."

In essence, this book presents the views of significant scholars discussing the nature, scope, and role of various theories in the practice of exemplary public relations study and practice. The editors of this book have worked with a number of highly respected scholars in presenting their findings and perspectives to the field of public relations education and practice. Readers will find that these authors give significant insight to the role of theory for the public relations profession.

In his preface to the *Encyclopedia*, Heath reviews a significant set of issues that are highly integrated in the practice of public relations. Included in his discussion are mission and vision, strategies, functions, and tools and tactics. While not following this discussion directly, this present book does focus on each of these areas, giving the practitioner, educator, and student varying theoretical perspectives related to each of the areas of critical interest.

In addition, this book focuses on many of the changes in the public relations field during the past decade. Recognizing the changes in the milieu in which public relations operates today, there are significant theoretical works relating to international and multicultural perspectives. As business, government, nongovernmental organizations, and education have become highly international in scope, the need to understand public relations in this sphere has become more significant.

The issue regarding the role of gender, especially in the United States, continues to be of importance. One section of this text provides significant theoretical understanding for those concerned with the progress and future of this area of study.

Perhaps no issue has been more central to the study of public relations in the past several decades than ethics. As Heath and many others have suggested, public relations is often defined in negative terms, especially related to ethical behavior in successful public relations. This text provides significant understanding of the role of ethics and theoretical applications of strong ethical stands that will serve the profession well in the minds of stakeholders and stakeseekers. As some have said, people who do not understand their history are doomed to repeat its mistakes. Lessons learned from the perspectives presented in this text will, I hope, help us to avoid the ethical lapses of the past.

Because of the broad scope of this undertaking, along with the contributions of significant scholars and researchers, this text will be of significant value to the practitioner, the student, and the scholar of public relations.

As Heath concluded in his preface, the *Encyclopedia* may be helpful in leading practitioners, students, educators, and researchers "onward into the fog—but with a lantern to lead." In this perspective, this text is one of the lanterns to follow through the fog.

John Madsen, Ph.D.
Associate Professor
St. Ambrose University

PREFACE

There is nothing as practical as a good theory. However, for many students (academic and professional) of public relations, attaining the theory-practice connection can be tough. It is not always an easy matter to take theoretical constructs and predictions and apply them to practice in what we call praxis. This is the purpose driving this book. We want to aid the process of using theory in public relations practice, making theory come alive as we work with our various publics, and with students, practitioners, or professional clients.

This text provides background on key theories; each theory presentation is followed by a case study and application questions. This allows you, the reader, to move back and forth between theory and practice. Often the theory may seem vague until the case is brought forth. Then as the case is discussed and related to the theory, the infrastructure of the theoretical concepts becomes clearer and the applications seem more relevant. Most important, the discussion reveals the true map value of theory in providing direction in the breadth and depth of idea development. With the many maps provided in this book, you will have the opportunity to better understand the nuances of communication as related to the practice of public relations.

Enjoy this venture into the theory-practice connection. The questions for application provide the incentive to challenge your thinking and application processes in a variety of ways.

Tricia Hansen-Horn
University of Central Missouri
Bonita Dostal Neff
Valparaiso University, Indiana

ACKNOWLEDGMENTS

The authors wish to acknowledge the following reviewers: Isaac A. Blankson, Southern Illinois University, Edwardsville; Samuel Coad Dyer, Jr., Southwest Missouri State University; Michael F. Smith, La Salle University.

SECTION I

EFFECTIVENESS MANAGEMENT
Engaging Systems of Power and Networks of Communication

Tricia L. Hansen-Horn

Bonita Dostal Neff

The pursuit of effectiveness in our professional lives is a notable endeavor. Speaking of effectiveness and management in the same context is not out of place. In the area of public relations scholarship, effectiveness management can be understood as power and control over stakeholders and stakeseekers, systemic and systematic interaction, issues monitoring and massage, and creative and heuristic use of technology, among many other concepts.

Heath addresses the wrangle among power and control in light of social responsibility and ethical practice. Weick's model of organizing resolves uncertainties and Kreps cites the bio terrorist threats as an effective application of this approach.

Heath continues to develop theoretical constructs to explore strategic perspectives. His concepts support issues management efforts. Hallahan, in turn, focuses on the conceptual nuances of relationships in a cyberspace environ, an area public relations must factor in when addressing effectiveness management.

CHAPTER ONE

POWER RESOURCE MANAGEMENT
Pushing Buttons and Building Cases

ROBERT L. HEATH

Power and control are two of the molar concepts in the theory, research, and best practices of public relations. In the current era of political correctness, religious conservatism, and normative theory building, theorists often downplay the role of these concepts. However, empirically based research flies in the face of what some thinkers want to pose as conventional wisdom. The question is not whether power and control are important, but rather how they can be exercised in a socially responsible and ethical way (Hansen-Horn, 2005).

The prevailing paradigm is that power and control are best handled when they are approached symmetrically rather than asymmetrically, bilaterally rather than unilaterally, and treated as a community resource rather than privileged to serve a narrow interest. Simply put, even though all players in this tussle do not seek mutually beneficial ends, one can argue that ultimately the best situation, one that does not demand constant power battles, features mutually defined solutions to shared problems and interests as the best way to exert power and control. That is the object of the exploration and understanding of power resource management theory.

In short, companies, nonprofits, and government agencies work to gain power, exert power to accomplish their mission, and attempt to use power to control their destiny. Crisis occurs when they appear to lose or misuse their power and control. Faced with the reality of social, financial, and political dimensions of change and sociopolitical order, some academics work to ignore and even denigrate the role power plays in the practice and theory of public relations. Ethics, among many other considerations, is important to this discussion because theorists and practitioners work for a view of public relations that allows and even encourages practitioners to think they can and should sit in judgment on the ethics and soundness of policies of their organization and its relationship with other parts of society. Positioning practitioners in such noble—and powerful—roles is laudable, but perhaps is quite unrealistic at times. Power is contestable and the ethics of how power should be exerted is in constant flux.

This chapter outlines a rationale for a power resource management philosophy of public relations. The analysis argues that change accomplished through power resource management is a continuing factor of human existence. Individuals and organizations are constantly engaged in creating and resisting change for many reasons, ranging from altruism to sound business practices, to solid public policy in the public interest, and to narrow self-interest that flaunts the public interest. The view in this analysis sees society as matrixed connections between multiple stakeholders and stakeseekers ranging in power from that held by individuals to that held by large business, government, and nonprofit organizations. At the heart of this discussion is the role of change through activism. As Smith and Ferguson (2001) advised, "Activism is such a part of public relations that some have suggested that public relations practitioners gain legitimacy and increase their utility to an organization primarily in the presence of active publics" (p. 291).

In the introduction to *Activists Speak Out,* Marie Cieri (2000) reported several interviews to capture the dynamics of this robust dialogue. She observed that activists, or at least engaged individuals:

> . . . are scattered throughout this country, coming from different backgrounds, walks of life, and points of view. They are known within their own communities and activist networks, but most are not famous and do not aspire to be. But they are heroes nonetheless. They are part of a little-recognized subculture, operating on the belief that dramatic, progressive change is needed in our society and willing to pay the often formidable price of being activist in America. (pp. 1–2)

Interviews reported by Cieri added depth to what other scholars of activism and power resource management had discovered. Activism is about the strategic use of the tools of change: "person-to-person organizing, employment of mass media, economic pressuring, public actions, skillful oratory, legal weaponry, quiet persuasion, education, steady vigilance, and even prayer" (p. 10). In the main, no one ever said the engagement of individuals and organizations in the management of issues is or will be easy. Noting how activists engage in the tactics and strategies of public relations, Smith and Ferguson (2001) stressed the reality that "the relationship between activists and organizations is tenuous, and the history of conflict between these two entities suggests that much can be learned from the studying of activism and responses to it" (p. 291).

Such perspective can be true and enlightening for the marketing—publicity and promotion—side of public relations. But it is even more fruitful and probably demanded for the public policy and issue debate aspects of the field. Based on this rationale, a case will be discussed and conclusions for best practices and a research agenda will be posed. In a nutshell, power resource management theory reasons that battles over the formation of public policy—the ways in which people collectively manage the circumstances and norms of their lives—entails advocacy and power pressure. Such pressure, in particular, and advocacy entails power resources, and acknowledges the requirement that sociopolitical and business norms often change only because some segment of society brings its weight to bear on the formation, change, and enforcement of public policy.

No better demonstration of the role of power as power can be offered than the weight of votes. A majority vote is the standard. If the opinion is that of an authorized power group, such as the U.S. Supreme Court, then even with a majority vote, five of nine people can impose their judgment as the law of the land. Advocacy—the rhetorical contest of the superiority of one position in competition with other views—is both process and content. It entails the clash of ideas as statement and counterstatement. In the best sense, the clash is done in public with citizens (natural and artificial) influencing the outcome by having weighed the merits of the points advocated for or against some policy of public interest.

HISTORICAL AND THEORETICAL PERSPECTIVES ON POWER

Power and control are universal aspects of the human experience and vital to the dynamics of society. As a gross simplification, one can argue that the essence of society and the history of human experience revolve around efforts to gain and exert power and control. Battles between individuals, groups, countries, and cultures carve out the situationally relevant amounts of power held and exerted by each side. Public relations by nature, if not name, has been part of this struggle since the beginning of human history.

Discussions of power often are an uncomfortable part of the literature of public relations because there is fear that such positions necessarily privilege large corporations and even government agencies. However, power resource management theory argues that the limits to one entity's power is the ability of a competing entity to exert opposing pressure. Indeed, even the most precise discussions of symmetry and asymmetry eventually center around when an organization, otherwise dedicated to symmetrical balances of power resources, can or must exert its power because its course is ethically or factually more correct than the position advocated by some group of opponents.

Part of the process of gathering and using power depends on individuals' ability to create a reputation and set of operating principles that are empowering to the relevant parties. Such reputation-building efforts have traditionally included the strategic attempts of government officials, leaders of governments (including kings, queens, regents, emperors, presidents, and people of similar rank and title), religious figures that are part of most cultures, commercial figures, and the dichotomy of the haves and have-nots. As will be seen below, reputation—at least in part—is crafted and used to legitimize the person's or organization's ability to have and exert power.

Public relations has been part of this process of reputation building, authority formation, and advocacy of competing positions since the dawn of civilization. The necessity of social coordination and normative behavior requires policies that prescribe and proscribe behavior. Public relations has, at least in modern times, been seen to privilege the already loud and influential voice of business, especially big business. However, as will be noted below, such advocacy has also traditionally been used by the have-nots to fight in power struggles against the haves.

Origins of Power Resource Management Theory

Interest in the power resource management approach to public relations, especially its connections with issues management—by that name—became a reality in the United States during the 1960s and 1970s. Some scholars interested in public relations brought to that era education that was steeped in the rhetoric and public address tradition of the communication field, especially speech communication. Practitioners such as R. P. Ewing recognized the tensions of power as the rationale for issues management. As Ewing (1987) concluded, issues management "developed within the business community as an educational task aimed at preserving the proper balance between the legitimate goals and rights of the free enterprise system and those of society" (p. 5). Such analysis, underpinned by knowledge of the history of industry, realized that issues management is at least as old as the U.S. industrial revolution. (See Chapter 2 in Heath [1997] for a brief discussion of this history.) If we trace the antecedents of public relations back (especially its engagement with issues), we will find its activities intertwined with the efforts of great monarchs in ancient and modern civilizations, the Roman Empire, the Catholic Church, governments, and influential business enterprises (Heath, 2005).

One primary source for understanding the tradition of power in society has been the study of rhetoric and public address—its history and criticism. During much of the twentieth century, classes at all categories of universities and colleges studied the history and criticism of public address. These classes chronicled the conditions under which notable speakers performed, the quality of their response to the rhetorical problems of their times, the rhetorical problems they raised in their times, and the manner in which they gave voice to issue positions of the public policy challenges of their times. These classes critically scrutinized the rhetorical efforts of speakers and writers whose words were associated with power and change, even if their individual influence on meandering currents of time could only be postulated and rarely proven with certainty. They were part of the process and the formation of meaning that shaped the course of society.

Almost invariably the voices studied were those of some minority position—or interest. Or, if they were the majority opinion, it needed to be claimed and proven because it might be at odds with the policies being formulated and implemented by the power elite, such as a monarchy. These voices, for instance, might ask for consideration of an alternative view to that being imposed or otherwise implemented by the will of a monarchy. The topics of these addresses might in total be considered as the evolution of the democratic will of the "people." Seminal, for instance, in British public address were the demands of the barons against King John at Runnymede. There, on June 15, 1215, he accepted the Magna Carta, a step toward a more collaborative form of government. Words crafted in speech and writing were the war of words that made for robust debates in the House of Commons by which the English people formed public policy, even against the will of the monarchy.

The public address of the United States began with a study of the words of colonial ministers and matured into the voices of the revolutionary patriots who debated the merits of supporting or rejecting the authority of the English monarchy and the House of Commons. Long after they were the subject of interest by theme, period, and genre of the speech communication discipline, public relations historians such as Cutlip (1994, 1995; see also Cutlip, Center, & Broom, 1996) claimed these voices for the public relations discipline.

Scholars of public address tended to study the arguments made by those who sought to change society. Advocacy was not only respected, but it was also explored as the defining quality of a democratic and progressive society. This discipline invested power in the people based on the spirit of the First Amendment of the U.S. Constitution. Individuals speaking in public took their cases to the people. The people have the right to hear and decide between competing perspectives. The corpus of public address was as interested in the advocacy of the secessionist southerners as in the claim advocated by Abraham Lincoln that a house divided against itself could no longer endure.

Every aspect of U.S. society was explored by these studies. They were keenly interested in religious rhetoric, that of women forging a new role in society and especially politics for the "weaker gender," and that of advocates against the peculiar institution of slavery. Voice was given to labor, to regions, to occupations such as farmers, to environmentalists, to consumer rights advocates, to advocates for higher standards of civil rights and human rights. No aspect of society was beyond the curiosity of these scholars who offered in-depth studies of the role of advocacy in the public policy arena. These studies focused primarily on the voices of change, those who felt the stain of finding problems and encountering circumstances that violated their expectations of what should be. They recognized problems and were involved with issues. They had the courage to recognize constraints and to empower followers to overcome them.

By the 1960s, hundreds of scholarly articles, theses, books, and dissertations had explored in meticulous detail the rhetorical strategies and proficient and ethical use of those strategies by competing advocates for and against a variety of social, political, and business policies. This well-developed rhetorical, critical heritage offered substantial insights for the discipline of public relations, especially for those interested in issues management. On the one hand, people who examined this era of public relations wrote in cautioning ways about advocacy and the power of persuasion taken to the public arena to forge public policy. They worried that dominant voices might prevail. Normative public relations, investing the senior practitioner with the sagacity of Plato's philosopher king, might be the answer. On the other hand, scholars and leading practitioners opted for a more Aristotelian view, that voices need to contest the relative merits of issues by taking their case to the people of society.

At the heart of this discussion is the need for organizations, perhaps most specifically companies, to gain support of key members of society. The fundamental outcomes and dependent variables in this situation are support or opposition. As the twentieth century matured, those interested in issues advocacy and power resource management began to focus their critical attention on the organizational (corporate entity) as a spokesperson in society, rather than on an individual speaker. Social movement groups and other voices became the sources of new ideas and conflicting

opinions. It was not surprising to scholars of this type that the practice of public relations began to feel pressures to change in the 1950s and 1960s as one of the most
robust eras of social movements of all kinds formed. Activists called for new policies
on which to form society.

Public relations has often tended to ignore this aspect of the discipline. It was
luxuriating in media releases as the primary tool of the practice. Publicity and promotion were the primary functions. Out of this gap arose public affairs and the modern
form of issues management, which in its nature was much closer to the tradition
of public address history and criticism than it was to the journalistic foundations of
public relations that invested great influence in the organization–reporter relationship. New forms of relationship were called for that redefined the tools, tactics, and
functions of public relations. For some academics in public relations, this era called
for substantial reinvestigation. For those steeped in the history and criticism of public
address, it was just another day at the office. They had long been interested in the
origins, rationale, and application of power in society.

Power and Its Resources

Power and control are problematic concepts in the discussion of public relations
practice, theory, and research. This topic brings quickly to the minds some of the
dangers of deep-pocket spending by the powerful corporate entity to dominate
and even manipulate society to its narrow interests. This corporate entity looms
even larger in the minds of some because of the loud voice that can be brought
to bear by businesses, especially large ones. This voice may be magnified through
trade associations.

Pearson (1992) realized that perspectives on business were vital to an understanding of ethical public relations. With this motivation, he discussed the prevailing
and conflicting perspectives on public relations that emerged in historical accounts
of the practice. His review of prevailing perspectives focused primarily as applied to
the interests of business and, through those interests, the public interest as it is
conceived in various ways, at various times, through various perspectives serving as
interpretive lens. In his analysis, Pearson emphasized the historian's truth that no
view of the history of public relations is privileged to be "truth"—that is more true
than other views. Each view focuses on facts and opinions and then imposes interpretive frames to explain and judge the phenomena at hand. Hitting at the essence
of perspectives and power resource management, Pearson succinctly concluded:
"From the left, public relations is seen as serving the private interests of individuals,
from the right public relations is seen as threatening these interests" (p. 130).

In this line of discussion, the eternal paradox is between the internal
and external influences as executive leadership seeks to make its organization
maximally effective to achieve its mission and serve its purpose—the reason for
which it was authorized as an "artificial citizen." It is axiomatic that activist
publics seek to change, correct, and guide the organization's future by applying
pressure from the outside. In this regard, activists bring to bear discussions of
propositions of fact, value, and policy in the discussion of issues relevant to the
operations, policies, and resource acquisition of the targeted organization.

The defining key to the relationship between organization and critic is the legitimacy of the efforts undertaken by the organization. Do those efforts meet or exceed the expectations of key publics who can at least work to exert influence for or against the future of the organization as it seeks its future? Analyzing and understanding this challenge requires a set of tools to address the nature and magnitude of any legitimacy gap that exists between the organization's operations and the expectations of its key publics (Heath, 1997, see especially p. 5; Sethi, 1977). The challenge is for each organization to be viewed as legitimate in its understanding of the situation in which it operates, the formulation of plans to accomplish its mission, and the crafting and accommodating means to implement plans to achieve that future. Public relations analysis, planning, and implementation is part of that strategic effort to be seen as legitimately operating in the public interest.

Stressing this point of expectation and legitimacy, Fraser (2003) asked: "Why do so many movements couch their claims in the idiom of recognition?" (p. 21). To explore this question central to power and its resources, the next section examines the resources of legitimacy, power resource acquisition, and power resource enactment.

Rationale: Legitimacy to Have and Exert Power.   Legitimacy, as noted above, is vital to any organization's success. Public relations has long been seen in theory, research, and application as a discipline that can or must help an organization to be, and be seen as, legitimate. To this point, Condit and Condit (1992) observed how antitobacco activists have used incremental erosion to diminish the legitimacy of the tobacco industry. This strategy entails slowly chipping away at premises that the industry would use to justify the legitimacy of its policies, products, and actions. The activists challenge the industry's legitimacy by focusing on and seeking to alter or eliminate premises that support the industry. Activists work to put premises into place or bring them to bear in ways that force the industry to alter its place and actions.

Here the connection with power resource management becomes well defined. It is in the nexus of legitimacy and power resource availability that we see the starting point for this discussion. Power has long and often been defined as the ability and will to achieve or affect outcomes. Thus, we might conclude that X organization has power to the extent that it can determine its future. By extension we can observe that Y has power to the extent to which it can affect X's ability to achieve its future.

Barnes (1998) perceptively noted that seeing such circumstances in this relationship between X and Y merely indicates the presence of power but does not actually define it conceptually or in practice. Barnes directed our attention to the key question in determining power resources: "Whether we talk of rights and obligations, or of roles and institutions, or of patterned social relationships, the import is much the same: we are talking of a presumed structure and orderliness in social activity, and a need to understand the nature and the basis of such structure and orderliness is implied" (p. 20). Power results from value premises and social norms—expected and accepted patterns of thinking and acting: "The normative order must reflect not internal pressures within the psyche but the pressures people exert upon each other" (p. 42).

Barnes continued his discussion of the essence of legitimacy—the rationale and systemic structures that bring power into being and become the arena for its exertion. He noted that meaning that guides interpretations and actions is the basis of society and social order. Stressing this point, Barnes concluded: "Every society possesses a shared body of technical, manipulation-related knowledge, knowledge of nature, and a shared body of social knowledge, knowledge of a normative order" (p. 55). Power, therefore, results from shared knowledge—the norms and expectations that are captured in this collective view of selves, social relationships, privileges, and obligations. As interest groups and organizations (public and private sector) contest assumptions and norms, they define and redefine power, "the structure of discretion" (p. 62). Power, in this sense, is the "capacity for action and the possession of power [is] the possession of discretion in the use of capacity for action" (p. 67).

Perhaps no current discussion has done more to refocus attention on legitimacy than has the "war on terrorism." At heart in that "war" is a definition of what constitutes as terrorist. Governmental definitions exist. President George W. Bush built the reputation of his presidency on terrorism as a global threat, one sufficient to require military and peacekeeping actions against Iraq. Stressing the rhetorical dimension of terrorism, journalists began to shift framing terminology soon after the resistance against U.S. and allied occupation of Iraq. No longer were those opposed to the U.S. and ally presence terrorists; they were redefined into the politically correct—perhaps semantically correct—terms of insurgents, local militia, and even freedom fighters. Military attacks on fighters in cities such as Fallujah, Iraq, could be seen by some observers as a parallel to the Battle of the Alamo where Texans resisted the army of Santa Anna.

Any examination of terrorism focused attention on strategic use of threats and actual force, including murder and injury to body and property. The assumption is, and probably continues to be, that terrorists are willing to try to force change through threats and actions by seeking to intimidate the authorities who are the target of their outrage.

The problem with that definition is that terrorists and terrorism are, like beauty, in the mind of the beholder. Long before the events of September 11, 2001, Dowling (1986) made the insightful observation: "Terrorism frequently has rhetorical ends. Critics of rhetoric have a duty to examine terrorism to determine what contributions they can make to understanding it and to evaluating proposed responses to the terrorist threat" (p. 12). In truth, that has long been the case. Clearly, by the operating definition of the analysts of terrorists, the revolutionary patriots in the American colonies who successfully opposed the rule of King George III of England and brought about the American War for Independence were terrorists. Now iconic heroes, they were in their own time traitors whose lives were on the line in what could have been a failed effort at achieving independence.

These patriots destroyed property, such as the tea in Boston Harbor and the residences of tax collectors and other British authorities. They threatened lives and actually engaged in armed rebellion. Even before the activism of the 1960s in the United States, Gipson (1954) characterized the years from 1763 to 1775 as a steady progression toward a conflict over the right and ability of the colonies to assert and achieve self-government. Colonists sought the right and ability to exert power over their interests. Gipson's study focused on this era "of the Revolution—marked at its worst by the disorder of mobs rather than by armed insurrection" (p. xi). During this period, buildings associated with tax collection and other aspects of British authority were burned or otherwise severely damaged. Tax collectors and other British authorities were threatened in effigy. It was not uncommon for the effigy to be beheaded and burned. British military authority often had to move quickly to avoid harm and even death to its representatives and sometimes their families. Although effective on specific incidents, British authority was being flaunted as being unable to prevent such occurrences. Members of government were forced out of office for fear of their lives.

Of the actions of some colonists during the Boston Tea Party, Chitwood (1961) observed, "The effect that this riot had on sentiment in America and England and on British policy gives it a significance out of all proportion to its character as an unfortunate act of an undisciplined mob" (p. 535). As such acts may lose supporters as well as gain them, one consequence of this "riot" was that it earned the condemnation by William Pitt, who had been a strong supporter of the colonial cause. If such events had happened in 2003, would CNN have reported the colonists' actions as the work of rioters, insurgents, or terrorists? Were they freedom fighters? Were they in revolt or rebellion? That question will go unanswered, but it demonstrates the rhetorical nature of terrorism. These appellations resonate with rhetorical implications from some of the seminal moments in U.S. history, especially the War for Independence and the Civil War.

Leading up to the Civil War, the career of John Brown, who was treated as a traitor (the older version of terrorist), was clearly defined today as the work of terrorism. Were the southerners who fired on a federal fort in Charleston Harbor terrorists, activists, or patriots attempting to restore states rights to the much-aggrieved South? Note also that the Southern Confederacy based its form of government on the Articles of Confederacy, which was the first form of limited federal authority and power following the treaty ending the American War for Independence.

Similar to the theme of defining terrorists, activists in the labor movements near the end of the nineteenth century were willing to destroy property and threaten lives. They had to achieve legitimacy to speak for others and against their foes. They needed facts, values, and policies that could energize their followers and challenge the legitimacy of those who opposed changes in labor policy. Recall also that industrial giants were also willing and able to engage agents who were skilled at bringing force down on labor protestors.

Such challenges are essential, as Hobson (2003) recently declared of social movement activism. Looking at the politics of contention, she observed that:

> One could say that POLITICS in the study is in capital letters, whereas politics in recognition struggles, in the lower case, involves confronting everyday institutionalized patterns and practices that deny social groups participatory citizenship, struggles that challenge the basic coding of rights and obligations in nation states and constitute different varieties of collective "we'" than the norms that emerged in the eighteenth and nineteenth centuries when those polities were formed. (p. 3)

First then, in the understanding of power resource management, is to understand the dynamics—systems and meaning—of legitimacy as part of the arenas in which organizations of various kinds obtain, exert, and counterbalance power. The next section extends this scrutiny of power and its resources to examine the enactment of power.

Ability to Influence Outcomes through the Enactment of Power.   Coupled to legitimacy is the need to obtain and exert power resources. One requirement is rhetorical resources, the justification of the cause of the activists and the condemnation of the course of action of the target. Another requirement is the ability to mobilize power, as a result of felt strains leading to mobilized moments of confrontation (Heath, 1997).

Once power is forming, it must be brought to bear in the name of change. It is the enactment of change leading to confrontation, conflict, negotiation, collaborative decision making, and even the defeat of the target of hostility. Part of this equation of power is the ability to raise and sustain the discussion of issues. Essential to these issues is not only the strength—persuasiveness—of any position advocated, but also its ability to gather and bring to bear stakes as power resources. The next section briefly discusses issues and the following focuses on stakes, stakeholder, and stakeseekers.

Issues: Contestable Matters of Fact, Value, and Policy

One standard way of defining issues draws on the rhetorical heritage. According to this body of literature, an issue is a contestable matter of fact, value, or policy. Nichols (1963) summed the essence of the rhetorical tradition as being committed to enlightened choice. Such choice can center on facts, values, and policies.

These types of issues typically may not be separate in the context of a specific controversy. For instance, the battle over global warming addresses that facts are known, which ones are relevant, and how best each fact in context should be interpreted. This in essence captures the traditions of legal argument and medical science, as well as the physical, behavioral, and social sciences. It is the essence of the humanities.

In addition to facts, especially in matters of interpretation, clashes occur over values. An argument may focus on the definition of one or more values, and its or their specific application to a specific decision. The rhetorical heritage presupposes that various controversies center on value priorities. Values may change slowly, but more often the controversy centers on which value, as defined, is most relevant to various interpretations. Environmentalists often disagree about the priority of a clean, safe, and healthy environment versus industrial or governmental progress. Labor policy focuses on definitions of workplace safety and humane working conditions and a living wage.

Policies center on the universal controversy over what ought to be done. What is best for the relevant interests? If private policy is believed to fail, social movements often work to change policies, ostensibly in the public interest.

One ideal approach to the practice and role of public relations in such controversies might advance the proposition that the organization, through the counsel of its top public relations people, should engage in research, communicate openly with activists, and respond to their needs and interests. This view assumes all too often that an organization is dealing with only one stakeholder or stakeseeker at a time, and that they concur in their preferences of policy, interpretation of fact, and value priorities. This ideal view also presupposes, perhaps naively, that all advocates deserve equal consideration. In truth, some advocates are dead wrong by various standards of good judgment.

For instance, on matters of diversity hiring, one can see advance in principle and best practice for listening to and responding to advocates for diversity. But what about the interests that oppose diversity? Do they deserve equal consideration? In matters of community planning, we would surely see the value of a planning and zoning commission listening to the pleas of homeowners that might be affected by some city policy or action by a developer. In listening to the citizens who voice concerns, should the commission also listen to and consider the views of the developer and citizens who favor the change opposed by their neighbors?

Stakes, Stakeholders, and Stakeseekers

The best way to conceptualize power is in terms of the stakes that are relevant to a controversy, an issue, and the legitimacy and ability of the players to use their stakes—those they hold as sanctions. It is also a reality in such circumstances to consider the role of the stakes sought. It may well be that stakeseeking is the essence of stakeholding. Large and powerful companies and governmental agencies must by necessity seek stakes. For businesses, they may be market choices—willing buyers, workers, and public policymakers. Politicians seek stakes, in the form of votes. Government agencies seek stakes as funding. The power of holding a stake is that it must be something valued and desired by a stakeseeker.

In his efforts to make sense of social movements, Crossley (2002) summarized the dynamics of social movement politics:

> The question of change, particularly change by way of movement politics, is a question about the difference which social agents themselves can make to the various structural dimensions of their life, a question about the form and distribution of power in society and the adequacy and limits of democracy. Social movements are, in effect, natural experiments in power, legitimation and democracy. (p. 9)

Most applicable to the discussion of power and public relations is the literature that discusses stakes and stakeholders. As noted above, power must be brought to bear as being legitimate and through the application of various resources. Simply put, one way to conceptualize and theorize these resources is as stakes that can be granted, sought, held, withheld, and otherwise used as rewards and constraints. The use of the stakes is the essence of power that entails being able to influence strategic outcomes. These terms are defined in various ways. Their definition seems to be important—more than a matter of semantics. How people define stakes and stakeholders seems central to the ways in which they study issues management and public relations, the assumptions that are made about best practices, and the logics of the discipline.

One view of stakes grows from the concept that stakeholders are people who have an *interest* in the policies, operations, and impact of any relevant organization. By this logic, a stake is an interest. One can infer that an interest might include ownership, such as is the case for stockholders of publicly traded companies, members of partnerships, citizens who have an interest in government operations, and donors and members of nonprofit organizations.

This interest concept can help us understand the logics of how and why individuals become concerned about the operations and policies of these types of organizations. The stakeholder is concerned that his/her/its interest can be positively or negatively affected. This view of interest carries us beyond the more pedestrian notion of interest as curiosity or concern, but it seems impoverished to suggest how we might understand and use the power resource approach to this subject. It also implies, perhaps, that the organization has "power" to affect the interest of the individuals. We then must ask if they, in turn, have power or would like to have power to affect the interest of the organization. Now we have advanced the concept of interest from curiosity of something more akin to view that features rewards/costs of the relationship between the individual stakeholder with an interest in the organization to something more substantial. Indeed, we are likely to see people who take an interest view as stakeholder to advance to the next step—to assert that organizations must be aware of and responsive to this interest because the organization needs the goodwill of these people to function as it wants, and even to continue to exist. By this extension, we are likely to realize that "goodwill" is a power resource.

A second view of stake—and therefore stakeholder—is developed and promoted by J. Grunig (1992). He viewed stakeholders as a general category of people who are "affected" by the decisions—strategic and important—made by an organization. He observed:

> An organization that practices public relations strategically develops programs to communicate with publics, both external and internal, that provide the greatest threats to and opportunities for the organization. These strategic publics fit into categories that many theorists have called *stakeholders.* (p. 12, emphasis in the original)

Grunig advised practitioners to "identify potential problems in the relationship" and "define the categories of stakeholders that are affected by the problem" (p. 13). Based on this logic, J. Grunig and Repper (1992) concluded: "People are stakeholders because they are in a category affected by decisions of an organization or if their decisions affect the organization" (p. 125). As did many other scholars and hordes of practitioners, L. Grunig (1992) noted how activists could limit the goals, aspirations, and choices of companies.

The logic in this analysis is partially in accord with the seminal analysis of Freeman (1984), who reasoned that a stakeholder "is any individual or group who can affect or is affected by the actions, decisions, policies, practices, or goals of the organization" (p. 25). Note that in this explanation, both sides of some "problem" can affect each other. They hold something—a stake—that the other wants or needs. For this reason, each side of a problem holds a stake or several stakes.

Applying this logic, Heath (1997) observed, "Stakeholders are any persons or groups that hold something of value that can be used as rewards or constraints in exchange for goods, services, or organizational policies and operating standards" (p. 28). That definition of stakeholder allows us to focus attention on the stakes that are or can be played in the conflict, power struggle, or controversy that surrounds a problem that is likely to be translated into one or more issues. If this is the case, what is a stake? In traditional conflict theory logic, Heath (1997) defined a stake as "anything— tangible or intangible, material or immaterial—that one person or group has that is of value to another person or group" (p. 28). That discussion is clarified by thinking that groups are also organizations or other types of collectivities. The discussion of power resource management focuses on constraints and rewards. Stakes can be used (granted, given, or withheld) as constraints and rewards as the case might be.

One of the most important stakes is identification (Burke, 1969). Activism often seeks to form new identities and identifications. It instantiates the rhetoric of definition and redefinition. It contests perspectives including those of definitions of humans. The list is huge but includes the rights based on definition of laborers, environmentalists, gay and lesbian activists, conservative Christians, and workers to end poverty and fight diseases such as AIDS. Its voices call for people to identify with the ridley turtle or giant redwoods, to battle industrial giants who may be defined as purveyors of toxic waste. In essence, social movements argue for a position and they ask potential followers and supporters: Who are you and what do you stand for (Stryker, Owens, & White, 2000)?

In these ways and because of these reasons, power is not granted, but earned. Its use depends on ideology and legitimacy, as well as the specific skill needed to bring it to bear for and against various interests. Power in the abstract comes to life in application.

Applications

Applications of power resource management theory are easy to identify but entail a broad range of efforts to change or mitigate efforts to change the meaning, expectations, and sociopolitical processes of a society, national or global. So dynamic and complex are these efforts that no player, however powerful, can manage many if any changes unilaterally and with indifference to the interests and power of others. Coalitions, alliances, and collaborations tend to be the standard operating strategies and tactics at this level. At the broadest societal level, power resource management occurs with societal redefinitions. One of the most important was the legendary effort of the utility industry in the twentieth century to convince the public to accept regulated monopolies as the preferred operating system for utilities.

At all levels, the processes of government, the dynamics of business, the legitimacy of social movement activism, and the serendipity of events are likely to predict how change occurs or is mitigated. For instance, efforts to elevate a population in terms of monetary and other infrastructural changes can be dramatically dampened and even defeated by an epidemic of AIDS that reduces the population, eliminates many of the most potentially productive citizens, and drains coffers for medical treatment.

All the options of issues management are available for those who engage in affecting change through power resource management (Heath, 1997). Media processes and policies, as well as the emerging nature of the new communication technologies, are among some of the most obvious ways in which the tactics and strategies of activists and other players in the public policy arena can communicate with audiences and be attacked by critics or championed by supporters.

One of the principles relevant to application that seems to endure is that the strength of the most powerful can actually be used against them. They can blunder in their efforts to influence policy. They can lose sight of the need to be embracing and collaborative. Exposure of their narrow self-interest is front-page news and catalyzes opposition from all order of stakeseekers and stakeholders.

Organizations, as do individuals, are wise to realize that stakes are the name of the game. They need to understand those they seek as well as those they hold. They must know that actions serve as stakes as well as words and opinions. In the order of things, a systems perspective that encourages ethical approaches to balanced exchanges can wisely guide executive—including public relations—best practices. As is so often the case in negotiation and other forms of conflict resolution, any exchange of stakes is predicated on what the players believe to be fair and potentially in the mutual interest of all. Power can be exerted when an activist can embarrass a company or government agency by getting news coverage of some offending action or misjudgment. Power is brought to bear when a committee is motivated to conduct hearings of some industry's operations. Activists have power when they can influence the hearings and even have their voice heard.

CONCLUSION

Implications of power resource management theory are a vital aspect of public relations. This theory is not only relevant to the circumstances of organizations and interests within a country; it is also applicable to the global marketplace and public policy arena. Writers such as Hamel, Lustiger-Thaler, Pieterse, and Roseneil (2001) have stressed the importance of recognizing globalization and multinational development as being coupled with social movements and power resource management. This struggle seeks a balance between individual and collective interests in the tensions between societal and environmental development and global modernization. The authors observed how "contemporary accelerated globalization refers to a new distribution of power and comes in a package together with other trends, of informalization, informatization, flexibilitization and the difficulty of sustaining community" (p. 11).

Change, strain, mobilization, confrontation, negotiation, and collective decision making are timeless aspects of the human experience. Public relations and issues management are functional approaches that organizations can take toward the evolution of policy. They are advocates and must also be listeners. They engage in finding and interpreting relevant facts, considering the best values, and developing the policies that most serve the public interest.

By definition and identity, social movements are integral to society, however muted or robust any might be at a specific moment. They always focus attention on the power resources of society because they call for change. As defined in this tradition, a social movement is "a collective, organized, sustained, and noninstitutional challenge to authorities, powerholders, or cultural beliefs and practices" (Goodwin & Jasper, 2003, p. 3).

CASE: CPSC VERSUS DAISY

Many cases of power resource management could be used to demonstrate the principles discussed above. Many such cases are so complex that they could consume the space allotted for the total discussion in this book of that topic. News outlets are replete with cases. For instance, much of the news in a publication such as the *Wall Street Journal* is all about power resource management. This case demonstrates how power resource management operates, whether to the satisfaction of all the parties engaged, and ways that demonstrate normative ethics and symmetry. Issues evolve because of power resource management in all its nuances.

One relevant case centered on action taken by the Consumer Produce Safety Commission (CPSC), which sued Daisy Manufacturing Co. in 2001 over an effort "to force Daisy to recall millions of allegedly defective guns" (Gruley, 2004, p. A1). Eventually, the agency made a settlement with the company that meant that it did not have to recall a single BB gun. Instead, the company was required to spend $1.5 million to publicize and promote safe BB-gun use. The dynamics of this power tussle reveal the strategies and vagaries—even serendipity—of power resource management.

A case that motivated concern by all parties arose when two sixteen-year-old boys who believed a specific BB gun was out of BBs engaged in horseplay that turned dangerous. The muzzle velocity of a fully charged gun is sufficient to propel a BB at 650 feet per second. The projectile under those circumstances can (and did) penetrate the skull. The product came with a warning: "Not a toy. Adult supervision required." The skull of one of the boys was penetrated, leading to serious damage that would have likely led to permanent disabilities if it had not resulted in death.

In past years, the company had made many design changes intended to increase the safety of the type of gun by reducing the chances that a BB could lodge, leading users to believe that the gun was unloaded. Later, the BB could be shaken loose and become a potentially lethal projectile. But the design changes were not part of a recall. Thus, older models still in use were not as safe as newer ones. Along with design changes, the company had made legal settlements over the years to those who had been harmed by these guns.

The complexities of this case and the array of efforts by the CPSC to deal with this problem and similar ones are not totally necessary to understand the relevance of this case to power resource management. Part of the trajectory of the issue depended on the membership of the CPSC. During the days surrounding efforts to file the suit, the membership of the CPSC changed. An appointee who had supported the suit was replaced by one who opposed it. The new member had been a supporter of George W. Bush for president. This person was a member of a nonprofit group called the Rio Grande Foundation, which is dedicated to limited government intervention and maximum economic freedom. With him voting against the suit and for a more favorable settlement, the CPSC case was withdrawn.

One of the strategic moves was brought to bear not by the company, but by the National Rifle Association (NRA). At a crucial moment during the CPSC deliberation, the NRA sent an alert to its members. Its intent was to defend the less-restricted rights of the company. The NRA feared that this case could open a floodgate of suits and other actions against gun manufacturers and marketers. Hostile e-mail messages flooded the CPSC, voicing concern about its regulatory and legal actions. Under pressures and with a more favorable committee, the moderate actions were taken against the company. The family continued its legal action against the company. Ultimately through a variety of moves that changed the power dynamics of the case, its nature and impact changed.

Here is a classic case of stakeseekers at odds with stakeholders. It demonstrates that multiple players often form alliances or work against one another. One stake the offended family thought it held was taken away with the appointment of a more favorable member to the CPSC. The NRA, long known for hardball politics, used its intimidating clout (stake) with its ever-present ability to work for and against political elections. In contrast to other government agencies, the CPSC is not as daunting in the exercise of its mission. The company held stakes, but also sought them from the CPSC. The CPSC held stakes that changed as its membership changed.

Several issues are at foot in this case. Facts seem to be relatively beyond contest. Values seem to be at odds, especially the usefulness of government consumer protection. This value is held to an even higher standard by the NRA, which elevated this case by implication to the defense of the Second Amendment of the U.S. Constitution and the belief that gun control is a tyranny. Clearly at odds is the policy that is most in the public interest, whatever the definition of the public and its interest. The CPSC had the legitimate power to make the decision it did. Other decisions by legitimate stakeholders may follow. All this will be played out in the public policy arena fraught with differences of opinion and conflicting senses of what is the public interest.

QUESTIONS FOR APPLICATION

Public relations engages in power resource management. Power is socially constructed. For this reason, public relations practitioners both help create and respond to that social reality, defined and applied to an array of interests, causes, and missions. To this end, several reflections are warranted. Respond to the following questions, drawing on the information contained in the case above, as well as other contemporary examples.

1. In what ways do principles develop and evolve that serve as the rationale for power—who has it and who can apply it? How do these principles support and justify power in action?

2. How are power resources generated through rhetorical discourse, systemic dynamics, and relationship management?

   a. How do statements and counter statements compete to define the nature and rationale of power, those who exert it, and the causes to which it can be put?

   b. In what ways and how does power resource management, once given legitimacy, depend on skilled and ethical use?

3. Do you agree or disagree with the following: Public relations practitioners help build reputations that deserve to use power in the public interest.

4. How might we understand stakes as the wages of power to be sought, granted, and exchanged?

5. Are power resources subject to ethical standards? If so, how and in what ways?

These reflections focus attention on the reality that power is an intrinsic element of society. Power constitutes both a tool and a challenge for public relations scholars and practitioners. It can neither be shaped nor long applied asymmetrically

REFERENCES

Barnes, B. (1988). *The nature of power.* Urbana: University of Illinois Press.

Burke, K. (1969). *A rhetoric of motives.* Berkeley: University of California Press.

Chitwood, O. P. (1961). *A history of colonial America* (3rd ed.). New York: Harper & Row.

Cieri , M. (2000). Introduction: You cross that line. In M. Cieri & C. Peeps (Eds.), *Activists speak out: Reflections on the pursuit of change in America* (pp. 1–14). New York: Palgrave.

Condit, C. M., & Condit, D. M. (1992). Smoking or health: Incremental erosion as a public interest group strategy. In E. L. Toth & R. L. Heath (Eds.), *Rhetorical and critical approaches to public relations* (pp. 241–256). Hillsdale, NJ: Lawrence Erlbaum Associates.

Crossley, N. (2002). *Making sense of social movements.* Buckingham, UK: Open University Press.

Cutlip, S. M. (1994). *The unseen power: Public relations, a history.* Hillsdale, NJ: Lawrence Erlbaum Associates.

Cutlip, S. M. (1995). *Public relations history: From the 17th to the 20th century. The antecedents.* Hillsdale, NJ: Lawrence Erlbaum Associates.

Cutlip, S. M., Center, A. H., & Broom, G. M. (1996). *Effective public relations* (8th ed.). Englewood Cliffs, NJ: Prentice-Hall.

Dowling, R. E. (1986). Terrorism and the media: A rhetorical genre. *Journal of Communication, 36*(1), 12–24.

Ewing, R. P. (1987). *Managing the new bottom line: Issues management for senior executives.* Homewood, IL: Dow Jones-Irwin.

Fraser, N. (2003). Rethinking recognition: Overcoming displacement and reification in cultural politics. In B. Hobson (Ed.), *Recognition struggles and social movements: Contested identities, agency and power* (pp. 21–32). Cambridge: Cambridge University Press.

Freeman, R. E. (1984). *Strategic management: A stakeholder approach.* Boston: Pitman.

Gipson, L. H. (1954). *The coming of the revolution: 1763–1775.* New York: Harper & Row.

Goodwin, J., & Jasper, J. M. (2003). Editors' introduction. In J. Goodwin and J. M. Jasper (Eds.), *The social movements reader: Cases and concepts* (pp. 3–7). Malden, MA: Blackwell.

Gruley, B. (2004, April 29). Teenage shooting opens a window on safety agency. *Wall Street Journal*, pp. A1, A6.

Grunig, J. E. (1992). Communication, public relations, and effective organizations: An overview of the book. In J. E. Grunig (Ed.), *Excellence in public relations and communication management* (pp. 1–28). Hillsdale, NJ: Lawrence Erlbaum.

Grunig, J. E., & Repper, F. G. (1992). Strategic management, publics, and issues. In J. E. Grunig (Ed.), *Excellence in public relations and communication management* (pp. 117–157). Hillsdale, NJ: Lawrence Erlbaum.

Grunig, L. A. (1992). Activism: How it limits the effectiveness of organizations and how excellent public relations departments respond. In J. E. Grunig (Ed.), *Excellence in public relations and communication management* (pp. 503–530). Hillsdale, NJ: Lawrence Erlbaum Associates.

Hamel, P., Lustiger-Thaler, H., Pieterse, J. N., & Roseneil, S. (2001). Introduction: The shifting frames of collective action. In P. Hamel, H. Lustiger-Thaler, J. N. Pieterse, & S. Roseneil (Eds.), *Globalization and social movements* (pp. 1–18). Hampshire, England: Palgrave.

Hansen-Horn, T. L. (2005). Power resource management theory. In R. L. Heath (Ed.), *Encyclopedia of public relations* (pp. 632–634). Thousand Oaks, CA: Sage.

Heath, R. L. (1997). *Strategic issues management: Organizations and public policy challenges.* Thousand Oaks, CA: Sage.

Heath, R. L. (2005). Antecedents of public relations. In R. L. Heath (Ed.), *Encyclopedia of Public Relations* (pp. 32–36). Thousand Oaks, CA: Sage.

Hobson, B. (2003). Introduction. In B. Hobson (ed.), *Recognition struggles and social movements: Contested identities, agency and power* (pp. 1–17). Cambridge: Cambridge University Press.

Nichols, M. H. (1963). *Rhetoric and criticism*. Baton Rouge: Louisiana State University Press.

Pearson, R. (1992). Perspectives on public relations history. In E. L. Toth and R. L. Heath (Eds.), *Rhetorical and critical approaches to public relations* (pp. 111–130). Hillsdale, NJ: Lawrence Erlbaum.

Sethi, S. P. (1977). *Advocacy advertising and large corporations: Social conflict, big business image, the news media, and public policy*. Lexington, MA: D. C. Heath.

Smith, M. F., & Ferguson, D. P. (2001). Activism. In R. L. Heath (Ed.), *Handbook of public relations* (pp. 291–300). Thousand Oaks, CA: Sage.

Stryker, S., Owens, T. J., & White, R. W. (Eds.). *Self, identity, and social movements*. Minneapolis: University of Minnesota Press.

CHAPTER TWO

A WEICKIAN APPROACH TO PUBLIC RELATIONS AND CRISIS MANAGEMENT

GARY L. KREPS

Public relations efforts help manage complex information demands in organizational life by framing important issues for key publics, especially in times of high uncertainty (Kreps, 1989, 1990). Karl Weick's model of organizing (Weick, 1969, 1979) is a contemporary theory of organizing that describes the process in terms of resolving uncertainties (Weick refers to these uncertain situations as equivocal inputs) that are inherent in the issues typically confronted in modern organizational life. For example, coping with rapidly changing market conditions, increased competition, inflation, access to raw materials, or scandal can all increase the uncertainties of organizing activities. According to Weick, equivocal organizational situations like these are best resolved through collective interdependent communication and information-processing activities that help reduce uncertainty and identify appropriate organizational response. He explains that in the process of organizing, organizational actors are confronted by many complex, difficult, unpredictable, and equivocal situations, and each of these issues presents an information-processing problem. Effective public relations efforts help to resolve equivocality by establishing meanings for complex situations and advocating appropriate responses for organizational representatives and key stakeholders.

Weick asserts that the more equivocal (difficult to interpret and respond to) the problems that organizational actors confront are, the more these actors need help from others to cope with these complex problems. In fact, it is Weick's contention that organizations have developed expressly as communication systems for resolving equivocality and increasing the certainty of life. Organizations are established to undertake many of the most difficult tasks that humans face. In essence, organizations exist because life is complex and public relations efforts are designed to help manage the complex information demands of social organization. This chapter will describe Weick's model of organizing, identify implications of this model for guiding effective public relations activities, and provide a case study example of crisis communication to illustrate how Weick's model can promote successful organizing.

WEICK'S MODEL OF ORGANIZING

In 1969, Karl Weick published the first edition of his influential book *The Social Psychology of Organizing,* in which he presented a process-oriented model stressing human interaction as the central phenomenon of organizing. He argued that organizations do not exist but are in the process of existing through continual streams of organized human activities. Communication is the crucial process performed by organization members to enable ongoing organization. In the theory, Weick traces the specific communicative activities used to accomplish organization and describes the information processing functions of organizing.

Weick's model is built on three primary theoretical foundations: sociocultural evolutionary theory, information theory, and systems theory. Weick adopts different pieces of each perspective and adapts them to organizational analysis. By combining aspects of these three theories, Weick derives the major themes of his model.

Sociocultural evolutionary theory describes the processes by which people adapt to changes in their social and cultural environments to survive. People change their behaviors in response to social pressures by devising strategies and social innovations that help them survive. The sociocultural evolutionary process involves the interrelated processes of variation, selection, and retention of socially advantageous behavioral innovations. The innovations that occur during the variation stage become the pool of potential adaptive responses from which the social group can choose when confronted with environmental changes. The most advantageous variations are selected by the cultural group for use and retained as functional attributes of the cultural group. Weick borrows this three-stage model of adaptation, modifying it into three phases of organizing: enactment, selection, and retention. Later in this chapter it will be shown how public relations processes can benefit from this three-stage approach, too.

Information theory is concerned with the efficiency of message transmission and reduction of information loss based on the structural relationships between message codes and channel capacities (Kreps, 1990). Information theory is concerned with eliminating message distortion between source and receiver, increasing the fidelity of message transmission, and increasing the predictability of future messages. Information helps to reduce the number of decisions an individual has to make, which increases certainty. This theory explains that different channels have differing capacities for handling ambiguity. To reduce the uncertainty in communication, appropriate message codes must be matched with specific channel capacities to provide the receiver with meaningful information. Weick integrates the concept of uncertainty from information theory into his theory of organizing, such that organizational actors attempt to reduce uncertainty by generating information through the use of organizational rules and communication cycles (interaction patterns that help people develop rules). Weick's concept of equivocality is virtually identical to the information theory concept of uncertainty, where specific rules and cycles are adapted to informational inputs to bring information to an optimal level of equivocality (certainty) for organizational actors. Different organizations (and organizational actors) have differing capacities for handling the equivocality inherent in different information inputs and must make use of appropriate rules and cycles in response to its capacities and message inputs. Public relations professionals must endeavor to help key audiences make sense of equivocal situations.

Systems theory attempts to explain complex organizational processes with different interdependent hierarchical levels of complexity: the system, the subsystem, and the suprasystem. Each level of organization is composed of interconnected and mutually influenced components, each of which performs a functional process for the system level of which it is a part. It is the combination of all the functional processes of these system components that allows the system to survive and adapt to its environment. If the performance of any component or group of components is impeded within a system, the performance of all other components will be influenced. This interdependence of system components indicates a need to view the system as a whole, because it is the joint efforts of all the system components that transforms system inputs into advantageous system outputs. Feedback among system components is a major part of systems theory, where positive and negative feedback loops provide a homeostatic mechanism for monitoring system activities, facilitating or inhibiting certain system processes according to the needs of the system as a whole. Weick adopts a great deal of systems theory in developing his model of organizing. Like the systems model of organizations, Weick's organizing model can be applied to a multitude of organizing contexts and hierarchical organizational levels. It is a model of the organizing process, not of a particular organization. The basic organizing processes that occur at one level of Weick's model occur at both higher and lower hierarchical levels. All the phases and subprocesses within Weick's model of organizing are mutually dependent. The whole process of organizing is more than the sum of the processes used in organizing. By creatively adapting organizational activities to specific information inputs, organization members can transform these inputs into appropriate functional outputs. Moreover, Weick identifies feedback loops that allow organization members to maintain a homeostatic balance in organizing processes. The systems issues of hierarchy and interdependence are critical issues for public relations efforts.

INFORMATION ENVIRONMENT AND EQUIVOCAL INFORMATION INPUTS

A central part of Weick's model is the role of information as the key components of organizational environment. The concept of information environment is a shift from the traditional structural, static view of physical surroundings to an action, process view of the messages that organization members perceive and the meanings that they create in response to these messages. Organizations rely on a variety of sources of information in organizing, including interviews, sales calls, letters, documents, telephone conversations, and group discussions. Public relations professionals rely heavily on gathering information from a variety of sources to identify emerging organizational issues and to develop appropriate responses to these issues. Weick's model is thus a representation of how organization members react to the information that surrounds their organization. The processes used by members to respond to the organization's information environment are communication processes.

A crucial part of Weick's model of organizing is the concept of information *equivocality*, or the level of understandability of messages to which organization members respond. Some aspects of equivocality are the levels of ambiguity, complexity, and obscurity of information inputs. The more equivocal a situation is, the more challenging it is to respond appropriately. For example, if profits margins in a business organization drop precipitously, without warning, it is very difficult to resolve the situation. Organizational actors have to make sense of the situation, and gather information about the causes of sudden profit loss, to reduce informational equivocality. Weick explains that organizational actors attempt to process equivocal information so they can predict future information and respond to information inputs with appropriate organizational actions. This is the central job of public relations professionals: making sense of complex organizational situations and developing appropriate communication strategies for responding to these situations.

Organizations strive to manage equivocality, to maintain a balance between highly equivocal and highly unequivocal messages. Each organization processes the messages it has to deal with in an attempt to transform these information inputs into understandable and predictable messages. Highly equivocal (very complicated) message inputs must be processed by the organization. The ambiguity of the information must be reduced so that the organization can create appropriate reactions to the information input. For example, in an uncertain (equivocal) product market, leaders of a manufacturing company must gather information to determine what types of products will sell and how their company can produce and sell these products at a profit. The uncertain market conditions are high-equivocality message inputs. If the production company is to survive, it must reduce the equivocality of the situation to predict the best possible business strategies.

Organizations must react to message inputs with the same amount of equivocality that is present in the messages themselves. This is known as the principle of requisite variety (Weick, 1969). To cope with a very complex situation (high-equivocality information input), organizational representatives should engage in intensive information-seeking and processing activities to make sense of the situation and learn how to handle the input adequately. Conversely, to deal with easily understandable information (low-equivocality inputs), an organization should react with very clear, simple, rule-governed behaviors, based on past experience with similar issues. Weick explains that "it takes equivocality to remove equivocality. This means that processes must have the same degree of order or chaos as there is in the input of these processes" (1969, p. 40). The implication of requisite variety for public relations is that practitioners need to develop appropriate public relations processes to match the equivocality of the organizational issues being addressed. It would be a major mistake to respond in a simple rule-governed manner to a highly charged and complex organizational issue. Such issues will demand a sophisticated public relations response. However, it would be a waste of time and effort to comprise a major public relations campaign in response to a routine organizational issue that can be easily and effectively addressed.

COMMUNICATION RULES AND CYCLES

Weick identifies two related communication processes used by organizations to cope with the level of equivocality of information inputs, rules, and cycles (Weick, 1969). Rules help organizational actors ascertain the level of familiarity, or equivocality, in any message input into the organization, as well as search the pool of standardized message responses available to the organization that are compatible with (appropriate to) the specific message input. Organizations can usually respond to simple (unequivocal) message inputs with preset rules. For example, form letters, catalogs, rate sheets, and printed directions are rules that are often used in formal organizations in response to common organizational inputs.

Communication behavior cycles are a series of interlocked communication behaviors among organization actors that allow the organization to process highly equivocal information by reducing the equivocality of complex inputs. Weick describes a cycle as a double interact, a three-part exchange of conditionally related messages: act, response, and adjustment. In essence, the communication cycle introduces an idea, responds to that idea, and adjusts to the response. It is a way to gather information and feedback. The more equivocal information inputs are for the organization, the more organization members must depend on performing communication cycles to cope with the input. Each cycle processes some equivocality out of the input, making it more understandable to the organization and enabling organization members to apply rules for responding to it. Not every cycle reduces the same amount of equivocality from an information input, but each cycle reduces some of the initial equivocality.

Three major relationships exist among the information equivocality, rules, and communication cycles posited in Weick's theory of organizing.

1. A direct relationship exists between the equivocality of information input into an organization and the organization's dependence on the performance of communication cycles to respond to the input. As equivocality increases, the organization will attempt to cope with these complex messages by acting out a series of communication cycles designed to process out enough equivocality from the messages to make them manageable (understandable) for the organization. As equivocality decreases, there is less need to cycle out equivocality. The more equivocality, the greater the need for communication cycles; the less the equivocality, the less the need for cycles.

2. An inverse relationship exists between the equivocality of information input into an organization and the organization's dependence on rules for registering and composing organizational responses to the input. The less equivocal the input, the more the organization can depend on rules to guide organizational behaviors. There is no need for communication cycles to reduce the equivocality of an already easily understandable information input. The more equivocal the input, the fewer the rules available to guide action, so communication cycles are needed.

3. An inverse relationship exists between the organization's use of rules and the organization's need for performing communication cycles. When rules for dealing with an input are available to the organization, communication cycles become superfluous. When there are few rules to guide the organization, communication cycles are needed to resolve equivocality and create rules.

In sum, if the organizational situation a public relations practitioner responds to is highly equivocal, the professional must rely on performing cycles to cope with the input; if the situation is unequivocal, the professional can apply rules to the input to guide organizational response. The more equivocal information situations are, the more the professional needs to engage in communication cycles to reduce the information equivocality to a manageable level. The less equivocal information inputs are, the more the professional can rely on communication rules to cope with the information situation. If information is very clear, it becomes easy for the public relations practitioner to register the amount of equivocality in the input and assign standardized behaviors to respond. The more rules the public relations staff has available to interpret and develop responses to message inputs, the fewer actual communication cycles have to be performed. This is why experienced public relations professionals are often more adept at handling a variety of organizational problems. Past experience provides the savvy practitioner with rules (strategies) for interpreting and responding effectively to many situations.

ENACTMENT, SELECTION, AND RETENTION

As mentioned earlier, Weick suggests that in the process of organizing, the organization goes through three major communication phases: enactment, selection, and retention. Rules and cycles are used in each of these phases, in which the level of equivocality of the input is ascertained and either appropriate rules are selected (if available to the organization) or communication cycles are performed (if the input is too complex to be handled by rules). In each phase of organizing, information is processed through subprocesses of appropriate rules and communication cycles.

In the enactment phase of organizing, the organization attends to the information environment that surrounds it. The organization recreates (or enacts) its environment in the sense that organization members assign meaning to information events through their decoding processes. During the enactment phase, the organization is made aware of changes in its information environment, the level of equivocality of information inputs is determined, and appropriate rules and cycles are called on to process the information inputs. It is during enactment that public relations professionals make sense of the issues facing the organization, registering the level of equivocality in each situation.

In the selection phase of organizing, decisions are made about how the rules and cycles used by the organization have affected the equivocality of the information inputs and which cycles should be repeated by the organization to process the inputs further. On the basis of decisions made in the selection phase, additional rules and cycles are chosen and repeated to continue reducing the level of equivocality of the messages imported into the organization, enabling the organization to understand the inputs better and react to them. In the selection phase of organizing the public relations professional develops the best communication strategies for addressing specific organizational issues.

In the retention phase of organizing, information about the ways the organization has responded to different inputs is gathered and stored. The various communication cycles developed and used by the organization to process equivocal information are evaluated for their usefulness to the organization, and if they are deemed to be successful strategies for coping with equivocal situations, they are made into rules for responding to similar future inputs. A repertoire of rules is developed in the retention phase to be used as a form of organizational intelligence to guide organizational actions. It is this organizational intelligence that makes experienced public relations professionals so valuable. They can use the wisdom they've developed from past experiences to guide future action and response.

The enactment, selection, and retention phases work together in the process of organizing, and feedback loops among the phases are used to coordinate their activities. Feedback loops are message systems connecting the phases, allowing coordinating communication among them. Weick identifies two feedback loops: one connects retention to enactment, and the other connects retention to selection. In this way, the retention phase, which contains the organization's intelligence, can be used to guide the enactment and selection activities. Positive feedback messages are used to elicit information from the retention phase for use in selection and enactment, and to seek information from enactment and selection for storage in retention. In public relations practice, positive feedback loops are used to gather information from past experiences (retention) to guide interpretation (enactment) and response (selection) to organizational issues. Negative feedback messages are used to stop the flow of information from retention to enactment and selection, halting the performance of new behaviors, and to check the flow of information about enactment and selection activities to the retention phase. In low-equivocality public relations situations, negative feedback loops are used to minimize over-responses, limiting the use of unnecessary and wasteful communication activities.

In the enactment phase of organizing, the organization evaluates message inputs for their level of equivocality. Feedback loops between enactment and retention allow the organization to use the information from retention to guide the evaluation of messages, and to store the information about the messages enacted for future reference. In the selection phase, during which rules and cycles are chosen and created in response to information inputs, feedback loops from retention are used to guide the organization in deciding how to process message inputs by drawing on organizational intelligence and the repertoire of rules stored in the retention phase. The retention phase constantly draws information from enactment and selection through feedback loops to update its information about message inputs and organizational response strategies.

During the course of organizational practice, public relations professionals must monitor the results of different strategies and activities to determine their effectiveness in accomplishing organizational goals. If a strategy does not accomplish its objectives, or if the strategy results in unpopular side effects, the practitioner must search for alternative strategies. These alternatives will be identified in the repertoire of rules the public relations staff has retained as part of organizational intelligence. If there are no rules to cover the problems that the organization is encountering, public relations professionals will have to develop new behavior cycles to address the problems. Advantageous cycles (those that adequately treat organizational demands) will become part of the public relations staff's repertoire of rules to be used in future organizing situations. Effective public relations activities depend on the coordination of selection and retention phases of organizing.

Organizational intelligence is often distributed throughout the organization. To make a knowledgeable decision about organizational practice, public relations professionals must rely on obtaining information from other organization members. Moreover, in highly equivocal organizational situations, practitioners may have to interact with knowledgeable others outside the organization—lawyers, accountants, consultants, and such—to process the equivocal information down to an understandable level through the performance of communication behavior cycles. Proactive public relations professionals must keep on top of changes in the organization's information environment by paying particular attention to its boundary-spanning mechanisms and personnel (often concentrated at the top and the bottom of the organizational hierarchy) (Kreps, 1990). For example, at the bottom of the hierarchy, boundary spanners might include receptionists, secretaries, and complaint department, security, and sales staff. Conversely, at the top of the organizational hierarchy, chief executives often have extensive contact with representatives from the environment. These organization members must be used as resources for public relations to help evaluate information from the environment and to help guide appropriate responses to different issues.

SUMMARY AND RECOMMENDATIONS

Weick's model of organizing stresses human interactions and information processing as the central activities of organizing. It is, in fact, a communication theory, representing communication interactions and collective information processing as the primary elements of organization. Interpretation and strategic reactions to environmental information inputs enable organizational adaptation and survival. Information is the major input and output of organization. The primary activity of organizations is to process this information through communication so that organization members can react to inputs, creating the primary output of organizations—processed information. This also models the public relations processes of interpreting challenging (current and future) organizational issues, developing appropriate communication responses to these challenging situations, and retaining the information about how to deal with similar situations to guide future organizational communication.

Weick's model of organizing identifies communication among organizational actors (both organization members and key external stakeholders) as crucial to organizational survival. Communication must be recognized as an indispensable organizational and public relations activity. This recognition can aid organizational adaptation by encouraging concern for the adequacy and accuracy of interaction in organizational life. From this perspective, it becomes the formal responsibility of all organization members to communicate actively on the job, giving and receiving messages in response to informational inputs.

Weick's model describes the way that human beings coordinate efforts (organize) to process equivocal information and direct organizational activities. Public relations professionals could benefit from knowledge of Weick's model of organizing by following these seven basic recommendations:

1. Public relations professionals should engage in regular communication contact with organizational boundary spanners and environmental representatives to identify key issues and process equivocal information inputs.

2. To remain viable and efficient, public relations professionals must process information with the same degree of equivocality as is present in the issue being handled. If they handle equivocal inputs as though they were unequivocal (without constructing appropriate communication behavior cycles), fatal mistakes are likely to occur because they will be unlikely to process the equivocal information into understandable information and will probably react inappropriately to the inputs. If they handle unequivocal inputs as though they were equivocal (by performing a variety of double interacts), they are likely to waste organizational energy.

3. Public relations professionals must endeavor to accurately register the level of equivocality in information inputs, construct appropriate communication behavior cycles in response to the inputs, and process the equivocal inputs into desired organizational outputs. Care must be taken to evaluate information inputs accurately.

4. Public relations professionals can facilitate organizational adaptation to informational equivocality by making connections throughout the organization and its relevant environment, and engaging in interaction with key organization members on difficult organizational tasks. The public relations practitioner must ask relevant questions when processing difficult information inputs, and work with others to deal with issues that are too complex for them to individually comprehend and easily perform.

5. Public relations professionals should concentrate less on individual organization actions and more on the interlocked communication behaviors of interdependent groups of organizational members, because the process of control within organizations is accomplished through relationships among individuals rather than by individuals.

6. Training programs can be developed in organizations stressing teamwork; daily and weekly meetings among organization members can be arranged; problem-solving organizational groups can be formed to provide the interlocked communication behaviors necessary for organizational adaptation.

7. Care must be taken to retain relevant information from the ways public relations situations have been handled in the past to use as organizational intelligence for guiding future public relations efforts. Every previous public relations activity is a point of comparison for future activities.

CASE: CRISIS COMMUNICATION AND ANTHRAX

The public may be more wary today about the dangers of bioterrorism and infectious diseases than in any other time in recent history (Kreps et al., 2005a). The possibility of bioterrorist threats has become a significant public concern. This context means that public health authorities and the public face a set of unique health risks, especially in a time of crisis. Public relations, crisis management, and emergency communicators also face major challenges in this era of bioterrorism (Kreps et al., 2005b).

One such public relations crisis occurred in October 2001 when anthrax spores were spread via the U.S. postal system, alarming a public already anxious due to the September 11 terrorist attacks (Hobbs, Kittler, Volk, Kreps, & Bates, 2004). Although investigation ultimately revealed that only four letters containing anthrax had entered the postal system, this relatively small-scale dispersion generated confusion and panic among the public and the media, and illustrated the challenge of communicating information about risk and reality to an alarmed public.

During the anthrax threat, the traditional media presented the public with an enormous amount of information on the emerging events, but the information provided was extremely variable, often shallow, and not always validated by health authorities. While some public health authorities endeavored to communicate evidence-based facts, other coverage simultaneously offered conflicting and often confusing accounts of what was happening, as well as varying advice on the dangers of anthrax and how to protect oneself. Such a context made it difficult for the public to decide which sources to trust and which advice to follow.

In some cases, inaccurate information about anthrax was disseminated to the public, serving to increase the complexity (equivocality) of this public health crisis. For example, Secretary of Health and Human Services Tommy Thompson, following the first inhalation anthrax case, suggested in an interview with national media that the anthrax contamination was probably of natural origin, based on something picked up by drinking from a South Carolina stream. Scientists who are knowledgeable about this health threat knew immediately that anthrax is not a waterborne organism and that it is impossible to contract inhalation anthrax by participating in these types of outdoor activities (Kreps et al., 2005a). Further, Thompson, a former Wisconsin governor with no in-depth scientific or medical training, issued orders that all anthrax-related information to the public and media come directly from his office, barring the most well-informed government scientists and health experts from providing expert advice or information. The secretary's errant comments haunted his department and the Centers for Disease Control (CDC) as credible sources of health information concerning anthrax.

This public relations breakdown could have been avoided by using Weick's model of organizing as a guideline for effective crisis communication. The spread of anthrax was undoubtedly a very unique and terrifying situation for the U.S. public (Hobbs, Kittler, Volk, Kreps, & Bates, 2004). Effective public relations efforts should have registered this issue as being highly equivocal. There were few precedents for this situation, and due to this equivocality there were minimal preset rules for governing effective public response. The principle of requisite variety suggests that in a high-equivocality situation like this, there should be concerted efforts to gather relevant information though the use of communication cycles, to clearly make sense of the problem (enactment) and to develop appropriate strategies for responding to the problem (selection). Unfortunately, this was not the way this crisis was handled. Secretary Thompson made public statements before gathering full and accurate information about anthrax. He also limited the input from leading experts on the situation. Thompson responded as though this was a low-equivocality situation and violated the principle of requisite variety. Luckily, a lot was learned about responding to bioterrorist threats based on the anthrax situation, and the CDC have developed elaborate information gathering and analysis systems for generating effective communication responses that follow the principle of requisite variety for guiding future crisis communication situations like this (retention) (Kreps et al., 2005a).

QUESTIONS FOR APPLICATION

1. Describe how Weick's model of organizing can inform public relations practices. Specifically, note how a professional's knowledge of communication during times of equivocality is key during a crisis.

2. How should the information equivocality of organizational issues influence public relations activities? How does information resolve equivocality?

3. What does the principle of requisite variety suggest about the kinds of communication activities that public relations professionals should engage in when responding to organizational issues with different levels of equivocality?

4. Describe the kinds of communication cycles that public relations professionals might engage in to reduce the equivocality of complex organizational situations.

5. How can public relations professionals develop appropriate rules for directing responses to future public relations demands in organizational life? Relate this question to the anthrax case.

6. Why is retention of organizational intelligence critically important for public relations professionals? How can organizational intelligence be gathered for future reference?

7. Identify several communication strategies for effectively retaining and utilizing organizational intelligence in public relations. Relate these strategies to stakeholders who are critical to the survival of an organization.

REFERENCES

Kittler, A., Hobbs, J., Volk, L., Kreps, G. L., and Bates, D. (2004). The Internet as a vehicle to communicate health information during a public health emergency: A survey analysis involving the anthrax scare of 2001. *Journal of Medical Internet Research, 6*(1), e8. www.jmir.org/ 2004/1/e8.

Kreps, G. L. (1989). Reflexivity and internal public relations: The role of information in directing organizational development. In C. Botan & V. Hazleton (Eds.), *Public relations theory* (pp. 265–279). Hillsdale, NJ: Lawrence Erlbaum.

——. (1990). *Organizational communication: Theory and practice* (2nd ed.). White Plains, NY: Longman.

Kreps, G. L., Alibek, K., Bailey, C., Neuhauser, L., Rowan, K., and Sparks, L. (2005a). The critical role of communication to prepare for biological threats: Prevention, mobilization, and response. In H. D. O'Hair, R. L. Heath, & G. R. Ledlow (Eds.), *Community preparedness and response to terrorism. Vol. 3: Communication and the media* (pp. 191–210). Westport, CT: Praeger.

——. (2005b). Emergency/risk communication to promote public health and respond to biological threats. In M. Haider (Ed.), *Public health communications utility, values, and challenges* (pp. 349–362). Sudbury, MA: Jones & Bartlett.

Weick, K. E. (1969). The social psychology of organizing. Reading, MA: Addison-Wesley.

——. (1979). The social psychology of organizing (2nd edition). Reading, MA: Addison-Wesley.

CHAPTER THREE

STRATEGIC ISSUES MANAGEMENT

Theoretical Underpinnings for Strategic Planning and Operations in the Public Policy Arena

ROBERT L. HEATH

The theory and practical application of strategic issues management (SIM) poses some substantial issues for practitioners and academics. However old this approach to organizational success has been in practice may well be a matter of contention, but the origin of its name as such is not. Issues management—or as some prefer, issue management—got its name in the 1970s at a time when corporate practitioners and those senior practitioners in high-profile agencies were struggling to recraft the discipline to address an era of hostility. The end of the Great Depression and the victory of World War II left American industry at a high point of public popularity and support. Measures of corporate leadership were high, both for effectiveness and ethics, as the 1960s started. But this age of deference was soon to end. The national poll data on corporate honesty and ethics would plummet. From a time when most people believed that corporate leaders were honest and ethical, the era would dawn when only 16 to 20 percent of the respondents would so believe.

The anti-Vietnam War sentiment coupled with the civil rights movement to spawn an era where every institution was scrutinized and most were found wanting. Under pressure from all sides, the corporate public relations leadership crafted the term public affairs and helped found the Public Affairs Council. Other leadership, especially the work of W. Howard Chase (1984), led to the issue(s) management process. Because Chase's book was published more than twenty years ago, as a hallmark of the issues management movement, this chapter is somewhat of a retrospective. To that end, the chapter first addresses the question of whether issues management is something unique in the practice of public relations or merely public relations. The chapter then progresses to discuss the dominant theoretical underpinnings that support its theory and practice. From that foundation, attention will focus on the four major functions that seem to give its uniqueness. Finally, observations will help readers see how to apply this theory. Throughout this chapter, emphasis will be given to the management part of the term.

Management can be interpreted as manipulation. In the context of issues management, this balance is important. Management entails choices that make or are selected to make organizations effective given near-term and long-term circumstances. After some initial false starts, issues management under CEO-level leadership began to feature the centrality of management and strategic business planning (regardless of whether the organization is a company, nonprofit, or government agency). Only the naive practitioner or overly ambitious critic ever believed that advocates of issues management believed that issues could be "managed" to the eternal preference of the sponsor of this organizational function. Most senior practitioners know that issues are multifaceted and that the playing field consists of multiple publics (stakeholders and stakeseekers) who compete to influence the direction and outcome of issues. One reality is that issues management must be part of strategic business planning. Issues management practitioners and experts such as Sawaya and Arrington (1988) argued that issues emerge and take many directions. For this reason, managements must consider issue implications, trajectories, and challenges when looking for opportunity and threat. The authors made the point that issues can often offer opportunity and should not be seen as necessarily threatening. For this reason, issues management was often seen by such experts as a way of thinking as well as a way of acting.

UNIQUENESS: OLD HAT OR A NEW BALL GAME?

Perhaps the best way to understand issues management theory results from a review of how it came about and the debate that occurred to create and refine the discipline. The debate ultimately reshaped the practice and influenced the research to increase the contribution of public relations. How should issues management be defined? What is it? Is it something new? Is it old hat—just another name for how public relations is and should be practiced?

One way to answer that question is to look at the history of public relations. Heath (1997) has argued that issues management as practice, but not by name, is at least as old as the industrial revolution—the era when the large corporation was fighting to dominate the business paradigm. This was the era, as it has been called, of the robber baron, the entrepreneur who worked to dominate a market and key elements of the economy and sociopolitical arena to his benefit. This section will consider whether issues management is something that was new to the practice of public relations in the 1970s and 1980s. Along the way, we will discuss whether issues management is the big picture and public relations is a part of it, or whether issues management is a subfunction or approach to public relations.

A point worth making in preparation for this discussion is that an active engagement in the public policy arena in support of business activities was certainly an important ingredient of the late nineteenth and early twentieth centuries in the

United States. As industry grew—often filled with buyouts and hostile takeovers—it needed a favorable public policy environment. One of the key issues was the creation of the trust as a business entity, an amalgamation of small businesses in an industry into one "business." Oil, steel, and tobacco are three industries that used this business model. Railroads were big and getting bigger by similar tactics. So it was not a stretch when U.S. congressmen proposed antitrust legislation and interstate commerce regulations. Battles also occurred within industries. None is more iconic than the battle of the currents, which pitted Thomas Edison against George Westinghouse over the issue of whether direct current or alternating current would be the standard of the electricity industry. Industries—telegraph, telephone, water, gas, and electricity—sought to organize as regulated monopolies. So public policy defined business as business defined industry and public policy. And activism was rampant and successful in this era.

Over the decades leading to the formal creation of issues management, practitioners engaged in this function. Cutlip's *The Unseen Power* (1994) focuses substantial attention on many practitioners whose work included much of what came to be the practice of issues management. The pioneers in public relations frequently engaged in counseling and communication to help clients and employers solve relationship problems between the business plan and the public policy climate of the time. These practitioners were willing and able advocates of cases on behalf of their clients. Some truly aspired to seek a mutual balance between public and private interests.

In every aspect of issues management, John W. Hill, principal founder of Hill and Knowlton, was a practitioner of issues management in the most complete sense. (See Heath & Bowen, 2002, for an extensive discussion of this topic.) Hill (1958, 1963) knew that no industry could long thrive, and perhaps could not survive, if its strategic business plan was not in harmony with the public opinion, public interest, public policy arena. Companies operated, he knew and counseled, at the will of the public. They must be in harmony with the public. If there is disharmony, then either the company (industry) must change or the public policy arena must be changed. The latter is hard to accomplish, Hill knew—and counseled. He therefore was attentive to the quality of each client's standards of corporate responsibility. In that sense, he was convinced that a company must have a good reputation, one that is honest and deserved. He scrupulously monitored issues. He often created libraries of issue-related materials and constantly engaged in research for his clients to see how the vagaries of issue development were offering threats or opportunities.

To properly position the client organization to be in harmony with its public policy environment, Hill (1958) recognized that:

> The corporate balance sheet is nowadays affected not only by conditions within the business—but also by the rules and regulations of government bureaus, the probings and acts of Congress, and the strategy of powerful labor unions. And, looking over the shoulders of management in its every important move, is Public Opinion. (p. viii)

Building from this philosophy, Hill (1958) recognized that public relations (as is issues management) is a function and an outcome. For this reason, it is a way of thinking and acting as guided by skilled professionals: "when a management decides to guard, improve, or develop this asset [public goodwill], 'public relations' becomes the label for *a function*. Here the term that took a plural verb becomes singular, so that now we say: 'Public relations is a function of top management in every well-managed corporation' " (p. 4). Viewed this way, issues management or corporate-level public relations is not merely a communication function. In fact, communication may not be the tool to use to deal effectively with an issue. As Sethi (1977) later observed, the strain between the company and its stakeholders may result from or produce a legitimacy gap. This gap can at times be closed through communication, but other strategies may be needed, most particularly a strategic business plan that is founded on better standards of corporate responsibility.

Conventional wisdom establishes the origins of issue(s) management with the ideas of James O'Toole and Chase. O'Toole (1975a, 1975b) recommended advocacy advertising to counterbalance challenges against corporate policy and actions by critical reporters and activists. Activism had grown considerably by the mid-1970s. One harbinger for the interest in issues management was the innovative use of op-eds by Mobil Oil Company to counter what it believed to be unfair and uninformed criticism of big business in general and the oil industry in particular (Schmertz, 1986). Eventually a laundry list of terms would be coined to capture the communication response to activism challenges.

Chase (1976, 1977, 1984) is usually credited with the development of issues management as a discipline. Along with Jones and Chase (1979) put the concept of managing issues into the public relations vocabulary. Chase (1982), speaking as the chairperson of the Issue Management Association, proposed a definition:

> Issues management is the capacity to understand, mobilize, coordinate, and direct all strategic and policy planning functions, and all public affairs/public relations skills, toward achievement of one objective: meaningful participation in creation of public policy that affects personal and institutional destiny. (p. 1)

Although limited in his sense of what the discipline would achieve, Chase added to its foundation.

Even though Chase can be credited as the founder of the issues management movement, this title could also be claimed by James K. Brown (1979), who conducted a research project for the Conference Board's Public Affairs Research Council. This study matured into what may have been the first comprehensive statement on issues management by that name. The principles of issues management Brown stressed in 1979 were current in the thinking of others, such as Raymond Ewing (1979, 1980, 1982). According to these experts, issues management is more than communication. It is a fully articulated program of situational analysis, strategic planning, and savvy responses based on efforts of the organization to achieve higher standards of corporate responsibility that reduce the rationale and motivation for external and internal critics.

This brief review leads to a telling question. Is issues management merely public relations revisited (Ehling & Hesse, 1983; Fox, 1983)? Is it a subfunction of public relations (Public Relations Society of America, 1987), or a program that companies use to improve their involvement in the public policy process (Public Affairs Council, 1978)?

Public relations entails publicity and promotion. Although issues may require responding to unfavorable publicity and publicizing certain facts, it is naive to assume that issues management requires nothing more than gaining favorable publicity. In that regard, efforts to engineer public opinion and consent (Bernays, 1955) are likely to fail because they are founded on a false understanding of the origin of issues and the reasons why they stay alive. If the part of public relations that goes well beyond publicity and promotion includes the correct assumptions, then Ehling and Hesse (1983) are potentially correct, but often such is not the case. Note also that Ehling and Hesse published their article before the best, most current thinking was published on the subject.

J. E. Grunig (1992) adopted the view of issues management that it is coupled with addressing emerging and effective communication. His view featured the role of strategic business planning and management: "Organizations use strategic management to define and shape their missions, but they do so through an iterative process of interacting with their environments" (p. 12). How is this done? "Organizations use the process of *issues management* to anticipate issues and resolve conflict before the public make it an issue. Organizations that wait for issues to occur before managing their communication with strategic publics usually have crises on their hands and have to resort to short-term *crisis communication*" (p. 13). We can assume, Grunig wrote, that public relations practitioners counsel and otherwise assist clients or employers in the following way: "Strategic public relations, then, begins when communication practitioners identify potential problems in the relationship with the organizations' stakeholders and define the categories of stakeholders that are affected by the problem" (p. 13). In this paradigm, issues management entails strategic management, early detection of problems in relationships, and communication, especially that of applying the skills and processes of conflict resolution.

In this way, public relations can be practiced using issues management strategies. If issues management is viewed as encompassing public relations, then public relations approaches issues, stakes, stakeholders, stakeseekers, and communication with a constructive, proactive problem-solving orientation. It brings the reality of external strains and opportunities to bear on internal planning. It is planning, including public relations planning.

However defined, the motive behind the innovation of issues management was to get planners and monitors engaged in the response options of an organization as early as possible. In 1979, *Business Week* reported on the fledgling trend by some companies to use environmental scanning to improve strategic business plans and to alert line managers to changes in public sentiments regarding operating procedures ("Capitalizing," 1979). An early effort to identify the key functions of issues management reasoned that it involved three activities: "issue identification, corporate proaction, and the inclusion of public affairs issues in established decision-making processes and managerial functions" (Fleming, 1980, p. 35). Business professors such as Fleming led this innovation while communication specialists and scholars joined later. Business faculty, in particular Post (1978, 1979) and Buchholz (1982a, 1982b, 1985), produced seminal studies to expose the need for companies to recognize the important role public policy plays in planning efforts and operations.

A milestone in this reasoning was the publication of *Issues Management and Strategic Planning* by W. L. Renfro (1993), a pioneer in the theory and practice of issues management. His work centers on the factors that predict how issues emerge and become worth consideration. He stresses the need to identify and monitor issues as preliminary to strategic planning. "The field of issues management emerged as public relations or public affairs officers included more and more forecasting and futures research in their planning and analysis of policy" (p. 23). In this sense, "issues management is an intelligence function that does not get involved in the 'operations side' unless specifically directed to do so" (p. 89).

Based on a 1990 literature review, Heath and Cousino (1990) concluded that issues management required the integrated and ethical application of four strategic functions: strategic business planning based on understanding public policy threats and opportunities; high standards of corporate responsibility; issues monitoring; and issues communication. Heath and Cousino noticed that management professors and executives were prone to think of issues management more in terms of corporate responsibility and effective, sensitive strategic planning than they were to feature communication strategies. And public relations scholars were more likely to feature communication as futurists were more likely to stress the role of issue monitoring and early response to emerging issues. Thus, one can argue that all four elements are essential for issues management.

UNDERPINNINGS OF ISSUES MANAGEMENT

Without doubt, one of the requirements of issues management—and one of its contributions to the effectiveness of an organization—is to make the organization more aware of its relationships with its publics and markets and more sensitive to whether its relationships with them are relatively free of strains and problems. With a new era of interest in public relations as relationship management, however, we should not be lured to believe that issues management is narrowly interested in the quality of relationships. Its focus is on issues that may foster or strain relationships.

The best continuing definition of an issue taps the rhetorical tradition. There we find a legacy of defining issues as contestable matters of fact, value, and policy. Framed this way, an issue—the different views that lead to parties's contesting, conflicting, or competing points of view—can result from problems that one or more parties see. The nature of these problems is a difference between what people believe to be true or best and what they see in operation. For instance, global warming is one of the major controversies dividing environmental groups, scientists, policymakers, and large oil and gas companies. Are the various gases produced in the combustion or other uses of hydrocarbons leading to increasingly elevated temperatures in all parts of the world? The contest of facts takes many forms—what is fact, which facts are relevant to the contest, and what are the most accurate interpretations of these facts. Thus, the controversy centers on the contest of fact.

This example probably does not divide on values, but oil companies and environmentalists have had substantial conflicts over value. Perhaps one of the more dramatic was the conflict between the Shell Oil Company and Greenpeace over the disposal of the oil tanker buoy named the Brent Spar. The sound science and due diligence studies funded by Shell brought together many of the leading scientists, engineering firms, and governmental regulators in the North Sea area. The conclusion was to scuttle the Brent Spar in the area where the oil had been extracted. The sediment in the buoy, so the scientists reasoned, would dissipate in quantities that would not be unfriendly to the wildlife that was native to that region. Conflict over facts divided Greenpeace and Shell and its associates. But the big conflict centered on a value premise that eventually affected the policy that was adopted. Greenpeace argued that, regardless of the soundness of the decision in scientific terms, it could not agree with the value premise of disposing materials by scuttling them. It argued emphatically that the ocean must not become a garbage dump or cesspool—a value position that has obvious policy implications. Issues of policy focus on difference of what should be done. In this case, the policy is not to scuttle the buoy but to remove and remediate the residues in the storage tank and to use the tank for some other purpose.

As will be seen in the next section, the trajectory of issues has implications for an organization's business plan, mission, vision, and strategic management. It has implications for the organization's standards of corporate responsibility. The wise organization strives to use all of its monitoring resources—well beyond those that public relations people can provide—to be vigilant of the emergence and evolution of issues that pose threats and opportunities for the organization. This latter point is vital to an understanding of issues management. At times issues do pose threats, but they also offer opportunities.

Issues management assumes that competing interests offer through their communication various platforms of fact, value, and policy. These platforms are sensitive to the nature of each issue and the preferred understanding, evaluations, and recommendations of the various interests. To exert influence, parties hold stakes as constraints and rewards. They seek stakes that other parties hold. For this reason, issues management can entail substantial differences of opinions, conflicts, competing interests, and power resource management.

Whereas the typical views of issues management may see businesses pitted against activist critics, this approach is narrow. Companies within an industry may be at odds with one another—intraindustry controversies. Companies in one industry may be at odds with those in another industry. For example, car insurance companies and automobile manufacturers may disagree over who should bear the cost of car safety—insurers or manufacturers. Companies may ally with activists against government agencies. Government agencies may ally with business against activists. Activists and government agencies may be allies in various controversies. The elegance of issues management is the variation of competing interests and points of view that work themselves out, in the best case, to the advantage of the public interest.

Because of these dynamics, issues management theory rests on the general principles of systems theory. This entire body of literature is too vast to review here, but it is safe to say that systems cannot long be at odds with other systems and closed to their influence. Interdependence, openness, and balance are three of the major features of systems. They lead to various predictions over how various systems are best at adapting to one another. All these variations have implications for the dynamics of issues management.

The rhetorical tradition grew out of the contest of ideas. If there were agreement, there would be no need for rhetoric. In the simplest, and perhaps the best, view of rhetoric, the dialogues of society consist of statement and counterstatement. Voices, individual and corporate, compete to demonstrate the soundness of their cases as the issues that are given voice are put into the public policy arena where they can best be resolved. This tradition is the essence of democracy. That democracy plays itself out in news stories that feature both or the many sides of a controversy. It is operating in talk-show debates, public hearings, legislative sessions, position papers, web sites, and myriad other contexts. Perhaps no one ever captured the essence and dynamics of the process better than did Kenneth Burke (1969a), who viewed society as a marketplace of competing ideas: "the Scramble, the Wrangle of the Marketplace, the flurries and flare-ups of the Human Barnyard, Give and Take, the wavering line of pressure and counter pressure, the Logomachy, the onus of ownership, the War of Nerves, the War" (p. 23).

This battle includes the use of courtship, through which the competing perspectives invite others to join them—to identify themselves with the views of the advocates (Burke, 1969b). This bridging and connecting can account for how publics form, change, dissipate, and reform. All of society, in this sense, looks to the evolution and change of ideas, as perspectives, by which circumstances are known and judged, and policies formed.

Social exchange is a third body of literature that supports issues management. It largely reflects thinkers from interpersonal communication who realize that relationships require normatively shaped positive behavior. When organizations violate the norms of key publics, those publics work to sanction the organizations to force them to no longer be in violation. Harmony is a goal. How it is created depends on the competing and cooperating dynamics among the various stakeholders. Crucial to this way of explaining the dynamics of change as association is the principle of rewards and costs, support and opposition, creation and dissolution of relationship. What drives these relationship dynamics is the occurrence of problems, the differences of opinions, and the awkward readjustment of various entities to one another.

The theory of issue management sees a subtle but powerful nexus among issues, crisis, and risk. As stated above, an issue is a contestable matter of fact, value, or policy. A crisis is the occurrence of an event that is predictable in nature, but not in time, that can threaten the organization because it can harm its relationships with its publics and markets. A crisis can be an event that strains the organization or it can be the slow progression of an issue that threatens it.

Crisis occurs when a negative risk manifests itself. A risk is a positive or negative outcome that can be managed—in occurrence, magnitude, and people who bear the consequence of the risk. One, in this sense, can argue that risk management is the rationale for societies. Societies organize and manage themselves for the collective management of risk.

Based on this logic, we have many permutations. An issue can become a crisis (e.g., the asbestos issue has put many individuals, businesses, and government agencies into a crisis mode). A crisis, such as the release of methyl isocynate (MIC) at Union Carbide's plant in Bhopal, India, became an issue that led to community right-to-know legislation. A risk that is poorly managed can become a crisis—as is the AIDS epidemic in Africa. Efforts to manage a risk—such as global warming—pose many issues. This line of analysis is especially powerful for connecting the dots to create a whole picture of the ways that issues management, crisis management, and risk management are not separate but interconnected disciplines. That logic is really made more compelling by the current interest in strategic management that is predicated on risk management.

Seen this way, issues management in its wholeness is probably more than what is typically viewed as the essence of the public relations discipline. Issues management is something organizations do, whether they do it well or not. By the same token, organizations have public relations—relations with publics—whether they do it well or poorly. But a solid issues management program is a way of thinking and operating that entails all the people of an organization. Public relations is only part of the issues management efforts of each organization. This view of public relations, however, is not taken to diminish the importance of public relations or its centrality in the issues management program. In fact, one can easily argue that any issues management program that is not based on sound public relations principles is bound to fail, or at least be less effective.

FOUR LEGS OF THE ISSUES MANAGEMENT STOOL

Based on the ideas explored above, four key functions seem to be essential for a fully developed and well-implemented issues management program. Such a program is not only a way of thinking and acting; it demands all the key disciplines of any organization to work together in a matrix. Issues management at its best is not something added on to an organization to reduce its friction or massage its image or reputation. Its goal is not reputation and relationship enhancement. Those factors are important, but more vital is the need for issues management to permeate the organization's culture. It is a way to make the organization smarter, more savvy in how it deals with itself and the world in which it operates. And, most important, issues management is more—much more—than getting positive press for an organization when it is engaged in an issue debate.

The centerpiece for issues management, the first pillar, is to integrate the process of issues management into every aspect of an organization's strategic planning and management. Its mission and vision are designed to help the orga-nization know where it is going and what its identity will be in its marketplace and in its public policy arena. Every kind of organization (business, nonprofit, and government agency) engages in strategic business planning. In essence, strategic business planning asks simple questions: How should money be generated and budgeted, and how should systems in the organization be designed and managed to maximize the organization's effectiveness? To answer those questions, issues management brings lots of insights and counsel to the management table. It guides as it keeps the organization alert to its environment—to look for threats and opportunities.

The second key element in the issues management arsenal is issue monitoring. An organization can plan and consider its choices only when it understands those choices, which are always influenced by trends that occur in the world around it. Monitoring entails issue scanning, identification, analysis, prioritization, and tracking. Some issues management promoters have tended to feature it as a monitoring, futurist discipline looking for issues as they emerge. Narrowly defined, many strategic issues management (SIM) programs failed or had to change. Merely seeing trends and observing issues is not enough. Those insights need to be integrated into strategic business planning, to avoid threats and take advantage of opportunities. Also, many issues have emerged. They are like the family dog, always underfoot. So, interest in emerging issues may not be as important as is the tracking of their trajectory: What's happening? What does that mean for the organization's future?

Part of what an issue means for an organization is its impact on the current standards of corporate responsibility, the third pillar. There are universal standards of corporate responsibility. For instance, will we ever not believe that an organization needs to be honest, truthful, and candid in its communication? However, many standards change over time. If we demand that an organization seek and implement the highest standards of environmental responsibility, we must acknowledge that those standards evolve and change. For this reason, issues monitoring can aid the organization's definition of corporate responsibility and determine how well it is satisfying its stakeholders' and stakeseekers' expectations in that regard. Is it a good organization? Does it meet or exceed the standards expected by key publics?

If being good is essential as a first step, then we are prone to say that the next step, or the fourth pillar, is to be an effective communicator. Here is where some practitioners stop in their issue communication. They merely focus on strategies and tactics selected and designed to achieve favorable publicity. Such efforts are not trivial or unimportant, but they are not enough to serve the needs of society in an issue debate. If issues are contestable matters of fact, value, and policy, the organization must be prepared to engage in this kind of dialogue. To do so also brings the reality that the organization may be wrong. Facts are facts as long as they cannot be disproved. Values are debatable as standards of operation. Policies are contested to determine which one best serves society.

Many types of communication and venues make up the dialogue (see Heath, 1997, p. 231, for a list of issue communication vehicles). As much as some public relations scholars do not like the concept of advocacy, it is a reality. It is even an expectation. Often, especially in a world where in the dialogue organizations have displaced individuals as such, each side of a controversy engages in advocacy. It asserts its point of view and is expected to support the wisdom of that view. One can argue that if organizations are stewards of the public interest, part of their stewardship is to be prepared to effectively and responsibly engage in debates where they have expertise that is useful to society. The best test of this observation is the continuing line of ruling by the U.S. Supreme Court. The Court has in many rulings believed that society needs responsible and accurate communication by companies. Restrictions tend to occur when the communication is narrow, self-interested, and capable of dominating the dialogue because of deep pockets.

These four pillars are needed for a fully developed issues management program. Having said that, we can consider how to apply this theory in practice.

APPLICATIONS

SIM is complex and detailed in its implication. However, some principles can be posed to suggest the kinds of applications that grow from the theory discussed above. To make the applications seem more systematic, they will be featured in association with each of the pillars (strategic business planning, issue monitoring, corporate responsibility, issue communication) of a fully developed issues management program.

Strategic Business Planning Through Integration

The purpose or rationale for issues management is to make the organization more effective by working to foster a favorable rather than hostile public policy arena.

■ Integrate all the vigilance of issue monitoring, grooming of standards of corporate responsibility, and the stewardship of issues communication into every aspect of strategic business planning.

■ Watch for trends that pose threats and opportunities.

■ Recognize that the debate over issues will affect the business plan. Accept this reality; know that no organization can dominate that conversation; and prefer a proactive involvement with issues.

■ Realize that interests and issues are inseparable; know that the organization's interests in its planning process must be legitimate in the minds of its stakeholders and stakeseekers.

Issue Monitoring

Issues monitoring is a process by which the organization stays vigilant to the subtle as well as dramatic shifts in issues because of the efforts of a dynamic system of interested parties.

■ **Scan:** Realize that issues often have been at work for a long time before they emerge into the popular press. Know that a matrix of specialists inside and outside of the organization will be needed to spot issues and bring them into the monitoring process. Make issue scanners of people who do not know that it is part of their responsibility. Create a process by which scanning can be orderly and not overwhelming. Don't isolate the organization, but open it to the outside world.

■ **Identify:** Know what issues are, know how they have life, and know the players who keep issues alive. Recognize each issue for its type. See that it is something being contested.

■ **Analyze:** Understand the issue, the rationale for the positions various voices take, and the implications for the strategic business plan. Use analysis as a part of developing or refining standards of corporate responsibility and various plans: business, public policy, and communication.

■ **Prioritize:** Often an organization finds many issues. Some will take on trajectories driven by forces too daunting for any organization to engage seriously. Choose the issues that pose the greatest threats and opportunities, a guideline that is often easier said than done.

■ **Tracking:** Once relevant and potentially relevant issues have been identified, they must also be followed. Issue development and organizational responses are important.

Corporate Responsibility

■ Constantly reevaluate the standards by which the organization should be operating. Know that expectations change. Realize that, because organizations find themselves in the company of multiple publics, the standards of responsibility can not satisfy everyone. Which standards are essential and what is the most responsible way to conduct the organization's activities to balance its interests and the public interest?

■ Recognize the high-potential and high-impact values and give them attention.

■ Realize that internal operating and management systems must reflect the organization's standards of corporate responsibility. These have more impact when they are integrated seriously into review procedures for personnel and departments.

Issue Communication

■ Understand the dialogue, who is saying what to whom and with what effect.

■ Engage where the dialogue can profit most by the organization's sense of fact, value, or policy, depending on the type of issue at foot.

■ Create multidimensional communication programs that take advantage of a wide array of vehicles. Know who is using these vehicles. See the communication process as something than cannot be controlled but will benefit if the organization participates.

■ Foster communication infrastructures that enhance the quality of the dialogue; don't deny opponents access to those infrastructures.

■ The web may be the most important issue communication vehicle of the future. It allows opportunity—twenty-four hours a day, seven days a week—for interested parties to see the facts, values, and policy positions advocated by the organization. Commit to being the first and best source of information on all matters relevant to the organization.

CONCLUSION

Issues management is a program and a way of thinking as a foundation for a way of acting. As it has matured, its proponents have seen it as adding to the practice of public relations by demonstrating the role that practitioners can play in effectively positioning organizations in their public policy arenas. For whatever kind of organization, a fully developed SIM program begins with focus on assisting in the development and management of the organization's business plan. That plan is made effective by the organization's public policy and communication plans.

The organization must strive for high standards of corporate responsibility to reduce the sense that its policies and activities create a legitimacy gap with the stakeholders and stakeseekers. The organization must not take itself for granted. Its concern for corporate responsibility must be kept alive, in part with issue monitoring. Issue monitoring allows the organization to scout the terrain where it operates, looking for threats and opportunities. The issue communication plan needs to address issues of fact, value, and policy where the organization believes it can add to the quality of the dialogue in the public interest.

CASE: THE WTO AND G8

Globalization of economies is not a new trend, but various interests are wrestling with the challenges of creating a global marketplace that reflects the values and marketplace dynamics of this era. That marketplace consists of products, impact of operations, and work issues. In various ways, the World Trade Organization (WTO) has been formed and meets with the purpose of working out as many details by agreement as possible. The WTO was added to economic summits of government leaders now called the Group of Eight (G8).

Critics of the WTO and G8 come from all aspects of society and the economy. The range of critics is dramatic, from ecoterrorists and anarchists on one end of the spectrum to well-established institutionalized labor unions. For this case, it is interesting to look not at the SIM efforts of the WTO, but to look at those of some activists who offer a counterstatement to WTO statements. One reason that this view is interesting is that many who think about issues management see it as a program only for the establishment, and not for those who critique the establishment.

The current statements and corporate responsibility standards adopted by the critics reflect the realities of the dialogue that has existed before. At times, the protests have become violent and destructive. In the face of such protests, WTO meeting organizers have created barriers to limit and control the contact of the protesters with citizens, media, police, and WTO members.

During the summer of 2004, as the protesters geared up to express reservations against globalization at the G8 conference to be held in Georgia, they adopted a new standard of corporate responsibility and new communication tactics. Carrns and Harris (2004), writing for the *Wall Street Journal*, described some of the new tactics.

The protesters began a campaign to reduce friction with local police and even foster cordial relations. They held a potluck supper with the invitation to "meet the protesters." They held the event in the fellowship hall of a local church. The meal consisted of spaghetti, sweet tea, and banana pudding. They fostered dialogue in a cordial and quiet manner. One of the tactics was to engage a local county commissioner to play a version of trivial pursuit. One of the questions asked how many windows had been broken during the 2002 G8 meeting in Canada? (Answer: zero.)

Knowing the history of violence at other conferences, this group of organizations adopted new standards of corporate responsibility and communication tactics that were more likely to invite and encourage their participation in the dialogue rather than lead to their marginalization as crazy activists. The Southeast Anarchist Network encouraged members to avoid violence and to demonstrate their values and those of globalization by repairing homes of poor people. This demonstration could still make the point that global economies must provide jobs and prosperity for people and not harm their interests. Such efforts could also dramatize the differences between ordinary people's living conditions and the multimillion-dollar cottages on the island where the conference would be held.

In these ways, the activists recognized the stewardship of first becoming *good* as the first step toward being effective communicators. This 2004 conference would be one moment in a long debate. In that debate, some of the protesters recognized the need for new standards of corporate responsibility to increase the potential impact of what they say. Their business plan has developed to continue their protests.

QUESTIONS FOR APPLICATION

1. At its best, public relations, as part of issues management, can help society to function more soundly. In what ways can it do this?

2. Reflect on how a SIM perspective can influence organizational communication activities and functions in the ways listed below. Come up with concrete examples of these from contemporary organizational functioning.
   - Help make strategic business planning and operations more in harmony with the interests of internal and external publics.
   - Strengthen relationships needed for mutual success and minimal crisis.
   - Keep organizations in tune with emerging and changing issues.
   - Raise the organization's understanding and compliance with prevailing standards of corporate responsibility.
   - Augment systemic analysis and adjustment.
   - Work with others for the social construction of reality through rhetoric.
   - Foster dialogue instead of monologue.

3. Explain the following: "This view of issues management features a holistic perspective that the smart organization believes, knows, and lives issues management. It is a process, and a way of thinking smart." How did this idea take shape in the WTO and G8 case?

REFERENCES

Bernays, E. L. (1955). The engineering of consent. Norman, OK: University of Oklahoma Press.

Brown, J. K. (1979). *The business of issues: Coping with the company's environments.* New York: Conference Board.

Buchholz, R. A. (1982a). *Business environment and public policy: Implications for management.* Englewood Cliffs, NJ: Prentice-Hall.

———. (1982b). Education for public issues management: Key insights from a survey of top practitioners. *Public Affairs Review, 3,* 65–76.

———. (1985). *The essentials of public policy for management*. Englewood Cliffs, NJ: Prentice-Hall.

Burke, K. (1969a). *A grammar of motives*. Berkeley: University of California Press.

———. (1969b). *A rhetoric of motives*. Berkeley: University of California Press.

Capitalizing on social change. (1979, October 29). *Business Week*, 105–106.

Carrns, A., & Harris, N. (2004, June 2). As Georgia gears up for G-8, protesters gear down rhetoric. *Wall Street Journal*, pp. A1, A2.

Chase, W. H. (1976). Organizing for our new responsibility. *Public Relations Journal, 32*(5), 14–15.

———. (1977). Public issue management: The new science. *Public Relations Journal, 32*(10), 25–26.

———. (1982, December 1). Issue management conference—a special report. *Corporate Public Issues and Their Management, 7*, 1–2.

———. (1984). *Issue management: Origins of the future*. Stamford, CT: Issue Action Publications.

Cutlip, S. M. (1994). *The unseen power: Public relations. A history*. Hillsdale, NJ: Lawrence Erlbaum.

Ehling, W. P., & Hesse, M. B. (1983). Use of "issue management" in public relations. *Public Relations Review, 9*(2), 18–35.

Ewing, R. P. (1979). The uses of futurist techniques in issues management. *Public Relations Quarterly, 24*(1), 15–18.

———. (1980). Evaluating issues management. *Public Relations Journal, 36*(6), 14–16.

———. (1982). Advocacy advertising: The voice of business in public policy debate. *Public Affairs Review, 3*, 23–29.

Fleming, J. E. (1980). Linking public affairs with corporate planning. *California Management Review, 23*(2), 35–43.

Fox, J. F. (1983). Communicating on issues: The CEO's changing role. *Public Relations Review, 9*(11), 11–23.

Grunig, J. E. (1992). Communication, public relations, and effective organizations: An overview of the book. In J. E. Grunig (Ed.), *Excellence in public relations and communication management* (pp. 1–28). Hillsdale, NJ: Lawrence Erlbaum.

Heath, R. L. (1997). *Strategic issues management: Organizations and public policy challenges*. Thousand Oaks, CA: Sage.

Heath, R. L., & Bowen, S. (2002). The public relations philosophy of John W. Hill: Bricks in the foundation of issues management. *Journal of Public Affairs, 2*(4), 230–246.

Heath, R. L., & Cousino, K. R. (1990). Issues management: End of first decade progress report. *Public Relations Review, 17*(1), 6–18.

Hill, J. W. (1958). *Corporate public relations: Arm of modern management*. New York: Harper & Brothers.

———. (1963). *The making of a public relations man*. New York: David McKay Company.

Jones, B. L., & Chase, W. H. (1979). Managing public issues. *Public Relations Review, 5*(2), 3–23.

Post, J. E. (1978). *Corporate behavior and social change*. Reston, VA: Reston Publishing.

———. (1979). Corporate response models and public affairs management. *Public Relations Quarterly, 24*(4), 27–32.

Public Affairs Council (1978). *The fundamentals of issue management*. Washington, DC: Public Affairs Council.

Public Relations Society of America. (1987). Report of special committee on terminology. *International Public Relations Review, 11*(2), 6–11.

O'Toole, J. E. (1975a). Advocacy advertising act II. *Cross Currents in Corporate Communications, 2*, 33–37.

———. (1975b). Advocacy advertising shows the flag. *Public Relations Journal, 31*(11), 14–16.

Renfro, W. L. (1993). *Issues management in strategic planning*. Westport, CT: Quorum Books.

Sawaya, R. N., & Arrington, C. B. (1988). Linking corporate planning with strategic issues. In R. L. Heath (Ed.), *Strategic issues management: How organizations influence and respond to public interests and policies* (pp. 73–86). San Francisco: Jossey-Bass.

Schmertz, H. (1986). *Good-bye to the low profile: The art of creative confrontation*. Boston: Little, Brown.

Sethi, S. P. (1977). *Advocacy advertising and large corporations: Social conflict, big business image, the news media, and public policy*. Lexington, MA: D. C. Heath.

CHAPTER FOUR

ORGANIZATIONAL-PUBLIC RELATIONSHIPS IN CYBERSPACE

KIRK HALLAHAN

With the widespread adoption of online communication, practitioners must consider the benefits and challenges of using the Internet to develop relationships between client organizations and their key publics. This chapter reviews the emergence of online communications as well as research related to organizational-public relationships. It then examines the issues related to the deployment and measurement of online communication within the context of five generally accepted measures of relationship quality: commitment, control mutuality, communality, trustworthiness, and satisfaction. The chapter suggests that three other measures of relationship building online also are important: cognitive learning, affective responses, and resulting behaviors.

Online communication has emerged as a major avenue for organizations to communicate with key publics. At the same time, fostering positive organizational-public relationships has become a major focus for examining public relations. Although practitioners now enthusiastically embrace the Internet, comparatively little theory exists about how technology fits into an organization's efforts to influence people's behaviors and or how technology is used to foster mutually beneficial relationships.

ONLINE COMMUNICATION'S POTENTIAL

Internet technologies (web sites, e-mail, instant messaging, discussion groups, live chats, blogs, etc.) enable organizations to communicate with key publics twenty-four hours a day, seven days a week (Cooley, 1999; Hume, 2001; Lordan, 2001; Pavlik & Dozier, 1996; Springston, 2001; Wright, 1998, 2001). Today, one-third of all customer-to-business contacts are mediated through online technology (Cooper, 2001, p. 111).

In the mid-1990s, practitioners viewed online communication as a tool for research and for professional interchanges (Gaddis, 2001; Neff, 1998; Thomsen, 1996) as well as for publishing information (Seybold, 1996). With the subsequent widespread adoption of both e-mail and web sites, and the subsequent emergence of e-commerce, online's promotional and relationship-building potential was quickly recognized. High tech and dot-com companies, in particular, enthusiastically embraced new media (Hamel & Sampler, 1998; High tech PR, 2001; Major, 1995; Newell, 2000; Park & Berger, 2002; Weill, 2001).

Spataro (1998) coined the term *net relations* to describe the establishment and maintenance of online relationships by organizations. Reflecting the heightened interest in e-commerce, he described net relations as the intersection of traditional direct marketing, public relations, and the Internet. Phillips (2001) soon thereafter raised the critical question of whether and how the Internet in general, and web sites in particular, could change relationships.

Early research suggests that public relations professionals did not fully understand technology's potential and were slow in getting involved (Hill & White, 2000; Johnson, 1997; White & Ramen, 1989). Practitioners were cautious despite the Internet's potential to enhance their role in organizations (Porter & Sallot, 2003, 2005; Porter, Sallot, Cameron, & Shamp, 2001; Sallot, Porter, & Acosta-Alzuru, 2004). Yet the Internet's inherent facility for two-way communication spawned hope among public relation theorists. Commentators envisioned the Internet's potential to create more-balanced exchanges in discussions about issues (Heath, 1998); to develop a true sense of community (Badarocco, 1998); to equalize power relationships in society (Coombs, 1998); and to encourage democratic discussions (Hiebert, 2005).

Today, that potential is widely recognized ("Exploring the New Century's," 2000; Gregory, 2004; Killoran, 1999; Lordan, 2001; Springston, 2001). For example, a sizeable number of later studies analyzed the presence of relationship-building components in web sites (Aikat, 2000; Esrock & Leichty, 1998, 1999, 2000; Ho, 2001; Hoffman & Novak, 1996; Kent, 1998/1999; Kent & Taylor, 1998; Kent, Taylor, & White, 2002, 2003; Liu, Arnett, Capella, & Beatty, 1997; Maynard & Tan, 2004; O'Malley & Irani, 1998; Park & Berger, 2002; Peng, 2001; Perry & Bodkin, 2000; Tamini, Rajan, & Sebestanelli, 2000; Taylor, Kent, & White, 2001; Vattyan & Lubbers, 1999).

Other public relations researchers have considered the relationship-building potential of the Internet in the context of organizational culture and effectiveness (Murgolo-Poore, Pitt, Berthon, & Prendegast, 2003; Murgolo-Poore, Pitt, & Ewing, 2002; Tindal, 2003), crisis management (DiNardo, 2002; Hearit, 1999; Perry & Taylor, 2002; Taylor & Perry, 2005); media relations (Callison, 2003; Duke, 2002; Hachigian & Hallahan, 2003; Middleberg & Ross, 2002; Shin & Cameron, 2003); politics (Curtin & Gaither, 2004; Len-Rios, 2004); and advocacy by nonprofit groups (Kang & Norton, 2004; Naude, Froneman, & Atwood, 2004).

Public relations is not the only management discipline concerned with relationships or using technology to foster them. Cooper (2001) argues that organizations today are relational enterprises that deploy technology three ways: to promote collaboration and interaction; to administer back-room support functions;

and as analytical tools in research (Springston, 2001). In an increasing number of organizations, Internet communications are linked to relational databases that permit individualized information exchanges and transactions (Bejou, 1997; Copulsky & Wolf, 1990; CRM and the Internet, 2001; Petrison & Wang, 1993). Online thus operates in tandem with automated customer relationship management (CRM) systems (Cooper, 2001; "CRM and the Internet," 2001; Rosenberger, 2001) and related self-service technologies (SSTs) such as automated tellers, kiosks, and self check-in/check-out machines at airports and retail stores (Barnes, Dunne, & Glynn, 2000; "CRM and the Internet," 2001; Meuter, Ostrom, Roundtree, & Bitner, 2000; Prendergast & Marr, 1993).

Managers in functional units such as marketing, sales, operations, and human resources today emphasize relationship building in much the same way as public relations (Chaudbury, Mallick, & Rao, 2001; Copulsky & Wolf, 1990; Duncan & Moriarty, 1998; Frazer & McMillan, 1999; Geyskens, Gielsens, & Dekimpe, 2002; Gronross, 2000). In information technology, for example, Sisosdia and Wolfe (2000, pp. 526, 551) describe a shift away from information management to relationship management. For them, new media technologies can facilitate dialogue and serve as "an agent of surrogacy" to rekindle the type of individual relationships organizations had diligently cultivated in the past. As one information technology professional put it, "Information itself offers value only when presented in the context of relationships" (M. Schrage, quoted in Sisodia & Wolfe, 2000, p. 552). Managers in other fields describe relationship building as efforts to become more intimate with customers (Barnes, 2001; Gordon 1998; Treacy & Wiersesa, 1993) and to create community (Hagel & Armstrong, 1997).

Research in other disciplines suggests that the adroit use of the Internet can help foster relationships. Supporting evidence has been provided in advertising (Salam, Rao, & Pegels, 1998), consumer promotions (Cross, 1994; Stauss, 2000; Zufryden, 2000) and business-to-business channels research (Parks, 1996; Reber & Fosdick, 2002; Steinfield, Kraut, & Plummer, 1996). Interestingly, many of these findings contradict earlier research from interpersonal communication and social psychology that suggested the imposition of technology reduces the quality of interpersonal relationships and social involvement (Barnes, Dunn, & Glynn, 1999; Kraut et al., 1998; Lea & Spears, 1995).

Today, many organizations have not fully deployed online communication to its maximum potential. Critics suggest that organizations fail to provide content that meets user needs, to fully engage or involve users, and to encourage and take advantage of user feedback (Callison, 2003; Esrock & Leichty, 1998, 1999, 2000; Flynn, 2001; Ha & James, 1998; Nielsen, 2001; Rewick, 2001; Shaw, 2001; Taylor, Kent, & White 2001). Explanations for the shortfall include a lack of awareness, technical expertise, and financial resources—and smug overconfidence in the sufficiency of technologies that are being deployed.

EXAMINING RELATIONSHIPS

Understanding relationships has been suggested as a framework for theory and research in public relations (Ferguson, 1984), for conducting applied research

(Broom & Dozier, 1990), for dealing with customers (McKenna, 1990), and for understanding how organizations negotiate and manage their external environments (Botan, 1992, 1997). Establishing quality relationships also has been identified as the basis for excellence in the field (Grunig, Grunig, & Dozier, 2002, pp. 548–554; Grunig, Grunig, & Ehling, 1992, p. 86) and for defining the field itself (Cutlip, Center, & Broom, 1994; Hutton, 1999; Ledingham & Bruning, 1998, 2000). Broom, Casey, and Ritchey (1997) synthesized much of the then-existing research to identify a model of antecedents, processes, and consequences of organizational-public relationships. Grunig and Huang (2000) later recast ideas from the IABC-sponsored Excellence Study (Grunig, 1992) to fit Broom, Casey, and Ritchey's three-phase model and labeled their parallel components situational antecedents, maintenance strategies, and relationship outcomes.

Four principal programs of relationship research followed. Grunig and Huang's relational outcomes were operationalized in six benchmark measurements developed by Hon and Grunig (1999). Huang (2001) then adapted and extended these scales for use in Eastern cultures in a study of conflict and relationships involving government in Taiwan. Separately, Ledingham and Bruning (2000) spearheaded a program of applied community- and customer-based research that identified three different types of relationship scales: professional, community, and personal. Their research showed that positive relationships can serve a variety of purposes, including customer retention (Bruning, 2002). Finally, Kim (2002; Kim & Jo, 2002) launched a separate research program that included the role of reputation and loyalty. This research was then extended to include an early study on web-based relationships (Jo & Kim, 2003).

Despite the construct's potential usefulness, researchers have yet to adequately define organizational-public relationship. Bruning and Ledingham (1999), for example, described an organizational-public relationship as the "state which exists between an organization and its key publics in which the actions of either entity impact the economic, social, political and other cultural well-being of the other entity" (p. 160). In a postscript to their seminal 1997 article, Broom, Casey, and Ritchey (2000) explained that organizational-public relationships are "represented by patterns of interaction, transaction, exchange and linkage between an organization and its publics" (p. 18). The authors went on to suggest these patterns have properties that are "distinct from the identities, attributes and perceptions of the individuals and the social collectivities in the relationships" (p. 18).

Contrary to Broom, Casey, and Ritchey's admonition against doing so, most research has defined and measured relationships using perceptions by one of the parties (usually the public) about the performance of the other (usually the organization). Even among those researchers who have focused on relationships as a process, rather than a static state, the focus of empirical research has been to develop valid and reliable measures to assess relationship quality at particular points in time (Huang, 2001; Hon & Grunig, 1999, p. 16; Kim, 2002, p. 804.)

A useful alternative definition for organizational-public relationships would be a routinized, sustained pattern of behavior by an individual in conjunction with his or her involvement with an organization (Hallahan, 2003). Behavior refers to what a person knows and feels and does—and thus incorporates the cognitive, affective, and conative dimensions of behavior found in psychology. Relationships thus involve both perceptions and actions (Donaldson & O'Toole, 2000, 2002, p. 102). Stated another way, a relationship constitutes all links (Vasquez, 1994), contacts or communications between an organization and stakeholders—and not only those created through public relations initiatives.

Organizational-public relationships are a part of everyday life and evolve out of a person's need to solve problems or desire to seek gratifications. These relationships are not necessarily contemplated—in the same way that many interpersonal relationships evolve and are not planned (Duck & Pittman, 1994). Organizational-public relationships frequently involve weak ties compared to the richer ties that people develop with families or friends (Preece 2001; Wellman & Guila, 1999). Behaviors are sustained or repeated (Czepiel, 1990, p. 15) as long as the benefits derived from a relationship outweigh the costs (Blau, 1964; Pfeffer & Salancik, 1978; Thibaut & Kelley, 1959) or are more efficient than alternative arrangements, such as free-market mechanisms (Williamson, 1985).

Members of publics do not necessarily seek long-term relationships with organizations (Bendapudi & Berry, 1997; Botan, 1997; Hallahan, 1999a). When people enter into relationships with organizations, their motivations are often short-term and not always readily evident (Bendapudi & Berry, 1997; Hennig-Tharau, Gwinner, & Gremler, 2000; Sheth & Parvatiyar, 1995). Organizational-public relationships develop over time, and in stages ("Caution: Biz Relationships," 2001; Gordon, 1998; Knapp, 1978; Tomlinson, 2000; Wilson, 2000). The burden for maintaining these relationships can fall to the organization, the individual, or a combination of the two (Dwyer, Schurr, & Oh, 1987). In most cases, however, organizations have a vested interest in taking the initiative to curry favor with customers, employees, investors, workers, voters, and so on.

MEASURES OF RELATIONSHIP QUALITY

Research in the offline environment has generally converged on five key concepts that can be used to assess the quality of organizational-public relationships Bruning (1998) (Bruning & Ledingham, 1999, Garabino & Johnson, 2000; Grunig & Huang, 2000; Hon & Grunig, 1999, Ledingham & Bruning, 1998). These are briefly summarized below:

■ *Commitment* is an enduring and demonstrated desire to maintain a valued relationship with another party. Commitment is most commonly demonstrated through exchanges involving either intangibles (information, social support, affection, etc.) or tangible items (transactions, gifts exchanges, etc.) (Moon, 2000). Commitment also is indicated by the parties being ready and willing to communicate. Their ability to do so, however, might vary.

■ *Control mutuality* involves determining among the parties who shall set relationship goals, who shall specify how interactions will occur, and who shall exercise the rightful power to influence the other. As suggested previously, most organizational-public relationships are asymmetric—versus symmetric—wherein one party (usually the organization) exercises enormous power over how communications and exchanges with publics will occur. This arrangement might be hegemonically (tacitly) accepted by members of constituent publics. After all, many members of publics have only a marginal interest or have limited time to devote to the relationship or organization. But increasingly, members of constituent publics seek both a greater voice and greater control over their interactions with organizations (Shostack, 1977).

■ *Communality* is the degree to which parties in a relationship share mutual concerns, values, and identities. This often includes a demonstrable concern for the welfare and care of the other—and involves providing benefits to the other without any quid pro quo. The creation of communal relationships with constituencies (versus merely exchange relationships) distinguishes public relations from marketing and forms the basis for many public relations communications.

■ *Trust* can be defined as whether one partner in a relationship believes that the other partner will behave as expected (inferred based on past performance) or as promised (explicitly or implicitly stated in past communications). Trust assumes a communality of values and interests and involves openness and honesty. Trust is important to relationship building because trust reduces fears of exploitation or risk.

■ *Satisfaction* is one party's overall assessment of the performance of the other party in light of one's expectations. In satisfying relationships, positive impressions are created and the rewards obtained outweigh the financial or psychological costs incurred. Satisfaction is generally considered a necessary condition for loyalty—the intention to repeat a particular behavior (such as buying a product) without considering alternatives (Jacoby & Chestnut, 1978; Oliver, 1981). Yet a person can maintain satisfying relationships with multiple organizations (Newell, 2000) and an exclusive commitment is not a necessary condition for satisfaction.

APPLYING THE MEASURES TO ONLINE COMMUNICATION

These benchmarks provide a valuable foundation for measuring relationships with key publics, but also provide useful guidelines for effective offline and online communications. These criteria suggest that successful communications involve commitment, control mutuality, communality, trust, and satisfaction.

Relationship research has generally recognized the importance of communication in the relationship-building process (e.g., Toth, 2000). Communication has been described it as a link (Broom, Casey, & Ritchey, 1997), as a maintenance strategy (Grunig & Huang, 2000), and as a strategic tool (Ledingham & Bruning, 1998; Wilson, 1994, p. 63). Research has documented major impacts of specific forms of communication, such as interpersonal communication with media effects. It is not possible to discuss here whether the Internet is truly a media form but it is worthwhile to mention the research from traditional media studies. The two-step-flow of communication, for example, identified the flow of ideas from gatekeepers of the media to opinion leaders to opinion followers. (Lazarsfeld & Katz, 1995). Later research documented the importance of social status in the flow of communication, thus revealing more of a horizontal than vertical flow of information (Baran & David, 2000, pp. 129–130).

Within an online context, the investigation of organizational-public relationships is a part of social informatics—an emerging field of study that focuses on how people work with technology and the social aspects of computerization (Preece, 2001). The use of technology is important in organizational-public relationships because organizations must rely on a variety of different communications media to maintain relationships effectively and efficiently. These include public media, controlled media, and interactive media, as well as group and interpersonal channels such as events and one-on-one communications (Hallahan, 2001a). *All* forms of communication can be used to foster relationships. However, medium theory posits that technological characteristics of a particular medium shape both communication content and processes (McLuhan, 1964).

Commitment

Clearly the fundamental building block for online relationship building is a user's willingness to use technology to engage in basic information (and possibly economic) exchanges. Various factors influence the likelihood that people will become users of online communication. These include accessibility to a system and the number and mix of alternative communications choices available. People also are influenced by their prior experience with an organization and by their prior exposure to organizational communications. Other factors include personality type (Eveland & Dunwoody, 1998; MacEvoy, 1997; Rogers, 2003); attitudes toward computing and technology in general (Kowlowsky, Lazar, & Hoffman, 1988; Loyd & Gressand, 1984; Loyd & Loyd, 1985; Pope-Davis & Twing, 1991; Postman, 1992; Stoll, 1995) and user skill and confidence or self-efficacy (Cassidy & Eachus, 1997; Compeau & Higgins, 1995; Heinssen, Glas, & Knight, 1987; Loyd & Gressand, 1984).

Users have different motives and derive various gratifications from using technology (Springston, 2001). Gollwitzer (1996) suggested users approach technology with either an implemental (goal-oriented) or exploratory (experiential-oriented) mind-set. Papacharissi and Rubin (2000) similarly outlined five key motives that drive Internet use: interpersonal utility, the passing of time, information seeking, convenience, and entertainment.

By merely making technology-based access available, organizations demonstrate their commitment to communicate with key constituents. Indeed, organizations today have a choice whether to provide access via the Internet. Whereas some organizations have shown a strong commitment, others have followed a more measured approach. Yet many people today expect organizations to provide some form of technological access and assume organizations are savvy in deploying technology (Kanoleas & Teigen, 2000). To do otherwise can signal a lack of commitment to constituents who have become dependent on online communication.

Committed organizations invest in up-to-date hardware and software and provide content important to users. They also actively promote and encourage use of systems (Chase, Shulock, & Hanger, 2001; Godin, 1999; Palmer & Griffith, 1998). The technology acceptance model (TAM) posits that acceptance of computer technologies by users is determined by both ease of use of the system and the perceived usefulness of content (Davis, 1989; Davis, Bagozzi, & Warshaw, 1989). Indeed, acceptance can be enhanced by following design principles that enhance the adoption of innovations in general (Barnes, Dunne, & Glynn, 2000; Ha & James, 1998; Hallahan, 2001b; Meuter, Ostrom, Roundtree, & Bitner, 2000; Rogers, 2003; Ryan, 2000).

Regrettably many organizations view online communications merely as a way to reduce costs and eliminate dependence on other, less-efficient (higher-cost) avenues of contact with publics. Obviously, exclusive reliance on online communication makes sense for dot-com companies that operate only online (McNaughton, 2001). For other organizations, however, placing too much emphasis on the efficiency and control benefits of online communication (Berger & Park, 2000) can appear to users as indifference and can actually harm relationships.

Control Mutuality

When designing online systems, organizations essentially determine how users will interact with the organization in cyberspace. They specify the topics that will be communicated, the context, and the options available to users. But organizations also can provide various choices that allow users to manage and share control of their online experience. To the degree the choices provided instill a sense of empowerment—a feeling that users exercise control—relationship building can be fostered (Kayany, Wotring, & Forrest, 1996). One major airline illustrates this point in an advertising headline for its online reservation system: "It may be our site, but you're in control" (Continental Airlines, 2004).

One of the strengths of online communication is that people are active users or producers of content—not merely passive processors or receivers of messages (Ha & James, 1998; Jo & Kim, 2003; Miller & Slater, 2000, p. 165). Online communications require users to initiate involvement. Then, with the possible exception of incidental exposure to advertisements that appear on web pages, the inherently interactive nature of online communications requires continued engagement.

Interactivity represents the critical component of control mutuality in online communications. Communications theorists schooled in interpersonal communication and symbolic interactionism would argue that, in fact, interaction is the essence of communication (Duck & Pittman, 1994; Blumer, 1969; Mead, 1934). From relatively crude beginnings, online interactivity has become increasingly sophisticated (Ha & James, 1998; Morris & Ogan, 1996; Palmer & Griffith, 1998; Rafaeli & Sudsweeks, 1997). Researchers point to various benefits of interactivity. These include increased speed, efficiency, and heightened user involvement in information processing (Cross & Smith, 1995; Hoogeveen, 1987; Roehm & Haugtvedt, 1999). Interactivity has already been recognized as an important element in online public relations (Jo & Kim, 2003; Springston, 2001) and online advertising (Ghose & Dou, 1998; Haeckel, 1998; Liu, Arnett, Capella, & Beatty 1997; Morris-Lee, 2000), and in integrated marketing communication more generally (Duncan, 2001; Kitchen & Schultz, 2001; Peletier, Schribrowsky, & Schultz, 2003; Rust & Varki, 1996; Schultz & Schultz, 2004; Stewart, Frazier, & Martin, 1996).

Two distinct types of interactivity empower users to share control of online relationships with organizations. The first form is system interactivity—the ability of users to modify the format and content of online communications without any other human contact. Here the user focuses on making choices and responding to a program (Springston, 2001). Examples include the use of hypertext links on web sites that enable people to conduct searches, take quizzes, or complete surveys. Other examples include protocols for playing online games. Customization and personalization also allow users to receive only individualized content tailored to their needs (Horton, 2001; Roehm & Haugtvedt, 1999).

The second form of interactivity involves verbal interaction—the capability of users to produce and send messages to others—a web site sponsor, participants in a discussion group, or friends via e-mail or instant messaging. Verbal interaction is a higher-order form of interactivity that requires users to compose their own thoughts (Roehm & Haugtvedt, 1999). Clearly the most robust form of verbal interaction online is dialogue or mutual discourse, where participants engage in two-way conversations. Indeed, engaging in dialogue and symmetrical communication have been deemed the most ethical form for conducting public relations (van Es & Meijlink, 2000). Yet lower-level forms of interactivity are also possible, such as responsive discourse and simple feedback. All three are superior to unidirectional monologues from organizations (McMillan, 2002; McMillan & Dowes, 2000).

Organizations that want to take advantage of the interactive capabilities of the Internet must be prepared to invest the human and financial resources necessary to respond when people send them messages via e-mail or other forms of feedback. Their responses also must be timely, pertinent, and authentic. But, surprisingly, despite the Internet's enormous potential for interactive two-way communication, research suggests that most organizations are not very responsive when they receive online queries from users (Galea, 1999; O'Connell, 1998; Taylor, Kent, & White, 1998; Weber, 1996). An automated, formulaic, or perfunctory response to a user concerned with a real problem or issue will serve only to aggravate—not enhance—an already stressed relationship.

Communality

Of special interest to many online theorists is how online communications might help form relationships in the absence of direct, face-to-face contacts. Cozier and Witmer (2001) draw on structuration theory to suggest that one unanticipated result of the Internet is to create entirely new publics for organizations. Rheingold (1993) popularized the notion that the Internet overcomes limitations created by time and space to create virtual communities or what might be defined as online communal relationships. His idea has been extended widely by others (Armstrong and Hagel, 1996; Boone, 2001; Hallahan, 2004c; Jones, 1995). Yet some critics dismiss online communities by saying discussion groups and chats are not really communities at all; at best, they are inauthentic pseudocommunities (Beniger, 1987). Parallel to theories about why individuals use the Internet, Hagel and Armstrong (1997) argue that online communities are organized to: conduct transactions; interact with others with similar interests; escape reality through fantasies or the creation of alternative personas; or obtain social support from others who share similar life experiences.

Organizations can serve either as sponsors of internal online communities (such as a discussion group for employees or customers) or as active and coequal participants in external virtual communities organized around topics important to the organization. Yet, organizational-public relationships differ from interpersonal relationships (Pierce, 1994). Organizations are unnatural people (Coleman, 1982). Although organizations strive to create personas and speak with a voice, people's expectations about organizations invariably differ from their expectations about other individuals. Distrust of powerful and complex organizations ("Caution: Biz Relationships," 2001), combined with comparatively lower involvement levels with organizations (Hallahan 1999a), might limit the extension of the community metaphor to build organizational-public relationships online. But if it is accepted that organizational-public relationships can function at low or superficial levels, technology might be sufficient to maintain such shallow relationships.

Community membership implies that users identify with others in the group. This can be based on perceived commonality of interests, values, and goals (Page, 2001) or what Burke (1950) called *consubstantiality.* Identification can involve whether the person recognizes that he or she plays a role in the organization (as employee, customer, investor, donor, etc.) or more generally as a stakeholder (someone who is impacted by the organization's actions, or vice versa). However, identification also can take the form of interest or involvement in an organization and its activities. Such interest can range from occasional enjoyment of an activity to fanatical involvement in ways that define a person's self and shape his or her lifestyle (Civin, 2000; Hickman & Kuhn, 1956; Littlejohn, 2002; Wood, 1995).

Research that directly examines the processes of forming organizational-public relationships is yet to be undertaken. At best, public relations researchers can make inferences based only on case studies and content analyses. However, the growing—albeit contradictory—research about how individuals develop impressions and form interpersonal relationships in online chatrooms and discussion groups suggests the following ideas.

■ Social cues provide guidance about who users should communicate with, about appropriate online conduct, and about what participants should disclose about themselves. Reduced social cues can lead to feelings of anonymity, lower self-awareness, and fewer behavioral inhibitions (*social influence model:* Sproull & Kiesler, 1986).

■ Mediated interactions take more time to develop relationships than face-to-face interactions (*social information processing theory of communication in computer media communication:* Walther, 1992).

■ Users who interact anonymously in groups tend to lose their personal identity in favor of a social or group identity, assume group norms, and generalize perceived attributes of certain group members to the group as a whole. This can result in less discriminating and more positive assessments of others in the group (*social identification/deindividuation [SIDE] theory:* Postumes, Spears, & Lea, 1998; see also Turkle, 1995; Wallace, 1999).

■ Users can experience intimacy, affection, and make assessments of other communicants that exceed those experienced in face-to-face encounters (*hyperpersonal communication theory:* Walther, 1996).

■ Once relationships are established, changes in social cues can alter assessments of others and extant relationships. For example, meeting or seeing a photo of another person for the first time can create discrepant perceptions and lower one's affinity with the other person (Walther, Slovacek, & Tidwell, 2001).

Trust

Because online communication remains comparatively new, many users remain unconvinced about the credibility of the Internet as an information source. Overall, research suggests the Internet enjoys about the same low level of credibility as television, radio, and magazines—which are all lower in trustworthiness than newspapers (Flanagin & Metzger, 2000; Johnson & Kaye, 1998). An important question related to measuring trustworthiness deals with whether perceptions of trust relate to the technology or the presumed source of online content. Regrettably, for example, most research on web credibility confounds the technology, the source, and the content (e.g., Amento, Terveen, & Hill, 2000; Bailey, Gurak, & Konstan, 2003; Burbules, 2001; Fogg et al., 2001; Fogg & Tseng, 1999; Friedman, 2001; Katerattanakul & Siau, 2000; Wathen & Burkell, 2002).

A closely related (and surprising) question involves whether users even recognize organizations as sources of online content. Evidence suggests that people think about technology as social actors (Deighton, 1999) and treat computers and related technologies in social and natural ways—as if the devices were human. Reeves and Nass (1996) found that interactions with computers are actually *more* satisfactory when users don't think about the people organizations behind them. Such thoughts only fatigue and frustrate users.

Other research suggests people act differently when online and differentiate between mediated and nonmediated reality. *Telepresence* is the ability of a person to interject oneself and develop a sense of his or her own identity online. The resulting mediated reality can often take precedence over perceptions about the nonmediated "real world" (Coyle & Thorson, 2001; Steuer, 1992). Escaping from reality in cyberspace in this way involves achieving a flow state, in which a person's attention and cognitive energies become so self-absorbed that users disconnect from the nonmediated, "real world" about them (Dholakia & Bagozzi, 2001). Although these concerns are not readily intuitive or widely recognized, public relations practitioners and others concerned with the trustworthiness of online communication need to consider them. These findings suggest that different rules might apply to offline and online assessments of trustworthiness.

If it is assumed that users are aware of the source of online content and don't leave everyday reality when using online communication, organizations must recognize that users often have limited information available to them. For example, a customer who walks into a retail store can gain valuable cues by looking at the décor, watching other customers, and asking questions of various people. In contrast, online users often must largely rely on what is provided them on the screen by the organization to: make sense of messages; make attributions about the organization's intent; and make judgments about appropriate actions to take.

Creating an environment of online trust can be achieved several ways. One is to assure that systems operate with reliability (without disruption) and integrity (avoiding security breaches and encroachments on user privacy). To do so, organizations must be vigilant to protect their digital assets (Hallahan, 2004b). Authenticity also is particularly important to create trust. To be authentic, online communications must be consistent, responsive, truthful, accurate, genuine, and open—even to the point of providing unexpected information that might expose an organization's vulnerabilities. A lack of authenticity only makes a mockery of attempts to build one-on-one relationships online (Shockley, Ellis, & Cesaria, 2000; Sisodia & Wolf, 2001, p. 560).

Satisfaction

Satisfaction is a summary measure of a person's experience—based on a user's perceptions about organizational commitment, control mutuality, communality, and trustworthiness. However, other factors also contribute to satisfactory online relationships. One of the most important keys to satisfaction is providing users a choice about whether to use online communications at all. Only two-thirds of Americans, for example, even have Internet access (Pew, 2002). Adoption rates are considerably lower elsewhere in the world (Franda, 2002). This so-called digital divide obviously limits online relationship building with the digital have-nots (Jung, Linchaun, & Kim, 2001).

Among those who are connected, not all constituents might want to use online communications or might not wish to do so all the time. In certain situations—such as resolving problems, negotiating arrangements, or addressing personal problems—constituents might prefer to communicate using correspondence, telephone calls, or personal visits. Surprisingly, however, as many as 40 percent of organizations with web sites never give online users any alternative means to communicate with them—a growing source of frustration for users.

Usability of a system is critical to satisfaction as well as adoption (discussed earlier). The higher the level of system sophistication and interactivity, the more difficult an online system can be to use. Thus it becomes critical to adhere to principles of effective computer-human interface design and navigation (Hallahan, 2001b; Nielsen, 2000) and to follow conventions consistent with users' expectations (learned cognitive rules) for using a technology (Len-Rios, 2002; Len-Rios & Cameron, 2001, 2002). Usefulness of content similarly contributes to satisfaction. In the mid-1990s organizations viewed web sites as generic electronic brochures. Today, people are increasingly seeking personalized and customized information only—a fact that enhances the utility of online information and heightens users' processing of organization-related content (Hallahan, 2001b, 2004a).

Adapting Conventional Measures to Online Research.   These five criteria for measuring relationships can be applied to the online environment and provide a basis on which relationship quality can be assessed by asking users questions in surveys or in-depth interviews. Examples of possible measures that can be compiled into reliable index measures include:

■ *Commitment* [Organization name] is committed to communicating with me online; invests resources to communicate with me; wants to develop a relationship with me; is available when it's important to me; makes an effort to communicate with me.

■ *Control mutuality* [Organization name] encourages me to participate online; gives me a lot of choices of content; lets me decide what's important; pays attention to my interests; is open to my ideas and feedback; responds to me when I ask questions.

■ *Communality* [Organization name] shares common values with me; understands me; is like me; makes me feel a part of a community; encourages sharing ideas with others; cares about users like me.

■ *Trust* [Organization name] is believable; competent; knowledgeable/expert; reliable; credible; trustworthy; consistent in what it says to me.

■ *Satisfaction* Overall, my online experience with [Organization name] exceeds my expectations; is good; satisfies me; compares favorably with other organizations; benefits me; is pleasing to me; meets my needs.

ADDITIONAL MEASURES OF RELATIONSHIPS

Although useful, these generally accepted measures of relationship quality extend beyond some of the basic psychological processes that underlie them. Thus, effective assessments of relationships (both online or offline) must also examine how communications influence people's knowledge, attitudes, and behaviors.

Cognitive Learning

Among the most important criteria is understanding the degree to which members of publics acquire a familiarity (general awareness) and a more in-depth knowledge (understanding) of an organization. Learning involves a user engaging in increasingly deep levels of psychological processing—beginning with preattention and focal attention, and progressing to comprehension (understanding) and elaboration (interpretation and evaluation) of content (Greenwald & Leavitt, 1984). In purely cognitive terms, the depth of an organizational-public relationship can be defined as the depth and complexity of cognitive elaborations and associations found in a person's memory.

Although researchers such as J. Grunig (1993; Grunig, Grunig, & Dozier, 2002, pp. 145–147) question the value of cognition measures such as organizational identity, image, brand, or reputation, in favor of the relationship quality measures outlined here, other researchers contend these perceptions shape an individual's understanding of an organization (Argenti, 2003; Argenti & Forman, 2002; Fombrun, 1996). These notions might be particularly important in an online environment, where a person's experience with an organization is limited.

Researchers outside public relations have generally recognized message learning as an important indicator of online effectiveness (Sundar, 2000; Tewksbury & Althaus, 2000). The depth and style of learning can vary significantly based on whether a user is an expert or a novice on a particular topic (Hallahan, 1999a, 1999b). For both groups, research suggests that the shift of content from what was traditionally labeled the sender to the receiver facilitates learning by enhancing the elaboration process (Eveland & Dunwoody, 1998, 2001a, 2001b, 2002; Schlosser, 2000).

Increasing processing involvement is particularly important for users who rely primarily on verbal, versus visual, information (Bezjian-Avery, Calder & Iacobucci, 1998; Scholsser, 2000). Indeed, the effectiveness of online communication is mostly grounded in the processing of textual messages (Nielsen, 2000). Although visuals can motivate users to pay attention to messages, the value of photos and more elaborate multimedia components have been questioned (Jo & Kim 2003; King & Xia, 1999). A notable exception involves advertising versus news (Heo & Sundar, 2000). One explanation is that fancy graphics distract attention or take up too much cognitive capacity to process information (Heller, 1990; Lang, 2000).

Providing a context for learning is important in online communications, because available information is often limited. The rationale for this axiom is simple: The more context provided, the more likely that people can create multiple associations (relationships) in memory. Context can include capitalizing on the nonverbal cues inherent in a particular online medium (*media richness theory:* Daft & Lengel, 1984, 1986; Trevino, Lengel, & Daft, 1987). Messages can also include cues that suggest that presence of people—an established away to capture attention and create positive affective (emotional) responses that stimulate more extensive cognitive processing (*social presence theory:* Short, Williams, & Christie, 1976; Wood & Smith, 2001). One approach for overcoming the sterile, nonpersonal nature of web sites, for example, is to prominently feature people. Another technique to instill social presence is the use of computer-generated avatars, synthetic voice recognition systems, and virtual customer service agents that exhibit humanlike qualities (Damer, 1998; Nowak, 2004; Spencer, 2005).

Clearly, learning is a necessary condition for relationship building. Knowledge about an organization can be assessed using traditional recognition and recall measures as well as thought-listing procedures that analyze the number and valence of discrete ideas that people can retrieve from memory (du Plessis, 1994; Petty, Ostrom, & Brock, 1981).

Affective Responses

Online communications also can arouse emotional or affective responses—feelings of exhilaration, hedonic pleasure, empathy, outrage, and so on. These can contribute to the formation of positive attitudes, or predispositions toward the subject of the communication. Attitudes are believed to lead to reasoned or planned action (Ajzen & Fishbein, 1980).

While engaged in online communications, users form attitudes about the content and about the online experience itself. Attitudes toward online content can be measured at least three ways.

- *Liking/disliking* refers to a user's general affective response, that is, whether the content is good versus bad, pleasant versus unpleasant, exciting versus dull, and so on.
- *Quality* refers to the perceived completeness, relevance, or usefulness of the content (Amento, Terveen, & Hill, 2000).
- *Believability* assesses the level of verisimilitude of the content, or whether it "rings true" with the user's offline and online experience.

Research in advertising suggests an important link exists between assessments of content—generally referred to as attitude toward the ad, A_{ad}—and assessments of the subject matter or brand featured in a communication—attitude toward the brand, A_{brand} (Mackenzie, Lutz, & Belch, 1986; Mitchell & Olson, 1981; Stevenson, Bruner, & Kumar, 2000).

Later parallel research suggests that attitudes toward people's experiences using technology shape their assessments. Researchers focusing on web sites, for example have conceptualized this attitudinal response as attitude toward the site, A_{site} (Chen & Wells, 1999, 2001; Eighemy, 1997; Stevenson, Bruner, & Kumar, 2000). Attitude toward the site complements other attitudinal measures that have been proposed, such as pleasantness (Nielsen, 2000).

Online experiences that generate positive (versus neutral or negative) assessments clearly contribute to relationship building. At least five attitudinal measures might be appropriate.

- *Liking/disliking* of the organization involves the degree to which an individual develops an overall positive predisposition toward the organization.
- *Relevance* measures the degree to which an individual feels that an organization's actions are involving or have consequences in their lives (Petty & Cacioppo, 1986).
- *Identification* involves the degree to which an individual believes an organization shares similar interests and values.
- *Affinity* analyzes the degree to which an individual wants to enter into or continue an affiliation with an organization.
- *Intent* measures the degree to which an individual plans to take a particular action (Sheppard, Hartwick, & Warshaw, 1988).

Resulting Behaviors

In the end, using technology to build and maintain relationships is valuable only to the extent that routinized, sustained patterns of behavior are created that benefit an organization. These include communication and behavioral actions that contribute to an organization's mission and goals.

Favorable communications behaviors include repeated use of online technologies. Revisiting a web site, for example, can result from the intrinsic value of the content (O'Malley & Irani, 1998), system design features (Kent & Taylor, 1998), or promotional incentives to build traffic (Chase, Shulock, & Hanger, 2001). Communications also include other offline interactions with organization representatives, attendance at events, attention to an organization's publicity or advertising, and so on. Finally, communication can involve sharing online content with others—whether offline (talking with friends) or online (e-mails, discussion groups, chats, blogs, etc.). Viral marketing employs word-of-mouth techniques to encourage and to make it easy for individuals to share e-mails or other online communications (Chase, Shulock, & Hanger, 2001; MacPherson, 2001; Silverman, 2001). Serving as a committed advocate in this way is probably the most powerful indicator of a strong relationship (Gordon, 1998).

The ultimate measure of organizational-public relationships is the user's engagement in behaviors that directly benefit the organization. Such behaviors commonly include buying, investing, donating, working, voting, or adopting beliefs and values advocated by the organization that contribute to one's spiritual, emotional, or physical well-being. Engaging in these behaviors, of course, can benefit individuals by fulfilling their needs, wants, concerns, or interests while helping the organization fulfill its purpose.

With increased frequency, organizations operate only in an online environment. For them, building and maintaining an online relationship is critical but comparatively easy to track, because all exchanges are conducted online. But similar to most traditional communications tools, it is often more difficult to identify and segregate the effects of online communications in an offline environment, because so many other influences can be at work

CONCLUSION

One of the pressing questions for public relations researchers and practitioners pertains to the quality of relationships that can be created in an online environment. If it is assumed that organizational-public relationships operate at lower thresholds than face-to-face or other person-to-person interactions, relationships primarily established or maintained online probably will be more limited and weaker than other kinds of multiplex relationships. Nonetheless, the creation or reinforcement of even weak relationships might be valuable for organizations.

As organizations further embrace online communications in the coming years, organizations need to better understand relationship building and create user-centered online communication systems that supplement other "touch points" where constituents come into contact with an organization. Organizations that want to use technology effectively must demonstrate commitment, share control, establish a sense of communality, build trust, and create satisfaction. But in doing so, they must also not lose sight of the fact that their ultimate goal is to influence people's knowledge, attitudes, and behaviors in ways that are conducive to the organization. Building effective online relationships is important, but relationship building is not an end in itself—it serves to help organizations fulfill their purposes.

CASE: INTEL'S 1994 PENTIUM CHIP CRISIS

In June 1994, as the Internet was beginning to be adopted on a widespread basis, officials at Intel discovered a division error in the Pentium chip it produced for use in IBM and other major brands of personal computers. Company managers thought the error would not affect many people and decided not to inform anyone outside the company—even though such a disclosure probably would have generated little public outcry.

In October, a mathematician at Lynchburg College in Virginia discovered the error. Dr. Thomas Nicely contacted Intel, whose representative duplicated and confirmed the error, but said it had not been reported before. A week later, after having received no further information from Intel, Dr. Nicely sent an e-mail message to a few friends. These friends, in turn, forwarded the message to what became a snowballing number of computer experts. Within a day, the story had circulated to major hardware and software producers and was posted to the Canopus discussion forum of CompuServe. The message asked still more users to test for the flaw.

Alan Wolfe, a reporter for *Electronic Engineering Times,* saw the posting and wrote computer guru Terje Mathisen in Norway, who both confirmed the flaw and posted another message on the comp.sys.intel Internet newsgroup. Within a week, hundreds of techies all over the world knew about the problem. The story soon spilled over into technical and business/investment newsgroups and began to be reported widely in the general press.

A furor ensued. Intel spokesperson Steve Smith dismissed the importance of the problem on CNN's *Moneyline.* But experts outside Intel soon developed models for predicting when the calculation error would occur. Other computer geeks engineered a fix for the problem. On Thanksgiving, the *New York Times* ran a damaging story that the company was still shipping flawed chips. Meanwhile, Ken Hendren, an applications support manager, posted a message online saying that no one at Intel was providing customer support. Instead of offering to replace the chip unconditionally, Intel begrudgingly agreed to replace the chip if users could demonstrate it would actually cause them a problem.

Customers became irate. The chip hit the fan. Intel CEO Andy Grove attempted to circumvent further problems by posting a personal message on comp.sys.intel. But his message bore someone else's return address, which led some newsgroup members to question whether the missive was a spoof. The company also failed to distribute the message to anyone beyond this one newsgroup.

By early December, Intel was flooded with thousands of messages and phone calls saying it had missed the point. The company was the laughingstock of the industry. One joke claimed, "At Intel, quality is job 0.999999998." By mid-December, IBM halted shipments of personal computers with Pentium chips. Eight product liability and two shareholder suits were filed, and Florida's attorney general threatened legal action. Finally, on December 20—two months after the first disclosure—Intel apologized. The company, whose stock price had already declined as result of the flap, announced it would replace all flawed Pentium chips at an estimated cost of $420 million. (For further background, see Emery, 1996; Hearit, 1999.)

QUESTIONS FOR APPLICATION

1. What is a *relationship?* Why are relationships important offline? Why would they be particularly important to organizations and publics in an online environment?

2. How do organizational-public relationships differ from the relationship between two people?

3. Interactivity is one of the inherent strengths of the Internet. What are examples of both economic and information exchanges that can take place online between an organization and members of key publics? How does the interactive nature of online communications encourage dialogue and what James Grunig termed *symmetrical two-way communication?*

4. What does Spataro mean when he defined *net relations* as intersection of direct marketing, public relations, and the Internet? In light of the current trend toward integrated communication among organizations, is the Internet primarily a marketing or public relations tool? In each case, why would developing and maintaining relationships be important? Under the circumstances, who should oversee an organization's online communication?

5. Do particular online technologies (web sites, e-mail, instant messaging, etc.) have inherently distinct characteristics that especially lend themselves to being used by organizations for relationship-building purposes? Based on your personal experience, which technology do you think has the greatest potential? Why?

6. Are relationships developed primarily through technology more short-term or long-term? How can technology contribute to the ability of organizations to cultivate quality, longer-term offline relationships with stakeholders in tandem with offline efforts? Why would this be important?

7. Which one of the five measures of relationship quality do you think are *most* important in sustaining the relationship between an organization and its publics? Explain.

8. Under what circumstances can online communication be effective in helping users learn about an organization, its products, services, causes, or candidates? In shaping positive attitudes toward an organization? In prompting online or offline behaviors? When would online communications *not* be effective?

9. Intel's Pentium chip fiasco was the first major online crisis. Do you think that Intel could (or would) handle the situation in the same way today? Why?

10. This case illustrates the potential importance of the Internet in crisis situations. How is a crisis a special case of maintaining organizational-public relationships? Explain. Why could the Internet be especially important in crisis management?

11. For each of the concepts identified in this chapter, discuss how Intel could have done a better job of using online communication to establish and maintain relationships with its key publics. Consider organizational commitment, control mutuality, communality, trust, and satisfaction.

12. The initial controversy was limited to a small group of experts in the computer industry. To what extent do you think they represented a *community?* How did that influence their response?

13. Do you think Intel's problems were uniquely related to online communications? Or were they a more general mishandling of organizational-public relations?

14. Based on this case, do you think an organization's online communications can be addressed without regard to other forms of public relations communications? Why or why not?

REFERENCES

Aikat, D. (2000). A new medium for organizational communication: Analyzing web content characteristics of Fortune 500 companies. *Electronic Journal of Communication, 10*(1/2). Retrieved September 1, 2004, from www.cios.org/getfile.aikat-v10n1200.

Ajzen, I. & Fishbein, M. (1980). *Understanding attitudes and predicting social behavior.* Englewood Cliffs, NJ: Prentice-Hall.

Amento, B., Terveen, L., & Hill. W. (2000). Does "authority" mean "quality"? Predicting expert quality ratings of web sites. Proceedings of the 23rd Annual International Conference on Research and Development in Information Retrieval (SIGIR, 2000). Athens, Greece, pp. 296–303.

Argenti, P. A. (2003). *Corporate communication* (3rd ed.). Boston: McGraw-Hill Irwin.

Argenti, P. A., & Forman, J. (2002). *The power of corporate communication. Crafting the voice and image of your business.* New York: McGraw-Hill.

Armstrong, A., & Hagel, J., III (1996, May–June). The real value of online communities. *Harvard Business Review, 74*(3), pp. 134–141.

Badaracco, C. H. (1998). The transparent corporation and organized community. *Public Relations Review, 23*(3), pp. 265–272.

Bailey, B. P., Gurak, L. J., & Konstan, J. A. (2003). Trust in cyberspace. In J. Ratner (Ed.), *Human factors and web development* (pp. 311–322). Mahwah, NJ: Lawrence Erlbaum.

Baran, S. J., & Davis, D. K. (2000). *Mass communication theory: Foundations, ferment, and future.* Belmont, CA: Wadsworth Thomas Learning.

Barnes, J. G. (2001). Close in customer relationships: Examining the payback from getting closer to the customer. In T. Hennig-Thurau & U. Hansen (Eds.), *Relationship marketing: Gaining competitive advantage through customer satisfaction and customer retention* (pp. 89–106). Berlin: Springer.

Barnes, J. G., Dunne, P. A., & Glynn, W. J. (1999). Self-service and technology. In T. A. Swartz & D. Iacobucci (Eds.), *Handbook of services marketing & management* (pp. 89–102). Thousand Oaks, CA: Sage.

Bejou, D. (1997). Relationship marketing: Evolution, present state, and future. *Psychology & Marketing, 14*(8), pp. 727–736.

Bendapudi, N., & Berry, L. L. (1997). Customers' motivations for maintaining relationships with service providers. *Journal of Retailing, 73*(1), pp. 15–37.

Beniger, J. (1987). Personalization of mass media and the growth of pseudo-community. *Communication Research, 14*(3), pp. 352–371.

Berger, B. K. & Park, D. (2000). Public relation(ships) or private controls? Practitioner perspectives on the uses and benefits of new technologies. Paper presented to the International Communication Association, Washington, DC.

Bezjian-Avery, A., Calder, B., & Iacobucci, D. (1998, July–August). New media interactive advertising v. traditional advertising. *Journal of Advertising Research, 38*, pp. 23–32.

Blau, P. (1964). *Exchange and power in social life.* New York: John Wiley.

Blumer, H. (1969). *Symbolic interactions: Theory and method.* Berkeley: University of California Press.

Boone, M. E. (2001). *Managing interactively. Executing business strategy, improving communication, and creating a knowledge-sharing culture.* New York: McGraw-Hill.

Botan, C. (1992). International public relations: Critique and reformulation. *Public Relations Review, 18*(2), 149–159.

———. (1997). Ethics in strategic communication campaigns: The case for a new approach to public relations. *Journal of Business Communication, 34*, 188–202.

Broom, G. M., Casey, S. & Ritchey, J. (1997). Toward a concept and theory of organization-public relationships. *Journal of Public Relations Research, 9*(2), 83–98.

———. (2000). Toward a concept and theory of organization-public relationships. In J. A. Ledingham and S. D. Bruning (Eds.), *Public relations as relationship management. A relational approach to the study and practice of public relations* (pp. 3–22). Mahwah, NJ: Lawrence Erlbaum.

Broom, G. M., & Dozier, D. M. (1990). *Using research in public relations: Applications in program management.* Englewood Cliffs, NJ: Prentice-Hall.

Bruning, S. D. (2002). Relationship building as a retention strategy: Linking relationship attitude and satisfaction evaluations to behavioral outcomes. *Public Relations Review, 28*(1), pp. 39–48.

Bruning, S. D., & Ledingham, J. D. (1999). Relationships between organizations and publics: Development of a multi-dimensional organization-public relationship scale. *Public Relations Review, 25*(2), pp. 157–170.

Burbules, N. C. (2001). Paradoxes of the web: The ethical dimensions of credibility. *Library Trends, 49*(3), pp. 441–453.

Burke, K. (1950). *A rhetoric of motives.* Englewood, Cliffs, NJ: Prentice-Hall.

Callison, C. (2003). Media relations and the Internet. How Fortune 500 company web sites assist journalists in gathering news. *Public Relations Review, 29*(1), pp. 29–42.

Cassidy, S., & Eachus, P. (1997). Developing the computer self-efficacy scale (CSE): Investigating the relationship between CSE gender and experience with computers. Accessed September 1, 2004, at www.salford.ac.uk/healthSci/selfeff/selfeff.htm.

Caution: Biz relationships are different from personal relationships, so require a different approach (2001). *pr reporter, 44*(6), p. 1.

Chase, L., Shulock, E., & Hanger, N. C. (2001). *Essential business tactics for the net.* New York: John Wiley & Sons.

Chaudbury, A., Mallick, D. N., & Rao, H. R. (2001). Web channels in e-commerce. *Communication of the ACM, 44*(1), pp. 99–104.

Chen, Q., & Wells, W. D. (1999). Attitude toward the site. *Journal of Advertising Research, 38*(5), pp. 27–38.

———. (2001). .Com satisfaction and .com dissatisfaction. One or two constructs? In M. C. Gilly & J. Meyers-Levy (Eds.), *Advances in consumer research, 28* (pp. 34–39). Valdosta, GA: Association for Consumer Research.

Civin, M. A. (2000). *Male, female, email: The struggle for relatedness in a paranoid society.* New York: Other Press.

Coleman, J. S. (1982). *The asymmetric society.* Syracuse, NY: Syracuse University Press.

Compeau, D. R., & Higgins, C. A. (1995). Computer self-efficacy: Development of a measure and initial test. *MIS Quarterly, 19*, pp. 189–211.

Continental Airlines (2004). It may be our site, but you're in control. Advertisement.

Cooley, T. (1999). Interactive communication. Public relations on the web. *Public Relations Quarterly, 44*(2), pp. 41–42.

Coombs, W. T. (1998). The Internet as potential equalizer: New leverage for confronting social irresponsibility. *Public Relations Review, 24*(3), pp. 289–305.

Cooper, K. C. (2001). *The relational enterprise: Moving beyond CRM to maximize all your business relationships.* New York: AMACOM.

Copulsky, J. R., & Wolf, M. J. (1990). Relationship marketing: Position for the future. *Journal of Business Strategy, 11*(4), pp. 16–20.

Coyle, J. R., & Thorson E. (2001). The effects of progressive levels of interactivity and vividness in web marketing sites. *Journal of Advertising, 30*(3), pp. 65–77.

Cozier, Z. R., and Witmer, D. F. (2001). The development of a structuration analysis of new publics in an electronic environment practitioner. In R. L. Heath (Ed.), *Handbook of public relations* (pp. 614–624). Thousand Oaks, CA: Sage.

CRM and the Internet (2001, October 22). *Business Week,* advertising supplement.

Cross, R., & Smith, J. (1995). Customer-focused strategies and tactics. In E. Forrest & R. Mizerski (Eds.), *Interactive marketing* (pp. 5–28). Lincolnwood, IL: NTC Business Books.

Curtin, P. A., & Gaither, T. K. (2004). International agenda-building in cyberspace. A study of Middle East government English-language web sites. *Public Relations Review, 30*(1), pp. 25–36.

Cutlip, S. M., Center, A. H., & Broom, G. M. (1994). *Effective public relations* (7th ed.). Englewood Cliffs, NJ: Prentice-Hall.

Czepiel, J. A. (1990). Service encounters and service relationships: Implications for research. *Journal of Business Research, 20*, pp. 13–21.

Daft, R. L., & Lengel, R. H. (1984). Information richness: A new approach to managerial behavior and organizational design. *Research in Organizational Behavior, 6*(2), pp. 191–233.

———. (1986). Organizational information requirements, media richness, and structural design. *Management Science, 32*(5), pp. 554–571.

Damer, B. (1998). *Avatars! Exploring and building virtual worlds on the Internet.* Berkeley, CA: Peachpit Press.

Davis, F. D. (1989). Perceived useful, perceived ease of use, and user acceptance of information technology. *MIS Quarterly, 13*, pp. 319–340.

Davis, F. D., Bagozzi, R. P., & Warshaw, P. B. (1989). User acceptance of computer technology: A comparison of two theoretical models. *Management Science, 35*(8), pp. 982–1003.

Deighton, J. (1999). Computers as social actors. In E. J. Arnold & L. M. Scott (Eds.), *Advances in consumer research, 26,* pp. 392–393. Valdosta, GA: Association for Consumer Research.

Dholakia, U., & Bagozzi, R. P. (2001). Consumer behavior in digital environments. In J. Wind & V. Mahajan (Eds.), *Digital marketing. Global strategies from the world's leading experts* (pp. 163–200). New York: John Wiley & Sons.

DiNardo, A. M. (2002). The Internet as a crisis management tool. A critique of banking sites during Y2K. *Public Relations Review, 28*(4), pp. 367–378.

Donaldson, B., & O'Toole, T. (2000). Classifying relationship structures: Relationship strength in industrial markets. *Journal of Business and Industrial Marketing, 15*(7), pp. 491–506.

———. (2002). *Strategic marketing relationships.* New York: John Wiley & Sons.

Duck, S., & Pittman, G. (1994). Social and personal relationships. In M. L. Knapp & G. R. Miller (Eds.), *Handbook of interpersonal communication* (pp. 676–695). Thousand Oaks, CA: Sage.

Duke, S. (2002). Wired science: Use of World Wide Web and e-mail in science public relations. *Public Relations Review, 28*(3), pp. 311–324.

Duncan, T. (2001). *IMC: Using advertising and promotion to build brands.* New York: McGraw-Hill.

Duncan, T., & Moriarty, S. E. (1998). A communication-based marketing model for managing relationships. *Journal of Marketing, 62*, pp. 1–13.

du Plessis, E. (1994). Recognition versus recall. *Journal of Advertising Research, 14*(3), pp. 75–91.

Dwyer, F. R., Schurr, P. H., & Oh, S. (1987, April). Developing buyer-seller relationships. *Journal of Marketing, 51*, pp. 11–27.

Eighemy, J. (1997). Profiling user responses to commercial web sites. *Journal of Advertising Research, 35*(3), pp. 59–66.

Emery, V. (1996). The Pentium chip story. A learning experience. Vince Emery Productions. Accessed September 1, 2004, at www.emery.com/1e/pentium.htm.

Esrock, S. L., & Leichty, G. B. (1998). Social responsibility and corporate web pages: Self-presentation or agenda-setting? *Public Relations Review, 24*(3), pp. 305–320.

———. (1999). Corporate World Wide Web pages: Serving the news media and other publics. *Journalism & Mass Communication Quarterly, 76*(3), pp. 456–467.

———. (2000). Organization of corporate web pages: Publics and functions. *Public Relations Review, 26*(3), pp. 327–344.

Eveland, W. P. Jr., & Dunwoody, S. (1998). Users and navigation patterns of a science World Wide Web site for the public. *Public Understanding of Science, 7*, pp. 285–311.

———. (2001a). Applying research on the use and cognitive effects of hypermedia to the study of the World Wide Web. In W. B. Gudyskunst (Ed.), *Communication Yearbook, 25* (pp. 79–113). Thousand Oaks, CA: Sage.

———. (2001b). User control and structural isomorphism or disorientation and cognitive load? Learn from the web versus print. *Communication Research, 28*(1), pp. 48–78.

———. (2002). An investigation of elaboration and selective scanning as mediators of learning from the web versus print. *Journal of Broadcasting & Electronic Media, 46*(1), pp. 34–53.

Exploring the new century's web-related possibility (2000). *Public Relations Tactics, 7*(1), p. 6.

Ferguson, M. A. (1984, August). Building theory in public relations: Interorganizational relationships. Paper presented to the Association for Education in Journalism and Mass Communication, Gainesville, FL.

Flanagin, A. J., & Metzger, M. J. (2000). Perceptions of Internet information credibility. *Journalism & Mass Communication Quarterly, 77*(3), pp. 515–540.

Flynn, L. F. (2001, March 26). Compressed data: Corporate sites seem to skimp on the facts. *New York Times*, p. C5.

Fogg, B., Marshall, J., Laraki, O., Osipivich, A., Varma, C., Fang, N., Paul, J., Rangnekar, A., Shon, J., Swani, P., & Treinan, M. (2001). What makes web sites credible? A report on a large quantitative study. *Computer Human Interface, 3*(1), pp. 1–68.

Fogg, B., & Tseng, H. (1991, May). The elements of computer credibility. Proceedings of Association for Computing Machinery Computer Human Interaction Conference, Pittsburgh, PA.

Fombrun, C. J. (1996). *Reputation: Realizing value from the corporate image.* Boston: Harvard Business School Press.

Franda, M. F. (2002). *Launching into cyberspace: Internet development and politics in five world regions.* Boulder, CO: Lynn Rienner.

Frazer, C., & McMillan, S. J. (1999). Sophistication on the World Wide Web: Evaluating structure, function and commercial goals of web sites. In D. W. Schumann & E. Thorson (Eds.), *Advertising and the World Wide Web* (pp. 119–134). Mahwah, NJ: Lawrence Erlbaum.

Friedman, M. (2001). Tips & tactics: Building trust online. Supplement to *pr reporter, 39*(9), pp. 1–2.

Gaddis, S. E. (2001). On-line research techniques for the public relations practitioner. In R. L. Heath (Ed.), *Handbook of public relations* (pp. 591–601). Thousand Oaks, CA: Sage.

Galea, D. (1999). Managing corporate e-mail and website feedback. In J. Keyes (Ed.), *Internet management* (pp. 513–522). Boca Raton, FL: Auerbach.

Garbarino, E., & Johnson, M. S. (1999). The different roles of satisfaction, trust, and commitment in customer relations. *Journal of Marketing, 63*(2), pp. 70–87.

Geyskens, I., Gielsens, K., & Dekimpe, M. G. (2002). The market valuation of Internet channel additions. *Journal of Marketing, 66*(2), pp. 102–119.

Ghose, S., & Dou, W. (1998). Interactive functions and their impacts on the appeal of Internet presence sites. *Journal of Advertising Research, 38*(2), pp. 29–43.

Godin, S. (1999). *Permission marketing: Turning strangers into friends, and friends into customers.* New York : Simon & Schuster.

Gollwitzer, P. M. (1996). The volitional benefits of planning. In P. M. Gollwitzer & J. A. Bargh (Eds.), *The psychology of action: Linking cognition and motivation to behavior* (pp. 287–312). New York: Guilford Press.

Gordon, I. (1998). *Relationship marketing: New strategies, techniques and technologies to win the customers you want and keep them forever.* Toronto and New York: John Wiley.

Greenwald, A. G., & Leavitt, C. (1984). Audience involvement in advertising: Four levels. *Journal of Consumer Research, 11,* pp. 581–592.

Gregory, A. (2004). Scope and structure of public relations: A technology driven view. *Public Relations Review, 30*(3), pp. 245–254.

Gronroos, C. (2000). Relationship marketing. The Nordic perspective. In. J. N. Sheth & A. Parvatiyar (Eds.), *Handbook of relationship marketing* (pp. 95–118). Thousand Oaks, CA: Sage.

Grunig, J. E. (Ed.). (1992). *Excellence in public relations and communications management.* Hillsdale, NJ: Lawrence Erlbaum.

———. (1993). Image and substance: From symbolic to behavioral relationships. *Public Relations Review, 19*(2), pp. 121–139.

Grunig, J. E., & Huang, Y. (2000). From organizational effectiveness to relationship indicators: Antecedents of relationships, public relations strategies, and relationship outcomes. In J. A. Ledingham & S. D. Bruning (Eds.), *Public relations as relationship management: A relational approach to the study and practice of public relations* (pp. 23–53). Mahwah, NJ: Lawrence Erlbaum.

Grunig, L. A., Grunig, J. E. & Dozier, D. M. (2002). *Excellent public relations and effective organizations. A study of communications management in three countries.* Mahwah, NJ: Lawrence Erlbaum Associates.

Grunig, L. A., Grunig, J. E., & Ehling, W. P. (1992). What is an effective organization? In J. E. Grunig (Ed.), *Excellence in public relations and communications management* (pp. 65–90). Hillsdale, NJ: Lawrence Erlbaum.

Ha, L., & James, E. L. (1998). Interactivity reexamined: A baseline analysis of early business web sites. *Journal of Broadcasting & Electronic Media, 42*(3), pp. 457–474.

Hachigian, D., & Hallahan, K. (2003). Perceptions of public relations web sites by computer industry journalists. *Public Relations Review, 29*(2), pp. 43–64.

Haeckel, S. H. (1998). About the nature and future of interactive marketing. *Journal of Interactive Marketing, 12*(1), pp. 63–71.

Hagel, J., III, & Armstrong, A. G. (1997). *Net gain. Expanding marketing through virtual communities.* Boston: Harvard Business School Press.

Hallahan, K. (1999a). Inactive publics: The forgotten publics in public relations. *Public Relations Review, 26*(4), pp. 499–515.

———. (1999b). Enhancing motivation, opportunity and ability to process public relations messages. *Public Relations Review, 26*(4), pp. 463–480.

———. (2001a). Strategic media planning. Toward an integrated public relations media model practitioner. In R. L. Heath (Ed.), *Handbook of public relations* (pp. 461–470). Thousand Oaks, CA: Sage.

———. (2001b). Improving public relations web sites through usability research. *Public Relations Review, 27*(2), pp. 223–240.

———. (2004a). Online public relations. In H. Bidgoli (Ed.), *The Internet encyclopedia* (Vol. 2.) (pp. 769–783). Hoboken, NJ: John Wiley.

———. (2004b) Protecting an organization's digital public relations assets. *Public Relations Review, 30*(3), pp. 255–268.

———. (2004c). "Community" as the framework for public relations theory and research. *Communication Yearbook, 28,* pp. 233–279.

Hamel, G., & Sampler, J. (1998). The e-corporation: More than just web-based, it's building a new industrial order. *Fortune, 138*(11), pp. 81–92.

Hearit, K. M. (1999). Newsgroups, activist publics and corporate apologia: The case of Intel and its Pentium chip. *Public Relations Review, 25*(3), pp. 391–308.

Heath, R. L. (1998). New communication technologies: An issues management point of view. *Public Relations Review, 24*(3), pp. 273–288.

Heinssen, R. K., Glass, C. R., & Knight, L. A. (1987). Assessing computer anxiety: Development and validation of the computer anxiety rating scale. *Computers in Human Behavior, 3,* pp. 49–59.

Heller, R. S. (1990). The role of hypermedia in education. A look at research issues. *Journal of Research on Computing in Education, 23,* pp. 431–441.

Hennig-Thurau, T., Gwinner, K. P., & Gremler, D. D. (2000). Why customers build relations with companies—and why not. In T. Hennig-Thurau & U. Hansen (Eds.), *Relationship marketing* (pp. 369–391). Berlin: Springer.

Heo, N., & Sundar, S. S. (2000, May). Visual orientation and memory for web advertising. Paper presented to the International Communication Association, Acapulco, Mexico.

Hickman, C. A., & Kuhn, M. H. (1956). *Individuals, groups and economic behavior.* New York: Dryden Press.

Hiebert, R. E. (2005). Commentary: New technologies, public relations, and democracy. *Public Relations Review, 31*(1), pp. 1–10.

High tech PR: Was it all froth and hype? (2001, May 14). *PR Week,* p. 10.

Hill, L. N., & White, C. (2000). Public relations practitioners' perceptions of the World Wide Web as a communications tool. *Public Relations Review, 26*(1), pp. 31–52.

Ho, J. (2001, January 28). Evaluating the World Wide Web. A global study of commercial sites. Accessed at jcmc.huji.ac.il/vol3/issue1/ho.html.

Hoffman, D. L., & Novak, T. P. (1996). Marketing in hypermedia computer-mediated environments. Conceptual foundations. *Journal of Marketing, 60*(3), pp. 50–68.

Hon, L., & Grunig, J. E. (1999). Guidelines for measuring relationships in public relations. Gainesville, FL: The Institute for Public Relations.

Hoogeveen, M. (1997). Toward a theory of the effectiveness of multimedia systems. *International Journal of Human-Computer Interaction, 9*(1), pp. 151–168.

Horton, J. L. (2001). *Online public relations: A handbook for practitioners.* Westport, CT: Greenwood.

Huang, Y. (2001). OPRA—A cross-cultural, multiple-item scale for measuring organization-public relationships. *Journal of Public Relations Research, 13*(1), pp. 61–90.

Hume, P. (2001). Online PR: Emerging organizational practice. *Corporate Communications: An International Journal, 6*(2), pp. 71–75.

Hutton, J. G. (1999). The definition, dimensions and domain of public relations. *Public Relations Review, 25*(2), pp. 199–214.

Jacoby, J., & Chestnut, R. W. (1978). *Brand loyalty.* New York: John Wiley & Sons.

Jo, S., & Kim, Y. (2003). The effects of web characteristics on relationship building. *Journal of Public Relations Research, 15*(3), pp. 199–224.

Johnson, M. A. (1997). Public relations and technology: Practitioner perspectives. *Journal of Public Relations Research, 9*(3), pp. 213–236.

Johnson, T. J., & Kaye, B. K. (1998). Cruising is believing? Comparing the Internet and traditional sources of media credibility measures. *Journalism & Mass Communication Quarterly, 75*(2), pp. 325–340.

Jones, S. G. (1995). *Cybersociety: Computer-mediated-communication and community.* Thousand Oaks, CA: Sage.

Jung, J., Qiu, J., & Kim, Y. (2001). Internet connectedness and inequality. Beyond the "divide." *Communication Research, 28*(4), pp. 507–535.

Kang, S., & Norton, H. E. (2004). Nonprofit organization's use of the World Wide Web. Are they sufficiently fulfilling organizational goals? *Public Relations Review, 30*(3), pp. 279–284.

Kanoleas, D., & Teigen, L. G. (2000, October). The technology-image expectancy gap: A new theory of public relations. Paper presented to the Educators Academy, Public Relations Society of America, Chicago.

Katerattanakul, P., & Siau, K. (2000). Measuring information quality of web sites: Development of an instrument. Proceedings of the 20th Annual International Conference on Information Systems, Charlotte, NC (pp. 279–285).

Kayany, J. M., Wotring, C. E., & Forrest, E. J. (1996). Relational control and interactive media choice in technology-mediated communications situations. *Human Communication Research, 22*(3), pp. 399–421.

Kent, M. L. (1998/1999). Does your web site attract or repel customers? Three tests of web site effectiveness. *Public Relations Quarterly, 43*(4), pp. 31–33.

Kent, M. L., & Taylor, M. (1998). Building dialogic relationships through the World Wide Web. *Public Relations Review, 24*(3), pp. 321–334.

Kent, M. L., Taylor, M., & White, W. J. (2002). Toward a dialogic theory of public relations. *Public Relations Review, 28*(1), pp. 21–37.

———. (2003). The relationship between web site design and organizational responsiveness to stakeholders. *Public Relations Review, 29*(2), pp. 63–68.

Killoran, J. B. (1999). Under construction: A "PR" department for private citizens. *Business Communication Quarterly, 62*(2), pp. 101–104.

Kim, Y. (2002). Searching for the organization-public relationship: A valid and reliable instrument. *Journalism & Mass Communication Quarterly, 78*(4), pp. 799–815.

Kim, Y., & Jo, S. (2002, August). The effects of relationships on satisfaction, loyalty and future behavior. A case of a community bank. Paper presented to the Association for Education in Journalism and Mass Communication, Miami, FL.

King, R. C., & Xia, W. (1999). Media appropriateness. Effectiveness of experience on communication media choice. In K. E. Kendall (Ed.), *Emerging information technology. Improving decisions, cooperation and infrastructure* (pp. 143–175). Thousand Oaks, CA: Sage.

Kitchen, P. J., & Schultz, D. E. (2000). The role of integrated communication in the interactive age. In P. J. Kitchen & D. E. Schultz (Eds.), *Raising the corporate umbrella. Corporate communication in the 21st century* (pp. 82–114). New York: Palgrave/St. Martin's Press.

Knapp, M. L. (1978). *Social intercourse: From greeting to good-bye.* Boston: Allyn & Bacon.

Koslowsky, M., Lazar, A., & Hoffman, M. (1988). Validating an attitude toward computer scale. *Educational & Psychological Measurement, 48* (2), pp. 517–521.

Kraut, R., Lundmark, V., Patterson, M., Kieser, S., Mukopadhyay, T., & Scherlis, W. (1998). Internet paradox: A social technology that reduces social involvement and psychological well-being. *American Psychologist, 53*(9), pp. 1017–1031.

Lang, A. (2000). The limited capacity model of mediated message processing. *Journal of Communication, 50,* pp. 46–70.

Lazarsfeld, P., & Katz, E. (1995). *Personal influence: The part played by people in the flow of mass communications.* Glencoe, IL: Free Press.

Lea, M., & Spears, R. (1995). Love at first byte? Building relations over computer networks. In J. T. Wood & S. W. Duck (Eds.), *Under-studied relationships. Off the beaten track* (pp. 197–233). Thousand Oaks, CA: Sage.

Ledingham, J. A., & Bruning, S. D. (1998). Relationship management in public relations. Dimensions of an organization-public relationship. *Public Relations Review, 24,* pp. 55–65.

———. (2000). Introduction: Background and current trends in the study of relationship management. In J. A. Ledingham & S. D. Bruning (Eds.), *Relationship management: A relational approach to the study and practice of public relations* (pp. xi–xvii). Mahwah, NJ: Lawrence Erlbaum.

Len-Rios, M. E. (2002). The Bush and Gore presidential web sites: Identifying with Hispanic voters during the 2000 Iowa caucuses and New Hampshire primary. *Journalism & Mass Communication Quarterly, 79*(4), pp. 887–904.

Len-Rios, M. E., & Cameron, G. T. (2001). Playing by the rules: Relationships with online users—RATES (Rules-Appropriate Testing Evaluation Scale) and implications for e-commerce and portal web sites. Gainesville, FL: The Institute for Public Relations. Accessed at www. institute-forpr.com.

———. (2002, July). Knowing what to say and when to say it: Rules for building relationships with online publics. Paper presented to the International Communication Association, Seoul, South Korea.

Littlejohn, S. W. (2002). *Theories of human communication* (7th ed.) Belmont, CA: Wadsworth.

Liu, C., Arnett, K. P., Capella, L. M., & Beatty, R. C. (1997). Websites of the Fortune 500 companies: Facing customers through home pages. *Information and Management, 31*(6), pp. 335–345.

Lordan, E. J. (2001). Cyberspin: The use of new technologies in public relations. In R. L. Heath (Ed.), *Handbook of public relations* (pp. 583–590). Thousand Oaks, CA: Sage.

Loyd, B. H., & Gressard, C. (1984). Reliability and factorial validity of computer attitude scales. *Educational & Psychological Measurement, 44* (2), pp. 501–505.

Loyd, B. H., & Loyd, D. E. (1985). The reliability and validity of an instrument for the assessment of computer attitudes. *Educational & Psychological Measurement, 45*(4), pp. 903–908.

MacEvoy, B. (1997). Change leaders and new media. In L. Kahle & L. Chiagouris (Eds.), *Values, lifestyles and psychographics* (pp. 283–298). Mahwah, NJ: Lawrence Erlbaum.

Mackenzie, S. B., Lutz, R. J., & Belch, G. E. (1986). The role of attitude toward the ad as a mediator of advertising effectiveness: A test of competing explanations. *Journal of Marketing Research, 23*(2), pp. 130–143.

MacPherson, K. (2001). *Permission-based e-mail marketing that works.* Chicago: Dearborn Trade.

Major, M. J. (1995). How tech-friendly companies communicate. *Public Relations Journal, 51*(1), pp. 24–27.

Maynard, M., & Tan, Y. (2004). Between global and glocal: Content analysis of the Chinese web sites of the top 500 global brands. *Public Relations Review, 30*(3), pp. 285–292.

McLuhan, M. (1964). *Understanding media: The extensions of man.* New York: Signet.

McMillan, S. J. (2002). A four-part model of cyber-interactivity. *New Media & Society, 4*(2), pp. 271–291.

McMillan, S. J., & Dowes, E. J. (2000). Defining interactivity: A qualitative identification of key dimensions. *New Media & Society, 2,* pp. 157–179.

McNaughton, R. D. (2001). A typology of web site objectives in high technology business markets. *Marketing Intelligence & Planning, 19*(2), pp. 82–87.

Mead, G. H. (1934). *Mind, self and society.* Chicago: University of Chicago Press.

Meuter, M. L., Ostrom, A. L., Roundtree, R. I., & Bitner, M. J. (2000, July). Self-service technologies: Understanding customer satisfaction with technology-based service encounters. *Journal of Marketing, 64,* pp. 50–64.

Middleberg, D., & Ross, S. (2002). The Middleberg/Ross media survey: Change and its impact on communications. Eighth annual national survey. New York: Middleberg Associates.

Miller, D., & Slater, D. (2000). *The Internet: An ethnographic approach.* Oxford, England: Berg.

Mitchell, A. A., & Olson, J. C. (1981). Are product attribute beliefs the only mediator of advertising effects on brand attitudes? *Journal of Marketing Research, 18*(3), pp. 318–332.

Moon, Y. (2000). Intimate exchanges: Using computers to elicit self-disclosure from customers. *Journal of Consumer Research, 26,* pp. 323–339.

Morris, M., & Ogan, C. (1996). The Internet as mass medium. *Journal of Communication, 46,* pp. 39–50.

Morris-Lee, J. (2000). Assessing web site effectiveness. *Direct Marketing, 63*(3), pp. 30–33.

Murgolo-Poore, M. E., Pitt, L. F., Berthon, P. R., & Prendegast, G. (2003). Corporate intelligence dissemination as a consequence of Intranet effectiveness: An empirical study. *Public Relations Review, 29*(2), pp. 29–42.

Murgolo-Poore, M. E., Pitt, L., & Ewing, M. (2002). Intranet effectiveness: A public relations paper-and-pencil checklist. *Public Relations Review, 28,* pp. 113–123.

Naude, A. M. E., Froneman, J. D., & Atwood, R. A. (2004). The use of the Internet by ten South Africans non-government organizations—a public relations perspective. *Public Relations Review, 30*(1), pp. 87–94.

Neff, B. D. (1998). Harmonizing global relations. A speech theory analysis of PR forum. *Public Relations Review, 24*(3), pp. 351–376.

Newell, F. (2000). *Loyalty.com: Customer relationship management in the new era of Internet marketing.* New York: McGraw-Hill.

Nielsen, J. (2000). *Designing usability.* Indianapolis: New Rider.

———. (2001, April 1). Corporate websites get a 'D' in PR. *Alertbox.* Accessed September 1, 2004, at www.useit.com/alertbox/20010401.html.

Nowak, K. L. (2004, January). The influence of anthromorphism and agency on social judgment in virtual environments. *Journal of Computer-Mediated Communication, 9*(2). Accessed September 1, 2004, at jcmc.indiana.edu/vol9/issue2/nowak.html.

O'Connell, P. L. (1998, July 6). We got your e-mail: Just don't expect a reply. *New York Times,* p. C1.

Oliver, R. L. (1981). Measurement and evaluation of satisfaction process in retail setting. *Journal of Retailing, 57,* pp. 25–48.

O'Malley, M., & Irani, T. (1998, August). Public relations and the web: Measuring the effect of interactivity, information and access to information in web sites. Paper presented to the Association for Education in Journalism and Mass Communication, Baltimore.

Page, K. (2001, May). Prioritizing relations: Exploring goal compatibility between organizations and publics. Paper presented to the International Communication Association, Washington, DC.

Palmer, J. W., & Griffith, D. A. (1998). An emerging model of web site design for marketing. *Communications of the ACM, 41*(3), pp. 44–51.

Papacharissi, Z., & Rubin, A. (2000). Predictors of Internet use. *Journal of Broadcasting & Electronic Media, 44*(2), pp. 175–196.

Park, D., & Berger, B. K. (2002, July). Korean and American companies in cyberspace: Comparing public relations models reflected in web sites. Working paper, College of Communication, University of Alabama, Tuscaloosa.

———. (2002, July). The asymmetry of cyberspace communications: Public relations models reflected in the web sites of Fortune 500 and dot-com companies. Paper presented to the International Communication Association, Seoul, South Korea.

Parks, M. R. (1996). Making friends in cyberspace. *Journal of Communication, 46,* pp. 80–97.

Pavlik, J. V., & Dozier, D. M. (1996). *Managing the information superhighway: A report on issues facing communications professionals.* Gainesville, FL: The Institute for Public Relations Research & Education.

Peletier, J. W., Schibrowsky, J. A., & Schultz, D. E. (2003). Interactive integrated marketing communication: Combining the power of IMC, the new media and database marketing. *International Journal of Advertising, 22,* pp. 93–115.

Peng, S. (2001, August). Investigating dialogic communication. A content analysis of Chinese corporate web pages. Paper presented to the Association for Education in Journalism and Mass Communication, Washington, DC.

Perry, D. C., & Taylor, M. (2002, July). Internet adoption of traditional and new media tactics in crisis communication. Paper presented to the International Communication Association, Seoul, South Korea.

Perry, M., & Bodkin, C. (2000). Content analysis of Fortune 100 company web sites. *Corporate Communications, 2,* pp. 876–896.

Petrison, L. A., & Wang, P. (1993). From relationships to relationship marketing: Applying database technology to public relations. *Public Relations Review, 19*(3), pp. 235–245.

Petty, R. E., & Cacioppo, J. T. (1986). *Communication and persuasion: Central and peripheral routes to attitude change.* New York: Springer-Verlag.

Petty, R. E., Ostrom, T. E., & Brock, T. C. (1981). *Cognitive responses in persuasion.* Hillsdale, NJ: Lawrence Erlbaum.

Pew Internet and American Life Project (2002). Accessed September 1, 2002, at www. pewinternet .org.

Pfeffer, J., & Salancik, G. (1978*). The external control of organizations. A resource dependence perspective.* New York: Harper & Row.

Phillips, D. (2001). *Online public relations.* London: Kogen Poge.

Pierce, G. R. (1994). The quality of relationships inventory. Assessing the interpersonal context of social support. In B. R. Burleson, T. L. Albrecht, & I. G. Sarason (Eds.), *Communication of social support. Messages, interactions, relationships and community* (pp. 247–266). Thousand Oaks, CA: Sage.

Pope-Davis, D. B., & Twing, J. S. (1991). The effects of age, gender, and experience on measures of attitude regarding computers. *Computers in Human Behavior, 7*(4), pp. 333–339.

Porter, L. V., & Sallot, L. M. (2003). The Internet and public relations: Investigating practitioners' roles and the World Wide Web. *Journalism & Mass Communication Quarterly, 78*(1), pp. 172–190.

———. (2005). Web power: A survey of practitioners' World Wide Web use and their perceptions of their effects on their decision-making power. *Public Relations Review, 31*(1), pp. 111–120.

Porter, L. V., Sallot, M., Cameron, G., & Shamp, T. (2001). New technologies and public relations: Practitioner use of online resources to earn a seat at the management table. *Journalism and Mass Communication Quarterly, 78,* pp. 172–191.

Postman, N. (1992). *Technopoly.* New York: Knopf.

Postumes, T., Spears, R., & Lea, M. (1998). Breaching or building social boundaries? *Communication Research, 25,* pp. 689–716.

Preece, J. (2001). *Online communities. Designing usability, supporting sociability.* Chichester, England: John Wiley & Sons.

Prendergast, G. P., & Marr, N. E. (1993). Disenchantment discontinuance in the diffusion of self-service technologies in the services industry. A case study in retailing banking. *Journal of International Consumer Marketing, 7,* pp. 25–40.

Rafaeli, S., & Sudweeks, F. (1997). Networked interactivity. *Journal of Computer Mediated Communication, 2*(4). Accessed September 1, 2004, at www.usc/edu/dept/annenberg/vol2,issue4/rafaeli .sudsweek.html.

Reber, R. H., & Fosdick, S. (2002, August). Building business relationships online: Relationship management in business-to-business e-commerce. Paper presented to the Association for Education in Journalism and Mass Communication, Miami Beach, FL.

Reeves, B., & Nass. C. (1996). *The media equation. How people treat computers, television and new media like real people and places.* New York: Cambridge University Press.

Rewick, J. (2001, February 22). Not all company web sites live up to their billing. *Wall Street Journal,* p. B10.

Rheingold, H. (1993). *The virtual community. Homesteading on the electronic frontier.* Reading, MA: Addison-Wesley.

Roehm, H. A., & Haugtvedt, C. P. (1999). Understanding interactivity of cyberspace advertising. In D. W. Schumann & E. Thorson (Eds.), *Advertising and the World Wide Web* (pp. 27–39). Mahwah, NJ: Lawrence Erlbaum.

Rogers, E. (2003). *The diffusion of innovations* (5th ed). New York: Free Press.

Rosenberger, G. (2001). Relationship marketing from a consumer policy perspective. In T. Hennig-Thurau & U. Hansen (Eds.), *Relationship marketing: Gaining competitive advantage through customer satisfaction and customer retention* (pp. 353–368). Berlin: Springer.

Rust, R. T., & Varki, S. (1996). Rising from the ashes of advertising. *Journal of Business Research, 37,* pp. 173–181.

Ryan, M. (2000). Gender, experience and public relations practitioner adoption of new technologies. *Southwestern Mass Communication Journal, 16*(1), pp. 49–60.

Salam, A. F., Rao, H. R., & Pegels, C. C. (1998). Content of corporate web pages as advertising media. *Communication of the ACM, 41*(3), pp. 76–77.

Sallot, L. M., Porter, L. V., & Acosta-Alzuru, C. (2004). Practitioners' web use and perceptions of their own roles and power. A qualitative study. *Public Relations Review, 30*(3), pp. 269–278.

Schlosser, A. (2000). Harnessing the power of interactivity: Implications for consumer behavior in online environments. In S. J. Hoch & R. J. Meyer (Eds.), *Advances in consumer research, 27* (p. 79). Valdosta, GA: Association for Consumer Research.

Schultz, D., & Schultz, H. (2004). *IMC: The next generation. Five steps for delivering value and measuring returns using marketing communication.* New York: McGraw-Hill.

Shockley, P., Ellis, K., & Cesaria, R. (2000). Measuring organizational trust. A diagnostic survey and international indicator. San Francisco: International Association of Business Communicators.

Seybold, P. B. (1996). Don't let PR control your web site! *Computerworld, 30*(15), p. 37.

Shaw, R. (2001, February 21). Using web-based customer feedback. *PR Week,* p. 24.

Sheppard, B. H., Hartwick, J., & Warshaw, J. R. (1988). The theory of reasoned action: A meta-analysis of past research with recommendations for modifications and future research. *Journal of Consumer Research, 15* (December), pp. 325–343.

Sheth, N. J., & Parvatiyar, A. (1995). Relationship marketing in consumer markets: Antecedents and consequences. *Journal of Academy of Marketing Science, 23*, pp. 255–271.

Shin, J., & Cameron, G. T. (2003). The potential of online media; A coorientational analysis of conflict between PR practitioners and journalists in South Korea, *Journalism & Mass Communication Quarterly, 80*(3), pp. 583–602.

Short, J., Williams, E., & Christie, B. (1976). *The social psychology of telecommunications.* London: John Wiley & Sons.

Shostack, J. (1977). Breaking free from product marketing. *Journal of Marketing, 41*, pp. 73–80.

Silverman, G. (2001). *The secrets of word-of-mouth marketing.* New York: Amacom.

Sisodia, R. S., & Wolfe, D. B. (2000). Information technology: Its role in building, maintaining and enhancing relationships. In J. N. Sheth & A. Parvatiyar (Eds.), *Handbook of relationship marketing* (pp. 525–564). Thousand Oaks, CA: Sage.

Spencer, J. (2005, February 8). The annoying new face of customer service. *Wall Street Journal,* p. B1.

Spataro, M. (1998). Net relations: a function of direct marketing and public relations. *Direct Marketing, 61*(4), pp. 16–20.

Springston, J. K. (2001). Public relations and new media technology: The impact of the Internet. In R. L. Heath (Ed.), *Handbook of public relations* (pp. 603–614). Thousand Oaks, CA: Sage.

Sproull, L., & Kiesler, S. (1986). Reducing social context cues: Electronic mail in organizational communication. *Management Science, 32*, pp. 1492–1512.

Stauss, B. (2000). Using new media for customer interaction: A challenge for relationship marketing. In T. Hennig-Thurau & U. Hansen (Eds.), *Relationship marketing: Gaining competitive advantage through customer satisfaction and customer retention* (pp. 233–253). Berlin: Springer.

Steinfield, C., Kraut, R., & Plummer, A. (1996). The impact of interorganizational networks on buyer-seller relationships. *Journal of Computer Mediated Communication, 1*(3). Accessed September 1, 2004, at www.ascusc.org/jcmc/vol1/issue3/steinfld.htm.

Steuer, J. (1992). Defining virtual reality. Dimensions determining telepresence. *Journal of Communication, 42*(4), pp. 73–93.

Stevenson, J. S., Bruner, G. C., III, & Kumar, A. (2000). Webpage background and viewer attitudes. *Journal of Advertising Research, 40*(1–2), pp. 29–34.

Stewart, D. W., Frazier, G. L., & Martin, I. (1996). Integrated channel management: Merging the communication and distribution functions of the firm. In E. Thorson & J. Moore (Eds.), *Integrated communication. Synergy of persuasive voices* (pp. 185–216). Mahwah, NJ: Lawrence Erlbaum.

Stoll, C. (1995). *Silicon snake oil. Second thoughts on the information highway.* New York: Doubleday.

Sundar, S. S. (2000). Multimedia effects on processing and perception of online news: A study of picture, audio and video downloads. *Journalism and Mass Communication Quarterly, 77*(3), pp. 480–499.

Tamimi, N., Rajan, M., & Sebastanelli, R. (2000). Benchmarking the home pages of Fortune 500 companies. *Quality Progress, 33*(7), pp. 47–51.

Taylor, M., Kent, M. L., & White, W. J. (2001). How activist organizations are using the Internet to build relationships. *Public Relations Review, 27*(3), pp. 263–284.

Taylor, M., & Perry, D. C. (2005). Diffusion of traditional and new media tactics in crisis communication. *Public Relations Review, 31*(2), pp. 209–218.

Tewksbury, D., & Althaus, S. L. (2000). Differences in knowledge acquisition among readers of the paper and online versions of a national newspaper. *Journalism and Mass Communication Quarterly,* 77(3), pp. 457–479.

Thibaut, J. W., & Kelley, H. H. (1959). *The social psychology of groups.* New York: John Wiley.

Thomsen, S. R. (1996). @work in cyberspace. Exploring practitioner use of the PR forum. *Public Relations Review, 22*(2), pp. 115–132.

Tindal, R. (2003). Building guanxi on the Web: 10 tips for creating an online presence in China. *Public Relations Tactics, 10*(7), p. 6.

Tomlinson, T. D. (2000). An interpersonal prime with implications for public relations. In J. A. Ledingham & S. D. Bruning (Eds.), *Public relations as relationship management: A relational approach to the study and practice of public relations* (pp. 177–204). Mahwah, NJ: Lawrence Erlbaum.

Toth, E. L. (2000). From personal influence to interpersonal influence. A model for relationship management. In J. A. Ledingham & S. D. Bruning (Eds.), *Public relations as relationship management: A relational approach to the study and practice of public relations* (pp. 205–219). Mahwah, NJ: Lawrence Erlbaum.

Treacy, M., & Wiersema, F. (1993). Customer intimacy and other value disciplines. *Harvard Business Review, 71*(1), pp. 84–96.

Trevino, L. K., Lengel, R. H., & Daft, R. L. (1987). Media symbolism, media richness and media choice in organizations. *Communication Research, 14*(5), pp. 553–574.

Turkle, Sherry (1995). *Life on the screen: Identity in the age of the Internet.* New York: Touchstone.

Van Es, R., & Meijlink, T. J. (2000). The dialogic turn of public relations ethics. *Journal of Business Ethics, 27*, pp. 69–77.

Vasquez, G. (1994). A *homo narrans* paradigm for public relations. Combining Bormann's symbolic convergence theory with Grunig's situational theory of publics. *Journal of Public Relations Research, 5*(3), pp. 201–216.

Vattyan, S., & Lubbers, C. A. (1999, August). A content analysis of the web pages of large U.S. corporations: What is the role of public and marketing? Paper presented to the Association for Education in Journalism and Mass Communication, New Orleans.

Wallace, P. (1999). *The psychology of the Internet.* New York: Cambridge University Press.

Walther, J. B. (1992). Interpersonal effects on computer-mediated interaction: A relational perspective. *Communication Research, 19*(1), pp. 52–90.

———. (1996). CMC: Impersonal, interpersonal and hyperpersonal interaction. *Communication Research, 23*(1), pp. 3–43.

Walther, J. B., Slovacek, C., & Tidwell, L. C. (2001). Is a picture worth a thousand words? Photographic images in long-term and short-term computer mediated communication. *Communication Research, 28*(2), pp. 105–134.

Wathen, C. N., & Burkell, J. (2002). Believe it or not: Factors influencing credibility on the web. *Journal of the American Society for Information Science and Technology, 53*(2), pp. 134–144.

Weber, T. E. (1996, October 21). Simplest e-mail queries confound companies. *Wall Street Journal,* p. B1.

Weill, G. (2001). PR repercussions from the Internet shakeout. *Public Relations Tactics, 8*(7), p. 6.

Wellman, B., & Guila, M. (1999). Net surfers don't ride alone: Virtual communities as communities. In P. K. Kollock & M. Smith (Eds.), *Communities and cyberspace* (pp. 167–194). New York: Routledge.

White, C., & Raman, N. (1999). The World Wide Web as a public relations medium: The use of research, planning and evaluation in web site development. *Public Relations Review, 25*(4), pp. 405–420.

Williamson, O. E. (1985). *The economic institutions of capitalism.* New York: Free Press.

Wilson, D. T. (2000). An integrated model of buyer-seller relationships. In J. N. Sheth & A. Parvatiyar (Eds.), *Handbook of relationship marketing* (pp. 245–270). Thousand Oaks, CA: Sage.

Wilson, L. J. (1994). The return to Gemeinschaft: A theory of public relations and corporate community relations as relationship building. In A. F. Alkhafaji (Ed.), *Business research yearbook. Global business perspectives, 1* (pp. 135–141). Lanham, MD: University Press of America.

Wood, A. F., & Smith, M. J. (2001). *Online communication. Linking technology, identity and culture.* Mahwah, NJ: Lawrence Erlbaum.

Wood, J. (1995). *Relational communication. Continuity and change in personal relationships.* Belmont, CA: ITP Wadsworth.

Wright, D. K. (1998). *Corporate communications policy concerning the Internet: A survey of the nation's senior-level corporate public relations officers.* Gainesville, FL: The Institute for Public Relations.

———. (2001). *The magic communication machine. Examining the Internet's impact on public relations, journalism and the public.* Gainesville, FL: The Institute for Public Relations.

Zufryden, F. (2000). New film website promotion and box-office performance. *Journal of Advertising Research, 40*(1–2), pp. 55–64.

FUNDAMENTAL PERSPECTIVES
Creating Action and Meaning Through Messaging

Bonita Dostal Neff

Tricia Hansen-Horn

All fields of scholar and application have roots in foundational perspectives. Public relations theory and scholarship have roots in understandings of the process of diffusion, dialogic and nondialogic, social constructs, dramatic interplay, and contingent positioning and choices.

One of the more well-known theoretical applications is based in diffusion theory. Carden brings to our attention the importance of innovation-decision theory when working with publics, a concept fundamental to the practice of public relations. Neff builds on the dialogic approach to establish the full contextual framework of interactivity. Culture, the self, the episode, the relationship, and the public relations act bind the process together for examining the foundational elements of public relations.

Social constructionism is examined by Gordon and Pellegrin as a way to understand the world though one's discourse. Based fully within the interaction process, these authors contend that the view of social constructionism is framed from both a dialogic and rhetoric perspective. Mickey adds sociodrama theory as a communication-based approach to the practice of public relations. Elements of drama create more of a contextual environ for public relations interrelationships, a factor that adds importance to the words we use. It is contingency theory that focuses on the use of language to move publics toward one or another stance. Cameron, Pang, and Jin demonstrate how one uses language to change the stance of a position. Noting the process of changing positions is important in understanding the movements between advocacy and accommodation.

....

CHAPTER FIVE

WORKING WITH INNOVATORS AND LAGGARDS

The Diffusion of Innovations Theory and Public Relations

ANN R. CARDEN

Imagine it is time for you to buy a new car. You will likely take a number of steps to complete the process. First, you need to become aware of the various choices you have. You may accomplish this by noticing commercials on TV, looking at ads in magazines, or asking your friends what they drive. Based on what you discover, you narrow your choices. This will probably be based on how much you can afford, the attractiveness of the choices, and how they fit your needs. This leads you to do additional research on your final choices—perhaps searching for safety ratings or reading *Consumer Reports*.

You finally find the perfect car. You go to the car dealership and take it for a test drive. Even though you love it, you decide to go home to think about it. A couple of days later you return to the dealership and purchase the car. You have just gone through the adoption phase of the diffusion of innovations process.

This chapter breaks down the various elements of the diffusion process, explains how they work together to disseminate messages, looks at how the process applies to both external and internal target publics, and, most important, why it is so important in the practice of public relations.

THE THEORY OF THE DIFFUSION OF INNOVATIONS

> Never doubt that a small group of thoughtful committed citizens can change the world. Indeed, it's the only thing that ever has.
>
> —Margaret Mead

The foundation for the diffusion of innovation theory was laid in 1903 when Gabriel Tarde plotted an S-curve to represent the rate at which ideas are adopted. In 1943, the adoption process was further explored by Bryce Ryan and Neal Gross when they studied the diffusion of hybrid seed among Iowa farmers. One of the most important findings from this study was the categorization of the farmers based on how long it took them to adopt the innovation ("Diffusion of Innovation" 2003, p. 16).

The theory as we know it today was introduced by Everett Rogers in the early 1960s. He defined the diffusion of innovations as "the process by which an innovation is communicated through certain channels over time among the members of a social system" (1983, p. 5). Four elements define the process: innovation, channels, time, and social system.

Innovation

Rogers (1983) defines an innovation as "an idea, practice, or object that is perceived as new by an individual or other unit of adoption" (p. 11). Innovations can take many forms. They may be a new product or service; a significant differentiation of an existing product or service; a change in market position, price, quality, or customer service; or a restructuring of the organization. The key here is that if something is *perceived* as new, it is an innovation to the person being asked to adopt it. According to Rogers, innovations have five characteristics:

> *Relative advantage* is the degree to which an innovation is perceived as better than the idea it superseded. . . . *Compatibility* is the degree to which an innovation is perceived as being consistent with the existing values, past experiences and needs of potential adopters. . . . *Complexity* is the degree to which an innovation is perceived as difficult to understand and use. . . . *Trialability* is the degree to which the innovation may be experimented with on a limited basis. . . . *Observability* is the degree to which the results of an innovation are visible to others. (pp. 15–16)

Innovations are diffused at different rates, partly because of these characteristics. For example, innovations that are perceived as being better than a current situation, compatible with existing values, simple, and easy to try with visible results are more readily adopted than those innovations perceived as being worse than the current situation, incompatible with existing values, and difficult.

Channel

As with any type of communication, a channel is necessary to relay the message from the sender to the receiver. In the diffusion of innovations theory, mass media and interpersonal communication are the most frequently used channels. While mass media is an effective vehicle to create or increase awareness of an innovation, decisions on whether to adopt the innovation are more likely to be affected by interpersonal communication (Cutlip, Center, & Broom, 2000).

Time

There are three factors involved in this element: the innovation-decision process; relative time (of adoption) with which an innovation is adopted by an individual or group; and the innovation's rate of adoption (Rogers, 1983).

A critical component of the diffusion of innovations theory is the innovation-decision process, during which an individual goes from becoming aware of an innovation to adopting or rejecting it. It is important to note the difference between this adoption process, which involves individual decision making, and the diffusion process as a whole, which occurs as a group process within society. There are five stages to the innovation-decision process:

> *Knowledge* occurs when an individual . . . is exposed to the innovation's existence and gains some understanding of how it functions. *Persuasion* occurs when an individual . . . forms a favorable or unfavorable attitude toward the innovation. *Decision* occurs when an individual engages in activities that lead to a choice to adopt or reject the innovation. *Implementation* occurs when an individual . . . puts an innovation into use. *Confirmation* occurs when an individual . . . seeks reinforcement of an innovation-decision that has already been made. (Rogers, 1983, p. 20)

These five stages are sometimes referred to as awareness, information, evaluation, trial, and adoption (Newsom, Scott, & Turk 1996).

Let's go back to the car-buying example at the beginning of this chapter. Knowledge (awareness) occurred when you noticed cars advertised on TV or in magazines and asked your friends what they drove. Persuasion (information) occurred when you narrowed your choices and conducted additional research. This led you to make a decision (evaluation) based on what you had learned. When you went to the dealership to test drive your selected car, you implemented your decision (trial), which was confirmed (adopted) when you bought it.

At any time during the innovation-decision process, an individual may choose to reject the innovation. A decision to reject an innovation *after* it has been adopted is referred to as *discontinuance*. Rogers (1983) defines two types of discontinuance: "A *replacement discontinuance* is a decision to reject an idea in order to adopt a better idea that supercedes it . . . A *disenchantment discontinuance* is a decision to reject an idea as a result of dissatisfaction with its performance" (pp. 186–187). Using the car example once again, possible choices were rejected for one reason or another throughout the entire process. When you finally selected a car and took it for a test drive, two things might have happened after you bought the car: you might have been *disenchanted* with your choice—perhaps it turned out to be uncomfortable, difficult to drive, or a lemon. Or you may have decided on a *replacement*. Perhaps you became aware of a more perfect car and decided to start the process all over.

In addition to the characteristics of the innovation, the characteristics of the public targeted for the innovation will influence the adoption process. Innovativeness is "the degree to which an individual . . . is relatively earlier in adopting new ideas than the other members of a system" (Rogers, 1983, p. 22).

In their 1943 study, Ryan and Gross categorized Iowa farmers based on their innovativeness. The researchers found that the farmers who were the first to adopt the innovation shared characteristics that were different from those groups that adopted the innovation at a later time (Rogers, 1983). Rogers (as cited in "Diffusion of Innovation") went on to label and characterize the groups involved in the adoption process:

■ *Innovators* are venturesome and like to take risks. They are able to cope with the uncertainty that often accompanies an innovation, are able to understand complex material, and are financially secure.

■ *Early adopters* are respectable members of a localized social system. They are opinion leaders, serve as role models, and are successful.

■ Those in the *early majority* are deliberate in nature. They interact frequently with their peers, but are seldom opinion leaders.

■ Those in the *late majority* tend to be skeptical and cautious. They usually adopt innovations because of pressure from peers or out of economic necessity.

■ *Laggards* are traditional people who are suspicious of innovations. Their point of reference is the past.

Tarde's S-shaped curve lends explanatory power here. The S-curve represents the rate of adoption for most innovations. The slant of the S-curve will vary, depending on the length of time it takes to adopt an innovation. Innovations that are adopted quickly will be reflected in a steep S-curve, while innovations that are adopted slowly will be reflected in an S-curve with a more gradual slope (see Figure 5.1). The five categories of adopters can also be traced on the S-curve, which forms a bell curve when the process is complete. Traditionally, innovators make up the first 2.5 percent; early adopters, 13.5 percent; the early majority and

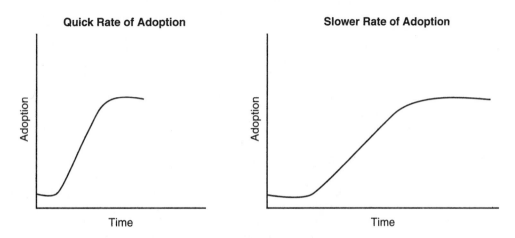

FIGURE 5.1   The variations of the S-curve during an adoption process

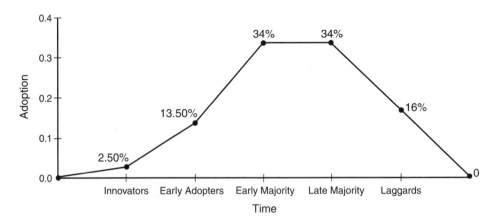

FIGURE 5.2   Distribution of adopter categories during the diffusion process

late majority, 34 percent each; and laggards, 16 percent (see Figure 5.2). An important point on the S-curve is the point of critical mass. This is where enough people have adopted the innovation that further adoption will not affect the diffusion of the innovation (Rogers, 1983).

Social System

A social system is defined as "a set of interrelated units that are engaged in joint problem solving to accomplish a common goal" (Rogers, 1983, p. 24). A social system—which may consist of organizations, informal groups, individuals, or subsystems—is the area within which an innovation is diffused. An examination of the social system includes looking at how diffusion affects the social structure, how the norms of the social structure affect the diffusion process, the role played by opinion leaders in the process, the decisions made about the innovation, and the consequences of the innovation (Rogers, 1983).

Of special note here are opinion leaders. Public relations practitioners have long known the importance of this group in influencing target publics. The role they play in the diffusion of innovations process, often as early adopters, is just as critical in spreading information and influencing the rest of the social system. Other integral roles in the diffusion process are change agents and change aides. Change agents are typically professionals with degrees in technical fields who enjoy a high social status. Their role is to influence the innovative decisions of the social system, or clients, based on what they think the agency spearheading the change wants (Rogers, 1983).

> The change agent functions are to develop a need for change on the part of the client, to establish an information-exchange relationship, to diagnose the client problems, to create intent to change in the client, to translate this intent into action, to stabilize adoption and prevent discontinuance, and to shift the client from reliance on the change agent to self-reliance. (Clarke, 1999, paragraph 14)

Assisting the change agent may be a change aide, a person with less training and, therefore, lower social status (Rogers, 1983). They have "more intensive contact with clients ... less competence credibility but more safety or trustworthiness credibility" (Clarke, 1999, paragraph 13).

DIFFUSING INFORMATION TO EXTERNAL PUBLICS

> This "telephone" has too many shortcomings to be seriously considered as a means of communication. The device is inherently of no value to us.
>
> —Western Union internal memo, 1897

The past fifty years have seen the ready adoption of tremendous technological advances; other innovations, however, have been adopted so slowly that the S-curve looked like a straight line. An example of quick adoption is the sticky yellow piece of paper that is probably marking an important page in this book. 3M's Post-it® notes were created by accident, but when they were introduced to the public in 1980, it took only one year for them to be named 3M's Outstanding New Product ("Art Fry," 1998). Today, with a product line of more than six-hundred items, Post-it® products are among the most popular available. A 1998 poll that surveyed more than thousand U.S. workers found that professionals use more than eleven Post-it® notes every day ("Post-it," 2003).

Another innovation that has quickly become part of our daily lives is the Internet. The Internet was developed in the mid-1960s as a resource to connect researchers at colleges and government facilities. The Internet as we know it today was introduced in 1982. In 1984, there were more than 1,000 hosts; three years later, there were more than 10,000 hosts. By 1990, the Internet was an essential tool for communication and had more than 300,000 hosts. Two years later, hosts exceeded the 1-million mark. By 1996, 40 million people were connected among 10 million hosts. Today, more than 605 million people are "wired" ("How Many Online," 2002).

Not all innovations catch on so quickly, however. Let's go back to the car-buying example, except the year is 1957. Since 1955, the media and public had been anticipating the introduction of Ford's new car division, Edsel. In September, when the new models were unveiled, 3 million people visited showrooms. Their response was underwhelming. Then a recession hit that had severe impact on all of Ford's car sales. Little more than 63,000 cars were sold in Edsel's first year of production, 1958; 45,000 were sold in 1959; and fewer than 3,000 were sold in 1960, the last year of production. Much has been written about what led to the failure. One possibility was its name. Following twelve months of market research to name the new Ford, a choice was made by company executives to name it after Henry Ford's only son, Edsel. It is interesting to note that the public relations director for the new division responded to the name selection in an internal memo, stating, "We have just lost 200,000 sales" (Young, 1989).

As already discussed, innovations are diffused at various rates, usually based on the characteristics of the innovation and the target publics. At the heart of the public relations process are the decisions practitioners make about their organization's target publics, the groups of people on which the success of the organization depends. Practitioners must not only correctly identify their target publics, but also analyze their wants, interests, and needs to construct effective messages for them. Public relations practitioners also are responsible for determining the best ways to communicate those messages, whether through mass media or interpersonal communication, such as the use of opinion leaders, or through a variety of other communicative means.

Because of these functions, it is critical that public relations be involved throughout the diffusion process. To introduce innovations in the most effective way, public relations practitioners often work with marketing and advertising professionals to develop a fully integrated communication plan aimed at creating awareness of an innovation and ultimately increasing sales through adoption ("Diffusion of Innovation," 2003).

DIFFUSING INFORMATION
TO INTERNAL PUBLICS

> Public relations is everybody's job.
>
> —Arthur W. Page

Even before innovations are diffused to external publics, they must be diffused internally. Employees are the most important customers an organization has and should be given at least the same attention as external publics. Yes, employees are customers, and when they receive poor service, they do what most dissatisfied customers do—they complain. Every dissatisfied customer tells about thirteen other people. Still, employees, an organization's most powerful selling force, are often overlooked.

Let's go back to the car dealership where you test drove your car. How would you react if the salesperson spoke negatively about the car dealership itself? Employees represent the organizations for which they work. They help create a public image of that organization, an image that may not be consistent with the one the organization thinks it has or would like to have.

Think about it. At the end of the day, employees go home to their family, friends, and neighbors, and they talk about their day at work—the good, the bad, and the ugly. When people have a question about products, programs, or services offered by a company, they often go to an employee of that organization for the "real story." As an organization's "front line," employees are seen as a more credible, interpersonal source of information. That's power, and it can make or break an organization.

Yet, according to some surveys, CEOs spend as little as 15 percent of their time talking with, rather than to, employees. This can result in low employee morale and poor attitude, which translates into low productivity and less-than-desirable messages going to external publics (Newsom, Scott, & Turk, 1996).

When employees are communicated with effectively, however, they respect management more, are happier, and take pride in the products they produce or services they offer, which results in positive messages going to external publics.

While employee satisfaction depends on a variety of things such as benefits, salaries, and work schedules, there is no doubt that good communication is one of the top factors of job satisfaction:

> A recent Gemini study showed two-thirds of workers worldwide would leave their current employer for a 10% increase in salary. The same survey showed that only 16% knew their company's mission. But interestingly, the survey indicated that employees who do see a connection between the company's mission and what they do are *17%* more likely to remain with their employer even if they are offered that 10% increase to go elsewhere. (Curley, 2001, paragraph 12)

Engaging Employees in Public Relations

Communicating with employees and educating them about the organization is more than a "feel good" endeavor—it is important to the organization's bottom line. Employees should be thought of as an extension of the public relations department. Organizational knowledge not only makes them feel more a part of the organization, it also helps to maintain the organization's reputation and to promote its products, programs, and services to customers.

A. Smith (1990) writes, "Maintaining or winning back the loyalty and commitment of employees—and gaining their cooperation in achieving corporate quality and productivity goals—will be the greatest challenge facing corporate communicators in the next few years" (p. 20). It still is. Since the 1990s, it seems that the one thing constant in business has been change—restructuring, reengineering, re-creating, reundertaking. Communication is an essential part of diffusing such change and innovation within an organization. "The fact that the failures of so many large-scale change projects has been attributed to weak communication has put a spotlight on this area" (Curley, 2001, paragraph 8).

> Today, the biggest growth opportunities lie in leveraging intangible assets, such as relationships; innovations; data; and employee skills and motivation. In other words, today's growth strategies depend on good communication. . . . Another driver is the growth focus on employee empowerment. To increase innovation and speed, power must be decentralized. Broader empowerment requires better information sharing and a new level of internal dialogue. (Curley, 2001, paragraphs 4–5, 9)

The five adopter categories—innovators, early adopters, early and late majorities, and laggards—can be found in any organization. The laggards are usually the easiest to pick out, because they are the ones who react negatively to change and protest the loudest ("But we've never done it that way before"), even though they are relatively small in number. The innovators and early adopters, on the other end of the scale, may sometimes be harder to identify. However, they are critical to achieving success in diffusing any innovation.

Success Stories

PNC Financial Services.   When a new chair came on board at PNC Financial Services, headquartered in Pittsburgh, he offered a challenge to employees. Chairman Jim Rohr, who wanted to establish a corporate culture that was driven by sales and marketing, issued the Chairman's Challenge ("PNC Financial Services," 2002).

Prior to the start of a campaign to increase sales referrals by employees, a survey of nearly two thousand staff members found that 30 percent of them did not think they had the knowledge they needed to adequately describe PNC products and services to family and friends. In addition, 72 percent of employees not working in sales said they had never referred a customer to PNC; however, six out of ten employees said they would. A key finding of the research was that employees would be willing to promote the company to friends and family if PNC provided them with consistent communication and education about products and services. The Chairman's Challenge sought to add PNC's 14,000 employees to the company's existing sales force and, as a result, "obtain 10,000 new customer accounts leading to new business sales totaling $40 million" ("PNC Financial Services," 2002, planning section, paragraph 1).

As part of the sales campaign, which followed a creative baseball theme, information was diffused in many ways, including through a Chairman's Challenge team that was made up of employees from various departments providing ongoing communication and support to employees ("PNC Financial Services," 2002).

> The Chairman's Challenge was the biggest employee sales success in PNC history. . . . Post-campaign research showed that 96% of employees rated the communications as "good-to-excellent.". . . 86% of employees believe they have the knowledge they need to initially sell PNC's products. . . . The campaign resulted in 12,563 new customer accounts with deposits of $85 million. ("PNC Financial Services," 2002, Evaluation section, paragraphs 1–5)

As part of the campaign's evaluation, one employee provided the following feedback: "The Chairman's Challenge serves as a useful reminder of what each of us can do to attract more customers" ("PNC Financial Services" 2002, evaluation section, p. 6). The campaign received a 2002 Silver Anvil Award for internal communications from the Public Relations Society of America (PRSA).

ALLTEL Communications.   The 2001 Silver Anvil Award for marketing consumer services went to ALLTEL Communications for its Project Splash. When ALLTEL acquired GTE Wireless properties, it was instantly faced with several business challenges: even though ALLTEL was now a major player in Cleveland, Akron, and Canton, Ohio, it was still thought of as a rural telephone company with no technological expertise; there was heavy competition; and aggressive third-quarter sales targets were set—the highest in either ALLTEL's or GTE's history ("Project Splash," 2001).

Even though employees were already trying to adjust to a new corporate climate resulting from the merger, they were expected to play a big role in meeting the sales projections. ALLTEL needed staff members to market from the inside out—to be a resource to customers, act as message carriers, and serve as ambassadors in the community. A multifaceted internal communications program engaged employees and led to a 45 percent increase in awareness of ALLTEL and a 39.5 percent increase in store traffic. The aggressive sales goals were exceeded by 6 percent ("Project Splash," 2001).

Effective Employee Communication

There are six fundamental principles that organizations should use to effectively communicate with employees, especially during the diffusion process: be honest; share the good, the bad, and the ugly; don't forget the "why"; speak with one voice; be timely; and say it, do it.

An organization must be honest with its employees. Trust and respect must exist as foundations for communication efforts; without them, any efforts will fail. Organizations must share the good, the bad, and the ugly. As humans, we all know that life isn't always a bed of roses, so organizations shouldn't try to sugarcoat bad information. In fact, sharing the bad news, as well as the good, helps an organization become more credible in the eyes of its employees. In general, people prefer hearing bad news to no news, seven to one. The worst thing that can happen to an organization is for employees to hear bad news from an outside source. It's embarrassing for the employees and disastrous for the organization.

While it is essential that employees are kept informed of decisions, changes, and developments affecting the company, it is just as important that they are told the reasons for those decisions—the "why" behind the "what." Such explanations help provide a big picture to employees and allow them to feel part of a team. Employees are first and foremost concerned with how change affects them directly. Organizations must explain how the big picture (the goals of the organization) links with each employee and the role he or she plays in reaching those goals. Organizations must speak with one voice. Public relations practitioners are well aware of the "one-voice principle," the goal of which is to disseminate consistent messages.

Communication must be timely. The lack of information creates a vacuum that will be filled, usually with rumors and inaccuracies. The longer it takes for accurate information to be communicated, the bigger the vacuum will become and the more difficult it will be to overcome the grapevine.

And finally, if you say it, do it. An organization's management team must model the behavior that it wants employees to follow. Also, management must do what it says it is planning to do. Lots of words but no action will result in a corrosion of credibility in the eyes of employees. In this type of environment, it will not take long for the latest innovation to be labeled the "flavor of the month."

CONCLUSION

This chapter takes a close look at the diffusion of innovations theory and its importance in the practice of public relations. When introducing anything that may be perceived as new by internal or external publics, keep in mind the four components of the diffusion process: the innovation itself, communication channels, time, and the social system. All this must be contextualized by a realistic attitude about the length of time it will take for the innovation to be adopted based on the innovation's characteristics—relative advantage, compatibility, complexity, trialability, and observability.

Five stages of the adoption process must be addressed—knowledge, persuasion, decision, implementation, and confirmation—in the strategic plan. All five adopter categories must be identified—innovators, early adopters, early majority, late majority, and laggards—in the social system in which the innovation will be introduced. Innovators and early adopters need to be engaged to help with the diffusion process.

Most important, the diffusion of innovations should start at home. Internal publics should be included in the process so that they, in turn, can assist in diffusing information to external publics. Ways to boost the flow and exchange of creativity, knowledge, and innovation within the organization must be sought. Learning more about employee empowerment, closed versus open systems, and proactive versus reactive public relations is a starting point for new ideas.

CASE: NATIONWIDE

The following information was taken from the nomination for "Employees and Agents Picture a Brand-new Way of Doing Business: Nationwide's Internal Branch Launch Campaign," which received the 2000 Silver Anvil Award for internal communications from PRSA.

> In 1998, Nationwide research revealed consumer perception of large insurance companies in general and Nationwide in particular did not reflect the kind of relationships it wanted with its customers. However, employees and agents were comfortable doing business the way they always had. They had helped Nationwide reach its current level of growth and profitability through their processes. . . . Nationwide was strong and powerful, an industry leader. Why tamper with success and risk its position of strength? (paragraphs 2–3, 6)

Because of changes occurring within the industry and the research findings regarding customer perceptions, Nationwide decided to pursue a new customer-focused brand strategy that would emphasize three principles: access, customization, and ease of use. However, it was clear that the strategy would fail unless employees and agents could be convinced to adopt it, and that wouldn't be easy.

Nationwide decided to launch an internal campaign prior to introducing the new brand publicly in an effort to gain support from employees and agents. To help develop the campaign, extensive research was conducted in the form of literature reviews, surveys, interviews, and focus groups. The research found that "although consumers wanted change, employees didn't believe Nationwide would embrace it. In focus groups they dismissed the brand initiative as the 'flavor of the month.'" (research section, paragraph 1).

Nationwide's communication staff was given the task of overcoming the internal resistance to change. To be successful, it would have to reach more than 40,000 employees and agents working out of nearly 10,000 locations. Campaign objectives included educating internal publics on the meaning and value of the new brand, their role in the new brand strategy, and building excitement about the new brand to enable its acceptance.

Among the many strategies and tactics included in the campaign were the training of brand coaches and the establishment of a Brand Builders program. Brand coaches were selected from the company's officer level and trained to train others in their departments. One nonmanagement employee was selected from every twenty-five to fifty employees to participate in the Brand Builders program, the goal of which was to help the staff "learn how to live the brand" and make it "an integral part of everyday life at Nationwide" (planning section, paragraph 5).

Evaluative research conducted following the internal campaign and the public brand launch revealed that "employee commitment to the brand was measured at 93 percent and agent commitment at 75 percent" (evaluation section, paragraph 3), compared to the expectations of 65 percent.

Using the three-month period between the internal launch and the public advertising launch proved an investment in employee and agent acceptance of the new brand and commitment to its success. The employees and agents actually became change agents for the brand. . . . Having been actively involved in the corporate culture change, Nationwide employees and agents now eagerly meet—even exceed—customers' expectations of doing business on their terms with access, customization, and ease of use. (evaluation section, paragraphs 4, 6)

QUESTIONS FOR APPLICATION

1. Identify and apply the various elements of the adoption process in one of the following scenarios:

   - College selection
   - Career choice
   - Product purchase

2. See if you can identify the five adopter categories in your workplace or other type of organization in which you are active by observing people's characteristics.

3. Select two types of innovations and compare their relative advantages, complexity, compatibility, trialability, and observability.

4. Identify the following elements of the diffusion process as presented in the Nationwide case:

   - The innovation and its characteristics
   - Communication channels used
   - The innovative-decision process
   - Adopter categories
   - Rate of adoption
   - The social system

5. Discuss the way in which the diffusion of an innovation to employees overlaps the diffusion of innovation to external publics. Use the Nationwide information as a starting place.

REFERENCES

Art Fry and the invention of Post-it® notes. (1998). Accessed April 6, 2003, at *www.3m.com/about3M/pioneers/fry.html.*

Clarke, R. (1999). A primer in diffusion of innovations theory. Accessed February 5, 2003, at *www.anu.edu.au/people/Roger.Clarke/SOS/InnDiff.html.*

Curley, A. (2001). Best practices: Communicating to align and engage employees. Accessed April 10, 2003, at *www.awpagesociety.com/protected/2001_seminar_pdf/curlspeech.pdf.*

Cutlip, S., Center, A. H., & Broom, G. M. (2000). *Effective public relations* (8th ed.). Upper Saddle River, NJ: Prentice Hall.

Diffusion of innovation theory. (n.d.). Accessed February 5, 2003, at *www.ciadvertising.org/studies/student/98_fall/theory/hornor/paper1.html.*

Employees and agents picture a brand-new way of doing business: Nationwide's internal brand launch strategy. (2000). Accessed April 9, 2003, at *www.prsa.org/_Awards/silver/html/ 6BW0012B04.html.*

How many online? (2002). Accessed April 10, 2003, at *www.nua.com/surveys/how_ many_online.*

Newsom, D., Scott, A., & Turk, J. V. (1996). *This is PR: The realities of public relations* (6th ed.). Belmont, CA: Wadsworth.

PNC Financial Services Group hits grand slam as employees "pitch PNC." (2002). Accessed April 10, 2003, at *www.prsa.org/_Awards/silver/html/6bw0212b23.html.*

Post-it® fun facts. (n.d.). Accessed April 6, 2003, at *www.3m.com/us/office/postit/learn_history_facts.jhtml.*

Project Splash. (2001). Accessed April 9, 2003, at *www.prsa.org/_Awards/silver/html/ 6BW0108C01.html.*

Rogers, E. (1983). *Diffusion of innovation* (3rd ed.). New York: Free Press.

Smith, A. (1990, November). Bridging the gap between employees and management. *Public Relations Journal,* pp. 20–21, 41.

Timeline: Life on the Internet. (n.d.). Accessed April 6, 2003, at *www.pbs.org/internet/timeline.*

Young, A. (1989). The rise and fall of the Edsel. Accessed April 6, 2003, at *www.libertyhaven.com/ regulationandpropertyrights/tradeandinternationalecomics/risefall.html.*

■ ■ ■ ■ ■ ■

CHAPTER SIX

SPEECH ACT THEORY

An Approach to Public Relations Leadership

BONITA DOSTAL NEFF

Theory is the map for the practice of public relations. The public relations discipline is inherently based on a theory-to-practice paradigm. As the psychologist Kurt Lewin once stated, "There is nothing as so practical as a theory" (Banks, 2000, p. 23). Poole and McPhee (1985) stressed the importance of paying "greater attention to the theory-technique linkage" (p. 157). Since theory is the clue to how public relations is practiced, the reality test is to view theories in terms of the real world.

Such professional links, however, exist in various forms between the academics and practitioners in the public relations discipline. As a profession, the academic and practitioner link becomes apparent as both groups respectively develop a variety of diverse curriculum and training modules based on theory, principles, and models.

The goal of this chapter is to review a theoretical approach that accommodates the connection between theory and practice while integrating the public relations profession's perspectives. The effort also emphasizes the importance of viewing the profession from a more holistic view, an approach that signals the transition to a more integrative as well as a mutually beneficial interactive concept for public relations.

LANGUAGE AS THE CORE CARRIER OF PUBLIC RELATIONS FUNCTIONS

Pearce (2001) quotes Deborah Tannen from her book *The Argument Culture*, where opposition is used "to accomplish <u>every</u> goal, even those that do not require fighting but might also (or better) be accomplished by other means, such as exploring, expanding, discussing, investigation, and the exchanging of ideas suggested by the word 'dialogue'" (p. 4). A most compelling statement describing the coordinated management of meaning (CMM) stated in this global summary reflects on an approach as emphasizing a more social interest than mere focus on some discourse.

The quality of our personal lives and of our social worlds is directly related to the quality of communication in which we engage. Thus CMM, as the foundational background for speech act theory, provides the societal connection when it is asked, "What events and objects in our social worlds are we making when we communicate like this?" (2001, p. 8).

Answering the Dilemma

Speech act theory focuses on natural language as based in tradition (the way of being). Searle (1987) stated that "speaking a language is engaging in a rule-governed form of behavior" (p. 4). Within this "rule-governed form of behavior," distinct characteristics of interaction are defined to depict the essence of the communication act and interact.

This movement away from cognition to the idea that "people create social reality through their language per se or 'speech acts' is a distinct shift from the idea that communication is information" (Neff, 1998, p. 354). The idea that thought is based on "social interaction" as a dialogic process is also a foundational or an essential part of rhetorical communication. As stated earlier, it is the intent or purpose of communication during interaction that drives the development of thought. Steve Banks and Patricia Riley describe intention as based on our reflection on vast number of social exchanges (Witmer, 2000, p. 66). Examining these social exchanges suggests a web of developing relationships and provides another opportunity for clarifying the focus of such sustained interactivity.

One has to pose the question: How does one initiate, develop, sustain, and so on these evolving relationships? The answer should bring one back to the fundamental process—communication. Such an approach was posed by Robyn Penman (2000):

> I first began . . . with a seemingly innocent and obvious question: What makes a good relationship? It soon became apparent, at least to me, that this question needed to be reworded to "What makes a good communication process?" Communication is the observable practice of a relationship, and so it was to the actual process of communicating that I had to attend. (p. 1)

Neff (1984) offers two major assumptions underlying the discussion on organizational communication through languaging. First, it must be noted that "the cumulative and concerted acts by members of the organization are what makes communication" and second, "the organization is the communication process" (p. 7). So where does that place the concept of relationship development (not only the concept of relationship)? Obviously, relationship lives in communication. The degree or the lack of a relationship is revealed by languaging. Studying the networks of communication (not the organizational structure) provides a broader picture of relationships and indicates the quality of the relationships. However, by viewing "organizational communication grounded in context" to "describe reality or organizational history . . . will keep an organization stuck in ritual, episodes, etc." (p. 7). So the contexts as descriptions are really perceptions that keep possibilities from happening. Neff further indicates there is not much usefulness to studying organizations as context. Organizations exist only in language. There is no usefulness to studying static concepts of relationships (present or historical), particularly in terms of public relations functions. This is why systems theory is described by Heath (2001) as "such a benign theory" (p. 34). One must acknowledge that only through languaging can one create organizational relationships. Relationships thus are grounded in communication and derive empowerment from expression. Similarly, as outlined earlier—context is powerless as present time or history. Neff (1984) notes that "a contextual shift is the ability to use language to create a new language for action" (p. 7).

Currently and traditionally, most public relations scholars support the idea of communication as fundamental to public relations. Kirk Hallahan presented and reinforced this idea in his prepared remarks for the public relations panel at the 2003 International Communication Association's annual conference on "Public Relations Crossing the Borders: What Are the Concerns and Benefits?" Hallahan stated: "I would agree with Elizabeth Toth and our European colleagues [e.g. Ruler & Verčič] that we should focus on *communication* activities in which organizations actually engage" (Hallahan, 2003). Similar agreement was reported by another International Communication Association panel supporting communication as the basis for public relations functions. (Panel on "What Should Be the Focus of Public Relations? Presenters were A. A. Betteke Van Ruler, Robert Heath, and Dean Kruckeberg with Guenter Bentele as respondent, San Diego, CA, May 2003). Ruler and Verčič (2002) noted in their research on "Communication but Not Mere Transmission of Information" that communication remains integral to the concept of public relations regardless of how one asks the question (pp. 6–8).

Academics and practitioners must "develop beyond a public relations expert skilled at 'handling' information" (Neff, 1985, pp. 8–10) to a more expanded role viewing public relations as networking, community relations, and developing communication infrastructure organizationally, including policymaking. Neff (1989) supported the concept of communication as central to public relations with specific reference to essential concepts that are grounded structurally by social interaction:

> Public relations, based in the communication process and developed through social interaction, is a process that is not rationalistic. Professionals must be trained to see that people live in their interpretation of experiences and actions (Burke, 1985). Public relations training must illustrate how language structures one's existence and how the languaging, as Flores (1982) wrote, is not mere "transmission or processing of information" (p. 1). (Neff, p. 165)

And again, Neff argues that:

> Public relations is necessarily based in social interaction and thus intricately tied to the communication process. Public relations is increasingly a boundary-spanning activity, and technology only increases the potential for interaction. The increased

> opportunities for languaging for action inherent in social interaction increases the responsibilities and potential effect of the public relations role. (p. 165)

In other words, the quality of communication in which we engage affects the quality of our public relations practice. This perspective provides a strong foundation for positing communication not only as central to the public relations process but also as the key criteria for evaluating outcomes (community relations, crisis communication, media relations, etc.). Communication, hence, is the foundation for theoretical development and the study of the public relations practice.

PUBLIC RELATIONS AS A DIVERSE COMMUNICATION FUNCTION

Pearce (2001) writes the "CMM works not only as a theory but as a set of tools for practitioners and as a worldview" (p. 1). This is exactly how CMM is presented here—as the backdrop to the focus on speech act theory. The organizational CMM theory provides the framework of elements important to the speech act. The public relations function is the foci for the application of this theory. Thus, CMM demonstrates communication embedded with key elements, presented in dialogic form, is fundamental to good communication. A public relations framework is one application of a theoretical perspective grounded in dialogic communication.

As stated earlier, it is the intent or purpose of communication during interaction that drives the development of thought. The speech acts are trim tabbed by the interlinking elements of culture, relationship, the self, and the episode. Through the dialogic process, these elements of culture, the self, the episode per se, and the relationship component all intersect via the speech act within a public relations environs to shape the interpretive potential. Communication then is uplifted beyond "only patterns of communication" to be viewed also "as textures of communication" (Pearce, 2001, p. 3).

Previous studies have not provided a comprehensive examination of the communication paradigm for public relations. Moving to a dialogic focus develops an understanding of the communication process necessary for an effective profession. The move to a dialogic focus is not easy because the urge to move toward a marketing and publicity model remains dominant in today's society. You hear of constant "branding" and "rebranding" as the answer to any kind of situation—low awareness, the need for having something to focus on or a "launching pad," so to speak, or an effort to shift perceptions. This false sense of imposing or dominating a community ignores elements shaping interactivity—the self (the organization and publics), the episode, the culture, and the relationship. The public is treated as if it is malleable and easily manipulated. Their involvement is superficial. This is deliberately orchestrated by those "doing" PR because the organization is so afraid of losing control. Thus, the urge to allow the media to dominate during campaigns blocks a deeper level of interaction, one that focuses more on publics. The idea that "spin" is considered a viable option further complicates the scenario. Chris Komisarjevsky (2003), former CEO of Burson-Marsteller, explains the usage of "spin" by misguided public relations professionals as not professional. Those who use spin "view the public as gullible and easily fooled." Spin essentially indicates the "lack of respect for the public" and thus violates the spirit of dialogue. Komisarjevky indicated one only develops a relationship through credible communication.

The Dialectic and Rhetorical Relationship: A Historical Partnership

Burke (1962) indicated that "rhetoric is thus made from fragments of dialectic," and he further amplified this point by stating that "dialectic could be treated as the ground of rhetoric, hence as not merely verbal, but in the realm of things, the realm of the universal order, guiding the rhetorician in his choice of purposes" (p. 584). Burke added other definitions of dialectic as well:

> Reasoning from opinion; the discovery of truth by the give and take of converse and redefinition; the art of disputation; the processes of "interaction" between the verbal and the non-verbal; the competition of cooperation or the cooperation of competition; the spinning of terms out of terms, as the dialectician proceeds to make explicit the conclusions implicit in key terms or propositions used in generating principles (the kind of internal development that distinguishes mathematical systems); the internal dialogue of thought. . . . or the progressive or successive development and reconciliation of opposites." (p. 403)

Obviously, the dialectical process is a partner of the rhetorical process. Yet little research in public relations indicates specifically how the dialectical mode is executed. Because the dialectical mode serves as the foundation for rhetoric as well and, in turn, the foundation for public relations practice, this chapter proposes speech act theory as a basis for examining what Burke calls dialectic: "the cooperative use of competition, progressing from division, to merger, to identification" (Heath, 2001, p. 40). Burke noted that dialectic is the foundation of rhetorical expression and that dialectic exchanges serve as the basis for a rhetorician's choice of expression.

Speech Act Theory: The Means of Expression in Public Relations Practice

Pearce and Cronen (2003, p. 74) discuss the communication process as dialogue in terms of four major elements—the self, relationship, episode, and culture. Integrating these contexts provides the fullest operational sense of how public relations functions. For example, Pearce and Cronen diagram these elements within the process of communication as central to the model and graphically present the contexts in sequences to display the centrality to the dialogic process as well. One needs only to insert the public relations function as the central foci in the series of interacts to fully illustrate the interactive process. The following is a hierarchical outline of these key levels.

Here the elements of culture, the self, the episode per se, and the relationship component all intersect via the speech act through a public relations medium to give full input into the communication process. Pearce (2001) writes the "CMM works not only as a theory but as a set of tools for practitioners and as a world-view" (p. 1). In this approach Searle "basically revises Austin's earlier contributions into simpler and more direct categories of speech acts. These acts were described and developed by Austin and Searle and later integrated into the works of the social philosopher Habermas" (Neff, 1998, p. 356).

Speech Act A

Culture   Episode
Public Relations Medium
Speech Act
Public Relations Medium
Relationship   Self/Public/Organization

Speech Act B

Culture   Episode
Public Relations Medium
Speech Act
Public Relations Medium
Relationship   Self/Public/Organization

Speech Act C

Culture   Episode
Public Relations Medium
Speech Act
Public Relations Medium
Relationship   Self/Public/Organizations

Searle hypothesizes that when one speaks a language one is behaving in a rule-governed approach. Neff (1998) claims that Searle would state that:

> Rule-governed language suggests communication outcomes vary in value of contribution focuses on the inherent characteristics which govern speech acts. The intent or purpose in the act of communicating during interaction becomes the focus of the analysis. Searle classified speech acts as *directives* (*requests*), *promises* (*commissives*) and *expressives* (*declarations*). These three speech acts comprise the

communication for action paradigm with each speech act having a specific role in the dialectic process. (p. 356; emphases added)

A dialogic approach illustrating the sequencing of speech acts with the intention of action is based on interactivity. The speech act in Figure 6.1 identified as a declaration provides the basis for all further speech acts. Unique to the speech act of declaration is its creative potential to open the space for other speech acts. The most particular aspect of the declaration is its disconnect with reality. There is no requirement for a declaration to be grounded in reality.

Once a declaration is offered or made, other speech acts can then be enacted. However, at this point the criteria of reality must be applied. The option possible, however, is to go back to the declaration act if the nondeclarative speech acts are not working.

There are three types of declarations essential to the speech act process: predictive, expressive, and verdictive. The predictive declaration "establishes the area of concern. The expressive declaration assures the speech acts are fully complied, an act of completion. Lastly, the verdictive declaration takes on a number of variations including legal, official, or the act of naming" (Neff, 1998, p. 356).

The speech act represented as a request is the source of enabling expression. If a request is not made, there is no act or action. In the request there are rules that govern (choices and engagement). Especially important is an underlying assumption that the request must "meet the test of reality" (Neff, 1998, p. 357). Partnering with the request is the speech act or a response to a request—the promise. The options are "yes" or "no" along with the possibility of offering another option, called a *counteroffer*, as a way to work out the conditions of satisfaction.

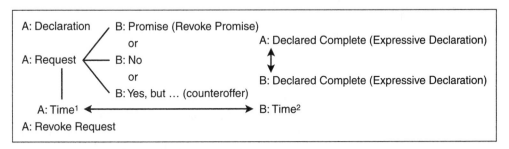

FIGURE 6.1   Model of speech act theory in dialectic form

Note: "A" is the first speaker; "B" is the second speaker.

[1]Countries participating in the *European Body of Knowledge Project* (EBOK) included: Austria, Belgium, Bulgaria, Croatia, Denmark, Finland, France, Germany, Hungary, Ireland, Italy, Latvia, Netherlands, Norway, Poland, Portugal, Russia, Slovakia, Slovenia, Spain, Sweden, Switzerland, Ukraine, United Kingdom, Yugoslavia, Greece, Malta, and Turkey.

[2] The more rhetorical communication based organizations established public relations divisions: International Communication Association in 1984; National Communication Association in 1987; Central States Communication Association in 1987; and Southern States Communication Association in 1989. The International and Interdisciplinary Research Conference was founded in the 1990s. Source: Bourland, P., & Neff, B. D. (2002). Networking: enhancing your academic success by association." In *Teaching Public Relations Handbook*.

What fully ties these speech acts together is the interactivity that brings forth each participant's conditions of satisfaction. The process includes the acknowledgment of timelines. As in Figure 6.1, the speech act as a declaration leads to an interactivity that is focused on requests and promises with the elements worked out within a timely framework. It is important to note that speech acts do not work in the domain of information. Speech act theory focuses on creating language for action. Speech acts that "are extrinsic are then valenced as to its contributive value toward creating language for action" (Neff, 1998, p. 357). Neff valenced the speech acts in later research to bring forth the value of the interactive exchange (p. 356).

Speech Act Theory as the Source of Leadership Potential for Public Relations

Speech act theory illustrates well the dialogic principles needed to conduct professional public relations actions. A key dimension in speech acts is also particularly of benefit to the public relations discipline. There is much research and discussion on public relations as a management function. Yet this often seems incompatible with top-level positions of leadership. Many believe public relations professionals should have a seat at the table where the decisions are made or even a more independent role in organizational influence. Yet management may be a suitable function for many and this may also be true for those who are involved in the more technical or tactical aspect of public relations. All these perspectives need the involvement of public relations practitioners. What may be often missing, yet also sought after, is the perspective of public relations as a leadership position, that it is the public relations professional most prepared for top-level decision making. This goes beyond the obvious leadership offered by an agency or firm in public relations. This approach asserts that the public relations professional should be in leadership positions—perhaps the head. If the public-relations trained individual is truly aware of the leadership dimension and understands how language does provide the leadership—then there are those who should be allowed to exercise that knowledge at the top level of influence.

In the speech act model, the concept of declaration is instrumental in providing this leadership component. If the public-relations trained professional has the ability to make these declarations, then the leadership potential is most fully articulated for that position in an organization. It seems logical that the capacity to provide this leadership may be most suitable for someone trained in public relations who has provided the research and evaluation for a board, who has implemented the primary projects, and who has been involved in setting the goals and objectives. It may well be the public relations professional who has the experience that is needed to make these speech acts that are viewed as emanating from a source of leadership. Of course, the skill in following up with the requests and promises, and the ability to negotiate the conditions as influenced by the timelines—all these speech act applications are similarly very vital. However, to be the source of declarations gives the public relations role a particularly powerful impact on the communication process.

Having expanded the leadership potential of the public relations function through speech act theory, one remaining issue needs to be addressed. It is also logical that the ethical dimension in dialogic communication is based on the speech act being expanded into the interact status allowing for the intersection of the "intent" of the participants to surface. Communication then is uplifted beyond "only patterns of communication" to be viewed also "as textures of communication" (Pearce, 2001, p. 3).

Speech Act Theory Offers an Ethical Basis for the Dialogic Process

The concept of ethics emerges as a central feature of the dialogic format. Moving the sense of ethics from a code to a dialogic process, Burber (as given in Griffin, 2003) talks about two types of relationships—I-It (lacks mutuality) versus I-Thou (one we are—created in the image of God and treat him or her as a valued end rather than as a means to our own end). This implies that we will seek to experience the relationship as it appears to the other person. Burber says we can do this "only through dialogue" (Griffin, 2003, p. 222). Thus ethics is inherent to the dialogic process and is available to the participants who adhere to the principles of dialogue. Burber reinforces this perspective when he defines dialogue as a "synonym for ethical communication; mutuality in conversation that creates the transaction through which we help each other be more human" (Griffin, 2003, p. A-3).

The above discussion seems quite substantial in establishing the ethical dimension of dialogue given the premises and assumptions. Yet Kent and Taylor (1998) questioned the ethical potential: "A final criticism of dialogue is that dialogue is often called 'more ethical' but no 'evidence' exists to support such a claim. However, it is evident at this point to note that Pearson indicated that there exists an equally ethical responsibility to assure dialogue" (Pearson, 1992, p. 129).

Perhaps this is why the communication model that places communication at the center needs to reflect fully the culture, the episode, the self, and the relationships, and be under authentic dialogic conditions of participation, time constraints, and completion agreements within speech acts. In this way the nuances critical to speech acts is interwoven into the public relations communication efforts as a dialogic approach. To not have all these critical factors could create gaps and thus a more unethical situation. The evidence is there but the larger question of ethicality shows when *intent* surfaces. So the concern underlining the entire process is the intention of the participants as to whether the dialogue will be an ethical exchange. Neff (1984) offered an analogy that might best clarify the situation: A knife is not inherently evil. A knife can be used to operate on someone to save a life or be used as a weapon to do great harm. Thus the ethical dimension is revealed by the intent of the communication exchange. What the human brings to the dialogic situation in terms of intent is what creates the ethical potential. Intent is ingrained in the process through the idea of allowing completeness in speech enactments, responses to speech acts, and the element of time. All are factors of much import revealed only as the exchanges progress. Therefore, dialogic approach is the means for allowing intent to be fully expressed when viewed within a speech act analysis, and these enactments bring the ethical dimension to full expression.

Neff (1984) also noted that "the ontological scheme for guiding communication is based in authenticity and openness to possibilities, a state of uncertainty" (p. 1). These standards are important to guiding the use of language and "communication must bring forth one's commitment through language" (Hermenet Inc., 1983). As a dialectical process, "the commitment must be acceptable to both the speaker and the listener or action does not take place" (Neff, May 1984, p. 3).

Scholars describe the ethical dimension in different ways. Buber uses such words reciprocity, mutuality, involvement, and openness as ethical values (Cissna & Anderson, 1995, pp. 11–45). Buber (1965) also suggests that "dialogic communication should be the goal of the interaction and not merely a means to an end such as marketing or advertising" (p. 204). Rogers, in his client-centered psychology, talks about "positive regard" with a healthy regard of another (Johnson, 1997, pp. 213–236). Johannesen (1971) discusses qualities that are genuine, accurate, empathetic, and understanding with an unconditional positive regard, a presentness, a spirit of mutual equality, with a supportive psychological climate (p. 373). Grunig (2001) believes communicating about issues as in dialogue is a basis for excellence (p. 15). Heath (2001) states that within the context of debate he calls rhetorical dialogue as a statement with a counterstatement (p. 31). Vasquez (2001) writes the "two-way symmetrical model conceptualizes public relations as a negotiation situation in which parties hold or perceive they hold compatible, rather than incompatible goals. Simply put, the compatible goal is a shared mission of social progress" (Pearce & Cronen, 2003). Evolve to CMM where the "concept of dialogue as the advocacy function of organizational communication in the public policy process" and, hence, the role of public relations via speech act theory allows for the fullest expression of these foundational principles; (Neff, 1998, pp. 351–376).

CASE: AMERIFLORA'92

AmeriFlora'92 evolved, from the creator's perspective, to "a world class exposition featuring international exhibits, popular attractions, cultural entertainment and exotic cuisine" (Neff et al., 1993, p. 5). Research conducted by the upper-level public relations class from Valparaiso University, however, indicated that the "average person" did not "know what AmeriFlora" was or considered AmeriFlora "a flower show" (Neff et al., 1993, p. 5). The horticultural group had the "image that AmeriFlora" was like the "Floriade Expo held in Holland every 10 years" that was, coincidently, also scheduled to open in 1992 (p. 5).

Columbus, Ohio, was chosen to host AmeriFlora'92 because its location is within a one-day drive from two-thirds of America's population and, therefore, accessible to a large portion of any potential public. Columbus is the state capital. At that time its composition was 74.5 percent Caucasian, 22.5 percent African American, Asian about 2.3 percent, and Native Americans about .2 percent. However, the Native Americans protested greatly that Columbus's namesake was being lauded in the celebrations and countered with the dark history of death and destruction brought upon their people when Columbus came to North America.

AmeriFlora'92 was held in Franklin Park, the largest park in Columbus, located in the minority district, the near east side of the city. In 1990, Columbus's near east side was 80 percent black. Tim Widman, a news reporter on AmeriFlor'92, explained, "What the 'south side' is to Chicago, this area of town is to Columbus" (Neff et al., 1993). The park was a central meeting place for the surrounding community, especially for youngsters. Area residents felt their park was stolen from them; in one day a fence appeared that actually kept the locals out of their public park. AmeriFlora'92 planners' decision to use Franklin Park ignited a nasty power struggle that not only produced a great deal of negative publicity, but also turned AmeriFlora'92 into a political battle filled with racial tensions.

Widman, editor of the *Mainstreet Business Journal* of Columbus, shared his opinions of how the African-American community around Franklin Park viewed the event. He said, "A bunch of downtown power brokers decided they were going to do it and didn't ask anybody's permission or advice." Widman added that "the most powerful man in town, John F. Wolfe (owner of the *Dispatch* newspaper, among other things) led the group and they decided to use Franklin Park" (Neff et al., 1993, p. 21).

Yolanda Robinson of the Black Student Organization in Columbus said the negative feelings the black community held toward AmeriFlora'92 were due to the lack of input they felt in the project. Widman was slightly more adamant: "The AmeriFlora people just said to hell with you and took over the park. They didn't listen and didn't care what the neighborhood wanted. . . . Long before any construction started AmeriFlora should have approached African-American community leaders and worked with them to try to establish grass-roots support for the event in the Franklin Park area" (Neff et al., 1993, p. 21).

The black neighborhood felt it had been railroaded by the powerful white downtown businesses. The resentment was felt strongly and caused a building fiasco after AmeriFlora'92 closed. AmeriFlora'92 was forced to tear down $17 million worth of permanent structures because the community refused to take them over. Widman phrased the community's feelings this way: "The area residents just said 'fine, since you didn't ever listen to us, we're going to fight you every step of the way.' The community . . . fought to make sure AmeriFlora'92 had to tear down every brick it put up in their park" (Neff et al., 1993, p. 21). However, later negotiations did save a large shelter that housed the German restaurant during Ameri-Flora'92.

AmeriFlora'92's local public relations efforts failed when it allowed what should have been an entertainment and flower event to become a symbol of the power struggle between races. White city leaders had the power to do what they wanted and arbitrarily decided to use Franklin Park. Black community leaders felt their park was stolen. Some black community leaders decided to show the "downtown power brokers" that the black community had political muscle, too. There was no organized public relations effort to pull the local perception of the event out of this vicious power struggle.

A large, one-time event such as this presents an opportunity for people who don't usually work together to do so. With a well-planned public relations campaign, AmeriFlora'92 could have been seen as an event that brought people together instead of a symbol of the racial power struggle in Columbus.

The racial tensions created around AmeriFlora'92 and general concerns about the safety of the area had some effect on local attendance. Local people received general information that was either negative or repetitive. "Within the 250-mile radius of Columbus was an informed public on major topics and events, yet there was little communication concerning entertainment and special exhibits. The citizens knew of AmeriFlora'92, but did not understand what was present at the Expo and what exactly AmeriFlora was" (Neff et al., 1993, p. 7).

The special role of Disney was not well promoted either. An AmeriFlora'92 video showed the Disney topiary characters and giant statues. The video indicated that this was the first time since the 1964 World's Fair in New York City that Disney participated in an exposition setting outside the Disney theme parks. *Ohio Magazine,* a free magazine provided by the Ohio Visitors Bureau, was one of the only publications to indicate that Disney was participating in AmeriFlora'92. The magazine noted that "Disney trained specialists were hired to provide the kind of knock-your-socks-off attractions that people expect at world class events" (*Ohio Magazine,* 1992, p. 18). Unfortunately, it was the $6 guidebook purchased at the park that "gave the greatest attention to the Disney impact on AmeriFlora'92" (p. 18).

Later in the year, when attendance was down and a financial crunch was felt, a desperate attempt was made to bring public relations and marketing together. The decision was to save money by not serving the markets in the outer ring (Chicago, Cleveland, Detroit, etc.). The results of public relations are of relatively low cost (some people argue they are free) but this was not understood because the marketing end dominated the decision making.

The following is a record of the progression of decisions and actions forming the AmeriFlora'92 event.

1980	John Reiner and the late Mel Dodge come up with an idea to have an extravagant flower show in Columbus, Ohio. The exhibit would be modeled after the International Exposition.
1985	Ohio's top flower man, John Peterson, is called in to set up foreign communication and to help with AmeriFlora'92.
1987	Tustin Management Resources becomes involved with AmeriFlora'92. Community begins to voice concerns about the event.
1990	Franklin Park closes for renovation to prepare for AmeriFlora'92.
1991:	
June	Borden Dairy, Coca-Cola USA, Coca-Cola Bottling company of Northern Ohio, and Xerox sign on as corporate sponsors and suppliers of AmeriFlora'92.
Aug.	General Motors announces the GM wide-screen film that was shown at Expo'92 in Seville, Spain, would be shown at AmeriFlora'92.

Sept.   Smithsonian Institute adds "Seeds of Change" exhibit for AmeriFlora'92. Susan Mowden is named special events and project manager. Rebecca Lusk resigns as director of communication.

Oct.   Val Patore is hired as director of media relations.

Nov.   Franks Nursery and Crafts is designated the official garden center of Ameri-Flora'92.

Dec.   Richard Frans, chairman of AmeriFlora, terminates a contract with Telemundi Worldwide, a Dutch company, which secured corporate sponsors for Ameri-Flora'92. Tustin Management Resources takes over.

1992:

April   500,000 annual and 150,000 perennials are planted in Franklin Park. Floriade opens in Holland. AmeriFlora'92 opens in Columbus. Massive freeze hits Columbus.

June   Public relations and marketing join to better AmeriFlora'92.

July   Massive downpours bombard the Columbus area.

Oct.   Floriade closes in Holland. AmeriFlora'92 closes.

Overall, a more positive interaction was needed between AmeriFlora officials and the community. AmeriFlora's first priority should have been to develop grassroots support in the Franklin Park community and the greater Columbus community. Both the internal and external publics were largely ignored and public relations was never fully understood or used. Because of this, AmeriFlora'92 was not the financial success it should have been. More than $100 million was spent on AmeriFlora'92 and an original agreement required the participating corporations to cover any deficit to balance the budget. Corporations did contribute to cover the losses.

QUESTIONS FOR APPLICATION

1. In the AmeriFlora'92 case study, what were the costs of ignoring the internal publics? What happens when power, rather than dialogic communication, is used to conduct community business?

2. What are the strengths and weaknesses of keeping public relations and marketing separate during a major event? What are the consequences if public relations and marketing are not brought together in the planning process? What happens often when the two areas are brought together in the planning process? How can one avoid such disconnects from happening? How can one avoid the dominance of one area over the other?

3. The vision and mission of AmeriFlora'92 evolved over the development of the event. How did this hinder the public relations and marketing efforts? How did this make the process much more difficult for the public to understand?

4. What is the nature of the U.S. culture in terms of this type of event—horticultural expositions? How did the location also contribute to the misunderstanding about an event intended to be international and exclusive (world's fair exhibits, other nations participating such as England, Taiwan, Russia, etc.)? Essentially, how do public relations professionals overcome the strongly held perceptions by members of various communities?

5. Speech act theory suggests communication is rule-governed. So what rules were violated in this case study? What implications does this have for non-Western cultures?

6. What happens when one does not use the speech act called *request*? Provide examples where this situation is important to public relations professionals.

7. This case study focused on fund-raising, an area of expertise important to public relations. Develop a plan for a nonprofit organization based on the critical speech acts outlined in this chapter. Integrate into your plan the thinking in terms of relationship, culture, episode, and self from a public relations perspective. Do enough research to have a good speech act theory (CMM-based) approach to your plan.

8. How do diversity and global public relations affect speech act theory? What insights do you have from other cultures that bring different nuances to the speech acts?

9. In what respect does the speech act theory provide more opportunity for the public relations functions to develop beyond the tactical and managerial level? How is leadership potential expressed through speech act theory?

10. The concern about ethics in dialogic communication seems to be an important concern when not linked to the rules-governed language possibilities. When one sees dialogic communication within the context of speech act theory, what elements of this theory build in rigor for an argument that dialogic communication is ethical?

11. How does dialectic serve the rhetorical aspect of communication? What is the relationship between dialectic and rhetoric in the process of working through the issues in society? How does this work when one takes these concepts to other cultures in the world?

REFERENCES

Banks, S. (2000). *Multicultural public relations: A social-interpretive approach.* Ames: Iowa State University Press.

Buber, M. (1965). *Between man and man.* New York: Macmillan.

Burke, J. (1985). *The day the universe changed.* Boston: Little, Brown.

Burke, K. (1962). *A grammar of motives and a rhetoric of motives.* New York: Meridian Books.

Cissna, K., & Anderson, R. (1995). The 1957 Martin Buber-Carl Rogers dialogue, as dialogue. *Journalism of Humanistic Psychology, 34,* pp. 11–45.

Flores, C. F. (1982). *Management and communication in the office of the future.* Report printed by Hermenet Inc., San Francisco.

Griffin, E. (2003). *A first look at communication theory* (5th ed.). Boston: McGraw-Hill.

Grunig, J. (2001). Two-way symmetrical public relations: Past, present, and future. In R. L. Heath (Ed.), *Public relations handbook* (pp. 11–30). Thousand Oaks, CA: Sage.

Hallahan, K. (2003, May 26). Public relations crossing the borders: What are the concerns and benefits? A competitive paper presented to the International Communication Association, Public Relations Division, San Diego.

Hazleton, V., & Botan, C. (1989). *Public relations theory.* Hillsdale, NJ: Lawrence Erlbaum.

Heath, R. L. (2001). Rhetorical enactment rationale for public relations: The good organization communicating well. In R. L. Heath (Ed.), *Handbook of public relations* (pp. 31–50). Thousand Oaks, CA: Sage.

Hermenet Inc. (1983). Transcripts of notes on Advanced Action Workshop. Chicago. July 30–31.

Johannesen, R. L. (1971). The emerging concept of communication as dialogue. *The Quarterly Journal of Speech, 57*(4), pp. 373–382.

Johnson, M. A. (1997). Public relations and technology: Practitioner perspectives. *Journal of Public Relations Research, 9*(8), pp. 213–236.

Kent, M. L., & Taylor, M. (1998). Building dialogic relationships through the World Wide Web. *Public Relations Review, 2*(3), pp. 321–324.

Komisarjevsky, C. (2003). CEO of Burson-Marsteller. Telephone interview with author, June 2.

Neff, B. D. (1984, May). Organizational communication in language. Refereed paper presented to the International Communication Association, San Francisco, CA.

Neff, B. D. (1985). State of the art in public relations: An international perspective. Paper presented to the International Communication Association, San Francisco, CA.

Neff, B. D. (1989). The emerging theoretical perspective in PR: An opportunity for communication departments. In C. Botan and V. Hazleton (Eds.), *Public relations theory* (pp. 159–172). Hillsdale, NJ: Lawrence Erlbaum.

Neff, B. D. (1998). Harmonizing global relations: A speech act theory analysis of PRForum. *Public Relations Review, 24*(3), pp. 351–376.

Neff, B. D., et al. (1993). *AmeriFlora '92: America's Celebration of Discovery.* Report developed by public relations seminar class at Valparaiso University, Indiana.

Ohio Magazine. (1992, February). Published by the state of Ohio.

Pearce, W. B. (2001, June 25). A brief introduction to "the coordinated management of meaning (CMM)." San Mateo, California.

Pearce, W. B., & Cronene, V. (2003). CMM in action—Stories from the field of mediation. In E. A. Griffin (Ed.), *A first look at communication theory* (5th ed.). Boston: McGraw-Hill.

Pearson, R. (1992). Perspectives on PR history. In E. L. Toth & R. L. Heath (Eds.), *Rhetorical and critical approaches to public relations* (pp. 111–131). Hillsdale, NJ: Lawrence Erlbaum.

Penman, Robyn. (2000). *Reconstructing communicating.* Mahwah, NJ: Lawrence Erlbaum Press.

Poole, M. S., & McPhee, R. D. (1985). Methodology in interpersonal communication research. In M. L. Knapp & G. R. Miller (Eds.), *Handbook of interpersonal communication* (pp. 100–170). Beverley Hills, CA: Sage.

Ruler, B. V., and Verčič, D. (2002). *The Bled manifesto on public relations.* Ljubljana, Slovenia: Pristop d.o.o.

Searle, J. R. (1987). *Speech acts: An essay in the philosophy of language.* London: Cambridge University Press.

Toth, E., & Heath, R. (1992). *Rhetorical and critical approaches to public relations.* Hillsdale, NJ: Lawrence Erlbaum.

Vasquez, G. (2001). Research perspectives on "the public." In R. L. Heath (Ed.), *Handbook of public relations* (pp. 139–154). Thousand Oaks, CA: Sage.

Witmer, D. (2000). *Spinning the Web: A handbook for public relations on the Internet.* New York: Addison Wesley Longman.

CHAPTER SEVEN

SOCIAL CONSTRUCTIONISM AND PUBLIC RELATIONS

JOYE GORDON

PETER PELLEGRIN

Social constructionism, as a theoretical perspective to explain how humans account for their worlds, offers both challenges and rewards to the practice and philosophy of public relations. These challenges and rewards simultaneously shake our foundations and provide a platform for propelling the practice and scholarship of the field. This chapter first explores the basic tenets of social constructionism. It then provides a brief historical background of the competing intellectual traditions influencing the development of public relations. Finally, it addresses implications of social constructionism for the practice and study of public relations. An orientation that focuses on the making of meaning through human interaction offers routes to redefine, refine, reformulate, and restructure ourselves and our methods relating to both the practice and study of public relations. While the roots of social constructionist thought have been around for centuries, it has been only in the last century that it has matured as a theoretical orientation and become a basis of inquiry within social and cultural studies.

THE BASIC TENETS OF SOCIAL CONSTRUCTIONISM

At its most rudimentary level, social constructionism is concerned with how people account for their world. Empiricist thought contends that language is a tool that can reflect the world that is knowable through observation. Social constructionism, in contrast, views language as an artifact of social interaction, not as a reflection of the world. Discourse, from the constructionist orientation, is both a product of human interaction and a mechanism through which social realities are constructed. Social reality may be described as the world of everyday life, what we commonly believe to be true about our environment. Berger and Luckmann

(1966/1980) argued that "the world of everyday life is not only taken for granted as reality by the ordinary members of society in the subjectively meaningful conduct of the lives" (p. 19); "it is a world that originated in their thoughts and actions, and is maintained as real by these" (p. 3). From the constructionist orientation, *knowledge* is itself a human product as well as an ongoing human production. Social constructionism, in short, contends that reality is a social construction that is created, maintained, altered, and destroyed through the process of human interaction.

Social constructionism does acknowledge a physical world independent of human interpretation. For example, Searle (1995), a noted philosopher of language, labels features of the world that exist independently of a perceiver, a mental state, or a human institution as *brute facts.* Everyday facts that can exist only within human institutions and through human interpretation are labeled by him as *institutional facts.* To borrow Searle's example, that hydrogen has one atom is a brute fact, but the fact that a $5 bill has value depends on human institutions and is an institutional fact. Searle, who approaches the question of how people account for their world from the perspective of philosophy of language, argues "the *fact stated* needs to be distinguished from the *statement* of it" (p. 3).

Some utterances themselves create the institutional fact. For example, when the preacher says, "I now pronounce you man and wife," the utterance creates the institutional fact of marriage where none had been before. Society is full of similar examples, such as the bestowing of citizenship, degrees, and divorces. These utterances are not reflecting the world but are actually creating a world that did not exist before in an objective, quantifiable manner.

Social constructionism, as Searle (1970, 1995) presents it, is not an argument that an objective environment does not exist or is unknowable, but is an argument that our understanding of that world (including of ourselves) is a product of human interaction. In addition, social constructionism posits that human institutions depend on discourse for their very existence and modification. Searle (1995) argues that human institutions such as nations, corporations, and the economic system in which a $5 bill has value are products of interaction; they are institutional facts in that they cannot exist independently of human agreement. Moreover, language is not only the mechanism that creates human institutions but also is constitutive of institutional reality, meaning that language forms the rules that not only regulate interaction but that also *create* the system of interaction. The process of creating institutional facts through social interaction is ultimately reflexive in that the development of new or altered institutional facts is influenced by preexistence of other institutional facts.

Three central tenets of social constructionism can form the basis of this perspective (Berger & Luckmann, 1966/1980; Blumer, 1969; Carroll, 1956; Gergen, 1985). One tenet is that conceptions of reality (including of ourselves) are created through social interaction. A second tenet is that human institutions are created through social interactions and cannot exist independently of human agreement. Finally, a third tenet is that the constructed world of everyday life is itself an important element in the maintenance and reconstruction of social reality, human institutions, and ourselves.

HISTORICAL PERSPECTIVE

Understanding the role of social constructionism in modern thought, particularly as it applies to the social sciences, illuminates its significance. It is also important to note that social constructionist thought is not new. Philosophical debates over the nature of knowledge and meaning solidly establish two major competing intellectual traditions that impact modern thought. Gergen (2002) labeled these two competing traditions as the exogenic and the endogenic perspectives. The exogenic perspective represents the orientation of empiricists in that knowledge does, or should, map or mirror the actualities of the real world. Moreover, the empiricist-based logical positivism that emerged from the Vienna School in the 1920s and 1930s asserted that observation and our senses are the *only* path to justify our beliefs and to explain the meanings of our words. The verification principle grew out of this school of thought and posits that any question that cannot be answered by experience is meaningless.

In contrast, the endogenic perspective posits that "Humans harbor inherent tendencies . . . to think, categorize, or process information, and it is these tendencies (rather than features of the world in itself) that are of paramount importance in fashioning knowledge" (Gergen, 2002, p. 10). In short, the world is not knowable as it exists, in actuality, independent of human interpretation. Therefore, social constructionism argues that humans construct knowledge rather than something discovered through rigorous observation and documentation. Knowledge and meaning are not something people hold in their memories or libraries; rather, knowledge and meaning (including knowledge/meaning of self and society) is a thing people do together (Gergen, 2002, p. 10).

Numerous scholars affiliated with the social sciences, especially psychology and sociology, during the last century have addressed the notions of the importance of human interaction and meaning. George Hebert Mead's writings in the early part of the 1900s addresses the self as being developed from social interaction and communication as essential to the human order (see Morris, 1934). Similarly, Herbert Blumer (1969), while acknowledging empiricism's respect for observation, developed his theory of social interactionism whereby meaning is seen as being developed through speech acts and interaction among people. In 1966, with Luckmann and Berger's *The Social Construction of Reality: A Treatise in the Sociology of Knowledge,* the theoretical perspective known as social constructionism matured to its current definition. Modern social constructionists generally accept no distinction between objective and subjective or between knowledge and reality. They view knowledge and/or reality as contingent on social relationships and as products of human activity and communication.

Kenneth Gergen, who is generally credited with being a pioneer and advocate for social constructionist thought in psychology, argued that the practice and study of psychology have been influenced heavily by the two competing traditions and that the field swings between the two perspectives. For example, that behaviorism had in many ways been overshadowed by the popularity of cognitive psychology in the 1950s and 1960s indicated to Gergen (1985, 2002) a shift toward the endogenic perspective during that time frame. The question for this analysis now is how the two competing traditions are reflected in the practice and study of public relations, particularly as they apply to the notions addressing the ethicality of persuasion and discrepancy of power.

INTELLECTUAL TRADITIONS IN PUBLIC RELATIONS

One could argue that the exogenic approach has dominated the majority of modern public relations. From public relations' early manifestation in Bernays's *Crystallizing Public Opinion* in 1923 until recently, it has been aligned with the social sciences. Through alignment with the social sciences of the early twentieth century, the empiricist school of thought—the dominant philosophy in both the physical and social sciences—was largely adopted without question. To Bernays and others, public opinion was an entity that existed in fact and could be changed by the introduction of variables of information and persuasion to create an outcome desired by some client. The very title of Bernays's 1955 text, *The Engineering of Consent,* implies that public relations can take on the character of tangible objects that can be augmented for desired effect. Indeed, in an earlier explanation, Bernays (1952) overtly said that engineering of consent means that public relations uses "action based only on thorough knowledge of the situation and on the application of scientific principles and tried practices in the task of getting people to support ideas and programs" (p. 159).

Bernays's desire to advocate public relations practioners to the status of professionals, rather than mere technicians, fueled his pursuit to develop theory for the field. In *The Engineering of Consent,* Bernays (1955) set to paper his theory of public relations. The theory advocated by Bernays, however, outlined three broad functions—adjustment, information, and persuasion—and proposed a sequential model of activities for performance of public relations. What was then presented as a theory of public relations now is generally considered the procedure of public relations activity.

Bernays did not shy from depicting public relations activity as inherently persuasive. To Bernays, the ethicality of swaying public opinion depended on the ethicality of the claim being made. Whether persuasion was good or bad, he said, "depends upon the merit of the cause urged, and the correctness of the information published" (Bernays, 1928, p. 20). As he once said in an interview, the ethical distinction is if propaganda is "proper-ganda." Bernays fully acknowledged that persuasion had the potential to be misused by those with evil intent, but in furthering his argument for the ethicality of persuasion, he maintained that persuasion was an essential ingredient in the democratic process, and that justified the activities of public relations practice. "These concerns noted by Bernays reflect the critics from the 5th century B.C., the era of Plato," who worried about vacuous statements, manipulation, and pander. However, these ancient critics, like Bernays, "supported rhetoric in its capacity to challenge pandering and to forewarn persons to watch for manipulative techniques" (Heath, 2001b, pp. 31–32).

Given that persuasion is a prerequisite to democracy and that its ethicality can be determined through statement and counterstatement—dialogue—how then did Bernays address the idea of symmetry? How did he address the criticism—the very criticism that drives much current thought regarding public relations theory—that dominant forces in society can, and do, dictate meaning for the less powerful sectors of society? About his *new propaganda* (renamed *public relations counsel*) Bernays (1928) says, "the minority has discovered a powerful help in influencing majorities . . . to mold the mind of the masses that they will throw their newly gained strength in the desired direction" (p. 13). In fact, he said the minority *needs* to make use of public relations. He maintained this view, stating that public relations "counteracts the tyranny of the majority and helps re-establish the inherent pluralism of America" (Bernays, 1952, p. 9). Beyond the acknowledgment that propaganda can have a bottom-up influence on societal decision making, the texts *Propaganda, The Engineering of Consent,* and *Public Relations* do not deal overtly with the symmetry dilemma in depth. In Bernays's writings, as long as the public interest was being served, who defined or promoted the public interest was not consequential.

Without overtly acknowledging symmetry or the issue of discrepancies of power, Bernays did advocate that public relations practitioners play a role in being listeners for their clients and facilitating the adjustment of organizations and their publics, even playing the role of conscience for client organizations. Bernays goes on to provide other examples of the need for symmetry. He cites that "a laudable movement may be lost unless it impresses itself on the public mind" (1928, p. 26). He noted that "nowadays the successors of the rulers, those whose position or ability gives them power, can no longer do what they want without the approval of the masses" (p. 26). He moves to more than a "bottom-up approach" when he describes the new public relations counsel as "it takes account not merely of the individual, nor even the mass mind alone, but also and especially of the anatomy of society, with its interlocking group formations and loyalties" (p. 28). It is in the summation of these numerous examples that Bernays demonstrates the interaction that is necessary to bring about this support. Bernays continues in his book to describe the various contexts in which this new discipline would work such as: psychology (individual's motives; p. 52), business (boards are "honorable in their private and public life"; p. 65), and political leadership (the political leader must be a creator of circumstances; p. 106). And in two other critical areas the dialogic potential is graphically outlined by Bernays. He argues, "Arts and Sciences: It is not merely a question of making people come to the museum. It is also a ques-tion of making the museum, and the beauty which it houses, go to the people" (pp. 146–147). In a second area he writes, "Education: Many of our leading universities rightly feel that the results of their scholarly researches should not only be presented to libraries and learned publications, but should also where practi-cable and useful, be given to the public in the dramatic form which the public can understand" (p. 129).

This latter comment sounds like today's effort to establish a dialogue between the public relations scholars and the practice. Unfortunately, Bernays's use of language in his books misled the public. It seems paradoxical and almost an oxymoron for such a leader in the field of public relations to use such misleading words. However, in historical context Bernays does trace the evolution of the word *propaganda*; at one time it was truly positive and meant "the spreading of the fait or an effort directed systematically toward the gaining of public support for an opinion or a course of action" (1928, p. 21). Unfortunately, the word "change took place mainly during the late war when the term took on a decidedly sinister complexion" and Bernays's use was caught by changing public opinion (p. 28). This is especially unfortunate since he had renamed the field early in his book as *public relations counseling* (an interactive perspective) (1928, p. 37).

Cutlip (1994) credits Bernays with introducing the two-way concept of public relations as opposed to pure one-way publicity tactics. Bernays's critics, however, seized on Bernays's use of the terms "propaganda" and "engineering of consent" and severely criticized him and the fledgling field of public relations for what they viewed as inherently manipulative (Cutlip, 1994). Like today, charges fly that public relations, as an agent of powerful sectors of society, can dictate meaning to less powerful sectors of society.

Bernays advocated that public relations practitioners should be listeners for their clients and facilitate the adjustment of organizations and their publics, even playing the role of conscience for client organizations. Most important, Bernays's elements of constructionist thought are detectable in his conceptualization of the public and/or public opinion. The constructionist conceptualization would *not* be that public opinion is simply an average of sum or individuals' opinions. To the constructionist, people interact to create knowledge/reality/opinion, and that creation is somehow greater than the sum of its parts. Indeed, Bernays's earliest writings depict acknowledgment of such an orientation. Citing Walter Lippmann and others, Bernays (1928) asserted "the group has mental characteristics distinct from those of the individual, and is motivated by impulses and emotions which cannot be explained on the basis of what we know of individual psychology" (p. 47). Bernays recognized that the study of group psychology was gaining strength. He also recognized the value of the newer techniques or empiricist-anchored social sciences and added these approaches to the repertoire of public relations.

> Theory and practice have combined with sufficient success to permit us to know that in certain cases we can effect some change in public opinion with a fair degree of accuracy by operating a certain mechanism, just as the motorist can regulate the speed of his car by manipulating the flow of gasoline. Propaganda is not a science in the laboratory sense, but it is no longer entirely the empirical affair that it was before the advent of the study of mass psychology. It is now scientific in the sense that it seeks to base its operations upon definite knowledge drawn from direct observation of the group mind, and upon the application of principles, which have been demonstrated, to be consistent and relatively constant. (Bernays, 1928, pp. 47–48)

Overall, through an analysis of Bernays's writing one can see how the foundations of public relations theory and practice evolved to represent both the endogenic thought and the increasingly scientific exogenic approaches. In the latter, it was assumed that the world, including social dynamics, was knowable through observation. The questions were "How is public opinion formed?" and "How can one apply the principles of empirical social science so that public opinion can be altered from a preexisting state to a more desirable state?" Within this foundation, the concern over the ethicality of persuasion was answered by using the rigorous and "true situation ethics" (as opposed to the misuse as a synonym for ethical relativism) (Curtin & Boynton, 2001, p. 419) and the belief that public relations provided a role in balancing power discrepancies.

MODERN VIEWS OF PUBLIC RELATIONS

Like Bernays's work, the modern practice of public relations receives harsh critical comments and accusations of manipulations. Popular books such as Rampton and Stauber's (1995) *Toxic Sludge is Good For You: Lies, Damn Lies and the Public Relations Industry* charge that public relations has the power to dictate meaning on unsuspecting publics in ways that serve corporate America. In response, modern scholars point to examples of minorities influencing majorities, just as Bernays did eighty years earlier. Criticisms also drive public relations professionals to police themselves through codes of conduct and condemnation of practitioners who knowingly employ deceptive tactics. Historically, the introductory public relations textbooks written by primarily journalism professionals emphasized information dissemination such as in news releases and public service announcements. More recently, these textbooks are incorporating rhetorical research or persuasion in their discussions on public relations. Rhetorical scholars provide the balance and understanding of rhetorical theory to better explain the critical role of persuasion in a democracy. The more formal training future public relations professionals receive before entering the workforce, the better the professional is prepared to provide a high standard of quality performance. As Crable and Vibbert (1986) state:

> The public relations person must know something about communication and persuasion in general, the construction of communication campaigns, writing strategies, oral communication strategies, and action strategies. These five crucial [abilities] are complex but they must be learned and applied. Knowing how to use communication is a major test of effectiveness of public relations work. (p. 17)

Many modern depictions of public relations also advocate symmetrical practice of the profession as a response to concerns that discrepancies of power exist that enable public relations to dictate meaning for sectors of society that are less powerful. Nowhere is this concern more evident than in the earlier works of James Grunig (1989), who argued that the two-way symmetrical model is a more moral and ethical approach to public relations than other models of public relations. Grunig wrote "the long-term effects of the asymmetrical models make it impossible for them to be an ethical and socially responsible approach to public relations" (p. 13). The two-way symmetrical model was described then as public relations practice that used "bargaining, negotiation, and strategies of conflict resolution to bring about symbiotic changes in the ideas, attitude, and behaviors of both the organization and its publics" (p. 13). In more recent works, Grunig and colleagues (Dozier, Grunig, & Grunig, 1995) have developed an elaborated symmetrical archetype whereby the two-way symmetrical model is conceptualized as mixed-motive communication that does not force an organization to sacrifice its interests.

The revised conceptualization envisions a three-model continuum with: (1) a pure asymmetrical model whereby the public is dominated by the organization; (2) a pure cooperative model whereby the organization is convinced to "cave in to" the public; and (3) a two-way model whereby communication is used to move both the public and the organization to a win-win zone as opposed to the zero-sum or win-lose scenarios of the other two models (Grunig, 2001). The new model of two-way communication does not advocate symmetry as the normative, or even necessarily the most effective, way to practice public relations, nor does it contend that an organization behaves unethically when it overtly protects or advances its own interests. Grunig (2001) writes the "new contingency model is an excellent two-way model of public relations that subsumes the former two-way symmetrical and asymmetrical models of public relations" (p. 16). "Depending on the situation," he adds, "asymmetrical tactics sometimes may be used to gain the best position for organizations within the win-win zone. Because such practices are bounded by a symmetrical world view that respects the integrity of long-term relationships, the two-way model is essentially symmetrical" (p. 16).

Whether observing earlier or later versions of the models of public relations practices, it is clear that concerns over discrepancies of power fuel the line of reasoning. While it seems that the symmetrical approach to viewing public relations has somewhat softened its stance against persuasion and an organization's need to protect/advocate selfish interest, an overriding concern that public relations can easily be a tool of domination is evident in the literature. Whereas Bernays was willing to rely on the ethicality of the persuasive claim to determine the ethicality of public relations efforts, modern models place the ethicality of public relations practice within the nature of the activity itself. The claim now made is that the dominant actors' willingness to somewhat, or sometimes, "cave in to" the public's position creates a desired way to practice public relations.

The concern over the discrepancy of power, we argue, is a symptom of the exogenic tradition and our literal understanding of power. Within that tradition of the world of things to be observed, power has become akin to a physical resource. The model approach to understanding public relations practice assumes some people have it and some people don't. It follows then that desirable public relations practice requires that those who have power must be willing to share it at times. By extension of this view of power, persuasion takes on the character of a dominating force and is viewed as somehow inherently unethical.

The exogenic tradition also implies that power is a finite resource. For me to have it, I must take it from you. For you to keep it, you must be stronger than I. Power conceptualized as a finite resource fuels a common theme in current public relations literature that public relations *should* be part of the organizational management. This theme reflects the assumption that public relations will gain power through or from existing holders of power—organizational management. Likewise, the idea of finite power often overrides practitioner-guided interactions between an organization and its publics, sometimes to the detriment of organizations.

Dozier and Lauzen (2000) argue that another limiting factor on public relations theory and research has been the inability of scholars to separate the practice of public relations from the intellectual domain. They propose to use critical theory and that "takes the public relations scholar outside the relationship between powerful organizations and publics with deep pockets, begging a different set of questions, raising different concerns, and employing different methodological approaches (p. 19).

However, these authors are driven to address the paradox presented when less-powerful groups gain influence—for example, activists. In this respect, Robert Heath (2001b) provides the defining description of the role of activists:

> Activism is a fight for rhetorical symmetry because some publics (individuals or groups) feel alienated (Cheney, 1992), strains (Smelser, 1963; Toch, 1965) and other incentives to resist a hegemony of community that denies the virtue of partisan statements (Brummet, 1995). Motivated by these feelings, "they may offer defensive responses to system encroachment or the colonization of the lifeworld," or they may take actions against the organization (Leitch & Neilson, 1997, p. 24). If no differences exist, then one has less reason to employ public relations. The best evidence of this is the absence of any discussion of rhetoric in Mores (1955) *Utopia*. In a utopia, people have what they need and have no reason for dispute—rhetoric or public relations. (p. 35)

The authors define the intellectual domain of public relations to be "the study of action, communication, and relationships between organizations and publics, as well as the study of intended and unintended consequences of those relationships for individuals and society as a whole" (Dozier & Lauzen, 2000, p. 18). Driven to address the paradox presented when less powerful groups gain influence (like Bernays's explanation that minorities can gain influences over the majority), such as in the case of activist groups, Dozier and Lauzen advocate a critical theoretical approach to the intellectual domain of public relations inquiry and theorizing.

Dozier and Lauzen (2000) overtly acknowledge that the "world view of the critical school—which sees the mass media (and, inferentially, public relations) as a means of protecting and extending the influences of the wealthy and powerful—does not fit comfortably with the prevailing world views of scholars who study public relations" (p. 18). In this statement, we see support of the thesis presented earlier in this essay that public relations has adopted a worldview of the haves and have-nots and, in response, has sought to disassociate itself from a self-image as an agent of domination through situational ethics and evaluative observations of practice.

Dozier and Lauzen's work is important on two counts. First, the proposal to liberate the intellectual from the professional activity contributes toward maturation. Second, the proposal to use critical theory in many ways represents a shift away from the orientation and methods of the logical positivists. "Critical theory takes the public relations scholar outside the relationship between powerful organizations and publics with deep pockets, begging a different set of questions, raising different concerns, and employing different methodological approaches" (Dozier & Lauzen, 2000, p. 19). Indeed, critical theory, while retaining a haves-and-have-nots view of power, does provide a platform of scholarly inquiry independent of the professional activity of public relations and provides a method of scholarly inquiry independent of the empirical methodologies associated with the exogenic tradition.

Several other public relations scholars have proposed or incorporated theoretical perspectives other than symmetrical-based orientations for the study of public relations. Adoption of games theories, for example, has been common (Murphy, 1987, 1989, 1991). Others have adopted orientations from negotiation and conflict-resolution literature (Plowman, 1998; Vasquez, 1996; Vasquez & Taylor, 2000). A strong trend toward relationship building and community as a basis for theoretical development is evident (Heath, 2001b; Kruckeberg & Starck, 1988; Leeper, 2000; Leitch & Neilson, 2000; Starck & Kruckeberg, 2001). Broom, Casey, and Ritchey (1997) propose a theory focusing on relationships. Murphy (1996) proposed chaos theory as a model to apply to issue management and crises. Some have proposed an orientation focused on community. Still others have focused on the publics as an element to build theory for public relations. Feminist theory, too, has been widely assimilated into public relations literature (Aldoory & Toth, 2002; Grunig, Toth, & Hon, 2000; Toth, 2001). Clearly public relationship scholarship is to be commended for the dedication and efforts of its scholars to engage in active contemplation and theory building.

Some research clearly indicates a swing away from exogenic thinking in the field. Notably is the work of rhetorical scholars who advocate rhetorical theory as a basis for the study of public relations (Cheney & Dionisopoulos, 1989; Heath, 2000). Other studies even indicate clear leaning toward social constructionism's tenet that meaning is formed through interaction. Some issue management study, for instance, views issues as being created and managed within a social system through communicative efforts (Vibbert & Bostdorff, 1988). Taylor's (2000) work on public relations as nation building, in essence the creation of human institutions, also shows how endogenic thought is becoming part of the public relations scholarship.

Moreover, the methods employed by public relations researchers indicate an increased understanding of the importance of endogenic thinking. Exogenic traditions dictate the strict observation methods of logical empiricism. Endogenic traditions are, at least for the time being, affiliated with more qualitative methodologies. The efficacy of the case study, an endogenic way of knowing, is widely accepted in public relations and indicates the value of understanding human behavior from the perspectives of the actors themselves. Likewise, focus groups are applauded because researchers can view how groups respond to information and come to conclusions, rather than studying the individual in isolation. Endogenic thinkers from the fields of psychology and sociology regularly incorporate methods such as ethnographic studies, which to date remain rare in the public relations literature. However, the shortcomings of strictly quantifying human behavior have been long noted in public relations research. Bernays (1928) overtly attacked the pitfalls of polling data and was known to frequent psychoanalysts for insights regarding his clients and their products (p. 21). A greater mix of the two traditions, exogenic and endogenic, with more inclusion of the orientation of social constructionism as representing the latter, can positively impact both the practice and stuffy of public relations in many ways, from adoption of methods to theories that have been useful to many other disciplines. One strong implication for social constructionism as a grounding for study of public relations will be an emphasis on the study of language itself.

SOCIAL CONSTRUCTIONISM AND LANGUAGE

In reviewing the works of Bernays, Grunig, and others, it becomes obvious that public relations often concerns itself with advocating specific meanings. Because meaning must be conveyed through language, epistemologists and social constructionists are naturally concerned about language, the medium with which public relations practitioners work. Questions naturally arise as to the exact nature and origin of language, but linguists generally agree that language is symbolic, meaning that a word signifies, or acts as a sign for, something else. The word can stand for a "concrete" objective item, such as a rock, or an abstract subjective item, such as love. This harkens back to Searle's (1995) distinction between brute and institutional facts.

On the surface the division seems to be relatively simple, just as the public relations practitioner can distinguish between a physical power plant and the "good" it brings to the community. It is not so simple, however. Because of its symbolic nature, language—and words especially—have no meaning other than those we give them. The only certain characteristic about language is that it will change. Though a process called perjuration, the Old English *ceorl* (meaning a free man) has over the years become *churl*, meaning someone who is crude or of low breeding with all its negative connotations. Similarly, through a process called amelioration, once-negative words can take on a positive context. For example, *knight* once meant *servant*, as the modern German "Knecht" still does (Pyles & Alego, 1993). These meanings are established in the social arena and are hence socially constructed. The public relations practitioner needs to be aware that he or she is only one of many partners in this linguistic dance.

Meaning is not the only fluid characteristic of language. Even the spelling and pronunciation of words will change, and in a relatively short time. For example, we know that "often" and "orphan" must have rhymed when Gilbert and Sullivan wrote *The Pirates of Penzance* because the authors often have the characters confuse the two words. Today no one would confuse their pronunciations. Spelling, too, has changed over time for various reasons. There is the famous example from Shakespeare's *King Lear* in which the fool refers to Lear as "my nuncle." The word *nuncle* actually derived from a butchering of the phrase "mine uncle." Perhaps due to the close proximity of the two nasal "n" sounds back to back, people chose not to distinguish between the two and shortened them, thus creating a new word.

In modern society people often create linguistic codes to distinguish themselves from other social groups. This linguistic coding, which we term slang, occurs in all segments of society from the lowest to the highest. Some popular American examples of this coding are the jive talk of the 1970s and the Valley Girl talk of the 1980s, as well as the slang/jargon to distinguish people of a particular profession, such as truckers. Slang words, although different in meaning from "mainstream" society, are nonetheless socially constructed by the group using them. Once slang is co-opted by the mainstream, however, it no longer serves its purpose and new slangs must be developed.

Language is so much more than how one describes the world. It is, in fact, the very basis of how we see the world. Edward Sapir and Benjamin Lee Whorf noted the inherent risks in arguing that language can be used to define a knowable world accurately reflected through observation (Sapir, 1949). The Sapir-Whorf theory proposes that the language we use affects the way we interpret and respond to the world. One famous example demonstrating this involves color. The English language breaks down color into eleven basic groups, pink being one of these. Other languages have fewer basic color groups, pink not being among them. So when speakers of English are given color chips to stack into groups, they invariably have a pink group. Because the other languages have no word for pink, they stack these "pink" chips in the red category. Language is full of such subtle yet powerful indicators of how we perceive the world. For example, in the English language, we must have a subject and a verb, even if the subject is understood or the verb is in the passive voice. This grammatical fact would seem to imply that we expect an actor for every action, that nothing simply happens of its own accord (Pyles & Alego, 1993, p. 24).

So knowledge and meaning are transmitted through language, and words are the building blocks of language, but words in and of themselves do not mean a thing. They have no meaning other than what we give them. This fact has important implications for the public relations practitioner who is in the business of nothing less than the formulation and transmission of words to create and convey meaning and knowledge. We must be aware, however, that this creation does not take place in a vacuum, and that once public relations specialists have placed a message in the market place of ideas, they literally have no more control over it. Publics are free to take the carefully crafted pieces of knowledge and redefine them any way they choose, and they often do. Like social constructionism, the study of language has much to offer both the practice and the study of public relations.

SOCIAL CONSTRUCTION: A BASIS FOR PRACTICE AND STUDY

When Dozier and Lauzen (2000) argued to separate the practice from the intellectual domain of public relations, they provided two definitions of public relations—one for the practice and another for the intellectual domain. We accept their argument for the need to separate the two arenas and follow their format in providing definitions to facilitate the social constructionist argument provided here. Gordon (1997) has already provided a definition of the practice of public relations based on a social constructionist orientation. She proposed a definition that viewed public relations as having a role in the social construction of meaning (Gorden, 1997, pp. 63–65). Here we argue that the definition of the intellectual domain of public relations is the study of the social construction of meaning.

The adoption of social constructionism as a basis for public relations presents distinct advantages in highlighting the underlying value also represented in the rhetorical tradition: the creation of dialogue. It is through dialogue that the demonstration of ethical construction (interpersonal or through messages) and the balance of power (all voices are represented) are negotiated. In social constructionism and rhetorical enactment, public relation practitioners learn language is dialogic representation. Within these schools of thought, persuasion is the very nature of humans: We make meaning. Persuasion is not seen as inherently unethical or a tool of domination. Within these schools of thought, meaning, like language itself, is inherently fluid and changing of meaning is not mere (not absolute) but a natural outcome of human interaction (Heath, 2001b, p. 32). Moreover, within the social constructionist worldview, "less powerful" segments of society are equally capable of forming meaning for themselves as is any other segment of society. In fact, social constructionism draws into question our very notion of power by forcing us to acknowledge that power exists as an institutional fact, not a brute fact, and that we have constructed the concept to represent a limited and finite resource. Social movements strategies of Gandhi and Martin Luther King Jr. demonstrate that "power" can be self-generated and that people can redefine themselves rather than accept the meaning proposed by others.

On an intellectual level, social constructionism offers a new sphere to develop public relations as an intellectual endeavor. Dozier and Lauzen (2000) argued in their proposal for critical theory as a basis for public relations study that critical theory begs a different set of questions, raises different concerns, and employs different methodological approaches (pp. 3–7). Those same arguments hold true for social constructionism. Social constructionism offers pathways to a dimension of scholarly inquiry that has yet to be explored.

By accepting the social constructionist tenets, we acknowledge that in proposing these definitions we are advocating a position and a direction for public relations inquiry and practice. While we maintain that it has great potential to contribute to both the theory and practice of public relations, we are not arguing that social constructionism offers the one and only unifying theory of public relations. Social constructionism offers only one way of explaining how we account for our world. Within this perspective, the intellectual domain of public relations is concerned with the study of socially constructed meaning. For that is essentially what undergirds all public relations practice: offering publics a particular meaning—promoting a particular way of understanding the world. Social constructionism then plants public relations onto a solid ground of philosophical inquiry while simultaneously providing a practical roadmap focused on the single most important aspect of public relations—communication. This should not be taken to mean that other perspectives, including empirical-based approaches, lack merit. If anything, this chapter shows that public relations is in a strong period of theoretical growth and development that can be only aided with the incorporation of alternative worldviews and opinions.

CONCLUSION

From the first halting steps at the beginning of the twentieth century to the first theoretical underpinnings of Bernays, modern public relations has been searching for a concept that can help define its identity within the legitimate field of academic inquiry while providing practical implications for practitioners. Social constructionism offers public relations the best of both worlds. First, it offers solid grounding for academic inquiry into the philosophical basis of public relations and the social construction of meaning. Second, it demonstrates from both a dialectic and rhetorical perspective when dealing with ethical dilemmas and illustrates the impact of persuasion on the balance of power issues. This approach provides a model for public relations practice.

CASE: OTPOR (1998 SERBIAN RESISTANCE)

On October 10, 1998, Otpor ("Resistance") was founded by twelve student protesters in Serbia, all veterans of the 1996–1997 student-led protests against Slobodan Milošević. Initially, Otpor limited its demands to a repeal of the University Law, which suspended academic freedom in Serbia, but the organization soon became more than just another student organization. The role of Otpor in the downfall of one of Eastern Europe's most powerful dictators provides an excellent case study of social constructionism at work. At the heart of the movement was a clear effort to redefine the concept of the everyday world in the minds of Serbians, particularly as it applied to the concept of the social institution of "government." The work of Otpor moved a nation to comprehend power, as Searle defined it, as an "institutional fact," not a "brute fact." In social constructionist terms, Otpor consciously moved from an exogenic tradition—power is a finite resource—to an endogenic tradition—power is self-generated—as exemplified in the works of Gandhi and King.

Milošević ruled Serbia by means of violent repression. Intuitively, Otpor leaders realized their movement must be defined by something other than violence, so they chose humor as a key component of their campaign. The organization was helped in part by U.S.-based Freedom House, which donated five thousand copies of Gene Sharp's *From Dictatorship to Democracy: A Conceptual Framework for Liberation.* They later obtained copies of Sharp's most influential work, *The Politics of Nonviolent Action* (1973), and adapted this work to their own situation. This initial decision to define themselves as nonviolent was crucial to success. An attempt by the government to label Otpor a "terrorist organization" in March 1999 failed because Otpor, through humor, demonstrated how ridiculous the charges were. Serbians saw Otpor members as "only kids," students, clearly not terrorists bent on destruction. The definition of Otpor did not take place in a vacuum but was, in fact, socially constructed by Otpor and Serbian citizens; thus the government's exogenic attempt to impose meaning from above failed.

Otpor uttered into existence a definition not only of itself but of its own scope. The group originally consisted of twelve members, but by means of flyers, it created the impression it was much bigger. Later, Otpor declared itself a national movement. At the time, it was only a small student organization, but in a year's time, it did indeed become a national movement in which the membership consisted of tens of thousands of ordinary Serbians, not just students.

On January 13, 2000, on the Orthodox New Year's Eve, Otpor invited Belgrade residents to a party to ring in the new year. Before midnight, thousands of people enjoyed a free concert, but at midnight Otpor turned off the music and instead played a video complete with names and pictures of many who had died under Milošević's rule. The group then told the crowd that there was no reason to celebrate and to go home and think about what to do. Otpor left them with a slogan: "This Is the Year," meaning the last year of Milošević's rule. And it was. Simply stating this concept of reality redefined the "proper" timeline for change. Otpor alone could not have constructed this reality; it took the belief of the masses to make it so.

Otpor's focus on nonviolence was a deliberate effort to present itself, and by extension all Serbians, as civilized. Colonel Robert Helvey, a close colleague of Sharp's, helped train Otpor in nonviolent resistance. His main message was "Eliminate the Authority of the Ruler." An exogenic approach to power would have called for revolution and "chopping off the head" of the regime. Otpor, however, rejected this view of power, adopted the endogenic approach that viewed power as self-generated, and focused on elections as a means to remove Milošević. Moreover, when the regime attempted to impose a definition of Otpor first as a terrorist organization and later as a puppet of the Western powers, it failed because Otpor's endogenic approach was more powerful at constructing meaning than was the regime's exogenic approach.

When the regime took over all independent sources of news in Belgrade (radio, TV, newspapers), Otpor led three days of protests in which literally thousands of people took to the street in Belgrade. Ten days after the protests, which were successful at forcing the regime to relinquish control over the seized media outlets, Otpor demanded a coalition be formed from the numerous opposition parties to back a single candidate who could defeat Milošević. When Milošević announced on July 27, 2000, that national elections would be held ten months ahead of schedule, the opposition parties answered. On September 1, 2000, a new coalition called the Democratic Opposition of Serbia (DOS) was unveiled, backing Vojislav Kostunica as its candidate. Again, Otpor socially reconstructed reality. Whereas before each opposition party was too suspicious of the others and of Otpor to work together, they could now rally behind a single candidate. This example also demonstrates another way in which Otpor helped to define the perceptions of everyday Serbians. Prior to this, most agreed that Milošević needed to be removed but answered that idea with a doubtful, "If not Milošević, then who?" Otpor redefined the perceptions of Serbians, arguing that the "who" could be settled afterward; getting rid of Milošević, that was important.

In an effort to oust Milošević, Otpor introduced yet another slogan, *Gotov Je*, "He Is Finished." As more people came to believe this socially constructed reality, Milošević was indeed finished. On September 24, 2000, Otpor had stationed trained poll watchers at every voting station to ensure that the votes were speedily counted so that when the regime claimed a false victory, Otpor would have proof otherwise. In fact, Kostunica and the DOS announced they were victorious, making it impossible to steal the election. They simply stated they had won and defined the political reality.

On May 15, 2000, after Milošević had stated the results were too close and demanded a run off, Otpor mobilized more than 20,000 Serbians from all over the country for a final facedown with the regime. Police were naturally told to stop them, but they refused to comply with orders. Otpor had trained the citizenry not to use violence against the police, arguing that the police were just as much victims of the regime as anyone else, thereby redefining police as victims sharing in a common oppression as opposed to being tools of a despotic regime. Only two people died this day: one as a result of a traffic accident, and another because of a heart attack. The crowd that descended on Belgrade chanted "Serbia Has Arisen," and the mere saying of it was a testament to the statement's truth.

In the end, Serbia ousted Milošević in a triumph of democracy and nonviolent resistance. Otpor socially reconstructed the perception of itself, of the Serbian public, of Milošević, and of power itself. This case study exemplifies social constructionism at its best, emphasizing the endogenic over the exogenic concept of public relations. Otpor was just another rhetor seeking to define the world, not a "power" imposing its views on others. Ethically, Otpor was able to define itself and ultimately all Serbians as civilized, peaceful people deserving of freedom and basic human dignity. The "institutional" facts—regime, power, freedom, and society— were redefined through the active participation of several groups, including Otpor, the opposition parties, the Serbian people, and Milošević himself.

QUESTIONS FOR APPLICATION

1. Define what Gergen means by "endogenic" and "exogenic." How do these terms apply to public relations?

2. What did Searle mean by "brute fact" and "institutional fact"? Give an example of each.

3. What are the three central tenets of social constructionism?

4. What did Bernays mean when he wrote, "Public relations counteracts the tyranny of the majority and helps re-establish the inherent pluralism of America"? Would Bernays's approach be classified as exogenic or endogenic? Why?

5. How do the concerns about methodology serve as the prime focus of this article? How do current philosophies agree and/or disagree with this concern about methodology?

6. What is the three-model continuum of public relations as presented by Grunig?

7. How does the endogenic approach view power?

8. What does the Sapir-Whorf theory argue?

9. What two public relations problems does social constructionism address? What is the role of public relations in dealing with this problem?

10. Cite three examples that demonstrate Otpor's endogenic approach to public relations. Cite two examples of the regime's exogenic approach.

11. Is there an ethical problem in the case study with the student group misleading the public about the number of people involved in their group? Is using a flyer to create the impression it was much bigger really deceptive? Or is the "means to an end" justified if there is a socially responsible goal?

REFERENCES

Aldoory, L., & Toth, E. (2002). Gender discrepancies in a gendered profession: A developing theory for public relations. *Journal of Public Relations Research, 14*(2), pp. 103–126.

Berger, P. L., & Luckmann, T. (1966/1980). *The social construction of reality: A treatise in the sociology of knowledge.* Reprint, New York: Irvington.

Bernays, E. L. (1923). *Crystallizing public opinion.* New York: Boni and Liveright.

———. (1928). *Propaganda.* New York: Horace Liveright.

———. (1952). *Public relations.* Norman: University of Oklahoma Press.

———. (1955). *The engineering of consent.* Norman: University of Oklahoma Press.

Blumer, H. (1969). Symbolic interactionism: Perspective and method. Englewood Cliffs, NJ: Prentice Hall.

Broom, G. M., Casey, S., & Ritchey, J. (1997). Towards a concept of theory of organization-public relationships. *Journal of Public Relations Research, 9*(2), pp. 83–98.

Carroll, J. B. (Ed.). (1956). *Language, thought, and reality: Selected writings.* Cambridge: Technology Press of the Massachusetts Institute of Technology.

Cheney, G., & Dionisopoulos, G. N. (1989). Symmetrical presuppositions as a framework for public relations theory. In C. Botan & V. Hazleton (Eds.), *Public relations theory* (pp. 135–157). Hillsdale, NJ: Lawrence Erlbaum.

Crable, R. E., & Vibbert, S. (1986). *Public relations as communication management.* Edina, MN: Bellweather Press.

Curtin, P., & Boynton, L. (2001). Ethics in public relations: Theory and practice. In R. Heath & G. Vasquez (Eds.), *Handbook of Public Relations* (pp. 411–422). Thousand Oaks, CA: Sage.

Cutlip, S. M. (1994). *The unseen power: Public relations. A history.* Hillsdale, NJ: Lawrence Erlbaum.

Dozier, D. M., Grunig, L. A., & Grunig, J. E. (1995). *Manager's guide to excellence in public relations and communication management.* Mahwah, NJ: Lawrence Erlbaum.

Dozier, D. M., & Lauzen, M. M. (2000). Liberating the intellectual domain from the practice: Public relations, activism, and the role of the scholar. *Journal of Public Relations Research. 12*(10), pp. 3–22.

Gergen, K. J. (1985). The social constructionist movement in modern psychology. *American Psychologist, 40*(3), pp. 266–275.

———. (2002). Construction in contention: Toward consequential resolutions. *Theory & Psychology, 11*(3), pp. 429–432.

Gordon, J. C. (1997). Interpreting definition of public relations: Self assessment and a symbolic interactionism-based alternative. *Public Relations Review, 23*(1), pp. 57–66.

Grunig, J. E. (1989). Symmetrical presuppositions as a framework for public relations theory. In C. Botan & V. Hazleton (Eds.), *Public relations theory* (pp.17–44). Hillsdale, NJ: Lawrence Erlbaum.

———. (2001). Two-way symmetrical public relations: Past, present, and future. In R. L. Heath & G. M. Vasquez (Eds.), *Handbook of public relations* (pp. 11–30). Thousand Oaks, CA: Sage.

Grunig, L. A., Toth, E. L., & Hon, L. C. (2000). Feminists values in public relations. *Journal of Public Relations Research, 12*(1), pp. 49–68.

Heath, R. L. (2000). Rhetorical perspective on the values of public relations: Crossroads and pathways toward concurrence. *Journal of Public Relations Research, 12*(1), pp. 69–91.

———. (2001a). Shifting foundations: Public relations as relationship building. In R. L. Heath & G. M. Vasquez (Eds.), *Handbook of public relations* (pp. 1–9). Thousand Oaks, CA: Sage.

———. (2001b). A rhetorical enactment rationale for public relations: The good organization communicating well. In R. L. Heath & G. M. Vasquez (Eds.), *Handbook of public relations* (pp. 31–50). Thousand Oaks, CA: Sage.

Kruckeberg, D., & Starck, K. (1988). *Public Relations and community: A reconstructed theory.* New York: Praeger.

Leeper, R. (2000). In search of a metatheory for public relations: An argument for communitarianism. In R. L. Heath & G. M. Vasquez (Eds.), *Handbook of public relations* (pp. 93–104). Thousand Oaks, CA: Sage.

Leitch, S., & Neilson, D. (2000). Bringing publics into public relations: New theoretical frameworks for practice. In R. L. Heath & G. M. Vasquez (Eds.), *Handbook of public relations* (pp. 127–138). Thousand Oaks, CA: Sage.

Morris, C. W. (Ed.). (1934). *Mind, self, and society from the standpoint of a social behaviorist.* Chicago: University of Chicago Press.

Murphy, P. (1987). Using games as a model for crisis communication. *Public Relations Review, 13*(4), pp. 19–28.

———. (1989). Game theory as a paradigm for the public relations process. In C. Botan & V. Hazleton (Eds.), *Public relations theory* (pp.173–192). Hillsdale, NJ: Lawrence Erlbaum.

———. (1991). The limits of symmetry: A game theory approach to symmetric and asymmetric public relations. In L. A. Grunig & J. E. Grunig (Eds.), *Public relations research annual* (vol. 3, pp. 115–131). Hillsdale, NJ: Lawrence Erlbaum.

———. (1996). Chaos theory as a model for managing issues and crises. *Public Relations Review, 22,* pp. 95–113.

Plowman, K. D. (1998). Power in conflict for public relations. *Journal of Public Relations Research, 10*(4), pp. 237–261.

Pyles, T., & Alego, J. (1993*). The origins and development of the English language.* New York: Harcourt.

Rampton, S., & Stauber, J. (1995). *Toxic sludge is good for you: Lies, damn lies and the public relations industry.* Monroe, ME: Common Courage Press.

Sapir, E. (1949). *Language, an introduction to the study of speech.* New York: Harcourt, Brace.

Searle, J. R. (1970). *Speech acts: An essay in the philosophy of language.* London: Cambridge University Press.

———. (1995). *The construction of social reality.* New York: Free Press.

Starck, K., & Kruckeberg, D. (2001). Public relations and community: A reconstructed theory revisited. In R. L. Heath & G. M. Vasquez (Eds.), *Handbook of public relations* (pp. 51–60). Thousand Oaks, CA: Sage.

Taylor, M. (2000). Toward a public relations approach to nation building. *Journal of Public Relations Research, 12*(2), pp. 179–210.

Toth, E. L. (2001). How feminist theory advanced the practice of public relations. In R. L. Heath & G. M. Vasquez (Eds.), *Handbook of public relations* (pp. 237–246). Thousand Oaks, CA: Sage.

Vasquez, G. M. (1996). Public relations as negotiation: An issue development perspective. *Journal of Public Relations Research, 8*(1), pp. 57–77.

Vasquez, G. M., & Taylor, M. (2000). Research perspectives on "the public." In R. L. Heath & G. M. Vasquez (Eds.), *Handbook of public relations* (pp. 139–154). Thousand Oaks, CA: Sage.

Vibbert, S. L., & Bostdorff, D. (1988). Issue management in the "Lawsuit Crisis." In C. Conrad (Ed.), *The ethical nexus: Values, communication and organizational decisions.* New York: Ablex.

CHAPTER EIGHT

SOCIODRAMA FOR PUBLIC RELATIONS PRACTICE

THOMAS MICKEY

Sociodrama is a language-based approach to public relations and as such is an interactional, interpretive, and cultural perspective. It explores the question of how as social participants in society we "make meaning." The theory calls attention to the discourse of public relations practice in such forms as speeches, press releases, brochures, and feature stories.

The theory of sociodrama relies on the major schools of thought referred to as dramatism (also called dramaturgy) and symbolic interactionism. This chapter discusses sociodrama's origin, principle concepts, focus on language, and usefulness in understanding public relations practice.

SOCIODRAMA

Sociologist Hugh Duncan (1985) found, in the field of literature, a preferable way to study the human condition. He combined his interest in language with his attempts to understand how society works. For Duncan, literary criticism became a source for understanding how society evolves.

Duncan was struck by the "drama" of human relationships. People are not born with relationships already in place. They create those relationships through form or symbol. Duncan sought to explain how people use words to interact with one another. He spent his life trying to construct a dramatistic image of social interaction. "Art," Duncan (1985) said, "like any basic social institution, constitutes social relations, because it creates the forms in which these relationships take place" (p. 51). The tradition of dramatism continues with the work of Young (1990) and Brissett and Edgley (1990). Perinbanaygam (1985), however, combines the symbolic interactionist tradition with dramatism.

In public relations there is growing interest in exploring connections between the practice of public relations and deconstruction, semiotics, feminist theory, and postmodernism. As a theory based on public relations discourse, sociodrama shares that same focus. Popovich and Popovich (1994) used socio-drama in their public relations study of a hospital. Sherman, Blanchard, and Kagel (1995) saw the theory as a way to explore the publics in a community theater. The theory is discussed in detail in Mickey's (1995) book.

Sources for Duncan

The MacCannells' (1982) work on signs and symbols in society argues for consideration of symbol and drama in everyday life. They argue that even everyday life proliferates cultural productions that serve as metasystems of interpretation: From below the level of the individual to the self and beyond, to class, and to any human system, we engage in a drama of interpretations that is the mechanism (secondary modeling systems) of cultural development.

Duncan studied the question of how we use language as a way to justify, explain, motivate, and understand one another. He approached the study of society through the use of forms, especially language, in our interactions with one another.

Duncan seems to write for the public relations practitioner when he says that the rise to power of the publicist (the modern Sophist) indicates that, as differentiation increases in large corporate structures, consensus will depend on our ability to think about communication as symbolic action. In solving the problem of how to establish favorable conditions for appeals to customers, American businesses, working in a free economy, have not been able to rely on monopolies of symbols (as in a priestly caste), of technical means of communication (as in a dictatorship), or of training in communicative skills (as in clerical orders). They have been forced to develop skills in persuasive techniques, always in competition with other businesses as well as with other agencies or institutions in the state.

Symbolic interactionism asserts that a person carves out his or her social existence. He or she does not merely conform to group norms. Cultural norms, status positions, and role relationships are only the framework within which social action takes place, not the crucial and coercive determinants of that action. Symbolic interactionism perceives the human as creating or remaking his or her environment with a course of action, rather than simply responding to normative expectations.

Concerning the question of communication, therefore, symbolic interactionists would say that we interact in communication. The participants or actors construct a relationship, or destroy it, through symbols used in communication. Duncan was concerned with the relationship among symbol, communication, and social order. He focuses on this concern in his model called *sociodrama* and leans heavily on Kenneth Burke's (1966) discussion of dramatism. Burke's work can be summarized in his dramatistic view of man. For Burke, a human in search of oneself and a better life is the universal situation, and the complex drama of this situation is a major part of all one's work.

Dramatism is the essence of Burke's work (1966). According to Burke, dramatism is a method of analysis and a corresponding critique of terminology designed to show that the most direct route to the study of human relations and human motives is via a methodological inquiry into cycles or clusters of terms and their functions. Note Burke's reference to *terms*. He stresses the importance of looking at the language we use to understand how we relate. It is the term we use that creates the relationship.

Mangham and Overington (1990) argue that for Burke and for ourselves, working and writing in a dramatistic key, people are actors who play characters; they are works of dramatic art. It is through language that we become self-conscious, capable of playing a number of characters to varying audiences and yet still retaining a grasp of an acting self. In this notion of the distinction between ourselves and our roles—a theatrical consciousness, if you will—exists links between dramatism and the tradition of symbolic interactionism that stretches from the work of James, Cooley, and Mead (1985) to the present.

As a method, dramatism addresses the empirical questions of how people explain their actions to themselves and others, and what the cultural and structural influences of these explanations might be. Burke's concern in dramatism is the persuasive or rhetorical link between motivation and action. Language is seen as social action. Language is not simply a way to express oneself, but a way to relate to both self and others. That self is as rhetorically defended as it is rhetorically constructed, and is the key to sociodrama (Perinbanaygam, 1985).

Unlike most positivistic social science, dramaturgical thinking is not a linear, sequential explanation of human behavior based on mechanistic assumptions. Its point of departure is Burke's (1966) profound assertion that the difference between a thing and a person is that a thing merely moves, whereas a person acts. The language of mechanism is therefore inapplicable to the study of human selves.

Those investigators (Burke, 1966; Duncan, 1968; Perinbanaygam, 1985) are bent on establishing the legitimacy of dramatism or dramaturgy as a distinctive form of social thought and subscribe to the view that life is drama. For them, dramaturgical understanding is that long-sought, clear window into human reality. Perinbanaygam (1985), whose work provides us with a most careful and detailed examination of the dramaturgical position, argues most forcefully for the idea of drama as reality.

Drama as an ontology begins with the premise that humans cannot help but communicate with symbols, and cannot help but be aware that others around them are interpreting those symbols. Such communication is achieved with selected features of communication media. The world consists of communication-worthy social facts or social objects that dramatically develop and present a theme. The theater is not something apart from society, or something that society invented. It is a crystallization and typification of what goes on in society all the time, or sharply, what a social relationship is.

Concepts

Language is a way to explain and to create motives that lead to a certain kind of action. The focus on language suggests a link with public relations practice. It is the language used that encourages the participants (e.g., the company's public relations professional and the company's audiences) to act in a certain way.

Dramatism emphasizes three key words: language, motives, and action. Dramatism is a systematic approach to understanding human action through an analysis of the motives—the explanations—that people offer for such action. How we verbalize about our work, our organizations, and ourselves both motivates and clarifies the action we perform. Symbolic interactionism and dramatism, therefore, are an interpretive/subjective view of society: The human world is an interpretive experience. The world does not reveal itself; we formulate it as interpretable through language and other symbols.

Language is the way roles are created in an effort to relate to one another, whether in a family or in a business. Unless we talk and write, we cannot understand our relationships or ourselves. Without language, we cannot act toward each other. It is Duncan who brought the schools of symbolic interactionism and dramatism together in what he called sociodrama.

Blyler (1992) studied language to understand public relations writing. She found that narratives were particularly important because they provided a comprehensive, compelling framework for belief and thus contributed greatly to the shared meaning created by writers and readers. Goodman (1978) sees science, art, and other cultural forms as "ways of worldmaking" through symbol. Edelman (1988) says the most incisive students of language, although working from different premises, collectively conclude that language is the primary creator of the social worlds people identify with, not a tool for describing an objective reality.

Sociodrama is not only concerned with content or agency in communication but also with how people use the words to define themselves. Gusfield (1976) describes how the social scientist acts as a dramatist—setting a stage and persuading his or her readers to treat his or her work as one type of production rather than another. He argues that if words, sentences, paragraphs, and larger units are a major tool for reporting and persuading, an analysis of how scientific knowledge leads to practical action cannot ignore the language and literary style of the field of science.

In writing about social and problem drinkers, for example, Gusfield (1976) shows the influence in the practice of writing. He specifically relates how a scientific report about the problem drinker not only explains but also creates the type of drinker that needs help. In the act of developing and presenting particular data, the theorizing and/or conclusion-making stems from acts of selection, of nomenclature, artistic presentation, and language. To be relevant or significant, data must not only be selected, but must also be typified and interpreted. In doing this, language and thought are themselves the vehicles through which such relevance is cast. In Burke's (1966) terms they are "modes of action." By writing and reading about problem drinkers, those in the helping profession recognize them in their work and recommend appropriate treatment. In classifying them as "the clients," the role of counselor is assumed. The language becomes the way to relate, not simply the means to talk about the problem.

Erving Goffman (1974) discusses everyday conversation as sociodrama when he says what talkers undertake to do is not to provide information to a recipient but to present dramas to an audience. Indeed, it seems that we spend most of our time not engaged in giving information but in giving shows. This theatricality is not based on mere display of feelings or faked exhibitions of spontaneity or any-thing else we might derogate by calling theatrical. The parallel between stage and conversation is much deeper than that. The point is that ordinarily when an indi-vidual says something, he or she is not saying it as a bald statement of fact on his or her own behalf. The person is recounting. The person is running through already determined events for the engagements of the listeners.

We speak in dramatic metaphor as a primary way to engage our listeners. We add our own interpretation in the process to portray the consummate actor—one who has an audience. Indeed, our dialogue then becomes the way to link with one another.

Perinbanaygam (1985) argues that systems of signs become the material out of which "selves" are constituted (p. 93). The relationship between selves is a relationship between one self and another in which the first is subject to him or herself and an object to the other, and the second is subject to him- or herself and an object to the first, simultaneously.

These examples show how linguistic analysis justifies certain behavior by creating a drama in which people participate. That is the crux of sociodrama. Sociodrama, like dramatism, seeks an analysis of the language used in discourse and its influence on human conduct.

Sociodrama is a way to enlist involvement and identification through the use of words. Duncan (1985) creates a meaning for sociodrama. He says that movies, radio, television, the popular press, all forms of modern mass communi-cation, reach their greatest power in their creation of sociodramas, which, like art drama, are staged as struggles between good and bad principles of social order. People do not want information about, but identification with, community life. In drama, they participate.

We create meanings as we communicate. Communication is not a message track in which symbols become objects passing through that track. With such a view we *transact* meanings that are already established, but do not create them. Sociodrama is concerned with creating meanings as we become involved. If a rela-tionship or group of people have no meaning for us, like a failing marriage or a company we no longer enjoy working for, it is because we do not identify our-selves as part of the social order. We talk as if that person or group no longer means anything to us, and, in that process, we become disconnected.

Duncan (1985) was concerned that students of human social behavior simply do not believe that how we communicate determines how we relate as social beings. Most people want to see some reality, such as power, authority, con-flict, or consensus, behind a symbol. However, words are used that determine their social meaning.

A more functionalist approach to public relations might view symbol-makers as ventriloquists' dummies. The speeches of political candidates—the ways in which they try to move people to vote—are considered a "reflection to interests" instead of ways to relate. In sociodrama, words express who we are and the way we are held together.

Communication is an act in itself, through the symbol of language. Perin-banaygam (1987) contends, "The production of meaning must be viewed as an act, albeit an act that demands completion from self and/or others, whether it is a speech act or a written act" (p. 12).

Sociodrama is not concerned with how society persuades us, but how words about society persuade us to act in certain ways in our social relationships. We do not relate and then talk; we relate as we talk, and the forms of speech available to us determine how we relate as social beings. What we read and with whom we speak determine what way we relate to ourselves and those who are significant to us.

The communication theory implicit in the theory of sociodrama is an active, self-determining, and creative one. It is concerned with how symbols are used to create and sustain social order. Many people have said that society exists within communication. Sociodrama shows how that happens by emphasizing that symbols constitute social order. The kinds of symbols we have—the ways in which they are used, for what purposes, by what kinds of people, and in what kinds of acts—structure our relationships with one another. If how reality is expressed has little to do with how it functions in creating social order, communication becomes a residual, not a constitutive, category of social experience.

In sociodrama, public relations is not *like* a drama. It *is* a drama that calls forth the active involvement of the participants, and the involvement takes place through identification. As members of an audience, we identify with one another just as elements in a machine mesh or separate. Which is more dialogical? We want to identify with others. We want to be part of something. If we can identify ourselves with an organization, we become a part of it. They no longer communicate to us; we communicate with one another.

Identification is our response or action in the dramatic process called sociodrama. Duncan (1985) contends that in times of transition, shifts in allegiance to symbols of authority are common. Problem of identity, not simply the need to belong but with whom to belong, become crucial. When people cannot act under one set of names they must choose others; how such choices are made is revealed in the symbolic phases of the struggle for new meanings. Identity is expressed as a glory, a mystical moment of belonging in which we commit ourselves to act under a certain name. These inner mysterious moments must be expressed to become acts or attitudes, which are incipient acts. Thus, identification is always dependent on objectification through communication.

The concept of identification is rooted in the symbolic interactionist tradition, which advocates the discovery of self in and through communication. One does not have an identity and then communicate. Instead, one finds his or her identity through communication.

Elements of the Drama

Also important in sociodrama is the concept of the presence of drama in our speech or writing. The drama is our link with others. Language takes on a dramatic metaphor that forms our understanding, interpretation, and attitude of the person, thing, or event about which we are speaking or writing. We relate to one another through written or spoken words that share the characteristics of drama.

Perinbanaygam (1987) sets the stage for looking at symbols as drama when he says that all discourses can be examined in terms of texture and dramatic structures (p. 22). Every cognition, is derived from a previous cognition, and in dramatic and narrative forms this derivation is the central defining principle (p. 125). Borrowing from Burke (1966), Duncan (1985) introduces the pentad, or the five elements that make up the drama of discourse. These five major dramatic concepts, called *dramatic elements,* are act, scene, actors, means, and purpose. As we talk or write, these elements are always present.

The act is what is done. It is society's celebration of social bonds; the transcendental occasions when society is reborn with an enactment of beliefs and values that its members, in general, accept. We talk about a family holiday dinner long before we assemble and long after we have left one another. The act—the dinner—is not only a word, but also a way of relating to one another. The scene symbolizes time and place as a dramatic setting, creating the proper conditions for social action. When we gather for a special dinner, the setting we want must be perfect: candles, china, wine, and flowers. We discuss the way things should look for the occasion.

The means is the form of communication we use. The medium can portray a certain message concerning the country, but can also, on occasion, bring the country together. A space shuttle success or disaster can do the same via media coverage. A handshake may provide a person with a sense of belonging. A memo, however, may provide a sense of isolation. A person interprets each form in terms of his or her relationship to a particular social order.

Actors refer to those who play certain roles for community purposes. The president of the United States presides over Memorial Day services at Arlington National Cemetery. Through him the country honors those who died during war. Elders often preside at family get-togethers. Their power gives meaning to the event for us and for others. As we arrange the seating at the table, we do not simply recognize the power line, we create it. Finally, purpose indicates the reasons why we do what we do in this drama. It involves belief in certain values that may be considered necessary to community survival. The Equal Rights Amendment struggle rallies around the premise that, in our society, women are equal to men.

The press portrays the news in dramatic form, highlighting conflict, familiar heroes, and villains. News reporters are involved in the creation of sociodrama, staging an eternal struggle between good and bad principles of social order. Edelman (1988) says a crisis, like all news developments, is a creation of the language used to depict it. The appearance of a crisis is a political act, not recognition of fact or of a rare situation. The drama is enacted, therefore, for the purposes of a particular social order. By acting in certain sociodramas, we uphold a particular order of human relationship. The enactment takes place through our choice of communication forms. Social interaction is not a process, but a dramatic expression, an enactment of roles by individuals who seek to identify with one another in their search to create social order.

Hierarchy

Language expresses a certain hierarchy. Perinbanaygam (1985) says that power, status, degrees of intimacy, and changes in the character of ongoing relationships are all indicated by the grammatical forms chosen for the exchange of significant acts between relevant actors (p. 58).

Social order involves people who communicate as superiors, inferiors, and equals, and pass from one position to another. We justify our rank to ourselves and to others at any particular time by enacting, in various kinds of community dramas, the value of some great transcendent principle of social order. One company, for example, expects us to act in a certain way. A company asks a communication professional to present this matter in a certain light. In complying, the professional seeks to uphold some great transcendent principle of social order.

The public relations person, who is a middle manager (hierarchy), has to report to a supervisor (hierarchy) and at the same time write a newsletter for the employees (hierarchy) so that they can serve clients (hierarchy) more effectively. Each person or group of people represents a certain positioning in regard to the organization. We are not the same audience and our needs are not the same in regard to the organization. The organization could not function without that hierarchy. A simple newsletter becomes a way to create, justify, and sustain a hierarchy through which the organization functions. McCarthy (1994) said public relations practitioners could use the newsletter as a vehicle of dialogue with new customers. Give the reader a chance to respond. *Relationship marketing* is sometimes used as a name for direct marketing. Each level recognizes the others, and that is done not telepathically, but through the newsletter as discourse. Sociodrama helps us see that the organization and its structure are born and sustained through an intricate system of communication forms with which the various constituents of the organization identify.

A communications study from a large corporation showed how various employees read the company newsletter according to their own needs: supervisors, to make sure their message is coming across; achievers, to find out if there are any new openings in the company; and socialites, to learn about events in the lives of other employees, such as births and weddings. Each audience reads the same newsletter differently because each level is creating and justifying its position in the organization through decoding the newsletter according to individual needs (McCarthy 1994).

Sociodrama proposes that we use forms to create a certain kind of social order, but that the forms are expressed in a hierarchical context. We appeal to a higher power and are part of that social order at the same time.

Public relations takes expression in the discourse of writing and speaking that, in turn, enables audiences to play a role in the organization. In a dramatistic study of firefighters, Cragan and Shields (1981) show that public relations and a good public image are synonymous with a higher power for firefighters. The style of writing shows a hierarchy that justifies and validates a certain social order—in this case, the fire department. More than a justification, the words can also create the kind of fire department it is. In this study, public relations activities are the means to an end, the road to salvation, and the way to expiate past sins, all rolled into one. The writing enables the organization to take a certain format, that is, we are a fire department that seeks to serve the public good, and in that service we find our reason for being.

THREE LEVELS OF SOCIODRAMA.

Public relations efforts result in the production and distribution of messages through multiple kinds of mediums, whether interpersonal or linked to technology. Discourse between participants can occur on three levels. Each level corresponds to where we see the drama being played, either behind the scenes (concerning the producers), onstage (concerning the audience), or outside the theater (concerning the outside actors with whom the audience later interacts).

The first level, behind the scenes, involves the actors in an organization making a decision regarding the message to be used. The actors could be the public relations director and the writer, who choose not only the content but also the form. The timing and setting for distribution is also up to them. Their reasons for choosing one piece of news over another is frequently based on editorial policy, but can also be based on their need to say something, even to themselves. Finally, they must decide to whom the messages should go.

What is important to notice in behind-the-scenes sociodrama is that the actors (public relations director, producers, writers, artists, photographers) attach meaning to their work. That meaning may be based on a desire to be number one in the market, or just a need to get the job done today. In other words, there could be any number of reasons why they choose to say one thing rather than another, but their motives are wrapped up in their communication. Actors justify their way of acting in communication.

We, the "audience" who receives the message, have images or ideas about what may have happened behind the scenes. We can imagine how the story in the newsletter originated, under what setting it was written, why it was written, why certain words were used, and why the writer talks about one person rather than another. All these are elements of the sociodrama called "newsletter."

The second level is onstage, which involves an audience paying attention to our message. The recipients of the message, either viewers or readers, hear or see the message and attach meaning to it. Sometimes that meaning can be quite different from what the public relations staff had in mind. The message is received at a certain time and place—within a certain context—that may be different from person to person. For example, the news serves different purposes for each person, ranging from entertainment to information or a combination of each. The audience uses the language of the writer to identify with the drama that is being created.

The recipients of our message need to make sense of their lives, and our communication media provide them with a vehicle. They acknowledge and absorb messages according to their needs. When they read the newsletter, they use the information as they need to, but not necessarily in the way the writer intended. Discussion of the newsletter is one expression of their use of that newsletter. Talk is necessary to be and stay an organization. Discussions happen because they express involvement and identification. A good question to research within sociodrama would certainly be "What kind of sociodramatic talk is going on within our organization—gossip, a newsletter, media coverage, a brochure, a meeting, or a speech?" Talking is the primary way in which our audiences create their image of the organization and the way they relate to it.

The third level of sociodrama is outside the theater. Here we view the relationships of the message recipients to the larger social order. The actors interpret the message for their own needs and then interpret it for others such as family, friends, the neighborhood, the city, the country, and so on. They relate the message to themselves and to others, thus creating a sociodrama. By talking about it, they give it value for themselves. They order their world in and through the message. By identifying with the message, they create their own drama of the organization in relation to the wider social environment. Writers and public relations professionals interact to produce a message; readers and viewers interact with the communication form; and viewers interact with their world of friends and associates. Sociodrama proposes that communication forms human relationships on each level. Television and the press do not impact us in the way a health-care worker injects an arm with a needle. Instead, they create sociodramas. Like all good drama, they portray struggles between good and bad principles of social order and we participate in that struggle. Perinbanaygam (1987) says that meaning is produced between reflective actors through discursive acts, and significances are waves that move between and among them (p. 20).

CONCLUSION

Communication, and public relations specifically, does not involve giving someone a message, but instead involves identification with others within a common drama. We need public relations to identify with an organization. Sociodrama explains the way we identify with it. We imagine, we talk, we write in dramatic forms, and these forms of communication become the way we relate to one another, not simply the way to get a message to others. Perinbanaygam (1987) says that in the discourses of everyday life, be they in the form of conversation, stories, or games, a self is created, its intentionalities experienced, announced, and asserted, and an effect is created in the world. This is achieved most parsimoniously and successfully, and often with a style and an élan, by using the resources of narrative and drama (p. 140).

Life is neither theater nor is it different from theater. It is "theater-like." Sociodrama is a description of the behavior of human beings who use theatrical (expressive) means to build their worlds. In many respects, they regard the world as so serious that the last thing they would call it is "theater." This is but one of the many paradoxes and riddles of sociodramatic thinking. Notwithstanding such criticism, sociodrama is a way for us to understand language and its relationship to social order. As such, it is a useful theory to help understand public relations practice.

CASE: CONCORD HOSPITAL

The public relations department of Concord Hospital, the only hospital in a suburban community of 30,000, wants to create a community relations campaign. Concord Hospital wants to use the theory of sociodrama to help it conduct preliminary research for the campaign. Concord wants publics to identify with the hospital. It needs to know the terms the public uses to talk about its hospital experiences. Concord also needs to correct any relevant misunderstandings the publics may hold about the hospital.

Recent events affecting the hospital include: an editorial published in a local newspaper describing how difficult it is for visitors to park at the facility; an ongoing malpractice suit (even though it looks as if the hospital is going to win) concerning a niece of the town's mayor; a recent van wreck (Concord was able to stabilize three of four seriously injured children and send them on for treatment at a large pediatric hospital); and plans to open an urgent care clinic on nights and weekends for the first time in the town's history.

Once the Concord public relations staff knows how the publics experience and talk about it, that information can be used in communication materials directed to the publics through a strategic public relations campaign.

QUESTIONS FOR APPLICATION

1. Give specific steps in this process and examples of any materials you think would be generated by Concord Hospital's public relations department. Finally, build a public relations plan with a timeline and evaluation process.

2. What in general is a language-based public relations theory?

3. Why is our publics' language about our organization important?

4. How does the language of our public(s) develop?

5. How, according to sociodrama, might we use the language of our public in the organization's public relations materials to reach those publics?

6. What is the relationship between identification and language?

7. How do we, organization and publics, build a common drama together?

8. How does sociodrama differ from other public relations theories, such as systems or two-step flow, that have become so important for public relations practice?

REFERENCES

Blyler, N. R. (1992). Shared meaning and public relations writing. *Journal of Technical Writing and Communication, 22*(3), pp. 301–318.

Brissett, D., and Edgley, C. (Eds.). (1990). *Life as theater: A dramaturgical sourcebook* (2nd ed.). New York: Aldine De Cruyter.

Burke, K. (1966). *Language as symbolic action: Essays in life, literature, and method.* Berkeley: University of California Press.

Cooley, C. H. (1918). *Social Process.* New York: C. Scribner's Son.

Cooley, C. H. (1902). *Human nature and the social order.* New York: C. Scribner's Son.

Cragan, J. F., & Shields, D. C. (1981). *Applied communication research: A dramatistic approach.* Prospect Heights, IL: Waveland Press.

Duncan, H. (1985). *Communication and social order.* New Brunswick, NJ: Transaction Books.

Duncan, H. (1968). *Symbols in society.* Oxford: Oxford University Press.

Edelman, M. (1988). *Constructing the political spectacle.* Chicago: University of Chicago Press.

Goffman, E. (1974). *Frame Analysis: An essay on the organization of experience.* Cambridge, MA: Harvard University Press.

Goodman, N. (1978). *Ways of worldmaking.* Indianapolis: Hackett.

Gusfield, J. (1976). The literary rhetoric of science: Comedy and pathos in drinking and driving research. *American Sociological Review, 41*, pp. 16–34.

James, Cooley, & Mead, H. (1985). *The foundation of symbolic interaction.* Sage.

MacCannell, D., and MacCannell, J. F. (1982). *The time of the sing: Semiotic interpretation of modern culture.* Bloomington: Indiana University Press.

Mangham, I. L., & Overington, M. A. (1990). Dramatism and the theatrical metaphor in *Life as Theater* (2nd ed.). In D. Brissett & C. Edgley (Eds.), *Life as Theater: A dramaturgical source book.* New York: Aldine de Gruyter.

McCarthy, B. (1994). Lecture: *Marketing communication in the information economy.* Sponsored by the Public Relations Society. Waltham, MA.

Mead, G. H. (1964). *The social psychology of George Herbert Mead.* Chicago: University of Chicago Press.

Mickey, T. (1996). *Sociodrama: An interpretive theory for the practice of public relations.* Lanham, MD: University Press of America.

Perinbanaygam, R. S. (1985). *Signifying acts: Structure and meaning in everyday life.* Carbondale: Southern Illinois University Press.

Perinbanaygam, R. S. (1987). Drama in everyday life. *Studies in Symbolic Interaction, 8*, pp. 125–140.

Popovich, K. & Popovich, M. (1994). "Use of Q Methodology by Public Relations. Practitioners for Strategic Hospital Planning". Operant Subjectivity, Number 17.

Sherman, R., Blanchard, C. Law, & Kagel, K. (1995, July–August). Local theater attendance: A scientific approach to audience recruitment. *Operant Subjectivity*, 108–120.

Young, T. R. (1990). *The drama of social life: Essays in post-modern social psychology.* New Brunswick, NJ: Transaction Books.

CHAPTER NINE

CONTINGENCY THEORY
Strategic Management of Confict in Public Relations

GLEN T. CAMERON

AUGUSTINE PANG

YAN JIN

Conflict is dynamic. So is strategic conflict management. Can you remember the last time you quarreled with a friend, a spouse, or a family member? How did you manage the conflict? In what manner was the conflict resolved?

Even as your thought processes begin stirring, let us throw you some other questions to help you focus your thoughts: How much did you have to give in, or how much did the other party give in to you? What made you give in, or even give up entirely? How did you deal with issues that remained in shades of gray?

While you are thinking, let us share a short story of how a conflict in public relations was managed, an illustration, perhaps, of how very often in conflicts we intuitively engage in a dynamic, and possibly concomitant process of arguing for and advancing our agendas on the one hand, while giving in and accommodating on the other hand. What course we take depends on many contingent factors.

Now here's the story. By all measures, C. Richard Yarbrough is a consummate, experienced, top-class public relations professional. As the managing director of communications of the Atlanta Committee for the Olympic Games (ACOG), Yarbrough knew all too well what it was like to be confronted with conflicts—even before the world descended on Atlanta, the venue of the 1996 Olympics, and the customary lighting of the torch to signal the start of the Games.

Management of conflicts was part of a day's job for Yarbrough, and among the myriad conflicts Yarbrough was confronted with, long before the Olympics began, was one involving a powerful newspaper that was concerned about possible financial excesses in the ACOG. The premier newspaper in Atlanta, the *Atlanta Journal-Constitution* (AJC), demanded full disclosure of salaries in the

ACOG team. Yarbrough had all along maintained that such highly sensitive and private information should not enter the public domain. This would create unnecessary jealousy in the unified team he was trying to foster and revelation could cause unhappiness among sponsors. With the help of the ACOG lawyers, he successfully negotiated with AJC that such information should forever remain confidential. In doing so, you could say that he was pushing his agenda here, arguing and advocating for what he believed.

Events beyond his control soon took a turn that caused Yarbrough to change his mind. Subsequent changes approved by the International Olympic Committee (IOC) mandated changes to be similarly made at ACOG, and that included disclosures of titles and salaries. Yarbrough was caught in a dilemma: How should he deal with an issue for which he had so strongly advocated?

He soon realized his hands were tied: He had to give in. He finally agreed to release details of the salaries—but only with the ACOG board's approval. The ACOG board was understandably concerned about the impact of its decision. At the same time, the AJC was adamant that such disclosures should be published sooner rather than later, and had even threatened to sue. To exacerbate matters, it had added ammunition in the form of support from the state's attorney general. AJC was determined to press relentlessly for the executive salary figures. The situation deteriorated to a stage where the ACOG–AJC relations became untenable, a public relations disaster for the ACOG, which was tasked with showcasing the best of Atlanta to the rest of the world through the media, and where it was so crucial to have the media as an ally rather than an adversary.

To strategically manage the conflict, Yarbrough knew he had to change his stance to reflect prevailing conditions. He had to assume a different stance with his different stakeholders. With the ACOG board, he moved from a position of advocating against the disclosure of salaries to one of accommodation—by threatening to resign if the ACOG board did not agree to release top salary figures to the newspaper. With AJC, he moved from a position of advocacy against the disclosure to one of accommodation, finally coming full circle to advocacy by setting boundaries of what he would and would not release. He insisted on terms for what the newspaper could and could not do with the information.

When the standoff was finally resolved, the media hailed this as "a turning point" in ACOG's "search for its own character," which it found by demonstrating the "very best of moral, ethical and responsible behavior" (Budd [1995], cited in Yarbrough, Cameron, Sallot, & McWilliams, 1998, p. 49).

Yarbrough was able to negotiate the conflict because he appreciated the concomitant, tangential, and always dynamic application of different stances: when to negotiate and when to confront; when to allow the dispute to escalate, and when to contain it; when to advocate, when to accommodate—all paramount challenges of high-level public relations. Yarborough did not enroll in a business class to learn this. It came naturally, just as it would to any of us with a lifetime of experience in public relations, experience in managing competition and conflict on behalf of our own organization. This management of competition and conflict is the crux of Glen T. Cameron's contingency theory (see below) and arguably the essence of what we do in public relations.

Certainly, life would be simpler if management of conflicts could be reduced to a formulaic principle where we always strive for a "win-win" communication. We can often arrive at win-win outcomes, but we have to realize the road that leads there is often littered with footprints of pushing our agendas and giving in to other people's agendas, with the position we take at any given point in time subjected to a confluence of factors that bear enormous weight on the decisions we make.

Conflict is dynamic—so is strategic management of conflict in public relations. This dynamism makes the field an exciting, but challenging, profession at the center of modern life and ever present in the news media that bathe our modern life with print, audio, and video stories derived from public relations efforts. Even as you are thinking about your own experiences in managing conflicts, allow us to present a theory that we have systematically and empirically tested to provide a framework for conflicts to be managed strategically using public relations tools.

THE STANCE WE TAKE IS INFLUENCED BY THE SITUATION WE ARE IN

Professor Glen T. Cameron from the Missouri School of Journalism offers a theory to understand how the inevitable competition and conflicts that occur in a complex world can be managed. A diametric theoretical perspective from the normative position taken in excellence theory (see the original excellence study in J. Grunig, 1992), the contingency theory offers a perspective to examine how one party relates to another through the enactment of a given stance toward the other party at a given point in time; how those stances change, sometimes almost instantaneously; and what influences the change in stance (Cancel, Cameron, Sallot, & Mitrook, 1997). Cameron's contingency theory argues for a realistic and useful model of how strategic public relations is practiced as a consequence of the organization's stance.

This stance can be measured and placed along a continuum, with advocacy at one extreme and accommodation at the other. Most of the time, organizations do not remain at the extreme poles while arguing for their own interests exclusively (pure advocacy) or making concessions to the other party exclusively (pure accommodation). Most organizations fall somewhere in between and, over time, their position usually moves along the continuum. At the same time, each public that an organization identifies will also be determining its stance toward others, changing in response to conditions.

Between the two ends are a wide range of operational stances that entail "different degrees of advocacy and accommodation" (Cancel, Cameron, Sallot, & Mitrook, 1997, p. 37). Along this continuum, the theory argues that any of the eighty-seven factors (see Appendix A) derived from public relations literature, excellence theory, observations, and grounded theory (Cameron, 1997), can affect the location of an organization on that continuum *at a given time regarding a given public*" (Cancel, Mitrook, & Cameron, 1999, p. 172; Yarbrough, Cameron, Sallot, & McWilliams, 1998, p. 40).

The theory seeks to understand the dynamics, within and without the organization, that affect an accommodative stance. By understanding these dynamics, the contingency theory specifies and elaborates on the conditions, factors, and forces that undergird such a stance, along a continuum, so that public relations needs not be viewed by artificially classifying public relations practice into only four or five models. It aims to "offer a structure for better understanding of the dynamics of accommodation as well as the efficacy and ethical implications of accommodation in public relations practice" (Yarbrough, Cameron, Sallot, & McWilliams, 1998, p. 41). Put simply, the stance we take is influenced by the circumstances we face.

The Circumstance—"It Depends"

Under the overarching "It Depends" philosophy, Cameron and his colleagues developed the contingency theory of accommodation by using a continuum from pure advocacy to pure accommodation to represent the stance movement of an organization toward a given public at a given time and in a given situation. Therefore, contingency theory is focused on the stance of the organization in dealing with a given public, not the outcomes of a public relations practice. The stance of the organization taken at a given time is found to be influenced by different factors. Cameron and his colleagues initially identified a matrix of contingent factors (see Appendix A) that were grouped into internal variables related to the characteristics of the organization and external variables regarding the environment and the characteristics of the publics. Other factors, such as CEO stock options and grassroots Internet activism, have been proffered by researchers or professionals in public relations.

Cameron takes the position that this welter of factors is not only a realistic portrayal of how complicated and sophisticated public relations practice is, but that any good theory in the twenty-first century should reflect the complexity of natural phenomena. He argues that, like our colleagues in the so-called hard sciences such as biochemistry or medicine, we should embrace complexity. Whether in the understanding of cancer or the more complex understanding of the management of conflict in public arenas, answers depend on multiple factors. Just as biomedical understanding, for example, is not a matter of one or two factors, social phenomena are similarly complex and multifactored.

The contingency variables are categorized into predisposing and situational factors: Predisposing factors include the characteristics of the dominant coalition, public relations' access to top management, organizational size and culture, and so forth. Situational factors include the characteristics of the external public, perceived urgency and threat, and the feasibility of accommodation. Predisposing variables determine the stance of an organization before it goes into a situation dealing with a given public, while the combination and variability of situational factors may shift the stance of the organization over time, depending on whether the situational factors are powerful enough to change the predisposition to a particular stance on the continuum.

One key argument of contingency theory is the disentanglement of stance from the cluster of strategies and tactics that follow from a given stance. Stance drives strategy and tactics in public relations, but is not synonymous with a style of communication. For example, an organization may decide to be munificent toward a public, using one-way communication to announce a new health plan for workers. One-way communication may be typically associated with manipulation or propagandizing, but in this instance offers information of benefit to a key public.

Another key contribution of the contingency theory is the proposition that it is not only acceptable to advocate aggressively in some cases for one's organization, but it may also be the only legal or ethical course to take. To understand why symmetrical or accommodative stances cannot be taken in some situations, Cameron, Cropp, and Reber (2001) conducted research on several key variables, which they call proscriptive factors. These are factors that prevent an organization from collaborating or communicating with a public. Bearing in mind that each public is also an organization that is determining its stance toward others, the proscription is sometimes mutual. For example, two companies operating in a regulated industry such as electrical power generation may not be allowed to communicate. Similarly, the moral conviction of an organization may preclude it from accommodative overtures. A religious group that opposes abortion may find it morally impossible to negotiate or collaborate with a pro-choice group. And an organization that identifies two publics who are diametrically opposed cannot make genuine accommodation of one public without by definition taking an adversarial stance toward the other. A zoning commission cannot accommodate both those opposing a Wal-Mart location and the Wal-Mart team seeking approval.

Cameron, Cropp, and Reber (2001) noted that often one hears platitudes about how an organization is willing to practice accommodative public relations by reaching out to a public. They argue that often these statements belie actual practice when these proscriptive factors preclude an organization to accommodate or even communicate with a public. It is concluded that for those situations, even though at the surface an organization seems to take an excellence approach, their stance swiftly changes and moves on the continuum of accommodation toward advocacy.

Given its nature and major application, contingency theory is a positive theory, which describes when and how different types of public relations are practiced, providing a more realistic view of the profession and the "It Depends" reality of PR practitioners' decision-making processes. Contingency theory takes a dynamic view of the continuum from the very beginning, in which the organization's stance is influenced by both predisposing and situational factors. In light of effectiveness and ethics, Cameron and his colleagues propose that true excellence lies in picking the most appropriate stance on the continuum at a given time toward a given public.

PILLARS OF CONTINGENCY THEORY—DYNAMISM AND REALISM

Dynamism in Conflict Management

Contingency theory takes the strategic communication management perspective, emphasizing the importance of managing the communication between an organization and its publics by using different strategies at different times. It also highlights the role of power control of dominant coalition in the public relations decision-making process with its characteristics, schema, and fear of threats. Both internal and external factors are identified as influencers of the public relations practice.

Recent studies using contingency theories have demonstrated its applications in the field of high-profile conflict resolution, health-related crisis communication, and the source-reporter relationship, to name a few. Shin, Cheng, Jin, and Cameron (2005) conducted content analyses of news coverage for high profile conflicts that provide a natural history of the use of the contingency theory in public relations. The content analysis tracked the changing stances of organizations moving on the continuum from pure advocacy to pure accommodation, in response to a number of contingent factors that can just as readily move an organization toward accommodation as it did toward advocacy. By integrating conflict resolution models from the conflict literature with the contingency theory in public relations, the research results confirmed that strategies as well as stances of an organization and its public change over time. Both parties in each conflict demonstrated overall advocacy and employed a contending strategy predominantly during the conflict management process responding to perceived threats.

Using content analyses of severe acute respiratory syndrome (SARS) news coverage in Singapore and China, Jin, Pang, and Cameron's series of studies (2004, 2006), and Pang, Jin, and Cameron (2004) integrated crisis communication strategies and contingency theory to identify the influential factors or conditions determining the stances and strategies of an organization toward multiple publics. The health-crisis related conflict studies examined how crisis was communicated at the macro levels by the two governments, what stances were taken, and what strategies were used to manage strategic publics. Findings showed that although both Singapore and China share similar cultures and media systems, and perceived the crisis similarly in terms of severity and attribution, the dominant factors and motivations influencing each of their stances and strategies between advocacy and accommodation were different. Singapore, perceiving SARS as threatening to its political and social fabric, was more internally motivated, and hence more advocating. China, anxious to downplay the pressure from its international detractors, was externally motivated, hence more accommodating. The differentiation of culture and political circumstance were accentuated in an examination of comparative approaches like this, highlighting the critical role culture plays in studies involving the government as the organization, as well as between governments in international public relations.

Shin and Cameron (2004) surveyed 641 public relations practitioners and journalists about their perceived conflict between the two professions. They found that the perceived conflict can be best illuminated by a bilevel of perceptual differences among agreement, congruency, and accuracy regarding the professional orientation of public relations practitioners and journalists. While the two professions demonstrated their perceptual discrepancies in terms of roles, values, independence, dyadic adjustment, and attitudes in conflict, both also revealed a tendency to escalate or minimize the conflict to strategically manage the degree of conflict in the interests of their own profession. Public relations practitioners sought to accommodate journalists, while journalists maintained professionalism by tending to the more adversarial.

Contingency theory has been applied to international settings as well. Choi and Cameron (2005) examined strategic conflict management in the Korean context to assess whether the two-way symmetrical model of public relations propounded in the excellence theory had universal or transcendent application across cultures. Results suggested that the way conflict and strategic communication were managed depended on many factors. This work resonated with a program of contingency research conducted by Zhang and Cameron (Zhang & Cameron, 2003; Zhang, Qiu, & Cameron, 2004) that merged international studies, diplomacy research, and public relations. Findings suggest that multinational companies and countries manage conflict strategically, moving in response to factors along the contingency continuum. Called public diplomacy, the application of contingency theory and a better understanding of the role of public relations offers promise for more effective and constructive solutions to global competition and conflict.

Realism in Litigation Public Relations

Using contingency theory, Reber, Cropp, and Cameron (2001) analyzed the long considered adversarial relationships between public relations practitioners and lawyers via Q methodology and depth interviews. Subjective attitudes were measured regarding strategies in dealing with the public in times of organizational crisis and how the individuals viewed their professional counterparts. It was found that lawyers more accurately projected the public relations response than vice versa. Relationships seem to be all-important and the proverbial law-public relations conflict may have taken on nearly mythic proportions. In actuality, it appears that legal and public relations teams very often work together to establish favorable antecedent conditions for both litigation and for quite frequent negotiation of differences with publics.

Reber, Cropp, and Cameron (2003) further applied the contingency theory of accommodation to advance the role of public relations beyond its publicity and media-relations roots to a crucial place in conflict management. Proscriptive variables (e.g., legal factors, regulatory agencies) further add parsimony to the theory by establishing ground rules that affect a stance toward a public at a given time. A case study out of an in-depth analysis of Norfolk Southern's hostile takeover of Conrail (Reber, Cropp, & Cameron, 2003) illustrates the dynamism of conflict management in public relations as well as the proscriptions on how an organization handles conflicts.

In advancing the theory in the field of litigation public relations, Cameron and his colleagues have identified a matrix of variables that might affect an organization's stance toward an individual public. Research evidence shows that contingency theory offers a richly complex and realistic portrayal of changing public relations activity along a continuum from pure advocacy to pure accommodation of a given public at a given time.

INSPIRATION OF CONTINGENCY
THEORY—EXPANSION AND EXTENSION

Expansion: Emotions and Threat Appraisal

Jin and Cameron (2004) called for attention to the role of emotions as central to public-relations theory building. Using an adapted appraisal model of emotion in public relations, crucial dimensions were added to Cameron's contingency theory that take into account emotional tone, weight, and temperature with regard to contingency factors (see Figure 9.1). An emotion-laden contingency model is presented on a multidimensional plane (see Figure 9.2), proposing that for a given public at a given time in a given public relations encounter, and across external and internal contingent factors, the public's emotional tone, temperature, and weight regarding encounter-related contingency factors will have strong effects on the public's stance toward the organization on the accommodation continuum.

The role of threat assessment—closely related to the new focus on the role of affective factors in the public relations decision-making process regarding the stance of an organization—the conceptual framework of threat assessment was introduced into the theory. Threats, both internal and external as identified in the original contingency factor matrix, have been commonly used to describe the state that a nation, organization, or individual endures during a crisis. Jin, Pang, and Cameron

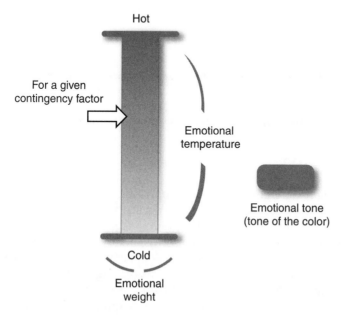

FIGURE 9.1   Emotional tone, weight, and temperature with regard to contingency factors

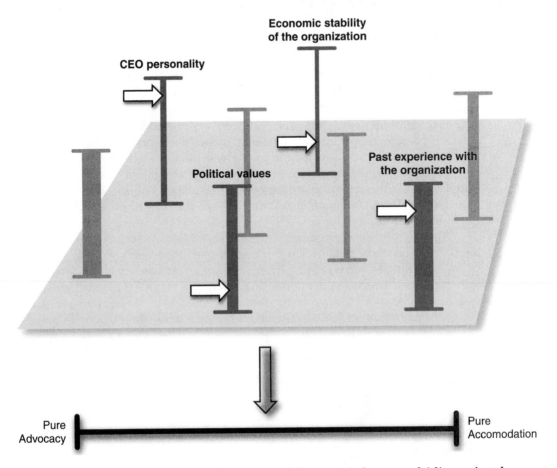

FIGURE 9.2 **Emotional-laden contingency model presented on a multidimensional plane**

(2005) conceptually differentiated threats from "risk," "fear," and "conflict," which are the cause and the effect of crisis. They proposed the explication of the concept by expanding, cross-fertilizing, and integrating ideas from an interdisciplinary review of literature and enumerated the dimensionality of threats (see Figure 9.3). A threat appraisal model within the contingency theory framework is based on the cognitive, affective, and conative levels of threats (see Figure 9.4).

Two empirical trials were conducted to test this threat appraisal model. Pang, Jin, and Cameron (2006) adapted this model to examine the fabric and faces of threat on an ongoing issue and to see how it can be communicated. The issuance of terror alerts by the Department of Homeland Security (DHS) was analyzed in terms of how the terrorism-related threat was appraised by the DHS, and the con-

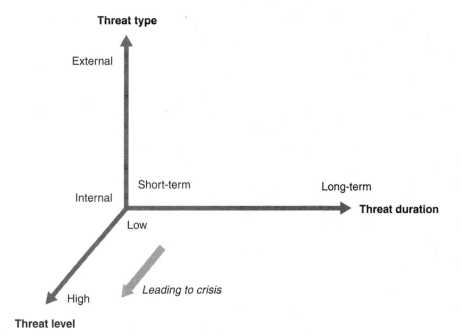

FIGURE 9.3   **Interdisciplinary view**

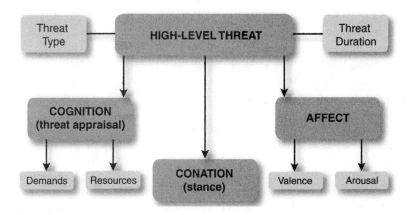

FIGURE 9.4   **Threat appraisal model based on cognitive, affective, and conative levels of threats**

servative and liberal audiences. Findings showed a shared view by the DHS and the conservative audiences, while the liberal audiences thought otherwise. Though there appeared to be consensus in threat communication, more internal consistency within the DHS is needed to optimize its effectiveness.

Jin (2005) conducted an online experiment on the effects of threat type and threat duration on public relations professionals' cognitive appraisal of threats, affective responses to threats, and the stances taken in threat-embedded crisis situations. Using a 2 (external versus internal threat type) x 2 (long-term versus short-term threat duration) within-subjects design, 116 public relations professionals were exposed to four crisis situation scenarios. Research findings revealed the main effects of threat type on threat appraisal, emotional arousal, and qualified-rhetoric-mixed accommodations, and the main effects of threat duration across all threat consequences. Interactions of these two threat dimensions revealed that external and long-term threat combination led to higher situational demands appraisal and more intensive emotional arousal. This study further examined the relationship between cognitive appraisal, affective responses, and stances as key aspects of threat consequences. High cognition and stronger affect regarding threats were found to be related to more accommodating stances.

These recent advances in contingency theory and its applications shed light on the feasibility and the imperative of integrating cognition, emotion, and conation in public relations research, and provided insights for public relations professionals on how to apply the theory to their daily strategic conflict management practice.

Extension: Conflict Positioning in Crisis Communication

Cameron introduced the term conflict positioning, which he defined as positioning the organization "favorably in anticipation of conflicts" (Wilcox & Cameron, 2006, p. 244). This, he argued, is the culmination of sound precrisis preparations, such as environmental scanning, issues tracking, issues management, and formulation of crisis plans, among the recommended measures organizations should engage in before crises erupt.

Taking this concept further, Pang (2006) argues that the key in organizational strategic thinking is to position itself favorably in anticipation of crisis. Practitioners must understand what factors are critical in determining an organization's position, or what Pang calls conflict stance.

The organization's conflict stance, or sometimes multiple stances for multiple publics, which encapsulates organizational assessment of threat, would in turn influence its crisis response strategies during the crisis, leading to outcomes that match what the organization had prepared for in the first place. For instance, if a standing rule in an organization's dominant coalition is to forbid communication with its publics, the conflict stance assumed would be one marked by obstinacy and dogged resistance, or advocacy, as described in contingency theory. The strategies the organization is most likely to employ during the crisis might be denial of, or evading of, responsibility. On the contrary, if an organization is predisposed to a more accommodative stance of engaging them with the aim of working through the crisis with the publics, it is most likely to employ accommodative strategies, like corrective action, to communicate during the crisis.

Favorable positioning in a crisis thus involves first understanding what factors, within and without the organization, play critical roles in the organization's ability to handle the crisis; second, based on the influence of these factors, what stance the organization is likely to adopt; and third, what strategies are likely to be used based on the stance. Knowing the conditions (factors) that facilitate its reaction (stance) that influence its action (strategies) enables the organization to understand what causes the effects of its actions. Therefore, a major premise is that crisis factors lead to conflict stance, which leads to response strategy selection.

Through an extensive literature review, drawn from a tapestry of literature from interdisciplinary fields, Pang (2006) has identified five key factors that influence organizational stance: involvement of the dominant coalition in a crisis; influence and autonomy of public relations in the crisis; influence and role of legal practitioners in the crisis; importance of publics to the organization during the crisis; and the organization's perception of threat in the crisis.

In conflict positioning, Pang (2006) argues for a plausible integration of contingency theory's stance perspectives with image repair theory's strategy analyses on a continuum. Pang (2006) argues that both these theories are complementary and supplementary in that contingency theory is based on analyzing an organization's stance before it enters into communication, while image repair theory is based on analyzing an organization's strategies as it enters into communication. As with contingency theory, image repair strategies can also be conceptualized as existing on a continuum. Since the offensiveness of an error and responsibility of the error might be regarded as "existing on a continuum" (Benoit, 2004, p. 265), message options can similarly be argued to exist on a continuum. Image repair theory's five general strategies—denial, evading responsibility, reducing offensiveness, corrective action, and mortification—can be seen as existing on a continuum, with denial sharing similar characteristics as advocacy (i.e., insisting on one's right and point of view), and mortification sharing similar characteristics as accommodation (i.e., giving in).

CONFLICT POSITIONING: INTEGRATING CONTINGENCY STANCE WITH IMAGE REPAIR STRATEGIES

With advocacy and accommodation set as opposite poles on a continuum, contingency theory advocates analyzing stance before an organization enters into communication. Likewise, with denial and mortification set as opposite poles on a continuum, image repair theory advocates analyzing strategies as an organization enters into communication.

Based on the factor-stance-strategy conceptualization, for instance, if the dominant coalition (factor) is predisposed to communication with the publics during a crisis, it is likely to adopt a more accommodative approach (stance), and the strategies the organization uses are likely to be reducing offensiveness, corrective action, and mortification. On the contrary, if the dominant coalition (factor) is bounded by moral, legal, regulatory, and jurisdictional constraints, it is likely to adopt a less accommodative approach (stance), and the strategies it is likely to employ are less accommodative, such as denial and evading responsibility.

In proposing this conflict-positioning conceptualization based on factor-stance strategy, Pang (2006) argues that three assumptions are critical. First, the stance an organization takes is based on factors that affect this stance. Second, the stance the organization takes will affect the strategies it employs. Changes in stance will, concomitantly, affect changes in strategies. Third, the stance will be consonant with strategies. An asynchronized, wildly differential stance from strategy is argued to jeopardize an organization's position during a crisis.

NEW FRONTIERS FOR CONTINGENCY THEORY

Measurement of Contingent Factors

The matrix of contingent factors, an essential component of contingency theory, provide a systematic spectrum of understanding the dynamics and stance movement in public relations practices and decision-making processes. Shin, Cameron, and Cropp (2002) conducted a national survey of public relations practitioners on the perceived importance of contingent factors and the influence in their daily public relations practice. Practitioners agreed that contingency theory did reflect their practice reality, and organization-related characteristics were found to be most influential.

Reber and Cameron (2003) developed a scale to measure some key dimensions of contingent factors to accord the theory some modicum of parsimony and applicability in daily practice. Via a survey of ninety-one top public relations practitioners, the authors quantified contingency theory by constructing scales of five theoretical constructs: external threats, external public characteristics, organizational characteristics, public relations department characteristics, and dominant coalition characteristics. Practitioners cited fear of legitimizing activist claims, credibility and commitment of an external public, and the place of public relations in the dominant coalition as contingencies impacting dialogue with contending publics. In the near future, this research will inform the development of expert systems and decision-support software to aid practitioners in assessing the internal and external communication environment as a stance for the organization is developed regarding a given public at a given time.

As more measurement and scale development research projects are executed, each identified contingent factor or cluster of factors will continue to be examined systematically. The interrelationship between contingency factors will also continue to be studied.

Further Elaboration on Stances

This chapter has emphasized the importance of stance as a key concept in understanding public relations practice. According to Cameron and his colleagues, stance moves along the continuum of accommodation, with organizations adopting a variety of stances with their publics at any given point, and these stances change, depending on the circumstances. The continuum has two poles, advocacy and accommodation, that represent the extent of willingness to make concessions or make changes within the organization on behalf of a public. One key argument of contingency theory is the disentanglement of stance from the cluster of strategies and tactics. Unlike strategies and tactics, stance is operationalized as the position an organization takes in decision making, which is supposed to determine which strategy or tactic to employ.

However, for public relations stances, there is a lack of any multiple-item scale or inventory being developed and tested in terms of its evaluative qualities. Jin and Cameron (2006) embarked on a study developing a multiple-item scale for measuring public relations stance (see Appendix B), which meets reliability and validity standards and can be applied in public relations practice. The area of public relations and stance is wide open for further study.

CONCLUSION

Building on this foundational work, future studies on stance and its measurement might focus on the explication of the client and employer advocacy facet of the continuum, corresponding to the aspect of accommodation to publics, so as to provide a full picture of the domain of contingency from pure advocacy to pure accommodation. Having established that the stance of an organization is dynamic in response to a complex set of factors, future work on how that particular stance is enacted through public relations strategies and tactics will advance contingency theory as a more complete theory of public relations.

CASE: THE SARS CRISES

For months in 2003, the world lay under siege by a strain of virus that masqueraded as pneumonia but inflicted a far more lethal effect. By all accounts, the mystery of how the virus in the severe respiratory acute syndrome (SARS) has come to be has remained largely unsolved (Bradsher & Altman, 2003). What began as routine fever and cough in a Chinese physician, who was later identified as a supercarrier, rapidly spread to people who had cursory contacts with him, spiraling into a worldwide crisis that spanned across Asia and North America (Rosenthal, 2003).

On March 18, 2003, Singapore, a cosmopolitan city-state nestled at the tip of Malaysia, entered the annals of the World Health Organization (WHO) as a casualty of the dreaded SARS. On April 2, 2003, after months of foot-dragging and denial, China reluctantly joined Canada, Singapore, Hong Kong, and Taiwan in the SARS hit list. It soon became apparent that China and Singapore were to take different approaches to resolve the crisis. Singapore, on the one hand, adopted a transparent approach. When it was finally cleared of SARS on May 31, it was praised by WHO for its "exemplary" (Khalik & Wong, 2003, p. 1) handling of the crisis. China, on the other hand, has been blamed for escalating the crisis through its failure to curb the disease earlier and for covering up news about the rapid outbreak (Eckholm, 2003). Except for a huge sigh of relief, China did not receive the same kind of reception that Singapore did when it was declared SARS-free on June 25.

Note: This case study is excerpted from the article that is first published by the authors in the Journal of International Communication.

The diametrically opposite approaches adopted by the two governments presented an intriguing opportunity to study how they communicated the crisis. To analyze the two countries' approaches, content analyses of reports published in key media outlets, as evidence of enactments of informational strategies, are used. To analyze Singapore's approach, data come from the population of SARS stories from *The Straits Times*, Singapore's newspaper of record (Turnbull, 1995). To analyze China's approach, data come from the population of SARS stories from *China Daily*, China's government-run *English Daily* (Marsden, 1990) throughout the duration of the crisis.

Due to the rapidity, abruptness, and volatility of the situation brought about by SARS, and the exigency and imperativeness to manage the crisis as efficiently and effectively as possible by the respective governments, analyses of the Chinese and Singaporean stances and strategies, as well as the publics' responses, through news coverage would provide a more accurate representation of what had happened than other sources, like press releases. Martinelli and Briggs (1998) argued that in a crisis, the media become an important tool to examine an organization's stances and strategies, and the effectiveness with which it gets its messages across to its publics, rather than other means, such as government-issued press releases.

With every quick turn of events during the crisis, the governments needed to communicate speedily. Arguably there is no better way that it could have done so, in rapid succession, than through the media, particularly the respective nations' prestigious newspapers, which the government trusted (Kuo, & Ang, 2000; Lecher, 2003). As subjective as the news reports may be, we believe that prestigious newspapers, as argued by both Krippendorf (2004) and Riffe, Lacy, and Fico (1998), would project fair representations of the government's efforts, intents, stances, and strategies. Martinelli and Briggs (1998) also argued that by examining the strategies, and possibly the factors and stances, that are evident in media accounts, it can be determined how effective the organization was in getting its messages across.

Discussion

The comparison between Chinese and Singapore governments shed light on different stances and strategies different organizations employ in a given crisis and how their respective publics respond cognitively and affectively.

Organizations' Perceptions of the Crisis: Similar Perceptions, Similar Motivations.   Given that both Chinese and Singapore governments perceived the severity of the crisis in a similar way, we surmise that both governments set their stances and strategies on the same baseline, which is: The SARS crisis was severe and largely internally controllable. In a common crisis where both governments were not culpable, and the locus of control was external, based on Coombs' (1998) typology, it was left to the respective governments to take responsibility instead of attributing blame to external parties. Perhaps this is a reflection of the conservative, collectivist (Schwartz, 1994) culture that Singapore and China come from. Such cultures are characterized by family security, restoration of social order, preservation of values, and national security (Schwartz, 1994, p. 102). In a scenario where the enemy was largely unknown, and dangerous, it appears that the respective governments took over the mantle of leadership, and galvanized its peoples toward restoration. There is a famous Chinese saying that has filtered into the psyche of Singaporeans, largely made of immigrant stock from China, as well: Your fate is in your own hands.

This is also consistent with the hallmarks of the two governments: The Chinese government is centrally controlled. As Wu (2002) argued, the Chinese Communist Party relies on effective leadership, undergirded by the dual social forces of traditional values and patriotism to reconstruct a new cohesive force. In that regard, it is possible that the media, which is neo-authoritarian (Merrill, 2000), would frame the government as capable of taking the full responsibility to handle the crisis. Singapore also has a neo-authoritarian media system. More than just a reflection of media framing, the Singapore government has been known to be extremely proactive when it is confronted with threats to the country's survival, particularly political threats (Sikorski, 1996). This can be extended to biological threats as well.

Organizations' Stances and Strategies: Advocacy to Galvanize, Accommodation to Steer.   Comparing the Chinese government's and Singapore government's stances toward their respective publics as evident in the news stories, our findings show that these two governments tend to move in a similar way. Compared to the Singapore government, the Chinese government, however, tended to be more accommodating when dealing with publics such as WHO, foreign countries, as well as the general publics. The differences are all found to be statistically significant respectively.

A crisis, like SARS, brings about a government public relations crisis for the Chinese government at all levels. It could be conjectured that the newly empowered Chinese central leadership under President Hu Jintao realized that government public relations programs, if executed properly, could help with the management of this kind of crisis.

Taking a cautious and proactive position, the new Chinese government seemed to put substantial efforts into building constructive and cooperative relationships with a variety of key publics threatened or damaged by the SARS crisis. Three reasons are proffered as to why the Chinese government found accommodation toward WHO, foreign countries, and its general public a better stance:

■ China was cooperating closely with WHO, a world body, to find the antidote for the disease. When the hallmark of a relationship is that of cooperation, accommodation almost always takes precedence over advocacy.

■ An accommodative stance toward foreign countries and businesses is consistent with China's well-embedded policies on building optimal international relations and encouraging foreign investment to support the domestic economic development, based on political realism, and national and diplomatic interests.

■ The government needed to steer its massive populace to follow its directions. While advocacy could galvanize its people, it is accommodation that will sway them over to its side. For a huge country like China, that would be important factor.

Compared to China, Singapore appeared to advocate more, particularly toward two publics, the quarantined public and general public. The rationale appears to be thus: The quarantined public has to be told what to do so that it does not infect the general public, and the general public has to be told what to do so that the virus is not spread. This may be due to overall decision-making abilities of the government to make crisis-time policies that required the adherence of the crucial publics.

Threat was found to be the dominant contingent factor undergirding both the countries' governments' stances. Threat, especially one as insidious as SARS, breeds fear. Fear can emerge as a dominant factor in the contingency theory. Even though threat was an underlying force affecting the organization's strategies, both countries appeared to respond differently. The most used strategy in the Chinese government's arsenal was cooperation while that of the Singapore government was attack. This could be because the new generation of Chinese government officials, characteristically younger, more energetic, better educated, and less ideology-driven, tend to back away from the use of traditional political propaganda in dealing with their publics, which paves way for a much more accommodating strategy. Singapore used a mix of strategies, ranging from cooperation with some publics, such as WHO, and attack on others, like the quarantined public. Advocating strategies like attack were softened with accommodating strategies, like cooperation.

Publics' Perception and Emotional Responses toward the Organizations: Same Perceptions, Different Motivations. The multiple publics in both countries appeared to agree with their respective governments in the perception and attribution of the crisis. There were no significant differences in the levels of emotions displayed, or the emotional temperature. One can surmise that the publics are generally supportive of the stances and strategies employed, as reflected in the media coverage. Foreign countries and businesses in China were, however, most supportive of the Chinese government's efforts, compared to the same groups in Singapore. This could be the result of the accommodative stance taken by the Chinese government in reaching out to them, or it could be the perception the Chinese government wished to project in its media after all the allegations of the initial cover-up of SARS.

Again, threats seemed to be the predominant motivation among the publics in the two countries. But that is where the similarities end. Compared to the Chinese, Singaporeans' response to the government seemed to be additionally driven by the external (namely, general political/social/cultural) environment inflicted by SARS, as well as the external public. What this may mean is that SARS was seen as an irritant that needed to be eradicated quickly because it was affecting the livelihoods and lifestyles of Singaporeans. This was reinforced by the government through the media, and because, as Hao (1996) argued, Singaporeans generally trust the government and what it tells them through the media.

Lessons from Crisis Communications: Dynamic Interaction of Contingency Theory Factors and the Emergence of Culture as a Key Factor. Based on the contingency theory and crisis literature, the stances of an organization and its publics are not static, but rather moving from advocacy to accommodation and possibly back to advocacy. An organization may begin with a predisposing stance of advocacy, but the collective demands of the public and the situation may be "powerful enough" (Cancel, Mitrook, & Cameron, 1999, p. 191) to force the organization to assume a position of accommodation as a way to resolve the crisis.

As the Chinese government—which assumed an initial stance of obstinate advocacy by covering up the extent of damage SARS had inflicted—backpedaled to salvage the situation, it embarked on accommodative strategies to manage its varied publics aimed at regaining their trust. This, however, did not mean that the Singapore government was less accommodating. It displayed traces of advocacy as a reflection of the threat and urgency of situation. As the contingency theory addresses, threat is a powerful factor that may cause oscillation on the continuum (Cameron, Cropp, & Reber, 2001).

The stance and strategies, as a reflection of the differentiation of cultures and political circumstances, is accentuated in an examination of comparative approaches like this study, even if both the Singaporean and Chinese cultures, right down to media systems, may appear to be similar. Both governments, reflecting their cultures, conservative collectivists (Schwartz, 1994) as they are, appeared to start off on the same footing: It's a collective problem; let's solve it together, and the media can help. The Chinese government, however, needed a little more prodding from the international community before it agreed to come to terms with the crisis. That is why while one of its key motivations was to eradicate the threats, it was also driven by the approvals of its foreign publics, namely WHO and foreign countries and businesses—the international community—to help it strategize.

In a setting where the organization is the government, and comparisons are made between cultures, the role culture plays should be elevated and further elucidated. In terms of theory building in contingency theory, culture, which was not a major factor of consideration in the movement of the organization's stance in previous studies of the theory, can be incorporated as a predisposing variable.

QUESTIONS FOR APPLICATION

1. What are the elements and dynamics in strategic management of conflict?

2. How do the twin concepts of advocacy and accommodation, central tenets in contingency theory, apply in your experiences in managing conflicts strategically?

3. To what extent does relationship management, based on mutually beneficial relationships and anchored on two-way symmetrical communication, help parties resolve conflicts?

4. Besides content analyses of news reports, how else can you capture the stance movements of an organization in conflict?

5. What are the similarities and differences between stance and strategies? Should there be a contradiction between the two, how do you reconcile them?

6. What other key variables, besides those identified by contingency theory, are critical in determining an organization's stance?

REFERENCES

Benoit, W. L. (2004). Image restoration discourse and crisis communication. In D. P. Millar & R. L. Heath (Eds.), *Responding to crisis: A rhetorical approach to crisis communication* (pp. 263–280). Mahwah, NJ: Lawrence Erlbaum.

Bradsher, K., & Altman, L. K. (2003, May 24). Strain of SARS is found in 3 animal species in Asia. *New York Times*, p. A1.

Cameron, G. T., Cropp, F., & Reber, B. H. (2001). Getting past platitudes: Factors limiting accommodation in public relations. *Journal of Communication Management, 5*(3), pp. 242–261.

Cancel, A. E., Cameron, G. T., Sallot, L. M., & Mitrook, M. A. (1997). It depends: A contingency theory of accommodation in public relations. *Journal of Public Relations Research, 9*(1), pp. 31–63.

Cancel, A. E., Mitrook, M. A., & Cameron, G. T. (1999). Testing the contingency theory of accommodation in public relations. *Public Relations Review, 25*(2), pp. 171–197.

Choi, Y., & Cameron, G. T. (2005). Overcoming ethnocentrism: The role of identity in contingent practice of international public relations. *Journal of Public Relations Research, 17*(2), pp. 171–189.

Eckholm, E. (2003, April 13). W.H.O. team visits hospital in Beijing to investigate disease. *New York Times*, p. A16.

Grunig, L. A. (1996). Public relations. In M. D. Salwen & D. W. Stacks (Eds.), *An integrated approach to communication theory and research* (pp. 459–477). Mahwah, NJ: Lawrence Erlbaum.

Grunig, J. E., and Hunt, T. (1984). *Managing public relations.* New York: Holt.

Hao, X. M. (1996). The press and public trust: The case of Singapore. *Asian Journal of Communication, 6*(1), pp. 111–123.

Jin, Y. (2005). Explicating "threat": The effects of threat type and threat duration on public relations professionals' cognitive, affective and conative responses in crisis situations. Doctoral dissertation published by the University of Missouri–Columbia.

Jin, Y., & Cameron, G. T. (2006, in press). Scale development of measuring stances as degree of accomodation. Public Relations Review, 32(4).

Jin, Y., & Cameron, G. T. (2004). *Rediscovering emotion in public relations: An adapted appraisal model and an emotion laden contingency plane.* New Orleans: ICA.

Jin, Y., Pang, A., & Cameron, G. T. (2004). *Different means to the same end: A comparative contingency analyses of Singapore and China's management of the*

severe acute respiratory syndrome (SARS) crisis. Toronto, CA: AEJMC.

Jin, Y., Pang, A., & Cameron, G. T. (2006). Strategic communication in crisis governance; Singapore's management of the SARS crisis. Copenhagen Journal of Asian Studies, 23, 81–104.

Jin, Y., Pang, A., & Cameron, G. T. (2005). *Explicating threats: Towards a conceptual understanding of the faces and fabric of threat in an organizational crisis.* New York City: ICA.

Khalik, S., & Wong, S. M. (2003, June 1). SARS-free, not to fine-tune crisis handling. *The Straits Times*, p. 1.

Krippendorff, K. (2004). *Content analysis: An introduction to its methodology* (2nd ed.). Thousand Oaks, CA: Sage.

Kuo, E., & Ang, P. H. (2000). Singapore. In S. Gunaratne (Ed.), *Handbook of the media in Asia* (pp. 402–428). New Delhi: Sage. Lecher. (2003).

Marsden, E. (1990). Letter from Beijing. *Columbia Journalism Review, 29*(4), pp. 46–51.

Martinelli, K. A., & Briggs, W. (1998). Integrating public relations and legal responses during a crisis: The case of Odwalla, Inc. *Public Relations Review, 24*(4), pp. 443–460.

Merrill, J. (2000). Social stability and harmony: A new mission for the press? *Asian Journal of Communication, 10*(2), pp. 33–52.

Pang, A. (2006). *Conflict positioning in crisis communication.* Doctoral dissertation, published by the University of Missouri–Columbia.

Pang, A., Jin, Y., & Cameron, G. T. (2004). *"If we can learn some lessons in the process": A contingency approach to analyzing the Chinese government's management of the perception and emotion of its multiple publics during the severe acute respiratory syndrome (SARS) crisis.* Miami, FL: IPRRC.

Pang, A., Jin, Y., & Cameron, G. T. (2006). *Do we stand on common ground? A threat appraisal model for terror alerts issued by the Department of Homeland Security.* Journal of Contingencies and Crisis Management, 14(2), pp. 82–96.

Reber, B., & Cameron, G. T. (2003). Measuring contingencies: Using scales to measure public relations practitioner limits to accommodation. *Journalism and Mass Communication Quarterly, 80*(2), pp. 431–446.

Reber, B. H, Cropp, F., & Cameron, G. T. (2001). Mythic battles: Examining the lawyer-public relations counselor dynamic. *Journal of Public Relations Research, 13*(3), pp. 187–218.

Reber, B. H., Cropp, F., & Cameron, G. T. (2003). Impossible odds: Contributions of legal counsel and public relations practitioners in a hostile bid for Conrail Inc. by Norfolk Southern Corporation. *Journal of Public Relations Research, 15*(1), pp. 1–25.

Riffe, D., Lacy, S., & Fico, F. G. (1998). *Analyzing media messages.* Mahwah, NJ: Lawrence Erlbaum.

Rosenthal, E. (2003, April 27). The SARS epidemic: The path. *New York Times*, Section 1, p. 1.

Schwartz, S. H. (1994). Beyond individualism/collectivism: New cultural dimensions of values. In Uichol Kim et al. (Eds.), *Individualism and collectivism: Theory, method, and applications* (pp. 85–119). New York: Sage.

Shin, J., & Cameron, G. T. (2004). Conflict measurements: An analysis of simultaneous inclusion in roles, values, independence, attitudes, dyadic adjustment. *Public Relations Review, 30*(4), pp. 401–410.

Shin, J., Cameron, G. T., & Cropp, F. (2002). *Asking what matters most: A national survey of PR professional response to the contingency model.* Miami, FL: AEJMC.

Shin, J., Cheng, I., Jin, Y., & Cameron, G. T. (2005). Going head to head: Content analysis of high profile conflicts as played out in the press. *Public Relations Review, 31*(3), pp. 399–406.

Sikorski, D. (1996). Effective government in Singapore: Perspective of a concerned American. *Asian Survey, 36*(8), pp. 818–903.

Turnbull, M. (1995). *Dateline Singapore.* Singapore: Singapore Press Holdings.

Wilcox, D. L., & Cameron, G. T. (2006). *Public relations: Strategies and tactics* (8th ed.). Boston: Allyn & Bacon.

Wu, X. (2002). Doing PR in China: A 2001 version—concepts, practices, and some misperceptions. *Public Relations Quarterly, 47*(2), pp. 10–19.

Yarbrough, C. R., Cameron, G. T., Sallot, L. M., & McWilliams, A. (1998). Tough calls to make: Contingency theory and the Centennial Olympic Games. *Journal of Communication Management, 3*(1), pp. 39–56.

Zhang, J., Qiu, Q., & Cameron, G. T. (2004). A contingency approach to the Sino-US conflict resolution. *Public Relations Review, 30*, pp. 391–399.

Zhang, J., & Cameron, G. T. (2003). China's agenda building and image polishing in the US: Assessing an international public relations campaign. *Public Relations Review, 29*, pp. 13–28.

APPENDIX A

MATRIX OF CONTINGENCY FACTORS: VARIABLES THAT AFFECT AN ORGANIZATION'S RESPONSE

External variables

Threats

- Litigation
- Government regulation
- Potentially damaging publicity
- Scarring of company's reputation in the business community and in the general public
- Legitimizing activists' claims

Industry environment

- Changing (dynamic) or static
- Number of competitors/level of competition
- Richness or leanness of resources in the environment

General political/social environment/external culture

- Degree of political support of business
- Degree of social support of business

The external public (group, individual, etc.)

- Size and/or number of members
- Degree of source credibility/powerful members or connections
- Past successes or failures of groups to evoke change
- Amount of advocacy practiced by the organization
- Level of commitment/involvement of members
- Whether the group has public relations counselors
- Public's perception of group: reasonable or radical
- Level of media coverage the public has received in past
- Whether representatives of the public know or like representatives of the organization
- Whether representatives of the organization know or like representatives from the public

- Public's willingness to dilute its cause/request/claim
- Moves and countermoves
- Relative power of organization
- Relative power of public

Issue under question

- Size
- Stake
- Complexity

Internal variables

Organization characteristics

- Open or closed culture
- Dispersed widely geographically or centralized
- Level of technology the organization uses to produce its product or service
- Homogeneity or heterogeneity of officials involved
- Age of the organization/value placed on tradition
- Speed of growth in the knowledge level the organization uses
- Economic stability of the organization
- Existence or nonexistence of issues management officials or program
- Organization's past experiences with the public
- Distribution of decision-making power
- Formalization: number of roles or codes defining and limiting the job
- Stratification/hierarchy of positions
- Existence or influence of legal department
- Business exposure
- Corporate culture

Public relations department characteristics

- Number of practitioners and number of college degrees
- Type of past training: trained in PR or ex-journalists, marketing, etc.
- Location of PR department in hierarchy: independent or under marketing umbrella/experiencing encroachment of marketing/persuasive mentality
- Representation in the dominant coalition
- Experience level of PR practitioners in dealing with crisis
- General communication competency of department
- Autonomy of department
- Physical placement of department in building (near CEO and other decision makers or not)
- Staff trained in research methods
- Amount of funding available for dealing with external publics
- Amount of time allowed to use dealing with external publics

- Gender: percentage of female upper-level staff/managers
- Potential of department to practice various models of public relations

Characteristics of dominant coalition (top management)

- Political values: conservative or liberal/closed or open to change
- Management style: domineering or laid-back
- General altruism level
- Support and understanding of PR
- Frequency of external contact with publics
- Departmental perception of the organization's external environment
- Calculation of potential rewards or losses using different strategies with external publics
- Degree of line manager involvement in external affairs

Internal threats (How much is at stake in the situation?)

- Economic loss or gain from implementing various stances
- Marring of employees' or stockholders' perception of the company
- Marring of the personal reputations of the company's decision makers

Individual characteristics (public relations practitioners, domestic coalition, and line managers)

- Training in diplomacy, marketing, journalism, engineering, etc.
- Personal ethics
- Tolerance or ability to deal with uncertainty
- Comfort level with conflict or dissonance
- Comfort level with change
- Ability to recognize potential and existing problems
- Extent to openness to innovation
- Extent to which individual can grasp others' worldview
- Personality: dogmatic, authoritarian
- Communication competency
- Cognitive complexity: ability to handle complex problems
- Predisposition toward negotiations
- Predisposition toward altruism
- How individuals receive, process, and use information and influence
- Familiarity with external public or its representative
- Like external public or its representative
- Gender: female versus male

Relationship characteristics

- Level of trust between organization and external public
- Dependency of parties involved
- Ideological barriers between organization and public

STANCE (DEGREES OF ACCOMMODATION)
MEASUREMENT SCALE

Given the situation, I will be _____ (1 = Completely Unwilling,
7 = Completely Willing)

AA: Action-based Accommodations:

1. To yield to the public's demands
2. To agree to follow what the public proposed
3. To accept the publics' propositions
4. To agree with the public on future action or procedure
5. To agree to try the solutions suggested by the public

QRA: Qualified-Rhetoric-mixed Accommodations:

1. To express regret or apologize to the public
2. To collaborate with the public to solve the problem at hand
3. To change my own position toward that of the public's
4. To make concessions with the public
5. To admit wrongdoing

NORMATIVE APPROACHES
Leveraging Constraints and Opportunities

Tricia Hansen-Horn

Bonita Dostal Neff

Questions of what is, and should and should not be, are of philosophical and complex discussion. Public relations practitioners and scholars alike are much a part of these important discussions.

Ethics reflects the evolution of public relations over time. As our society confronts undeniable concerns with social responsibility and the complexity of issues, the question of an ethical basis for public relations is a critical criterion. Bowen demonstrates how public relations is fully engaged in the intricacies of a moral philosophy, articulating many of the concerns, constructs, and implications associated with complex social and moral engagements and disengagements.

Len-Rios asks us to examine the communication rules that "dictate what is socially acceptable." She focuses on rules within the interpersonal context as well as the organizational context, extending her discussion to organizational and public relationships.

Rentner brings to life social norms theory through a case study on alcohol education programs on college campuses. The lack of a theoretical foundation providing support for these programs makes obvious the need for it. Rentner urges readers to pursue the development of theoretical constructs that can anchor campaigns such as these or other outreach efforts.

CHAPTER TEN

FOUNDATIONS IN MORAL PHILOSOPHY FOR PUBLIC RELATIONS ETHICS

SHANNON A. BOWEN

> I hope I shall always possess firmness and virtue enough to maintain what I consider the most enviable of all titles, the character of an Honest Man.
>
> —George Washington (on being offered the title "king")

To provide a framework for the consideration of public relations ethics, larger questions of moral philosophy must first be addressed. Do objective good and evil exist outside of human experience, or are these concepts created, or imposed, by moral judgments? Are there such things as absolute good and absolute bad? Truth and falsehood? Right and wrong? And if so, how are we to recognize them? How are we to know when an action crosses the line from one to the other? What standards can we use to judge these situations? And are those standards the same for everyone? Or should they vary by culture, training, religion, age, education, or some other criterion?

Good versus evil is an age-old question. The forces of evil attempt to destroy the forces of good in countless sagas from literature to pop culture. Should these questions remain in the realms of philosophy and literature, or do these types of questions apply to public relations?

There is little doubt that public relations holds negative connotations among journalists as an unethical occupation (Kopenhaver, 1985; Ryan & Martinson, 1988; Spicer, 1993). Even those who choose to study public relations often hold negative misconceptions of the function (Bowen, 2003). Some critics (Stauber & Rampton, 1995) argued that public relations is inherently evil, equating the practice with propaganda, manipulation, and even espionage. In every occupation there are people who intend to cheat, steal, manipulate, and deceive. But is public relations, by its very nature, an inherently unethical practice?

IS PUBLIC RELATIONS UNETHICAL?

Through reasoning based on moral philosophy, this chapter argues that public relations is not an intrinsically unethical pursuit. Public relations helps hold society together by facilitating a free flow of information and communication between various groups, including publics and organizations. Dialogue is a social good, according to philosophers (Habermas, 1984; Kant, 1785/1964) and ethics scholars (De George, 1995; Pearson, 1989c). Encouraging the open flow of information is an intrinsically good pursuit, because, as Francis Bacon observed, knowledge provides power (Goodman, 1997). For this reason, public relations is not an amoral activity. Every communication holds power; therefore, public relations must be approached with a sense of ethical responsibility (Grunig & White, 1992). Public relations is at risk of losing its status as a management counseling function if practitioners approach the responsibility amorally, not only immorally.

Helping an organization and publics communicate is a valuable function in maintaining an informed society (Bowen & Heath, forthcoming; Heath & Ryan, 1989). Allowing a dialogue between publics with vastly disproportionate amounts of power and resources is an ethical function that lets society debate ideas and progress in its understanding, achieving a workable level of consensus that allows society to exist and function. Through public relations, social debate progresses based on the merit of ideas (Heath, 2001a) and information—rather than on who can afford to have an opinion, or who has the political or military might to enforce their opinion on others. Public relations professionals often educate people on matters of public policy and why they should, or should not, support a cause. These causes can be as broad as fighting terrorism on a global level, or as specific as the campaign by People for the Ethical Treatment of Animals (PETA) to boycott chicken producers because of poor animal conditions in that industry.

Normatively, public relations management functions with the intent to create understanding rather than to deceive, to facilitate dialogue, education, collaboration, and understanding is a noble pursuit. This pursuit must be handled with a sense of responsibility and ethics, because the choices made in communicating influence not only the communication, but also how it is received (Goffman, 1974). The public relations function holds great power to facilitate discussion (Grunig & Grunig, 1992; Heath, 2001b; Huang, 2004), resolve problems (Grunig & Repper, 1992; Heath, 1997), create and build relationships (Ledingham & Bruning, 2000; Toth, 1992), and frame issues (Bowen, 2005a; Hallahan, 1999). With that power comes the responsibility for ascertaining when to use ethical analyses and how the resulting decisions should be implemented.

Public Relations as Ethical Conscience of the Organization

Historical public relations figures Ivy Lee and John W. Hill argued that public relations needs to act as the "ethical conscience" of the organization (Heath & Bowen, 2002). Scholars (Bowen, 2004b; Grunig & Grunig, 1996; Ryan & Martinson, 1983) continue to argue that public relations serves the organization best when it acts as an ethical conscience. The legal department advises the dominant coalition only on what it can do legally, rather than what it should do ethically. If public relations does not fill the role of ethical conscience in an organization, this role is often deferred to the legal department, with poor or problematic relations with publics resulting (Bowen & Heath, 2003). For example, Enron had corporate legal counsel in charge of general ethics, and no one to oversee its finance and accounting practices, resulting in a disastrous inattention to matters of ethics (Sims & Brinkman, 2003).

Public relations professionals are often best suited to the role of ethical conscience in an organization, because other management functions (such as finance, legal, and operations) often do not stop to consider how a decision will be perceived by many publics outside the organization. For instance, the marketing department is concerned with how consumers will see the organization, not the many, varied publics that public relations addresses (Ehling, White, & Grunig, 1992; Grunig & Grunig, 1998). As professional communicators, public relations professionals are ideal for the role of problem-solving process facilitators (Broom, Lauzen, & Tucker, 1991), in which collaborative decisions are constructed. They can also communicate effectively about the outcomes of the decision-making process and why a certain avenue was chosen over alternatives (Bowen, 2004a).

Systems Theory Support for Acting as Ethical Conscience

Systems theory explains that, as boundary spanners, public relations managers are in a position uniquely suited to understanding the values and beliefs of strategic publics. Public relations practitioners are sometimes the only voice in an organization that can accurately represent the interests and values of publics to the dominant coalition (L. A. Grunig, 1992b; Lauzen, 1992). These types of policy decisions are often made in concert with top decision-makers from finance, legal, operations, and other relevant departments in an organization. The CEO must rely on the ethical counsel of the public relations professional alone for a connection to the values, beliefs, and views of varied publics, because other organizational functions will see the issue from their own particular perspective. Although no function in an organization can predict the future with accuracy, the familiarity of public relations managers with the beliefs, attitudes, and values of publics allows them to understand how those publics will potentially assess the morality of the organization's behavior.

It is common for the public relations professional and the legal counsel to have conflicting or even opposing opinions about how to resolve dilemmas (Fitzpatrick & Rubin, 1995; Lee, Jares, & Heath, 1999). Public relations serves to communicate with publics whereas the legal department often wants to communicate very little for reasons of legal liability. Attorneys often see any communication on a problematic issue as a potential complication of cases or an admission of responsibility or guilt. This tension is understandable, but the dominant coalition must keep in mind that ethical and legal actions are not synonymous. Legal actions refer to what can be done, while ethical considerations refer to what should be done. The legality of an action has no bearing on its moral worth. The example of slavery illustrates this concept.

Even though the work of public relations is often intangible, the price of unethical activity is high. Once public trust is lost, it can rarely be earned back Huang, 2001a; Plowman, 1999), and attempting to do so, although uncertain, is extremely costly. Trust is a vital component of maintaining a relationship between an organization and its publics (Grunig, Grunig, & Ehling, 1992; Huang, 1997). In exploring the antecedents of effective relationships, J. E. Grunig and Huang (2000) explained that "trust is essential to promoting and maintaining a relationship, whereas suspicion undermines favorable growth in a relationship" (p. 45). Other factors—such as mutual control, access, and commitment—are important to maintaining a relationship between organizations and publics. Attention to ethics can establish and enhance both credibility and trust, and these factors appear to be necessary to encourage the later formation and growth of other relational dimensions.

Public relations executives hold a great deal of power and responsibility when acting as ethics counselors in organizations (Bowen, 2002). Acting as the ethical conscience of an organization implies that a practitioner is able to rationally (Grossman, 1988) and thoroughly analyze the moral choices available to her or him. The required rational analysis of moral dilemmas calls for public relations managers to study moral philosophy (L. A. Grunig, 1992c). Through moral philosophy, the ethical implications of decisions can be rigorously studied and decisions are then rationally defensible. To advise the dominant coalition on ethical dilemmas, a general understanding of the various approaches to ethical analyses provided by moral philosophy is essential when public relations acts as the ethical conscience of an organization.

MORAL PHILOSOPHY

Moral philosophy attempts to ascertain and explain what actions are right, or morally worthy, versus what actions are wrong, or morally unworthy. Moral philosophy studies questions such as why an action is considered morally sound and what makes one act more moral than an alternative. Moral philosophers investigate ethical questions by looking for underlying ethical principles and the justification for why they are ethical (De George, 1995). These underlying moral principles are the maxims that should guide behavior (Kant, 1785/1964). If philosophers discover general or universally applicable moral maxims, ethical decision making is simplified in theory and in implementation. For instance, "do not murder" is a generally accepted moral maxim based on the principle of the value of life. However, there are instances in which moral philosophers can counter this maxim, such as in the case of self-defense. Moral maxims provide generally applicable guidelines that govern ethical behavior based on the moral worth of an action.

Most methods that philosophers use to determine what should constitute moral maxims or principles are based on using a rational or analytical decision-making process. An ethical outcome must be logical rather than based on bias, self-interest, personal preference, or capriciousness (De George, 1999; Sullivan, 1989). Public relations must base its ethics on moral philosophy to have the best ability to analytically evaluate the ethics of its decisions (Bowen, 2004a). Only through an analytical and rational evaluation can one even come close to the objective vantage required by moral philosophy (Sullivan, 1989, 1994). In this approach, all viewpoints are considered; similar to systems theory, various publics have equal import in ethical decision making. Additionally, the concept of fairness (Rawls, 1971) is maintained by using a rational moral analysis. If the decision is logical rather than based on fiat, it should produce less rancor among opposed publics than one in which their concerns were dismissed.

Ethics

The employment of moral philosophy is called ethics. Ethics is the study of how we should live our lives, or what constitutes right or wrong, fair or unfair (Jaksa & Pritchard, 1994). Normative ethics is the study of what rules and principles should be used to guide ethical decision making (De George, 1999). Applied ethics is the application of normative rules to ethical circumstances in an area or industry (Day, 1997), such as medical ethics or business ethics. Descriptive ethics simply describe what people believe is morally acceptable or unacceptable, such as in a survey of CEOs regarding corporate accountability (Beauchamp & Bowie, 2004). Just as normative theory is ideal and positive theory is how things occur in practice, normative and applied ethics are, respectively, ideal and practical.

The focus of this chapter is on normative ethics, because normative ethics seeks to identify what moral principles should be used to guide behavior. Public relations theory can be extended by incorporating normative ethics into the approaches we bring to scholarship and management. The two-way symmetrical model is an example of normative ethics because it encourages dialogue, mutual understanding, and collaboration (J. E. Grunig, 2001). This normative principle is also "applied" when the symmetrical model occurs in actual public relations practice (Grunig, Grunig, & Dozier, 2002) and descriptive when identified in a particular case. One example meeting all three forms of ethical criteria is the case of pharmaceutical giant Merck donating supplies of ivermectin, its river-blindness drug, to African countries (Donaldson & Gini, 1995). Their unprecedented donation of a new, breakthrough drug based on need illustrates normative, applied, and descriptive ethics, as well as normative and positive use of the two-way symmetrical model of public relations.

Public relations and ethics intersect in the areas of organizational decision making and communication surrounding both the decision and its implementation. Communication within an organization is used for interpreting and creating meaning of social contexts, and the ethical norms in that system are an important component of meaning (Cheney, 1983; Daft & Weick, 1984). The created meaning is evidenced in organizational culture (Eisenberg & Riley, 2001). Organizational culture provides guidance, in both subtle and overt senses, in ethical decision making (Bowen, 2004b).

To simplify applying ethical approaches to public relations, scholars (Grunig &

Grunig, 1996; L. A. Grunig, 1992c; Wright, 1985) divide moral philosophy into two approaches: utilitarianism and deontology. These approaches to ethics are normative, applied, and descriptive philosophies (Donaldson & Werhane, 1999). Although these schools of thought provide decision tests that use opposing measures, both utilitarianism and deontology are of tremendous value in helping public relations practitioners analyze ethical dilemmas (Curtin & Boynton, 2001). Knowing when to use each decision test is a key component of moral analysis for the public relations practitioner. Each type of philosophy lends itself to certain situations, and brings certain strengths and weaknesses to the analysis, as discussed below.

Utilitarian Philosophy.   The utilitarian approach to moral philosophy was originated by Jeremy Bentham (1780/1988) and his protégé, John Stuart Mill (1861/1957). This type of philosophy looks at the "utility"—or the expected outcome—of a decision (Biswas, 1997) to decide what is the morally correct course of action. This paradigm is a form of consequentialist philosophy because moral actions are defined by their consequences. Utilitarianism seeks to maximize the benefit of decisions for the largest number of people and minimize any negative consequences (Schick, 1997). The goal and subject of the utilitarian test can be divided into three utilitarian test types. This school of philosophy originated with a hedonistic approach valuing pleasure, but this measure was problematic and little researched. Eudaimonistic utilitarianism defines happiness as the ultimate test of utility, whereas ideal utilitarianism holds that all intrinsically valuable qualities can be of value in the utilitarianism test, such as knowledge, health, or friendship (De George, 1999).

Utilitarianism defines an ethical action as one providing the greatest utility, in most cases defined as creating the greatest amount of good for the greatest number of people. This type of philosophy emphasizes serving the public good, or the majority of people in society. Utilitarianism performs a cost-benefit analysis of moral situations, so that many public relations practitioners are familiar with making judgments in utilitarian terms. A cost-benefit approach to ethics is more intuitive in decision making than other, learned philosophies (Kohlberg, 1969). Many people employ a basic utilitarian analysis when they base their decision on the outcome that maximizes good and reduces bad outcome, weighing the pros and cons of a situation. In its normative form, utilitarianism is more complex than in this example, but the basic idea is the same.

Producing the greatest good for the greatest number is a seemingly simple decision-making guideline. However, defining "good" is more difficult than it might initially appear. Some utilitarians define good as anything that promotes happiness; others define good as something promoting benefit; still others define good as any intrinsically valuable concept. DeGeorge (1999) argued that the differing values in utilitarian philosophy were ultimately not problematic because, "Most calculations will come out the same, whether we use the ideal utilitarian approach, which allows for a plurality of intrinsic values; or the hedonistic approach, which reduces all values ultimately to pleasure; or the eudaimonistic utilitarian approach, which reduces them to happiness"(p. 59).

Further complexity is introduced when one considers "what" should actually be submitted to the utilitarian test. Act utilitarians assert that only a particular instance in all of its specificity should be submitted to the utilitarian test because no two cases are exactly alike. Rule utilitarians argue that only a general type of action should be submitted to the test since moral philosophy seeks to discover underlying principles or rules. Act utilitarians classify each specific decision as ethical based only on the projected outcomes in that unique instance; therefore, each act must be considered individually, implying that there are no rules that can govern across situations. On the contrary, rule utilitarians apply a type or class of action to the utilitarianism test in an effort to discover the moral utility of the consequences. This type of moral principle could be used to guide behavior based on consequences in large types or classes of similar decisions, eliminating the need for subjecting each and every decision to a utilitarian analysis. In either case, the morality of an action depends entirely on its projected consequences rather than on a principle inherent in the issue itself.

Employing Utilitarianism in Public Relations.   In utilitarianism, the moral judgment is made that an action is ethical if it produces a greater amount of good than bad. In situations in which two actions produce equal good, the choice resulting in the least amount of bad is the ethical action. Utilitarianism poses a collectivist ethic that is useful in public relations when dealing with large publics. Stakeholders are tied to the organization by consequences (J. E. Grunig, 1989), and this ideology allows for a thorough evaluation of potential consequences, both positive and negative, before action is taken. The utilitarian idea, "the greatest good for the greatest number," can be helpful in ethical decisions involving large publics and stakeholder groups, philanthropy, social responsibility, internal relations, and managing safety or health risks. Implementation of utilitarian analyses in public relations affords the opportunity to consider the affect of organizational decisions on publics in the environment, concordant with a systems theory approach (Roth, 2005).

To determine the morality of an act from a utilitarian perspective, the public relations manager would consider all decision alternatives in light of the potential consequences each option holds for strategic publics and stakeholders. Using the maxi-mins rule, the practitioner would pick the alternative that maximizes positive outcomes for the larger public and minimizes negative outcomes to a smaller number. For example, clinical trials testing a vaccine on humans are required by governmental agencies to develop and market a drug. Clinical trials carry an inherent risk of adverse reactions, even death, to participants. The benefit of the vaccine trial is that large numbers of people can be protected from an illness if a few people take the risk of being study subjects. Is the potential benefit worth the potential harm? Utilitarianism would hold that the greater good for the greater number (protecting the larger population from an illness) warrants the risk of harm to a smaller number of study subjects (who might be harmed by the vaccine). Therefore, utilitarianism would warrant the ethical choice as testing the vaccine on a study group because the good consequence for a larger population outweighs the risk to the smaller group. This simple example is logical, but utilitarian theory is not without problems and dangers in its implementation.

Pitfalls of utilitarianism.   Utilitarianism is arguably the most common approach to ethical decision making in business (De George, 1999) but the theory has several problem areas that limit its usefulness. Although utilitarianism has value in helping public relations professionals solve ethical issues, it requires that caution be exercised in its use as an analysis tool (Bowen, 2004a). Public relations managers should be wary of these caveats:

1. Utilitarianism always serves the interests of the majority. Serving the "greater good" or "happiness of the greater number" numerically quantifies the people on opposite sides of a decision. This theory determines that the majority is correct. Therefore, utilitarianism runs the risk of ignoring and alienating the minority on an issue. Utilitarianism can be used to justify or reinforce a status quo in which the majority is satisfied but the minority is not, either purposefully or inadvertently. Although utilitarianism does not advocate silencing the minority, it advocates that a majority makes a decision moral.

2. Utilitarianism can work against helping an organization adapt to a changing environment. Ignoring the needs of a small public is a genuine risk when using utilitarian ethics in public relations. Always giving the majority preference prevents the organization from adapting to a change impetus initiated by smaller publics and stakeholders. To ignore pressure to change from the environment could allow an organization to lose support from publics if competitors serve their needs better.

3. Relying only on utilitarianism runs a risk of governmental regulation and forced change. Dissatisfied publics can escalate issues to the point in which government steps in to regulate an industry (L. A. Grunig, 1992a; Heath, 1997; Reber, Cropp, & Cameron, 2003). The organization loses autonomy in its decision making and government regulation is often very expensive (Buchholz, 1988; Buchholz, Evans, & Wagley, 1994; Grunig & Repper, 1992; Grunig, Gruning, & Ehling, 1992; Heath, 2001a; Heath, Seshadri, & Lee, 1998). Boycotts are unofficial forms of regulation because they often force the organization to pay attention to the needs of a minority public without government regulation (Murphy & Dee, 1992). In either case, change can be expensive and the reputation of an organization can suffer.

4. A concern with utilitarianism's majority approach is that it "counts" people. Reducing humans to numbers is a concern for many philosophers because it ignores basic humanistic concerns in favor of a numerical approach to moral issues. Can people be reduced to numerical units? Or do they have a worth that lacks quantification? Are highly successful people worth more than people who contribute little to society or drain public resources? The argument can be made that the opinion of fifty-one people is not morally superior to the opinion of forty-nine opposing people simply based on their number. Further, if two members of the majority change their mind and join the minority, the ethical judgment also changes. The issue has not changed and the moral principles remain the same, only the count of people is altered; however, a new ethical conclusion is drawn.

5. The decision-maker, in our case the public relations manager, is required to accurately prognosticate the future consequences of each decision alternative. He or she must anticipate the reactions of numerous publics and choose among options based on which alternative has the highest probability of producing the greatest good and the least negative repercussions. However, many consequences are unexpected and unpredictable, creating the potential for severe and costly miscalculations in a utilitarian analysis. Decision making under conditions of risk and uncertainty is, at best, a tenuous process (Bowen, 2005b).

Benefits of utilitarianism. If applied carefully with attention to avoiding its pitfalls, utilitarianism can be a valuable approach to ethical decision making in public relations because it provides focus on the consequences of an organization's actions on publics. Most publics can be satisfied through using a utilitarian approach to organizational decision making. If effort is made not to alienate a minority public, utilitarianism can prove useful in helping to forecast and plan for the future of an organization. Attention to the consequences an organization has on publics and stakeholders helps to build and maintain relationships with those publics (J. E. Grunig, 1992a; Huang, 2001a; Ledingham & Bruning, 2000; Toth, 1992).

Difficulty often arises when deciding whether to use a utilitarian analysis or another form of ethical test. Understanding the strengths and weaknesses of various approaches in moral philosophy can help resolve this dilemma by using the decision test most appropriate to the moral question to be decided. For example, utilitarianism can be useful in deciding how to handle a majority issue. But it would not be wise to apply a utilitarian analysis to sexual harassment complaints from one or two employees due to the majority preference in utilitarianism—clearly, the minority has a valid complaint. Such a situation dictates a principle-based, rather than consequence-based, approach. However, utilitarianism can be successfully used to negotiate the minefield of ethical consequences on large numbers of people in which the organization wishes to serve the greater good.

Weighing the benefits versus the negative consequences of a decision is not a new idea. However, the strength of utilitarianism lies in that it explicitly states what value should be used to determine good—happiness, pleasure, or any concept of intrinsic worth. Once the guideline for determining what is of value is established, good is easier to recognize and quantify. Utilitarianism gives the decision-maker a logical guideline as to how to determine what is good and who is served by a decision. When applied in public relations, utilitarian analyses can be used with precision to satisfy the needs of specific publics. Although this language is biased in favor of the organizational perspective to maintain a consistent link to systems theory, it should also be noted that a utilitarian perspective is equally applicable from the perspective of small publics, such as activist groups.

What a utilitarian analysis lacks in predictive ability, it compensates for in the specificity of its analysis. A utilitarian analysis leaves little question about what values are defined as good or morally worthy, and which publics will be affected by the consequences of a decision. The direct link to consequences on publics provides a reliable mechanism for moral analysis of the impact of decision alternatives on the organization's environment.

Deontological Philosophy.   Deontological ethics focuses on the moral principle involved, rather than basing the morality of the decision on its projected outcomes. It maintains that there are moral principles that are right or wrong independent of their consequences (De George, 1999). This approach is also called "nonconse-quentialist" because it maintains that ethics should be guided by duty rather than consequence. Deontology was developed by German philosopher Immanuel Kant (1724–1804) as an attempt to find the underlying principles of morality that are universal, or the same for all people, and based on rational analysis rather than personal preference (Kant, 1785/1964). This approach defines that which is ethical as a decision based on rational moral principles. Deontology seeks to discover over-arching moral principles that do not change situationally or with the numbers of people served by a decision. Deontology is arguably the most exhaustive approach in ethics and is defined as "the ethical theory taking duty as the basis of morality" (Flew, 1979). In deontology, the ethical nature of an action does not depend on its outcome (as in utilitarianism) because this theory states that predicting the exact outcome is beyond human capability or control.

Deontological ideology is reliant on two core concepts: rationality and auton-omy (Sullivan, 1989). Through the use of a rational, logical, methodical, and objec-tive analysis of the situation, the public relations professional is asked what is the ethical course of action from a non-self-interested perspective. The decision must be considered from the vantage of multiple sides and interests, with only logical rationality being used to guide the process, so that any other rational decision-maker would arrive at a similar conclusion. By virtue of one's rationality and ability to conduct an objective analysis, the universal moral principles beneath the issue can be revealed.

Autonomy, or decision-making freedom, is a necessary factor when conduct-ing a deontological moral analysis (Sullivan, 1989). A moral agent cannot be focused on subjective concerns, appearances, fear of retribution, or other personal considera-tions that might bias the decision-making process and cause it to be made subjec-tively rather than rationally or objectively. A rational analysis should come as close to the objective ideal as humanly possible to ascertain the universal moral principle underlying the decision. Examples of subjective concerns that should not enter the rational analysis of decision alternatives are pressure to generate results for an organ-ization or client, and fear of the reaction of a superior. Moral autonomy implies that the person conducting the ethical analysis can consider all points of view as having equal right to enter the decision-making process, and make an ethical decision based on the analysis of what any other rational being would also consider a logical deci-sion. In this role, public relations practitioners are sometimes called the ethical con-sciences of the organization (Ryan & Martinson, 1983). Autonomy is a necessary condition to enact the role of ethical conscience in the organization because it pro-vides the freedom to conduct an impartial moral analysis.

Deontology holds that duty based on moral principle indicates what is the ethical course of action. How we determine where that duty lies—and, therefore, what is ethically correct—is clarified by the decision test of this ideology known as the categorical imperative. The categorical imperative moves deontology from being a normative ethical theory to being useful in positive application.

Employing Deontology: The Categorical Imperative.   Universal moral principles are defined by decision tests in the form of the categorical imperative. There are three forms of Kant's categorical imperative: measuring universal duty, dignity and respect, and good intention (Sullivan, 1989). The primary form of this test is based on universal duty. It advises: "Act only on that maxim through which you can at the same time will that it should become a universal law" (Kant, 1785/1964, p. 88). The categorical imperative asks the moral agent to measure what every other rational decision-maker would do in a similar situation, regardless of their "side" or stake in the issue.

The categorical imperative is a universal one in that it asks the decision-maker if he or she could make a certain decision a universal law that would apply in all similar situations. If the decision could still be rationally defended in all similar situations, it is deemed universal and ethical. The categorical imperative is also reversible in that the decision-maker could possibly be on the receiving end of the decision (such as a member of a public affected by the decision) and can view the issue from a completely different perspective. Deontologist Rawls (1971) conceptualized this state as a "veil of ignorance," meaning that the decision-maker should imagine that he or she did not know his or her place in the outcome of a decision or in society, so that all interests are accorded equal weight. Therefore, De George (1999) explained, the decision could be made based on principle rather than by what serves one's interest or role in society. After considering what all other rational people might do and putting herself or himself in all positions around the issue, the option is deemed ethical if it still appears the right thing to do. Thus, the concept of universal duty means what all moral agents would rationally surmise is ethical from any perspective on the issue.

The second form of the categorical imperative describes the autonomous person as the "repository of all value" (Kant, 1785/1964, p. 70) and commands that people not be used simply as means to an end in a decision. This second form of the categorical imperative asks if dignity and respect for others is maintained by the decision. If so, then the decision is ethically acceptable. Maintaining the dignity and respect of others is a crucial component of deontology because of the high value this ideology accords to rationality. All autonomous and rational decision-makers are entitled to have that rationality respected, even if their conclusions are different from our own. Rationality is what separates higher-order thinking from instinct. The human conscience arises from the analytical ability to know the difference between moral and immoral actions. Therefore, this philosophy views the capability for rational thought as the highest achievement of society, and worthy and deserving of respect.

The third and final form of Kant's categorical imperative is a test of the intention behind a decision, maintaining that only intentions made from a morally good will are truly ethical (Kant, 1793/1974). By intention, Kant meant the underlying motivation of the moral agent involved in making the decision. Motivations such as selfishness or doing what is best for the decision-maker are not moral, according to this philosophy. Deontology argues that "a good will" is the only true moral decision-making guide, since all other motivations can be corrupted (Kant, 1785/1993). For instance, pride can be corrupted into arrogance, happiness into complacency, frugality into selfishness, and so on. A goodwill stands alone as an incorruptible decision-making basis.

An example of a deontological decision is the well-known 1982 Tylenol case in which Johnson & Johnson made a decision to recall Tylenol from the U.S. market because of poisonous pills in Chicago. This recall was expensive to the organization, but public relations executives believed it was the right thing to do, regardless of the consequences to the company in cost or lost market share. Their first concern was protecting the health of the public, a moral principle valuing human life over cost or expediency. In this example, you can see that the intention of the company was indeed a goodwill, that the dignity and respect of publics was maintained, and that the decision could be universalized to all others in a similar situation. According to the most-senior public relations executive at Johnson & Johnson, "The first thing we consider is doing the right thing. Yes, consequences are present, but we do the right thing and then handle the consequences of that later" (W. D. Nielsen, personal communication, December 3, 2004).

Pitfalls of deontology.   Deontology provides a rigorous decision-making guide for examining the ethics of decisions from many angles but, like utilitarianism, it is not without potential problems.

1. Deontology is complex, arduous, and often time-consuming. This philosophy has the reputation for being difficult to implement because so much objective analysis is required, and many viewpoints must be considered to determine an underlying moral principle. Considering these factors takes time, which is sometimes in short supply in public relations dilemmas, especially crises. For this reason, ethicists and consultants are often needed to help an organization implement a deontological analysis.

2. Deontology requires training in ethics. Determining universal moral principles does not come naturally to most people (Kohlberg, 1969). Although considering the intention behind a decision is common, the rational objectivity, duty, and dignity or respect required in a deontological analysis often necessitate training in moral philosophy and ethics. Practitioners must make the effort and take the time to learn the process. Further, the organization must make a financial commitment to training decision-makers in the use of deontology.

3. Rationality is required. Deontology, in successful application, depends on the ability of the decision-maker to logically and impartially weigh all aspects of the moral principle involved in a decision. This means that it cannot be used by young children, the mentally challenged, or those with any impairments in their ability to make a rational judgment.

4. Deontology can be misapplied if goodwill and rationality are not maintained. For example, some soldiers have attempted to justify war crimes using the maxim "I was just doing my duty" or "following orders." However, this statement is *not* deontological because it denies autonomy by deferring analytical responsibility from the self to a superior. Autonomy and rationality are always linked in deontology. For example, U.S. military policy requires soldiers not to follow orders that they consider ethically objectionable, and to use a reporting process to have the orders reviewed by higher-level superiors. All components of deontology must be employed for the analysis to be successful and ethically sound.

Benefits of deontology.   One public relations executive described the usefulness of deontology as making decisions based on principles of right or wrong, not which group "benefits the most" (Bowen, 2000). This statement is a good descriptor of the inherent fairness and universal nature of deontology. It allows a communicator to consider the perspectives of multiple publics and to understand the values they hold. It takes bias toward what the organization desires out of the decision-making process and allows public relations to advise the dominant coalition on what is the right course of action based on moral principle, rather than cost or profit, self-interest, or expedience. This type of symmetrical decision making contributes to keeping an organization in balance with the desires of its publics (J. E. Grunig, 1992b).

In systems theory terms, deontology promotes a state of moving equilibrium—give and take—between the organization and publics. Dialogue is furthered, so that deontology is a valuable basis for supporting two-way symmetrical communication (Heath, 2001a; Pearson, 1989a, 1989b). Using a deontological approach in public relations allows the organization to be highly responsive to changing trends or issues via open-communication with many publics. This type of environment-focused orientation allows the organization to react to change pressures from the environment regardless of how many members constitute a public or who is in the majority. Deontology consistently allows the minority to have just as much impact on an issue as the majority: an important consideration for activist groups and demographic minorities alike (Grunig, Toth, & Hon, 2001; Hon, 1997). The power differential between the organization and its publics might still exist, but it is less pronounced when using a deontological approach to ethics than using other approaches because all publics have an equal right to a voice in the decision-making process.

Another benefit of the rigorous approach of deontology is that it leads to consistency in organizational decision making, allowing publics to build trust in an organization as reliable, and vice versa. The maintenance of long-term relationships is furthered when both publics and organizations know what to expect of each other, and feel that the other party reliably delivers on that expectation. The principle of building consistent relationships applies to both internal and external publics. In fact, organizational effectiveness can be enhanced through the development of a consistent organizational culture supporting ethical values (Bowen, 2004b) because internal publics have improved, stable relationships with the organization.

Trust between organization and publics is furthered by consistency, and trust is an essential component of ongoing relationships (Huang, 2001b). Consistency, met expectations, and reliability build stable relationships between organizations and publics. Parties are satisfied with the process rather than the more unstable alternative of being satisfied (Fisher & Ury, 1981; Plowman, 1999). Thus, the application of a deontological paradigm can result in long-enduring and effective resolutions to problems (Bowen, 2005c). Deontology is a complex philosophy, but will be summarized below by conceptualizing the theory's key components in a schematic.

ETHICAL CONSIDERATION TRIANGLE

A Deontological Approach to Organizational Decisions

The ethical consideration triangle (ECT) (see Figure 10.1) was developed as a decision aid for issues managers and senior public relations executives at two global organizations. This analytic tool is based on deontology but also requires the decision-maker to consider the consequences of decision alternatives on publics. Main tenets of deontology are summarized for ease of use in the ECT, making the theory easier to apply in public relations practice, even by those with little ethics training.

According to research findings (Bowen, 2004a; Pratt, Im, & Montague, 1994; Wright, 1985), deontological analysis is a useful aid in problem solving and issues management. A utilitarian perspective is also helpful when thinking about the impact of decisions on various publics due to its emphasis on consequences and serving the greater good for the greater number. The ECT includes the categorical

FIGURE 10.1   Ethical consideration triangle

Adapted and used by permission, courtesy of Shannon A. Bowen. Shannon A. Bowen, A practical model for ethical decision making in issues management and public relations, *Journal of Public Relations Research 17* (2005).

imperative considerations of duty, intention, and dignity or respect, therefore it is highly based on deontology. It also considers the consequences of decision alternatives on various publics, stakeholders, the decision-maker, the organization, and society. Consequences are not used to determine ethical or unethical actions in this model, but are used as considerations in determining duty, intention, and dignity and respect toward these groups.

To conduct an analysis of decision options using the ECT, consider the perspectives of each public inside the triangle with each consideration at the corner of the triangle. Remember that publics inside the triangle often might represent many other, smaller publics who should also be considered. Analysis of the decision options with each of these strategic publics (Grunig & Repper, 1992), through each of the three concepts of the triangle, provides a thorough means for evaluating decision options. Here are some questions to guide analysis of an ethical dilemma based on the deontological "points" of the ECT with the utilitarian consequences on publics in mind:

1. *Duty.* Could I (we) obligate everyone else who is ever in a similar situation to do the same thing I am (we are) about to do? What is my larger responsibility as an ethical person? What universal moral principles might be involved in this decision (consider truth, human life, fairness, equality, knowledge, freedom, justice, liberty, and other concepts of intrinsic value)?

2. *Dignity and respect.* Is dignity and respect maintained for each of the publics inside the ECT? Have I (we) considered their perspectives on the issue? Even if their values conflict with mine (ours), can they understand the logical basis (or rationality) of the decision? Can I be proud of myself as an autonomous moral agent? Do publics know and understand that their values were taken into account in the organization's decision making? Has an open and collaborative communication process been maintained and employed?

3. *Intention.* Are we as an organization (or I as an individual) proceeding from a basis of goodwill alone? Or are we allowing subjective concerns and desires to bias our decision making? What is the moral intention behind each decision alternative under consideration? Judgment cannot be rational if it is clouded by self-interest, but should be guided by the desire to do the right thing. We must examine our intention in this situation to make sure our objective rationality has been maintained.

The two-way symmetrical idea of public relations (Grunig & Hunt, 1984) enters the ECT when integrative or collaborative input is used in the analysis of decision alternatives. Input from publics is vital in a thorough analysis of decision options, or in inventing new options. Two-way dialogue among the organization and the groups in the ethical consideration triangle can construct more enduring solutions to ethical issues than the organization might be able to construct alone. Such dialogue and collaboration often lead to mutually beneficial solutions or behavior in which the integrity of a long-term organization/public relationship is a central decision-making focus, rather than focusing on expedient but short-term outcomes (Huang, 2001b; Plowman, 1998).

In a deontological paradigm, that which is ethical is that which is a person's moral duty. This moral duty is a higher calling than simply advocating an organization's position—one based on integrity of character, astute and rational analysis, and a responsibility to serve the public interest by facilitating a productive dialogue with truth as the ultimate goal. Using such a principled approach based on rational analyses allows the public relations professional to truly act as the ethical conscience of the organization (Bowen & Rawlins, 2005; Ryan & Martinson, 1983). The public relations executive can objectively evaluate the ethics of options independently of the outcome the organization desires, so that the role of ethics counsel to the dominant coalition is valued as distinct, expert input into strategic decision making. In this way, the excellence of the public relations function is encouraged and the autonomy of the public relations manager is realized.

CONCLUSION

There can be little doubt that public relations intersects with the communication process in ways that persuade and wield influence, whether by design or unintended consequence. Such power brings a responsibility to communicate ethically, in the interest of truth—before communicating in the interests of organizations, clients, or self-interest. By communicating ethically, with the interest of truth foremost, public relations can truly serve the public good (J. E. Grunig, 2000; Heath, 2005; Heath & Ryan, 1989; Kruckeberg & Starck, 2001; Leeper, 1996).

The social role of public relations has evolved over time. The function grew from press agentry and puffery into more sophisticated models of persuasion and, eventually, mutual understanding (Cutlip, Center, & Broom, 2000; Grunig & Grunig, 1992; Grunig & Hunt, 1984). To take the next step in the development of public relations theory, we must recognize the social role of the function, along with the responsibilities inherent in that role. As a social function, communication serves as the glue that binds society together through interaction and the creation of meaning. Public relations facilitates the interaction among parts of a social system, and allows disparate groups to communicate, work interdependently, and resolve conflict when it arises. Providing information and adjusting to input from publics holds an enormous ethical responsibility to communicate in the public interest.

Facilitating the flow of information is a powerful social role for public relations to fulfill, as explained in the agenda-setting and framing literature that explore how public communication selectively creates and interprets issues. Furthermore, advising an organization or client as the conscience of that organization calls for tremendous autonomy and analytical acumen, as well as complex problem-solving adroitness, precise research skills, the ability to enact a boundary-spanning role and maintain relationships with publics, articulate advising and communication skills, and so on. Knowledge of the rigorous ethical decision-making guidelines provided by moral philosophy can support a public relations executive in facing complex moral dilemmas with integrity, autonomy, rationality, and a sense of earnest responsibility to communicate in the public interest.

CASE: GOVERNMENT CONTRACTOR

As a public relations executive for a major government contractor, you learn of a situation involving a senior executive and a new member of your management. The new employee was, until recently, part of a government office that awarded contracts. You hear rumors and you fear that the senior executive offered employment to the new manager in exchange for that person awarding a multimillion-dollar government contract to your company.

You talk to the senior executive, who explains: "There are instances like this in which a win-win scenario helps everyone; the company got a major contract and the manager got a more lucrative job." The legal department says any such story would be "hearsay" and would not be provable, so it is nothing to worry about. However, you are concerned that this action violates the mission statement and code of conduct of your organization. Moreover, you are concerned about how this might look if the media were to write a story on it. What do you do?

QUESTIONS FOR APPLICATION

1. You believe you have identified an ethical dilemma. You begin to collect information and do research to determine the facts. What types of questions would you ask?

2. Who benefited from the contract? How many people were helped or could be hurt by the action?

3. What moral principles are involved here?

4. Which of those moral principles were upheld and which were violated?

5. What would a utilitarian analysis say to do?

6. What would a deontological analysis determine to be the correct course of action?

7. Which school of moral philosophy will you ultimately use to analyze the situation? Which is most applicable? Why?

8. What are the potential consequences if this transaction becomes public?

9. What does the organization value (as defined in the mission statement, ethics statement, or code of conduct) and reward? (You can speculate here since the case is intentionally vague, but in a real dilemma these would be vital considerations.)

10. What have you determined is the right thing to do? The wrong thing to do?

11. How would you explain your ethical analysis to the CEO?

12. How would you explain your ethical analysis to your publics and stakeholders?

Resolution

The above case is based on a recent factual occurrence, but identifying factors have been removed to protect the interests of the organization. However, the organization decided that its ethical principles had been violated and dismissed both the senior executive and the new manager. The situation was heralded as the company holding true to it ethical standards and commitment to fair business practices.

REFERENCES

Beauchamp, T. L., & Bowie, N. E. (2004). *Ethical theory and business* (7th ed.). Upper Saddle River, NJ: Pearson Prentice Hall.

Bentham, J. (1780/1988). *The principles of morals and legislation.* Reprint; Amherst, NY: Prometheus.

Biswas, T. (1997). *Decision-making under uncertainty.* New York: St. Martin's Press.

Bowen, S. A. (2000). *A theory of ethical issues management: Contributions of Kantian deontology to public relations' ethics and decision making.* Unpublished doctoral dissertation, University of Maryland, College Park.

———. (2002). Elite executives in issues management: The role of ethical paradigms in decision making. *Journal of Public Affairs, 2*(4), pp. 270–283.

———. (2003). "I thought it would be more glamorous": Preconceptions and misconceptions of public relations among students in the principles course. *Public Relations Review, 29,* pp. 199–214.

———. (2004a). Expansion of ethics as the tenth generic principle of public relations excellence: A Kantian theory and model for managing ethical issues. *Journal of Public Relations Research, 16*(1), pp. 65–92.

———. (2004b). Organizational factors encouraging ethical decision making: An exploration into the case of an exemplar. *Journal of Business Ethics, 52*(4), pp. 311–324.

———. (2005a). Communication ethics in the wake of terrorism. In G. Ledlow (Ed.), *Communication, communities, and terrorism.* Westport, CT: Praeger.

———. (2005b). Decision theory. In R. L. Heath (ed.), *Encyclopedia of public relations* (vol. 1, pp. 240–242). Thousand Oaks, CA: Sage.

———. (2005c). A practical model for ethical decision making in issues management and public relations. *Journal of Public Relations Research, 17.*

Bowen, S. A., & Heath, R. L. (2003, May). *Melting the distinction between ethical and legal guidelines: A case examination of Enron Corporation.* Paper presented at the meeting of the International Communication Association, San Diego.

———. (in press). Issues management, systems, and rhetoric: Exploring the distinction between ethical and legal guidelines at Enron. *Journal of Public Affairs.*

Bowen, S. A., & Rawlins, B. L. (2005). Corporate moral conscience. In R. L. Heath (Ed.), *Encyclopedia of public relations* (vol. 1, pp. 205–210). Thousand Oaks, CA: Sage.

Broom, G. M., Lauzen, M. M., & Tucker, K. (1991). Public relations and marketing: Dividing the conceptual domain and operational turf. *Public Relations Review, 17*(3), pp. 219–225.

Buchholz, R. A. (1988). Adjusting corporations to the realities of public interests and policy. In R. L. Heath (Ed.), *Strategic issues management: How organizations influence and respond to public interests and policies.* San Francisco: Jossey-Bass.

Buchholz, R. A., Evans, W. D., & Wagley, R. A. (1994). *Management responses to public issues: Concepts and cases in strategy formulation* (3rd ed.). Upper Saddle River, NJ: Prentice Hall.

Cheney, G. (1983). The rhetoric of identification and the study of organizational communication. *Quarterly Journal of Speech, 69,* pp. 143–158.

Curtin, P. A., & Boynton, L. A. (2001). Ethics in public relations: Theory and practice. In R. L. Heath (Ed.), *Handbook of public relations* (pp. 411–422). Thousand Oaks, CA: Sage.

Cutlip, S. M., Center, A. H., & Broom, G. M. (2000). *Effective public relations* (8th ed.). Upper Saddle River, NJ: Prentice Hall.

Daft, R., & Weick, K. (1984). Toward a model of organizations as interpretations systems. *Academy of Management Review, 9,* pp. 284–295.

Day, L. A. (1997). *Ethics in media communications: Cases and controversies* (2nd ed.). Belmont, CA: Wadsworth.

De George, R. T. (1995). *Business ethics* (4th ed.). Englewood Cliffs, NJ: Prentice Hall.

———. (1999). *Business ethics* (5th ed.). Englewood Cliffs, NJ: Prentice Hall.

Donaldson, T., & Gini, A. (1995). *Case studies in business ethics* (4th ed.). Upper Saddle River, NJ: Prentice Hall.

Donaldson, T., & Werhane, P. H. (1999). *Ethical issues in business: A philosophical approach* (6th ed.). Upper Saddle River, NJ: Prentice Hall.

Ehling, W. P., White, J., & Grunig, J. E. (1992). Public relations and marketing practices. In J. E. Grunig (Ed.), *Excellence in public relations and communication management* (pp. 357–393). Hillsdale, NJ: Lawrence Erlbaum.

Eisenberg, E. M., & Riley, P. (2001). Organizational culture. In F. M. Jablin & L. L. Putnam (Eds.), *The new handbook of organizational communication: Advances in theory, research, and methods* (pp. 291–322). Thousand Oaks, CA: Sage.

Fisher, R., & Ury, W. (1981). *Getting to yes: Negotiating agreement without giving in.* New York: Penguin.

Fitzpatrick, K. R., & Rubin, M. S. (1995). Public relations vs. legal strategies in organizational crisis decisions. *Public Relations Review, 21*(1), pp. 21–34.

Flew, A. (1979). *A dictionary of philosophy* (2nd ed.). New York: St. Martin's.

Goffman, E. (1974). *Frame analysis: An essay on the organization of experience.* Cambridge, MA: Harvard University Press.

Goodman, E. C. (Ed.). (1997). *The Forbes book of business quotations.* New York: Black Dog & Leventhal.

Grossman, B. (1988). *Corporate loyalty: A trust betrayed.* Markham, Ontario: Penguin.

Grunig, J. E. (1989). Publics, audiences and market segments: Segmentation principles for campaigns. In C. Salmon (Ed.), *Information campaigns: Balancing social values and social change* (pp. 199–228). Newbury Park, CA: Sage.

———. (1992a). Communication, public relations, and effective organizations: An overview of the book. In J. E. Grunig (Ed.), *Excellence in public relations and communication management* (pp. 1–30). Hillsdale, NJ: Lawrence Erlbaum.

———. (1992b). What is excellence in management? In J. E. Grunig (Ed.), *Excellence in public relations and communication management* (pp. 219–250). Hillsdale, NJ: Lawrence Erlbaum.

———. (2000). Collectivism, collaboration, and societal corporatism as core professional values in public relations. *Journal of Public Relations Research, 12*(1), pp. 23–48.

———. (2001). Two-way symmetrical public relations: Past, present, and future. In R. L. Heath (Ed.), *Handbook of public relations* (pp. 11–30). Thousand Oaks, CA: Sage.

Grunig, J. E., & Grunig, L. A. (1992). Models of public relations and communication. In J. E. Grunig (Ed.), *Excellence in public relations and communication management* (pp. 285–325). Hillsdale, NJ: Lawrence Erlbaum.

———. (1996, May). *Implications of symmetry for a theory of ethics and social responsibility in public relations.* Paper presented at the meeting of the International Communication Association, Chicago.

———. (1998). The relationship between public relations and marketing in excellent organizations: Evidence from the IABC study. *Journal of Marketing Communications, 4*, pp. 141–162.

Grunig, J. E., & Huang, Y. H. (2000). From organizational effectiveness to relationship indicators: Antecedents of relationships, public relations strategies, and relationship outcomes. In J. Ledingham & S. Bruning (Eds.), *Public relations as relationship management: A relational approach to the study and practice of public relations* (pp. 23–53). Mahwah, NJ: Lawrence Erlbaum.

Grunig, J. E., & Hunt, T. (1984). *Managing public relations.* New York: Holt, Rinehart and Winston.

Grunig, J. E., & Repper, F. C. (1992). Strategic management, publics, and issues. In J. E. Grunig (Ed.), *Excellence in public relations and communication management* (pp. 117–157). Hillsdale, NJ: Lawrence Erlbaum.

Grunig, J. E., & White, J. (1992). The effect of worldviews on public relations theory and practice. In J. E. Grunig (Ed.), *Excellence in public relations and communication management* (pp. 31–64). Hillsdale, NJ: Lawrence Erlbaum.

Grunig, L. A. (1992a). Activism: How it limits the effectiveness of organizations and how excellent public relations departments respond. In J. E. Grunig (Ed.), *Excellence in public relations and communication management* (pp. 503–530). Hillsdale, NJ: Lawrence Erlbaum.

———. (1992b). How public relations/communication departments should adapt to the structure and environment of an organization . . . and what they actually do. In J. E. Grunig (Ed.), *Excellence in public relations and communication management* (pp. 467–481). Hillsdale, NJ: Lawrence Erlbaum.

———. (1992c). Toward the philosophy of public relations. In E. L. Toth & R. L. Heath (Eds.), *Rhetorical and critical approaches to public relations* (pp. 65–91). Hillsdale, NJ: Lawrence Erlbaum.

Grunig, L. A., Grunig, J. E., & Dozier, D. M. (2002). *Excellent public relations and effective organizations: A study of communication management in three countries.* Mahwah, NJ: Lawrence Erlbaum.

Grunig, L. A., Grunig, J. E., & Ehling, W. P. (1992). What is an effective organization? In J. E. Grunig (Ed.), *Excellence in public relations and communication management* (pp. 65–90). Hillsdale, NJ: Lawrence Erlbaum.

Grunig, L. A., Toth, E. L., & Hon, L. C. (2001). *Women in public relations: How gender influences practice.* New York: Guilford.

Habermas, J. (1984). *The theory of communicative action: Reason and the rationalization of society* (T. McCarthy, Trans. vol. 1). Boston: Beacon Press.

Hallahan, K. (1999). Seven models of framing: Implications for public relations. *Journal of Public Relations Research, 11*(3), pp. 205–242.

Heath, R. L. (1997). *Strategic issues management: Organizations and public policy challenges.* Thousand Oaks, CA: Sage.

———. (2001a). A rhetorical enactment rationale for public relations: The good organization communicating well. In R. L. Heath (Ed.), *Handbook of public relations* (pp. 31–50). Thousand Oaks, CA: Sage.

———. (2001b). Shifting foundations: Public relations as relationship building. In R. L. Heath (Ed.), *Handbook of public relations* (pp. 1–10). Thousand Oaks, CA: Sage.

———. (2005). Preface. In R. L. Heath (Ed.), *Encyclopedia of public relations* (Vol. 1, pp. xxiii–xxvii). Thousand Oaks, CA: Sage.

Heath, R. L., & Bowen, S. A. (2002). The public relations philosophy of John W. Hill: Bricks in the foundation of issues management. *Journal of Public Affairs, 2*(4), pp. 230–246.

Heath, R. L., & Ryan, M. (1989). Public relations' role in defining corporate social responsibility. *Journal of Mass Media Ethics, 4*(1), pp. 21–38.

Heath, R. L., Seshadri, S., & Lee, J. (1998). Risk communication: A two-community analysis of proximity, dread, trust, involvement, uncertainty, openness/accessibility, and knowledge on support/opposition toward chemical companies. *Journal of Public Relations Research, 10*(1), pp. 35–56.

Hon, L. C. (1997). "To redeem the soul of America": Public relations and the civil rights movement. *Journal of Public Relations Research, 9*(3), pp. 163–212.

Huang, Y. H. (1997). *Public relations strategies, relational outcomes, and conflict management strategies.*

Unpublished doctoral dissertation, University of Maryland, College Park.

Huang, Y. H. (2001a). OPRA: A cross-cultural, multiple-item scale for measuring organization-public relationships. *Journal of Public Relations Research, 13*(1), pp. 61–90.

———. (2001b). Values of public relations: Effects on organization-public relationships mediating conflict resolution. *Journal of Public Relations Research, 13*(4), pp. 265–302.

———. (2004). Is symmetrical communication ethical and effective? *Journal of Business Ethics, 53*(4), pp. 333–352.

Jaksa, J. A., & Pritchard, M. S. (1994). *Communication ethics: Methods of analysis* (2nd ed.). Belmont, CA: Wadsworth.

Kant, I. (1785/1964). *Groundwork of the metaphysic of morals* (H. J. Paton, Trans.). Reprint; New York: Harper & Row.

———. (1785/1993). Metaphysical foundations of morals (C. J. Friedrich, Trans.). In C. J. Friedrich (Ed.), *The philosophy of Kant: Immanuel Kant's moral and political writings* (pp. 154–229). New York: Modern Library.

———. (1793/1974). *On the old saw: That may be right in theory but it won't work in practice* (E. B. Ashton, Trans.). Reprint; Philadelphia: University of Pennsylvania Press.

Kohlberg, L. (1969). Stage and sequence: The cognitive developmental approach to socialization. In D. A. Goslin (Ed.), *Handbook of socialization theory of research* (pp. 347–480). Chicago: Rand McNally.

Kopenhaver, L. L. (1985). Aligning values of practitioners and journalists. *Public Relations Review, 11*(1), pp. 34–42.

Kruckeberg, D., & Starck, K. (2001). Public relations and community: A reconstructed theory revisited. In R. L. Heath (Ed.), *Handbook of public relations* (pp. 51–60). Thousand Oaks, CA: Sage.

Lauzen, M. M. (1992). Public relations roles, intra-organizational power, and encroachment. *Journal of Public Relations Research, 4*(1), pp. 61–80.

Ledingham, J., & Bruning, S. (Eds.). (2000). *Public relations as relationship management: A relational approach to the study and practice of public relations.* Mahwah, NJ: Lawrence Erlbaum.

Lee, J., Jares, S. M., & Heath, R. L. (1999). Decision-making encroachment and cooperative relationships between public relations and legal counselors in the management of organizational crisis. *Journal of Public Relations Research, 11*(3), pp. 243–270.

Leeper, K. A. (1996). Public relations ethics and communitarinism: A preliminary investigation. *Public Relations Review, 22*(2), pp. 163–179.

Mill, J. S. (1861/1957). *Utilitarianism.* Reprint; New York: Liberal Arts Press.

Murphy, P., & Dee, J. (1992). Du Pont and Greenpeace: The dynamics of conflict between corporations and activist groups. *Journal of Public Relations Research, 4*(1), pp. 3–20.

Pearson, R. (1989a). Albert J. Sullivan's theory of public relations ethics. *Public Relations Review, 15*(2), pp. 52–62.

———. (1989b). Beyond ethical relativism in public relations: Coorientation, rules, and the idea of communication symmetry. In J. E. Grunig & L. A. Grunig (Eds.), *Public relations research annual* (vol. 1, pp. 67–86). Hillsdale, NJ: Lawrence Erlbaum.

———. (1989c). Business ethics as communication ethics: Public relations practice and the idea of dialogue. In C. H. Botan & V. Hazleton Jr. (Eds.), *Public relations theory* (pp. 111–131). Hillsdale, NJ: Lawrence Erlbaum.

Plowman, K. D. (1998). Power in conflict for public relations. *Journal of Public Relations Research, 10*(4), pp. 237–261.

———. (1999, June). *Strategic management, conflict, and public relations.* Paper presented at the meeting of the Public Relations Society of America Educators Academy, College Park, MD.

Pratt, C. B., Im, S. H., & Montague, S. N. (1994). Investigating the application of deontology among U.S. public relations practitioners. *Journal of Public Relations Research, 6*(4), pp. 241–266.

Rawls, J. (1971). *A theory of justice.* Cambridge, MA: Harvard University Press.

Reber, B. H., Cropp, F., & Cameron, G. T. (2003). Impossible odds: Contributions of legal counsel and public relations practitioners in a hostile bid for Conrail Inc. by Norfolk Southern Corporation. *Journal of Public Relations Research, 15*(1), pp. 1–25.

Roth, W. F. (2005). *Ethics in the workplace: A systems perspective.* Upper Saddle River, NJ: Pearson Prentice Hall.

Ryan, M., & Martinson, D. L. (1983). The PR officer as corporate conscience. *Public Relations Quarterly, 28*(2), pp. 20–23.

Ryan, M., & Martinson, D. L. (1988). Journalists and public relations practitioners: Why the antagonism? *Journalism Quarterly, 62*(2), pp. 131–140.

Schick, F. (1997). *Making choices: A recasting of decision theory.* New York: Cambridge University Press.

Sims, R. R., & Brinkman, J. (2003). Enron ethics (or, culture matters more than codes). *Journal of Business Ethics, 45*(3), pp. 243–256.

Spicer, C. (1993). Images of PR in the print media. *Journal of Public Relations Research, 5*(1), pp. 47–61.

Stauber, J., & Rampton, S. (1995). *Toxic sludge is good for you: Lies, damn lies and the public relations industry.* Monroe, ME: Common Courage Press.

Sullivan, R. J. (1989). *Immanuel Kant's moral theory.* Cambridge: Cambridge University Press.

———. (1994). *An introduction to Kant's ethics.* New York: Cambridge University Press.

Toth, E. L. (1992). The case for pluralistic studies of public relations: Rhetorical, critical, and systems perspectives. In E. L. Toth & R. L. Heath (Eds.), *Rhetorical and critical approaches to public relations* (pp. 3–16). Hillsdale, NJ: Lawrence Erlbaum.

Wright, D. K. (1985). Can age predict the moral values of public relations practitioners? *Public Relations Review, 11*(1), pp. 51–60.

CHAPTER ELEVEN

FOLLOWING COMMUNICATION RULES

A Communication-Centered Theory for Public Relations

MARÍA E. LEN-RÍOS

Imagine the following scenario: You work as a public relations adviser to a U.S. representative in Washington, D.C. You are working on the representative's reelection campaign. One of the congressman's speechwriters is worried because spending is being cut, which might mean a loss in positions such as hers. You are going to meet her for lunch. If you have a close relationship with her, what is the appropriate thing for you to say?

After lunch you are back at the office. You receive a call from CBS's *60 Minutes*. A producer wants to arrange an interview with the representative about rumors that his former business partners handled some questionable financial investments. You know that you should call the reporter back as soon as possible, but you need to talk to the representative first. You know that saying "No comment" to the journalist is not a good option.

Meanwhile, a group of the representative's constituents is organizing a local protest at the state capital against one of the many bills the representative supports. Your boss has asked you to handle the situation and meet with his constituents. What response should you provide? What will constituents expect?

Aside from facing several challenges, there is something that ties together all the situations that you have just encountered. What is the commonality? Each situation had an "appropriate" or "preferred" response—communication rules for situations.

Communication rules are norms that dictate what is socially acceptable communication based on the cultural values and norms of the communicators. So in the opening scenario, there are expectations for how a public relations adviser should communicate and interact with a coworker, a television journalist, a supervisor, and a group of protesters.

Organizations and individuals who engage in public relations need to be aware of communication rules. Part of the function of public relations is to communicate with publics to elicit positive attitudes toward your organization or client and to avoid negative ones. Rules theory suggests that communication is an essential factor in establishing, maintaining, and ending relationships. When communication rules are understood, communicators can decide to follow or break rules to achieve their relational goals. An understanding of communication rules theory can enable practitioners to do their jobs more effectively and to learn better techniques to manage public relations relationships.

This chapter explores communication rules theory and describes how this theory pertains to public relations and the power of public relations to affect organization-public relationships.

COMMUNICATION RULES THEORY

Communication rules theory has its origins in sociolinguistics. While linguists have examined the rules for how words are ordered and placed in sentences, sociolinguists have grown interested in how language is used to create cultural meaning in communication exchanges within social groups. According to Grimshaw (2000), sociolinguists study how speakers use language to achieve their goals in certain communication situations. Sociolinguists also study how groups and cultures work to maintain their language systems.

Sociolinguists' interest in rules led them to examine rules that govern communication differences based on the age, gender, and occupation of communicators, as well as the formality of language within cultures and situations. For example, in the United States it is acceptable to refer to others as "you" no matter their social status. However, in many Spanish-speaking cultures, when addressing another person, the more formal "usted" (for "you") is used to address superiors, older individuals, or people you do not know. The familiar form, "tu," is reserved for individuals who are of equal status or those with whom you are familiar. Market researchers have found that the use of Spanish can also differ based on the level of acculturation (Valdés, 2000).

S. Ervin-Tripp (1972), a sociolinguist who studies rules, says that different occupations call for a particular set of communication rules. For example, doctors communicate with patients differently than public relations professionals communicate with journalists. Distinct rules exist for a variety of interactions and communication partners or groups. Even in communications with journalists, a public relations practitioner may have different communication rules for interacting with a reporter who works at a magazine versus a reporter at a television station because each communication channel has lead time and format differences.

D. Cushman and G. C. Whiting (1972) are often credited with introducing rules theory to communications. They used the theory to understand interpersonal interactions and how we, as humans, construct and communicate meaning.

They suggested that individuals have rules that they bring to a communications situation and that the more closely individuals' rules match, the more likely they will be to reach consensus. The authors also noted that, "When one focuses upon the analysis of communication rules the outcome of such an analysis informs us about the process of communication itself, as well as the consequences of that process" (p. 234).

Cushman's later research with B. Kovacic (1994) shows that in interpersonal communication—or communication between two individuals—creating friendships and mate relationships are outcomes of following (or not following) communication rules. They found that when mate relationships break down, it is often because partners do not follow rules governing conflict. Partners who destroy their relationships approach conflict by blaming, being defensive, and confronting their partner instead of agreeing on a solution. Public relations practitioners can apply these findings to conflict resolution (e.g., helping organizations come to negotiated agreements with striking workers).

S. B. Shimanoff (1980) was the first communications scholar to thoroughly differentiate rules theory from other communication concepts and theories used at the time. Her book combines work in the areas of linguistics, sociolinguistics, and ethnography to provide a comprehensive analysis of the research in these fields as it applies to a communication theory of rules. Shimanoff identifies types of rules and offers suggestions on how researchers can uncover rules. According to Shimanoff, a rule is a rule if it is followable, prescriptive, and contextual. A rule is followable because it is something you can choose to do—you must have free will and physically be able to do it. Rules are prescriptive in that they govern what a person must or must not or should or should not do. Rules are contextual because what one must or must not, or should or should not do varies according to who is communicating and the situation.

In media relations, for example, when a public relations practitioner is preparing to pitch a story to a reporter about a political candidate's issue stance, he or she may follow slightly different communication rules than when a reporter is calling him or her to interview the political candidate because of a scandal. The two contexts require the practitioner to follow the communication rules most appropriate for the situation.

Rules are culturally bound and change over time. Rules may change from culture to culture. A media relations practitioner in Korea may follow decidedly different rules than those who practice in the United States. For example, Shin and Cameron (2003) found that Korean journalists and public relations practitioners value and tend to prefer informal interpersonal communication to online communication in comparison to many U.S. journalists and public relations professionals.

Shimanoff also links rules with communication behavior. In other words, communication rules govern or guide what public relations practitioners do. For a practitioner's behavior to be governed or guided by rules, it must be controllable, criticizable, and contextual. We've already discussed how rules are contextual. Rule-generated behavior is controllable because you, as a public relations practitioner, can decide whether to follow the rule. The communicator can follow or break the rule. It is possible that a practitioner may break a rule on purpose (e.g., tell a reporter "No comment" to keep the media speculating about a celebrity marriage). A rule is criticizable because others can evaluate it as appropriate or inappropriate.

Types of Rules and Their Force

Communication rules theorists believe communication rules are enforced by social pressure. *Social pressure* is the real or perceived idea that if one deviates from expected standard group behavior, there will be real, expected, or imagined consequences from other group members. No doubt as a teenager in high school you noticed real or imagined social pressure from your peers to look and act in certain ways. Similarly, organizations and public figures are also subject to social pressure, and public relations departments or agencies are often charged with providing an organization's response to social pressure. For example, in August 2004, N.J. Governor James McGreevey held a press conference to announce publicly that he was gay, had cheated on his wife, and planned to resign. Apparently, McGreevey felt he had violated social rules, believed that there would be personal and professional consequences, and so concluded that the appropriate response would be to leave office ("McGreevey's bombshells; New Jersey politics," 2004).

In her work, Shimanoff (1980) wrote that rules can be explicitly identified or implicitly observed by how others behave or by how they are punished. Organizations may provide formal oral or written statements to employees of what constitutes appropriate professional, workplace behavior in their organizations. These oral or written statements are *explicit rules*. The U.S. House of Representatives currently has a forty-nine-page rulebook that governs House communication and behavior. The book even contains a rule that prohibits the use of cell phones, personal computers, and cigarettes on the House floor (Trandahl, 2005).

Implicit rules are unstated, but you can infer them from the situation. For example, Knepprath (1985) examined communication rules of the Ways and Means Committee of the U.S. House of Representatives and determined it was a House rule to "yield the floor when asked, even to members of the opposition" (p. 205).

The social pressure to conform to explicit rules may come from the knowledge that there are legal or established consequences for noncompliance. While following and exceeding rules can lead to rewards, the penalties for not following the rules are called *sanctions*. The Public Relations Society of America (PRSA) has developed a code of conduct, titled "PRSA Member Code of Ethics 2000." It provides ethical guidelines for its members. Members who violate these guidelines may be expelled from the organization if reprimanded by the U.S. government or found guilty in court.

There also may be sanctions, or consequences, for not conforming to implicit rules—for instance, embarrassment and loss of employment. CBS television asked singer Justin Timberlake to publicly apologize for his part in Super Bowl 2004's Jackson-Timberlake "wardrobe malfunction." Because Timberlake had broken implicit communication rules for his part in broadcasting content inappropriate for family viewing, he was required to apologize to a worldwide audience during the Grammy Awards on February 8, 2004. For his apology, he said, "Listen, I know it's been a rough week on everybody and . . . what occurred was unintentional, completely regrettable and I apologize if you guys were offended" (Brand, 2004). Timberlake was sanctioned for his behavior.

In addition to explicit and implicit rules, communication rules may be general or specific. A *general rule* is one that applies in a wide variety of situations. In public relations, a general rule is to never communicate a lie. This applies across the board in public relations communications situations. Rules with greater *specificity* apply only under certain circumstances or contexts. For example, undergraduate journalism students believe more strongly that a company's web site should feature the prices for a company's products more so than the company's earnings information (Len-Ríos, 2003). However, a financial reporter may value equally the company's earnings information and its prices. In this situation, the rule is specific to the communication audience, that is, who is involved in the communication context. It does not matter whether a rule is general or specific; both have sanctions and rewards attached to whether they are followed.

Several scholars have categorized rules according to their prescriptive and proscriptive force. The term *prescription* refers to a recommendation or command to produce a particular action or result. *Proscription* is an order to prohibit an action. In the area of rules, *force* is the degree of social pressure or perceived social pressure that is operating in the communication context. The stronger the social pressure, the greater the practitioner may feel the need to follow the rule. Originally Shimanoff (1980) introduced three kinds of rules classified by their force: "prohibitive," "obligatory," and "preferred." Prohibitive rules define what one *must not* do or say and obligatory rules define what one *must* do or say. Preferred rules describe what one should or should not do or say.

In political communication, rules govern what U.S. presidential candidates can say. For example, during a U.S. presidential campaign today it appears that it is still a prohibitive rule for candidates to go too far in name-calling or cursing. It is considered unpresidential. An obligatory rule today might be for the candidate to express one's patriotism and allegiance to the United States. A preferred rule might be that the candidate should be able to debate well with challengers and present his or her ideas clearly.

Cushman and Whiting (1972), in their discussion of rules, also used similar concepts and defined rules as either "formal," or more permanent, or "informal," or more flexible. The authors also proposed that rules be presented in the form "in context X, Y is required or permitted" (p. 228). For example, in the context of a political party convention, the candidate is usually required to appear on the final day with his family. Rules that are required are considered formal rules, and those that are permitted are perceived as informal because the social pressure for rule compliance is less rigorous.

Following, or meeting, communication rules means complying with the rules and is often referred to as communication rule *compliance*. When a rule is not followed, or met, the communicator has either violated (not met) or surpassed (met and exceeded) the rule-governed behavior. Recent research suggests that rule compliance be viewed on a continuum with violating and surpassing rules as

FIGURE 11.1   Range to Rule Compliance Continuum

A diagram of the continuum (Len-Ríos, 2005) shows that there is a range to rule compliance.

the two extremes (Len-Ríos, 2002, 2005). Having followed and met the communication rule prescription serves as a zero point on the compliance continuum (see Figure 11.1).

The effects of rule compliance vary by strength. According to communication rules theory, violating a prohibitive or obligatory rule can lead to stronger consequences, perhaps terminating public relations relationships. There may be no reward for following or simply meeting the rule. In other words, rules have a range of effects, with violating and surpassing rules at the two extremes of the continuum.

For example, in media relations, it is unacceptable to lie to a reporter. A public relations practitioner who violates the rule and lies to a reporter would be sanctioned for doing so (very publicly, or at least professionally). Lying to a reporter is a prohibitive rule. In another instance, a reporter may prefer to receive her news releases from public relations practitioners via e-mail; however, if he or she receives a well-written release by postal mail, he or she may still consider using it. This latter situation illustrates a *preferred* rule. Although the practitioner violated the reporter's rule by sending the release in the mail, the sanction, or penalty, will most likely be less severe than the sanction applied for lying to a reporter.

In summary, rules are followable, contextual, and prescriptive or proscriptive (obligatory, prohibitive, or preferred). They may be explicitly stated or implicitly inferred in situations. People follow communication rules because of social force and to meet their relational goals. Communication-generated behavior may violate, meet, or surpass rule prescriptions and has varying consequences.

COMMUNICATION RULES AND RELATIONSHIPS

Communication Rules—In the Interpersonal Context

Theorists in interpersonal communication have used rules theory to examine interpersonal relationship development and dissolution. As noted previously, Cushman and colleagues have examined how communication rules enhance or inhibit relationship growth. With the growing emphasis of public relations as relationship management (see Ledingham & Bruning, 2000), looking at what rules theory tells us about relationships may be particularly fruitful.

Cushman, Valentinsen, and Dietrich (1982) looked at a large array of studies about communication rules to explain how people form friendships and romantic relationships. One important rule for relationship development, they found, is that partners communicate to their partners that they find them physically attractive. Other necessary rules include communicating to your partner that he or she has qualities that match what you would consider qualities of your ideal mate. In other words, following specified communication rules aids the development of a mate relationship.

Communication rules have also been studied in interactions between strangers. For example, Schlenker and Darby (1981) identified social rules for providing apologies in cases where an individual, walking along the street or a hallway, collided with a stranger. They found that people provide (and expect) more complete apologies when accidental collisions result in injury.

R. Pearson (1989) has reviewed studies about reporter-source relationships. He suggests that when reporters and sources operate from different sets of rules, the reporter-source relationship suffers. As an example, Pearson writes that scientists have communication rules for when the terms "breakthrough" and "cure" are to be used in information reported to the public. Using the words breakthrough and cure carry particular meaning, and scientists believe these words are appropriate to use only in specific conditions. If a reporter uses these words inappropriately to describe a scientist's research in a story, the scientist is less likely to speak with the reporter the next time the reporter needs a source for a story. The reporter thus alienates a source by not adhering to the rule. Pearson notes that scientists can come to distrust reporters who do not stick to the rules and will sever their relationships with reporters. It is easy to see how communication rules become important in media relations situations.

Communication Rules—In an Organizational Context

Scholars in organizational communication began studying rules theory in the 1980s and were involved in studying how communication rules influenced internal organizational communication. Researchers have since examined communication rules in supervisor–subordinate communication, employee selection, and the appropriateness of emotions in the workplace.

College students anticipate looking for professional jobs. They must know the communication rules for applying for a job. A study by Ramsay, Gallois, and Callan (1997) examined the communication rules for the interview situation. They found that a poor interview presentation was attributed to the person's competence (e.g., lack of preparation), but that nervousness demonstrated by the interviewee was attributed to the situation rather than the person. This means that it is expected a candidate may be a little nervous in a job interview. However, it is unacceptable to be unprepared. Thus, the communication rules are that an applicant must appear prepared; it is preferred that the applicant show confidence.

Other studies examine communication rules in employer–employee relationships. Eisenberg, Monge, and Farace (1984) compared the perceptions of supervisor and subordinate pairs to find out whether perceptions of compliance with communication rules met actual behavior. They found that it was perceptions of noncompliance with communication-generated behavior (e.g., the employer felt the employee did not meet performance expectations) that led supervisors or employees to sanction each other—and *not* the actual behavior (e.g., how hard the employee actually worked). This, of course, is an important point for public relations practitioners—it is not always what a client does that generates negative feedback, but rather what the client is *perceived* to have done.

Verbal behavior is not the only type of behavior in an organizational setting that requires rule compliance. Kramer and Hess (2002) studied rules for the display of emotions in work settings. They found that "the most common rule given was to express emotions professionally" (p. 72). Professional expression of emotion means workers are expected to contain emotion. When employees express emotion, it is preferred that it be masked or neutral or positive.

A combination of verbal and emotional expression hurt former 2004 presidential front-runner Howard Dean. When speaking to his supporters after a disappointing third-place finish in the January 19, 2004, Iowa caucuses, Dean delivered an impassioned motivational speech that was dubbed "Dean's 'Iowa Yell'" (Marinucci, 2004), "Rebel Yell" and the "screech heard 'round the world'" (Shiflett, 2004). What appeared to have caught the attention of the news media, and Dean's political opponents, is that his behavior and emotional expression violated communication rules for how presidential candidates should express themselves. Some political consultants suggested that this reinforced the idea that Dean was not quite presidential material (Marinucci, 2004). Although Dean's speech appeared to play well to supporters who saw him in person, it did not play well on national television. One's profession, or the profession one aspires to, is associated with certain expectations or rules for emotional displays.

COMMUNICATION RULES IN THE PUBLIC RELATIONS CONTEXT

It is easy to see how communication rules theory affects the practice of public relations. Public relations is about building relationships between an organization and its publics. This is achieved primarily through an organization's communications and behaviors. All aspects of an organization's communications (e.g., brochures, e-mailed news releases, ads, press conferences, etc.) follow communication rules. Although rules theory can be applied to many areas of public relations, we will focus specifically on communication rules for media relations in crisis communications and Internet communications, because most of the research that pertains to rules has been conducted in these domains.

Rules for Media Relations in Crisis Communication

The scenario that opened this chapter suggested that a reporter from CBS's *60 Minutes* wanted to interview your representative about his or her former business associates (and most probably about the representative's former business dealings). You know that you should avoid telling the reporter "No comment," and should say you'll get back to him or her with the answer (and then do). How do you know that? It is a communications rule. Reporters expect that if the representative has something to hide, he or she will say "No comment." However, if you instead provide the reporter with a response to a question, you may surpass the reporter's expectations and thus you may be evaluated more favorably—rewarded.

In crisis situations, when a company quickly takes responsibility for a crisis and offers compensation to those affected, the company often surpasses public expectations. For example, when Johnson & Johnson recalled its Extra-Strength Tylenol products in 1982 and introduced the new Tylenol caplets and product packaging, the company surpassed expectations for its handling of the crisis, and the situation is now a classic case for good crisis communication.

However, not taking action in a crisis can be harmful in more ways than one. In May 2001, a young woman, Chandra Levy, was reported missing by her parents. She had served as an intern with the Federal Bureau of Prisons in Washington, D.C. The young woman was thought to have a boyfriend. U.S. Congressman Gary Condit received tremendous media scrutiny when it was discovered he was the one who had had a relationship with Levy. And although Levy's parents reported her missing in May, Condit remained publicly silent. In addition, Levy's parents stated in interviews that Condit had been uncooperative in the search for their daughter. For his part, Condit did not address public speculation until late August. By then, more than two months had passed since Levy's disappearance. In an analysis of this case, Len-Ríos and Benoit (2004) suggested that Condit did not communicate the appropriate concern and cooperation expected by social convention, which led the public to mistrust his motives and intentions. There are expectations for action when a person is missing, especially when you are close to them.

Rules for Internet Communication

When you are online and one of your friends signs on to his e-mail account, you might expect that your friend will send you a quick instant message to say hello. If he doesn't, you may assume he is busy or you may assume that he is ignoring you. In corporate communication, there are also rules for appropriate online communication. In fact, many organizations have developed protocols for using office e-mail. Some organizations contain disclaimers in the signatures of the e-mails saying that if confidential information was inadvertently sent to the wrong person, the recipient should discard it and immediately tell the sender.

In public relations, Internet-based messages for internal and external communication are governed by certain rules. This not only includes e-mail, but also web site communications. An organization's web site is its public face on the Internet.

Researchers at the University of Missouri–Columbia developed a series of studies to identify communication rules for communicating with publics via the Internet. An exploratory study of college students by Len-Ríos (2003) identified communication rules for consumer web sites. She found people had different expectations of consumer goods web sites compared with news and informational web sites. More specifically, she found that news and information web sites were visited more frequently, yet were viewed as more replaceable. Consumer goods web sites, however, were expected to offer personalization and to provide customer service. For all consumer web sites, it was not considered obligatory that companies provide public relations information on their sites, but it was preferred that the companies did.

In earlier studies, Len-Ríos and Cameron (2001, 2002) also identified website rules for providing product information corrections, attribution of information sources, and promotional e-mail communications. The authors identified some preferred rules for e-commerce sites: "Web sites should contain referral pages for outdated links" and "If a customer buys an item online, the customer should be able to return the item via mail carrier" (2001, p. 49).

In a study using an experimental design of six web sites, Len-Ríos (2002) found that when an organization's web site surpassed communication rules for providing information online, participants perceived they had better relationships with the organization and identified themselves more closely as customers of the company than if the organization violated or simply met certain communication rules. Participants also felt that the web site that surpassed communication rules had increased goodwill toward its users than web sites that did not. This suggests that surpassing communication rules for communication helps to build a more favorable image of an organization and strengthens organization-public relationships.

CONCLUSION

Communication rules theory was introduced to the field of communication studies nearly thirty years ago. It has been applied to examine interpersonal communication, organizational communication, and communication between an organization and its publics. Rules guide our communications and behaviors. An understanding of rules can help us become better communicators and public relations professionals. The theory is evolving and as scholars continue to test and refine its predictions and assumptions, we can expect that the theory will be developed further. Some important questions will be raised as the theory is developed: What are the best ways to measure rules? How can rules theory be used to predict the success of a public relations program? Can communication rules be used to test the acceptance of messages? Perhaps after reading this chapter you will decide to use communication rules theory to guide your own research.

CASE: A SENATOR IN HOT WATER

Communication by politicians is governed by communication rules. How politicians handle communication when their public image is damaged is vital to image repair and, in some cases, saving their job. Only fifteen days after Senator Trent Lott

(R-Miss.) made a comment on December 5, 2002, at the hundredth birthday party for former Senator Strom Thurmond (R-S.C.), Lott resigned and forfeited his leadership position as Senate Majority Leader. What happened?

On the evening of Thurmond's party, Lott made the statement, "I want to say this about my state. When Strom Thurmond ran for president, we voted for him. We're proud of it. And if the rest of the country had followed our lead, we wouldn't have had all these problems over all of these years either" (Tierney, 2002). When Thurmond ran for the U.S. presidency, he was on the 1948 segregationist party's ballot (Shepard, 2002).

As a result of his statement, Lott found that he violated communication rules for addressing the African American community, some of his constituents, some members of the public, his fellow senators, and the president. What was the general rule? "People (especially politicians who represent 'the people') must not make insensitive comments about historical injustices." How would Lott try to fix the perceptions of these publics? If you were Lott's public relations adviser, what would you recommend he do?

Lott issued a series of statements. One of his first statements was: "This was a lighthearted celebration of the hundredth birthday of legendary Thurmond. My comments were not an endorsement of his positions of over 50 years ago, but of the man and his life" (Welch, 2002). However, this apology did not prove good enough for many. Lott's comments could be classified as comments used to evade responsibility. The general rule for an apology is to take responsibility. The rule might be stated as: "When you have made a mistake, you should make a sincere apology and take responsibility for your error."

In a later statement, in another effort to repair his image, on December 9 Lott said: "A poor choice of words conveyed to some the impression that I embraced the discarded policies of the past. Nothing could be further from the truth, and I apologize to anyone who was offended by my statement" (Shepard, 2002). Again, another general rule for apologizing is not to blame the person who was wronged. Lott's latter comment is worded as such that it suggests that only certain people were offended, and that they were offended because they got the wrong impression from his comments. Again, Lott avoided taking responsibility, even though he voiced his concern.

Other politicians made statements about whether Lott should resign. Congressman J. C. Watts (R-Okla.), an African American, defended Lott early on, but Jesse Jackson, a political leader, and the Congressional Black Caucus had already called for Lott's resignation. President George W. Bush was equivocal in his support for Lott. John Kerry (D-Mass.) was the first senator to call for Lott's resignation (Tierney, 2002).

One problem Lott had to overcome was the perception that his previous public support for segregation early in his career was reflected in his public comment. Another was the eventual loss of support from the White House. On December 13, Bush stated, "Any suggestion that the segregated past was acceptable or positive is offensive, and it is wrong" (Nagourney & Hulse, 2002). Another complication facing Lott was his appearance on Black Entertainment Television (BET) on December 16, 2002. Reactions to his apology to BET viewers were negative and brought up another issue—Why hadn't a prominent politician ever before offered to be interviewed on BET? A writer for the *St. Petersburg Times* wrote, "Lott's attempts to shift the furor into some generalized, nationwide dialogue on race galled me most" (Deggans, 2002, p. 2B).

On December 20, 2002, Lott resigned his position as the Republican leader of the U.S. Senate. He had lost the political support of his party and the White House. This appeared to be the ultimate sanction for violating a communication rule.

QUESTIONS FOR APPLICATION

1. If you were counsel to Lott, what communication rules would you suggest he should have followed to repair his image? Do you believe it was possible to repair his image? Could the sanction he received for violating communication rules have been lessened? What other implicit rules can you infer from this situation?

2. If you were counsel to the U.S. president, also of the Republican Party, how would you advise the president to handle the situation? What rules govern how a president should respond in such a situation?

3. Imagine that the context was different. Would the sanction have been applied differently if the politician were a Democrat? How would the communication rule be different if the senator were African American or Latino and had made an insensitive comment about another racial group? Would the rules be different? How about the sanctions? How might you have

to handle it differently as a public relations adviser?

4. How do you think an organization's status or power within an industry affects how it is expected to comply with communication rules?

5. Would a person's status or position give the person more flexibility in complying with rules?

6. A theory is considered useful when it is parsimonious (simple). Is communication rules theory parsimonious?

7. Communication rules theory is considered culturally bound. How can communication rules theory help practitioners who are trying to reach multicultural audiences?

8. When are communication rules more helpful to practitioners? When they are general rules? When they are more specific?

REFERENCES

Brand, M. (2004, February 9). Justin Timberlake's apology for the Super Bowl show at last night's Grammy Awards. *National Public Radio*. Accessed February 23, 2004, at Lexis-Nexis Academic Universe.

Cushman, D. P., & Kovacic, B. (1994). Human communication: A rules perspective. In F. L. Casmir (Ed.), *Building communication theories: A socio/cultural approach* (pp. 269–295). Hillsdale, NJ: Lawrence Erlbaum.

Cushman, D. P., Valentinsen, B., & Dietrich, D. (1982). A rules theory of interpersonal relationships. In F. E. X. Dance (Ed.), *Human communication theory: Comparative essays* (pp. 90–119). New York: Harper & Row.

Cushman, D. P., & Whiting, G. C. (1972). An approach to communication theory: Toward a consensus on rules. *The Journal of Communication, 22,* pp. 217–238.

Deggans, E. (2002, December 18). Lott represents BET high and low. *St. Petersburg Times,* p. 2B.

Eisenberg, E. M., Monge, P. R., & Farace, R. V. (1984). Coorientation on communication rules in managerial dyads. *Human Communication Research, 11,* pp. 261–271.

Ervin-Tripp, S. (1972). On sociolinguistic rules: Alternation and co-occurrence. In J. J. Gumperz & D. Hymes (eds.), *Directions in sociolinguistics: The ethnography of communication.* New York: Holt, Rinehart and Winston.

Grimshaw, A. D. (2000). Sociolinguistics. In E. F. Borgatta, & R. J. V. Montgomery (Eds.), *Encyclopedia of Sociology* (2nd ed.) (pp. 2894–2912). New York: Macmillan Reference USA.

Knepprath, H. E. (1985). A test of Shimanoff's procedures for determining communication rules from behavior. *Central States Speech Journal, 36,* pp. 201–207.

Kramer, M. W., & Hess, J. A. (2002). Communication rules for the display of emotions in organizational settings. *Management Communication Quarterly, 16,* pp. 66–80.

Ledingham, J. A., & Bruning, S. D. (2000). *Public relations as relationship management: A relational approach to the study and practice of public relations.* Mahwah, NJ: Erlbaum.

Len-Ríos, M. E. (2002). *Communication rules and corporate online communication.* Unpublished doctoral dissertation, University of Missouri–Columbia.

———. (2003). Consumer rules and orientations toward corporate web sites: A pilot study. *Journal of Promotion Management, 9,* pp. 125–143.

———. (2005). Rules theory. In R. L. Heath (Ed.) *Encyclopedia of Public Relations* (pp. 758–761). Thousand Oaks, CA: Sage.

Len-Ríos, M. E., & Benoit, W. J. (2004). Gary Condit's image repair strategies: Determined denial and differentiation. *Public Relations Review, 30,* pp. 95–106.

Len-Ríos, M. E., & Cameron, G. T. (2001, February). *Playing by the rules: Relationships with online users— RATES (rules-appropriate testing evaluation scale) and implications for e-commerce and portal web sites.* Gainesville, FL: Institute for Public Relations.

———. (2002, July). *Knowing what to say and when to say it: Rules for building relationships with online publics.* Paper presented at the annual meeting of the International Communication Association, Public Relations Division, Seoul, South Korea.

"McGreevey's bombshells; New Jersey politics." (2004, August 21). *The Economist.* Available: Lexis-Nexis Academic Universe.

Marinucci, C. (2004, January 21). "'Iowa yell' stirring doubts about Dean," *San Francisco Chronicle,* p. A1.

Nagourney, A., & Hulse, C. (2002, December 13). Divisive words: The Republic leader; Bush rebukes Lott over remarks on Thurmond. *The New York Times,* p. A1.

Pearson, R. (1989). Beyond ethical relativism in public relations: Coorientation, rules, and the idea of communication symmetry. In J. E. Grunig & L. A. Grunig (Eds.), *Public Relations Research Annual* (vol. 1, pp. 67–86). Hillsdale, NJ: Erlbaum.

Ramsay, S., Gallois, C., & Callan, V. J. (1997). Social rules and attributions in the personnel selection interview. *Journal of Occupational and Organizational Psychology, 70,* pp. 189–203.

Schlenker, B. R., & Darby, B. W. (1981). The use of apologies in social predicaments. *Social Psychology Quarterly, 44,* pp. 271–278.

Shepard, S. (2002, December 10). Lott sorry for "poor choice of words." *The Atlanta Journal-Constitution,* p. 1A.

Shiflett, D. (2004, January 30). "Old Yeller," National Review Online. Available: Lexis-Nexis Academic Universe.

Shimanoff, S. B. (1980). *Communication rules: Theory and research.* Beverly Hills, CA: Sage.

Shin, J., & Cameron, G. T. (2003). The interplay of professional and cultural factors in the online source-reporter relationship. *Journalism Studies, 4,* pp. 253–272.

Tierney, C. (2002, December 22). How political pressure built on Sen. Trent Lott. *St. Louis Post-Dispatch,* p. A13.

Trandahl, J. (2005, January 4). *Rules of the House of Representatives: One hundred ninth Congress.* Accessed June 14, 2005, at www.house.gov/rules/house_rules.htm.

Valdés, M. I. (2000). *Marketing to American Latinos: A guide to an in-culture approach.* Ithaca, NY: Paramount Marketing.

Welch, W. M. (2002, December 11). Black caucus unforgiving after Lott's apology. *USA Today,* p. 6A.

ADDITIONAL REFERENCES

Doorbar, R. (1971). Meaning, rules and behavior. *Mind, 80,* pp. 29–40.

Morgan, J. M., & Krone, K. J. (2001). Bending the rules of "professional" display: Emotional improvisation in caregiver performances. *Journal of Applied Communication Research, 29,* pp. 317–340.

Philipsen, G. (1975). Speaking "like a man" in Teamsterville: Culture patterns of role enactment in an urban neighborhood. *Quarterly Journal of Speech, 61,* pp. 13–22.

Rose, R. A. (1985). Organizational adaptation from a rules theory perspective. *The Western Journal of Speech Communication, 49,* pp. 322–340.

White, J. (2002). Fee setting in public relations consultancies: A study of consultancy and client views of current practice in the UK. *Journal of Communication Management, 6*(4), pp. 355–367.

CHAPTER TWELVE

INTEGRATING SOCIAL NORMS THEORY IN PUBLIC RELATIONS CAMPAIGN DEVELOPMENT

TERRY L. RENTNER

For researchers and practitioners, integrating theory into practice is much like trying to pat your head, rub your stomach, and chew gum at the same time. It can be done, but not without a lot of thought and coordination. Scholars would explore the theoretical implications of patting, rubbing, and chewing, while practitioners would develop the tactics to meet this objective. But when it comes to execution, scholars and practitioners know that the best way to accomplish this challenging task is to integrate theory with application.

For scholars, theories in public relations are developed and debated to advance the field, which in turn helps practitioners to develop more effective campaigns. One of the common themes within the scholarly literature in public relations is an argument for ongoing theory-building in the discipline. Ferguson (1984) was one of the first to conduct a study of theory-building by public relations scholars. Her conclusions were quite dismal—only 4 percent of the articles analyzed in a content analysis of public relations academic journals contributed to theory development in the discipline (Ferguson, 1984). More recently, an expanded study of Ferguson's work found that 20 percent of articles analyzed in public relations journals contributed to theory development in the field (Sallot, Lyon, Acosta-Alzuru, & Jones, 2003). Specifically, this study found that excellence theory and theory of public relationships appeared most often (Sallot, Lyon, Acosta-Alzuru, & Jones, 2003, p. 51). This study also notes other theories appearing in the literature, including role theories, risk communication, and organizational communication theories.

Practitioners, however, often disregard theory, citing it as too difficult and much too complex to incorporate in practice. As a result, most theories in the public relations discipline never see their way into the practitioner's world. Obviously, the best case scenarios are found when theory and practice merge. Social norms is one such theory that may help bridge the gap between theory and application.

SOCIAL NORMS THEORY

The premise of social norms theory lies in one's *perceptions* of reality, not reality itself. Evolving throughout the 1990s, Berkowitz and Perkins, leading scholars in alcohol research, developed this theory as a model for understanding human behavior. Their research began in the late 1980s with criticisms of traditional alcohol-education programs on college campuses. They argued that these programs lacked a theoretical orientation and ignored a critical component—perceptions of alcohol use (Berkowitz & Perkins, 1986). As a result, Berkowitz and Perkins focused their studies exclusively on alcohol use among college students in the 1990s and began challenging traditional information campaigns. Other researchers followed in developing and applying this "new" approach to combating alcohol abuse on college campuses.

The tenants of social norms theory are embedded in the psychology and sociology disciplines, most notably attribution theory (Heider, 1958) and social learning theory (Bandura, 1977). Attribution theory focuses on social perceptions, arguing that attributions are necessary to meet a number of needs—the need to explain, to predict, and to protect oneself and one's social identity. That is, a person in a social situation observes another individual's behavior, and based on that observation, the person infers motivation and intentions. In turn, this inference is used to explain the observed behavior. Many times, however, these attributes are incorrect. This happens because a person simply does not know, or cannot explain, the context of the individual's behavior, and therefore fills in the gap with explanations, many of which are erroneous. Furthermore, a person will associate these observed behaviors as part of the individual's characteristics, thereby concluding that this is the individual's usual behavior when, in fact, it may not be.

Bandura's social learning theory argues that social behavior is learned by observing others' behaviors and by reinforcing specific behaviors. Individuals learn of these behaviors through both direct and indirect experiences with their environment. In the case of alcohol use, students may learn about drinking behaviors through direct experiences, such as those with their family. Or they may learn through indirect experiences, such as observing other college students' behaviors. For example, when a first-year college student enters an unfamiliar campus environment, he or she will learn about the consequences or rewards of his or her behavior more indirectly. The student will observe how other individuals act. An example of this would be the "next-day" stories in which students gather around to hear others brag about drinking experiences the night before. By observing the positive reinforcements of those listening to the stories, the behavior is then reinforced. This type of observation influences an individual to think and act based on how his or her peers think and act, especially with those in close proximity and with whom he or she has extended interaction (Perkins, 1991). Perkins further explains that this is because "peers set and maintain the normative standards and definitions of acceptable and valuable behavior" (p. 12). In this case, a student who finds heavy drinking unacceptable may actually embrace this behavior because it is in some way rewarded by his or her peer group. Furthermore, the student who does participate in heavy drinking feels validated, or what

Toch and Klofas (1984) refer to as "false consensus," meaning they justify their behaviors by buying into misperceptions.

Individuals also learn through direct experiences with their environment, such as a college campus. Students observe the number of alcohol-related messages displayed in residence halls, bookstores, and the campus newspaper, for example. These types of observations allow students to reconcile their concept that "everybody drinks" with the expectations, beliefs, and choices about drinking. Social learning theorists would argue that a reduction in the direct experience with the campus environment might also lead to a reconciliation of an individual's belief about the environment.

Social learning theory also helps illustrate the importance of differentiating between objective and subjective perceptions. Past studies of alcohol use among college students, for example, have focused heavily on the objective conditions—a descriptive analysis of actual drinking patterns and behaviors—while ignoring subjective conditions, such as perceived norms. Perkins (1991) argues that subjective perceptions are important because people act on their perceptions of the world in addition to acting with the real world. Therefore, to best understand peer norms, researchers need to consider both objective and subjective perceptions. Perkins theorized that the study of both objective and subjective components may be useful in helping researchers understand the importance of distinguishing between actual and perceived norms within any peer-intensive environment. This, in turn, will provide practitioners with a solid theoretical foundation for developing effective health-related campaigns.

Research in the area of high-risk drinking among college students has shown that peers provide the strongest influence on college-aged drinking, and the "development of individual drinking patterns during college takes place in the context of norms for alcohol use established and maintained within immediate peer groups" (Berkowitz & Perkins, 1987, p. 71). As a result, social norms theory postulates that an individual's behavior often is influenced by his or her perception of how those in that social group behave. That is, individuals tend to misperceive, or exaggerate, the negative health behavior of their peers. If individuals think a harmful behavior is typical, they may be more likely to engage in that behavior (Berkowitz, 1997). But social norms theory argues that these perceptions are often wrong. That is, an individual may overestimate the harmful behavior while underestimating the healthy behaviors of their peers. The theory predicts that "overestimations of problem behaviors will increase these problem behaviors, while underestimations of healthy behaviors discourage individuals from engaging in them" (Berkowitz, 2003b, p. 2).

The focus on *actual* norms is the basis of social norms theory. Social norms theory is described as a science-based method with the following assumptions:

- Misperceptions of norms reinforce negative behavior.
- Accurate perceptions increase healthy behavior.
- Multi-faceted intervention strategies are incorporated to dispel these misperceptions and to provide accurate information about a particular behavior (Likenbach, 2002).

Social norms theory can best be understood as an environmental approach, one that does not focus specifically on the individual but on perceptions a group may have about itself. This science-based method documents behaviors through survey research and focus group methodologies. Data collected through the survey research are then used to reinforce the "correct" information though social norms public relations campaigns. The communication efforts focus on the accurate information to dispel the misperceptions. In other words, if individuals understand what the true normative behavior is of their social group, they may conform more closely to the behavior of their peers.

What is being suggested for public relations practitioners is that social norms theory provides a foundation for developing intervention campaigns that focus on positive normative behavior. Social norms strategies provide students with data that illustrate the actual norms for a particular college campus. Actual norms would include statements such as, "Most students at this university drink three or fewer drinks in one sitting." The emphasis is on the use of data that yields "most" or "majority" results. Practitioners also have used social norms in large-scale efforts such as creating media coverage and affecting policy development (Linkenbach, 2002). Put simply, if a public relations message can convey that a certain behavior is the norm among peers, then behavior can be positively affected.

At this point, social norms programming has focused most notably on alcohol use (see Agostinelli, Brown, & Miller, 1995; Baer, 1994; Carter & Kahnweiler, 2000; Clapp & McDonnell, 2000; Far & Miller, 2003; Johannessen, Collins, Mills-Novoa, & Glider, 1999; Keeling, 2000; Perkins, 1997; Perkins, Meilman, Leichliter, Cashin, & Presley, 1999; Perkins & Craig, 2003; Rentner & Sadowski, 1997; Wechsler, Nelson, & Weitzman, 2000; Wechsler et al., 2002). It has also been the basis of other health-related campaigns, such as other drug use, cigarette smoking, eating disorders, and attitudes about sexual assault (Berkowitz, 2003a). Social norms programming has recently ventured out of the health field and has been used in campaigns on effective parenting (Linkenbach, Perkins, & Dejong, 2003) and social justice issues (Berkowitz, 2003a).

APPLICATION OF SOCIAL NORMS THEORY

In recent years, media coverage has been abundant in documenting how high-risk, or binge drinking, is a problem on college campuses nationwide. According to the 1999 Core Survey results, the percentage of students who had engaged in binge drinking—defined as men having five or more drinks and women four or more drinks in a row—at least once within a two-week period is 42 percent. Similarly, the 2001 update of the College Alcohol Study conducted by Wechsler found that 44 percent of students were binge drinkers (Wechsler et al., 2002). What is even more alarming, according to Wechsler, is that the frequency among binge drinkers increased from 20 percent in 1993 to 23 percent in 1999.

Recent studies also have been able to identify high-risk segments within the college student population. Among those at most risk are first-year residents, athletes, and members of Greek organizations (see Perkins & Craig, 2003;

Wechsler, Davenport, Dowdall, Grossman, & Zanakos, 1997; Kidorf, Sherman, Johnson, & Bigelow, 1995; Martin, 1998; and Leichliter, Meilman, Presley, & Cashin, 1998). For example, DeJong and Linkenbach (1999) argue that first-year students entering college are particularly vulnerable as they seek information on how to act in their new role away from home. Among athletes, 57 percent of male and 48 percent of females reported binge drinking, compared to 49 percent male and 40 percent female nonathletes, according to an alcohol-usage study (Nelson & Wechsler, 2001). Those who are members of Greek organizations report significantly higher rates of binge drinking than other students, have more tolerant views about getting drunk, and hold more positive beliefs about drinking (Borsari & Carey, 1999; Presley, Meilman, & Lyerla, 1995; Wechsler, Davenport, Dowdall, Moeykens, & Castillo, 1994). Even more staggering is that half of those students who participate in binge drinking had also done so in high school (Wechsler, Austin & DeJong, 1996).

Although researchers have been successful in identifying these high-risk segments, prevention programs have fallen short. A national survey on alcohol policies at college campuses revealed a large increase in the number of alcohol education programs at colleges and universities in the late 1970s and early 1980s (Gonzalez & Broughton, 1986). Although Gonzalez (1980) found that a few programs were successful in increasing knowledge among students, most researchers found that few of these programs were able to boast long-term successes in changing the perceptions of alcohol use by students (Bukoski, 1986; Hanson, 1982; Kraft, 1988; Oblander, 1984).

During the 1990s, most universities had policies and educational programs addressing alcohol issues in place, but very few have been able to claim success in altering perceptions and behaviors associated with drinking among college students. For example, Wechsler and colleagues (1997) found that of the 94 percent of schools with athletic programs, only 59 percent provided programs that targeted athletes. This is because most campus health and prevention centers disseminate traditional information to students that convey the physical and psychological effects about alcohol. Furthermore, the information is generally disseminated to a mass audience—an assumption that all college students share the same characteristics—while ignoring characteristics of particular audience segments. There has been little evidence indicating positive results from these approaches.

Michael Haines, a leading researcher in alcohol prevention, conducted a study that illustrated the limitations of such traditional programming. Haines described how, in the late 1980s, Northern Illinois University increased its prevention efforts through such mass media appeals as posters and flyers. Program evaluation at NIU in 1989 showed that the binge drinking rates and alcohol-related injury rates were statistically unchanged (Haines, 1996). This led Haines and his associates to a new direction in alcohol prevention programming, using social norms as the theoretical underpinning for campaign development.

The first step in campaign development, using social norms theory, is to document the gap between reality and misperceptions. This involves data collection through survey research. Questions are designed to elicit responses about actual patterns and behaviors as well as perceptions of peer groups. Analysis of these data will indicate what misperceptions occur among targeted groups.

Table 12.1 is an example comparing actual behavior and misperceptions. In this study, social norms research was conducted using a random sample of the university population. In addition, peer-intensive groups, such as first-year students, athletes,

TABLE 12.1   Perceptions and Actual Drinking Patterns Among Groups

ORGANIZATION	PERCENTAGE OF GROUP MEMBERS WHO "BINGE" DRINK (5 OR MORE DRINKS IN ONE SITTING)		
	Actual	*Perception of Group*	*Perception of Campus**
First-year students—women n = 15	33	73	93
First-year students—men n = 20	65	70	63
First-year students male/female A n = 16	50	56	75
First-year students male/female B n = 17	47	59	50
Sorority A n = 48	21	33	43
Sorority B n = 49	29	47	57
Sorority C n = 28	50	64	71
Sorority D n = 58	40	67	72
Fraternity A n = 33	55	67	70
Fraternity B n = 23	78	87	74
Athletic male team A n = 12	75	75	100
Athletic male team B n = 13	85	85	69
Athletic female team A n = 6	50	67	100
Athletic female team B n = 11	36	82	82
Athletic female team C n = 12	50	64	67
Athletic female team D n = 9	22	67	44

*Binge-drinking rate among all students at this university is 57.6 percent, according to the 1999 Core Alcohol and Drug Survey. (n = 704) Sample of each first-year student group was taken from one floor of a resident hall.

and members of Greek organizations, also were surveyed. As indicated in the table, misperceptions about binge drinking occur in each of these groups.

Once survey results of each group were analyzed, focus group discussions with members of each group were conducted to assess the "why" and "how" these misperceptions occur within the peer groups. The data collected from the universitywide survey, peer group surveys, and focus group discussions enabled campaign planners to develop social norms messages for each peer-intensive group, as well as for the overall university community. All messages emphasized the healthy behaviors of the target audiences.

Other universities have shown success using the social norms approach. For example, Hobart and William Smith colleges have shown a 40 percent reduction rate in high-risk drinking during a four-year period (Linkenbach, 2002). Other institutions—including Northern Illinois, University of Arizona, University of Missouri, and Rowan University—also have shown 12–40 percent reduction rates in high-risk drinking over two- to four-year spans (Linkenbach, 2002).

CONCLUSION

While social norms theory is not being offered here as a magic bullet to bridge the gap between theory and application, it certainly provides scholars and practitioners with a new approach for integrating theory and application. Social norms theory, best described as an environmental approach, provides a breakthrough in how practitioners develop campaigns to influence attitudinal and behavioral changes. This theory advances Bandura's (1977) social learning theory in that, while acknowledging the impact of both direct and indirect experiences as influences on attitude and behavioral changes, both researchers and practitioners must also consider the perception of these experiences. The theory predicts that those who overestimate their peers' drinking behaviors are more likely to engage in such behavior themselves. The practical implications of this are tremendous. By developing campaigns that focus on the normative behavior, target audiences are more likely to adjust their behaviors to fit the "true" norms.

Built into this process is one of the most crucial components of the public relations process—evaluation. Through the use of follow-up surveys and focus group discussions, evaluations of social norms interventions have shown decreases in high-risk drinking and increases in healthy behaviors.

While it appears to have practical and promising implications for the public relations field, social norms is in its infancy. Further application of this theory is needed, particularly in health-related campaigns. Although successes have been noted in social norms alcohol-reduction campaigns throughout the country, most programs have been in existence less than five years. Longitudinal studies should be conducted to better assess the long-term impact of public relations campaigns based on social norms theory.

For now, the challenge continues to integrate theory into practical application. The introduction of social norms theory allows both scholars and practitioners an opportunity to explore a new theoretical model for developing effective campaigns, particularly campaigns that seek to evoke positive social change.

CASE: BINGE DRINKING

As described earlier, social norms theory has most often been tested in the health communication field, particularly in the area of high-risk drinking. High-risk, or binge, drinking is defined by the Harvard School for Public Health as consuming five or more drinks in a row for men, four or more drinks in a row for women (Meilman, Cashin, McKillip, & Presley, 1998; Wechsler & Kuo, 2000). Haines, a prevention specialist at Northern Illinois University, was one of the first to apply social norms theory in a longitudinal intervention that resulted in reductions in misperceptions and were associated with increases in safe, or moderate, drinking (Haines & Spear, 1996). Since then, more than thirty studies have been published in the area of social norms programming and alcohol reduction on college campuses (see Agostinelli, Brown, & Miller, 1995; Baer, 1994; Barnett, Far, Maus, & Miller, 1996; Berkowitz, 1998; Clapp & McDonnell, 2000; Fabiano, 2001; Far & Miller, 2003; Glider et. al, 2001; Likenbach, 2003; Perkins & Craig, 2003; Rentner, 2001, Rentner & Sadowski, 1997; Scher, Bartholow, & Nanda, 2001; Thombs, 2002; Wechsler, Kelley et al., 2000).

Procedures

This case study is one of the author's ongoing research projects in the area of high-risk drinking and social norms programming. Data collection took place in 1997 and 1999 using the Core Alcohol and Drug Survey developed in 1989 by the Core Institute at Southern Illinois University. Data collected in 2000 and 2002 used the American College Health Association–National College Health Assessment Summary (ACHA) developed in 1998 by the American College Health Association. Both survey instruments contain questions ranging from actual drug and alcohol pattern and behaviors, to perceptions of others' drinking and drug-use patterns and behaviors. Samples for each survey were randomly drawn from the university listing of courses offered in the spring semesters for the Core survey and fall semesters for the ACHA survey, and were representative of the university population.

Campaign Development

Social norms campaigns began in 1997 at Bowling Green State University (BGSU), a mostly residential, rural Midwestern university of approximately 18,000 undergraduate and graduate students. Using the results from the 1997 Core survey, a social norms campaign was developed using the theme "I Don't Drink as Much as You Think." The campaign focused on positive messages that dispelled alcohol-related attitudes and behaviors of students. Comparisons of the 1997 and 1999 results showed a 2.5 percent decrease in the overall high-risk drinking rate (Rentner, 2001). Various other social norms messages also were incorporated.

In 1999, The U.S. Department of Education named BGSU as one of seven leading alcohol-reduction model programs in the nation and awarded a $78,000 grant to continue social norms research and programming. This allowed for an even more comprehensive social norms public relations campaign at this university. Data were analyzed using the 1999 Core survey, and the development of a comprehensive public relations campaign using social norms began in early 2000. Feedback from focus group discussions led to the development of the "Rise above High-Risk Drinking" campaign that incorporated posters, fliers, table tents, a speakers bureau, campus media, and faculty social norms kits. It should be noted that just prior to implementation of this new campaign, the ACHA survey was given to provide a benchmark for comparison in 2002.

Results

Results from the 2002 ACHA study conducted in the fall showed an additional 2.3 percent decrease in the high-risk drinking rate at this university (Rentner, 2003). Other changes from 2000 included:

- 4.3 percent more students reported not having had an alcohol drink at all in the previous thirty days;
- 2 percent increase in those who chose not to drink the last time they socialized and, of those who did drink, a 4 percent decrease in the number who consumed five or more drinks at a time;
- 2.8 percent decrease in students letting alcohol affect their academic performance.

The following example provides an illustration of some of the misperceptions reported in the survey: *On this campus, 1.2 percent of students drink daily. The perception is that 52.1 percent of students on this campus think their peers are drinking daily.* Correction of this misperception and others were addressed in an updated campaign in 2003. Some of these messages included:

- When BGSU students drink, *most* choose a designated driver (70 percent).
- When BGSU students drink, *most* eat before and/or during drinking (70 percent).
- *Most* BGSU students keep track of how many drinks they consume.
- As a result of their own drinking, *most* BGSU students have never experienced the following negative consequences:
    - Never been physically injured (74 percent)
    - Never been involved in a fight (87 percent)
    - Never have done something they later regretted (57 percent)
    - Never have forgotten where they were or what they had done (58 percent)
    - Never had unprotected sex (79 percent)

Evaluation

One of the most important components of any public relations campaign is evaluation. Both formative and summative evaluations are the keys to determining success of a social norms campaign. Formative evaluation is used to define the trends, attitudes, beliefs, and perceptions within a targeted population. Once surveyed, summative evaluation is used to look at the patterns across the target population and also within specific target audiences. Identification of true norms becomes the basis for a social norms campaign, and as the results of the above study indicate, social norms campaigns can successfully reduce high-risk drinking rates and other unhealthy behaviors associated with drinking.

QUESTIONS FOR APPLICATION

1. If the data were to indicate that the unhealthy behavior *is* the norm, how does this affect campaign planning?

2. Outside of health-related campaigns, what other areas might benefit from a social norms campaign?

3. What concerns, if any, should campaign planners have in using self-reported data on attitudes, behaviors, and perceptions?

4. What is the benefit of incorporating social norms theory into practice?

5. What are the benefits of questioning perception, especially when designing an informational campaign?

REFERENCES

Agostinelli, G., Brown, J. M., & Miller, W. R. (1995). Effects of normative feedback on consumption among heavy drinking college students. *Journal of Drug Education, 25*(1), pp. 31–40.

Baer, J. S. (1994). Effects of college residence on perceived norms for alcohol consumption: An examination of the first year of college. *Psychology of Addictive Behaviors, 8*, pp. 43–50.

Bandura, A. (1977). Social learning theory. Englewood Cliffs, NJ: Prentice-Hall.

Barnett, L. A., Far, J. M., Maus, A. L., & Miller, J. A. (1996). Changing perceptions of peer norms as a drinking reduction program for college students. *Journal of Alcohol and Drug Education, 96*, pp. 39–61.

Berkowitz, A. D. (1997). From reactive to proactive prevention: Promoting an ecology of health on campus. In P. C. Rivers & E. R. Shore (Eds.), *Substance abuse on campus: A handbook for college and university personnel* (chap. 6). Westport, CT: Greenwood.

———. (1998). The proactive prevention model: Helping students translate healthy beliefs into healthy actions. *About Campus (September–October)*, pp. 26–27.

———. (2003a). Applications of social norms theory to other health and social justice issues. In H. W. Perkins (Ed.), *The social norms approach to preventing school and college age substance abuse: A handbook for educators, counselors, clinicians* (pp. 259–279). San Francisco: Jossey-Bass.

———. (2003b). The social norms approach: Theory, research and annotated bibliography. A paper posted on the Higher Education Center for Alcohol and Other Drug Prevention's web site, accessed at www.edc.org/hec/.

Berkowitz, A. D., & Perkins, H. W. (1986). Problem drinking among college students: A review of recent research. *Journal of American College Health, 35*, pp. 21–28.

———. (1987). Current issues in effective alcohol education programming. *Alcohol policies and practices on college and university campuses, 7*, NASPA Monograph Series.

Borsari, M. S., & Carey, K. B. (1999). Understanding fraternity drinking: Five recurring themes in the literature, 1980–1998. *Journal of American College Health, 48*, pp. 30–37.

Bukoski, W. J. (1986). School-based substance abuse prevention: A review of program research. *Journal of Children in Contemporary Society, 18*, pp. 93–115.

Carter, C. A., & Kahnweiler, W. M. (2000). The efficacy of the social norms approach to substance abuse prevention applied to fraternity men. *Journal of American College Health, 49*, pp. 66–71.

Clapp, J. D., & McDonnel, A. L. (2000). The relationship of perceptions of alcohol promotion and peer drinking norms to alcohol problems reported by college students. *Journal of College Student Development, 41*(1), pp. 20–26.

DeJong, W., & Linkenbach, J. (1999). Telling it like it is: Using social norms marketing campaigns to reduce student drinking. *AAHE Bulletin 11–13,* p. 16.

Fabiano, P. (2001). The integration of social norms interventions into personalized feedback profiles with heavy, frequent (high-risk) college drinkers. A paper presented to the Fourth National Conference on the Social Norms Model in Anaheim, CA, July 18–20.

Far, J., & Miller, J. (2003). The small group norms-challenge model intervention: A social norms intervention with targeted high-risk groups. In H. W. Perkins (Ed.), *The social norms approach to preventing school and college age substance abuse: A handbook for educators, counselors, clinicians* (pp. 111–132). San Francisco: Jossey-Bass.

Ferguson, M. A. (1984). Building theory in public relations: Interorganizational relationships as a public relations paradigm. A paper presented to the annual meeting of the Association for Education in Journalism and Mass Communication, Public Relations Division, in Gainesville, FL, August.

Glider, P., Midyett, S., Mills-Novoa, B., Johannessen, K., & Collins, C. (2001). Challenging the collegiate rite of passage: A campus-wide social marketing campaign to reduce binge drinking. *Journal of Drug Education, 31,* pp. 207–220.

Gonzalez, G. M. (1980). The effect of a model alcohol education module on college students' attitudes, knowledge and behavior related to alcohol use. *Journal of Alcohol and Drug Education, 25,* pp. 1–12.

Gonzalez, G. M., & Broughton, E. A. (1986). Status of alcohol policies on campus: A national survey. Paper presented at the ADPA Higher Education Conference in San Antonio, Texas, April.

Haines, M. P. (1996). A social norms approach to preventing binge drinking at colleges and universities. U.S. Department of Education, Higher Education Center for Alcohol and Other Drug Prevention.

Haines, M. P., & Spear, S. F. (1996, November). Changing the perception of the norm: A strategy to decrease binge drinking among college students. *Journal of American College Health, 45,* pp. 134–140.

Hanson, D. J. (1982). The effectiveness of alcohol and drug education. *Journal of Alcohol and Drug Education, 27,* pp. 1–13.

Heider, F. (1958). *The psychology of interpersonal relations.* New York: Wiley.

Hildebrand, K. M., Johnson, D. J., & Bogle, K. (2001). Comparison of patterns of alcohol use between high school and college athletes and non-athletes. *College Student Journal, 35*(3), pp. 358–366.

Johannessen, K. J., Collins, C., Mills-Novoa, B. M., & Glider, P. (1999). *A practical guide to alcohol abuse prevention: A campus case study in implementing social norms and environmental management approaches.* Newton, MA: Higher Education Center for Alcohol and Other Drug Prevention.

Keeling, R. P. (2000). Social norms research in college health. *Journal of American College Health, 49,* pp. 53–56.

Kidorf, M., Sherman, M., Johnson, J., & Bigelow, G. (1995). Alcohol expectancies and changes in beer consumption of first-year college students. *Addictive Behaviors, 20*(2), pp. 225–231.

Kraft, D. P. (1988). The prevention and treatment of alcohol problems on a college campus. *Journal of Alcohol and Drug Education, 34*(1), pp. 37–51.

Leichliter, J. S., Meilman, P. W., Presley, C. A., & Cashin, J. R. (1998). Alcohol use and related consequences among students with varying levels of involvement in college athletics. *Journal of American College Health, 46*(6), pp. 257–262.

Linkenbach, J. (2003). The Montana model: Development and overview of a seven-step process for implementing macro-level social norms campaigns. In H. W. Perkins (Ed.), *The social norms approach to preventing school and college age substance abuse: A handbook for educators, counselors, clinicians.* (pp. 182–208). San Francisco: Jossey-Bass.

Linkenbach, J. (Ed.). (2002). The main frame: Strategies for generating social norms news. Montana State University. Retrieved Oct. 18, 2006, from http://alcohol.hws.edu/THE%20MAIN%20FRAME.pdf.

Linkenbach, J., Perkins, H. W., & Dejong, W. (2003). Parents' perceptions of parenting norms: Using the social norms approach to reinforce effective parenting. In H. W. Perkins (Ed.), *The social norms approach to preventing school and college age substance abuse: A handbook for educators, counselors, clinicians* (pp. 247–258). San Francisco: Jossey-Bass.

Martin, M. (1998). The use of alcohol among NCAA Division I female college basketball, softball and volleyball athletes. *Journal of Athletic Training, 33*(2), pp. 163–167.

Meilman, P. W., Cashin, J. R., McKillip, J. R., & Presley, C. A. (1998). Understanding the three national databases on collegiate alcohol and drug use. *Journal of American College Health, 46*(4), p. 16.

Nelson, T. F., & Wechsler, H. (2001). Alcohol and college athletes. *Medicine & Science in Sports & Exercise, 33*(1), pp. 43–47.

Oblander, F. W. (1984, October). A practice oriented synthesis: Effective alcohol education strategies. *ACU-I Bulletin,* pp. 17–23.

Perkins, H. W., (1991). *Confronting misperceptions of peer drug use norms among college students: An alternative approach for alcohol and other drug education programs* (pp. 1–29). Washington, DC: U.S. Department of Education (Fund for the Improvement of Post Secondary Education, Drug Prevention Program).

————. College student misperceptions of alcohol and other drug use norms among peers. In *Designing alcohol and other drug prevention programs in higher education: Bringing theory into practice* (pp. 177–206). Newton, MA: Higher Education Center for Alcohol and Other Drug Prevention.

Perkins, H. W., & Craig, D. A. (2003). A multi-faceted social norms approach to reduce high-risk drinking: Lessons from Hobart and William Smith Colleges. Newton, MA: Higher Education Center for Alcohol and Other Drug Prevention.

Perkins, H. W., Meilman, P. W., Leichliter, J. S., Cashin, J. R., & Presley, C. A. (1999). Misperceptions of the norms for the frequency of alcohol and other drug use on college campuses. *Journal of American College Health, 47*(6), pp. 253–258.

Presley, C. A., Meilman, P. W., & Lyerla, R. (1995). *Alcohol and drugs on American college campuses: Use, consequences, and perceptions of the campus environment.* Carbondale, IL.: Core Institute.

Rentner, T. L., (1999a). 1999 Core alcohol and drug survey. Funded by the U.S. Department of Education. Unpublished raw data, Bowing Green State University, Ohio.

————. (1999b). Survey and focus group research. Unpublished raw data.

————. (2000). Developing an alcohol misperception campaign: A nationally recognized model for college campuses. Paper and poster presented at the annual meeting of the International Communication Association, Public Relations Division, in Acapulco, Mexico, June.

————. (2001). BGSU peer-based misperception program. In D. S. Anderson & G. G. Milgram (Eds.), *Promising practices: Campus alcohol strategies sourcebook* (p. 78). Fairfax, VA: George Mason University.

————. (2003). ACHA survey research. Unpublished raw data.

Rentner, T. L., & Sadowski, R. (1997). Altering misperceptions on college campuses through peer-based programming. *Peers and Prevention, 1*(2), pp. 11–15.

Sallot, L. N., Lyon, L., Acosta-Alzuru, C., & Jones, K. O. (2003). From Aardvark to zebra: A news millennium analysis of theory development in public relations academic journals. *Journal of Public Relations Research, 15*(1), pp. 27–90.

Scher, K., Bartholow, B. D., & Nanda, S. (2001). Short- and long-term effects of fraternity and sorority membership on heavy drinking: A social norms perspective. *Psychology of Addictive Behaviors, 15,* pp. 42–51.

Toch, H., & Klofas, J. (1984). Pluralistic ignorance, revisited. In G. M. Stephenson and J. H. Davis (Eds.), *Progress in Applied Social Psychology* (vol. 2, pp. 56–82). New York: Wiley.

Thombs, D. L. (2002). A test of the perceived norms model to explain drinking patterns among university student athletes. *Journal of American College Health, 49,* pp. 75–83.

Wechsler, H., Austin, B., & Dejong, W. (1996). *Secondary effects of binge drinking on college campuses.* Newton, MA: Higher Education Center for Alcohol and Other Drug Prevention.

Wechsler, H., Davenport, A. E., Dowdall, G. W., Grossman, S. J., & Zanakos, S. I. (1997). Binge drinking, tobacco, and illicit drug use and involvement in college athletics: A survey of students at 140 American colleges. *Journal of American College Health, 45*(5), pp. 195–200.

Wechsler, H., Davenport, A. E., Dowdall, G. W., Moeykens, B., & Castillo, S. (1994). Health and behavioral consequences of binge drinking in college: A national survey of students at 140 campuses. *Journal of American College Health, 272,* 1672–1677.

Wechsler, H., Kelley, K., Weitzman, K., San Giovanni, E. R., Paul, J., & Seibring, M. (2000). What colleges are doing about student binge drinking. *Journal of American College Health, 48*(5), pp. 219–226.

Wechsler, H., & Kuo, M. (2000). College students define binge drinking and estimate its prevalence: Results of a national survey. *Journal of American College Health, 49,* pp. 57–64.

Wechsler, H., Lee, J. E., Kuo, M., Seibring, M., Nelson, T. F., & Lee, H. (2002). Trends in college binge drinking during a period of increased prevention efforts. *Journal of American College Health, 50*(5), pp. 203–217.

Wechsler, H., Nelson, T., & Weitzman, E. (2000). From knowledge to action: How Harvard's college alcohol study can help your campus design a campaign against student alcohol abuse. *Change, 32*(1), pp. 38–43.

RHETORICAL PERSPECTIVES— COMMUNICATION AS RELATIONSHIP

Bonita Dostal Neff

Tricia Hansen-Horn

Rhetoric has a long tradition and contributes to public relations from both an ethical and a process perspective. As one of the three pillars of public relations, Heath presents rhetorical theory as the essence of the profession.

Viewing public relations through the rhetoric of social invention, Opt uses rhetoric as a means to interpret change and the consequences of such. It is the use of the rhetorical perspective that allows one to interpret communicative impact on organizations and publics. Ultimately, as relationships are redefined the language for the relationships changes.

CHAPTER THIRTEEN

RHETORICAL THEORY, PUBLIC RELATIONS, AND MEANING
Giving Voice to Ideas

ROBERT L. HEATH

Much of public relations research, especially that by academicians in the past thirty years of the twentieth century, has focused on processes. Some of the these processes fall under the broad umbrella of media relations and other aspects of how public relations affects and is affected by the mass media, especially news reporting and commentary. Often when advice is given (but rarely research is conducted) academics focus on the need for openness and even candor, not persuasion, to be symmetrical in dealing with publics and markets. This focus on process and lack of insight regarding the content of communication begs a huge question: What should or do public relations practitioners communicate about, or what is the content of that communication?

The Grunig and Hunt (1984; Grunig, 1992) legacy of two-way symmetrical communication as the essence of excellent public relations features the concept of communication management and rests on the processes of communication best appreciated through the eyes of systems theory. Simply put, this view of public relations rests on the powerful assumption that systems do not like imbalance. If a relationship between an organization and any of its publics is asymmetrical, there is an inherent tension that is predicted to lead to corrective actions. Systems theory advises openness, the ease of information flow into and from one system to another. But what is the content of that information?

Systems theory is aethical. For instance, if some cataclysmic event, such as a massive asteroid or huge volcanic eruption, caused the end of some massive lineage of animal species, so be it, says systems theory. If a species cannot compete and becomes extinct, so be it. The fact that meat-eating predators kill and consume small bunnies and deer fawns, so be it. That's the nature of the system. Enter rhetoric and its companion, ethics: Rhetorical theory invests the human character and judgment explicitly into the meaning of communication. Also, ethics believes that the credibility of the statements of an organizational spokesperson is vital to the social usefulness of the communication.

As humans intrude into natural systems, they bring imbalance, ethics, and meaning. Human intellect and value systems can upset and even destroy a system. Environmentalists, for instance, inject values and meaning into those circumstances. Thus, rhetoric and ethics enter the equation. Environmentalists may call on one another and seek regulatory or legislative change (even judicial intercession) to prevent damage to a system. For centuries, rhetoricians—theorists and practitioners of rhetoric—have known that the first step toward being an effective communicator is to demonstrate high standards of character.

Once we have judgment, the potentiality for enlightened choice, we have seen the need for and invitation to understand, critique, and engage in rhetoric and ethical decision making. Enlightened choice assumes that people must have information—facts—and the interpretative frames needed to appropriately understand how well the information informs various conclusions. Facts do not come prepackaged into conclusions. Enlightened choice assumes that people think about and contest the accuracy, adequacy, relevance, and usefulness of facts at hand. They consider the best values to use in making a specific decision and the wisdom of various policies. This contest, simply conceptualized as statement and counter statement, is the essence of the rhetorical tradition. This chapter explores the three pillars of public relations theory, the rhetorical heritage, and the usefulness of this heritage for public relations theory.

THREE PILLARS OF PUBLIC RELATIONS THEORY

Messages and the meaning they produce are an essential result of public relations. Practitioners believe they are in the *message and meaning business,* the first pillar. Among other concerns, public relations theory and professional best practices require a solid understanding of messages and the meaning they can create—as well as how they can fail to adequately address rhetorical problems confronted by their employers and clients. Practitioners are paid to influence what people know, think, and do. The rhetorical heritage provides a long-standing and constantly developing body of strategic and critical insights to help practitioners be effective and ethical in the way they create messages and participate in the process by which society creates meaning. Rhetorical theory more recently has combined with organizational communication theory to feature the reality that all actions—the enactment of meaning—by organizations is rhetorical (Heath, 2001, 2005).

Systems theory, the second pillar, is useful for understanding and improving the processes of public relations, but it fails to help practitioners and scholars understand which messages are strategically and ethically relevant to each task. For more than two thousand years in Western civilization, the rhetorical heritage has examined the nature of messages and the strategic challenges in addressing rhetorical problems that demand the formation of shared meaning—socially constructed reality (Palenchar, 2005).

Critical studies that have been heavily influenced by European thinkers complete the troika of pillars for public relations. Some lines of critical investigation grow from the rhetorical heritage. Other approaches to criticism draw heavily on social theory to investigate and critique the roles large organizations play in the quality of the discourse of society. Critical studies centers its attention on hegemonies that dominate social thought, communication processes, and power resource management.

Rhetorical theory features the role information, or fact, plays in shaping knowledge and opinions as well as motivating actions. It addresses the ways that evaluations are debated and confirmed or challenged through discourse. It contests the wisdom and expedience of various policies. Rhetoric is a form of courtship (or courtship is rhetorical) by which individuals invite one another to evaluate and accept interpretations of fact, value, and policy, and to form identifications of various kinds. People compete through public debate to assert the strength of their ideas, their interpretations of facts. They know that others may disagree. Rhetoric is inherently dialogic. It assumes multiple voices. If one view is widely accepted, then alternative views are not voiced. Assuming that alternative views have merit, they are set before interested parties for consideration. Voices respond because they disagree or agree with one another. This spirited debate is the essence of the rhetorical heritage that believes in the right and ability of people to get messages and make judgments accordingly.

Rhetoric ultimately instantiates the democratic process because it presumes that one position voiced in public must be sufficiently compelling to withstand the logical critique voiced by other rhetors who believe their competing ideas have merit. Tyrants may speak without overt opposition, but in so doing they distort the rhetorical process, not apply it in its best tradition.

RHETORICAL HERITAGE: MEANING AND THE GOOD ORGANIZATION COMMUNICATING WELL

Rhetoric, as a term, has fell on hard times in the past four decades. During the antiwar and activist protest era of the 1960s, the cry of the agitator, in response to any establishment statement, was, "That is pure rhetoric." In this way, rhetoric, instead of signaling informed and reasoned discourse, came to be associated with sham and hollowness. Media reporters picked up this meaning of the term.

By this influence, many people acquired a narrow and limited understanding of rhetoric, as deceptive and shallow statements made falsely in an effort to manipulate and control rather than to reveal or debate fact, value, and policy. It is associated with spin, vacuous statements, propaganda, and pandering to audiences' base interests. Some may see it only as telling people what they want to know or are willing to accept, rather than relying on judgments of knowledge, truth, and good reasons.

Adhering to the best Western rhetorical heritage, academic programs in English and speech communication include courses in rhetoric and rhetorical studies. Studied and taught in that context, the term refers to the strategic options of communication influence within ethical standards. It is the rationale for suasory discourse. As a discipline, it addresses the ways people persuasively appeal to assert and challenge fact, value, and policy. It recognizes that humans deal with their lives through words and other influential symbols. They create collective action by appealing to one another. They dispute, cajole, agree, identify, challenge, and confirm. All of this is the domain of rhetoric, the rationale for forging conclusions and influencing actions. Rhetorical theory explains how people cocreate meaning through dialogue that can define and build mutually beneficial relationships.

Rhetoric is the rationale for effective discourse. It consists of a well-established body of strategic guidelines regarding how messages need to be proved, structured, framed, and worded. It is interested in how each message needs to be designed to be informative and persuasive. Because rhetorical theory arises out of disputes, doubts, and differences of opinion, it offers guidelines on how people can negotiate differences and work together in collaborative decision making. It informs, creates divisions, and bridges divisions. It motivates people to make one choice in preference to another. If people everywhere shared the same information, opinion, and motives, there would be no need for rhetoric. At its best, it is founded on the substance of good reasons and can help make society better for all. At its worst, it can engage in deception, manipulation, slander, character assassination, distortion, misinformation, and disinformation.

Champions of the rhetorical heritage believe that freedom of discourse is the best answer to the misuse of the art. The best corrective for deception, for instance, is public debate. In this format, a demonstrated case that one side of a controversy is engaging in can be discovered to be false, manipulative, or deceptive. Public discourse, the forum of rhetoric, allows for combatants to challenge, correct, and elevate the discourse of society.

Society, according to Kenneth Burke (1969a), is a marketplace of competing ideas. This marketplace requires rhetoric which addresses "the Scramble, the Wrangle of the Marketplace, the flurries and flare-ups of the Human Barnyard, Give and Take, the wavering line of pressure and counter pressure, the Logomachy, the onus of ownership, the War of Nerves, the War" (p. 23). For society to function at its best, actions of the people of society need to be coordinated based on shared, cocreated meaning.

Cooperation, even competition, requires rhetoric to foster shared perspectives and coordinated ways of acting in concert. Each perspective is a way of thinking. It is based on a set of facts and an interpretation of those facts. Each perspective offers its unique way of viewing reality. The terms of the perspective focus attention in unique ways and feature some alternatives as being preferable to others. For instance sports enthusiasts share a perspective whereby athletic competition is entertaining. That perspective might clash with one that is based on the fine arts. We can easily imagine the perspective of a sports enthusiast leading to different motives than one that prefers the fine arts. One person, by this logic, would want to see a ball game rather than attend the opera or symphony.

Family feuds come from competing perspectives. Religions constitute different perspectives. Perspectives are fostered and countered by marketing, advertising, and publicity. Some people want pickups, and others prefer sports cars. Some individuals support the unlimited possession of guns; others call for restraint, reflecting a different perspective. Activists—concerned citizens in a community—might argue with school board officials to avoid cuts in spending for the arts while athletics remains fully funded. Thus, rhetoric gives voice to competing preferences.

Championing the role of rhetoric in society, Lentz (1996) reasoned: "Truth should prevail in a market-like struggle where superior ideas vanquish their inferiors and achieve audience acceptance" (p. 1). The rhetorical heritage, Kennedy (1963) noted, rests largely on the thoughts that formed ancient Greek and Roman societies. "In its origin and intention rhetoric was natural and good: it produced clarity, vigor, and beauty, and it rose logically from the conditions and qualities of the classical mind" (p. 3).

Rather than being vacuous or hollow, rhetoric is best when it puts information and thoughtful interpretations before audiences for their consideration. Rhetoric is enlivened with facts, as well as values and policy recommendations. It deals with choice (Nichols, 1963). Which choice is best, most correct, wisest, and preferable? Rather than featuring rhetoric as vacuous statements, Aristotle (1952c) believed that the communicator is obliged to prove any point he or she asserts. Proofs of several kinds are the substance of rhetoric. These proofs are logical when they deal with facts and employ sound reasoning. They feature emotions as part of human nature. They reveal the character of the speaker. In this way, audiences can assess the credibility of all speakers by considering the values on which they base their life and build their messages. The end to which all discourse should be aimed, Aristotle (1952c) reasoned, was what was good for society. He worked to inspire people who used rhetoric to do so because it advanced the quality of society. Values and good reasons have been a classic ingredient of rhetorical discourse, along with a scrupulous interest in the soundness of arguments based on fact and flawless reasoning (Wallace, 1963; Weaver, 1953).

Ethics is a fundamental ingredient in rhetoric. Drawing from the work of Aristotle and other Greeks, a Roman teacher, Quintilian (1951) was firm: "My ideal orator, then, is the true philosopher, sound in morals and with full knowledge of speaking, always striving for the highest" (p. 20). He continued: "If a case is based on injustice, neither a good man [nor woman] nor rhetoric has any place in it" (p. 106). Such advice should inspire organizations using public relations to seek first to be ethical as a prerequisite for sound communication. For more than 2,500 years, people who consider the nature and societal role of rhetoric have recognized the need to be ethical as a first step toward being an effective communicator. Any organization that does not aspire to the highest levels of corporate responsibility is likely to find that its actions discredit its statements. Actions speak, and they speak louder than words.

One of the easy connections to make between systems, rhetoric, and ethics is based on the challenge issued by Quintilian (1951). As Grunig (1992) and others have argued, the excellent organization not only becomes so through communication but also communicates in ways that foster and demonstrate its excellence because of its character, its adherence to higher rather than narrow and self-interested standards and values.

Appeals to join one point of view, make one choice in preference of another, is the rationale for rhetoric. People identify with one another as they share perspectives. Thus, perspectives become the basis of rhetorical appeals. Advocates reason that one perspective is superior to its competitors. They court others to agree, to see the world in a particular way and to prefer some actions instead of others. Public relations uses identification in publicity. It informs, evaluates, and recommends. For instance, practitioners might publicize a baseball team, an amusement part, or a brand of exercise equipment.

Burke (1969b) argued that rhetoric is a form of courtship—or perhaps courtship is a form of rhetoric. Either way, it is easy to see public relations functions, such as publicity and promotion especially, as being organizational forms of courtship based on appeals to identification. In its best sense, rhetoric is invitational, asking people to consider alternative points of view (Foss & Griffin, 1995). Rhetoric appeals to people to make adjustments to one another and to ideas that can foster consensus and coordination (Bryant, 1953). Skilled communicators adapt ideas to people. They know that if ideas are too foreign, they will be rejected. Ideas change slowly.

A nonprofit organization might, for this reason, ask that donors adapt to the ideals and mission of the organization by giving modest amounts of money to support its charity. The nature of its charity has to be adapted to the people, by demonstrating that it fits with their values and preferences. Rhetoric also asks that people adjust to ideas. They might not at first accept the rationale for giving, but over time they can be convinced that this charity makes the community a better place to live.

Where there is agreement, rhetoric is not needed. Its rationale comes from uncertainty, doubt, difference of motive, and difference of opinion. In ancient Greece and Rome, individuals spoke in public to advocate one point of view in contest with competing views. Today, in an increasingly global society, organizations, instead of people, tend to speak or otherwise communicate. Even when individual voices stand out, they do so because they speak for an institution, an organization and even a nation. The newsworthiness of their case is not only where they agree with others, but also where they disagree. This is as true for the promotion of products as it is for the advocacy of going to war or seeking peace. The voice might be a publicist for a small company advocating the virtues of its product, or the president of a mighty nation seeking support for some policy or course of action.

Rhetoric can emphasize difference. Public relations practitioners may communicate to differentiate one product or service from another. Activists offer publics a choice between one vision of the future versus another. They might ask audiences to support them for increased sanctions against drunken driving as an enlightened choice to save lives and reduce injuries.

Rhetorical statements create narratives that give meaning to people's lives. We can imagine that narrative is one of the most characteristic forms of rhetorical statement. From childhood, we are taught that stories begin with "once upon a time" and may end "happily ever after." They might also have tragic endings. Narrative gives form and substance to rhetorical statements. Reporters use the form and substance in news reports. If the report is a crisis, then responding organizations engage in the narrative so that society eventually learns the "story" to account for what happened, why it happened, and what will be done to prevent its recurrence. Events, a standard public relations tool, are designed to have narrative form and content. Practitioners want audiences to pay attention to see who is doing what, why, how, when, and where. One of the major publicity events each year in the United States is the Academy Awards ceremony. Prior to the big night—and following it—stories are told about actors and other artists to attract audiences to see who won, why they won, what they wore, how they reacted to victory or defeat, and where the movie will be playing next.

Large organizations and activists often engage in advocacy and counteradvocacy regarding narratives of the future. The focal question is whether certain products or services as well as operations will lead to a tragic end or a "happily ever after" outcome. This competition asks listeners, readers, and viewers to adopt one narrative, one vision of the future, and make choices based on that preference. Activists often use the rhetorical tactic of comparing a picture of a dire future to one that is better. They advocate changes to avoid the dire future and achieve the better one.

Society cannot function without rhetoric. When it is working at its best, rhetoric serves society to foster enlightened choice. Its vitality originates from the reality that facts require interpretation, some values are better than others when making specific decisions, and policies always require contingency and expedience.

Each rhetorical statement is a strategic response to a rhetorical problem. A rhetorical problem is an exigency that must be addressed because it raises doubt on some matter relevant to the actions and choices made by an organization. This problem sets the conditions for an appropriate response. A crisis, for instance, might constitute a rhetorical problem. This problem is different depending on the cause of the crisis.

A rhetorical enactment view of public relations acknowledges that all of what each organization does and says becomes meaningful because of interpretations—meaning—people place on those actions and statements (Heath, 2001, 2005). Markets can be influenced, as well as activist publics, by what the organization does and says—and by what it does not do or does not say.

Publics offer competing perspectives through their rhetorical efforts that challenge the views and actions of organizations. For instance, community activists might be concerned about soot emitted from a manufacturing facility. They may call for higher standards of environmental aesthetics as well as public health and safety. These calls might include letters to opinion leaders, speeches and rallies, and lobbying efforts with appropriate regulators. Disgruntled customers vote with their feet and credit cards. They support one business by making a purchase from it. At the same time, this choice makes a statement of a lack of support for competitors.

Rhetorical theory champions the spirit and principles of the First Amendment to the U.S. Constitution. The right to speak is testimony to the positive role that public discourse plays in society. Rhetoric is a body of principles and strategies that strengthens the voice and enlivens the ideas of competing points of view. As it informs the way individuals communicate for themselves, it also is relevant for the practice of public relations. It offers strategies and challenges, but ultimately rests on the principle that to be effective each individual or organization needs first to be ethical, good. The next section examines the heritage of the connection between rhetoric and ethics.

"PR" THEORY AND PRACTICE: THE NEXUS OF RHETORIC AND ETHICS

Popular interpretations and uses of the word rhetoric treat the term narrowly and tend not to understand the problems of making discourse ethical as well as effective. This challenge is not new. Debate over the factors that make ethical and effective discourse reaches back at least to the time of Plato.

Plato: A Critic of Rhetoric and Ethics

Few critics have issued a sharper review of rhetorical ethics than did Plato. He challenged scholars of the rhetorical tradition to consider how discourse must be based on truth and high ethical appeals. He doubted that rhetoric could avoid using false accusations and contrived evidence that can lead to unethical ends. In the grounding of his indictment, he was pained by what he thought were contrived charges that had led to the false condemnation of his mentor, Socrates, and the order that he commit suicide for the good of society. In place of rhetoric, Plato preferred dialectic as a way to decide truth and favored the judgment of the philosopher who could use wisdom to be king.

Despite Kennedy's (1963) sense of ancient Greeks' love for public discourse logically crafted and eloquently presented, Plato (1952) caustically cautioned that "rhetoric is not an art at all, but the habit of a bold and ready wit, which knows how to manage mankind: this habit I sum up under the word 'flattery'" (p. 262). In modern terms, Plato might reason that rhetoric is spin, where truth is not as important as its appearance. In his estimation, rhetoric was an art similar to cookery, the use of ingredients to prepare a meal, not a means to discover the truth or improve knowledge.

Plato's challenge forced theorists and practitioners to be mindful of ethics, but his narrowing distortion of the sociopolitical role of the rhetorical tradition denied people access to means by which to engage in public discourse to share information, propose opinions, and seek mutually beneficial solutions to collective problems. Thus, rather than enriching the robust body of literature concerning the confluence of rhetorical and ethical theory, he essentially skirted the problem by denigrating public discourse as a potential means for ethical public policy decision making.

Whereas rhetoric could lead people to draw unfortunate conclusions, dialectic, Plato's preferred mode of learning the truth, could be used to disclose truth through focused exchange. But it assumed that one party in that exchange was more knowledgeable leading the other party to a predetermined truth. Those who oppose this view, that one party knows the truth and uses dialogue, prefer open dialogue, rhetoric, through which higher standards of truth and ethical judgment arise. Through rhetoric (see, Brummett, 1995; Burke, 1969a; L'Etang, 1996; Lentz, 1996), each voice in the dialogue can enrich this search for truth and right judgment.

Cynics doubt that conclusion. In the Platonic tradition, some critics believe that ethics cannot be forged through dialogue, but are predetermined and a priori to discussions and decisions. Plato's assessment of rhetoric, which is also voiced today, extends to public relations if it is vacuous, manipulative spin-doctoring. To support socially responsible ends, public relations must put into play the best information evaluated by the most ethical observations in support of mutually beneficial choices.

Aristotle: A Full Step Forward toward Blending Rhetoric and Ethics

Aristotle, a pupil of Plato, built an extensive rationale for rhetoric and documented strategies that could advance the good of society. His investigation enriched the rhetorical tradition by focusing on the ethics of the process and substance of public discourse as contributing to the good of society.

Three themes emerge from Aristotle's writing that are vital to the discourse of public relations: the need to demonstrate the merits of each case, to establish the character of the communicator, and to foster the good of society. Aristotle investigated ethics, politics, and rhetoric, and explored the interconnectedness of these disciplines that he believed were inseparable. By his demonstration, people favorably disposed to rhetoric have come to believe that its theory and practice must rest on a profound understanding of the role of discourse in a society, preferably one more disposed to democratic dispute rather than to royal proclamation.

Two lines of analysis support this conclusion. One reason is that rhetorical discourse must search for ideas that truly reflect the interests of people in society, that which is good for them. This search for good is never independent of ethics. The character of each speaker, that person's credibility, depends largely on the values that drive the person's life choices as well as underpin the reasons for or against any proposed action. Rhetorical scholars have argued that the substance of rhetoric is good reasons (Wallace, 1963) that promote the search for a higher vision of ourselves (Weaver, 1953, 1970).

Aristotle believed that the character of public speakers—the predominant form of communication in the golden age of Greece—was vital to their success or failure. Concern for character has underpinned 2,500 years of interest in what increases or decreases communicators' credibility. The term *ethos* in Greek was the ancient predecessor of the contemporary term for source credibility and the term *ethics*. Both considerations focused attention on the extent to which some person's action or statement demonstrated varying degrees of morality or virtue and character.

The rhetorical tradition concludes that people with higher credibility are more believable because they associate their lives and the cases they make with higher order values. Audiences are more trusting, rightly so, of those whom they exhibit character based on higher standards of morality and virtue.

Aristotle set two high ethical standards for those who engage in rhetoric. One is the need to demonstrate through evidence the factual basis for any claims advocated. The second is to demonstrate through the values espoused that the person has a high sense of what is good. What is it that distinguishes a speaker's character? Aristotle (1952c) answered, "good sense, good moral character, and goodwill" (p. 623). Standards of the "good" are basic to rhetoric that "exists to affect the giving of decisions" by listeners (readers or viewers) who then decide among the positions presented to them (p. 622).

Aristotle thought that public discourse in and of itself motivated communicators to seek the best—strongest and ethically best—points of view because these were contested in public where they received penetrating analysis. Aristotle believed the process entailed the seeking of truth through the process of public advocacy rather than leaving truth to be known (in the Platonic sense) by the singular analytic efforts of any "philosopher king." Thus, Aristotle took a stand that was comfortable with the current preference for two-way symmetrical communication. As Aristotle would argue, each side is neither inherently correct nor morally right, but the process of exchange can reveal the interests of both sides so they can achieve a win-win, integrative outcome based on collaborative decision making.

Responding to Plato's challenge, Aristotle (1952c) defended rhetoric as "the counterpart of dialectic" (p. 593). Dialectic was devoted to the discovery of sound ideas. Rhetoric was used to form, assert, and dispute ideas in public forums to achieve socially relevant ends. As Aristotle viewed this relationship between the discovery and exposition of ideas, he concluded that rhetoric is "the faculty of observing in any given case the available means of persuasion" (p. 595). The essence of persuasion is demonstration "since we are most fully persuaded when we consider a thing to have been demonstrated" (p. 594). Truth as it can best be known emerges through proof and reasoning presented for others to consider.

With rhetoric, people collectively make decisions and form policy for the public good. In the opinion of Aristotle (1952b) regarding politics, "If all communities aim at some good, the state or political community, which is the highest of all, and which embraces all the rest, aims at good in a greater degree than any others, and at the highest good" (p. 445). Thus, rhetoric is judged by the quality of the process and its outcomes: "A man [or woman] can confer the greatest of benefits by a right use of these [techniques], and inflict the greatest of injuries by using them wrongly" (p. 594). "Every state is a community of some kind, and every community is established with a view of some good; for mankind always acts in order to obtain that which they think 'good'" (p. 445). Good can either be prescribed by one philosopher king (elitism) or decided by the populace (democracy).

The First Amendment of the U.S. Constitution sees free expression as a way to discover the public interest, will, and ethic. Society calls for rhetoric to steward the mutual benefit of those who have an interest in the resolving differences and making enlightened choices. What, according to Aristotle (1952c), is the source of persuasiveness? "A statement is persuasive and credible either because it is directly self-evident or because it appears to be proved from other statements that are so" (p. 596). Aristotle believed that "Persuasion is achieved by the speaker's personal character when the speech is so spoken as to make us think him [or her] credible. We believe good men [and women] more fully and more readily than other" (p. 595).

Whether in a person or an organization, character is central to the rhetorical process because outcomes have consequence. For Aristotle (1952c), rhetoric served to give counsel "on matters about which people deliberate; matters, namely, that ultimately depend on ourselves, and which we have it in our power to set going" (p. 599). What do people rely on as they draw conclusions of that sort? Aristotle thought bad character undoes persuasion:

> False statements and bad advice are due to one or more of the following three causes. Men [or women] either form a false opinion through want of good sense; or they form a true opinion, but because of their moral badness do not say what they really think; or finally, they are both sensible and upright, but not well disposed to their hearers, and may fail in consequence to recommend what they know to be the best course. (p. 623)

This challenge asks whether knowledge and sound choice exist independent of the rhetorical process. Is rhetorical dialogue engaged by ethical people the best way to discover truth and make sound judgment?

When a rhetorician recommends a conclusion or action, he or she does so "on the ground that it will do good; if he [or she] urges its rejection, he [or she] does so on the ground that it will do harm" (Aristotle, 1952c, p. 598). People and societies are evaluated by the ends to which they aspire (Aristotle, 1952c, p. 608). Rhetoric is used to explore ways of achieving happiness by making choices that will do good and avoid or at least minimize harm. Aristotle (1952c) observed that, "When we know a thing, and have decided about it, there is no further use in speaking about it" (p. 639).

Centering attention on the connection between communication and ethics, Aristotle (1952a) began his *Nichomachean Ethics* by noting that "Every art and every inquiry, and similarly every action and pursuit, is thought to aim at some good; and for this reason the good has rightly been declared to be that at which all things aim" (p. 339). "Therefore, virtue is a kind of mean, since, as we have seen, it aims at what is intermediate" (p. 352). For Aristotle, the higher ethical position was one that struck an appropriate balance between ethical extremes. Thus, ethics in theory and application must recognize "that moral virtue is a mean, then, and in what sense it is so, and that it is a mean between two vices, the one involving excess and the other deficiency, and that is such because its character is to aim at what is intermediate in passions and in actions" (p. 354). He firmly believed that some actions and morals were bad in and of themselves: "But not every action nor every passion admits of a mean; for some have names that already imply badness, e.g. spite, shamelessness, envy, and in the case of actions adultery, theft, murder" (p. 352).

For Aristotle (1952a), "It is no easy task to be good. For in everything it is no easy task to find the middle" (p. 376). For him, ethics is a balance between excess and deficit. It is something that is learned, one might suggest, through thoughts and actions that pit extremes against one another. The search is for the middle between the extremes, a win-win midpoint. He was interested in justice and the search for justice: "We see that all men [and women] mean by justice that kind of state of character which makes people disposed to do what is just and makes them act justly and wish for what is just; and similarly by injustice that state which makes them act unjustly and wish for what is unjust" (p. 376). Thus, the tug of ethics is the process of knowing a state and its contrary state. Thus, the state of lying is known as a contrast to the state of telling the truth.

This view lays a foundation for his *Politics,* which frames his thoughts on rhetoric. Aristotle (1952b) began his treatise on politics:

> Every state is a community of some kind, and every community is established with a view to some good; for mankind always act in order to obtain that which they think good. But, if all communities aim at some good, the state or political community, which is the highest of all, and which embraces all the rest, aims at good in the greater degree than any others, and at the highest good. (p. 445)

"Virtue, then is a state of character concerned with choice. Lying in a mean, i.e. the mean relative to us, this being determined by a rational principle, and by that principle by which the man [or woman] of practical wisdom would determine it" (Aristotle, 1952a, p. 352).

In his *Rhetoric* (1952c), Aristotle argued that "rhetoric is useful (1) because things that are true and things that are just have a natural tendency to prevail over their opposites, so that if the decisions of judges are not what they ought to be, the defeat must be due to the speakers themselves, and they must be blamed accordingly" (p. 594). In this statement, Aristotle blends advocacy and symmetry (the essence of his ethics) in all rhetorical processes. The essence of rhetoric is statement and counterstatement in search for the truth. Aristotle's view, similar to symmetrical public relations, assumes that each voice deserves to be heard and judged for the merits of what is said. The voice of big business or government is not inherently superior to others. One voice should not drown out others. Appeals should be made in what can be seen as an asymmetrical approach to critical publics.

> No other of the arts draws opposite conclusions: dialectic and rhetoric alone do this. Both these arts draw opposite conclusions impartially. Nevertheless, the underlying facts do not lend themselves equally well to the contrary views. No: things that are true and things that are better are, by their nature, practically always easier to prove and easier to believe in. (p. 594)

Thus, for Aristotle, the strength of the case was not its deceit but its demonstration. Through demonstration the judges of claims could determine which is best. This seems to be two-way symmetrical, and even lays the foundation for his definition of persuasion: "Persuasion is clearly a sort of demonstration, since we are most fully persuaded when we consider a thing to have been demonstrated" (Aristotle, 1959c, p. 594). Great good can be done by using rhetoric ethically. The opposite can lead to harm. Aristotle (1952c) reasoned:

> Persuasion is achieved by the speaker's personal character when the speech is so spoken as to make us think him [or her] credible. We believe good men [and

women] more fully and more readily than others; this is true generally whatever the question is, and absolutely true where exact certainty is impossible and opinions are divided. This kind of persuasion, like the others, should be achieved by what the speaker says, not by what people think of his [or her] character before he [or she] begins to speak. (p. 595)

The rhetorician "must, it is clear, be able (1) to reason logically, (2) to understand human character and goodness in their various forms, and (3) to understand the emotions." Thus, "rhetoric is an offshoot of dialectic and also of ethical studies" (p. 595).

In these ways, Aristotle offered two important themes that help us understand and appreciate the connection between ethics and communication as a foundation for public relations practice and scholarship. Each communicator, Aristotle believed, puts his or her character on the line by the content of what is said and the ends to which statements are made. People must prove their claims and demonstrate that they aspire to the highest values in all that they do and say. This challenges the communicator to know and work for what is good for the community. The rhetorical tradition features as its most enduring standard that communicators need to be ethical in purpose and means seeking to advocate positions that advance the good of each community where they speak and operate. This standard is amplified by others in the rhetorical tradition such as Isocrates and Quintilian.

Isocrates: Rhetorical Training Depends on Social Responsibility

Isocrates' opinions on rhetoric coupled with his sense of how citizens need to prepare to serve society. He recognized the need for civic education, since each generation hands on to each following generation the reins of governance. How men and women are educated will shape how they govern. If they are educated to understand the power of persuasion and its responsible role for collective decision making in the public interest, they will act accordingly when it is their turn to lead society.

Isocrates (1929) observed that the first requirement of the effective communicator is "a mind which is capable of finding out and learning the truth and of working hard and remembering what it learns" (p. 293). Communication is not an art where a facile mind and a quick wit should be the rule; rather, the best rhetorician is a thinker devoted to truth in service to society.

As did Aristotle, Isocrates (1929) observed that rhetoric was a responsibility of each citizen and an essential element of an effective and ethical society. To this end, he reasoned:

> Because there has been implanted in us the power to persuade each other and to make clear to each other whatever we desire, not only have we escaped the life of wild beasts, but we have come together and founded cities and made laws and

invented arts; and, generally speaking there is no institution devised by man [or woman] which the power of speech has not helped us to establish. For this it is which has laid down laws concerning things just and unjust, and things honourable and base; and if it were not for these ordinances we should not be able to live with one another. It is by this also that we confute the bad and extol the good. Through this we educate the ignorant and appraise the wise; for the power to speak well is taken as the surest index of a sound understanding, and discourse which is true and lawful and just is taken as the surest index of a sound understanding, and discourse which is true and lawful and just is the outward image of a good and faithful soul. (p. 327)

The key to discourse is not its nature alone, but its role in the service to society. Sham and deceit may occur in the substance and strategies used by rhetoricians, but time will reveal those devices and their deficiencies (Isocrates, 1929).

In Isocrates' view, society is the benefactor of people trained to be effective and ethical communicators. Each citizen—today, even corporate citizens—must learn and apply the principles of strategic and ethical communication. That end must not narrowly be the service of some participant's self-interest, but the collective interest of all. Through robust dialogue, as Isocrates argued, a better, more ethical society can be crafted. "With this faculty we both contend against others on matters which are open to dispute and seek light for ourselves on things which are unknown; for the same arguments which we use in persuading others when we speak in public, we employ also when we deliberate in our own thoughts" (p. 327). To achieve this end, Isocrates knew that the study of what is good for society is the essence of improving the ethical standards of communicators.

In contrast to Plato, Isocrates reasoned that no one can know with certainty what is best or what is the best path to achieve the most desirable outcomes. Reasoning, knowledge, and the ability to communicate were, in his opinion, essential tools to that end: "I hold that man [or woman] to be wise who is able by his [or her] powers of conjecture to arrive generally at the best course" (p. 335). Education in communication theory and skills is essential to be a worthy citizen:

When anyone elects to speak or write discourses which are worthy of praise and honour, it is not conceivable that he [or she] will support causes which are unjust or petty or devoted to private quarrels, and not rather those which are great and honourable, devoted to the welfare of man or woman and our common good; for if he [or she] fails to find causes of this character, he [or she] will accomplish nothing to the purpose. (pp. 337–339)

Not only the ends, but the means of communication rest on sound ethical purpose. In the matter of means, character counts:

The man [or woman] who wishes to persuade people will not be negligent as to the matter of character; no, on the contrary, he [or she] will apply himself [or herself] above all to establish a most honourable name among his [or her] fellow-citizens;

> for who does not know that words carry greater conviction when spoken by men [or women] of good repute than when spoken by men [or women] who live under a cloud, and that the argument which is made by a man's [or woman's] life is of more weight than that which is furnished by words. (p. 339)

The ethical challenge, one can assume Isocrates would argue, has not changed over the past two thousand years: "Therefore, the stronger a man's [or woman's] desire to persuade his hearers, the more zealously will he [or she] strive to be honourable and to have the esteem of his fellow-citizens" (p. 339).

Citizens, Isocrates advised those of his age, need to be effective communicators. One can argue the same is true today, including corporate citizens using public relations. Ours is an age of organizational rhetoricians, instead of individuals themselves speaking or writing for public evaluation. It is a citizenship responsibility to participate in dialogue.

Quintilian: A Teacher of Ethical Rhetoric and Ethical Speakers

Greek philosophers realized two basic facts: People must be good and they must be effective communicators to be excellent citizens, enjoying the privilege of engaging in discourse and knowing how to meet the burden of responsible communication. They offered this legacy of learning and citizenship to the Romans who followed.

Picking up this tradition, Marcus Fabius Quintilian took a perspective that supports the paradigm for public relations as the good organization communicating well. Each organization should strive to be moral and communicate well to satisfy the interests of their markets, audiences, and publics. Only propositions that are justifiable and ethical can sustain themselves against the scrutiny of counter rhetoric.

On this point, Quintilian (1951)—scholar of rhetoric in ancient Rome—was firm: "My ideal orator, then, is the true philosopher, sound in morals and with full knowledge of speaking, always striving for the highest" (p. 20). Quintilian's mission was clear and relevant to public relations' ethical standards: "My aim is to educate the true orator, who must be a good man [or woman] and must include philosophy in his [or her] studies in order to shape his [or her] character as a citizen and to equip himself [or herself] to speak on ethical subjects, his [her] special role" (p. 20).

Toward a definition of rhetoric, Quintilian reviewed the ideas of his predecessors. Among them was Plato, who disparaged rhetoric when it is used for base outcomes and developed through false reasoning. Plato, Quintilian (1951) believed, "regarded rhetoric in itself as a honorable thing to be used by a just man [or woman] in securing what is just" (p. 98).

Quintilian (1951) considered social values to be an implicit or explicit part of each statement: "If a case is based on injustice, neither a good man [nor woman] nor rhetoric has any place in it" (p. 106). The quality of discourse is inseparable from the character of the person who chooses the side of an issue as well as the form and substance with which to address it. For the ancients, rhetoric took vitality not from what could be said to win some point of view, but how public dialogue could make society better by assisting the people to make sound choices.

This brief review of the heritage of ancient Greek and Roman thought on rhetoric offers a firm foundation for the theory and practice of public relations. It endures the test of the centuries.

APPLICATION

The descriptions of the excellence of rhetoric in service of society offered by the Greeks and Romans is worthy of our consideration today. A list of principles of that body of work may seem platitudinous, but it can inform the ethical practice of public relations.

- Acknowledge and affirm the virtue of symmetry brought to life through the public advocacy of claims based on fact, value, or the wisdom of competing policies.
- Commit to demonstrating claims by advocating the facts and by reasoning to justify those claims.
- Know that by public contest ideas can be made better, values can be advanced, and policies can be improved.
- Public relations raises and addresses rhetorical problems that pose choices that are basic to the quality of relationships in society.
- The essence of public relations is the good organization that knows how and is willing to communicate well in the public interest.

CONCLUSION

Classical treatises on rhetoric do not tell the whole story of how rhetoric can support and guide the practice and scholarly of rhetoric. Modern theories can offer substantial refinement to that legacy. However, understanding the nature of discourse and ethics today cannot ignore a legacy of more than two thousand years. Current distortions of the term "rhetoric" ignore the rich heritage of concern for the ways people, those wordy humans, engage in courtship, identification, and the wrangle (Burke, 1969a, 1969b).

Process is valuable. Ethics are never separate from the communication act. The choices of fact, value, and policy are guided by character. Public relations practitioners can learn from the past and build their practice on a rich rhetorical heritage that is as vital today as it was in the golden ages of Greece and Rome. It is a story of the good organization communicating well—in the interest of society.

CASE: THE WAR IN IRAQ

One of the fascinating case studies of rhetoric and public relations started in the days leading up to the initiation of war against Saddam Hussein's Iraq by the United States, Great Britain, and other allies in 2003. The rationale for this war was controversial at its initiation and was revisited during the 2004 U.S. presidential campaign. The rhetorical problem facing the Bush administration was whether sufficient justification existed for the United States to lead a war to topple a head of a sovereign nation.

The initial rationale for this action was voiced by President George W. Bush (State of the Union Address) and Secretary of State Colin Powell (before the United Nations). The case was predicated on the administration's ability to demonstrate a clear and present danger to the citizens of the United States (and the world) because of weapons of mass destruction that were alleged to still be in part of Hussein's arsenal, despite the best efforts of the weapons inspectors. The rhetorical problem for the administration changed as the troops found little or no evidence of these weapons.

Still needing a compelling rationale for the war, the administration took up another line of reasoning. It alleged that Iraq was part of the international terrorist conspiracy against many nations, most particularly the United States. Efforts were made to demonstrate the link between Al-Qaeda and Saddam. The evidence seemed to many authorities to be tenuous at best. Some argued that indeed for many reasons Al-Qaeda was an enemy of the Iraq regime rather than its allies. Experts were prone to demonstrate, however, that during the occupation of Iraq it because a *magnet* to terrorists who supported the insurgents fighting against occupation. Thus, the claim of the case seemed tenuous at best.

During the 2004 presidential campaign, the administration found a position more convincing to those willing to believe, but certainly insufficient to create consensus. It focused on the tyranny and evil character of Saddam as the reason for the need to topple his government. Substantial evidence was offered of grave sites of mass murder, tales of torture, and corruption. This case had merit; it could be demonstrated. However, critics of the war pointed out how the case continued to slip and slide—perhaps be spun—by the administration as prior claims were found wanting. And, these critics suggested, other governments were as bad and dangerous or worse than the one in Iraq, but had either not been attacked or were indeed seen as allies of the United States. Thus, although character and virtue were contested as rationale, they were not found to be fully compelling reasons for the actions against Iraq.

Time will tell how this case turns out. The 2004 presidential election supported the hypothesis that a majority of the Americans believed President Bush had a sound rationale and policy for fighting and winning the conflict in Iraq. Partisan politics will play a substantial role in the development of policy and the telling of history. Nevertheless, this is a fascinating case study in the rhetorical challenges of public relations for an administration.

QUESTIONS FOR APPLICATION

Instead of suggesting ways that words can deceive, the rhetorical heritage offers sound advice for public relations practitioners and scholars. It addresses discourse, the shaping of meaning that enlightens choice. Whether devoted to publicity, promotion, image building, or issue communication, public relations practitioners engage in meaning. They can benefit from reflecting on the rhetorical heritage. Draw on the case study about the war in Iraq when answering the following questions:

1. How might we argue that rhetoric and ethics are partners, not enemies or strangers?

2. Explain how public relations engages in competition, courtship, and identification.

Explain also how public relations suffers the challenge of the wrangle for enlightened choice.

3. How do public relations practitioners foster perspectives that result from socially constructed meaning?

4. How can character and the substance of discourse serve society, the public interest?

5. How do higher-order principles and sound argument combine to make society more sound?

6. How can public relations, by applying principles of rhetoric, serve society rather than some narrow interest?

REFERENCES

Aristotle. (1952a). *Nichomachean ethics* (W. D. Ross, Trans.). In R. M Hutchins (Ed.), *Great books* (vol. 2, pp. 333–436). Chicago: Encyclopaedia Britannica.

Aristotle. (1952b). *Politics* (B. Jowett, Trans.). In R. M Hutchins (Ed.), *Great books* (vol. 2, pp. 445–548). Chicago: Encyclopaedia Britannica.

Aristotle. (1952c). *Rhetoric* (W. R. Roberts, Trans.). In R. M Hutchins (Ed.), *Great books* (vol. 2, pp. 593–675). Chicago: Encyclopaedia Britannica.

Brummett, B. (1995). Scandalous rhetorics. In W. N. Elwood (Ed.), *Public relations inquiry as rhetorical criticism: Case studies of corporate discourse and social influence* (pp. 13–23). Westport, CT: Praeger.

Bryant, D. C. (1953). Rhetoric: Its function and its scope. *Quarterly Journal of Speech, 39*, pp. 401–424.

Burke, K. (1969a). *A grammar of motives*. Berkeley: University of California Press.

———. (1969b). *A rhetoric of motives*. Berkeley: University of California Press.

Foss, S. J., & Griffin, C. L. (1995). Beyond persuasion: A proposal for an invitational rhetoric. *Communication Monographs, 62*, pp. 2–18.

Grunig, J. E. (Ed.). (1992). *Excellence in public relations and communication management*. Hillsdale, NJ: Lawrence Erlbaum.

Grunig, J. E., & Hunt, T. (1984). *Managing public relations*. New York: Holt Reinhart and Winston.

Heath, R. L. (2001). A rhetorical enactment rationale for public relations. In R. L. Heath (Ed.), *Handbook of public relations* (pp. 31–50). Thousand Oaks, CA: Sage.

———. (2005). Rhetorical theory. In R. L. Heath (Ed.), *Encyclopedia of public relations* (pp. 749–752). Thousand Oaks, CA: Sage.

Isocrates. (1929). *Antidosis* (G. Norlin, Trans.). *Isocrates* (Vol. 2, pp. 181–365). Cambridge, MA: Harvard University Press.

Kennedy, G. (1963). *The art of persuasion in Greece*. Princeton, NJ: Princeton University Press.

Lentz, C. S. (1996). The fairness in broadcasting doctrine and the Constitution: Forced one-stop shopping in the "marketplace of ideas." *University of Illinois Law Review, 271*, pp. 1–39.

L'Etang, J. (1996). Public relations and rhetoric. In J. L. L'Etang & M. Pieczka (Eds.), *Critical perspectives in public relations* (pp. 106–123). London: International Thomson Business Press.

L'Etang, J., & Pieczka, M. (Eds.). (1996). *Critical perspectives in public relations*. London: International Thomson Business Press.

Nichols, M. H. (1963). *Rhetoric and criticism*. Baton Rouge: Louisiana State University Press.

Palenchar, M. J. (2005). Social construction of reality theory. In R. L. Heath (Ed.), *Encyclopedia of public relations* (pp. 780–783). Thousand Oaks, CA: Sage.

Plato. (1952). *Gorgias* (B. Jowett, Trans.). In R. M. Hutchins (Ed.), *Great books* (vol. 7, pp. 252–294). Chicago: Encyclopaedia Britannica.

Quintilian, M. F. (1951). *The institutio oratoria of Marcus Fabius Quintilianus* (C.E. Little, Trans.). Nashville, TN: George Peabody College for Teachers.

Wallace, K. R. (1963). The substance of rhetoric: Good reasons. *Quarterly Journal of Speech, 49,* pp. 239–249.

Weaver, R. M. (1953). *The ethics of rhetoric.* Chicago: Henry Regnery.

———. (1970). *Language is sermonic* (R. L. Johannesen, R. Strickland, & R. T. Eubanks, Eds.). Baton Rouge: Louisiana State University Press.

CHAPTER FOURTEEN

PUBLIC RELATIONS AND THE RHETORIC OF SOCIAL INTERVENTION

SUSAN K. OPT

As organizations enter an era that writers and critics label postmodern, one constancy in the study of the organizations is change. Public relations theorists emphasize the need to understand organizational and social change processes as a way to be proactive rather than reactive in the life of the organization. Holtzhausen (2000) writes, "Practitioners' ability to deal with changes in society will enable those who work in institutions to contribute to their organizations' survival and effectiveness" (p. 110). Sellnow, Seeger, and Ulmer (2002) see understanding change as key to managing organizational crisis situations. Murphy (1996) notes that "monitoring change and interpreting its context may be more realistic public relations goals than prediction or control" (p. 108).

This chapter examines change from a rhetorical perspective and illustrates how this stance might be applied to interpreting organizational/social change. It describes a rhetorical model of social intervention (RSI) that could be used to understand and intervene in attempts to promote and prevent organizational/social change. The chapter begins with a brief overview of related public relations theory. Next, it details the communicative assumptions underlying the RSI model and then describes the model's framework, connecting it with current theory. Finally, the chapter closes with RSI model applications.

CURRENT PUBLIC RELATIONS PERSPECTIVES ON CHANGE

Traditionally public relations practitioners have attempted to prompt change via a linear process—first, doing research; then setting strategies, goals, and objectives; next, determining communication tactics; then implementing the campaign; and finally, evaluating the results to refine the process. While this framework has provided a means of action, critics note that it assumes that the processes of organizational and social change are controllable and outcomes knowable. These theorists point out that many examples in public relations literature illustrate how, despite careful planning, the end result did not match expectations (Murphy, 2000). Others, such as Holtzhausen (2000, 2002), view this perspective as reinforcing modernist principles of command and control and maintaining capitalistic and often unjust value structures.

More recently public relations theorists have advocated examining organizational and social change from a nonlinear, holistic perspective that assumes that systems "do not unfold in a linearly predictable, conventional cause-and-effect manner over time" (Murphy, 1996, p. 96). Complexity and chaos theories exemplify what some name as postmodern approaches to understanding public relations experiences such as issues management and crisis communication (Murphy, 1996, 2000; Sellnow, Seeger, & Ulmer, 2002). Uncertainty, open-endedness, unpredictability, uncontrollability, and paradox characterize the assumptions underlying this perspective of change.

In this shift from linear, predictive theories to holistic, chaotic theories, little emphasis has been given to viewing communication as the driver of change, an assumption key to understanding change from a rhetorical viewpoint and a point that distinguishes communication from other fields of inquiry. Skerlep (2001) notes that the dominant linear public relations paradigm has had little interest in "rhetoric as an integral part of public relations" (p. 177), something the alternative paradigm risks sharing. Theorists such as Heath (1992a, 1992b, 2001), Toth (1992, 2000), and Elwood (1995) have highlighted insights that can be gained from examining and critiquing public relations from a rhetorical perspective. Besides a rhetorical focus, Holtzhausen (2002) points to the need for research methods that encourage activism and diversity in postmodern public relations.

One model that focuses on the symbolic nature of change and provides a framework for understanding, promoting, and impeding change is Brown's (1978, 1982) rhetorical model of social intervention. This model blends traditional rhetorical perspectives with assumptions found in chaos and complexity theories to create an approach that can be used as a tool to analyze patterns of change, construct rhetorical interventions to attempt to promote or forestall change, and increase awareness of diversity. To be considered next are the assumptions from which the model emerges.

Assumptions: Naming

Underlying the rhetorical model of social intervention (Brown, 1978, 1982) is the assumption that naming is the fundamental human activity. That is, humans name or symbolically categorize sensed and nonsensed experiences in order to communicate, think about, organize, and share these experiences—what Langer (1963) calls a symbolic transformation of experience. A name can range from a word or phrase to a narrative, frame, scenario, or ideology. For example, meat from swine could be named "dead pig" or "pork." Irradiated meat could be named "public health threat," just as "technology is progress" is a name. From this perspective, what scholars call ideology, such as the "American dream," is an overarching name for human experience.

This perspective assumes that as we learn language—learn to name—we learn to associate particular criteria, or defining attributes, with a name (Bruner, Goodnow, & Austin, 1956). For example, a child is taught that a criterial attribute for distinguishing cats from dogs or horses from cows is the noise that the animals make. The RSI model assumes that naming is a constant, ongoing process in human experience, with humans often dialoging about the criterial attributes that constitute a name. Public relations practitioners are often involved in constituting names (images) for their clients by showing how clients fit particular criterial attributes. For example, a company might be named "good citizen" by showing how its actions fit the criterial attributes associated with that name—donating funds to the community, avoiding harm to the environment, and so forth.

Brown identifies "differences that make a difference" as the "one major name generator" (Makay & Brown, 1972, p. 379), or universal topic of message invention. In other words, to constitute and maintain any name, we must show how our name is the same as and/or different from culturally accepted categorizations of present and past experience. The similarities to and differences from accepted symbolic categorizations point to approach or avoidance behaviors toward a categorization of experience. For example, naming the act of removing a fetus from a womb "freedom of choice" suggests approach behavior while naming it "murder" suggests avoidance behavior in U.S. American culture.

Key, however, is that naming requires abstracting or paying attention to some features of experience and backgrounding other features (Makay & Brown, 1972). Burke (1966) calls this emphasis in attention "terministic screens": "Even if any given terminology is a *reflection* of reality, by its very nature as a terminology it must be a *selection* of reality; and to this extent it must function also as a *deflection* of reality" (p. 45). Heath (1992b) illustrates this abstracting experience in his analysis of competing names for Alaska after the Exxon oil spill: "What some rhetors played up, others played down" (p. 44). Because our names for experience are grounded in symbolic abstraction, they categorize only some attributes of "reality" and not others. This abstracting process seems unavoidable; at the same time, it leads to the rhetorical functions of naming.

> Once a name is learned its application to a new instance carries with it the expectancies toward that instance shared by the language community. This makes possible the *rhetorical* functioning of names: as *names* for an entity shift, so to some extent do the perceptions of it. For *new* or *unfamiliar* phenomena, therefore, the name given them can go far toward determining attitudes toward them. (Makay & Brown, 1972, p. 371)

Names, then, in directing attention, create expectations about needs, relationships, and experience. Bruner and colleagues (1956) note that this symbolizing process provides us with a way to cope with the apparent complexity of experience, make experience predictable, reduce the need for constant learning, and order and relate classes of events.

Brown (1978) argues that we maintain our symbolic categorizations as long as they seem to explain and make predictable experience. When anomalies that are nonfitting with the expectancies created by the name are stressed, then individuals and organizations potentially face a renaming of experience to make it once again predictable. Experience itself is assumed not to change, but rather the way of symbolically categorizing changes. These changes, though, suggest new expectations about experience. For example, Sellnow and colleagues (2002) describe how during the 1997 Red River Valley floods, regional leaders continued to name water measuring instruments "reliable" until the name no longer accounted for or predicted the floods they were experiencing.

Renaming involves simultaneous shifts in our perceptions of relationships and needs, which form the underpinnings of the rhetorical model of social intervention. Brown (1978) argues that what occurs at microlevels of human experience (naming) also occurs at macrolevels of human experience (ideology), as will be shown in the RSI model.

MODEL DIMENSIONS: NEED, RELATIONSHIP, ATTENTION

The RSI model directs attention to the *superordinate* names we create communicatively to explain all of experience, or "ideology" (Brown, 1978). Brown defines ideology as "any symbolic construction of the world in whose superordinate 'name' human beings can comprehensively order their experience and subsume their specific activities" (p. 124). Chaos theorists might label ideology an "attractor," an "organizing principle, an inherent shape or state of affairs to which a phenomenon will always tend to return as it evolves, no matter how random each single moment may seem" (Murphy, 1996, p. 98). Specifically, naming/ideology could be viewed as "strange" attractors, about which chaotic systems, or in this instance, symbol systems, organize. Murphy explains that "chaotic situations are characterized by *strange attractors* where outcomes wander constantly and unpredictably within a bounded range" (p. 98).

An example of a strange attractor could be the ideology by which many people in the United States traditionally have made sense of specific experience, named by various scholars as the "American dream." In stories, discourse, narratives, and such, Americans communicatively constitute and maintain an understanding of their purpose and place in the world that is specific to U.S. society. The American dream, in turn, provides an overarching scenario by which Americans make sense of specific experience. Robertson (1980), Bormann (1985), Hochschild (1995), and others summarize the dream as a quest to re-create or return to paradise and describe its current dimensions as emphasizing freedom, change, science, progress, democracy, equality, individualism, success, manifest destiny, and frontierism. These tenets suggest behaviors toward realizing and recognizing achievement of the dream. Brown (1978) views ideology as emerging from and constituting three dimensions of human symbolizing activity—our naming of needs, relationships, and worldview—or what one might view as microlevel strange attractor patterns.

Need

In the RSI model, human beings are assumed to have growth-and-survival needs that are expressed in communication. At the same time, we symbolically create needs that we attribute to ourselves and others through communication (Brown, 1987). Ideology creates expectancies for human needs just as we symbolically attribute needs to self and others that constitute the ideology. For example, the American dream tenet "all human beings are created equally" (a) satisfies the assumed human need for order and provides identity by stating humans' relationship with one another and, at the same time, (b) attributes to humans the need to be "equal." Along with attributing needs, we also communicatively advocate needs. For example, via marches, antiwar protesters both attribute and advocate a need for alternatives to war as a way to resolve conflict, a need that arises out of and promotes an ideology to create a better world. The meeting of needs, however, requires the constituting or naming of relationships with those we perceive as needs-meeting. Brown (1978) calls this advocacy toward others "open-channel" behavior. For example, antiwar protesters might turn to the media and courts as needs-meeters. Interdependencies might shift from cooperative to competitive with government officials advocating a war perspective as a way to create a safer and better world.

In general, then, humans are assumed to always have needs, whether physically or rhetorically created. What changes are perceptions of a specific need's importance, how it should be met, whether it is being met, and who best can meet it. This latter aspect of need is intertwined with the relationship dimension of the RSI model.

Relationship

As human beings symbolically constitute need, they simultaneously constitute relationships, creating order in the form of roles and social hierarchy. Heath (1992a) writes, "Through rhetoric, individuals and organizations negotiate their relationships. To do so, they form opinions of one another, decide on actions, set limits, and express obligations that influence how each is to act toward the other" (p. 18). For instance, naming a relationship "supervisor/employee" creates expectations about behaviors and interactions for that relationship. By symbolically categorizing relationships, we satisfy the assumed human need for order and predictability by making sense of our and others' behavior.

Furthermore, relational names carry with them expectancies about hierarchy and the nature of the relationship. For example, in the rhetorical constitution of "supervisor/employee," we act as if "supervisor" is above "employee," and "employees" act as if the "supervisor" is over them, thus creating hierarchy. Brown (1986) writes, "Persons make power real by ascribing it interdependently to one another" (p. 186). Brown adds that all relationships are based on interdependence—without employees, there would be no supervisors and vice versa. A supervisor cannot meet organizational needs without employee cooperation. Supervisors and employees must act together to create and maintain "organizations," cooperating and simultaneously competing to enact hierarchy.

Finally, Brown (1978) argues that in negotiating names for relationships, humans are also negotiating choices or "futures," which he summarizes as follows:

> By abstracting entities such as "self," "others," "relationship," "role," and "status," and by attributing to one another—through action corollaries—ideological "motives" or "beliefs" that would account for their behavior, human beings act as though the world makes comprehensive sense to them. Thus they appear to live out a particular worldview. (p. 132)

In other words, in naming relationships, we constitute narratives and stories about experience and our roles within that experience, creating and enacting ideology.

In general, then, human are assumed to always have relationships, necessary for meeting needs and for constituting explanations about human experience. What changes are perceptions of the needs-meeting ability of a relationship, the hierarchical nature of a relationship, and the future-choosing role of a relationship. This latter aspect of relationship is intertwined with the worldview dimension of the RSI model.

Attention

As humans symbolically constitute need and relationship, they simultaneously create macrolevel categories for experience in the form of gestalts, templates, narratives, or worldviews that explain and make experience predictable. Yet because worldviews arise from the abstracting of abstractions, they, too, have gaps in them. Experiences occur that do not "fit" or cannot be explained by the worldview. A "difference" is emphasized between what the worldview predicts and what seems to happen in experience. For example, Cahill (1995) describes how funeral directors' beliefs about their occupation—that it is "an honorable profession deserving of social respect, authority, and handsome remuneration" (p. 116)—were constantly being challenged by the nonfitting experiences of increasing Federal Trade Commission regulation and dropping profit margins. Brown (1978) calls these nonfitting relations "anomalies." Awareness of anomalies creates discomfort for the human who is assumed to have a need to order and make sense of experience, to simplify the apparent complexity of all experience. When gaps are featured, the worldview no longer seems to explain or predict human experience. Adherents face what some have labeled a cosmology episode: "all existing forms of sensemaking fail to account for experiences" (Sellnow, Seeger, & Ulmer, 2002, p. 27).

The RSI model focuses not on whether humans can avoid such episodes, but rather on how we attempt to avoid or compensate for these anomalies inherent in the naming process. Brown (1978) argues that we adhere to a particular symbolic categorization of need, relationship, and/or worldview as long as it appears to explain and make predictable human experience. But when its adherents become aware of anomalies, they potentially face either a system collapse or an attention switch, defined as a "periodic refocusing of attention . . . compensatory to symbolic gaps and vicious circles" (p. 135). This refocusing of attention is similar to the chaos theory concept of bifurcations, or "sudden changes in the system's direction, character, or structure" (Murphy, 1996, p. 97). Murphy explains, "at such points the system rearranges itself around a new underlying order, which may come to resemble, or be very different from, the prior one" (p. 97). For attention switches to occur, Brown (1982) suggests that the following must be in place:

> Conceptually, an attention-switch requires that (1) at least two patterns or interpretative "templates" always be potentially involved in our sizing up a situation; (2) each pattern itself be capable of rendering the situation coherent, and (3) *movement* from one to another—with a consequent reconstituting of the situation—be necessary before a "switch" will have occurred. (p. 18)

Attention switching can also be linked to the complexity theory characteristic of "punctuated equilibrium." Murphy (2000) explains that systems "tend to organize into fairly stable periods that are ruptured, often unpredictably by periods of turmoil, which, in turn subside into new stable periods where radically different values may prevail" (p. 453). These radically different values may come about because an attention switch potentially shifts a person's way of knowing, way of being, and/or way of valuing (Brown, 1982).

In general, the model assumes that all change, whether individual, organizational, or social, arises out of the symbolic abstraction process. Transformations occur not because of historical, economic, or technological influences, but because expectations created via the rhetorical naming process are not fulfilled, and humans seek explanations for this lack of fulfillment. Change emerges out of how the historical, economic, and technological developments are symbolically categorized. The attention-switching process is constant; what changes is the content of the attention switch.

So far, the dimensions of the rhetorical model of social intervention have been viewed as "static" elements or parts that can be separately described. Next the model's dimensions are viewed as a dynamic, systemic, and interventional process.

INTERVENTION: CREATING, MAINTAINING, CHANGING

The systemic nature of the RSI model becomes apparent in its assumption that concurrent with an attention switch are shifts in people's perceptions of interdependencies with others (relationship) and of needs. Shifts in perceptions of relationship bring about simultaneous shifts in worldview and needs, just as shifts in perceptions of needs bring about corresponding shifts in relationships and worldview. For example, Holtzhausen (2000) attempts to promote an attention shift from a modernist to postmodern approach to public relations. Inherent in that switch is a shift in needs (new knowledge and skills) and a shift in relationships (from organizational promoter to community activist). Thus, as our names for experience change, so do our overall understandings of that experience. Like chaos theory, the RSI model leads the critic to search for underlying patterns of change in the human symbolizing process. In addition, although shift patterns, such as more/less advocacy, more/less interdependency, and anomaly-featuring/masking communication, can be identified, the timing and outcomes of the shifts are presumed unpredictable.

The systemic nature of the RSI model is also reflected in its focus on deviance-amplifying, deviance-compensating, and trend reversals (Brown, 1982), or what chaos theory would label "feedback" (Murphy, 1996). As adherents to a particular symbolic categorization continue to experience anomalies, the system becomes deviance-amplifying. In other words, deviance (or difference) is intensified between the expectations created by the name and experience itself. As awareness of gaps increases, the adherents potentially encounter a vicious circle in which "members of an ideological community act as if hiatuses in worldview would invalidate it" (Brown, 1978, p. 134), which might lead to system collapse. Trend reversal occurs when adherents find ways to fill the gaps or make the expectations generated by the name "fit" the experience, thus impeding system collapse. For example, an attention switch creates trend reversal, and the system becomes deviance-compensating. The world seems to make sense and be predictable once more, or in chaos terms, self-organization or order reemerges out of randomness (Sellnow, Seeger, & Ulmer, 2002). However, the system does not "return" to the same "space" after trend reversal. Rather, the system is assumed to "move" like a spiral "since events/ contexts change and do not by analogy occupy the same 'space'" (Brown, 1987, p. 13). This, too, is similar to a chaotic system. Murphy (1996) explains, "[A]s a chaotic system evolves, each step's output provides the material for a new formulation and outcome" (p. 97).

The systemic perspective of the RSI model points to a communicative conception of side effects resulting from rhetorical interventions. This aspect of the model is much like chaos theory, in which "minuscule changes in some systems' initial conditions may actually amplify exponentially as their effects unfold so the end result bears little resemblance to the beginning" (Murphy, 1996, p. 97). Side effects are assumed to occur whenever need, relationship, and/or attention shift, for a shift in one brings corresponding change in the other two. In general, when analyzing change, the critic tends to superordinate one dimension of the model. But the model provides a way to search for changes occurring in the other two aspects. Information gleaned from one dimension creates expectancies about change in the other aspects; the model is holographically conceived (i.e., "every part of the whole contains or implies the whole" (Brown, 1987, p. 2).

Related to side effects is another aspect of the RSI model—intervention. The model assumes that human beings *intervene* into, rather than *control*, the symbolic constitution of needs, relationship, and worldview. Human beings *affect*, but do not control, the development of the communicatively constituted human social system. They *interact* with, rather than act on, others. As we attempt to intervene in an organizational or social system, others are also simultaneously intervening; hence, the specific outcome of any intervention is unpredictable. The model, then, focuses attention on the processes by which we attempt to intervene in the creation, maintenance, and change of our symbolically constructed systems.

The dimensions of the RSI model—need, relationship, and attention—suggest starting points for intervention.

A need intervention occurs when we (a) become aware of unmet needs and/or accept the attribution/denial of "new" needs, and (b) advocate and/or disadvocate needs, toward others perceived as mediators of those needs (Brown, 1987). While these aspects of needs are described separately, they are assumed to occur concurrently. As awareness of a need increases, so do advocacy behaviors toward those perceived as being able to meet the need. The system becomes deviance amplifying until the need is met, which then reduces awareness of the need and advocacy behavior. Yet the model predicts that as saliency of one need diminishes, then awareness of a need previously in the background increases. For example, the public relations director of a grocery chain becomes aware from reading letters to the editor that certain publics are naming the chain as "lacking a community consciousness" because of its recent decision to close a poorly performing store in a lower-income area that is being revitalized. For the affected public, this is a nonfitting experience in an ideology that dreams of a better world. The public advocates needs via these letters and creates a relationship with the media as a way to promote its need. The director now has awareness of a need, although perhaps not the same one as the public, but rather the need to take action to recoup the grocery chain's image as a "community citizen." Grocery chain officials may have advocated the need to close the store as a way to maintain the organization's profit margins in line with the ideological quest toward paradise. The model suggests that we typically will advocate needs via socially accepted channels and in socially accepted ways (e.g., courts, grievances committees, customer complaint desks). However, if needs go unmet, advocates may turn to more extreme communication techniques that become damaging and costly for the organization. For example, the above public might organize a protest or cause physical damage to a store. In advocating needs, we are reminding others of their interdependency with us, especially when extreme measures are used. For instance, a grocery store can operate peacefully only as long as its publics cooperate to leave it in peace.

A relational intervention occurs when we (a) perceive that we need or no longer need specific others to mediate our needs and goals, and/or (b) perceive interdependency in advocating or disadvocating the choosing of specific futures. A renaming of the relationship occurs. At the same time, the rules that govern the relationship shift. Thus, simultaneously with a shift in needs comes a shift in perceptions of interdependence. We may perceive ourselves as more or less interdependent with other people and groups in the enacting of roles that lead to promoting organizational and social change or maintaining the system as is. These fluctuations in relationships are similar to those predicted in complexity theory, which assumes that "players" do not make decisions based on "conscious strategy to maximize their long-term gains. . . . Rather, the *players are adaptive*, simply adjusting to their immediate circumstances" (Murphy, 2000, p. 451). Hence, interdependencies evolve and change. Sellnow and colleagues (2002) describe how interdependencies shifted from competitive to cooperative among city and regional officials as their names for the 1997 Red River Valley flood experience shifted. In the earlier instance, in advocating a future in which the grocery store remains open, the store's constituents turn to the media and perhaps the city council to mediate their needs and goals. The media and city council assume roles in future-choosing, perhaps promoting the view of the constituents, promoting the view of the grocery store chain, or perhaps offering an alternative future. If the grocery store chain accepts the view of the future promoted by the public, then its needs and relationships will change. If the grocery store chain's vision overrides that of the publics', then the publics' needs and relationships will change. For example, residents might perceive a need to find housing elsewhere and constitute cooperative relationships with realtors and house builders.

This future-choosing, then, links to attention. An attention intervention occurs when we attempt to promote or impede a symbolic recategorization for experience. We rhetorically promote or impede attention switches by naming outcomes of experience as "fitting" or "nonfitting" with expectancies associated with a particular name (Brown, 1978, 1982). Anomaly-featuring communication *stresses* or features attention to nonfitting relations or anomalies between expectations and outcomes (differences). Anomaly-masking communication *de-emphasizes* or masks attention to nonfitting relations or anomalies between expectations and outcomes (similarities). To *promote* an attention switch, then, communicators (a) *emphasize* anomalies, flaws, contradictions, shortcomings, gaps, and lack of pattern in the *currently held* worldview, and (b) *de-emphasize* any anomalies, flaws, and so forth in the *new* symbolic categorization being promoted. To *impede* an attention switch, communicators (a) *emphasize* anomalies, flaws, and so forth, in the *new* worldview promoted by those who would bring about change, and (b) *de-emphasize* anomalies, gaps, and inadequacies in the *current* symbolic categorization. For example, Holtzhausen (2002) attempts to promote an attention switch to a postmodern view of public relations by featuring anomalies in the modernist perspective.

Regardless of whether one is promoting or impeding an attention switch, the overall end is to minimize anomalies and contradictions in our symbolic abstractions. Murphy (1996) notes, "As long as events adhere to a strange attractor, change will be very difficult to implement. However, when sufficient deviance has amplified through the system, change will be very difficult to arrest" (p. 108). Humans are able to adhere to a strange attractor because of the inherent abstracting nature of their symbolic categorization process. Via rhetorical strategies and maneuvers, we mask attention to experience that is nonfitting with the strange attractor. For example, the grocery store public relations director might account for the "anomaly" of the letters to the editor by naming the letter writers "troublemakers" who do not represent the general public. Sellnow and colleagues (2002) recount how city officials attempted to mask anomalies to maintain the name "normal flooding situation" to prevent the shift to "novel flooding incident" until their names no long accounted for experience.

An understanding of the rhetoric of change, then, is important to the everyday practice of public relations. As Holtzhausen (2000) remarks, "Public relations is about change or resistance to change" (p. 110). On a daily basis, public relations practitioners use rhetorical strategies to intervene, to attempt to create, maintain, and/or change their organizations' and the public's symbolic categorizations for experience.

APPLICATION

The rhetorical model of social intervention has been used to examine a wide variety of organizational and social/cultural change (Gonzalez, 1989; Gring, 1998; Leroux, 1991; Opt, 1988; Opt, 1997; Opt, 1998; Snyder, 2000; Stoner, 1989). Little attention has been given to its possible use in or contributions to public relations theory and practice.

As applied specifically to public relations, the RSI model suggests that the role of public relations practitioners is one of "intervener." They attempt to intervene in the ongoing symbolic categorizing process of human experience to create, maintain, and/or change the organization's relationship with its internal and external publics. The model focuses attention on the naming patterns being promoted and impeded by and within an organization, and those ongoing within publics perceived as interdependent and/or potentially interdependent with the organization. As Holtzhausen (2000) notes, "Publics view organizations from a perspective imbedded in their own realities" (pp. 96–97). The model assumes mutual influence and interdependency in future-choosing and emphasizes examining and understanding multiple perspectives.

As previously noted, chaos theory suggests that the public relations practitioner's role is one of monitoring and interpreting change. The RSI model provides a communicative methodology for that task. It leads the practitioner to research the patterns of naming ongoing within and about an organization and within and about its publics. The practitioner would attempt to identify the "dominant" name, or strange attractor, and the alternative names being offered for needs, relationship, and worldview by monitoring organizational/public discourse and analyzing it across time for patterns of anomaly-featuring and anomaly-masking communication to determine (a) if talk primarily is featuring nonfitting relations within the dominant name and to fitting relations with an alternative name (moving the organization/public in the direction of change), or (b) if talk primarily is masking gaps in the dominant name and featuring anomalies in the alternative names (moving the organization/public in the direction of homeostasis). In other words, it is not enough to know *what* is being said, but practitioners need to examine *how* the particular organizational/public "names" are being constructed. This rhetorical analysis could lead to predictions about change. For example, if the practitioner observes primarily anomaly-featuring communication and little anomaly-masking communication occurring, this might suggest that change is near. If the naming patterns point to change, then the practitioner could consider the side effects inherent in the renaming process—the simultaneous shifts in being, knowing, and valuing, and in internal and external relationships and needs—and outcomes of organizational/public response to the change.

Besides providing insight into organizational and social change, however, the RSI model might also offer a framework to guide interventional activities. For example, after completing the rhetorical analysis, the public relations practitioner would consider how the organization's message fits into the ongoing naming discourse and communication strategies for promoting or impeding change. This is not to suggest, however, that the practitioner's goal should be one of intervening to attempt to bring public opinion in line with the organizational view. Rather, the model promotes reflectivity and lends itself to the postmodern perspective that as boundary-spanners, practitioners should "recognize and respect differences on the side of both the organization and its publics" as well as "encourage the sides to change by making them aware of the depth of their conflict" (Holtzhausen, 2000, p. 108). The model points to the abstractive nature of the symbolizing process as a way to understand the conflict. Furthermore, the RSI model potentially provides a way to consider side effects of an organization's intervention attempts. For example, in analyzing possible worldview shifts, the practitioner could also examine whether the relationships and needs-meeting ability that would be predicted to change with the worldview shift are in place.

CONCLUSION

Holtzhausen (2000) writes, "In a world defined by continuous change, public relations practitioners need to play an important role in activating and defining change in organizations and societies" (p. 110). The RSI model offers a way to reflect on and enact rhetorical interventions. The model arises out of the assumption that naming is the fundamental human activity and the primary driver of change. Via naming, we share sensed and nonsensed experience, and constitute macrolevel names for experience in the form of ideologies and microlevel names in the form of need, relationship, and worldview. Constant in the model is the assumption that we all have needs, relationships, and explanations for experience. What changes is the content of needs, relationship, and worldview. Thus, the process of change becomes a constant of the symbolic abstraction process.

CASE: FRIENDS-TOGETHER

Friends-Together Inc. is a Florida-based nonprofit organization that is involved in HIV/AIDS awareness education. One of its target publics is college students. According to the national Centers for Disease Control and Prevention (CDC), AIDS is one of the leading causes of death among twenty-five- to forty-four-year-old Americans. It has been the leading cause of death among African American men in this age group since 1991 and the third leading cause of death among African American women in this age group since 1999. The CDC believes that many of these adults became infected in their teens and twenties. It estimates that at least half of all new HIV infections in the United States occur in people under age twenty-five, and the majority are infected sexually. Florida ranks third nationally in the number of HIV cases, hence one reason Friends-Together is targeting college students. Specifically, Friends-Together is attempting to convince students to take these kinds of actions: get HIV/AIDS testing, reduce their number of sexual partners, and use safer sexual practices. Most of all, the organization wants the students to understand that they are at risk for contracting HIV anytime they engage in any form of sex.

The organization has attempted to communicate the message in several ways. During the past year, it has run a publicity campaign that promotes the message "Only men, women and children get AIDS." The campaign features three poster and billboard designs showing a variety of people and the message. The billboards were posted around the city and the posters in classrooms around the campuses. The message was also promoted in a newspaper ad, which included the line "They've finally proven that only three categories of people get HIV. . . ." A radio public service announcement (PSA) featuring a male, a female, and a child singing about the message was distributed. The radio PSA emphasized that it was not who one was or where one lived but what one did that determined whether one contracted AIDS. The campaign included a brochure that described the organization's main speaker and organizer and facts about HIV/AIDS infection. Besides the publicity campaign, the adult organizational speaker, who is HIV-positive, visits college wellness courses and shares her experience (she was infected when raped) along with facts about the spread of HIV. The speaker also distributes fact sheets that include information about the percentage of infections, ways HIV is contracted, groups likely to be infected, and testing accuracy. The organization sponsors free monthly HIV testing on campuses and at locations around the community. It organizes special events on college campuses, such as panel presentations featuring medical experts during HIV/AIDS Awareness Week and displaying pieces of the national AIDS quilt. It also hosts workshops, camps, and retreats for families with members who have HIV/AIDS. The organization provides a web site (www.friendstogether.org) with information on local HIV/AIDS events.

Despite efforts of organizations such as Friends-Together, statistics show little change in the infection rate of college students, which suggests little change in their sexual practices. Informal interviews with students who come for repeat HIV/AIDS testing indicate no reduction in the numbers of sexual partners. The number of students getting tested has not increased significantly. In addition, students who do get tested often do not return to get their test results, which are confidential.

Consider how this situation would be approached through the lens of the rhetorical model of social intervention and how the RSI model would guide your analysis of the situation faced by Friends-Together.

QUESTIONS FOR APPLICATION

1. What do you see as the underlying ideology reflected in Friends-Together's concerns about the HIV/AIDS infection rates?

2. How would you describe Friends-Together's attempted intervention (e.g., how it has tried to reach the students and the messages it has been promoting)? How is it attempting to influence students' perceptions of needs, relationship, and worldview?

3. What kind of research would you suggest to further understand the situation—from both the organization's perspective and the target public's perspective?

4. How might the RSI model guide your interpretation of research findings and the development of communication strategies and/or changes that you would recommend to Friends-Together?

5. What other potential interveners (e.g., other HIV/AIDS organizations, student peer groups, media, parents) might be important to examine for possible competing messages or for the building of cooperative relationships?

6. What ethical issues should concern public relations practitioners as they attempt to influence organizational or social change?

7. View several television commercials and analyze them as need interventions. Discuss these questions:

   a. Who is the public for this intervention? Who is the intervener?

   b. To what physical and/or cultural needs is the intervener appealing or attributing to the public? Are these felt or created needs?

   c. How does the intervener attempt to align those needs with the public's ideology?

   d. If the public accepts the renaming of needs, how might it advocate those needs?

   e. To whom might the public turn for needs-meeting responses?

8. Analyze the editorial pages of newspapers as relational interventions. Discuss these questions:

   a. Who is the public for this intervention? Who is the intervener?

   b. How would you describe relationships and hierarchy before the attempted intervention (e.g., perceptions of interdependency, roles, competitive/cooperative, threat/exchange/connectedness)?

   c. How does the intervener attempt to shift perceptions of relationship?

   d. How does the intervener attempt to align relationships with the public's ideology?

   e. How might relationships and hierarchy appear after the intervention?

9. Collect samples of promotional materials from an organization (e.g., recruiting materials from your college campus) and analyze these materials as an attention intervention. Discuss these questions:

   a. Who is the public for this intervention? Who is the intervener?

   b. How would you describe the worldview ("name") being given to experience by the public before the attempted intervention?

   c. How would you describe the worldview being promoted by the intervener?

   d. How does the intervener attempt to promote the attention switch (e.g., anomaly-masking/featuring communication)?

   e. How might the public attempt to forestall the attention switch?

   f. How might needs and relationships shift if the public's attention shifts?

REFERENCES

Bormann, E. (1985). *The forces of fantasy.* Carbondale: Southern Illinois University Press.

Brown, W. R. (1978). Ideology as communication process. *Quarterly Journal of Speech, 64,* pp. 123–140.

———. (1982). Attention and the rhetoric of social intervention. *Quarterly Journal of Speech, 68,* pp. 17–27.

———. (1986). Power and the rhetoric of social intervention. *Communication Monographs, 53,* pp. 180–199.

———. (1987). *Need and the rhetoric of social intervention.* Unpublished manuscript, Ohio State University.

Bruner, J., Goodnow, J., & Austin, G. (1956). *A study of thinking.* New York: Wiley.

Burke, K. (1966). *Language as symbolic action.* Berkeley: University of California Press.

Cahill, S. E. (1995). Some rhetorical directions of funeral direction. *Work and Occupations, 22*(2), pp. 115–136.

Elwood, W. (1995). Public relations is a rhetorical experience. In W. Elwood (Ed.), *Public relations inquiry as rhetorical criticism* (pp. 3–12). Westport, CT: Praeger.

Gonzalez, A. (1989). "Participation" at WMEX-FM: Interventional rhetoric of Ohio Mexican Americans. *Western Journal of Speech Communication, 53*, pp. 398–410.

Gring, M. A. (1998). Attention, power, and need: The rhetoric of religion and revolution in Nicaragua. *World Communication Journal, 27*(4), pp. 27–37.

Heath, R. L. (1992a). Critical perspectives on public relations. In E. Toth & R. Heath (Eds.), *Rhetorical and critical approaches to public relations* (pp. 37–61). Hillsdale, NJ: Lawrence Erlbaum.

———. (1992b). The wrangle in the marketplace: A rhetorical perspective of public relations. In E. Toth & R. Heath (Eds.), *Rhetorical and critical approaches to public relations* (pp. 17–36). Hillsdale, NJ: Lawrence Erlbaum.

———. (2001). A rhetorical enactment rationale for public relations. In R. L. Heath (Ed.), *Handbook of public relations* (pp. 31–59). Thousand Oaks, CA: Sage.

Hochschild, J. L. (1995). *Facing up to the American dream.* Princeton, NJ: Princeton University Press.

Holtzhausen, D. (2000). Postmodern values in public relations. *Journal of Public Relations Research, 12*(1), pp. 93–114.

———. (2002). Towards a postmodern research agenda for public relations. *Public Relations Review, 28*, pp. 251–264.

Langer, S. (1963). *Philosophy in a new key: A study in the symbolism of reason, rite, and art.* Cambridge, MA: Harvard University Press.

Leroux, N. (1991). Frederick Douglass and the attention-shift. *Rhetoric Society Quarterly, 21*(2), pp. 36–46.

Makay, J., & Brown, W. R. (1972). *The rhetorical dialogue: Contemporary concepts and cases.* Dubuque, IA: Wm. C. Brown.

Murphy, P. (1996). Chaos theory as a model for managing issues and crises. *Public Relations Review, 22*(3), pp. 95–113.

———. (2000). Symmetry, contingency, complexity: Accommodating uncertainty in public relations theory. *Public Relations Review, 26*(4), pp. 447–462.

Opt, S. (1988). Continuity and change in storytelling about artificial intelligence: Extending the narrative paradigm. *Communication Quarterly, 36*, pp. 298–310.

———. (1997). The earth summit: Maintaining cultural myth. *Journal of the Northwest Communication Association, 25*, pp. 1–22.

———. (1998). Confirming and disconfirming American myth: Stories within the suggestion box. *Communication Quarterly, 46*(1), pp. 75–87.

Robertson, J. O. (1980). *American myth, American reality.* New York: Hill & Wang.

Sellnow, T. L., Seeger, M., & Ulmer, R. (2002). Chaos theory, informational needs, and natural disasters. *Journal of Applied Communication Research, 30,*(4), pp. 269–292.

Skerlep, A. (2001). Re-evaluating the role of rhetoric in public relations theory and in strategies of corporate discourse. *Journal of Communication Management, 6*(2), pp. 176–187.

Snyder, L. L. (2000). Invitation to transcendence: The book of Revelation. *Quarterly Journal of Speech, 86*(4), pp. 402–417.

Stoner, M. R. (1989). Understanding social movement rhetoric as social intervention. *The Speech Communication Annual, 3*, pp. 27–43.

Toth, E. (1992). The case for pluralistic studies of public relations: Rhetorical, critical, and systems perspectives. In. E. Toth & R. Heath (Eds.), *Rhetorical and critical approaches to public relations* (pp. 3–15). Hillsdale, NJ: Lawrence Erlbaum.

———. (2000). Public relations and rhetoric: History, concepts, future. In D. Moss, D. Vercic, & G. Warnbay (Eds.), *Perspectives on public relations research* (pp. 121–144). London: Routledge.

CRISIS COMMUNICATION— GIVING VOICE IN THE PROCESS

Tricia Hansen-Horn

Bonita Dostal Neff

Organizational crises are inevitable. Public relations professionals' need to successfully address crises is also inevitable. Their success can be enabled by establishing a body of knowledge dedicated to helping professionals approach crises from multiple understandings and strategies.

Benoit and Pang, and Coombs expand the present body of knowledge. Benoit and Pang urge us to accept the inevitability of needing to redress tainted images with the goal of image repair. Coombs addresses the need for continued development of crisis communication theory as a lens from which to explore, understand, and successfully enact crises.

CHAPTER FIFTEEN

CRISIS COMMUNICATION AND IMAGE REPAIR DISCOURSE

WILLIAM L. BENOIT

AUGUSTINE PANG

A corporation's image, or reputation, is a very important asset. Customers are, and should be, reluctant to do business with companies with tarnished reputations. We must be able to trust that products and services, from prescription drugs and food to investment advice and airline travel, are safe and effective. Therefore, when a business's product or service does not live up to expectations, unpleasant consequences can occur for consumers, ranging from death to inconvenience. Obviously, such adverse effects can be expected to make other customers reluctant to do business with that company. Furthermore, a firm's reputation is important for other reasons beyond the need to have consumers willing to purchase its goods and services. For example, a firm's image could influence how closely the government regulates its actions. Reputation can influence the price of a company's stock. It can even influence how other companies deal with it (e.g., terms offered for loans or credit; how long a supplier is willing to wait for payment or how much of a discount will be offered on a purchase). Clearly, image is important to companies large and small.

Threats to image are ubiquitous. Pinsdorf (1987) acknowledged that public relations crises "are no longer a matter of if, but when; no longer the exception, but the expected—even the inevitable" (p. 37). Companies recognize that their reputation is vital and, accordingly, they take preventive (Heath & Nelson, 1986; Olaniran & Williams, 2001) as well as restorative approaches to image threats (Allen & Caillouet, 1994; Hearit, 2001; Millar & Heath, 2004). This chapter explicates the theory of image repair discourse as a perspective for both developing and understanding messages used to respond to corporate image crises.

First, we want to define *image*. A company's (or person's or organization's) image is a subjective impression of that business held by other people. A corporation's image, or reputation, is subjective because it arises from the information held by people about that corporation. Our perceptions of an organization (or person or group) are formed from the words and deeds of that organization—and from what others say and do about that organization. So an image is a subjective impression of an organization formed through one's experience with that organization and inter- preted are based on other past experiences.

One implication of the fact that an image is a subjective impression is that a corporation's image will vary from one person to another. It is unlikely that two people will have identical experiences with or information about a company. They will have read, or seen, or heard different information about it. Furthermore, even if they did have exactly the same experiences with a given company, their other unique experiences are likely to color their own interpretations of the information they share about the company. Different people will often have similar impressions of a company, but it is unlikely that any two people will have precisely the same impression of a company. Some people, of course, will have widely disparate impressions of a firm. So different people can be expected to have different images of a given corporation (Moffitt, 1994).

This analysis also reveals the importance of communication in understand- ing and influencing images. Our image of a company is based on what we have seen, heard, and read about that company. The company's words and deeds are one source for our impression. This means a company whose image has been threatened can, at least in theory, use communication to repair that image. How- ever, this analysis also reveals that our image of a firm is also influenced by what other people do with and say about that company. This means an image can be influenced (and threatened or damaged) by the accusations, complaints, and behavior of others. Because a business's image is such an important asset, when image is threatened, it is often considered essential to take action to repair that image.

Observing that an image is an impression also means that an image may be at odds with reality. A company may be seen in a bad light even when a complete and clear understanding of the situation does not support that perception. Images may be at odds with reality. This does not mean that reality is irrelevant to image. If a company is falsely (or mistakenly) accused of wrongdoing, the truth (reality) of its innocence can be employed to repair the firm's image. However, it is vital to keep in mind that reality by itself is unlikely to repair an image. Perceptions can be more important than reality. The company inappropriately accused of wrong- doing must use communication to correct this mistaken image. Furthermore, sometimes people see what they want to see and fail to see what they do not want to see. The truth *can* repair an image, but if the relevant audience refuses to accept the truth, reality can not help the unfairly damaged image. So image and image repair both arise from reality but must be shaped through communication. Reality clearly influences images, but rarely do people have a complete knowledge of the facts, and what they do know is filtered or interpreted by their personal attitudes and experiences.

As we will see, some of the theory and research on image repair concerns individuals as well as corporations. We must acknowledge that there are differ- ences in the repair efforts of individuals and companies. For example, companies might use different appeals than do individuals, or employ those appeals in different configurations. Most companies will have more resources to expend in image repair efforts than do most individuals. Lawyers may suggest that the companies they represent avoid some appeals to minimize the risks of litigation, a constraint that is less likely to apply to individuals. Nevertheless, the basic options are the same for both individual and corporate image repair efforts. Furthermore, at times a corporate official may need to respond as an individual rather than as a proxy for the entire company. Thus, writing on both corporate and individual image repair can be useful.

IMAGE REPAIR THEORY

Benoit and his colleagues have developed the theory of image repair discourse and applied it in a variety of contexts: corporate (Benoit 1995a, 1995b; 1998; Benoit & Brinson, 1999; Benoit & Czerwinski, 1997; Benoit & Hirson, 2001; Blaney, Benoit, & Brazeal, 2002; Brinson & Benoit, 1996); political (Benoit 1995a, 1999; Benoit, Gullifor & Panici, 1991; Benoit & McHale, 1999; Benoit & Nill, 1998a; Benoit & Wells, 1998; Kennedy & Benoit, 1997; Len-Ríos & Benoit, 2004); international (Benoit & Brinson, 1999; Drumheller & Benoit, 2004; Zhang & Benoit, 2004; Zhang & Benoit, in press); and other contexts (Benoit, 1997a; Benoit & Anderson, 1996; Benoit & Hanczor, 1994; Benoit & Nill, 1998b; Blaney & Benoit, 1997, 2001). This section explains the basic concepts of this theory.

To understand how to respond to an image crisis, we must consider what causes such a threat. The key to understanding an image repair effort is to understand the nature of the accusations, attacks, or complaints that threaten corporate images (Benoit & Dorries, 1996; Benoit & Harthcock, 1999). An attack on a person's or organization's image has two basic elements (Pomerantz, 1978):

1. An offensive act has occurred.
2. The accused is responsible for that act.

Let us consider each of these two components. First, if nothing bad has happened, there is no threat to image. Only when an offense has occurred is there a potential threat to an image. If something good has happened, that is grounds for praise, not criticism. If nothing has happened, ordinarily there can be no potential threat to an image. An exception, of course, occurs when we are expected to do something and we fail to do it. So criticism and threats to image can arise when an act is committed with harmful consequences, or when an act is performed ineptly, or when an expected action is not performed. There must be a state of affairs that is considered undesirable for a potential threat to an image to arise.

Second, even when an offensive act has occurred, it is unreasonable to form a negative impression of a company unless that company is responsible for the offensive act. We must understand that responsibility for an act can take several forms: A company can be blamed if it performed, ordered, encouraged, facilitated, or permitted the act to occur—as well as for acts of omission or poorly performed acts. A salient audience (or audiences) must hold the firm responsible for the offensive act for its image to be threatened.

It is important to realize that just as an image is a perception, threats to image are perceptions as well. Images are threatened when another person obtains information that creates an unfavorable impression about another person or organization. As noted above, images can be damaged undeservedly, when false accusations are made (or suspicions arise) either maliciously in disregard of the truth or inadvertently through mistakes. Threats to image that are not based in reality can be just as damaging as threats arising from the accused's harmful actions. Hopefully, effective communication can repair those false threats, but it would be a mistake to ignore a threat simply because we believe it is untrue. However, it is also important to realize that some acts are viewed as offensive by some people but not everyone; people may vary in whether they perceive an act as offensive. For instance, advocates for the poor are offended when loans are denied to those in poverty. Stockholders of the bank, however, may view denial of loans to the poor as a desirable action because that policy limits the risk of loan defaults. Image, and threats to image, arise from the perceptions of the audience.

This leads to another important observation: It is vital to realize that businesses frequently must deal with several audiences. For example, a business might face such diverse audiences as local residents, stockholders, government regulators, employees, interest groups, and politicians. Identification of the key audience or audiences is important because different audiences often have diverse interests, concerns, and goals. If a business, for instance, is accused of polluting the environment, residents and environmental interest groups, on the one hand, would want the company to spare no expense to eliminate the pollution. Company stockholders, on the other hand, would surely prefer the most frugal approach. Government regulators may be unconcerned with expenses so long as the level of pollution conforms to regulations. So it is necessary for the crisis communicator to identify the most important audience or to prioritize the important audiences in a crisis situation.

TYPOLOGY OF IMAGE REPAIR STRATEGIES

Other writers have identified the kinds of crisis situations an organization can face (Dutton, 1986) or the stages though which a crisis passes (Fink, Beak, & Taddeo, 1971). However, image repair theory focuses on the content of crisis communication messages. Image repair theory (Benoit, 1995a, 1997b) is more exhaustive than the earlier theories (Ware & Linkugel's 1973 *apologia* or Burke's 1970 concept of mortification). Image repair theory offers five broad categories of image repair strategies, some with subforms, that can be used to respond to image threats (see Table 15.1). Reducing offensiveness and corrective action, the third and fourth broad category of image restoration, address the first component of accusations, reducing offensiveness of the act attributed to the accused. Denial and evasion of responsibility concern the second component of accusations rejecting or reducing the accused's responsibility for the act in question. The last general strategy,

TABLE 15.1 Image Restoration Strategies

STRATEGY	KEY CHARACTERISTIC	ILLUSTRATION
Denial		
Simple denial	Did not perform act	Phillip Morris: less nicotine after processing
Shift the blame	Act performed by another	Firestone: Ford underinflated tires
Evasion of responsibility		
Provocation	Responded to act of another	Firm moved because of new state laws
Defeasibility	Lack of information or ability	Executive not told meeting changed
Accident	Act was a mishap	Sears' unneeded repairs inadvertent
Good intentions	Meant well in act	Tobacco Institute: Voluntary actions to reduce teen smoking
Reducing offensiveness of event		
Bolstering	Stress good traits	Dow cares about women
Minimization	Act not serious	Sears: Thousands of repairs, few problems
Differentiation	Act less offensive than similar ones	RJ Reynolds: Cigarettes more like coffee and chocolate than heroin
Transcendence	More important considerations	Dow: Women feel the need for implants
Attack accuser	Reduce credibility of accuser	Sears attacked repair fraud report as flawed
Compensation	Reimburse victim	Firm gives discount on other products
Corrective action	Plan to solve or prevent problem	Texaco will punish, prevent racism
Mortification	Apologize for act	AT&T apologized for interruption

mortification, tries to restore an image by asking forgiveness without attempting to reduce blame for or offensiveness of the act. The following discussion explains and illustrates these strategies (note that we are not claiming these are necessarily effective or persuasive examples of the strategies; our only purpose is to use these examples to help understand the nature of the image repair strategies).

Denial. This approach has two variants, simple denial and shift the blame. One potential strategy for responding to an image threat is simply to deny the wrongful act. For example, the tobacco industry was attacked in the 1990s on ABC's *PrimeTime Live* and NBC's *Day One* on several grounds, including having "spiked" cigarettes with an addictive additive, nicotine. Philip Morris published newspaper ads responding to these accusations. Philip Morris observed: "In every case, with every brand we manufacture, the nicotine level in the finished cigarette is lower than the nicotine level of the original, natural tobacco leaf" (Benoit, 1998, p. 221). The clear implication is that if Philip Morris was adding nicotine, the levels of this chemical would be higher rather than lower. Simple denial can deny that the act occurred *or* that the accused committed the act.

A second format for denial is to shift the blame. This strategy admits that the act occurred but declares that another person or organization is really responsible for the offensive act. Firestone was blamed for 271 deaths from tire blowouts. One of the responses employed by Firestone was to shift the blame for these unfortunate incidents, suggesting that the problems occurred "only for Ford Explorers" because the Ford Motor Company recommended that tires be underinflated (Blaney, Benoit, & Brazeal, 2002, p. 383). This suggests that the problem was not caused by the tires themselves (when properly used) but by another company that gave dangerous instructions for using the otherwise safe products. If accepted by the audience, this explanation would move the blame for these deaths from Firestone to Ford.

Evasion of Responsibility.   This group of image repair strategies has four forms. Provocation explains that the firm's offensive act was a (reasonable) response to a prior offensive act. For instance, a company might claim it moved its plant to another state because the first state passed a new law reducing its profit margin. Part of the blame may be allocated on the person or organization that provoked the offensive act instead of having all the blame on the accused.

A second option for evading responsibility is defeasibility. Here, the accused explains that a lack of information about or control over key aspects of the situation contributed to the offensive act. To illustrate, an executive who missed a meeting might argue that "I was not informed of the meeting." Lacking important information may partially excuse the offensive act, reducing responsibility for it.

A third form of evading responsibility is to argue that the offensive action occurred by accident. One of the defenses offered by Sears when it was accused of overcharging customers for unneeded auto repairs was the claim that the auto repair mistakes were "inadvertent," rather than intentional (Benoit, 1995b, p. 97). Greater blame should come from an offensive act that occurred purposefully rather than inadvertently. If the firm persuades the audience that the offensive act in question happened accidentally, it should be held less accountable and the damage to the company's image should abate.

Stressing one's good intentions is another way to evade responsibility. Just as performing an offensive act accidentally (without malice) may reduce responsibility, when we do wrong while trying to do something good may help reduce blame. The tobacco industry was also defended by a lobbying group, the Tobacco Institute. In response to the accusation that cigarette companies were targeting young people with their deadly product, the Tobacco Institute argued that the industry had good intentions: "No other industry in America has taken such direct—and voluntary—actions to steer its product away from young people" (Benoit & Hirson, 2001, p. 287). Stressing the fact that these were *voluntary* actions may help create the impression that the industry's intentions were good, which in turn could reduce blame.

Reduce Offensiveness.   A firm that has been accused or suspected of wrongdoing may attempt to reduce the perceived offensiveness of that act. Obviously this strategy is meant to deal with the offensiveness of the act in question rather than with responsibility for that act. This approach to image repair has six variants.

One option for reducing offensiveness is bolstering. This strategy attempts to strengthen the audience's positive feelings toward the accused so as to offset the negative feelings arising from the wrongful deed. Dow Corning was criticized for manufacturing dangerous breast implants. The company attempted to show its concern for women: "Our overriding responsibility is to the women using silicone mammary implants" (Brinson & Benoit, 1996, p. 37). This statement does not argue either that implants are not harmful or that Dow Corning is not responsible for its breast implants. The point is to foster favorable feelings toward the company by declaring its concern for women, hoping that this positive attitude will counterbalance the negative feelings about the firm's breast implants.

A second form of reducing offensiveness is to directly lessen the negative feelings associated with the wrongful act, minimizing offensiveness. When accused of auto repair fraud, Sears also used minimization, suggesting that "with over two million automobile customers serviced in California alone," the instances of over-charging were few (Benoit, 1995b, p. 97). The suggestion is that these offensive acts were isolated examples rather than a widespread pattern of abuse.

Differentiation is a third image repair strategy used to reduce offensiveness. The basic idea is to distinguish the offensive act from similar but more offensive actions. In comparison, the offensive act does not look so bad. The classic example is to tell a friend, "I did not steal your car; I only borrowed it (without asking)." Both actions are offensive; however, stealing is clearly worse than borrowing without permission. The R. J. Reynolds Tobacco Company attempted to differenti-ate the addictiveness of cigarettes, suggesting, "Cigarette smoking is more like drinking coffee and eating chocolate than like using cocaine, heroin, or any truly addicting hard drug" (Benoit, 1998, p. 222). This strategy does not eliminate offensiveness, but it uses a comparison to reduce the perceived offensiveness of the firm's action.

A fourth method of reducing offensiveness is to employ transcendence. This strategy tries to put the act in a more favorable context, thereby making it appear less offensive. Dow Corning used this strategy by suggesting that there are "mil-lions of women who have had a compelling need for these implants" (Brinson & Benoit, 1996, p. 35). The point is that women's "need" for implants should be bal-anced against the potential risks.

A fifth variant of reducing offensiveness is to attack one's accuser. This strat-egy may help repair an image in two ways. First, it may suggest that the victim of the offensive act deserved what he or she received, thus lessening offensiveness. Second, criticizing the accuser can undermine the credibility and effectiveness of the attack. One of Sears' responses to the accusations of auto repair fraud was to criticize the California Consumer Affairs Department (which promulgated the accusations of auto repair fraud) for relying on a flawed investigation. Sears also claimed that the accusations were politically motivated, again attempting to reduce the credibility of the attack (Benoit, 1995b).

The last form of reducing offensiveness is compensation. If the compensation is acceptable to the victim, the firm's image should be improved. For example, if a company supplies defective parts to another firm, the offender may offer a discount on other goods to alleviate the ill will (the company might also want to replace the defective parts with good ones, but that would be an example of the next strategy).

Corrective Action.   One of the most effective image repair strategies is corrective action, in which the company promises to correct the problem. It can take two forms: restoring the state of affairs existing before the offensive action (fixing the problem), and/or promising to prevent the recurrence of the offensive act. For example, Texaco was accused of racism when a tape recording surfaced of one of its executives saying that African American employees were "black jelly beans" who were "glued to the bottom of the jar" (Brinson & Benoit, 1999, p. 484). Peter Bijur, chair of Texaco, promised that the company would "do everything in our power to heal the painful wounds that the reckless behavior of those involved have inflicted" (p. 494). This action attempts to repair the damage from the executive's remarks. He also announced that "I have directed today that all of our diversity and equal employment opportunity programs be reviewed" to prevent future problems (p. 493). Corrective action is an important option for repairing an image. Sometimes identifying and punishing the guilty is important, but people also want problems to be resolved and prevented.

Mortification.   The other general form of image repair strategy is to admit wrongdoing and ask for forgiveness, an approach Kenneth Burke labels mortification (1970). AT&T's long-distance service was interrupted in 1991. Among other problems, this grounded air travel in many parts of the country because the air traffic controllers relied on long-distance lines. AT&T's chairman, Robert Allen, published a letter of apology in newspapers. In it, he accepted responsibility for the disruption of service ("I am deeply disturbed that AT&T was responsible for a disruption in communications service") and offered a direct apology ("I apologize to all of you who were affected, directly or indirectly") (Benoit & Brinson, 1994, pp. 81–82). This is a very clear example of mortification or apology.

SUGGESTIONS FOR IMAGE REPAIR MESSAGES

It is important to realize that this typology of image repair strategies lists options available for those with damaged images. There is no guarantee that any strategy or combination of strategies will necessarily repair an image. For example, the Tobacco Institute employed denial: "The tobacco industry does not want young people to smoke" (Benoit & Hirson, 2001, p. 286). It is not at all clear that this denial would have persuaded many in the audience. The various case studies that have been conducted on image repair discourse are providing suggestions for effectively using the strategies emerging from this research. These suggestions are arranged here under three topics: preparing for crisis, identifying the nature of the crisis, and coping with crisis.

Preparation for Crisis

It is important to anticipate potential crises and prepare a contingency plan. Before a crisis emerges, careful planning can help to reduce response time and may avert mistakes in an organization's response to a crisis. It would be useful for the firm to identify a key executive who will be responsible for developing and then implementing a crisis response, someone who is able to take quick action when the need arises. For example, Tylenol acted quickly in the first poisoning episode (Benoit & Lindsey, 1987), whereas Exxon's reaction to the oil spill was too slow, hindering its attempt to repair its damaged image (Benoit, 1995a).

As suggested, the responsible executive should anticipate potential crises and prepare contingency plans. Of course, crises can take a variety of forms and an individual crisis is typically unexpected. However, some possible threats to a company's image can be anticipated. For example, restaurants should prepare a plan in case of food-poisoning. An airline should prepare a crisis contingency plan for a plane crash. These contingency plans should be reviewed periodically and updated as necessary. Furthermore, they must be implemented thoughtfully and flexibly; elements of the actual crisis may differ from the anticipated crisis, so crisis response plans should be modified as needed. However, having a ready plan that can be modified should both speed up the response and help avoid mistakes.

Identifying the Nature of the Crisis

When a crisis arises, it is important to understand both the nature of accusations and the relevant audience(s). First, what are the accusations or suspicions? A firm must know the nature of the crisis to respond appropriately. For example, arguing that accounting mistakes were accidents should be a more effective response to the accusation that a company "cooked" the books than the accusation that it engaged in careless bookkeeping. Second, it is important to know the perceived severity of the alleged offense. The response should be tailored to the offense. A more serious offense may require a different response than a minor offense.

Identifying the Relevant Audience(s).   It is extremely important to identify the most important audience(s). A vital part of persuasion is adapting a message to the intended audience. We noted earlier that a company in crisis may need to address several audiences; it is important not to design a message for the wrong audience! For example, suppose a company is accused of polluting the environment. At least five audiences are part of this situation. First, the company may wish to persuade the attackers, environmentalists. Second, the opinions of the firm's stockholders are obviously important, if they are aware of the controversy. A third audience consists of government regulators who may fine or otherwise sanction the company. Customers are yet another potential audience. People who live in the vicinity of the polluting plant are a fifth audience. It is important to realize that the interests of these various groups differ widely (e.g., environmentalists would care most about nature and extent of the pollution; stockholders about profits; regulators about environmental laws; customers about product performance and image; voters about their quality of life in their community). This means that strategies that might be effective with one audience could fail utterly with another. A crisis communicator must select the most important audience and tailor messages to the needs and interests of that group.

Of course, a firm facing a crisis may want to persuade more than one audience. In that case the communicator should decide which audience is most important. Then he or she can make sure that the most important audience is appeased, devoting as much time and effort to the other audiences as possible. It is possible to craft different messages for different audiences (keep in mind that separate messages may stress different points depending on the intended audience; it is risky to develop contradictory messages). It is also possible to devote different passages or parts of a message to different audiences. In any event, the crisis communicator must identify the most important audience(s) and adapt messages to be most persuasive with those intended audience(s).

Coping with Crisis

Once one has identified the accusation(s) and audience(s), what is next? First, it may be possible to redefine the attack. Differentiation is an example of this approach. Second, instead of altering the nature of the accusations, the business may attempt to refocus attention on other issues. A counterattack may shift the audiences' attentions away from the accusation. A company takes a risk when it ignores an accusation; however, if the key audiences shift their focus to the issues that the company decides to emphasize in an image repair message, that can benefit the company. Furthermore, one must not attack accusers whom the audience could view as sympathetic victims (e.g., children, elderly). Third, it is possible that each accusation is not important to the audiences. One may be able to ignore or slight an accusation that is less important to a specific audience. In other words, one may treat one accusation strategically different when addressing one audience than when addressing another, even to the point of not addressing the accusation at all.

It is important to keep in mind that image restoration rhetoric is a form of persuasive discourse, which means that recommendations for effective responses to crisis can be derived from our understanding of persuasion generally. The analysis of the ad wars between Coke and Pepsi (Benoit, 1995a) stressed such advice: Do not make false claims, provide adequate support for claims, develop themes throughout a campaign, avoid arguments that may backfire. Analysis of Exxon's discourse on the *Valdez* oil spill (Benoit, 1995a) indicated that once Exxon made self-serving statements that were at odds with other information available to the audience (their allegedly swift and competent cleanup), this may have damaged Exxon's credibility and undermined other arguments. Coke's response to Pepsi's accusations appropriately used a clearly identified and prominent company spokesperson (Benoit, 1995a), which was probably more effective than Sears' initial reliance on a lawyer from outside the company (Benoit, 1995b). However, other suggestions for image repair discourse are specific to various crisis communication strategies.

First, when a company is at fault it should probably admit this immediately (note, however, that image repair concerns may conflict with other goals, such as not providing evidence for the other side of a lawsuit). Apart from the fact that admitting wrongdoing is the morally correct action, attempting to deny true accusations can backfire. An organization that falsely denies being at fault for offensive action risks damaging its credibility if and when the truth emerges. For example, AT&T initially tried to shift the blame for the disruption to long-distance service, but it eventually accepted responsibility and apologized for the problem. This confession, along with corrective action, probably helped to repair its image (Benoit & Brinson, 1994). In the cola wars, Pepsi should have apologized for making false accusations against Coke (Benoit, 1995a); it had alleged that Coke charged its largest customer, McDonald's, less than it did other customers.

Of course, we know that those who are accused of wrongdoing are, at times, completely innocent. For example, Tylenol successfully denied that it had been responsible for deaths of customers (Benoit & Lindsey, 1987). As just suggested, Coca-Cola argued effectively that Pepsi's charges that Coke's other customers subsidized McDonald's were false (Benoit, 1995a). When innocent, a persuasive denial may be able to thwart the threat to image.

Third, at times it is possible to successfully shift the blame. For instance, Tylenol was able to shift blame for the poisonings to an unknown person, a madman (Benoit & Lindsey, 1987). This exonerated the company. In contrast Exxon tried to shift the blame for the *Valdez* oil spill to Captain Hazelwood, however, given that this captain had been hired and given command of the *Valdez* by Exxon, Exxon at the very least had to share responsibility with Hazelwood. Exxon also tried to blame the delay in the cleanup on the Coast Guard and the state of Alaska (Benoit, 1995a). These were not plausible targets for blame. The person or organization to whom one shifts the blame must be seen as a reasonable candidate for blame by the audience for this strategy to be successful.

Related to this is the strategy of defeasibility. For example, Exxon could have done a more effective job emphasizing the poor ocean conditions, which was beyond its control, as a hindrance to cleaning up the oil spill. If factors beyond one's control can be shown to have caused, or contributed to, the offensive act, defeasibility may alleviate responsibility and help restore a tarnished image.

Fifth, it is often very important to announce plans to correct and/or prevent recurrence of the problem. A firm commitment to correct the problem can be an effective component of image repair discourse. Corrective action is particularly important for those who admit responsibility for the offensive act. For instance, AT&T described in some detail plans for insuring reliability (Benoit & Brinson, 1994). Even those who are innocent of wrongdoing can benefit from plans for preventing recurrence of the problem. For example, while Tylenol denied responsibility for the deaths from poisoned capsules, they introduced tamper-resistant packaging after the first incident and phased out capsules altogether after the second incident (Benoit & Lindsey, 1987). The idea was to prevent another mad-man from adulterating its products.

Of course, use of corrective action cannot guarantee success. For example, although Exxon boasted of its "swift" and "competent" actions, newspaper reports revealed that these descriptions were inaccurate. There is a risk that this strategy will fail—and possibly even make things worse—if a company's actions do not redeem its promises.

Sixth, minimization cannot always be expected to improve one's image. An attempt to make a serious problem seem trivial can create a backlash in the audience.

It is possible that multiple strategies can work well together, a seventh suggestion. Union Carbide's plans to alleviate suffering were consistent with the attempts at bolstering, portraying the company as concerned with victims of the tragedy. Similarly, the strategy of defeasibility can identify the causes of the problem, which are then addressed by suitable corrective action. However, some strategies are incompatible. Saying "I deny that I committed this offense but I did so with good intentions" is unlikely to improve a damaged image. It can be important to offer a message that is consistent.

Finally, we must recognize that the powers of persuasion are limited. Other than corrective action, there was probably little that Exxon could do to repair its image after the *Valdez* oil spill—other than wait until most consumers had forgotten the incident. Some offenses are so heinous that forgiveness is impossible, excuses ineffectual. Indeed, earlier versions of this theory were called "image restoration." However, we prefer "image repair" because it is often unrealistic to believe that a tarnished image can be completely restored. It is often possible to repair an image, alleviating some of the damage.

CASE: VIOXX

Vioxx is a popular pain and arthritis drug that was consumed by millions world-wide after it launched in 1999, and chalked up global sales amounting to 2.5 billion in 2003 alone. It was withdrawn from the market on September 30, 2004. Merck & Co., which manufactured the drug, withdrew it after a trial showed that those who took 25mg of Vioxx daily for more than eighteen months were twice as likely to suffer a heart attack or stroke as those on a placebo. The withdrawal was described as the largest voluntary drug recall in history (Kaufman, 2004). A public opinion poll in February 2005 revealed that 56 percent of respondents said they had followed the Vioxx incident very or fairly closely (Kaiser, 2005).

Merck said it withdrew the drug based on results of a three-year clinical study that it had received days earlier. It said the withdrawal was to protect patients from further risks. However, allegations of cardiovascular risks associated with the drug surfaced as early as 2000. Though Merck said it was aware of some of the possible risks involved, the results were not positively conclusive. Significantly, the withdrawal coincided with a study released by a Food and Drug Administration (FDA) researcher about a month earlier, claiming that a database analysis of 1.4 million patients found that Vioxx users were more likely to suffer a heart attack or sudden cardiac death than those taking another drug, Celebrex, or an older nonsteroidal anti-inflammatory drug (NSAID) (Rubin, 2004). The key accusations were that Merck had sold a dangerous prescription drug (Vioxx) and that it had known about the side effects long before it recalled the drug.

Against the onslaught of criticism leveled at Merck from the medical fraternity, lawsuits by patients, and investigations by the U.S. Justice Department and the Securities and Exchange Commission, Merck maintained all along that it had acted appropriately. In February 2005, an FDA panel supported Vioxx's eventual return to the market (Schmit & McCoy, 2005). In May 2005, CEO Raymond Gilmartin, who, by far, had been Merck's most prominent defender in the controversy, resigned abruptly (McCoy & Appleby, 2005).

The dramatic twists in this case provide an intriguing opportunity to study the strategies Merck used to defend its position. Two key questions are asked: First, what were the predominant image repair strategies used by Merck in its defense? Second, how effective were these strategies? To analyze Merck's strategies, texts were obtained from two sources. Press releases, speeches, and statements made by Merck officials, particularly its CEO, from September 30, 2004, to May 6, 2005, were obtained from Merck's web site, downloaded from the "Newsroom" link. Stories, and replies by Merck officials in the letter-to-the-editor pages regarding the Vioxx withdrawal, published in three national dailies, *The Washington Post, New York Times,* and *USA Today,* were searched in Lexis-Nexis from September 30, 2004, to May 30, 2005. These were screened and those that quoted Merck officials were used.

Image Repair Efforts

Merck's image repair strategies can be analyzed in three phases. Each will be discussed separately here.

Phase 1: Withdrawal of Vioxx—bolstering, corrective action, and defeasibility. This period ran from September 30, 2004, to November 7, 2004. Right from the beginning, Merck employed the key strategy of bolstering its reputation. In its first press statement, Raymond Gilmartin, Merck's chairman, president, and CEO, stressed that the withdrawal was "voluntary" because the company believed that "best serves the interests of patients." At the same time, it had taken the necessary corrective action to inform the FDA, pharmacists, and physicians of its decision. It also offered to reimburse users with unused Vioxx (Merck, 2004).

Bolstering and defeasibility appeared to be the key strategies used to counter the allegations that it had known about the cardiovascular risks all along: Merck argued that prior research yielded no conclusive results and that only recently had the risks become clear. Bolstering was used when Merck argued that it had been transparent and proactive in rigorously subjecting the drug to repeated tests, and keeping the regulatory and medical community abreast of the developments. For instance, the president of Merck Research Laboratories, Dr. Peter S. Kim, argued that even though tests were inconclusive, the company had made all the test results public, including publication in a respected medical journal.

"We worked diligently with FDA to review these data and develop revised prescribing information," he said (Kim, 2004).

Bolstering of its actions extended to bolstering of its reputation and its belief in its products in news interviews and the three open letters Gilmartin wrote, presumably addressing shareholders, employees, and patients. Responding to speculation that Merck might sink into financial deep waters as a result of the withdrawal, Gilmartin reinstated: "Our business prospects are strong . . . we have a strong balance sheet, with cash and reserves that well exceed debt. We have high performing products . . . we have depth and breadth in our pipeline . . . we are well prepared to meet the challenges ahead and extremely confident in our financial strength and excellence of our science" (Merck, 2005).

Phase 2: Initial investigations—bolstering, defeasibility, partial blame shifting. This period lasted from November 8, 2004, to January 2005. During this phase Merck maintained its strategy of defeasibility to justify earlier inaction and bolstering (Gilmartin even observed that his wife was a Vioxx user). However, Merck increasingly began to shift the blame to the FDA. Even though it did not explicitly blame the FDA for the debacle, it suggested that part of the blame ought to be shared by the FDA. After all, the FDA was the regulatory body that approved Vioxx, and Merck had kept it informed at every stage of the research into Vioxx (Gilmartin, 2004a, 2004b). In this case, shifting the blame did not claim intentional wrongdoing by another party, but instead the company suggested the other party should share part of the responsibility for the wrongdoing.

Phase 3: Possible reinstatement—bolstering, partial shifting blame, bolstering. This period extended from February to May 2005. The possibility of reinstating Vioxx, described as "an unusual but not unprecedented event" (Schmit, 2005), was raised by an FDA panel in February 2005. Kim continued to bolster Merck's product by saying that "if the advisory committee and FDA conclude that the benefits of this class outweigh the risks in some patient populations, then we would have to consider the implications of these new data given the *unique* benefits Vioxx offers" (2005; emphasis added). Yet at the same time, when wrongdoing was pinned on Merck, the firm continued to engage in moving some of the blame to the FDA. In response to a front page story in the *New York Times* on April 24 that suggested that Merck knew of the risks, Kenneth C. Frazier, Merck's general counsel, further bolstered Merck's transparent practice of making its tests public, and subtly suggested the inescapable fact remained that the FDA had "analyzed the relevant information in its decision on the Vioxx label" (Frazier, 2005). In his testimony to the U.S. House of Representatives, Dr. Dennis Erb, Merck's vice president in global strategic regulatory development, maintained that the "FDA and an independent advisory panel agreed that Vioxx was safe and effective when used in accordance with its prescribing information" (Erb, 2005).

Evaluation of Image Repair Strategies

Merck's campaign throughout the eight-month period, from October 2004 to May 2005, appeared to have been about shaping the image of the company as one that was "diligent," "responsible," "prompt," "rigorous," "open," and "displayed integrity" in the saga. Its strategies had been consistent, and the statements issued by different Merck officials echoed the same message. Benoit (2004) and Brinson and Benoit (1999) argued such consistency is a hallmark of a confident campaign. More than just spewing savvy sound bites, Merck fortified its defense by bringing out an armory of evidence to support its case. For instance, the firm countered allegations that it had known about the cardiovascular risks by citing evidence of the inconclusive tests on Vioxx, while at the same time it took the opportunity to bolster its image as open, ethical, and honest.

In the first phase, bolstering was used along with corrective action and defeasibility. Corrective action was used to inform patients how they could be reimbursed. Defeasibility was used when Merck explained why it had not taken preventive action earlier. Bolstering and corrective action have been proven to be effective strategies in earlier studies (Brinson & Benoit, 1999), and pleading defeasibility (it lacked the necessary knowledge to make informed decisions) also proved to be effective. Consequently, feedback on the first phase of its campaign had been positive. The FDA praised Merck for its prompt action (Khalik, 2004), and others noted that the crisis was handled in "an exemplary manner" (Jones, 2004). Despite that, reservations remained. A *Chief Marketing Officer* magazine poll showed 56 percent of respondents believed Merck waited too long to take Vioxx off the market, with a follow-up poll showing that 57 percent of the respondents believed Merck was responsible for the continued sale of Vioxx after the health risks became apparent ("CMO Poll," 2004).

Merck's use of bolstering and defeasibility, with the strategic introduction of partial blame shifting in the subsequent two phases, further reinforced the message and image it aimed to convey, and the message that any imputation of liability should be referred to the regulatory authority, the FDA, which had approved the product. By doing so, besides subtly shifting the burden, Merck had also shifted the spotlight to the FDA, leading to calls from the scientific community and legislators to question the FDA's role in this saga. During this time, another poll—the *Wall Street Journal* Online/Harris Interactive Health Care Poll—that surveyed two classes of respondents, adults as well as Vioxx users, found that half believed Merck had acted responsibly. For the FDA, most of the adults (43 percent) as well as Vioxx users (51 percent) believed the FDA acted responsibly ("Nearly Half of Adults," 2004). A CNN/*USA Today*/Gallup poll reported that 70 percent had confidence in the FDA to ensure prescription drugs were safe (Appleby, 2004). By March 2005, however, an Associated Press/Ipsos Public Affairs poll found that consumers were more confident in the safety of prescription drugs than they were in the FDA's ability to ensure safety with use (Ipsos, 2005).

Thus far, Merck had been able to argue its case and reduce its liability. Whether these proved to be effective strategies in the long-term remain to be seen, especially when there was a cloud hanging over its head with the unexpected resignation of Gilmartin in May 2005, in the light of fresh revelations released by the House Committee on Government Reform (Kaufman, 2005) that Merck used hard sales tactics to market Vioxx.

QUESTIONS FOR APPLICATION

1. Which audience was it most important for Merck to address and why?

2. If Vioxx was safe, why "voluntarily" withdraw it? In other words, was the withdrawal of the drug truly voluntary?

3. Merck argued that earlier tests were "inconclusive." Is that enough, or should the drug be marketed when tests are inconclusive? Why or why not?

4. In phase two, was the FDA a plausible "target" for shifting the blame? If so, how much should that reduce Merck's blame?

5. If the company had tried to deny that Vioxx was harmful, how might that have affected the image repair effort?

REFERENCES

Allen, M. W., & Caillouet, R. H. (1994). Legitimation endeavors: Impression management strategies used by an organization in crisis. *Communication Monographs, 61,* pp. 44–62.

Appleby, J. (2004, November 23). Poll: Confidence in FDA still strong despite blunders. *USA Today.* Accessed June 29, 2005, www.usatoday.com/news/health/2004-11-23-fda_x.htm.

Benoit, W. L. (1995a). *Accounts, excuses, apologies: A theory of image restoration discourse.* Albany: State University of New York Press.

———. (1995b). Sears' repair of its auto service image: Image restoration discourse in the corporate sector. *Communication Studies, 46,* pp. 89–105.

———. (1997a). Hugh Grant's image restoration discourse: An actor apologizes. *Communication Quarterly, 45,* pp. 251–267.

———. (1997b). Image restoration discourse and crisis communication. *Public Relations Review, 23,* pp. 177–186.

———. (1998). Merchants of death: Persuasive defenses by the tobacco industry. In J. F. Klumpp (Ed.), *Argument in a time of change: Definition, frameworks, and critiques* (pp. 220–225). Annandale, VA: NCA.

———. (1999). Clinton in the Starr chamber. *American Communication Journal.* Accessed at www.americancomm.org/~aca/acj/acj.html.

———. (2000). Another visit to the theory of image restoration strategies. *Communication Quarterly, 48,* pp. 40–43.

———. (2004). Image restoration discourse and crisis communication. In D. P. Millar & R. L. Heath (Eds.), *Responding to crisis: A rhetorical approach to crisis communication* (pp. 263–280). Mahwah, NJ: Lawrence Erlbaum.

———. (2005). Image restoration theory. In R. L. Heath (Ed.), *Encyclopedia of public relations* (vol. 1, pp. 407–410). Thousand Oaks, CA: Sage.

Benoit, W. L., & Anderson, K. K. (1996). Blending politics and entertainment: Dan Quayle versus Murphy Brown. *Southern Communication Journal, 62,* pp. 73–85.

Benoit, W. L., & Brinson, S. (1994). AT&T: Apologies are not enough. *Communication Quarterly, 42,* pp. 75–88.

Benoit, W. L., & Brinson, S. L. (1999). Queen Elizabeth's image repair discourse: Insensitive royal or compassionate queen? *Public Relations Review, 25,* pp. 145–156.

Benoit, W. L., & Czerwinski, A. (1997). A critical analysis of USAir's image repair discourse. *Business Communication Quarterly, 60,* pp. 38–57.

Benoit, W. L., & Dorries, B. (1996). *Dateline NBC's* persuasive attack of Wal-Mart. *Communication Quarterly, 44,* pp. 463–477.

Benoit, W. L., & Drew, S. (1997). Appropriateness and effectiveness of image repair strategies. *Communication Reports, 10,* pp. 153–163.

Benoit, W. L., Gullifor, P., & Panici, D. (1991). President Reagan's defensive discourse on the Iran-contra affair. *Communication Studies, 42,* pp. 272–294.

Benoit, W. L., & Hanczor, R. (1994). The Tonya Harding controversy: An analysis of image repair strategies. *Communication Quarterly, 42,* pp. 416–433.

Benoit, W. L., & Harthcock, A. (1999). Attacking the tobacco industry: A rhetorical analysis of advertisements by the Campaign for Tobacco-Free Kids. *Southern Communication Journal, 65,* pp. 66–81.

Benoit, W. L., & Hirson, D. (2001). *Doonesbury* versus the Tobacco Institute: The Smoke Starters' Coupon. *Communication Quarterly, 49,* pp. 279–294.

Benoit, W. L., & McHale, J. P. (1999). Kenneth Starr's image repair discourse viewed in *20/20. Communication Quarterly, 47,* pp. 265–280.

Benoit, W. L., & Nill, D. M. (1998a). A critical analysis of Judge Clarence Thomas's statement before the Senate Judiciary Committee. *Communication Studies, 49,* pp. 179–195.

———. (1998b). Oliver Stone's defense of *JFK. Communication Quarterly, 46,* pp. 127–143.

Benoit, W. L., & Wells, W. T. (1998). An analysis of three image restoration discourses on Whitewater. *Journal of Public Advocacy, 3,* pp. 21–37.

Blaney, J. R., & Benoit, W. L. (1997). The persuasive defense of Jesus in the Gospel according to John. *Journal of Communication and Religion, 20,* pp. 25–30.

———. (2001). *The Clinton scandals and the politics of image restoration.* Westport, CT: Praeger.

Blaney, J. R., Benoit, W. L., & Brazeal, L. M. (2002). Blowout! Firestone's image restoration campaign. *Public Relations Research, 28,* pp. 379–392.

Brinson, S., & Benoit, W. L. (1996). Dow Corning's image repair strategies in the breast implant crisis. *Communication Quarterly, 44,* pp. 29–41.

———. (1999). The tarnished star: Restoring Texaco's damaged public image. *Management Communication Quarterly, 12,* pp. 483–510.

Burke, K. (1970). *The rhetoric of religion.* Berkeley: University of California Press.

CMO Poll. (2004). Accessed June 29, 2005, from www .cmomagazine.com/poll/results.html? ID=669.

Drumheller, K., & Benoit, W. L. (2004). USS *Greeneville* collides with Japan's *Ehime Maru:* Cultural issues in image repair discourse. *Public Relations Review, 30,* pp. 177–185.

Dutton, J. E. (1986). The processing of crisis and non-crisis strategic issues. *Journal of Management Studies, 23,* pp. 501–517.

Elwood, W. M. (Ed.) (1995). *Public relations inquiry as rhetorical criticism: Case studies of corporate discourse and social influence.* Westport, CT: Praeger.

Erb, D. (2005, June 27). Testimony of Dennis Erb before the U.S. House of Representatives. Accessed June 27, 2005, from www.merck.com.

Fink, S. L., Beak, J., & Taddeo, K. (1971). Organizational crisis and change. *Journal of Applied Behavioral Science, 7,* pp. 15–37.

Frazier, K. C. (2005, May 1). Merck and Vioxx. *New York Times,* p. 13.

Gilmartin, R. V. (2004a, November 18). Prepared testimony of Raymond V. Gilmartin before the U.S. Senate Committee on Finance. Accessed May 14, 2005, from www.merck.com.

———. (2004b, December 14). Opening remarks of Raymond V. Gilmartin at the 2004 Annual Business Briefing. Accessed May 15, 2005, from www.merck.com.

Heath, R. L., & Nelson, R. A. (1986). *Issues management: Corporate policymaking in an information society.* Beverly Hills, CA: Sage.

Hearit, K. M. (2001). Corporate apologia: When an organization speaks in defense of itself. In R. L. Heath (Ed.), *Handbook of public relations* (pp. 501–511). Thousand Oaks, CA: Sage.

Ipsos. (2005, March 9). Vioxx recall hurt Americans' confidence in FDA, not prescription drugs. Ipsos news release. Accessed June 29, 2005, from www .ipsos-na.com/news/pressrelease.cfm? id52591.

Jones, D. (2004, October 1). Experts give CEO's reaction top marks. *USA Today,* p. 2B.

Kaiser Family Foundation. (2005, February 2–6). Poll. Accessed July 1, 2005, from web.lexisnexis. com/universe/document?_m=2eafd5a9ba4 372af8c42de7488bf7b4b&_docnum=5&wchp= dGLbVtb-zSkVA&_md5=1cc9016c4a042d4e3ff7b 994466c7f2b.y.

Kaufman, M. (2004, October 1). Merck withdraws arthritic medication; Vioxx maker cites users' health risks. *The Washington Post,* p. 1A.

———. (2005, May 6). Merck CEO resigns as drug probe continues. *Washington Post,* p. A01.

Kennedy, K. A., & Benoit, W. L. (1997). The Newt Gingrich book deal controversy: A case study in self-defense rhetoric. *Southern Communication Journal, 63,* pp. 197–216.

Khalik, S. (2004, October 2). Arthritis drug Vioxx taken off the market. *The Straits Times,* p. 1.

Kim, P. S. (2004, October 13). Remarks of Peter S. Kim, Ph.D., President, Merck Research Laboratories, at a press conference, New York City. Accessed May 14, 2005, from www .merck.com.

———. (2005, February 17). Statement issued by Dr. Peter S. Kim at the FDA Advisory Committee Meeting. Accessed May 14, 2005, from www .merck.com.

Len-Ríos, M., & Benoit, W. L. (2004). Gary Condit's image repair strategies: Squandering a golden opportunity. *Public Relations Research, 50,* pp. 95–106.

McCoy, K., & Appleby, J. (2005, May 6). Company veteran replaces Merck CEO. *USA Today*, p. 1B.

Merck. (2004, September 30). Merck voluntarily withdraws Vioxx. Accessed October 3, 2005, from www.merck.com.

———. (2005). Our future, our strength. Accessed May 14, 2005, from www.merck.com.

Millar, D. L., & Heath, R. L. (Eds.). (2004). *Responding to crisis: A rhetorical approach to crisis communication*. Mahwah, NJ: Lawrence Erlbaum.

Moffitt, M. A. (1994). Collapsing and integrating concepts of "public" and "image" into a new theory. *Public Relations Research, 20*, pp. 159–170.

Nearly half of US adults closely followed news coverage of Vioxx withdrawal. (2004, December 10). *Wall Street Journal Online*. Accessed June 29, 2005, from www.harrisinteractive.com/news/newsletters/wsjhealthnews/WSJOnline_HI_HealthCarePoll2004vol3_iss24.pdf.

Olaniran, B. A., & Williams, D. E. (2001). Anticipatory model of crisis management: A vigilant response to technological crises. In R. L. Heath (Ed.), *Handbook of public relations* (pp. 487–500). Thousand Oaks, CA: Sage.

Pinsdorf, M. K. (1987). *Communicating when your company is under siege: Surviving public crisis*. Lexington, MA: Heath.

Pomerantz, A. (1978). Attributions of responsibility: Blamings. *Sociology, 12*, pp. 115–121.

Rubin, R. (2004, October 12). How did Vioxx debacle happen? *USA Today*, p. 2D.

Ryan, H. R. (1982). *Kategoria* and *apologia:* On their rhetorical criticism as a speech set. *Quarterly Journal of Speech, 68*, pp. 256–261.

Schmit, J. (2004, February 22). Return of Vioxx would be unusual, not unprecedented. *USA Today*, p. 3B.

Schmit, J., & McCoy, K. (2005, February 21). FDA panel supports return of Vioxx. *USA Today*, p. 1B.

Ware, B. L., & Linkugel, W. A. (1973). They spoke in defense of themselves: On the generic criticism of *apologia*. *Quarterly Journal of Speech, 59*, pp. 273–283.

Zhang, J., & Benoit, W. L. (2004). Message strategies of Saudi Arabia's image restoration campaign after 9/11. *Public Relations Review, 30*, pp. 161–167.

———. (in press). Former Minister Zhang's discourse on SARS: Government's image restoration or destruction? In Center of Media and Communication Research (Ed.), *Social construction of SARS*. Hong Kong: Hong Kong Baptist University Press.

CHAPTER SIXTEEN

THE DEVELOPMENT OF THE SITUATIONAL CRISIS COMMUNICATION THEORY

TIMOTHY COOMBS

The development of public relations theory has been historically sparse. In 1987, J. V. Pavlik (1987) noted that very little of the preceding decade's research in public relations was dedicated to developing theory. Two years later the trend was the same. C. Botan (1989), too, noted the general lack of theory development in public relations and a dearth of social scientific research in public relations. His observation was part of his own and V. Hazleton's efforts to begin focusing academic efforts on public relations theory development; to that end they edited the first book devoted entirely to public relations theory, titled *Public Relations Theory* (1989). The challenge to develop a theoretical base in the field of public relations was taking form. In 2003, Sallot, Lyon, Acosta-Alzuru, and Jones's analysis of 748 published articles in the main public relations journals found that 19.8 percent (148) were devoted to theory. While the smallest percentage in the authors' three categories, it is evidence that some progress is being made in public relations theory development.

Crisis communication, a subset of public relations, has been further behind the research and theory curve than the main field itself. For too many years crisis communication research was simply practitioner truisms and tales from the field: "What I did during our crisis." Botan's (1989) statement on the public relations field is a perfect fit for crisis communication today: "Theory does not develop automatically out of a large body of practical research. Systematic application of the theory development process is needed" (p. 107). Crisis communication has created a large body of practical research but scant theory has emerged. In a review of the crisis communication literature, Seeger, Sellnow, and Ulmer (1998) noted the lack of theory-based approaches. In Heath's (2001) *Handbook of Public Relations,* two different chapters noted the *recent* emergence of theory in crisis communication (Olaniran & Williams, 2001; Seeger, Sellnow, & Ulmer, 2001). One of the theory-driven approaches recognized in recent crisis management reviews is the situational crisis communication theory (SCCT) (Coombs & Holladay, 2002). This chapter articulates the theory, reviews the development of SCCT, and presents a case study of crisis communication for its application. Both crisis communication and the term *theory* are broad concepts with multiple definitions. It is useful to clarify how the term *theory* is used as well as to indicate the scope of crisis communication covered by SCCT.

CLARIFYING THEORY

Crisis communication is a diverse field that draws researchers and ideas from management, psychology, public relations, and rhetorical theory. It is also a very pragmatic, applied field. Crisis managers look to the literature for ideas on how to improve their crisis responses (Barton, 2001). Hence, crisis communication theory needs to go beyond the explanatory function of theory to prediction and control functions. Prediction involves the ability to anticipate outcomes while control provides suggestions for which actions should be the most effective or appropriate (Anderson & Ross, 2002; Neuliep, 1996). Crisis communication theory should be able to tell crisis managers what to expect in a crisis and how best to respond communicatively to the crisis. As an applied social science, prediction and control ideas do not net desired public relations results with 100 percent certainty—we do not have laws as are found in the physical sciences. People complicate our theories because it is human to sometimes act irrationally or unexpectedly. Even the science of economics is beginning to recognize the variability of humans with the development of behavioral economics, a field that moves away from the overly rationale mathematical absolutes of mainstream economics. Crisis communication theory seeks to offer guidelines that crisis managers can adapt to their own, unique circumstances.

CLARIFYING THE SCOPE

Crisis communication is embedded within the larger rubric of crisis management. Crisis management includes efforts designed to prevent and to detect potential crises, and to learn from crisis experiences (Caponigro, 2000; Cohn, 2000; Coombs, 1999b; Mitroff, 2001). Crisis communication has emphasized postcrisis communication and the use of crisis response strategies—what organizational leaders say and do after a crisis hits. SCCT seeks to map out postcrisis communication as does Benoit's (1995) image restoration and Hearit's (1994) corporate *apologia*. More specifically, SCCT is interested in how crisis response strategies can be used to protect reputational assets after the presentation of instructing information, which is the first communication priority in a crisis (Sturges, 1994). Instructing information tells stakeholders what to do to protect themselves from the crisis, the basics of what happened, and what the organization is doing to fix the situation and to prevent a recurrence of the problem

(Bergman, 1994; Coombs, 1998; Sturges, 1994). SCCT assumes the instructing information has been disseminated in order to protect people linked to the crisis.

Expressing compassion for victims should be taken as a corollary to instructing information. Some crises produce victims, people who are injured in some way by a crisis. People harmed by defective products or forced to evacuate a neighborhood are examples of victims. Victims place unique demands on crisis managers (Ogrizek & Guillery, 1999). In addition to instructing information, many crisis experts recommend including an expression of compassion for victims as a standard part of the initial crisis response (Augustine, 1995; Carney & Jorden, 1993; Mitchell, 1986; Sen & Egelhoff, 1991; Wilson & Patterson, 1987). An expression of compassion involves acknowledging and expressing sympathy for victims without accepting responsibility or stating remorse. Responsibility and remorse open up liability issues, issues covered later in this discussion. J. Cohen (1999), a legal expert on apologies, recommends compassion be used when fault is unclear. Most accidents and product recalls (either human or technical error) have unclear fault at the onset of the crisis and may take weeks or months to clarify (Ray, 1999). An expression of compassion should be automatic in a crisis that involves victims.

SCCT argues that the crisis situation determines which crisis response strategies will be most effective in protecting the organization's reputation. Reputational assets are important to an organization and are threatened by a crisis. It follows that crisis managers should try to maximize the reputational protection afforded by crisis response strategies.

SCCT'S CURRENT ARTICULATION

J. A. Benson (1988) wrote that there are a set number of crisis types and crisis response strategies. He challenged crisis communication research to find a way to match the crisis types of the appropriate crisis response strategy(ies). SCCT was developed to address this challenge. While it is easy to find lists of crisis types (categories of crises) and crisis response strategies, prior to SCCT there was no theoretical link between the two lists. Meaningful matching is possible only if there is some correspondence/link between the crisis types and crisis response strategies. SCCT drew on attribution theory and neoinstitutional theory to create the link.

Attribution theory is used to explain how people attribute causes to events. The focus is on negative, unexpected events (Weiner, 1985; Weiner, Amirhan, Folkes, & Verette, 1987). A number of researchers have noted the applicability of attribution theory to crises as people naturally try to establish responsibility for a crisis (Bradford & Garrett, 1995). Neoinstitutional theory holds that stakeholders expect organizations to behave in particular ways, and to act in ways that are consistent with societal norms/expectations. An organization is considered legitimate when it conforms to norms and/or meets expectations, and is judged worthy of operating in society while avoiding conflict with stakeholders. A crisis can be considered a violation of societal norms/expectations, thus creating a need to reestablish the meeting of expectations (Allen & Caillouet, 1994; Finet, 1994; Fuchs-Burnett, 2002; Massey, 2001; Sellnow, Ulmer, & Snider, 1998). The way SCCT uses attribution and neoinstitutional theories is woven through the remainder of this discussion. SCCT is presented by dividing it into three parts: the crisis situation, crisis response strategies, and the matching recommendations.

The Crisis Situation

A crisis situation will generate particular attributions of crisis responsibility, the degree to which the organization is perceived to be responsible for the crisis event. The crisis manager must assess the amount of responsibility a crisis will generate as part of the threat assessment process. The level of crisis responsibility is a primary indicator of how much of a threat the crisis is to the organization's reputation and what crisis response strategies are necessary to address that threat. The crisis situation is a combination of crisis type and the threat intensifiers. A crisis type is simply a category for a crisis. Each crisis type represents a frame for how stakeholders will view the crisis. The crisis type serves as the foundation for crisis responsibility assessment. Each crisis type will generate a specific level of crisis responsibility. SCCT is built on a list of thirteen crisis types, which have been divided into three clusters. Each of the crisis types in a cluster shares a similar level of crisis responsibility with the others (Coombs & Holladay, 2002). Table 16.1 defines the crisis types and indicates the general level of crisis responsibility each type should generate.

TABLE 16.1   Crisis types by level of crisis responsibility

Attributions of crisis responsibility, high: Preventable cluster

Human breakdown accidents: Human error causes an industrial accident.
Human breakdown recalls: Human error causes a product to be recalled.
Organizational misdeed with no injuries: Stakeholders are deceived without injury.
Organizational misdeed management misconduct: Laws or regulations are violated by management.
Organizational misdeed with injuries: Stakeholders are placed at risk by management and injuries occur.

Attributions of crisis responsibility, moderate: Accidental cluster

Challenges: Stakeholders claim an organization is operating in an inappropriate manner.
Megadamage: A technical accident where the focus is on the environmental damage from the accident.
Technical breakdown accidents: A technology or equipment failure causes an industrial accident.
Technical breakdown recalls: A technology or equipment failure causes a product to be recalled.

Attributions of crisis responsibility, low: Victim cluster

Natural disaster: Acts of nature that damage an organization, such as an earthquake.
Rumors: False and damaging information about an organization is being circulated.
Workplace violence: Current or former employee attacks current employees onsite.
Product tampering/malevolence: External agent causes damage to an organization.

From the foundation of crisis type, the crisis manager uses the threat intensifiers to complete the crisis threat assessment. The threat intensifiers serve to intensify the reputation damage a crisis type can inflict on an organization and include crisis history, relationship history, and severity. *Crisis history* lists similar crises an organization has had in the past. News stories often include reports if an organization has experienced similar crises. *Relationship history* indicates if the organization has had a record of good works or bad behavior. Relationship history is concerned with how the organization has treated its stakeholders in the past. Organizational behavior is a key factor in determining reputations. Stakeholders feel it is important for an organization's words and deeds to match (Herbig, Milewicz, & Golden, 1994). Together, crisis and relationship history are known as performance history because they are indicators of how the organization has acted in the past. *Severity* is the amount of damage inflicted by the crisis, including injuries, loss of lives, financial loss, and environmental destruction.

If an organization has a negative crisis history, negative relationship history, and/or the crisis damage is severe, the reputational damage of the crisis type is intensified. In Table 16.1, the crisis types are divided into three clusters based on similar, initial attributions of crisis responsibility: preventable, accidental, and victim. Any individual or combination of threat intensifier should move a crisis type into the next higher cluster. For instance, a victim crisis type would be treated like an accidental crisis and an accidental crisis would be treated as a preventable crisis. The threat intensifiers alter the reputational damage a crisis can inflict and the type of crisis response strategy needed to address it. The discussion of matching the situation and crisis response strategy will elaborate on this shift.

Crisis experts have speculated that favorable precrisis relationships with stakeholders should benefit an organization (Birch, 1994; Fearn-Banks, 1996; Siomkos & Shrivastava, 1993). A favorable relationship history should produce a halo effect, acting as a shield that protects the organization from the reputational damage of a crisis (Balzer & Sulsky, 1992). "In a crisis, stakeholders may ignore negative implications from the crisis or unfounded speculation about the causes of the crisis, or be more receptive to the organization's interpretation of the crisis" (Coombs & Holladay, 2001, p. 324). A favorable relationship history should affect attributions of crisis responsibility and the organization's reputation.

Crisis Response Strategies

SCCT works from a list of ten crisis response strategies that are grouped into three postures. A posture represents a set of strategies that share similar communicative goals and vary in terms of their focus on protecting the crisis victims (victim-orientation) and taking responsibility for the crisis. Note that responsibility is the link between the crisis types and crisis response strategies. The three postures represent the three basic communicative options available to the crisis manager and reflect attribution and neoinstitutional theory. Table 16.2 presents the crisis response strategies that comprise the three postures. The *deny* posture represents a set of strategies that claim that either no crisis occurred or that the accused organization has no responsibility for the crisis. If there is no crisis, there can be no

TABLE 16.2   Crisis response strategies by postures

Deny posture (low concern for victim and responsibility acceptance)

Attack the accuser: Crisis manager confronts the person or group claiming something is wrong with the organization.

Denial: Crisis manager claims that there is no crisis.

Scapegoat: Crisis manager blames some person or group outside the organization for the crisis.

Diminish posture

Excuse: Crisis manager minimizes organizational responsibility by denying intent to do harm and/or claiming inability to control the events that triggered the crisis.

Justification: Crisis manager minimizes the perceived damage caused by the crisis.

Deal posture (high concern for victim and responsibility acceptance)

Ingratiation: Crisis manager praises stakeholders and/or reminds them of past good works by the organization.

Concern: Crisis manager expresses concern for the victims.

Compensation: Crisis manager offers money or other gifts to victims.

Regret: Crisis manager indicates the organization feels bad about the crisis.

Apology: Crisis manager indicates the organization takes full responsibility for the crisis and asks stakeholders for forgiveness.

organizational responsibility for a crisis (attribution theory) and no violation of legitimacy (neoinstitutional theory).

The *diminish* posture reflects a set of strategies that attempt to alter stakeholder attributions by reframing how stakeholders should interpret the crisis (attribution theory). Crisis managers might try to place distance between the organization and the crisis, thereby seeking to reduce responsibility for the crisis. The *deal* posture represents a set of strategies that seek to improve the organization's reputation in some way. By protecting victims and accepting responsibility, crisis managers encourage stakeholders to judge the organization more positively or less negatively. An organization in an intentional crisis would be expected to address victim concerns, so the crisis response strategy must demonstrate the organization is meeting expectations/adhering to social norms (neoinstitutional theory).

The deal posture includes the concern strategy that is an expression of compassion. Although automatically used when there are victims, the concern strategy is optional when no one seems to be harmed. Moreover, the grouping shows that an expression of concern is viewed very similarly to apology and regret, the two crisis response strategies that can open an organization to legal liability.

Modeling the Process.   One valuable aspect of any theory is that it provides an organizing framework for the various concepts it uses. At this point it is useful to place the various concepts from SCCT into a model that shows their relationship to one another. Figure 16.1 presents a model of SCCT. To explain the model, the various relationships in SCCT are presented as propositions.

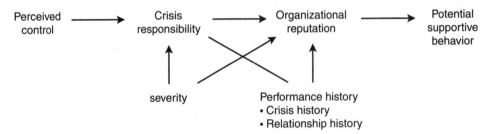

FIGURE 16.1 Situational crisis communication theory model

1. *Organizational reputation proposition:* There is a strong, negative correlation between organizational reputation and crisis responsibility. Attributions of crisis responsibility have a strong effect on perceptions of organizational reputation. The stronger the attributions of crisis responsibility, the more the crisis can damage the organizational reputation and, in turn, affect future interactions with the organization (potential supportive behavior).

2. *Potential supportive behavior proposition:* A strong, positive correlation exists between organizational reputation and potential supportive behavior, intentions to engage in acts that would help an organization. A negative reputation should result in less supportive behavior from stakeholders, while a positive reputation should engender more.

3. *Severity proposition:* Severity has a significant intensifying effect on crisis responsibility and damage to organizational reputation. As the crisis increases in severity (inflicts greater damage), attributions of crisis responsibility will intensify. Severity of an incident tends to increase perceptions of responsibility among individuals. The same dynamic is believed to hold true for organizations in crisis. Severity is also an indication of deviation from the norm. Greater severity suggests a greater violation of the expected norms and could result in direct damage to the organization's reputation.

4. *Crisis history proposition:* An unfavorable crisis history has a significant intensifying effect on crisis responsibility and damage to organizational reputation. Organizations that have experienced similar crises in the past will be attributed greater crisis responsibility and suffer more direct reputational damage than an organization with no history of crises. The history of crises indicates that the crisis is part of a pattern of behavior by the organization, another negative act by the organization and not an anomaly.

5. *Relationship history proposition A:* An unfavorable relationship history has a significant intensifying effect on crisis responsibility and damage to the organizational reputation. An organization that has treated stakeholders badly in the past will be attributed greater crisis responsibility and suffer more direct reputational damage than an organization with a neutral or positive relationship history.

6. *Relationship history proposition B:* A favorable relationship history has a significant reducing effect on crisis responsibility and damage to the organizational reputation. Organizations that have maintained favorable relationships with stakeholders will see weak attributions of crisis responsibility and less reputational damage for a crisis than those with neutral or unfavorable ones.

7. *Crisis response strategy selection proposition:* Organizations will suffer less reputational damage from a crisis and experience greater potential supportive behavior if they match the crisis response strategy to the reputational threat of the crisis. See Table 16.3 for a list of general recommendations.

Matching Crisis Situations to Crisis Response Strategies and Limitations

SCCT maintains that as attributions of crisis responsibility and/or the threat of reputational damage increases, crisis managers must use crisis response strategies that reflect a greater concern for victims and take more responsibility for the crisis. Table 16.3 provides a summary of the guidelines provided by SCCT. For instance, a technical-error accident (accidental cluster) would require a simple excuse, such as "We try to operate safely but technology does fail and accidents do happen." However, if the same technical error has happened three or four times, the crisis manager needs to use strategies from the deal posture because stakeholders will perceive the crisis as a form of organizational misdeed (preventable cluster) rather than a technical-error accident (accidental cluster). As noted earlier, the concern crisis response strategy should be added to any crisis with victims in order to express compassion for the victims.

All theories have limitations. Crisis managers cannot always use the optimum crisis response strategy recommended by SCCT. Legal and/or financial liabilities can restrict what an organization can and cannot say. Apologies, and in some states expressions of regret, will result in significant legal liabilities and financial costs (France, 2002). An organization may not be able to take on the liabilities and remain operational (Coombs, 2002a). Thus, a crisis manager may opt for a less-effective diminish strategy to protect a legal position or fiduciary responsibilities.

TABLE 16.3   List of crisis response recommendations

Rumor: Use any of the denial strategies.

Natural disaster: Use instructing information.

Workplace violence: Use instructing information.

Product tampering: Use instructing information.

Product recall, technical error; megadamage; and Accidents, technical error: Use excuse and/or justification.

Product recall, technical error; accidents, technical error; and megadamage, if there is a negative crisis history, relationship history, and/or severe damage: Use any of the deal strategies.

Product recall, human error and accidents, human error: Use any of the deal strategies.

Organizational misdeeds: Use any of the deal strategies.

When victims occur: Use the concern crisis response strategy in combination with other recommended strategy(ies).

SCCT allows crisis managers to understand the effect of choosing a nonmatching strategy by indicating why the effectiveness of the response is reduced.

HISTORICAL DEVELOPMENT OF SCCT

Theories evolve over time as research tests various aspects of them. SCCT has gone through a number of changes since first appearing as a decision flowchart in 1995. This section highlights the key changes and findings in SCCT. The historical development is divided into terminological changes, research-driven changes, and theory testing.

Terminological Changes

The most obvious terminological change in SCCT is the shift from symbolic to situational. The "S" stood for symbolic (Coombs & Holladay, 2001) when the approach was first articulated. The term symbolic was chosen because the crisis response strategies were viewed as *symbolic resources* that could be employed during a crisis. Words are symbols, hence, crisis response strategies were symbolic resources. However, many researchers thought the term *symbolic* carried too much baggage—symbolic is often used as an insult in that an action is symbolic rather than substantive—and would serve to undermine the value of SCCT. Symbolic was replaced with situational because the theory is premised on the crisis situation.

The threat intensifiers began as modifiers. However, research showed that negative performance histories drove the effect of the modifiers, the Velcro effect (Coombs & Holladay, 2001). The negative performance history served to intensify the attributions of crisis responsibility and the damage to the organizational reputation, so the name was changed. Another change was the shift from technical breakdown and human breakdown to technical error and human error in the naming of crisis types. Breakdown was too cumbersome and error captured the essence of the crisis types more parsimoniously.

Research-Driven Changes

The most significant change resulting from the tests of SCCT was the reconfiguration of crisis types from a grid to a continuum. Originally, crisis types were viewed as a 2-by-2 grid using personal control (whether the organization could control the source of the crisis) and external control (whether an external agent was in control of the source of the crisis) (Coombs, 1995; Coombs, Hazleton, Holladay, & Chandler, 1995). However, research found that external control contributed nothing to the explanation of variance for SCCT (Coombs, 1998). You could place the crisis types cleanly in to the grid but it was not useful in explaining the effects of the crisis types.

Later research showed that personal control and crisis responsibility were essentially the same variable (Coombs & Holladay, 2001, 2002). At first personal control was presented as an antecedent and predictor of crisis responsibility

(Coombs, 1998, 1999a). The two variables were collapsed into crisis responsibility (Coombs & Holladay, 2002).

Theory Testing

Overall, the research results have been supportive of the propositions of SCCT. This section will review the results, including validation of the scales and testing of the propositions.

To test SCCT, measures had to be developed for the central concepts of organizational reputation, crisis responsibility, and potential supportive behavior. The organizational reputation measure was built from McCroskey's (1966) measure of character. The focus is on trust, a central concept in past and current conceptualizations of reputation (Baskin & Aronoff, 1988; Fombrun, 1996; Winkleman, 1999). The items were revised to reflect the organization rather than an individual speaker. The original ten-item version was reduced to five items with the reliability remaining in the acceptable range of .80 to .92.

The crisis responsibility measure used two extant scales as a base: McAuley, Duncan, and Russell's (1992) Causal Dimension Scale II (CDSII) and Griffin, Babin, and Darden's (1992) blame scale. CDSII assesses attributions of controllability of an event while the blame scale assesses who is responsible for the event. The items went through a series of modifications to refine their wording and to reflect the evaluation of an organization (Coombs & Holladay, 2002). The final seven-item scale demonstrated reliabilities in the .80 to .91 range. Potential supportive behavior is the only scale developed from scratch with no prior psychometric examination. Potential supportive behavior is an assessment of behavioral intentions—how a stakeholder might act toward the organization after the crisis. Respondents are asked if they would be willing to engage in any one of eight behaviors, such as sign a petition in support of some action by the organization or say nice things about the organization (Coombs, 1999a). The idea is to determine if people intended to behave in ways that are favorable to the organization after the crisis. The potential supportive behavior scale demonstrated reliabilities between .81 and .87.

The organizational reputation proposition has been the most widely and thoroughly tested. Five studies have found a significant negative correlation between crisis responsibility and organization reputation. The average correlation is r = −.43. The correlations were found across the entire range of crisis types, including organizational misdeeds, human-error accidents, technical-error accidents, technical-error recalls, workplace violence, and product tampering (Coombs, 1998, 1999a; Coombs & Holladay, 2001, 2002; Coombs & Schmidt, 2000).

The crisis history proposition has been tested in three studies using organizational misdeeds, human-error crises, technical-error crisis, workplace violence, product tampering, and technical-error recall. Crisis history was found to have a significant effect on organizational reputation for all but the technical-error recall and a significant effect on crisis responsibility for all but product tampering and technical-error recall (Coombs, 1998, 2002b; Coombs & Holladay, 2001). This finding was termed the Velcro effect, as the unfavorable condition attracted and snagged additional reputational damage (Coombs & Holladay, 2002). Generally, the crisis history proposition held across a wide range of crisis types. Technical-error recall seems to be the main exception and should be studied further to determine why.

The relationship history propositions A and B were tested in one study using a human-error accident crisis. The unfavorable relationships history was found to have a significant effect on organizational reputation and crisis responsibility—support for A. A favorable relationships history was no different than having no relationship history, hence B was not supported. As with crisis history, a Velcro effect was observed; only the negative condition had an effect (Coombs & Holladay, 2001). This finding runs counter to the thinking that positive, precrisis relationships with stakeholders should serve to protect an organization from reputational damage. This concern needs further research, as the current manipulation of relationship history may be too limited to produce the desired positive effect. The relationship history proposition needs to be tested across a wide array of crisis types and with a stronger manipulation of relationship history.

The severity proposition was tested in one study using technical-error accident and organizational misdeed crisis types. The results were negative; the severity of the crisis damage did not effect either organizational reputation or crisis responsibility as anticipated (Coombs, 1998). Further testing across a large range of crisis types is needed to determine the viability of the severity proposition.

The potential supportive behavior proposition has been examined in two studies using organizational misdeed and human-error accident crisis types. Organizational reputation and potential supportive behavior correlated a $r = .46$ (Coombs & Schmidt, 2000) and $r = .48$ (Coombs & Holladay, 2001). The study of potential supportive behavior must be conducted across a wider variety of crisis types and regression analyses used to determine if organizational reputation is the best predictor of potential supportive behavior from among the various concepts used in SCCT.

The crisis response strategy selection proposition was tested in two studies using organizational misdeed and technical-error accident crisis types. In both studies the matched strategies (those recommended by SCCT) performed better than the mismatched strategies. The mismatched conditions included using responses that accepted greater responsibility than recommended by SCCT, to prevent finding an effect by simply using lower, less-effective crisis response strategies (Coombs & Holladay, 1996; Coombs & Schmidt, 2000). The testing of the crisis response strategy selection proposition has just begun as many more of the recommendations from the matching guidelines need tested.

CONCLUSION

Theory does not emerge from research by chance; it must be developed and tested. Situational crisis communication theory is an attempt to broaden the limited theoretical foundation of crisis communication. The core concepts and relations in SCCT have been developed over a number of years. Moreover, empirically based research has been used in the initial tests of SCCT. Thus far the results have been promising, as most the SCCT propositions have withstood scrutiny. Some have not, leading to modifications of SCCT. Any good theory is heuristic and SCCT offers a number of avenues for future research (Littlejohn, 1992). While still early in the testing, SCCT is a promising addition to theory building in crisis communication and public relations. Each crisis is unique and no crisis communication principles should be followed in a lockstep manner (Barton, 2001). SCCT's prescriptive guidelines give crisis managers organized and tested recommendations for protecting reputational assets during a crisis—an informed starting point for action.

CASE: THE PLANT EXPLOSION

The following case study represents an actual event. Use SCCT to:

1. Map the crisis situation and assess both the crisis responsibility and reputational threat presented by the crisis. With no cause listed, assume the crisis is technical error.

2. Identify gray areas in the crisis where different frames might be applied.

3. Evaluate West Pharmaceutical's early crisis response—their use of crisis response strategies. Would you recommend any additional crisis response strategies based upon SCCT?

West Pharmaceutical

Fox and CNN both covered the event live on January 29, 2003. Fox reporter Jane Skinner described the event as "Enormous plumes of jet black smoke filling the sky for miles and devastating flames, the result of some sort of explosion at the West Pharmaceutical Company in Kinston North Carolina." Live video footage and news photographs posted online showed smoke, walls missing from buildings, and people running from the scene. Initial reports placed the death toll at eight and estimates of sixty to hundred people inside the building during the blast with only thirty accounted for. Many news reports noted that West Pharmaceutical had recently been fined $10,000 by the Occupational Safety and Health Administration (OSHA) for violations at the Kinston facility. The West Pharmaceutical officials were unavailable for comments during the live coverage. Fox's John Gibson asked a resident to comment on West Pharmaceutical's good reputation in the community. "Yes it really does—it's been the community . . . it's always had a very good reputation in our community, a sponsor of different community events and baseball, Little League teams, so it's a very reputable business here in eastern North Carolina." The live reports noted it was too early to establish a cause.

A day later, the death toll was revised down to three with a fourth employee dying later in the hospital. There were twenty-seven injuries, nine of which were critical. Don Morel, the president and CEO, arrived in Kinston the next day. Morel noted the need to address the catastrophe and to maintain the supply of goods to its customers. Ten other West Pharmaceutical operations could make the parts and were going to pick up the slack. This focus on the customers was a result of West Pharmaceutical stocks dropping 10 percent, or $1.93, the day after the crisis. Trading was suspended the day of the crisis. The Kinston facility makes rubber syringe plungers and intravenous equipment parts. Morel noted that the OSHA transgressions were twenty-two safety violations and that early indications were that none played a role in the accident.

West Pharmaceutical began posting material about the crisis to its web site the day of the event. The home page contained a link identified as "Kinston Updates." The link contained the company statement quoted at the end of this case, company news releases, information on an employee trust fund, and information on third-party liability claims. The blast did disrupt other businesses so they could file claims for losses, third-party liability claims. The West Pharmaceutical statements noted the company was working with investigators to find the cause of the accident.

The federal investigation was spearheaded by the U.S. Chemical Safety and Hazard Investigation Board, known as the CSB. The CSB has the jurisdiction to investigate chemical accidents anywhere in the United States. The CSB believed the explosion was the result of dust buildup in the air at the facility. The leading cause of the dust was identified as the rubber dust from the mixing machines because the blast centered in the mixing area. Part of the CSB's statement is included at the end of this case. The CSB explained that dust explosions are not unusual but are most often associated with grain silos. The CSB also indicated that it did not believe any of the OSHA violations were responsible for the explosion.

The following is a statement from Dr. Donald Morel, president and chief executive officer of West Pharmaceutical Services Inc.:

> On behalf of West Pharmaceutical Services employees around the world, I would like to express our deepest sympathies to the families, friends and loved ones of our four fallen co-workers who lost their lives in the Kinston plant tragedy on January 29. The sudden loss of James Byrd, Lenni "Faye" Wilkins, William Gray, and Kevin Cruiess creates a void that can never be filled in the many lives that they touched.
>
> To the many fire fighters, police, emergency workers, doctors, nurses, clergy and community volunteers who have more than risen to the occasion at a time of acute need, we offer our gratitude. Your skill, courage and generosity of spirit under the most stressful and challenging conditions are a monumental tribute to the collective strength and character of this community.
>
> While we grieve, West also stands together with the community in prayer for the injured. We pray for a fast and complete recovery, and wish strength and comfort to your families during this most difficult time.

The following is an official CSB statement on Kinston:

A volatile mix of air and suspended dust caused the explosion and fire that killed four workers at the West Pharmaceutical Services plant last week, federal investigators said Monday. What sparked the blast remained a mystery. Investigators said the explosion began in a mixing area where small fires had occurred in the past. They also said they had identified several possible sources of dust, but could not say which was responsible. The plant, which made synthetic rubber stoppers and other medical supplies, used a variety of chemicals to cure rubber. Officials of the Bureau of Alcohol, Tobacco, Firearms and Explosives said they had ruled out a bomb or other criminal act and would surrender the investigation to the state Department of Labor and the U.S. Chemical Safety and Hazard Investigation Board, known as the CSB. CSB investigators first theorized last week that a dusty byproduct from rubber-making triggered the explosion. Board investigators said Monday that the explosion was centered on the lower level of the plant's rubber compounding area, where workers mixed crude rubber with chemicals, then rolled, coated, dried and cut the finished rubber. They said several chemicals used in the process could produce explosive dusts. Stephen Selk, the CSB's lead investigator, said the dust could have been ignited by a spark from static electricity, from machinery, a tool or smoking, though smoking is prohibited inside the plant. "It doesn't actually take very much energy to ignite a flammable fuel-air mixture," Selk said. CSB investigators said they were examining whether a mixing machine on the upper level of the compounding area could have caught fire or exploded, setting off the massive blast below. Workers told investigators that the mixer had caught fire before and that one fire was strong enough to blow off the mixer's door.

QUESTIONS FOR APPLICATION

1. How might a crisis manager "corrupt" ideas from SCCT to his or her advantage in a crisis?

2. What criteria should a crisis manager use when trying to balance financial concerns against the need to address victim concerns and accept responsibility?

3. In reviewing SCCT, can you identify an underlying social-financial tension that can emerge in postcrisis communication?

4. How might a crisis manager try to rectify a situation where organizational management believes a situation is one crisis type/frame while key stakeholders see a different crisis type/frame?

5. Why should researchers continue to try to find the existence of a halo effect from a positive relationship history?

6. Which aspects of SCCT would be the most difficult for a crisis manager to apply in actual crises?

7. Do you agree or disagree that victims constitute a unique stakeholder group? Why or why not?

8. What additional concepts should be added to enrich SCCT?

REFERENCES

Allen, M. W., & Caillouet, R. H. (1994). Legitimation endeavors: Impression management strategies used by an organization in crisis. *Communication Monographs, 61,* pp. 44–62.

Anderson, R., & Ross, V. (2002). *Questions of communication a practical introduction to theory* (3rd ed.). New York: Bedford/St. Martin.

Augustine, N. R. (1995). Managing the crisis you tried to prevent. *Harvard Business Review, 73*(6), pp. 147–158.

Balzer, W. K., & Sulsky, L. M. (1992). Halo and performance appraisal research: A critical examination. *Journal of Applied Psychology, 77,* pp. 975–985.

Barton, L. (2001). *Crisis in organizations II* (2nd ed.). Cincinnati, OH: College Divisions South-Western.

Baskin, O., & Aronoff, C. (1988). *Public relations: The profession and the practice* (2nd ed.). Dubuque, IA: Wm. C. Brown.

Benoit, W. L. (1995). *Accounts, excuses, and apologies: A theory of image restoration.* Albany: State University of New York Press.

Benson, J. A. (1988). Crisis revisited: An analysis of the strategies used by Tylenol in the second tampering episode. *Central States Speech Journal, 38,* pp. 49–66.

Bergman, E. (1994). Crisis? What crisis? *Communication World, 11*(4), pp. 9–13.

Birch, J. (1994, Spring). New factors in crisis planning and response. *Public Relations Quarterly, 39,* pp. 31–34.

Botan, C. H. (1989). Theory development in public relations. In C. H. Botan and V. Hazleton Jr. (Eds.). *Public relations theory* (pp. 99–110). Hillsdale, NJ: Lawrence Erlbaum.

Botan, C. H., & Hazleton Jr., V. (1989). *Public relations theory.* Hillsdale, NJ: Lawrence Erlbaum.

Bradford, J. L., & Garrett, D. E. (1995). The effectiveness of corporate communicative responses to accusations of unethical behavior. *Journal of Business Ethics, 14,* pp. 875–892.

Caponigro, J. R. (2000). *The crisis counselor: A step-by-step guide to managing a business crisis.* Chicago: Contemporary Books.

Carney, A., & Jorden, A. (1993, August). Prepare for business-related crises. *Public Relations Journal 49,* pp. 34–35.

Cohen, J. R. (1999). Advising clients to apologize. *S. California Law Review, 72,* pp. 1009–131.

Cohn, R. (2000). *The PR crisis bible.* New York: St. Martin's.

Coombs, W. T. (1995). Choosing the right words: The development of guidelines for the selection of the "appropriate" crisis response strategies. *Management Communication Quarterly, 8,* pp. 447–476.

———. (1998). An analytic framework for crisis situations: Better responses from a better understanding of the situation. *Journal of Public Relations Research, 10,* pp. 177–191.

———. (1999a). Information and compassion in crisis responses: A test of their effects. *Journal of Public Relations Research, 11,* pp. 125–142.

———. (1999b). *Ongoing crisis communication: Planning, managing, and responding.* Thousand Oaks, CA: Sage.

———. (2002a). Deep and surface threats: Conceptual and practical implications for "crisis" vs. "problem." *Public Relations Review, 28,* pp. 339–345.

———. (2002b, November). *Further testing of the situational crisis communication theory: An extended examination of crisis history as a modifier.* Paper presented at the annual meeting of the National Communication Association, New Orleans, LA.

Coombs, W. T., Hazleton, V., Holladay, S. J., & Chandler, R. C. (1995). The crisis grid: Theory and application in crisis management. In L. Barton (Ed.), *New avenues in risk and crisis management* (Vol. 4, pp. 30–39). Las Vegas, NV: UNLV Small Business Development Center.

Coombs, W. T., & Holladay, S. J. (1996). Communication and attributions in a crisis: An experimental study of crisis communication. *Journal of Public Relations Research, 8,* pp. 279–295.

———. (2001). An extended examination of the crisis situation: A fusion of the relational management and symbolic approaches. *Journal of Public Relations Research, 13,* pp. 321–340.

———. (2002). Helping crisis managers protect reputational assets: Initial tests of the situational crisis communication theory. *Management Communication Quarterly, 16,* pp. 165–186.

Coombs, W. T., & Schmidt, L. (2000). An empirical analysis of image restoration: Texaco's racism crisis. *Journal of Public Relations Research, 12*(2), pp. 163–178.

Fearn-Banks, K. (1996). *Crisis communications: A casebook approach.* Mahwah, NJ: Lawrence Erlbaum.

Finet, D. (1994). Sociopolitical consequences of organizational expression. *Journal of Communication, 44,* pp. 114–131.

Fombrun, C. J. (1996). *Reputation: Realizing value from the corporate image.* Boston: Harvard Business School Press.

France, M. (2002, August 26). The mea culpa defense. *Business Week, 3796,* pp. 76–78.

Fuchs-Burnett, T. (2002, May/July). Mass public corporate apology. *Dispute Resolution Journal, 57,* pp. 26–32.

Griffin, M., Babin, B. J., & Darden, W. R. (1992). Consumer assessments of responsibility for product-related injuries: The impact of regulations, warnings, and promotional policies. *Advances in Consumer Research, 19,* pp. 870–877.

Heath, R. L. (2001). Handbook of public relations. Thousand Oaks, CA: Sage.

Hearit, K. M. (1994, Summer). Apologies and public relations crises at Chrysler, Toshiba, and Volvo. *Public Relations Review, 20,* pp. 113–125.

Herbig, P., Milewicz, J., & Golden, J. (1994). A model of reputation building and destruction. *Journal of Business Research, 31,* pp. 23–31.

Littlejohn, W. (1992). *Theories of Human Communication* (4th ed). Belmont, CA: Wadsworth.

Massey, J. E. (2001). Managing organizational legitimacy. *Journal of Business Communication, 38,* pp. 152–182.

McAuley, E., Duncan, T. E., & Russell, D. W. (1992). Measuring causal attributions: The revised causal dimension scale (CDII). *Personality and Social Psychology Bulletin, 18,* pp. 566–573.

McCroskey, J. C. (1966). *An introduction to rhetorical communication.* Englewood Cliffs, NJ: Prentice-Hall.

Mitchell, T. H. (1986, Autumn). Coping with a corporate crisis. *Canadian Business Review, 13,* pp. 17–20.

Mitroff, I. I. (2001). *Managing crises before they happen: What every executive and manager needs to know about crisis management.* New York: AMACOM.

Neuliep, J. W. (1996). *Human communication theory: Applications & case studies.* Boston: Allyn & Bacon.

Ogrizek, M., & Guillery, J. M. (1999). *Communicating in crisis.* New York: Aldine De Gruyter.

Olaniran, B. A., & Willimas, D. E. (2001). Anticipatory model of crisis management: A vigilant response to technological crises. In R. L. Heath (Ed.), *Handbook of public relations* (pp. 487–500). Thousand Oaks, CA: Sage.

Pavlik, J. V. (1987). *Public relations: What research tells us.* Newbury Park, CA: Sage.

Ray, S. J. (1999). *Strategic communication in crisis management: Lessons from the airline industry.* Westport, CT: Quorum Books.

Sallot, L. M., Lyon, L. J., Acosta-Alzuru, C., & Jones, K. O. (2003). From aardvark to zebra: A new millennium analysis of theory development in public relations academic journals. *Journal of Public Relations Research, 15,* pp. 27–90.

Seeger, M. W., Sellnow, T. L., & Ulmer, R. R. (1998). Communication, organization, and crisis. In M. E. Roloff (Ed.), *Communication yearbook 21* (pp. 231–276). Thousand Oaks, CA: Sage.

———. (2001). Public relations and crisis communication: Organizing and chaos. In R. L. Heath (Ed.), *Handbook of public relations* (pp. 155–166). Thousand Oaks, CA: Sage.

Sellnow, T. L., Ulmer, R. R., & Snider, M. (1998). The compatibility of corrective action in organizational crisis communication. *Communication Quarterly, 46,* pp. 60–74.

Sen, F., & Egelhoff, W. G. (1991, Spring). Six years and counting: Leaning from crisis management at Bhopal. *Public Relations Review, 17,* pp. 69–83.

Siomkos, G., & Shrivastava, P. (1993). Responding to product liability crises. *Long range planning, 26*(5), pp. 72–79.

Sturges, D. L. (1994). Communicating through crisis: A strategy for organizational survival. *Management Communication Quarterly, 7,* pp. 297–316.

Weiner, B. (1985). An attributional theory of achievement motivation and emotion. *Psychology Review, 92,* pp. 548–573.

Weiner, B., Amirkan, J., Folkes, V. S., & Verette, J. A. (1987). An attribution analysis of excuse giving: Studies of a naive theory of emotion. *Journal of Personality and Social Psychology, 53,* pp. 316–324.

Wilson, S., & Patterson, B. (1987, November). When the news hits the fan. *Business Marketing, 72,* pp. 92–94.

Winkleman, M. (1999, April). The right stuff. *Chief Executive, 143,* pp. 80–81.

■ ■ ■ ■ ■

CONTEXTUAL PARAMETERS— UNDERSTANDING AND CREATING THE BIG PICTURE

Bonita Dostal Neff

Tricia Hansen-Horn

The contexts of public relations demand a broad view of the elements in the public relations process. Here international public relations, the feminist perspective, and an overview of the status of theoretical development provide an understanding of the challenges that remain for the public relations profession—both practitioner and academic.

International public relations, for example, offers an opportunity to integrate theoretical frameworks within a variety of cultures. Gaither and Curtin note the importance of a theoretical construct that addresses the diverse and cultural intricacies of interest to public relations. In a review of the various theoretical perspectives, these authors note how various theories contribute to an overarching interest in culture as a factor in theoretical development.

Okay and Okay examine theory usage by interviewing award-winning practitioners from the International Public Relations Association. The results, unfortunately, established that theory is not a major part of practitioner training.

Russell-Loretz incorporates the feminine perspective as a particularly fruitful approach to understanding public relations theory. With public relations viewed as largely a feminine field, the author quotes those who note that women are particularly well-suited for public relations. Most important, this chapter indicates the gender inequity issue is not unique to the public relations profession.

Sallot, Lyon, Acosta-Alzuru, and Jones provide a replication of an earlier study reviewing the status of public relations theory. By reviewing the articles in a more recent period from two leading public relations journals, the authors concluded that much remains to be done to develop theoretical perspectives essential to public relations.

CHAPTER SEVENTEEN

INTERNATIONAL PUBLIC RELATIONS

Toward an Integrated Theoretical Base

T. KENN GAITHER

PATRICIA A. CURTIN

> . . . the approach taken to diversity is to speculate on how a systems view of symmetric communication can be carried out within differing national cultures. In fact, to date, no comprehensive theory-driven and systematic treatment of multicultural communication in public relations has appeared. (Banks, 2000, p. 5)

Despite a limited theoretical base, both the practice and scholarship of international public relations are thriving (Botan, 1992; Culbertson & Chen, 1996; Kruckeberg, 1989). The proliferation of public relations associations in countries around the world and the reach of multinational corporations, or MNCs, from homelands to host countries provide convincing evidence (Botan, 1992; Kruckeberg, 1995–1996). As early as 1989, Modoux and Paluszek viewed international public relations as a growing subarea of public relations.

More recently, industry leaders have called international public relations one of the "hot PR specialties" (Van Hook, n.d.) and one of "the specialty areas that will rule the public relations world after the year 2000" (Greenberg, n.d.). David Drobis, chair and CEO of Ketchum Public Relations Worldwide, has called for a "new breed of practitioners" who are attuned to cross-cultural differences and issues (Greenberg, n.d.). Yet the rapid growth of the field has brought with it a host of challenges for practitioners, who are often poorly prepared for the rigors of communicating internationally and undertaking public relations work in cultures and societies different from their own (Kruckeberg, 1995–1996). In turn, there has been a steady rise in the amount of scholarly literature attempting to cross-culturally identify best public relations practices and examine the implications of "doing" public relations in various countries, cultures, and international settings.

Banks (2000) notes, however, there is not yet an overarching theory-driven approach to multicultural public relations,* which is hardly surprising given that public relations theory in general has long lagged behind other social sciences (Sallot, Lyon, Acosta-Alzuru, & Jones, 2003). The greatest challenge to existing theory is the introduction of culture to practice. Toth and Trujillo (1987) suggested a cross-disciplinary approach was needed to develop an "overbridging theory of public relations" (p. 159). More recently, Wakefield (1996) noted a base of scholarly research was necessary to form "theory building on what comprises effective practice in international public relations" (p. 19). This chapter builds on these treatments to suggest a new theoretical framework for considering the role of public relations in the international arena. It seeks to address two salient questions posed by Taylor (2001, p. 636): "How will public relations be different in other parts of the world?" and "How will we have to adapt to communicate with international publics?"

This chapter is a preliminary approach to answering these questions and to forming at least an inchoate understanding of what a unified theory of international public relations might encompass. The strengths and weaknesses of current approaches are reviewed, including the heavy dependence on case studies and on Western theoretical models, which limit their scope and explanatory value. More culturally situated approaches are then reviewed and serve as a springboard for proposing the "circuit of culture" (du Gay, Hall, Janes, Mackay, & Negus, 1997) as an integrative model to develop a theory of international public relations practice that captures its inherent dynamism while permitting practitioners to apply it in cross-cultural contexts.

SYMMETRICALISM AND EXCELLENCE IN THE CENTURY OF PUBLIC RELATIONS

If this century is, as Kruckeberg (1995–1996) posits, the "century of public relations," implicit in this notion is the need for perpetual activity to enhance public relations practice and extend public relations theory in an international context. Most scholarly literature in these areas falls into three streams: viewing public relations practice in a country or region through a comparative case study; focusing on multinational corporations and the relationship between the host culture and management style with the home norms, which are often Western-based; and the application of Western models, most prominently the Grunig and Hunt (1984) models, in other cultures. These research streams are summarized in the

---

*In this chapter, multicultural refers to public relations practice or scholarship that includes issues specifically related to, or relevant in, multiple cultures. Cross-cultural is the application of theory or practice internationally. "International public relations" subsumes both terms by assuming that public relations is not just a Western practice, and its definition, roles, and challenges are influenced by cultural factors.

following sections to undergird the issues and challenges of developing international public relations theory.

THE CASE STUDY

Case studies have provided a glimpse into public relations in countries around the world. Despite the sheer number of public relations case studies, several regions of the world are understudied, among them Africa and the Middle East (Taylor, 2001). Recent case studies include a study of the diffusion of public relations through China (Chen, 1996); the fit between Saudi Arabian public relations practices and Western models (Alanazi, 1996); links between Latin American and U.S. public relations scholarship (Molleda, 2002); and the need for theory to account for differences between public relations in New Zealand and the West (Motion & Leitch, 2001).

Many case studies use the West as a reference point, noting departures and/or similarities between public relations practices (Turk & Scanlan, 1999). While these approaches have yielded innumerable clues to the worldwide variation of public relations practice, they often ostensibly validate Western theories rather than generate new, more globally sensitive theories. Taylor and Kent (1999) wrote, "Many of the assumptions that guide Western theories and practices are not applicable in other regions of the world" (p. 131). Despite the challenges of applying Western-based models to other cultures, most case studies tend to find some semblance of Western theory in countries around the world (Rhee, 2002; Sriramesh, Kim, & Takasaki, 1999; Vasquez & Taylor, 2000).

CORPORATE PUBLIC RELATIONS

The study of corporate public relations—often by examining multinational corporations (MNCs)—has driven much international public relations research (Banks, 2000; Botan, 1992; L. Grunig, 1992; Signitzer & Coombs, 1992; Wilson, 1990), although corporations are only one site for public relations practice (Kunczik, 1997; Signitzer & Coombs, 1992; Taylor & Kent, 1999).

The need for corporate practitioners who are able to effectively carry out their work across international lines is considered paramount in the literature. Epley (1992), who suggests the United States is losing its leadership role in public relations, states "overcoming language and cultural nuances will continue to be perhaps our greatest challenge" (p. 114). Accordingly, corporate public relations practitioners are roundly criticized for ignoring the cultural implications of their international work. Kinzar and Bohn (1985) identified four possible models for public relations in MNCs. According to these authors, the two most common are ethnocentric and polycentric models—the former suggesting home country assumptions of public relations should drive its practice, the latter that practitioners are autonomous enough to implement initiatives that are culturally bound (see also Botan, 1992).

Three issues take precedence in the study of MNCs and public relations: the normative nature of most studies—that is, an ideal perspective of how public relations should be studied in a corporate setting (Verĉiĉ, Grunig, & Grunig, 1996; Wakefield, 1996); the varied definitions of the public relations function in different countries (Simöes, 1992; Van Leuven & Pratt, 1996); and the ongoing debate on whether a "one size fits all" approach to public relations practice is feasible (Botan, 1992; Illman, 1980; Rhee, 2002). Verĉiĉ and colleagues argued for an intermediate global public relations theory comprising generic features of effective public relations practices with specific applications.

APPLYING WESTERN THEORIES AROUND THE GLOBE

At the heart of most discussions is the relationship between public relations practice and culture. Many scholars have argued that too much research may be looking at the practice of public relations through ethnocentric lenses (Banks, 2000; Botan, 1992; Nessmann, 1995; Wilson, 1990). For example, Sriramesh and White (1992) have cautioned that Western public relations theory might not be extensive enough to account for worldwide cultural variance. These studies underscore that culture *does* matter in international public relations (Freitag, 2002; Sriramesh, 1996; Sriramesh, Kim, & Takasaki, 1999). While the United States might have the longest history of formal public relations training and scholarship, its basis for public relations is steeped in democracy and capitalism (Karlberg, 1996; Kruckeberg, 1995–1996; Pearson, 1989; Taylor & Kent, 1999). The role of public relations in lesser-developed countries or countries with different political structures and economic conditions forms a contentious area that clouds the development of integrated international public relations theory. Botan (1992) developed a matrix that borders on establishing such a theory by considering legal/political contexts, freedom of the press, and current international events, such as the global tendency toward democratization.

Research has demonstrated that public relations is not a unified discipline. Although it might have some generic similarities internationally, its practice is influenced by innumerable cultural factors. In the United Arab Emirates, for example, public relations is "vague, superficial and misunderstood" by Western standards (Creedon, Al-Khaja, & Kruckeberg, 1995, p. 65). In Africa, Van Leuven and Pratt (1996) observed "there is little opportunity for practicing public relations in the Western sense of the term" (p. 95). Chen (1996) reported a marked difference between public relations in China and the West. Poetry and oral traditions, such as storytelling, often ignored by Western public relations practitioners, are crucial to its practice in parts of Africa and the Middle East (Alanazi, 1996; Riley, 1991). These studies collectively form a patchwork mosaic predicated on difference, in which factors of development, governance, technology, cultural values, and power structures interact—and often conflict—to influence public relations practice.

Public relations theory has not accounted for these gaps of difference. One of the most evident trends is the extension of Western-based models, often the Grunig and Hunt (1984) models, to inform international public relations practice. These treatments ground public relations practice in Western roots, eliminating the possibility of theory development on terms other than Western ones. One of the more common methods is to test the models in other cultures, confirm or reject their relevance in a host culture, and then add or subtract based on the research findings. Huang (2001) added a fifth element—face and favor—to the excellence model to account for Eastern culture in her study of organization and public relationships in China. Rhee (2002) similarly added Confucian dynamism to the excellence models to increase the explanatory power of public relations in South Korea. Ekachi and Komolsevin (1996) suggested Thailand could benefit by moving toward a two-way symmetric model.

Underlying Assumptions and a New Integrated Framework

Identifying the underlying assumptions that inform theory and assist practitioners' understanding of public relations internationally is central to the successful evolution of an integrated framework. As L'Etang (1996) notes, public relations has "become fossilized at the systems theory stage" (p. 24). Hutton (1999) has considered this relationship between assumptions and the functional models of practice:

> Grunig and Hunt's "four models" typology is the basis for numerous articles and the largest sponsored research project in the field's history, yet there is little evidence that the underlying dimensions—direction of communication (one-way or two-way) and balance of intended effects (asymmetrical or symmetrical)—discriminate among the many public relations theories or practice philosophies, or are causally related to any substantive measure of organizational success. (p. 204)

Or as Brown (2002) notes, "Symmetricalism is an 'either-or' theory in a 'both-and' world" (p. 128).

The hazards of assumptions have not obfuscated the widely held belief that symmetrical communication is the gold standard of public relations practice. Even when the models are applied to the relatively similar political and economic structures of Western Europe, however, they have been called "utopian, illusory, and useless in practice" (Nessmann, 1995, p. 158). The evidence points to a fundamental lack of explanatory power underlying this theoretical approach, even when it is applied within similar socioeconomic environments.

Thus the idea that functional, normative models are feasible and indeed desirable is open to considerable debate. Taylor and Kent (1999) pose this question: How can the two-way symmetric model be the most ethical model of communication in an environment where it is often not possible or necessary? Yet non-Western descriptive models are often labeled unethical by scholars exhibiting a Western ethnocentrism that devalues and disempowers the contributions of other cultures (J. Grunig, 1993). As a result, Botan (1992) suggests that these Western-based normative approaches should be known as transborder public relations rather than international public relations. In turn, L. Grunig, J. Grunig, and D. Dozier (2002) have argued for the reconstruction of the models of public relations to include communication modalities, information flow, and ethical considerations.

To address these issues, research that deconstructs practice into features has informed some recent models. Zaharna (2001) developed three tiers to drive international public relations—systematically developing a country profile, cultural profile, and communications profile. Such an approach meshes with Sriramesh and White (1992), who believe international public relations must reflect the norms of the host nation. Botan (1992) and Wilson (1990) developed matrices to explore aspects of practice, a method that allows for some degree of variance of cultural and societal norms and other socioeconomic and political issues. Freitag (2002), who developed an ascending cultural competence model for practitioners, has suggested that cultural-specific and situation-specific training is needed for public relations practitioners. Such studies offer some modicum of flexibility to a scholarly base that is often not reflexive enough to consider what is lost in the translation of Western models to non-Western countries. These studies provide alternate ways of viewing public relations as a process that requires an ability to eschew Western models when necessary, extend them when appropriate, and adopt them if applicable. This is no easy task for scholars or practitioners; McDermott (1997) has compared international public relations to three-dimensional chess, where practitioners are no longer playing on a two-dimensional board.

THE NEED FOR A MACROLEVEL, CULTURAL APPROACH

The literature points to the need for development and application of macrolevel theory that extends beyond the instrumental (Karlberg, 1996; L'Etang & Pieczka, 1996) but still provides practical value (Toth, 2002). Common to these calls is the need to recognize public relations as a process rather than a product (Ferguson, 1984; Leichty & Springston, 1993). Some recent scholarship has centered on critical/cultural and postmodern paradigmatic approaches because of their inherent emphases on cultural processes, relationships, meanings, and conflicts. Such approaches extend well beyond the functional and have the breadth necessary to address public relations as a situated cultural process and product, making them particularly relevant for development of international public relations theory.

Holtzhausen (2000) suggests the postmodernist emphasis on situated relationships and the continuous conflict over meaning and identity that takes place within these relationships lends itself to informing international public relations practice:

> Postmodernism's understanding of the loss of a single truth is not rooted in relativism or in the individual's choice of moral codes but is based on the reality that

people with different ethnic, cultural, social, class, and economic frames of reference have very different realities. (p. 96)

She believes public relations can emancipate individuals from the reified social constructs that constrain thought and behavior (i.e., metanarratives) and perform an inherently democratizing function at the microlevel. Underlying this emancipatory function is Foucault's (1980) notion of power as inherent in relationships and not in things themselves. For example, Coca-Cola may be a powerful source for U.S. news media, which depend on corporate information subsidies for information (Gandy, 1982), but it lacked relative power in the summer of 1999, when the Belgian and French governments summarily banned sales after suspected cases of food poisoning. Foucault's concept of relational power stands in direct opposition to J. Grunig's claim that power resides in the dominant coalition and that to have power one must be part of top management.

But the postmodernism perspective has not been well-developed enough to be constructively used by practitioners (Toth, 2002). The unlimited number of individual relations and perspectives often results in a practical quagmire similar to that of contingency theory, which posits eighty-six possible variables that practitioners should consider in any given situation (Cancel, Cameron, Sallot, & Mitrook, 1997). For both postmodernism and contingency theory, what sounds promising in theory may be impractical in application.

Mickey's (2003) structuralist approach is more narrow, drawing on Jacques' work to deconstruct the material text of public relations campaigns. The goal is to apply critical thinking to public relations practice to question underlying ideas and assumptions, thus contributing to extant theory the role of cultural beliefs, or ideology, in informing practice. But given the sole focus on the product of public relations, the campaign text, only limited explanatory power can be achieved. Mickey counters that the exercise is valuable in and of itself because it promotes critical thinking, but without studying how and why practitioners produce those texts and how and why publics consume them, what can be said theoretically excludes any notion of public relations as an inherently relational process.

A more inclusive critical/cultural stance is provided by Berger (1999), who also calls for the inclusion of ideology in public relations theory to better explain the role of power, conflict, and struggle over meaning that informs the public relations process: ". . . public relations provides organizations with dynamic and comprehensive methods and processes of intentional representation in contested sites in which information is exchanged, meaning constructed and managed, and consensus, consent, and legitimation gained or lost with others" (p. 186). Berger focuses on three elements: production, where ideology serves to distort by creating a dominant world view through encoded meaning; the resulting texts or tactics, which form a terrain of struggle in which competing world views intersect; and consumption of those texts by publics, in which organizations gain consent when their ideology is legitimized. Berger's approach captures public relations as a situational process, but, like many discussions based in neo-Marxist thought, its dependence on economic determination makes it ultimately defeatist, leaving little room for ethical public relations practice.

The Circuit of Culture as an Integrating Framework

To develop a comprehensive basis for international public relations theory that realizes the potential of these postmodern and critical/cultural approaches, du Gay and colleagues' circuit of culture (1997; see Figure 17.1) provides a conceptual and organizational framework that places international public relations practice at the nexus of process, relationships, and culture. The purpose of the circuit is to establish the relationship between meaning and culture because "the production of social meanings is . . . a necessary precondition for the functioning of all social practices and an account of the cultural conditions of social practices must form part of the sociological explanation of how they work" (p. 2). In other words, we can understand the practice of public relations only if we understand how social meaning is produced and reproduced in the different spaces and moments of the circuit. Culture within this model is understood both as a whole way of life and as the production and circulation of meaning. These aspects remain in constant tension and interplay within the model, providing a bridge between public relations practice and the international or cross-cultural realm.

The circuit presents five moments or sites where meaning is constructed: representation (the "texts" of a public relations campaign), identity (the segmentation of publics and creation of organizational image and national identity), production (the work of public relations practitioners), consumption (how publics makes sense of campaign materials), and regulation (the cultural values that underlie how public relations campaigns are produced, packaged, and consumed). Although the moments are presented as individual entities, in practice they are intertwined in "complex and contingent ways" (du Gay et al., 1997, p. 4). Their connections form the operational realm for what Bourdieu (1984) termed *cultural intermediaries:* entities that help formulate cultural currency by providing form and or recognition to products or issues. Public relations practitioners are cultural intermediaries who

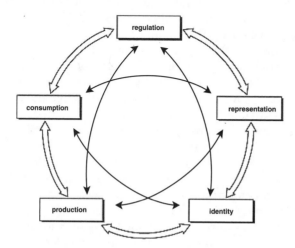

FIGURE 17.1   The circuit of culture

Source: Dara Curtin, 2006.

fulfill boundary spanning and agenda-building roles by shaping and packaging issues at the nexus of culture, meaning, and power. This conceptualization of boundary spanning stands in contrast to that of Holtzhausen (2000), who claims it is a dichotomous function that forces practitioners into an either/or situation. The circuit of culture framework allows for multiple boundaries and perspectives. It also provides for the maintenance of boundaries and not just their dissolution as a key function (see L'Etang, 1996).

The process does not start at any one point of the circle but is continuous. Only by studying the production of meaning within the whole circuit as a synergistic process can an integrated conceptual basis for international public relations theory be formulated. But to understand the whole, an understanding of the parts is necessary.

Representation.   Representation is the text—the language, images, signs, or, in public relations terms, the content and format of public relations campaigns and efforts. A semiological approach is used to unpack its meaning. For example, meaning can be extended from the known to the new through semantic networks in which meanings are expanded through associations, much as when practitioners use a transfer technique to create an attitude toward a previously unknown or dormant issue. When animal protection agencies were faced with publics who did not consider animal abuse a salient issue, practitioners produced a cause-related ad showing a child's face morphing into that of a dog. The tagline suggested that people who abuse animals will abuse children next. By extending the abhorrence for child abuse to that of animal abuse, meaning was created through extension and association.

Meanings are also created by how things are positioned as being similar to or different from other things. Labeling something an issue immediately infers that it is not a nonissue; a less-subtle example is labeling foreign military action a conflict as opposed to a war. At times the differentiation is made explicit, as in Habitat for Humanity's slogan "A hand up, not a hand out," which was designed to shed any negative connotations of welfare that might otherwise be implied. And meaning can be articulated through larger cultural themes and categories, such as at Scottish festivals in the United States where everyone wears a tartan, although this same practice is never seen in Scotland itself. But the tartan signifies an inherent Scottishness and thus stamps the event as culturally "authentic": it creates a representation of what it means to be Scottish.

Practitioners encode dominant meanings within their representations based on strategic goals and on underlying organizational and cultural ideologies, but as any practitioner can testify, publics do not always decode meanings in the same way. When the Centers for Disease Control and Prevention tried to put the necessity of childhood vaccinations on the media agenda through newsworthy and well-researched information subsidies, the *Atlanta Journal/Constitution* used the information to spark a long-running series on the controversies surrounding childhood vaccination. Representations, then, are often sites of contested meanings, and a study of representations in and of themselves does not capture the pluralism of the public relations process.

Identity. Identity is "... who we are and where we are placed in time and space. Identities create meanings as they are produced, consumed, and regulated within culture" (Acosta-Alzuru & Kreshel, 2002, p. 143). Although identity is partially biologically determined (e.g., sex), identity is also socially constructed (e.g., gender), particularly by those in power. An example is the identification of "welfare queens," which created a groundswell of support for welfare reform, even though it would have been hard to find anyone on welfare living like royalty.

It is in the moment of identity that definitions of publics are negotiated and defined. But publics in this model must be viewed as fluid because identities are not immutable (Pieczka, 1996). Possible identities are created through representation and contested within situated relationships among producers and consumers (Holtzhausen, 2000; Taylor & Kent, 1999). In turn, it is within the moment of identity that organizational cultures are accorded identities in part through their chosen representations and how those efforts at reputation, image management, and brand development are received and used by publics. (see Holt, 2002; Hutton, Goodman, Alexander, & Genest, 2001, for more work in this area.) On a national scale, du Gay and colleagues (1997) note:

> One of the most frequent ways in which companies and individuals are referred to during everyday discussions is through the discourse of national identity—the idea that people and things from within specific national borders possess very particular, idiosyncratic, national characteristics. When attempting to make sense of practices or sounds and images from other places in the world, one of the most common tactics is to attribute an identity in terms of national distinctiveness. (p. 48)

The creation of a national identity, then, often has its basis in stereotyping, manufacturing an authenticity for itself, as in the example noted above of what it means to be "Scottish." This problem further emphasizes the need to examine the intertwining moments of the circuit of culture as a synergistic whole if an integrated and practical theory of international public relations is to result.

Production. The moment of production encompasses the technical aspects and constraints of practice (i.e., client deadlines, budget constraints, available communication channels, and technology infrastructure) and also the ideological informing of practice. Production is "an integral part of the company way of life that informs intra-organizational decisions and activities. . . . But it also informs the perceptions of outside observers" (du Gay et al., 1997, p. 43).

The processes of production originate at many levels, including the talent of individuals, the organizational culture, and even the level of serendipitous, situational happenstance (du Gay et al., 1997). Production can be, and is often, gendered; this aspect of public relations practice has led to a productive, informative research stream in public relations theory regarding the feminization of the field (Aldoory, 2002; Grunig, Toth, & Hon, 2001). When applied internationally, the power inherent in production relationships often leads to an emphasis on the organization. Many MNCs, including large public relations firms, espouse making use of local talent while being sensitive to local cultural differences. But often inherent in that business philosophy is the underlying notion that the global is dominant and the local dependent, creating a new form of colonization (du Gay et al., 1997; Kinzar & Bohn, 1985).

The moment of production, then, includes the process by which practitioners create an identity for a public and create messages for that public encompassing organizational goals and ideology. Of import, however, is that producers subsequently monitor consumption of those messages, for the message constructed and encoded is often not the message consumed. Meaning does not reside in an object, such as a campaign tactic, but in how that object is used (Baudrillard, 1998).

Consumption.   Production and consumption do not exist in binary opposition. Consumers appropriate meanings and change them: "the processes of production only provide a series of possibilities that have to be realized in and through consumption" (du Gay et al., 1997, p. 8). Botan and Soto (1998) argue that "publics ought to be understood primarily as self-actuated and interactive social entities with values and internal dynamics at least as complex and important to communication campaigns as are message content or client/practitioner intentions" (p. 21). Depending on the situation, publics may "develop an interpretation that is more sophisticated, insightful, and socially linked than the understanding with which the practitioner/client started" (p. 38).

The Sony Walkman was produced in Japan so that a consumer could listen to music while not disturbing others, allowing social harmony to be maintained. In the United States, consumers often use it to block out external noise, which gave rise to the criticism it was creating asocial behavior. Criticism in the United States also centered on the device as promoting meaningless entertainment, yet many individuals used it for personal enrichment, such as listening to books on tape while exercising. The Walkman is used by du Gay and colleagues (1997) as an extended example of how the circuit of culture is realized—and in this instance how consumers and cultures appropriate and create meanings other than those of the producers.

The implications for public relations practice, particularly international practice, are clear: issues monitoring and environmental scanning are necessary to track newly created meanings so that campaigns may be adjusted on an ongoing basis and not just at some prespecified point at the end of the campaign. Yet tracking and identifying meanings are often not well accomplished through the standard quantitative methods of evaluating campaign effectiveness, such as collecting media clips and surveying publics. Qualitative methods are better suited for capturing meaning, particularly when cultural context is taken into account (du Gay et al., 1997; Rhee, 2002).

Regulation.   The moment of regulation is where the public and private spheres collide, and for this reason it is of particular importance to international public relations practice. Here, cultural classification systems, social assumptions, and mores reside. The moment of regulation, then, is crucial in helping form the representations and identities created by both producers and consumers. In any given situation, anything that does not fit an individual's system is rejected.

Practitioners consequently must evaluate both their own and their publics' regulatory systems. Such a move may have helped determine why Spanish-speaking audiences would construct a meaning of "no go" (*no va*) from the Chevy Nova rather than the intended meaning of "new" (*nova*).

Cancel, Mitrook, and Cameron's (1999) contingency theory is helpful in conceptualizing the regulatory process. The variables in contingency theory are divided into predisposing and situational variables. The cultural values and mores inherent in the moment of regulation may be seen as predisposing factors because they are the unexamined cultural assumptions that guide behavior: they "form a background that may become invisible" (p. 189). An important distinction is that although contingency theory focuses on the practitioner and how these factors influence production, the circuit also applies them to production of meaning by all actors in all other moments.

To inform international practice about these regulatory aspects, some researchers have suggested using Edward Hall's or Geert Hofstede's cultural indices (Freitag, 2002; Kanso & Nelson, 2002; Wakefield, 1996). Hall's (1977) focus is language, and his most well-known contribution is his categorization of communication as high or low context. In high-context cultures, such as those of the Middle East, much is left implicit and unstated, and relational prestige is more important than logical arguments. In low-context cultures, such as the United States, communication is explicit and information flows freely. The degree of context also dictates preferred message forms, with different cultures having different preferences for whether a message comes as words, numbers, or pictures. For example, in Ghana, dance, songs, and storytelling have been among the most important channels for conducting public communication campaigns in towns (Riley, 1991). As this example illustrates, interpersonal communication has much more import in some cultures, and the tendency for practitioners in the United States to rely on mediated channels of communication may not prove effective cross-culturally (Hall & Hall, 1995).

Another helpful construct is that of monochronic versus polychronic time (Hall & Hall, 1995). In monochronic cultures, such as much of the United States, deadlines and schedules are considered firm, privacy is respected, and promptness is expected and rewarded. In polychronic cultures, such as much of Latin America, plans are changed easily and often, schedules and budgets are guidelines but not strictures, and furthering relations is more important than property rights or privacy. From this aspect, it is easy to see how the dominant culture in the United States has defined public relations practice according to management by objective and following a systematic formula such as Marston's (1979) RACE acronym (research, action/planning, communication, evaluation). It is also not difficult to see, however, how public relations will have developed along quite different models in other countries. In these areas, trying to enforce the U.S. model of practice could be counterproductive to effective international public relations practice.

Hofstede (2001a) proposed five major cultural constructs: power distance (PDI), uncertainty avoidance (UAI), individualism (IDV), masculinity (MAS), and long-term orientation. PDI is defined as "the extent to which the less powerful members of institutions and organizations within a country expect and accept that power is distributed unequally" (p. 98). In high-PDI cultures, practitioners could employ more coercive strategies, whereas in low-PDI cultures, rewards or premiums would bring better results. UAI measures how intolerant or ethnocentric a culture is; a culture that is high on the uncertainty avoidance scale will resist anything seen as an "outside effort," and practitioners would be wise to hire a local firm and acquire a local sponsor for a campaign.

Individualism refers to how much the culture tends to think in terms of individual rights and responsibilities versus those of society. The classic example is the difference between the United States, a very individualistic culture, and Japan, which is guided by social norms. In Japan, shame is a powerful norm because it ostracizes one from the group; in the United States, guilt is more powerful because of the individual responsibility implied (Benedict, 1967; Feiler, 1991). Hofstede's construct of masculinity measures how much the culture values assertiveness versus nurturing and has obvious implications for humanitarian aid campaigns. Long-term orientation refers to how forward-looking a culture is. This measure may be of particular import for environmental issues, which often have inherent long-term goals and objectives.

Some case studies have used these constructs to examine values of practitioners within a culture (i.e., Rhee, 2002—South Korea; Vasquez & Taylor, 1999— United States; Verĉiĉ, Grunig, & Grunig, 1996—Slovenia; Kanso & Nelson, 2002, and Zaharna, 1995—Arabic countries) or the particular dimensions of import for a type of practice (Taylor & Kent, 1999—power distance in government relations work). These cases omit two important considerations: (1) an examination of how values come into play for publics as they create meaning, and (2) cross-national comparisons showing how to bridge cultural differences. Many scholars have updated and refined Hall's and Hofstede's indices (e.g., Morosini, 1998; Trompenaars, 1994), forming a ripe foundation for extending study.

Care must also be taken, however, that future studies purporting to develop holistic international public relations theory do not rely solely on measures of practitioners' cultural values or from basing all international public relations practice on cultural norms. To do so is to privilege one moment of the circuit to the exclusion of the others. Although the theory and practice of international public relations demand that the cultural values inherent in the moment of regulation be considered, they also demand that scholars take into account how practitioners produce meaning, how publics and organizations are constructed and identified, how publics create and re-create themselves and their meanings, and how public relations texts are formed. Culture as a way of life is not distinct and privileged; it operates in synergy with the notion of culture as the production and circulation of meaning throughout the circuit.

The Circuit as a Basis for Theoretical Development

Looking again at the model of the circuit of culture (Figure 17.1), it should be apparent that although the figure is static on the page, in practice it is spinning and pulsing along the points of connection within the circuit, also known as articulations (du Gay et al., 1997). The model is not tight and linear because international public relations is not a tight, linear practice. Key to further theoretical development is the dynamic tension that exists throughout the model: It does not privilege any one moment or any one actor, or even the totality of the moments. It emphasizes the points of articulation, where public relations practitioners operate as cultural intermediaries. Extant scholarly work has provided insightful glimpses into different moments, such as production or regulation from the practitioners' perspective. But until more work is done that takes into account the circuit as a whole and the positioning of public relations practice within the articulations of the model, practitioners will have little guidance when they venture into the international realm.

How the model can inform practice is best answered by returning to the two questions posed by Taylor (2001) at the beginning of this chapter: How will public relations be different in other parts of the world? How will we have to adapt to communicate with international publics? Because cultural assumptions, classifications, and values lie in the moment of regulation, this aspect of the circuit informs the first question. Building from case studies and using schemas such as those of E. Hall and G. Hofstede, it is possible to construct a contingency matrix of cultural factors that provide guidance on how public relations as a meaning-making practice will differ around the globe. But that matrix, while providing guidance and a useful jumping-off point, is not wholly predictive. A major lesson of the circuit of culture is that not every member of a culture inculcates cultural meaning and values in the same way. Sony may be a Japanese company, but those who work with Sony soon learn that it is also a global company (du Gay et al., 1997). The guidance obtained from a contingency matrix based on national characteristics provides only part of the picture, and it must be constantly updated to retain its value.

The model, then, is neither deterministic, nor is it entirely relative. And this aspect helps answer Taylor's second question, concerning how practitioners will have to adapt to communicate with international publics. Taking into account the moment of regulation, practitioners can structure messages and deliver them in culturally appropriate ways. But the construction of meaning is an active process, and publics the world over are an integral part of the process. Perhaps the main way that practitioners will have to adapt is to become more vigilant about monitoring how publics are using messages and more adept at continuously refining and reshaping campaigns. That campaign structure and content have to be culturally sensitive is a given; what is more difficult is to change how we view the process and practice of public relations and change our own behavior accordingly.

The circuit is not a normative model. Instead, it examines values from Hofstede's (2001b) perspective: "Cultural relevance does not imply normlessness for oneself or for one's own society. It does call for one to suspend judgment when dealing with groups or societies different from one's own" (p. 15). The model suggests that international ethics codes will prove meaningless in that they will be used to support a conflicting plethora of meanings. For practitioners looking for ethical guidance, the model suggests that self-reflexively examining the process as a holistic dynamic will provide ethical sensitivity. Whereas Cancel, Mitrooh, and Cameron (1999) criticized the two-way symmetric model for privileging the communication process over ethical principle, the circuit of culture suggests that every communicative act is a statement of ethical principle; the two cannot be viewed in separation, but neither must they be viewed as inherently embracing a particular normative stance.

Much work remains to be done to take the circuit of culture model and develop it into robust theory that informs practice. But what the model provides is an integrated framework to build comprehensive theory with predictive and explanatory power. Extant research has developed our understanding of particular moments on the circuit. What is needed now is research that focuses on the circuit in its totality, qualitative research that elicits meaning and the meaning-making process at all points of the circuit, and quantitative and qualitative longitudinal studies that capture the inherent dynamism of the practice of international public relations.

CASE: IVORY COAST*

The Ivory Coast (Cote d'Ivoire in French) is a sub-Saharan country the size of New Mexico (in the United States) located on the North Atlantic coast of West Africa. Long considered one of the economic success stories of Africa, the country has recently moved into a period of political upheaval and economic instability. In 1999, the country faced its first military coup, which tarnished almost four decades of tranquility. After the coup, presidential elections in 2000 resulted in widespread violence from political parties that felt excluded in the democratic process. A failed military coup in 2002 refocused international attention on the Ivory Coast. These recent political events have been compounded by the country's sagging economic performance. As one of the world's largest exporters of cocoa and coffee, the country has suffered from unpredictable price fluctuations worldwide.

These factors have made the country far less stable than at any other point since its independence from France in 1960 and have resulted in civil war. The Ivory Coast has more than sixty ethnic groups that have splintered across ethnic and religious lines, leading to the formation of ethnic militias and rebel groups vying for power held by the presidency. The Ivory Coast has maintained close ties with France since its independence, and France has often interceded to smooth over political unrest and broker fleeting peace agreements. France and other international coalitions are working with the Ivory Coast government to quell unrest in the country and to find diplomatic alternatives to war.

Situation Analysis

In 2002, the Ivory Coast government turned to a U.S. public relations agency for assistance in attracting MNCs to the country, generating increased tourism, and assisting with domestic public relations efforts. The government is hopeful that

---

*Based on a case written by Miller (1992). The background and situation analysis are based on information obtained from the *2002 World Factbook, O'Dwyer's PR Daily,* and the *New York Times.*

peace will prevail through negotiation sessions with groups trying to overthrow the president and that the Ivory Coast can recapture its international image as a progressive African country attractive to investors and accommodating to tourists.

A former U.S. diplomat identified these areas in which the cultural norms differ from those in the West: different concepts of family, the position of women in society, village customs and traditions, and belief in animistic forces that absolve the individual from responsibility for his or her actions. Additionally, 51.5 percent of the population over the age of fifteen is illiterate. The government has traditionally controlled much of the media, comprising fourteen radio stations and fourteen television stations. Journalists have been jailed for reporting antigovernment stances, drawing the ire of worldwide media watchdog groups and civil rights organizations.

The Assignment

If the government of the Ivory Coast asked your public relations agency based in your home country to handle public relations activities associated with its quest for modernization, stability, and a better international image, how would you proceed? Because the government is preoccupied with governance and the restoration of peace, it is relying on your public relations counsel to give it direction and provide effective communications to its various publics.

QUESTIONS FOR APPLICATION

1. How would you suggest to your firm's management that you structure a team to work on the Ivory Coast account?

2. What are some underlying assumptions about the Ivory Coast you can make and apply to the theories discussed in this chapter?

3. What are some cultural values you can cull from the case study that might affect your public relations work?

4. What are some public relations materials, or texts, that might be effective to communicate various government policies and messages to the following audiences:
   - The people of Ivory Coast?
   - Other governments?
   - MNCs?
   - Tourists?
   - Investors?

5. How might the government be represented to these audiences?

6. How might du Gay and colleagues' circuit of culture help establish a public relations strategy for the government of the Ivory Coast?

7. What conclusions can you draw from the public relations challenges the Ivory Coast faces about the universality—or lack thereof—of effective public relations practices?

REFERENCES

Acosta-Alzuru, C., & Kreshel, P. J. (2002). "I'm an American Girl . . . whatever *that* means": Girls consuming Pleasant Company's American Girl identity. *Journal of Communication, 52*(1), pp. 139–161.

Alanazi, A. (1996). Public relations in the Middle East: The case of Saudi Arabia. In H. Culbertson & N. Chen (Eds.), *International public relations: A comparative analysis* (pp. 239–255). Mahwah, NJ: Lawrence Erlbaum.

Aldoory, L. (2002, August). *Leadership and gender in public relations.* Paper presented to the annual meeting of the Association for Education in Journalism and Mass Communication, Miami, FL.

Banks, S. P. (2000). *Multicultural public relations: A social-interpretive approach* (2nd ed.). Ames: Iowa State University Press.

Baudrillard, J. (1988). *Selected writings.* Cambridge, England: Polity Press.

Benedict, R. (1967). *The chrysanthemum and the sword: Patterns of Japanese culture.* Cleveland, OH: Meridian Books.

Berger, B. K. (1999). The Halcion affair: Public relations and the construction of ideological world view. *Journal of Public Relations Research, 11*(3), pp. 185–203.

Botan, C. (1992). International public relations: Critique and reformulation. *Public Relations Review, 18*(2), pp. 149–159.

Botan, C. H., & Soto, F. (1998). A semiotic approach to the internal functioning of publics: Implications for strategic communication and public relations. *Public Relations Review, 24*(1), pp. 21–44.

Bourdieu, P. (1984). *Distinction* (R. Nice, Trans.). London: Routledge.

Brown, R. E. (2002). The physics of public relations. *Public Relations Review, 28*(1), pp. 125–129.

Cancel, A. E., Cameron, G. T., Sallot, L. M., & Mitrook, M. A. (1997). It depends: A contingency theory of accommodation in public relations. *Journal of Public Relations Research, 9*(1), pp. 31–63.

Cancel, A. E., Mitrook, M. A., & Cameron, G. T. (1999). Testing the contingency theory of accommodation in public relations. *Public Relations Review, 25*(2), pp. 171–197.

Chen, N. (1996). Public relations in China: The introduction and development of an occupational field. In H. Culbertson & N. Chen (Eds.), *International public relations: A comparative analysis* (pp. 121–155). Mahwah, NJ: Lawrence Erlbaum.

Chen, N., & Culbertson, H. M. (1992). Two contrasting approaches of government public relations in mainland China. *Public Relations Quarterly, 37*(3), pp. 36–41.

Creedon, P. J., Al-Khaja, W. A., Kruckeberg, D. (1995). Women and public relations education and practice in the United Arab Emirates. *Public Relations Review, 21*(1), pp. 59–77.

Culbertson, H., & Chen, N. (Eds.). (1996). *International public relations: A comparative analysis.* Mahwah, NJ: Lawrence Erlbaum.

du Gay, P., Hall, S., Janes, L., Mackay, H., & Negus, K. (1997). *Doing cultural studies: The story of the Sony walkman.* London: Sage.

Ekachai, D., & Komolsevin, R. (1998). Public relations education in Thailand. *Public Relations Review, 24*(2), pp. 219–234.

Epley, J. S. (1992). Public relations in the global village: An American perspective. *Public Relations Review, 18*(2), pp. 109–116.

Feiler, B. S. (1991). *Learning to bow: Inside the heart of Japan.* Boston: Houghton Mifflin.

Ferguson, M. A. (1984, August). *Building theory in public relations: Interorganizational relationships as a public relations paradigm.* Paper presented at the Association for Education in Journalism and Mass Communication, Gainesville, FL.

Foucault, M. (1980). *The history of sexuality.* New York: Vintage.

Freitag, A. R. (2002). Ascending cultural competence potential: An assessment and profile of U.S. public relations practitioners' preparation for international assignments. *Journal of Public Relations Research, 14*(3), pp. 207–227.

Gandy, O. (1982). *Beyond agenda setting: Information subsidies and public policies.* Norwood, NJ: Ablex.

Greenberg, K. E. (n.d.). *Job outlook 2000: A forecast for the next century.* Accessed April 8, 2003, from www.prsa.org/_Resources/profession/6c029820.html.

Grunig, J. E. (1993). Public relations and international affairs: Effects, ethics. *Journal of International Affairs, 47*(1), pp. 137–162.

Grunig, J., & Hunt, T. (1984). *Managing public relations.* New York: Holt, Rinehart and Winston.

Grunig, L. (1992). Strategic public relations constituencies on a global scale. *Public Relations Review, 18*(2), pp. 127–136.

Grunig, L. A., Grunig, J. E., & Dozier, D. (2002). *Excellent public relations and effective organizations:*

A study of communication management in three countries. Mahwah, NJ: Lawrence Erlbaum.

Grunig, L. A., Toth, E. L., & Hon, L. C. (2001). *Women in public relations: How gender influences practice.* New York: Guilford Press.

Hall, E. T. (1977). *Beyond culture.* New York: Anchor Press/Doubleday.

Hall, E. T., & Hall, M. R. (1995). *Understanding cultural differences.* Yarmouth, ME: International Press.

Hofstede, G. (2001a). *Culture's consequences: Comparing values, behaviors, institutions and organizations across nations* (2nd ed.). Thousand Oaks, CA: Sage.

———. (2001b). Differences and danger: Cultural profiles of nations and limits to tolerance. In M. H. Albrecht (Ed.), *International HRM: Managing diversity in the workplace* (pp. 9–23). Malden, MA: Blackwell.

Holt, D. B., (2002). Why do brands cause trouble? A dialectical theory of consumer culture and branding. *Journal of Consumer Research, 29*(1), pp. 70–90.

Holtzhausen, D. R. (2000). Postmodern values in public relations. *Journal of Public Relations Research, 12*(1), pp. 93–114.

Huang, Y. (2001). OPRA: A cross-cultural, multiple-item scale for measuring organization-public relationships. *Journal of Public Relations Research, 13*(1), pp. 61–90.

Hutton, J. (1999). The definition, dimensions, and domain of public relations. *Public Relations Review, 25*(2), pp. 199–214.

Hutton, J. G., Goodman, M. B., Alexander, J. B., & Genest, C. M. (2001). Reputation management: The new face of corporate public relations? *Public Relations Review, 27*(3), pp. 247–261.

Illman, P. E. (1980). *Developing overseas managers and managers overseas.* New York: AMACON.

Kanso, A., & Nelson, R. (2002, March). *Overcoming biases, stereotypes, and false inferences: Cross-cultural frameworks for Arab and American public relations practitioners.* Paper presented to the Public Relations Educator's Research Academy, Miami, FL.

Karlberg, M. (1996). Remembering the public in public relations research: From theoretical to operational symmetry. *Journal of Public Relations Research, 8*(4), pp. 263–278.

Kinzar, H. J., & Bohn, E. (1985, May). *Public relations challenges of multinational corporations.* Paper presented to the meeting of the International Communications Association, Honolulu, HI.

Kruckeberg, D. (1989). The need for an international code of ethics. *Public Relations Review, 15*(2), pp. 6–18.

———. (1995–1996). The challenge for public relations in an era of globalization. *Public Relations Quarterly, 40*(4), pp. 36–40.

Kunczik, M. (1997). *Images of nations and international public relations.* Hillsdale, NJ: Lawrence Erlbaum.

Leichty, G., & Springston, J. (1993). Reconsidering public relations models. *Public Relations Review, 19*, pp. 327–339.

L'Etang, J. (1996). Public relations as diplomacy. In J. L'Etang & M. Pieczka (Eds.), *Critical Perspectives in Public Relations* (pp. 14–34). London: International Thomson Business Press.

L'Etang, J., & Pieczka, M. (Eds.). (1996). *Critical perspectives in public relations.* London: International Thomson Business Press.

Marston, J. E. (1979). *Modern public relations.* New York: McGraw-Hill.

McDermott, P. M. (1991, November). *International public relations.* Workshop conducted at the annual meeting of the Public Relations Society of America, Nashville, TN.

Mickey, T. J. (2003). *Deconstructing public relations: Public relations criticism.* Mahwah, NJ: Lawrence Erlbaum.

Miller, R. H. (1992). Political dynamics in Cote d'Ivoire. In R. H. Miller (Ed.), *Inside an embassy: The political role of diplomats abroad* (pp. 33–34). Washington, DC: Congressional Quarterly.

Modoux, A. (1989). The growing role of public relations in a changing world. *International Public Relations Review, 12*, pp. 4–9.

Molleda, J. C. (2002, August). *International paradigms: The social role of Brazilian public relations professionals.* Paper presented at the annual meeting of the Association for Education in Journalism and Mass Communication, Miami, FL.

Morosini, P. (1998). *Managing cultural differences: Effective strategy and execution across cultures in global corporate affairs.* New York: Pergamon.

Motion, J., & Leitch, S. (2001). New Zealand perspectives on public relations. In R. Heath (Ed.), *The Handbook of Public Relations* (pp. 659–665). Thousand Oaks, CA: Sage.

Nessmann, K. (1995). Public relations in Europe: A comparison with the United States. *Public Relations Review, 21*, pp. 151–160.

Paluszek, J. (1989). Public relations in the coming global economy. *Vital Speeches of the Day, 56*, pp. 22–26.

Pearson, R. (1989). Beyond ethical relativism in public relations: Coorientation, rules, and the idea of communication symmetry. In J. E. Grunig & L. A. Grunig (Eds.), *Public relations research annual* (vol. 1, pp. 67–87). Hillsdale, NJ: Lawrence Erlbaum.

Pieczka, M. (1996). Paradigms, systems theory, and public relations. In J. L'Etang & M. Pieczka (Eds.), *Critical perspectives in public relations* (pp. 124–156). London: International Thomson Business Press.

Rhee, Y. (2002). Global public relations: A cross-cultural study of the excellence theory in South Korea. *Journal of Public Relations Research, 14*(3), pp. 159–184.

Riley, M. (1991, May). *Indigenous resources in a Ghanaian town: Potential for health education.* Paper presented at the annual meeting of the International Communication Association, Chicago.

Sallot, L. M., Lyon, L. J., Acosta-Alzuru, C., & Jones, K. O. (2003). From aardvark to zebra: A new millennium analysis of theory development in public relations academic journals. *Journal of Public Relations Research, 15*(1), pp. 27–90.

Signitzer, B. H., & Coombs, T. (1992). Public relations and public diplomacy: Conceptual convergences. *Public Relations Review, 18*(2), pp. 137–147.

Simões, R. P. (1992). Public relations as a political function: A Latin American view. *Public Relations Review, 18*(2), pp. 189–200.

Sriramesh, K. (1996). Power distance and public relations: An ethnographic study of Southern Indian organizations. In H. M. Culbertson & N. Chen (Eds.), *International public relations: A comparative analysis* (pp. 171–190). Mahwah, NJ: Lawrence Erlbaum.

Sriramesh, K., & White, J. (1992). Societal culture and public relations. In J. E. Grunig (Ed.), *Excellence in public relations and communication management* (pp. 597–614). Hillsdale, NJ: Lawrence Erlbaum.

Sriramesh, K., Kim, Y., & Takasaki, M. (1999). Public relations in three Asian countries: An analysis. *Journal of Public Relations Research, 11*(4), pp. 271–292.

Taylor, M. (2001). International public relations: Opportunities and challenges for the 21st century. In R. Heath (Ed.), *The handbook of public relations* (pp. 629–637). Thousand Oaks, CA: Sage.

Taylor, M., & Kent, M. L. (1999). Challenging assumptions of international public relations: When government is the most important public. *Public Relations Review, 25*(2), pp. 131–144.

Toth, E. L. (2002). Postmodernism for modernist public relations: The cash value and application of critical research in public relations. *Public Relations Review, 28*(3), pp. 243–250.

Toth, E. L., & Trujillo, N. (1987). Reinventing corporate communications. *Public Relations Review, 13,* pp. 42–53.

Trompenaars, F. (1994). *Riding the waves of culture: Understanding cultural diversity in global business.* New York: McGraw-Hill.

Turk, J., & Scanlan, L. H. (1999). *The evolution of public relations: Case studies from countries in transition.* Gainesville, FL: Institute for Public Relations.

Van Hook, S. R. (n.d.) *PR business is booming.* Accessed April 6, 2003, from http://aboutpublicrelations. net/aa042901a.htm.

Van Leuven, J. K., & Pratt, C. B. (1996). Public relations' role: Realities in Asia and in Africa south of the Sahara. In H. Culbertson & N. Chen (Eds.), *International public relations: A comparative analysis* (pp. 93–107). Mahwah, NJ: Lawrence Erlbaum.

Vasquez, G. M., & Taylor, M. (1999). What cultural values influence American public relations practitioners? *Public Relations Review, 25*(4), pp. 433–449.

Verčič, D., Grunig, L. A., & Grunig, J. E. (1996). Global and specific principles of public relations: Evidence from Slovenia. In H. Culbertson & N. Chen (Eds.), *International public relations: A comparative analysis* (pp. 31–65). Mahwah, NJ: Lawrence Erlbaum.

Wakefield, R. I. (1996). Interdisciplinary theoretical foundations for international public relations. In H. Culbertson and N. Chen (Eds.). *International public relations: A comparative analysis* (pp. 17–30). Mahwah, NJ: Lawrence Erlbaum.

Wilson, L. J. (1990). Corporate issues management: An international view. *Public Relations Review, 16*(1), pp. 40–51.

Zaharna, R. S. (1995). Understanding cultural preferences of Arab communication patterns. *Public Relations Review, 21*(3), pp. 241–255.

———. (2001). "In-awareness" approach to international public relations. *Public Relations Review, 27*(2), pp. 135–148.

CHAPTER EIGHTEEN

THE PLACE OF THEORY IN PUBLIC RELATIONS PRACTICE

AYDEMIR OKAY

ALYA OKAY

This chapter explores the possible theoretical relationships between the academic and professional worlds of public relations. This research also seeks to shed light on the ways in which academic knowledge, theories, and approaches are used in public relations practices as viewed by public relations practitioners. Many public relations practices appear to be based on intuitive or experimental learning rather than academic knowledge. This chapter examines a focal issue in the field of public relations, the way that practitioners view public relations theories and approaches in their practices.

Practitioners (project managers) of forty campaigns were identified as the population to be studied. Each practitioner, as project manager, was awarded a 2002 Golden World Award from the International Public Relations Association (IPRA) for most successful practices in 2003. A questionnaire was designed to focus on the theoretical public relations knowledge of these managers, especially their use and/or understanding of select public relations theories and approaches in their practices.

Collaboration between public relations practitioners and the academic world is an important area in public relations. It provides a framework that helps professionalize public relations, helps serve organizations' self-interests (Kent & Taylor, 2002), and demonstrates academics' and practitioners' agreement on the key public relations principles or outcome variables derived from an academic education (Neff, Walker, Smith, & Creedon, 1999).

Most existing public relations theories have been developed more recently within the context of public relations as a management function (Grunig, 1992; Dozier, Grunig, & Grunig, 1995; Heath, 2001). This might be a cyclical phenomenon, however; over time theories seem to evolve and/or leave their place to new ones. Holtzhausen (2002) quotes Lyotard's words: "Theories themselves are concealed narratives (and) we should not be taken by their claim to be valid for all times" (p. 253).

Heath (2001), for example, outlines the variety of approaches when "defining the practice." Heath states "the practice of public relations is a work in progress" and cites key areas such as "the forces of change, the challenge of organizational legitimacy, the education of practitioners, and the advances in ethical practices" that continually play a role in redefining the practice (p. 183). Cornelissen (2000) says that one of the major issues in the field of public relations is the insight into the extent to which thoughts and activities of practitioners are founded on or at least influenced by academic knowledge and research. However, it is important to determine first how aware public relations professionals are about developments in the field.

Neff (1989) documented inaccurate perceptions on where public relations was taught in the U.S. academic institutions, for example, and thus provided a clue to "the missing theoretical perspective in public relations" (p. 161). This analysis of the curriculum officially published in university and college catalogs established public relations as no longer dominated by academics from mass media. Many programs had shifted to nonjournalism departments represented primarily by public communication and rhetorical studies. This is one major reason why the public relations field suffers from a lack of accurate understanding of academic theories along with the public relations knowledge and tools stemming from them (Botan, 1989). Some public relations scholars, such as J. V. Pavlik, C. Salmon, and E. Toth, have argued that this absence of a strong academic foundation to guide the work of many practitioners directly affects a further "professionalization" of the discipline (Cornelissen, 2000).

A national study of U.S. public relations educators and practitioners provided a significant amount of data on the relationship of education to outcomes for the entry-level positions, advanced-level positions, and the academic requirements for educators teaching in public relations. On a scale of 1 to 7 with 7 expressing high agreement, these professionals surveyed agreed entry-level practitioners should be aware of social trends (6.31-educators and 6.04-practitioners on a scale of 7), have a high degree of critical thinking/problem-solving ability (6.63-E and 6.49-P) and research abilities (5.99-E and 5.79-P), in addition to many other key personal and professional characteristics necessary to the practice (Neff et al., 1999, p. 32). This same report established high agreement between educators and practitioners on desired advanced-level practitioner outcomes and these included: reads professional public relations publications (5.71-E and 5.41-P), research skills (6.21-E and 6.06-P), and skilled in issues tracking (5.55-E and 5.43-P) and included twenty-eight other outcome areas surveyed (Neff et al., 1999, p. 37). These results indicate a high agreement between practitioners and educators on the importance of research and theory as desired characteristics. Practitioners and educators agreed also on outcomes for educators (high involvement of practitioners in the academic institutions in the United States is a significant factor). Educators and practitioners agreed that the desired outcomes included: reads research in public relations and related areas (6.24-E and 6.22-P); uses theory in teaching and research (6.30-E and 5.54-P); and uses different research methods (6.10-E and 5.93-P). The doctoral level of desired outcomes included: advances public relations theory (6.27-E and 5.85-P) and publishes public relations research (6.26-E and 5.88-P). Again, educators and practitioners agreed on desired outcomes. Another question asked if these outcomes are also "found" in the practice. Both practitioners and educators agreed there is no strong evidence (all found outcomes rated less than 5.00).

Now, the found outcomes for educators were quite different in overall direction of support. These outcomes included: reads research in public relations and related areas (4.86-E and 5.20-P); uses theory in teaching and research (4.87-E and 5.22-P); uses different research methods (4.27-E and 4.79-P); uses advanced public relations theory (4.55-E and 5.23-P); and publishes public relations research (4.54-E and 5.03-P). Although educators could not rate found outcomes above a 5.00, practitioners did rate all outcomes above 5.00 with the exception of one question on methodology, and this outcome was still higher for practitioners than for the educators (Neff et al., 1999, p. 40). Definitely practitioners seem more confident than educators about theory and research being found as outcomes for public relations educators.

Thus the data on outcomes solidly support practitioners and educators agreeing on desired outcomes from an academic experience. Both groups also agreed strongly that these outcomes are not found significantly. Only when the public relations educators are rated for outcomes is there a trend toward finding results that are significant. Educators ranked all five found outcomes for educators lower than practitioners, with the latter reporting found outcomes *above* 5.00 except for the outcome "uses different research methods," which was rated at 4.79. Thus the premise of this study acknowledges that data on found outcomes focusing on theory and research for educators indicate neither group is seeing results or outcomes at a significant level. Educators and practitioners agree on outcomes and agree that these outcomes are largely not found except for educator outcomes as viewed by practitioners.

In sum, the higher desired ratings by educators could be due to the "reward structure inherent in most academic departments, where the ability to conduct theoretically grounded research is essential to tenure and promotion" (Neff et al., 1999, p. 43). However, discovering higher "found outcomes" by practitioners for educators suggests other factors are intervening. This finding "raises interesting questions about how educators and practitioners define research and theory" (p. 43).

PUBLIC RELATIONS' TRANSITION TO THEORY-BASED SCIENCE: AN ENDEAVOR

Arguments associated with whether public relations is a science started long ago. The idea of public relations as a social science was suggested in 1978 following the "First World Assembly of Public Relations Associations" held in Mexico: Public relations practice is "the art and social science of analyzing trends, predicting their consequences, counseling organizational leaders, and implementing planned programs of action which will serve both the organization and public interest" (Gordon, 1997, p. 60; Newsom, Vanslyke Turk, & Kruckeberg, 1996, p. 4).

After establishing degrees and degree emphases in public relations in various universities, especially in the United States, academic researchers began a rigorous dialogue about public relations' place as a social science. Academic journals such as *Public Relations Review* (the oldest academic publication dedicated to public relations), *Public Relations Quarterly,* and the *Journal of Public Relations Research,* have become domains in which a wide range of research and ideas are published. Organizations and divisions of public relations were established in academic associations during this period: The Association for Education in Journalism and Mass Communication's Public Relations Division of nearly five hundred members, founded over thirty years ago; the International Communication Association's Public Relations Division, founded in 1985 (approximately three hundred members and awards the Robert Heath Top Paper Award); the National Communication Association's Public Relations Division, founded in 1987 (approximately five hundred members and awards top research publications with the PRide Awards); the Central States Communication Association's Public Relations Division, founded in 1988 (approximately 195 members); the International Academy of Business Disciplines' Public Relations Track, founded in 1988; and the International and Interdisciplinary Public Relations Research Conference, founded in 1997 (Bourland and Neff, 2000). The latter group is a stand-alone organization with an affiliation to the Institute for Public Relations in the United States. Establishing public relations divisions within associations and special research organizations allows practitioners and scholars to present research and to discuss ideas with a major focus on public relations. Other major research efforts developing over the past five years or more include the annual research conferences held in Bled, Slovenia, and Dubrovnik, Croatia.

Also, books developing a scientific approach to public relations understanding and practice have increased in numbers. The field of public relations now has a *Handbook of Public Relations* and an *Encyclopedia of Public Relations*—two volumes (both edited by Robert Heath). Several basic texts emerged during the 1980s, establishing public relations as grounded in a body of literature. *Managing Public Relations,* published by Grunig and Hunt in 1984, attempted to characterize public relations as one-way and two-way communication flow patterns. The four models of public relations developed by Grunig and Hunt, although static in concept, do provide a framework for much discussion on the nature of communication from a public relations perspective. Crable and Vibbert's basic text on *Public Relations as Communication Management* in 1986 focused on identification, analysis, and performance within an organizational concept. Their text was based on a large body of scholarship emanating from the social sciences and focused on the process of research, analysis, communication, and evaluation (RACE). The most theoretical discussion of public relations on diversity appeared in the scholarly text by S. Banks, titled *Multicultural Public Relations: A Socio-Interpretive Approach* (2000). This theory outlined the diversity challenges from an organizational, an ethical, and a communication perspective for the public relations practitioners.

Today, the arguments over whether public relations is a science have been replaced by the question "Which theory works best?" This study suggests that the intersection of theory and practice is very important to the continued successful development of the public relations field.

THE IMPORTANCE OF THEORY DEVELOPMENT

Theory comes from some sort of practice and practice comes from some sort of theory. According to Hançerlioğlu (1986), there is no theory without practice, or practice without theory. One turns into the other and both constantly interact. Such thought manifests itself in public relations efforts in which theories are tested and/or developed through comprehensive analysis of practice. In this way, science is able to contribute to practice. Theories that are not examined through practice are not easily applied by public relations practitioners. The point that we stress here is that public relations is an "applied discipline." In public relations, practice and theory should be in constant interaction, and such interaction should be viewed as a cycle that forms science.

A number of theories have the potential to help us understand the process of public relations. They are not specific theories of public relations, but they serve as a guiding element of introduction to the matter for us, for example systems theory, situational theory, or an approach through conflict resolution (Fischer, 1997). These theories give us opportunities to observe public relations from different points of view. According to F. Ronnenberger (1987), "What should be expected from a public relations theory is that it links public relations activities to social institutions and processes, and designates its importance for the social existence" (p. 426). Rühl advocates that a well-suited public relations theory does not deal with the universal question of "what" but instead with "a function peculiar to the society" (Signitzer, 1997, p. 189). Signitzer has divided theories with a direct relation to public relations into three groups. These theories give us social theoretical perspectives, organizational theory perspectives, and other viewpoints such as rhetorical theory.

The theories listed in Signitzer's categories guide this study. This case study of award-winning campaign directors summarized each theory and used those summaries as a way to organize questions and responses.

Practitioners' Views of Public Relations Theories

This study investigated the idea that public relations theories are not known [by names] by practitioners but many public relations practices find their place in theories. The data collected was based on a survey of practitioners in charge of campaigns winning 2002 Golden World Awards from the (IPRA). IPRA has awarded this prize since 1990 to recognize the most successful public relations campaigns with a view of supporting ethical standards and social responsibility in the field of public relations. Each year, referees deal with a large number of applications in different categories, and assess campaigns for their quality of research, planning, application, and results.

Since the prize is awarded in different categories, our selection covered only winners and honorary mentions throughout all categories for two primary types of organizations: agency and corporate. The distribution of 2002 award winners by country, in-house campaign, or agency-driven campaigns, was as follows:

As shown in Table 18.1, most awards went to the United States, where public relations as an academic discipline and practice are highly developed, followed

TABLE 18.1   IPRA 2002 Golden World Awards, winning countries and their campaign

COUNTRY	AGENCY/OTHER ORGANIZATION	IN-HOUSE	TOTAL
Australia	2	1	3
Brazil	1	-	1
China	1	-	1
Germany	2	-	2
France	1	-	1
England	1	-	1
Hong Kong, China	-	1	1
Indonesia	1	1	2
Kenya	1	-	1
Switzerland	1	-	1
Serbia & Montenegro	1	-	1
Spain	1	-	1
Turkey	1	1	2
Hungary	2	-	2
USA	19	1	20
Total	35	5	40

by Australia, Germany, Indonesia, Turkey, Hungary, and other countries. A quick overview of the award-winning campaigns shows agencies most frequently conducted campaigns (thirty-five campaigns) with in-house campaigns representing only five campaigns. This yielded a potential population of forty campaigns for the initial research contact.

Methodology.   E-mail addresses and fax numbers of campaign supervisors of the forty 2002 Golden World Awards winners were obtained. A letter of introduction and a three-page questionnaire were e-mailed to each member of our selected population. If e-mail transmissions were returned as undeliverable, the questionnaires were faxed. Surveys were sent to participants twice with a three-week interval between electronic transmissions. Those responding to the first transmission were not sent the survey a second time. A total of sixteen usable questionnaires were returned yielding a 40 percent response rate. The results reflected the profile of the original pool of award winners.

The questionnaire contained sixteen questions. Fourteen questions were close-ended and two open-ended. The questionnaire consisted of three sections. Section 1 included questions aimed at exploring the demographics of respondents, as well as some information on their agencies and corporations. In Section 2, respondents were asked questions enabling them to indicate their knowledge of public relations theories. The final section of the questionnaire was intended to reveal the respondents' opinions about some public relations-related propositions, and to what extent they agreed with ideas advocated by specific (yet unnamed) public relations theories. SPSS (Statistical Package for the Social Sciences) was used to calculate responses on the fourteen close-ended questions. The open-ended questions addressed in this study focused on the academic knowledge and insights used by practitioners in their practice.

Population Profile. Of the sixteen practitioners responding, 56.3 percent of the target group was female and 43.8 percent was male. Ages of the respondents were grouped in the following way: 31.4 percent fell in the twenty-eight to thirty-eight years of age category, 37.7 percent in the forty-two to forty-six years of age category, and 25 percent in the forty-nine to fifty-nine years of age category. One respondent did not specify age.

Forty-four percent of the public relations supervisors had been active in the field for six to ten years, 50 percent fifteen to twenty years, while 6 percent had more than twenty-five years of experience. The different positions held by the respondents were as follows: 25.1 percent held the title of president/director/ CEO/senior, 25.1 percent served as consultant managing director, 25 percent held the position of vice president, 12.5 percent served as press and public relations officer, 6.3 percent served as public affairs manager, and 6.3 percent held the role of partner.

Of those who responded, 68.8 percent were university graduates, 18.8 percent had a master's degree, while 12.5 percent held a doctoral degree; 56.3 percent of the respondents received education in public relations or communications at the university level; and 37.5 percent graduated from a college department other than public relations. Of those having a university diploma in public relations/ communications, 44.4 percent stated that they had heard about public relations theories during courses they took, while 55.6 percent stated that they were given no information on public relations theories.

Of those who responded, 43.8 percent indicated that they regularly follow the literature in the field through such things as books and journals, while 37.5 percent indicated that they do it occasionally, and 18.8 percent stated that they do not keep up with it at all.

Assessment of Sample. Seven structured statements were used to assess the IPRA award winners' opinions or knowledge of public relations theory and practice. These statements focused on education, learnable practice, practice follows theory, theory follows practice, science develops more rapidly than practice, theory develops more rapidly than practice, and the impact of theory on practice. Each question was rated on a 5-point continuum of agree to disagree. The results are presented in Table 18.2.

The results established that 37.6 percent of the respondents felt public relations-related education was important. However, 62.5 percent did not agree with this statement. With the majority of respondents not agreeing on the importance of education, one notes this corresponds with a population profile that is older (56 percent with fifteen or more years of experience). The more recent academic developments in public relations have occurred within the last five to ten years. So the findings from a population (56.3 percent) with a diploma in public relations/ communications (55.6 percent given no information on public relations

TABLE 18.2   Campaign supervisors' views about the theory and the practice: IPRA award-winners' responses to theory and practice relationships

STATE YOUR OPINIONS ON THE FOLLOWING STATEMENTS	I TOTALLY AGREE (5)	I AGREE (4)	I PARTLY AGREE (3)	I DO NOT AGREE (2)	I DO NOT AGREE AT ALL (1)	UNANSWERED
Public relations practitioners should have received public relations-related education.	18.8	6.3	12.5	50	12.5	-
Public relations is a profession that is learnable by following a practical process, not by following a formal educational process.	18.8	31.3	31.3	12.5	6.3	-
Public relations practices follow theoretical developments in the field of public relations.	-	18.8	12.5	50	12.5	6.3
Public relations theories follow developments in the public relations practices.	-	68.8	25	-	-	6.3
The science of public relations evolves more rapidly than the practice does.	6.3	12.5	37.5	33.3	6.3	6.3
Theoretical progress in public relations finds rapidly its reflections in the practice.	6.3	25	25	37.5	6.3	-
Theory has no significance in public relations practices at all.	6.3	-	31.3	25	37.5	-

theory and 44.4 percent heard about public relations theory) establishes that having a university degree related in the area of public relations is no guarantee that public relations theory will be covered.

When 50 percent of the respondents indicated that public relations can be learned through practice rather than formal education, these respondents were speaking primarily from the experience of their own career development—not formal education. The percentage of those somewhat in partial agreement with this point of view (an additional 31.3 percent) yielded a total of 81.4 percent supporting public relations as a learnable practical response. However, one has to keep in mind that this finding represents 31.3 percent that only partly agree. Again, removing the partly-agree representation brings the numbers into balance with those in the minority receiving an academic education in public relations/communication. Yet as indicated earlier only 44.4 percent of the respondents with a diploma heard about public relations theory.

Very significantly, the majority of the respondents (62.5 percent) disagreed with the statements that "theory has no significance in public relations practices at all." With only 37.6 percent partially agreeing with this statement and a very minor percentage (6.3 percent) totally agreeing with this statement, the *support for theory* is very promising. These responses provide a strong base for the integration of theory into the practice of public relations.

What may be another interesting perspective to analyze further is that 68.8 percent of the respondents agreed that theory development comes only after developments in public relations practice. (So theory is needed but what comes first: theory or practice?) One also needs to note that an additional 25 percent partly agreed with this statement. A further 6.3 percent did not answer this question (indicating much uncertainty about this issue). So where does theory come from? It is very difficult for one to say the academic side when one has not experienced this opportunity. Yet even the few who heard about theory in public relations classes (44.4 percent) also seemed to find the practice as the "source" of theory modeling (100 percent supported or did not answer this question on "public relations theories follow development in the public relations practiced"). This probably indicates that theory presented in the academic realm is really very minor and has not been a central focus of educational experience. Again, one has to remember that the initial home for public relations was in departments supporting the publicity model and, therefore, theory or research approaches were not a priority.

Yet when the question about "the science of public relations evolves more rapidly than the practice does" was asked, the results were in opposition to the earlier stance of theory following practice. Nearly 56.3 percent agreed that the science is faster than the practice. And 6.3 percent had no response. Only 39.3 percent disagreed with this statement. The question is whether the statement using the word "science" rather than "theory" might have changed the meaning of the question. Regardless, this does suggest that the respondents do see the academic offerings progressing in public relations faster than the practice, and thus indicates a strong potential for valuing more academic training as a viable career option.

The thrust of the question on "theoretical progress in public relations finds rapidly its reflection in the practice" is the more-focused question on theory. Here the same 56.3 percent level of agreement as the previous "science" question is evident. So perhaps the "science" versus "theoretical" wording is not an issue or considered the same question by the respondents. There is a 43.8 percent response level that does not agree with this statement (again, similar to the previous question with only a 4-percentage-point difference and with all respondents choosing to answer this question the responses indicate the theoretical approach is supported by over 50 percent of the respondents).

With so few respondents trained in theory or only 43.8 percent following the literature in the field through books and journals, it is not surprising that the practice is not following theoretical developments in the field of public relations. So when the respondents say public relations theories follow developments in the public relations practice—there is another discussion one needs to have. First, one needs to know the theories first to assess the impact in either direction. So it is unlikely that the practice-to-theory connection is understood by a population that does not have adequate exposure to theoretical developments in the field. Second, the idea that theories follow developments in the public relations practices relates no doubt to the endless workshops, seminars, and now virtual sessions offered on writing and other tactics. The confusion of "learning" tactics as academic "theory" is obviously a stretch in meaning and thus inaccurate. The problem is this perceptual gap presents a quandary that needs to be explored further.

It is obvious that practice cannot affect theory if one does not know theory. Thus with little theory practiced, the challenge is now to translate this body of knowledge to the practice. Theory presently is borrowed and tested from the many other disciplines with a vested interest in theoretical approaches. These theories are brought to the field of public relations to "test" and "analyze" practice. (Note, the theories are already developed and not necessarily derived from public relations but more to advise and counsel practitioners.) This also suggests that "borrowed" theory is not as likely to be developed from practice but brought to practice for "fit" or analytical usefulness.

Theory is used to assess the practice of public relations. Since data from actual practice represents problems, experimental approaches and experience from other disciplines is needed to fully address the challenges in public relations. The theoretical approach is needed to overcome the inherent bias within a profession and to provide the fullest explanation possible of the issues being studied.

Theory development is a long-term effort. Obviously, the respondents indicate that theory does have significance in practice, the highest response rate of all questions asked with only 6.3 percent totally disagreeing. Because of the lack of academic training and inadequate academic training in theory, there has been little integration of theory into practice. Now with public relations programs offering public relations theory courses, graduate programs in public relations (both master's and doctoral levels) there are signs indicating public relations may be headed for a more solid theoretical foundation. Although this is not true for all programs, the increasing complexity of societal problems emphasizes the push for new practitioners to be better prepared for integrating theory with practice. So in the future, more theory development in the professional activities of award-winning practitioners should be expected (see Figure 18.1).

According to the data based on sixteen respondents, only eight received public relations or communications at the university level, and the latter category is too general to assure a public relations focus. It is not surprising to find ten respondents (62.5 percent) do not think a public relations education is necessary.

This continues when nearly 81.4 percent feels the practice can be learned. It further makes sense when the respondents continue to indicate that public relations practices do not follow theoretical developments (50 percent agreeing; 12.5 percent

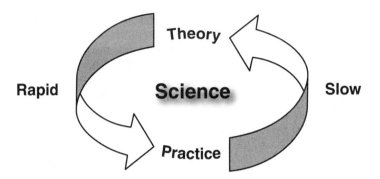

FIGURE 18.1   Relation between the theory and the practice as to time

partially agreeing; 6.3 percent no answer). But at this point 31.3 percent indicate they support the statement that practice follows theory. In contrast, 93.8 percent agree that theories do follow practice. So there is somewhat of a disconnect there. The respondents seem to think that the science of public relations does move more rapidly than practice (that makes one think that the practice should be reflecting more the theoretical research). Also, more than half agree that theory is "rapidly reflected in practice." And then their the "trump card": Nearly 62.5 percent supporting the importance of theory to public relations practice. In a sense, one feels like one comes full circle on these questions.

Conclusion: The need for theory is supported. *The difficulty:* How does one get to this level—how do the two ends connect to take advantage of the theoretical and research offerings? How do award-winning practitioners' professional activities improve when a greater theoretical and research base is incorporated into their campaigns?

Responses to Specific Theories.   Section 2 of the questionnaire assessed respondents' opinions and knowledge about public relations theories or approaches named in the survey. The theories included in the questionnaire were chosen from the categories identified by Signitzer (1997) and were also judged by this study as having application for public relations practice. Table 18.3 contains the question asked, the theories and approaches named, and response tallies.

Only four of fifteen different theories and approaches (conflict resolution, public relations as communication management, Grunig and Hunt's models of public relations, and excellent public relations research) were known by all sixteen respondents. The rate of familiarity with the additional theories and approaches was close to nonexistent. A closer assessment of responses revealed that 38.8 percent of the respondents had no idea about the included theories and approaches, 16.7 percent had heard theory or approach names but knew nothing about them, 13.8 percent knew the names and felt they "partly knew them," 18.8 percent knew them well, and 10.8 percent were "completely familiar with such theories." In general, the participating practitioners were unfamiliar with the names of the theories and approaches, and the propositions included in this study.

TABLE 18.3   Campaign supervisors' opinions on theories

WHAT ARE YOUR OPINIONS ABOUT THE FOLLOWING THEORIES AND APPROACHES? (%)	I AM FAMILIAR WITH (5)	I KNOW WELL (4)	PARTLY KNOWN TO ME (3)	I HEARD ABOUT IT BUT HAVE NO IDEA (2)	HAVE NO IDEA (1)	UNANSWERED
Systems theory	6.3	12.5	-	12.5	68.8	-
Situational theory	12.5	12.5	12.5	31.3	31.3	-
Approaches to conflict resolution	6.3	50.0	25.0	6.3	12.5	-
Action assembly theory	-	6.3	6.3	43.8	43.8	-
Social exchange theory	-	12.5	6.3	25.0	56.3	-
Diffusion theory	12.5	12.5	18.8	12.5	43.8	-
Social learning theory	6.3	6.3	43.8	18.8	25.0	-
Elaborated likelihood model	6.3	6.3	6.3	6.3	68.8	6.3
Public relations as a theory of public affairs of modern society (the theory of Ronnenberger and Rühl)	-	12.5	18.8	18.8	50.0	-
Constructive approaches	6.3	18.8	12.5	6.3	56.3	-
Consensus-oriented public relations approaches	6.3	25.0	12.5	12.5	37.5	6.3
Public relations as communication management	31.3	56.3	-	6.3	6.3	-
Grunig and Hunt's model of public relations	31.3	-	25.0	25.0	18.8	-
Dialogic theory	12.5	6.3	-	18.8	56.3	6.3
Excellent public relations research	25.0	43.8	18.8	6.3	6.3	-

A cross assessment of respondents' experience in the business (in terms of years) and their degree of familiarity with the theories and approaches indicated that 49.5 percent of those having six to ten years experience in the public relations industry were completely unfamiliar with them, and 18.1 percent had heard about them but had no idea about what they represented. So, we can suggest that the percentage of those completely unfamiliar with the study theories and approaches was 68 percent. Only 18.1 percent stated that they know the theories well or very well. Of respondents with 15 to 20 years experience in the public relations business, 42.5 percent stated that their knowledge on the theories was at a good or very good level, while 29.2 percent rated their knowledge as "have no idea," and 12.5 percent as "I heard about it but have no idea." Interestingly, the percentage of those familiar with the theories was almost equal to that of those unfamiliar with them.

Of the public relations officers with experience of more than twenty five years in the industry, 80 percent had no "idea" about any of the theories or approaches.

This means that public relations officers having less experience in the industry (six to ten years) were less knowledgeable in public relations theories than those with slightly more experience (fifteen to twenty years), and professional training could be a factor in this increase.

A comparison of the respondents' tendency to keep up with scientific publications in the field and their knowledge of theories and research approaches revealed an interesting breakdown of data. Of those stating that they followed public relations publications on regular basis, 53.4 percent had no idea what the theories and approaches mentioned meant. Only 27.6 percent from this group responded that their knowledge on the theories was at a high or very high level. On the contrary, only 37.8 percent of the respondents who occasionally follow publications could be included in the "I am familiar" classification, and 46.7 percent had information on the theories. The percentage of those who do not follow publications in the field at all was relevant, as 73.3 percent of them have no idea about the issue of theory and research approaches. In light of this data, one could postulate that the few reading journals and other academic publications are not reading the research or literature reviews and simply going to the findings.

Another cross assessment focused on whether the educational background of the respondents in public relations related to the level of their knowledge on theories and approaches. Of the 54.1 percent of the respondents with a public relations/communications-related educational background, 28.2 percent had a high or very high knowledge of theory and research approaches. Of the 65.6 percent of those who do not have formal training in public relations, 21.1 percent had a high or very high knowledge of public relations theories and approaches. While this represents only four or five respondents at most, it does indicate interest in theory and research. With so few respondents, one cannot conclude the impact of education. The few with public relations education are the younger professionals, and the study established that 80% of the public relations officers with experience of more than 25 years in the industry had no idea about any of the theories or approaches.

CASE: AWARD-WINNING PRACTITIONERS

This case study of award-winning practitioners probes their knowledge of specific theoretical and conceptual domains relevant to public relations. Such an analysis allows one to assess high-level practitioners' knowledge with specific reference to current thinking in the discipline.

Results

Sixteen award-winning public relations professionals were asked a series of questions to determine if these leaders were using theoretical and research practices. It was not important for the respondents to identify the theories, models, or research approaches.

Systems.   Although campaign supervisors stated that they had no idea about systems theory, 75.1 percent were found to view their working environment as a system. Most mentions focused on interaction of their corporation with other corporations (Grunig & Hunt, 1984).

Situational.   Only 25 percent identified situational theory by name. The rest of the respondents, 62.5 percent, agreed with the notion that "in determining emerging target groups a) one identified problems that such groups are likely to face with respect to the organization, b) noted whether targeting groups can be effective under particular situations, and c) identified their interest level in certain problems." In short, respondents agreed that use of this theory will help determine what groups emerge as a target groups under certain situations (Cutlip, Center, & Broom, 1994, pp. 245–246).

Public Affairs.   Ronnenberger and Rühl advocate that public relations is the product of modern societies rather than an ancient science, the roots of which go back to ancient times (Okay & Okay, 2002). Their theory constructs public relations as a theory of public affairs of modern societies. The theory of public affairs was known by name to 12.5 percent of the respondents. However, the percentage of those who agreed with the thesis of this theory was 68.8 percent.

Constructivist.   Only 25.1 percent of respondents knew, by name, the constructivist approach advocating the primary mission of public relations as building image. The percentage of those who support the idea of this theory is 43.8 percent, and 50 percent do not see this approach in their practice. Also asked was the degree to which the element of "accuracy" should be taken as the basis on which images should be built. According to Merten and Westerbarkey (1994), "an image's obligation to be based on accuracy is not binding" (p. 207). Of those who responded, 87.5 percent suggested that accuracy should be the basis on which images are built. When the constructivist approach was assessed as a whole, practitioners were found to agree with some of its notions, while they were against the other portions of the concepts beyond the theory.

Conflict Resolution.   When dealing with target groups, public relations practitioners are likely to face conflicts and differences of opinions. In their approach to conflict resolution, Fisher and Ury discussed how public relations practitioners handle problems in such cases (Fischer, 1997). A majority of our respondents (56.3 percent) stated that they knew this approach, and stressed that they did not adopt the first three suggestions of this theory (i.e., keep individuals away from problems; focus on the basic problem; and focus on interests, not positions). They did agree, however, that one should create mutual interests and benefits, and be insistent in objective criteria when dealing with target publics.

Action Assembly Theory.   Anticipating human behaviors requires knowing beforehand how others think. Although this is hard to achieve, communicative scientist John O. Greene believes that thinking can be exemplified by means of three structures (cognitive structure, content, and process) at an abstract level (Fischer, 1997). The percentages of respondents who knew/did not know this theory by name were 6.3 and 87.6 percent respectively. According to this theory, "in the cognitive process, specific actions yield predictable results in similar situations, and expect such results and fail to notice when the outcomes vary" (p. 51). Of those who responded, 31.3 percent agreed with this view, while 50 percent were hesitant to agree. In our opinion, the more percentage of people against the content of a theory, the less probability that such theory is implemented in practice.

Diffusion Theory.   Diffusion theory looks into how humans process information and how they communicate their response, and this suggests that a notion or thought is adoptable through a process made up of five steps (awareness, interest, evaluation, trial, and adaptation) (Lattimore, Baskin, Herman, Toth, & Van Leuven, 2004, p. 60). Although the theory was known to 25 percent of the respondents, 75.1 percent agreed with the notion that "being aware of how individuals process and admit information in their minds . . . explains how we reach important decisions" (p. 54).

Social Learning Theory.   Social learning theory suggests a different approach to individuals' cognitive process. It attempts to anticipate and exemplify behaviors. It argues that personal examples and mass media play important roles in the adoption of new behaviors, and new behaviors can be adopted only by observing others (Okay & Okay, 2002). Of those who responded, 12.6 percent knew the theory by name, while 50 percent admitted "rewards and positive behaviors of others are beneficial to individuals and organizations and lead to adoption of new behaviors." The percentage of those who partly agreed with this point of view was 43.8 percent.

Elaborated Likelihood Model.   The percentage of the respondents who knew the elaborated likelihood model by name was 12.6 percent. However, 81.3 percent of the respondents agreed with the opinion that "celebrities, reliable spokespersons, or various rewards are used to attract the attention of the publics," a contention forwarded by Richard Petty and John Cacioppo (Lattimore et al., p. 55). This model was not well known by name, but many public relations practitioners were found to share the notion of it in practice.

Communication Management.   The percentage of the respondents who regarded public relations as communication management was 87.6 percent. In regards to the effect of public relations on various organizational functions, respondents stated that public relations generally influences an organization's distribution system, personnel management, development and planning departments, and operational management. However, they also thought that public relations was not likely to support the production system of an organization.

Public Relations Models.   Finally, we asked the respondents which one of the four public relations models, formulated by Grunig and Hunt in the 1980s, they preferred to include in their campaigns. We found that the press agentry model was not preferred at all, while the preference for the public information model was 6.3 percent, the two-way asymmetric model 18.8 percent, and the two-way symmetrical model 56.3 percent. In addition, 18.3 percent of the respondents stated that they preferred to use more than one of these models in their campaigns.

CONCLUSION

This study revealed that award-winning public relations campaigns supervisors from all around the world use a number of public relations theories and approaches, or at least tenets of them, in their practices, but know few by name.

Public relations practitioners might find public relations theories and approaches hard to understand and often irrelevant to the problems on their agendas. If so, one might argue along with Cornellisen (2000) that the academic world provides only general visions and frameworks and not specific and concrete solutions to public relations problems. However, one might also argue that practitioners short themselves when they choose to not stay current with academic theory and approaches to development. And it may be that more education and praxis simply need to take place.

QUESTIONS FOR APPLICATION

1. What major theories have a direct relationship to public relations? How do the tenets of these theories shed light on public relations practices?

2. How will university-educated public relations professionals train in research and evaluation?

3. How do theory and research change public relations practices?

4. Since theory guides practice, how does one integrate theoretical constructs into global public relations practice?

5. How do the public relations associations support and develop the public relations practitioners in the areas of theory and research? Should practitioners be involved in both regional and global public relations associations?

REFERENCES

Banks, S. P. (2000). *Multicultural public relations: A social-interpretive approach.* Thousands Oaks, CA: Sage.

Botan, H. (1989). Theory development in public relations. In C. H. Botan & V. Hazleton (Eds.), *Public relations theory* (pp. 99–110). Hillsdale, NJ: Lawrence Erlbaum.

Bourland, P., & Neff, B. D. (2003). Networking: Enhancing your academic success by association. *Teaching public relations handbook.* Educators Academy Public Relations Society of America New York.

Commission on Education. (1999). *Port of entry: Commission on undergraduate and graduate education.* Public Relations Education of the 21st Century: A Port of Entry. The report of the Commission on Public Relations Education, October 1999.

Cornelissen, J. P. (2000). Toward an understanding of the use of academic theories in public relations practice. *Public Relations Review, 26*(3), pp. 315–326.

Crable, R., & Vibbert, S. (1986). *Public relations as communication management.* Edina, MN: Bellwether Press.

Cutlip, S. M., Center, A. H., & Broom, G. M. (1994). *Effective public relations* (7th ed.). Englewood Cliffs NJ: Prentice-Hall.

Dozier, D. M., Grunig, L. A., & Grunig, J. E. (Eds.). (1995). *Manager's guide to excellence in public relations and communication management.* Mahwah, NJ: Lawrence Erlbaum.

Fischer R. (1997). A theoretical basis for public relations. In O. Baskin, C. Aronoff, & D. Lattimore (Eds.), *Public relations: The profession and the practice* (pp. 54–62). New York: McGraw Hill.

Gordon, J. C. (1997). Interpreting definitions of public relations: Self assessment and symbolic interactionism-based alternative. *Public Relations Review, 23*(1), pp. 57–66.

Grunig, J. E. (Ed.). (1992). *Excellence in public relations and communication management.* Hillsdale, NJ: Lawrence Erlbaum.

Grunig, J. E., & Hunt, T. (1984). *Managing public relations.* New York: Holt, Rinehart and Winston.

Hançerlioğlu, O. (1986). *Toplumbilim sözlüğü.* Istanbul: Remzi Kitabevi.

Heath, R. (2001). Defining the practice: The dynamics of change in public relations practice. In R. Heath (Ed.), *Handbook of public relations* (pp. 183–188). Thousand Oaks, CA: Sage.

Heath, R. (Ed.). (2005). *Encyclopedia of public relations.* Thousand Oaks, CA: Sage.

Holtzhausen, D. R. (2002). Towards a postmodern research agenda for public relations. *Public Relations Review, 28*(3), pp. 251–264.

Kent, M. L., & Taylor, M. (2002). Toward a dialogic theory of public relations. *Public Relations Review, 28*(1), pp. 21–37.

Lattimore, D., Baskin, O., Heiman, S., Toth, E., & Van Leuven, J. (2004). *Public relations: The profession and the practice.* Boston: McGraw-Hill.

Merten, K., & Westerbarkey, J. (1994). Public opinion und public relations. In K. Merten and S. J. Schmidt (Eds.), *Die Wirklichkeit der medien.* Siegfried Weischenberg, Opladen: Westdeutscher Verlag.

Neff, B. (1989). The missing theoretical perspective in public relations. In C. H. Botan & V. Hazleton (Eds.), *Public Relations Theory* (pp. 159–172). Hillsdale, NJ: Lawrence Erlbaum.

Neff, B., Walker, G., Smith, M., & Creedon, P. (1999). Outcomes desired by practitioners and academics. *Public Relations Review, 25*(1), pp. 29–44.

Newsom, D., Vanslyke Turk, J., & Kruckeberg, D. (1996). *This is PR: The realities of public relations* (6th ed.). Belmont, CA: Wadsworth.

Okay, A., & Okay, A. (2002). *Halkla İlişkiler: Kavram, Strateji ve Uygulamalar* [Public relations: Concept, strategy and practices]. İstanbul: Der Yayinlari.

Ronnenberger, F. (1987). Theorie der public relations. In D. Pflaum and W. Pieper (Eds.), *Lexicon der public relations.* Landsberg/Lech: Verlag Moderne Industrie.

Signitzer, B. (1997). Einige Linien der aktuellen Public Relations-Theorieentwicklung. In R. Renger & G. Siegert (Eds.), *Kommunikationswelten: Wissenschaftliche Perspektiven zur Medien-Informationsgesellschaft.* Innsbruck; Wien: Studien Verl.

CHAPTER NINETEEN

WORKING THE SYSTEM

The Evolution of Feminist Perspectives in Public Relations Scholarship

THERESA RUSSELL-LORETZ

Recently, a student expressed succinctly the initial perceptions that many have come to associate with a feminist perspective. "I always thought being a feminist meant you had to hate men . . . and all that reproductive stuff. I didn't realize that it could be so much more." Her comments echoed my own fears and personal challenges in writing about a feminist perspective on public relations scholarship for this book, though for different reasons. First, feminist public relations scholarship already has identifiable matriarchs—Toth, L. Grunig, Hon, Creedon, Aldoory, and others. Second, the variety of feminist perspectives in the feminist literature is challenging, if not daunting, for all save the seasoned scholar in this area. And finally, because feminist scholarship is so personal. I have struggled to find my own voice and direction amid the literature, and have wrestled with my own feelings of vulnerability in describing a perspective that is avoided by some and is an attachment for others. I further recognize that my representation of a feminist perspective on scholarship in public relations makes choices that others would not make, and excludes far more than I wish. But I do find, as my young student expressed, that "there is so much more" that a feminist perspective might offer to advance scholarship *in* and *of* public relations. My hope is that future scholarship in our discipline takes hold of this mantra.

The confusion over and avoidance of feminism makes it all the more important that this chapter be included in a book on public relations theory, limited though my own perspective may be. Precisely because there is no monolithic "feminism," but rather, "feminismS," feminist scholarship provides many perspectives through which to understand and explore public relations practice (Rice, 1999, p. 1). At the same time, the task presents several challenges, not the least of which is to overcome alienation from the term *feminist*. Such alienation has been identified by scholars who have described individuals' reluctance to identify as feminists, as in "I'm not a feminist, but . . ." (Ashcraft, 1995), and the propensity to clarify one's feminist position, for example, "I AM a feminist, but . . ." (Renegar & Sowards, 2003). Lately, some scholars have noted that this alienation has become exacerbated, as the gap grows between boomers and a younger generation of women. Many of these women who identify themselves as "third-wave" feminists have not been barred from enrolling in college, or relegated to taking only secretarial courses, or isolated by peers after selecting the "wrong" career, or asked by potential employers how many babies they plan to have. Rather, these feminists have multiple perspectives on their relationships with themselves, with each other, and with men, and they seek an inclusive feminism that recognizes these different perspectives that do not align neatly with prescribed notions of "feminism."

This chapter will describe how feminist scholarship might move beyond studies that focus on women's experiences *in* public relations practice as professionals. Although I will briefly overview this work, I counsel readers to turn to the thorough reviews of the literature in feminist public relations scholarship (see Aldoory, 2003; Grunig, Toth, & Hon, 2000; Hon, 1995; and Toth, 2001). My goal is to locate their work as a touchstone to suggest future directions in feminist public relations scholarship that seeks to create awareness of how the practice might overcome inequities in human experiences.

I first address three challenges in feminist scholarship as it pertains to public relations. Next, I briefly overview previous work by feminist public relations scholars to illustrate the progression of feminist research topics in the public relations discipline and suggest future directions for research. Third, I utilize a case study to demonstrate how a feminist perspective of public relations might broaden scholarly inquiry. My underlying contention is that public relations scholars have not yet tapped the yield that feminist inquiry might provide.

CHALLENGES IN FEMINIST SCHOLARSHIP

Several challenges confront the feminist scholar. The first, the "denotative" challenge, asks the researcher to define her terms. What is feminism, anyway? Different scholars answer the question differently, causing some of the confusion and controversy over guiding questions and assumptions in terms of who is included and who is excluded from the definition. Inevitably, the denotative challenge results in confronting a second challenge—the connotative challenge to both definitions and labels, as feminism/womanism* involves a worldview about a topic that touches on beliefs about identity, social roles, and cultural mores. Negative images of feminists in mainstream media, and contrasting discourses about what it is to be feminine or a *real* woman, as well as heated discussions about gender

---

*Here I call attention to the African American movement that is not to be seen as separate from feminism, but does suggest feminist scholarship requires acknowledgment of various cultures that fall under the feminist umbrella and reminds us one perspective does not fit all.

boundaries and what is *natural* and what is *constructed*, belie the risks of violating the norms of a particular group. Related to this connotative challenge is the credibility bias, a third challenge that feminist scholars face. This challenge stems from using research methods that glean insights from outside traditional social scientific approach, where objectivity and replication are the goal. Personal accounts, for instance, are deemed "anecdotal" from a social science perspective, but considered a valid means by which individuals share their knowledge and experience from a feminist perspective. Further clarification of a feminist perspective necessitates a discussion of the challenges and the implications these may have for public relations scholarship.

No Monolithic Feminism

Though review of literature in feminist thought is too plentiful to take up here, feminist scholarship in general and feminist public relations scholarship in particular reveal various feminist perspectives, rather than a singular "feminist theory." The common focal point would seem to be "women." However, women can be studied from perspectives that are not feminist, as men can be studied from feminist perspectives. Further complicating definitions, different feminist scholars align themselves with different theoretical and philosophical orientations. Rice (1999, p. 1) refers to "feminismS" to denote the diversity of thought, while Tong (2003, pp. 1–9) refers to diverse "schools" of feminist thought that might include liberal, Marxist, radical, socialist, multicultural, global, ecological, existentialist, psychoanalytic, cultural, and postmodern. Aldoory and Toth (2007) as well as Grunig, Toth, and Hon (2000) focus their reviews of feminist scholarship in public relations on two perspectives: liberal and radical. However, they caution that this dichotomy oversimplifies the broader range of feminist scholarship.

While a thorough description of the diversity of feminist thought is beyond the purpose of this chapter—for such an explanation, readers may turn to Tong (1998, 2003)—a starting point for a feminist perspective is offered by Eisenberg and Goodall (2004). These organizational communication scholars assert that two concepts, ideology and power, focus feminist scholarship and parallel the work of critical scholars. They assert ideology is the "basic, often unexamined assumptions about how things are or, in some cases, how they should be" (p. 152) and definitions of *power* range from domination of one group over another to the way in which vocabulary frames characterization of a particular group. Others (Aldoory, 2003; O'Neil, 2003; Tong, 2003, 1998; and Toth, 2001) assert feminist thought, no matter its variation, has as its central purpose the illumination of women's oppression and proposed solutions for its elimination. To clarify feminism, Aldoory (2003) cites DeVault: "a movement and a set of beliefs that problematize gender inequality whereas . . . . Feminists believe that women have been subordinated through men's greater power" (p. 222). Additionally, for Aldoory *empowerment*, or overcoming domination, is paramount in feminist scholarship, and Grunig, Toth, and Hon (2000) note that solutions are as important as *consciousness raising* in a feminist perspective.

Toth (2001) explains feminist researchers are united in "considering feminism to be the means to interpreting phenomena in a way that values the socially ascribed attributes and actions of women" (p. 238). Indeed, for Martin (2003), one focus of feminist theorists has been "the reification and dichotomization of such concepts as male and female, objectivity and subjectivity, competition and cooperation, and rationality and emotionality" (p. 67). She asserts that the dichotomies typically align one concept as "desirable," while its opposing concept is "undesirable" and, hence, invalid.

Further complicating the understanding of feminism are differences among feminist schools in concepts such as "feminine," "masculine," "sex," and "gender," which carry different operational definitions for different scholars. Cleveland, Stockdale, and Murphy (2000) define sex as "biological differences in genetic composition and reproductive anatomy and function" (citing Unger & Crawford, 1992), whereas "gender reflects a society's or culture's interpretations or constructions based on the characteristics associated with biological sex" (p. 27). In contrast to these scholars in organizational communication, Grunig, Toth, and Hon (2000) write that they recognize "the complexity and interchangeability of the terms," and opt to use "gender to mean predetermined physical traits" (p. 21). Moreover, Cleveland, Stockdale, and Murphy (2000) observe that whereas masculinity and femininity are conceptualized as dichotomous, "androgyny suggests an individual can possess both feminine and masculine traits" (p. 27). The terms ground feminist scholarship that grapples over nature (biology) and nurture (experiences and socialization) and the part these play in societal expectations about the roles and characteristics of men and women in a variety of contexts.

Feminist orientations also focus research topics and proposed solutions to problems faced by women in public relations. In reviews by Aldoory (2003) and Grunig, Toth, and Hon (2000), feminist research in public relations is situated within either of two feminist perspectives, liberal feminism or radical feminism. Aldoory (2003) explains that for the liberal feminist, "equality is the goal" (p. 223). Tong (1998) posits that, while a liberal perspective can still be felt in such groups as the National Organization for Women, much of current feminist scholarship has developed in opposition to a liberal feminist perspective. Tong locates liberal feminism's origins in Mary Wollstonecraft's "Vindication of the Rights of Woman," John Stuart Mill's "Subjection of Women," and the Woman's Suffrage Movement, and posits that liberal feminists believe "female subordination is rooted in a set of customary and legal constraints blocking women's entrance to and success in the so-called public world" (p. 2). For the most part, liberal feminists focused on solutions to the empowerment of women that relied on exposing barriers women face, such as their inability to enroll in college, and then using coalitions of support to overcome the barrier (e.g., opening admissions to women, providing day care, offering women's support groups and mentors). Additionally, liberal feminists assert women should be seen first as individuals, rather than as women; however, other feminists argue that this is an androcentric perspective that denies differences between men and women. Moreover, liberal feminism has been accused of having a white, heterosexual, middle-class bias that excluded the voices and experiences of people of color, the poor, and lesbians.

In contrast, radical feminists range in their views with regard to androgyny, which includes approaches toward personal identity and public performances of identity. In areas such as sexuality and conceptions of professionalism, some radical feminists embrace androgyny, such that "No human being should be forbidden the sense of wholeness that comes from combining his or her masculine and feminine dimensions" (Tong, 2003, p. 3). Other feminists reject such androcentric thinking in the workplace, arguing that it implies a woman should "be more like a man." This, they argue, is not a solution that values the feminine; they assert femininity is not the problem, but should be embraced and valued, with radical-cultural feminists going so far as to claim biological motherhood as the ultimate source of a woman's power and focus (Tong, 2003, p. 4; see also Ruddick, 1995). Still others claim that femininity as it is currently understood has been created by men for their pleasure at the expense of women—that is, the Barbie syndrome, wherein many women have unrealistic expectations about their bodies, based on media depictions that work to socially construct the "ideal" woman.

Tong (2003) describes still other perspectives, and a truncated version of her work does not do it justice; yet a quick overview reveals additional focal points and proposed solutions for feminist scholars. "Socialist feminists agree with Marxist feminists that capitalism is the source of women's oppression, and with radical feminists that patriarchy is the source of women's oppression. As they see it, therefore, the way to end women's oppression is to kill the two-headed beast of capitalist patriarchy" (p. 5). Still other feminists use psychoanalytical approaches to individuals' conceptions of self, and describe how these self-conceptions might be changed to further self-empowerment; others call for changes in society, such as women's and men's dual participation in the workforce and at home, as a way to understand and assimilate the traits often associated with these environments—that is, love and dependence from home life, and authority and autonomy associated with the workplace (Toth, 2003). These differing perspectives explain why some feminists would align with social conservatives to end pornography as an industry and practice that exploits and objectifies women, while for other feminists, exhibition of the body allows for uninhibited self-expression and liberation.

The denotative challenge in underscoring an identity as a feminist scholar, then, is first to raise one's own awareness about the specific ideological perspective one takes. This involves a journey beyond the public relations literature into contemporary feminist literature, which at this point is quite vast. Additionally, a feminist scholar needs to be empowered to overcome the challenge of negative reactions to the "feminist scholarship" label, from nonfeminists as well as from feminists.

The Connotative Challenge of Feminism

Unfortunately, there are still negative associations with the term "feminist." Such negative labels as "bra-burner," "femi-Nazi," "man-hater," and others clearly link the feminist to a particular, monolithic set of ideological values with which few today identify. Dow (2004) argues that in general, television network depictions of the women's movement worked to frame the movement in a negative way, whereas alternative depictions of the women's movement were limited. Indeed, the negative images are often associated with media depictions of the history of the women's movement: Clearly women marched (and still do) and won the right to vote during the Suffrage Movement (the first wave). And women did gain advances into the workforce, in equal employment opportunity, and in reproductive rights, and gained entry into sports in college during the 1960s and 1970s with activist tactics (the second wave).* However, the images are inconsistent with the variety of perspectives taken with regard to feminism. Friedlin (2002) and Renegar and Sowards (2003) discuss controversies among feminists over "single issue" feminism. Indeed, current feminist thought has begun to assimilate the experiences of third-wave feminists who work alongside men, whose husbands and fathers have often shared more of the child-care responsibilities than any other generation of men in history, and who have seen female dentists, successful women legislators, and so on.

Then too, the third-wave generation has had more single and divorced mothers and fathers than any other generation in history, and same-sex partners are not a novelty. Their perspectives with regard to the roles of women and men in the home and in the workplace have been shaped by these experiences. This is not to deny the worth of feminist scholarship that uncovers the inequities women face in the workforce and on the home front, but instead to remind theorists that the feminism of the third-wave is not your mother's feminism (Renegar & Sowards, 2003).

Many women and men are vocal about their alienation from feminism—a phenomenon noted by Faludi (backlash; 1991) and other feminist scholars. Hon (2001), for instance, noted many of her public relations students did not see sexual discrimination as a problem they would face upon entry into the workforce; Ashcraft (1995) mentions her own initial distance from assuming the label of a "feminist." Wrigley (2002) also notes a generation of students who failed to connect with feminist issues.

For the most part, identifying public relations scholarship as "feminist" tends to marginalize its relevance away from mainstream issues in the field. Observe the rationale used to justify the appropriateness of a feminist perspective in public relations research and education: 70 percent of enrollees in undergraduate programs in public relations are female (Toth, 2001; Hon, 1995; Grunig, Toth, & Hon, 2000). For the feminist, a majority is not the criterion for justification of topic examination; rather, investigation gives voice to the issues faced by the underrepresented or oppressed. To suggest that feminist scholarship is worth the effort only when

---

*Like Renegar and Sowards, I also recognize the controversy in identifying "first wave," "second wave," and "third wave" feminist eras along chronological time lines. Dow (2004) identifies 1970 as the crucial year for the second wave of U.S. feminism. Some attribute third-wave feminism to the awareness of the women's movement's exclusion of people of color and the working class, while others attribute it to the 1990s. Renegar and Sowards (2003) use it to describe feminists born in the 1960s and 1970s and describe it as "an emerging movement" that is distinguishing itself in popular culture and academic writing. Friedlin (2002) identifies the first wave as the movement to obtain the right to vote, while the second wave is the women's movement of the 1960s and 1970s, and the more recent efforts of those in their 20s and 30s constitute the third wave.

women become an overwhelmingly majority, or a "threat" to the profession, suggests feminist public relations research still answers to a traditional scholarship
model of empirical generalizability. Yet exploration of minority issues—regardless
of gender, race, or class—affords examination that may improve the practice.
Indeed, a feminist perspective would be useful for examination of the issues
involved when men enter an all-female environment in public relations. Such was
the experience of one of my former students during an internship experience,
where he was excluded from the "in group" at work based on his gender and age.

However, women still face an implicit directive not to call attention to their
gender. One headhunter cautioned a former female student *not* to reveal her
"feminist" leanings, as this would have detrimental effects on her opportunities in
the professional public relations world. She had hoped to ask interviewers, "How
many women occupy top positions in your firm?" which, in itself, reveals the
assumptions that men will be in top positions. For the student, the question was
to reassure her that opportunities for advancement existed regardless of gender;
for the headhunter, this question raised red flags for the interviewer that she was
"one of those."

Credibility Bias

Besides denotative confusion and negative connotations, the feminist scholar
frequently faces criticism with regard to research questions, focus, and method.
While all scholars must be prepared to justify research topics as worthy and methods as sound, often implicit in criticism of feminist scholarship is the assumption
that such work is of interest only to women, unless it "threatens" the entire profession, or that the scholarship uses methods that violate "statistical soundness"
(see Aldoory, 2003; Riessman, 1993). This positivistic epistemological orientation is
grounded in understandings about knowledge traced back to the Enlightenment,
when "rationality" was favored over "emotion" and few women had access to a
classroom. Such a standard favors methods and approaches that are objective,
often neglecting the richness of data collected via alternative means—that is, narrative analysis, ethnography, semiotics, and rhetorical interpretation. Qualitative
research is not the sole method used by feminists. Indeed, feminist research in public relations has used both quantitative and qualitative methods, and frequently
uses both to triangulate the results. Still, recommendations that undergraduates
become familiar with statistical research methods to enhance the credibility of the
field would seem to discourage methods that stem from alternative approaches
often used by feminist scholars.

One facet of credibility bias that works against public relations research
grounded in a feminist perspective is that the perspective itself is outside of the
systems perspective that is the dominant paradigm in public relations (Creedon,
1993). Like critical theory with which feminist theory has been compared, a feminist perspective challenges the assumptions of systems theory, drawing on subjective experiences as valid observations with insightful yields, and working
toward the goal of egalitarianism versus sustaining a hierarchy (Martin, 2003). An
additional challenge in using a critical feminist perspective in public relations is

the corporate mentality that seeks results that give practitioners a quantifiable level of probability for a return on their investment. The questions derived from either the systems perspective or the practitioner's need for quantification are most likely to require the scientific method of inquiry where objectivity and generalizability are valued.

Moreover, one feminist tenet calls for revelation of one's personal perspective in scholarship, such that the reader can evaluate the conclusions given the scholar's stance. This approach to scholarship asserts that objectivity is its own selective worldview and is qualitatively different from the scientific method of "distancing the object" under study. The denotative, connotative, and credibility challenges notwithstanding, feminist scholarship in public relations has evolved over the years, though slowly.

THE LEGACY OF FEMINIST SCHOLARSHIP IN PUBLIC RELATIONS

The evolution of feminist scholarship in public relations has been traced by thorough reviews by Aldoory (2003), Grunig, Toth, and Hon (2000, 2001), and Toth (2001). A review of public relations scholarship from 1984 to 2000 in its key academic outlets by Sallot, Lyon, Acostsa-Alzuru, and Jones (2003) sketches the evolution and points to new directions in feminist public relations research. In their review, they found seventeen articles published under a subcategory of "women and minorities" that reflected on public relations education, and nine that were classified under "theory development" in a new subcategory of women's studies/feminist school/gender/diversity/minority theories. Absent were any studies on practice/application of public relations that used a feminist perspective.

Indeed, it appears that the legacy of feminist scholarship in public relations centers on descriptive studies focused on gender inequities in the workforce (see Aldoory 2003; Toth, 2001; Grunig, Toth, & Hon, 2001). Toth (2001) traces the origins of feminist public relations scholarship to three benchmark publications: the 1988 special issue of *Public Relations Review,* edited by L. Grunig, and two studies on women in public relations funded by the Public Relations Society of America's (PRSA) Research Foundation: "The Velvet Ghetto" and "Beyond the Velvet Ghetto" (Toth & Cline, 1989), which grew out of the women's task force of the PRSA. Both studies examined the impact of the increasing numbers of women in the field.

Toth (2001) acknowledged early feminist research in public relations used "few theoretical perspectives" beyond "human capital theory" that looked at the return on investment faced by an increasing number of women entering college to major in public relations programs. Echoing labor studies in other disciplines, this scholarship focused on issues faced by women in the workforce and, Toth notes, put gender on the academic agenda. Scholars examined: "threats" to the status of the field as a result of feminization of the profession; salary and corporate status inequities; and tokenism. Early research, Toth explained, presumed that factors such as job opportunities, job training, job tenure, and educational preparation were gender neutral, and that individual choices led to specific outcomes (pp. 237–238).

Later research revealed that these factors were often gender laden. For instance, Toth cites work by Toth and Cline that found women faced perceptions by others about their motivation to achieve managerial status, their willingness to sacrifice work over family demands, and their ability to command top salaries. Furthermore, research by Hon (1995) revealed women often lacked self-esteem and organizational mentors, found few female role models, and struggled to balance work and family while simultaneously facing exclusion from formal and informal networks that led to career advancement.

Toth and other public relations scholars (Hon, 1995; Grunig, Toth, & Hon, 2000), have suggested that perhaps women are drawn to the public relations profession because they have a natural inclination to perform well in the skill areas important to the profession—as good listeners and good communicators. And yet this assertion is not without its detractors. Whether the attributes of women and men are or should be considered "natural," or whether such skills might be learned competencies, is at the crux of a number of scholarly and public policy debates (see, e.g., Barnett & Rivers, 2004).

Additional topics of interest to feminist scholars in public relations included studies on sexual harassment and occupational segregation, which again reflect a labor studies focus. Scholarship in women's studies that moved feminism beyond white, middle-class experiences in the workforce has enhanced this line of questioning, as Aldoory has acknowledged previous research excluded the experiences of women of color, minorities, people with disabilities, and gays and lesbians (2001b). Her scholarship has incorporated the tenets of a multicultural feminist approach, and in her research she actively seeks to gain insights from women of varying ages, socioeconomic classes, ethnic backgrounds, and sexual orientation. More recently, Pompper (2004) has examined female African American practitioners' experiences, grounded in the assumptions that the experiences of these women are unique and vary from experiences of Caucasian female practitioners.

Though this early descriptive work narrowly focused on labor issues, both Aldoory (2003) and Toth (2001) point to its importance for, first, giving voice to women's issues and, second, building theoretical explanations that further the potential for future research in public relations. However, thus far the development of feminist theory has centered on women's roles in the public relations profession, again centering discussion on women's work in public relations occupations. Early roles research asserted that public relations practitioners could fit into one of four "levels" of roles, beginning with an entry-level technician and advancing to communication manager (see Toth, 2001, p. 237). Much of the research found women were more likely to take on the technician role—writing, editing, and layout—while men took on managerial roles. Additionally, women continued to "do it all" for less money, even when promoted to the position of manager. Role theory suggested this "feminization" of the field would lower the status of women managers in public relations departments, and facilitate the encroachment of the public relations function by managers of other departments, such as marketing (see Lauzen, 1992). Creedon (1993) countered the assumptions of roles research needed to be deconstructed. She argued that the dichotomy of manager/technician was reductionistic, and that the theory demonstrated an alpha bias, presenting "management" as the preferred occupation (p. 79). Moreover, Creedon critiqued the implication that women were to blame for and should overcome their "shortcomings"—the lack of mentors, isolation from dominant coalition networks, the tendency to remain technicians, and so on—a solution that Martin (2003) refers to as "Fixing the Women" (p. 71).

More recently, O'Neil (2003) has situated role research within a structuralist perspective, grounding assumptions about women's lack of power in system variables rather than individual attributes, such as professionalism and expertise. She used a questionnaire to determine whether formal structural power or relationship power best explained differences between men and women, and found female public relations practitioners have a lower amount of formal structural power, which would contribute to lessening their overall organizational power. Further, a lower proportion of females reported directly to the chairman, CEO, or president of a corporation, exacerbating their diminished power. She suggests that scholars direct attention to the impact of organizational dynamics on individual behavior in organizations and that female practitioners may need to work harder to develop long-term relationships with members of the dominant coalition—an ironic directive. Wrigley (2002), who was interested in women's views of the glass-ceiling phenomenon, conducted in-depth interviews and focus groups using a snowball sample of twenty-seven women. She posited a theoretical concept of negotiated resignation, wherein women resolve the cognitive dissonance they experience with regard to the glass ceiling through a psychological process that includes strategies to overcome the glass ceiling. These include: going along and fitting in; working harder and building consensus; and serving as peacemaker to resolve conflicts with coworkers. Women use different strategies to cope: denial of a glass ceiling; eschewing the attractiveness of promotion and adapting to their environments; questioning their competencies; channeling their resentment against other women; selecting a work culture that matches their own goals, objectives, and values; building coalitions with men and allowing them to be part of the solution; and working within the system to adapt the culture to be more hospitable to women. She also suggests that time is viewed as a woman's best friend: Through attrition, men will leave positions of power in the dominant coalition and more women will rise through organizational ranks, and as men take on more domestic responsibilities, they will become more sensitized to feminist issues—particularly when their daughters confront the issues.

O'Neil's (2003) and Wrigley's (2002) research was published after the date of the research reviewed by Sallot and colleagues (2003), demonstrating that scholars continue to examine gender inequities experienced by women *in* public relations with differing assertions about how the status quo might change. One could place suggestions to alleviate inequities along Martin's (2003) continuum of change strategies. Martin has synthesized feminist scholarship and critical scholarship in communication to derive an evolution of thought on such solutions, the first three of which are aligned with liberal feminist thought: fixing individual women, through training and socialization; valuing the feminine, or working to gain respect for the attributes women bring to the organization, such as nurturing, consensus and relationship building, and so on; and simply adding women to previously closed professions with minimal change in hierarchy or division of labor. Critics have charged these "fixes" have their problems, from women's self-blame to reification of harmful gender stereotypes and universalizing women's experiences without regard to race, culture, or class. Simply adding women to organizations results in failure due to continued gendered norms and standards that fail to adapt to women's experiences (Martin, 2003). More radical change strategies along Martin's continuum include making small, deep cultural changes, such as allowing employees to work from home; creating new organizational structures, such as feminist organizations; and transforming gendered society, all of which take time, as Wrigley (2002) notes.

The continuum helps illustrate room for changes beyond the dichotomous liberal or radical feminist perspective. Faced with the various perspectives—and an array of change options and a wealthy tradition of feminist research focused on women in public relations practice—it is tempting to conclude this tradition constitutes feminist public relations research. However, as Aldoory (2003) has observed, empowerment in public relations impacts audiences as well as scholars and professionals. Hence, feminist scholars may want to turn attention to different areas of the field for additional yields. For instance, few studies have investigated the impact of public relations practices *on* women, the inclusion *of* women in public relations research or campaign planning, or depictions of women in public relations materials. As feminist scholarship, rather than only examinations of women, such studies would critique patriarchal forms of hegemony (Martin, 2003). And, in keeping with critiques of hegemony, Martin points to "plentiful" feminist work on discourse, communication and textual analysis (p. 69).

Few such feminist studies exist in public relations outside a "reflective" focus on workforce issues. The few that have turned attention to more discursive practices include studies that have critiqued the exclusion of women's contributions to public relations from historical accounts (Creedon, 1989; Toth & Grunig, 1993), but even these were introspective in that they focused on public relations education. Postmillennial studies that will work to fill the gap in feminist scholarship focused on public relations applications/practices in Sallot and colleagues' (2003) framework might include campaigns that use health-care messages targeted to women. Such studies might resemble Anderson's (2004) analysis of the Women's Field Army campaign against breast cancer and the means by which women communicated with one another using interpersonal and media communication, and Straughan's (2001) historic account of the work of women volunteers to educate other women about pre- and postnatal care. These scholars suggest new questions and directions that might further feminist insights.

Aldoory (2003) also worked to bring health-care messages for women out of obscurity. She has taken to heart the counsel by Toth and Cline (1991) that feminist scholarship use qualitative approaches to listen more fully to individuals' interpretations of meaning (Aldoory, 1998, citing Toth & Cline, 1991; also see Aldoory, 2001b). In her work, Aldoory uses research methods to ensure diversity in race, class, sexual orientation, age, and educational background. She also moved beyond description, using the situational theory of publics to frame her study of how women create meaning with health-care messages and how these messages gain their involvement.

In other studies, Aldoory (1998) and Aldoory and Toth (2004) have focused on the discursive dimension of public relations practice in leadership styles and communication. Because leaders serve in communities to represent organizational interests, they serve a public relations role as boundary spanner (Aldoory & Toth, 2004). Aldoory (1998) has examined female public relations leaders and their language and communication strategies. Aldoory and Toth (2004) provided additional insights regarding transformational versus transactional leadership styles, using a multimethodological approach—questionnaires and focus groups. They found support for gendered styles of leadership and preferences for transformational leadership as "an appropriate fit for accomplishing public relations goals" (p. 179). Relying on management literature, Aldoory and Toth explain that transformational leaders are marked by "unique qualities surrounding charisma" distinguished by risk taking, goal articulation, high expectations, emphasis on collective identity, self-assertion, and vision that serves to create meaning and symbols for followers to further change (p. 159). In contrast, a transactional leader, most effective in stable conditions, works to establish and maintain a "right" position and is characterized by certainty, clear direction, personal oversight, and just treatment, and offers rewards for quality performance, hence the "transaction" (p. 159). Furthermore, they note women leaders often exhibit "interactive" and "pluralistic" leadership styles, characterized by participative decision making, working to enhance others' sense of self-worth, valuing others' opinions, energizing staff, and sharing power and information (p. 162). Results indicated women rated themselves lower in terms of being a leader than men did when rating themselves, but overall, there were few sex differences in perceptions of leadership style. Aldoory and Toth produced a leadership preference index and demonstrated how multimethodological approaches to studying perceptions could serve feminist goals, in addition to working to build theory that demonstrates leadership is situation and gender contingent.

Indeed, one premise of Aldoory and Toth's work is adherence to two-way symmetrical communication, the normative model for public relations presented by J. Grunig (Ed.) (1992), that frames the dominant paradigm in public relations. L. Grunig, Toth, and Hon (2000) describe implications of the normative model for ethical communication, noting that for some scholars, "the most effective public relations grows out of an entire world view that is feminine. That is, public relations that is practiced as balanced, two-way communication between an organization and its stakeholder groups stands to make the greatest contribution to organizational effectiveness" (p. 24). Their discussion of feminine values in public relations focuses on cooperation, diversity, justice, sensitivity, nurturance, empowerment, and honesty as feminist values that help to define a feminist ethic (especially pp. 95–108 and 355–360). Any suggestion to adopt a feminist ethic of public relations begs the question: Is there a public relations campaign that serves to illustrate a feminist ethic? Then, too, might one assess notable differences in ethical dimensions between campaigns generated by women and those generated by men? Might there be conflicts between a masculine ethic of justice versus an ethic of care exhibited in competing campaigns? In fact, Cheney and Christensen (2001) have pointed out, the ideal of symmetry is much more complex and fails to capture a power imbalance that may represent itself as two-way dialogue. To capture fully the complexities and nuances of the impact of power and ideology and the challenges faced by feminists to define and challenge the system, feminist theorists rely on multidisciplinary scholarship to gain insight.

FUTURE DIRECTIONS: MULTIDISCIPLINARY FEMINIST PUBLIC RELATIONS

An indication of the limited focus of feminist scholarship in public relations is the number of studies in Sallot and colleagues' (2003) "introspective" category, with few in the "theory" category and none in the "practice" category that pertain to feminist perspectives. In part, the slow growth of feminist studies, besides the challenges mentioned earlier in this chapter, could be due to the phenomenon noted by McKie (2001) that "the traffic in ideas between public relations and other areas of knowledge is . . . restricted" (p. 75). He attributes this, in part, to the observation by Olasky (1989) that "public relations practitioners had developed a comfortable paradigm and did not want to give it up" (p. 79, citing Olasky, p. 94). Additionally, when it comes to examining public relations practice, feminist work, especially that which is grounded in critical theory, often faces reactions that such scholarship is not "productive." In other words, critical feminist scholarship does not work to further the financial objectives of corporate public relations—that is, how to be more "effective"—but rather questions and challenges those objectives and the value of hierarchies of current practices (German, 1995, Martin, 2003; Holtzhausen, 2001; McKie, 2001; Toth, 1992; and Cheney & Christensen, 2001). It might be time to turn to other disciplines to help public relations scholars explore the feminist terrain and investigate the yields of other focal points.

Feminist research in other fields has produced scholarship that might be emulated in public relations. For insight and tutelage, feminist scholars in public relations might turn to Tetreault (1985), who has examined the evolution experienced in feminist scholarship across several disciplines. Her feminist phase theory evaluation model overviews the evolution of thinking about women posed in curricula during various phases of feminist scholarship in a variety of fields, notably anthropology, history, literature, and psychology. She identified five common phases: male-defined; contribution or "compensatory"; bifocal; feminist, or women's; and gender-balanced or multifocal or relational scholarship. Briefly, each phase is defined by the questions generated and the focus of inquiry. Whereas male-defined scholarship did not recognize the absence of women's experiences in its investigations, "compensatory scholarship" searched for missing stories of women's contributions in a discipline or scholarship by women. The work of Creedon (1991) and Toth (1992) exemplifies this phase in public relations, as does the work of Anderson (2004) and Straughan (2001).

The bifocal phase describes scholarship that examines the asymmetrical experiences of women and men and seeks to explain gender inequities and differences—as in how and why women and men are different. The bifocal approach examines dualist categories of human experience: male and female, public and private. Much of the roles studies in public relations that seek explanations for differences in women's and men's experiences would fit here. For Tetreault (1985), a more advanced phase of scholarly inquiry is the feminist scholarship phase, in which scholars pursue "new questions, new categories and new notions of significance which illuminate women's traditions, history, culture, values, visions and perspectives" (p. 367). This scholarship embraces a pluralistic view of women, acknowledging that race, ethnicity, and social class contribute to diversity rather than to universality of women's experiences. In scholarship, multidisciplinary, inductive approaches allow personal experiences to voice insights, and public and private is viewed not as a dichotomy, but as a continuum. Further, "experience exists within social, cultural, historical, political and economic contexts" (p. 367) . Furthermore, "disciplinary standards of excellence are questioned" and scholarship is evaluated with regard to the insights it provides into "any aspect of human experience, rather than according to how [it] measure[s] up to a predetermined canon derived from the experience of a privileged few" (p. 370).

Beyond the feminist phase, Tetreault (1985) identifies "multi-focal, relational scholarship" (p. 371), the final phase of her model. This type of scholarship affords a gender-balanced perspective that "serves to fuse women's and men's experiences into a holistic view of human experience" (p. 371). Like scholarship in the feminist phase, disciplinary standards of excellence are challenged, and work that spans disciplines is evaluated based not against a formal genre, but on insight into a reconceptualized "holistic" view of human experience (p. 371).

Using Tetreault's phase model, feminist scholars might derive an agenda for public relations research that stands on the shoulders of the scholars who have readied the field for the next fruits to be planted, nurtured, and harvested. Clearly, our work should continue to cultivate insights from public relations campaigns produced by and targeted to women, to gain insights into what women contribute to the field, but a more holistic approach would be to reclaim the lost stories of forerunners in building organizational relationships. If women, indeed, have served as the "conscience" of an organization, how has that manifested itself? Personal ethnographies that relay accounts of decision making and intervention that resulted from insights and awareness would profit younger professionals. And, borrowing from rhetorical scholars who have examined a feminist rhetoric, is there a genre of feminine or feminist corporate campaigns (see Campbell, 1973, 1989)? What of a genre of maternal appeals, as identified by Hayden (2003) or Ruddick's (1995) campaign for a politics of peace? And do depictions of people of color, gays and lesbians, women and men, the young, the elderly, and those with disabilities in campaign messages uphold the dignity, respect, nurturance, and encouragement we expect from a feminist ethic? Given the challenges presented earlier in this chapter, other studies focused on the application and practice of public relations might examine the representations of feminists in a campaign to build membership or further explanations and understandings about feminism. Do feminist organizations manifest communication strategies that are inclusive? Do all-female agencies adhere to feminist orientations in their work environments? And to which perspective do they adhere? How do they resolve tensions among feminist goals? How has the feminization of the field changed the agency or freelance environment? Have men become more sensitive to gender inequities? Can we, in fact, define universal feminist topoi for public relations scholars given the variety of perspectives? These are but a few of the questions that might offer future yield to the evolution in feminist scholarship in public relations.

CONCLUSION

This chapter has focused on the challenges feminist scholars face, as well as previous studies in public relations that have employed a feminist perspective. Additionally, I have offered two frameworks that might provide insights into the variety of inquiry that might be guided by a feminist perspective. My aim has been to demonstrate an evolution in feminist research that reflects the evolution in the feminist movement. Clearly, while a set of consistent goals is shared among "feminismS" (to empower the oppressed, in Aldoory's [2001a, 2001b] words), a fresh look reveals additional questions and methods that remain to be used to advance understanding of public relations practice from a feminist perspective. This evolution has prepared public relations scholars to move toward insights beyond traditional scholarship in the field, relying primarily on an integration of understandings gleaned from other disciplines and led by previous feminist scholars in the field.

It may be that it was necessary initially for feminist scholarship in public relations to politely call attention to women's presence in the profession so as not to alienate the men who set the rules of the game. And indeed, evidence still suggests some resistance and skepticism regarding the gender issues that confront individuals in the public relations practice (Leyland, 2001a, 2001b). Yet our research has not yet captured all the options that exist for women as they negotiate their careers and advocate for causes of interest to them as they work toward a meaningful life. Clearly, in practice women negotiate change and make their presence felt in a way that is not quite captured in current research, and for many more than liberal or radical alternatives exist. In fact, as my enthusiastic student observed, there is *so much more* to be investigated.

Tong (1998, 2003) observes that the multiple perspectives of feminist thinking, rather than being fodder for frustration, is an indication that feminist scholarship has matured to the point that it has a past, present, and future. One sign that feminist scholarship focused on workforce issues has advanced is the discontinuation in 1997 of the Women and Work series after a twelve-year run because, the editors claimed, such investigations have proliferated beyond the series into mainstream academic journals in a variety of disciplines. It is gratifying to see that the two mainstream journals (*Journal of Public Relations Research* and the *Public Relations Review*) in public relations have a history of including feminist scholarship, focused on questions of women in the workforce. My hope is that eager students begin joint ventures alongside colleagues in disciplines such as those identified by Stromberg et al. to pose new questions and new directions for feminist public relations scholarship.

CASE: WORKING THE SYSTEM

Consider the case of St. Bernadette's Catholic Elementary School, which faced a transition of leadership and parents' dissatisfaction with disciplinary actions directed at middle school students. (St. Bernadette's is a composite. The name and circumstances have been changed to protect the identity of the school.) The case uses feminist theoretical lenses to frame the case and demonstrate insights that may be gleaned for future public relations research and practice. In this case, a group of parents "worked the system"—or worked around the system, if you will—to accomplish an objective they believed would satisfy the needs of the school and its children.

The Setting

St. Bernadette's, an urban Catholic school at the edge of Metropolis, population 150,000, is one of four Catholic schools in an area known for educational excellence. Besides the public school system, several academic and religiously oriented private schools provide a variety of choices for education that best fits individual families' values.

St. Bernadette's is a diocesan school, which means any decisions about curriculum and personnel are made by the diocesan administration, which includes a secretary of education, the superintendent of Catholic schools, along with a director of curricular development. At the local level, the pastor of St. Bernadette's church answers to the diocese and oversees the principal, who implements policy set by the diocese and a school board. Board members are elected by parents, but their role is limited to an advisory position to the school administration. The local board's role is to support the mission of Catholic education, and to direct school policy, specifically to set tuition, and to oversee operating expenses, development, and recruiting activities.

The brick complex that houses the school also surrounds the parish church and rectory. The main church entrance faces a busy city street with limited parking. Underneath the church in the basement are some additional classroom space, the cafeteria, and the "gymatorium." The facility housing the church and school resembles to some degree other inner-city schools without grass or playgrounds, and uses the parking lot as recess space when school is in session.

The Situation

St. Bernadette's has seen its share of leaders, but many agreed that Mrs. Rodriguez was a special person—approachable, sincere, dynamic, energetic, empathetic, spiritual, interested in children, and focused on problem solving. She approached parents as equals, and lived the cliché about parents and teachers serving as "partners" in education.

Mrs. Rodriguez invited parents into the church for the daily school assembly, which included an enthusiastic daily welcome, scripture readings and reflection, announcements about the day's events and faculty and student birthdays, the pledge of allegiance, and a closing song. The students' processional from the schoolyard into the assembly was a cherished ritual. Parents brought children into the throng of schoolyard noise to join classmates as they chatted with other parents waiting for the procession—children lined up by grade following their teachers into the school after the whistle blew, waving good-bye to their parents. The ritual was broken only when it rained and children went directly into the gym, or when the schedule was altered.

Though feelings were positive about the school, the development committee recommended an audit to determine the school's strengths and weaknesses as it attempted to assess its communication, recruitment, and development practices. Consultants with public relations backgrounds working pro bono first assessed the principal's vision of the school's image, and assessed perceptions of the school's image during five focus groups that involved parents and students. The principal emphasized that while she believed the school had an excellent reputation for its academics, she did not want the school to be known as a "private" school, where people came merely for the academic rigor and discipline. Later, questionnaires generated from comments made during the focus groups were distributed and over 55 percent of families with children in the school responded. They identified the key attractions of the school as its faith-based education, the discipline of the students, the sense of community in the school, and the strength of the faculty. Weaknesses were the school's location and run-down facilities, as well as some comments about "old school" disciplinary approaches by some of the teachers in the upper grades. Additionally, the public relations role of Mrs. Rodriguez's leadership emerged both during parent focus groups and the open-ended responses on the questionnaire. The focus groups revealed that the principal embodied the energy of the school, and was the "face" of the school. As one parent put it, "Mrs. Rodriguez IS the school, and she is the reason many parents send their children to the school."

Mrs. Rodriguez welcomed the audit results, and worked to implement recommendations, which included maintenance of the rituals important to parents, and working harder to include newcomers into the school setting. The following year, however, St. Bernadette's pastor announced Mrs. Rodriguez had been hired by the diocese as a lay adviser for school administrators. After six years, the school would be getting a new principal.

Changing of the Guard: Crisis or "Growth"?

Leadership change is always difficult, but at St. Bernadette's the year was especially rough. Mrs. Venice, a twenty-six-year veteran Catholic school teacher in her first administrative position, was hired to fill Mrs. Rodriguez's shoes two weeks before the start of the new school year. Because parents had been without word all summer, they began calling the school and one another to learn about their children's homeroom teacher. However, the principal was unavailable, attending workshops for new administrators. Several parents of middle-school students began to voice concerns about some teachers, offering both negative and positive reports: She's strict, knows her stuff, yells at the kids, teaches to different learning styles, is unapproachable, prepares students well for high school, uses outdated discipline methods, and kids with special needs struggle under her.

Mrs. Venice addressed parents for the first time at back-to-school night one week after the start of school. She gave a brief introduction of herself that focused on her qualifications, and announced a number of changes she said were based on the diocese's concerns about safety. Already a letter had come home with a vague hint of change, without any specifics. Among the changes—the morning drop off and afternoon pickup procedure, which she said jeopardized children's safety, was to end. Parents were to drive straight through the parking lot, and their children were to go into the building immediately, waiting in the gym for their teacher to lead them to the church. Mrs. Venice also changed the arrival time, explaining the children were being left at school way too early, and that it was unfair to the faculty to supervise the children in the morning prior to the start of school. Before giving directions about parents' visiting the classrooms, she reminded parents how hard the faculty worked on behalf of their students and that parents should not call teachers at home.

Parents were stunned and curious. Working parents who relied on leaving children among friends and teachers in the morning worried about how they would now manage early morning child supervision. One faculty member who had always had parents call her at home seemed surprised and told parents they could continue to contact her at home.

Mrs. Venice's morning school assemblies also contrasted in many ways with previous assemblies, and some mothers expressed unhappiness. Gone were birthday announcements and clear information on the day's activities. The focus of Mrs. Venice's assembly was on ritual prayer, the pledge of allegiance, and directions to the children; parents were not part of the conversation.

Difficult as it now was with the new rules, parking-lot talk among parents escalated. Though the parking-lot community had disintegrated into a line of cars that had to "keep moving," stories spread about new rules the children had to follow—some true and some untrue: walking the hallways in complete silence with six inches between their bodies and the hallway walls. One of the stories was that the feared middle-school teachers had cornered the new principal and told her "the way it oughta be." At the first board meeting, the president announced that he was a bit concerned about several phone calls he had received from parents with regard to policy. A board member asked about some changes he noticed in the handbook, and the principal said she had made some "slight" changes to "your" book.

Phone calls to board members increased. Parents were upset that changes had been communicated after the fact, without input or feedback. Parents were also increasingly unhappy about adults' communication with children; yelling and blowing whistles were especially mentioned. At the second board meeting, twenty parents, mostly mothers of middle-school students, showed up to express their discontent. One father spoke passionately that "the life has gone out of the school" and that his children now came home solemn. Three mothers spoke about their concerns that their children with special needs were being ostracized by teachers and left to fend for themselves, amid an environment that punished difference as failure. One new policy, dubbed the "potty pass"—a hole punch card that allowed middle-school students thirty restroom visits per month—especially disturbed mothers of middle-school girls. The new principal was charged with responsibility for the unhappiness, yet was silent, only to say, "I'm listening and learning." Those who attended wanted answers, saying the stories were hurting the image of the school. "It's bad PR," one mother said. Others countered that their children had not had the negative experiences being expressed. The pastor of St. Bernadette's acknowledged the concerns of the parents and pledged to develop a task force to study and resolve the issues.

Task forces formed around school communication, ideas for students in the primary grades, students in middle school, students with learning differences, and recommendations for discipline. The committees were responsible for meeting and making recommendations to the school board for implementation by the principal. Almost every faculty member served on a committee, and some parents served on more than one committee. The committee with the largest number of volunteers was the middle school committee. Each committee met two or three times, working around the holidays and board meetings. The push was on to recommend and implement changes because several families indicated they may not return to the school the following year.

Mother Bears

After the recommendations had been amended and adopted, a board member who cochaired the middle school committee with his wife asked at the end of the meeting, "What happens now? We passed these policies, but what really has changed? How do we know the policies will be implemented?" The pastor and the principal explained that the principal was responsible for implementing policy, and some of the recommendations would not be put in place until the following year. "It takes time." A woman from the visitors' seats asked, "Do we have a timeline?" Other attendees said, "We've run out of time" and "We've spent six months on this and all we have is talk." One board member announced, "I don't think it's a secret that people are making calls to other Catholic schools in the area to see if they have openings." Indeed, one board member told the board president that her daughter would not be coming back.

After the meeting, some parents called board members to offer a solution: "Get rid of the teachers." Others with backgrounds in education suggested that the teachers were owed due process, and alternatively could be rehabilitated with "training" in newer discipline methods. Some offered advice, providing books and articles on appropriate disciplinary methods for adolescents. When a board member explained to one mother that the board did not hire or fire teachers, she snapped, "Well, who does? I'll tell you what. I've talked to Mrs. Venice. Nothing. I've talked to the pastor. Nothing. We worked on these task forces. I have a call in to the superintendent. I'm going to get some answers." Another board member received a phone call from a distraught mother whose daughter had learning disabilities. She tearfully explained a teacher had refused to play a tape recorder during review for a unit test. "I spoke with the teacher and Mrs. Venice and nothing.

You talk about a task force? I put my own task force together to help my daughter. She's not dumb. She just needs help. And we're going to a place where she can get it." In all, five board members had heard from the woman. One member, who heard about the incident from his wife, said, "My wife is furious. What can we do?"

After one mothers group gathering in April, members were advised to call the pastor and the superintendent of schools with additional complaints: the school was not clean; uniform infractions were punished, but bullying of other students went unpunished; teachers' communication showed a lack of respect toward students and parents; and the principal delayed responding to parents' calls. Throughout the following week, the diocesan superintendent came into school and met with the principal and with families who had complained about the principal's leadership. The board president told parents he fully expected the principal's contract would not be renewed; however, he was told the diocese was committed to honoring its three-year contract with the principal. He presented to the board a petition asking Mrs. Venice to resign that had been signed by twenty-two other families, including one faculty member, representing over sixty students who were committed to leaving the school if the principal returned. All but three board members signed the petition, which was presented to the principal the day before the last board meeting of the year.

At the school board meeting the following night, approximately sixty people showed up. Mrs. Venice did not arrive. The pastor called for the resignation of all the board members, admonished the school board for their actions, and expressed disappointment in some of the faculty for their unfair treatment of the principal. On Friday of that week, the principal resigned.

In July, a new principal was hired, Mr. Sirius, who had experience in school administration. His initial actions on hiring were to call all parents on the petition and ask them to come back to "my" school. Some did; some suggested they wanted to see whether the key issues had changed. He involved a variety of parents in decision making with regard to the school, and immediately did away with the notorious "potty pass" and worked to change the disciplinary process. At his first board meeting, he told members, "I learned long ago that you never get between a mama bear and her cubs. And I told the faculty this. It's the number-one rule for dealing with the students."

Case Analysis and Interpretation

Indeed, a public relations scholar could point to a number of factors that led to the crisis at St. Bernadette's, and many lessons were learned. However, two feminist lenses frame this analysis. Feminist perspectives (note the plural) at least raise the question: How does gender play a role in the situation?

The first helps to explore the means by which the parents of St. Bernadette's students raised their voices to empower themselves in a structure that clearly delineates who does and does not have authority to make choices on behalf of the children. In fact, the parents worked the system by using the school board to pressure the administration, and by "lighting up the switchboards at the diocesan office," as one board member described it.

The first feminist perspective used for examination stems from Ruddick's (1995) feminist perspective articulated as "Maternal Thinking," wherein she claims that maternal work—the work of being a mother—demands "preservation, growth, and social acceptability of one's children . . . to be a mother is to be committed to meeting these demands by works of preservative love, nurturance, and training" (pp. 17, 19). This work involves physical and emotional protection of one's child, as well as work to ensure emotional growth and that a child is accepted and respected in the world. This feminist perspective is not without its detractors. For instance, Barnett and Rivers (2004) claim that assertions about "maternal instinct" and "natural differences" between men and women mask a backlash against feminism that bolsters claims about the propensity of men to excel in leadership roles and excuses fathers from parental obligations (see also Faludi, 1991). Rather than engage in clarifications about "natural distinctions" however, Ruddick's (1995) feminist standpoint offers "a superior vision produced by the political conditions and distinctive work of women" (p. 129). She notes that while men can and do perform the work of protection, nurturing, and socialization, it is primarily women who do so.

I do not address the nature/nurture theory here. Instead, I examine the gendered nature of the relationships between school and home, which involves at least gendered expectations that surround parent/child, teacher/parent, child/teacher relationships. Indeed, Ruddick argues the perception and expectation is that mothers bear the "burden of expertise" when it comes to attending to their children's emotional and intellectual growth, while fathers can routinely attend to protection and training (p. 19). The more educated a mother is, the more she will attend to the emotional and intellectual needs of children, over and above "training" needs. At St. Bernadette's, mothers were predominantly professional women with advanced college degrees and experience who had chosen to stay at home at least for some time with their children, making that their primary "work." They clearly had a heavy investment in their roles as mothers and as school stakeholders/volunteers; their proximity allowed them to view up close the relationships of their children among peers and school professionals. Their involvement also afforded them some input into the collective discussion about the relationship between values in the home (a private place) and in school (a public space). Indeed, bridging the private/public distinction offered them legitimacy in an egalitarian setting under Mrs. Rodriguez, when they believed their voice was heard. Under the new principal they saw their roles challenged, or at least silenced. When opportunities to "oversee" the parking lot in the morning were cut off, when their opportunities to call teachers at home were discouraged, and when their suggestions about appropriate discipline were ignored, the mothers worked to regain their own legitimacy and sought a leader who would acknowledge as much. It is also interesting to note the mothers' role in approaching the situation. The women pleaded their case directly, but when these efforts failed, they relied on the male-dominated school board to appeal to a male-dominated administration. When that failed, they relied on strength in numbers.

The situation at St. Bernadette's is not unlikely to occur at a public school, and indeed it has, with parents working to oust a principal who fails to respond to concerns over children's needs. However, public school board members do have power to hire and fire, and the media often attends to offer its own version of events, allowing others to air their opinions on the issues presented. Additionally, private schools' needs to recruit and to solicit financial contributions place a heavier burden on courting relationships that public schools in the past have taken for granted—however numbered those days may be. If nothing else, the situation raises questions about how well our public relations theories address the challenges of gender roles that define key publics. As another of my students once related, "at my house mom was always at the school doing something. But when dad showed up, it meant there was trouble." A feminist perspective would question why women often feel the need to call in male reinforcements and point out that this is not an option available to single mothers.

A feminist perspective would also urge that we examine the positions of other women in the situation, and the gendered nature of their perspective on the situation. While mothers of unhappy children worked to gain legitimacy for their perspectives, the teachers worked to regain their own legitimacy in the face of challenges. The result was that frequently board meetings and task force meetings became a contest of constructed realities. Where one teacher would suggest "I see happy children," another would confide, "Things aren't what they used to be." A feminist read of the situation would caution that there is not one monolithic perspective, but would encourage us to recognize that gender plays a role in the meaning given these constructed realities. A female teacher's communication is often perceived based on our expectations about how women should communicate, or whether they violate these expectations. And in school settings, as this case has revealed, instances of interpersonal teacher/student or teacher/parent communication promote or damage public relationships.

But what of Mrs. Vincent? Did she also face at least some challenges to her authority because of her gender? It was clear at times she was not comfortable exposing her "private" role as mother in the "public" arena of the school community—though her disclosure may have garnered her at least some empathy. At one school event, she left early and was heavily criticized afterward, but remained tight-lipped about the reason: She had attended a religious ceremony for her son—ironic, given the school's raison d'être.

This leads to a second theory informed by feminist perspectives that may offer some insights into the situation. A study conducted by Aldoory and Toth (2004) sought to determine preference for leadership styles and to determine whether there was a gendered nature of leadership in public relations. They identified three leaderships styles based on the literature: transactional or authoritative leadership, focused on the authority of the leader; transformational leadership, likened mostly to charisma, where the leader uses "his or her vision to create meaning" (pp. 159–160); and pluralistic leadership "characterized by participative decision making, the recognition of other people, and the placing of value on others' opinions" (p. 160). A fourth style, which is not a pure "type," is situational leadership, which Aldoory and Toth claim marks those who change their style to fit the situation "depending on the circumstances and the environment" (p. 160).

Aldoory and Toth (2004) conducted a quantitative survey that showed a strong preference for transformational leadership over transactional leadership, which the authors speculate may be due to the ability of transformational leaders to best meet public relations goals for organizations that must constantly adapt to turbulence. With a change in leadership, one could argue that St. Bernadette's had undergone major turbulence—a drastic change in its identity. In terms of which gender relates to which leadership style, Aldoory and Toth's survey results showed no significant sex differences in perceptions of leadership style. However, focus group comments underscored distinctions regarding feminine and masculine forms of leadership: "Overall focus group participants perceived women as making better leaders in public relations due to the socialized traits they have acquired, that is, empathy and collaborative efforts, which in turn create a transformational leadership style" (p. 179). From this perspective, Mrs. Rodriguez offered a clear vision for the school and embodied not only the "face" of the school, but the persona of a transformational leader. Mrs. Vincent, perhaps due to inexperience, offered a more transactional approach to leadership, cautious to maintain authority and resist quick implementations of changes recommended by "outsiders"—parents who were not employees of the school. She relied more heavily on the hierarchy and the rules, rather than on fostering relationships, which would involve more self-disclosure and more collaborative investment in the school—the handbook being "our" book, rather than "yours."

At first glance, the failure of the task forces seems to contradict the preference for collaborative efforts. Clearly, the pastor worked to involve parents in a collaborative enterprise via the task forces to implement solutions. Why did these not work? Was impatience the explanation? Or did parents at some point recognize that their suggestions and recommendations were falling on deaf ears? Did recognition of a lack of position and power to implement the policy impede the process? As Aldoory and Toth note (2004), at times, "organizational culture [as well as] socialized gender stereotypes all work to constrain leadership style and women in leadership positions" (p. 179). Indeed, recall Grunig, Toth, and Hon's (2004) (see also Kowalski, 2000) admonition that two-way symmetrical communication involving empathy and collaboration is the heart of effective organizations. Their advice might inform and be informed by St. Bernadette's, particularly in the analysis of why collaboration backfired, especially when all entered into the discussion with a genuine sense of problem solving.

The approach of the St. Bernadette's parents is not without its fallout and criticism. To this day there are hurt feelings among parents supportive of Mrs. Vincent and those calling for her resignation, and among teachers and the school administration who saw the principal as the scapegoat for a few parents who usurped their authority. Nevertheless, when parents offered alternative suggestions for key problems, especially after their efforts at dialogue resulted in little change, they then took matters into their own hands, approaching the principal directly and demanding her resignation. In their view, lack of leadership allowed the issues to fester, and though "listening and learning" were to be admired, action was demanded. Several families left the school regardless of the administrative change because they did not believe the children's needs for nurturing, discipline, and learning differences had been addressed. However, the petition signers felt a sense of validation when the next new principal's energy and positive communication reinvigorated the school, when he made some changes at the middle-school level, and actively consulted parents prior to making decisions.

QUESTIONS FOR APPLICATION

1. What additional insights about the St. Bernadette's case might be gleaned from feminist perspectives?

2. Can you think of alternative feminist perspectives that might shed clarity on the school's situation and on why many in the school community believed the principal had to leave?

3. In thinking about public relations for schools, both public and private, where does gender play a role in building and maintaining relationships?

4. How do these insights inform your thinking about relationships between an organization and key stakeholders?

5. How would you have suggested the situation be handled had you been asked to serve on the school board?

6. Would your gender play a role in your decisions or in how you communicated your decisions? Imagine the same question posed to you as principal or as director of development at the school. How would you approach parents? How would you approach donors?

REFERENCES

Aldoory, L. (1998). The language of leadership for female public relations professionals. *Journal of Public Relations Research, 10*(2), pp. 73–101.

———. (2001a). The standard white woman in public relations. In E. L Toth & L. Aldoory (Eds.), *Diversity challenge to media: Voices from the field* (pp. 105–152). Cresskill, NJ: Hampton.

———. (2001b). Making health communications meaningful for women: Factors that influence involvement. *Journal of Public Relations Research, 13*, pp. 163–185.

———. (2003). The empowerment of feminist scholarship in public relations and the building of a feminist paradigm. *Communication Yearbook, 27*, pp. 221–255.

Aldoory, L., & Toth, E. (2004). Leadership and gender in public relations: Perceived effectiveness of transformational and transactional leadership styles. *Journal of Public Relations Research, 16*(2), pp. 157–184.

Anderson, W. B. (2004). "We can do it": A study of the women's field army public relations efforts. *Public Relations Review, 30*, pp. 196–197.

Ashcraft, K. L. (1995, November). *I wouldn't say I'm a feminist, but . . . : A tale of reluctant identity.* National Communication Association. Paper presented to the Organizational Communication Interest Division, San Antonio, TX.

Barnett, R., & Rivers, C. (2004). *Same difference: How gender myths are hurting our relationships, our children, and our jobs.* New York: Basic Books.

Bui, L. S. (1999). Mothers in public relations: How are they balancing career and family? *Public Relations Quarterly, 44*(2), pp. 23–26.

Campbell, K. K. (1973). The rhetoric of women's liberation: An oxymoron. *Quarterly Journal of Speech, 59*, pp. 74–86.

———. (1989). *Man cannot speak for her: A critical study of early feminist rhetoric.* Vol. I. New York: Praeger.

Cheney, G., & Christensen, L. T. (2001). Public relations as contested terrain: A critical response. In R. L. Heath (Ed.), *Handbook of public relations* (pp. 167–182). Thousand Oaks, CA: Sage.

Cleveland, J. N., Stockdale, M., & Murphy, K. (2000). *Women and men in organizations: Sex and gender issues at work.* Mahwah, NJ: Lawrence Erlbaum.

Condon, H. S. (1999). Feminist image campaign: Beyond the old stereotypes. *Fall 1999 NOW Times.* National Organization for Women, (Ed.). Accessed March 28, 2004, from www.now.org/nnt/fall-99/adcampaign.html.

Creedon, P. J. (1989). Public relations history misses "her story." *Journalism Educator, 44*, pp. 26–30.

———. (1991). Public relations and "women's work": Toward a feminist analysis of public relations roles. In J. E. Grunig and L. A. Grunig (Eds.), *Public relations research annual* (vol. 3, pp. 67–84). Hillsdale, NJ: Lawrence Erlbaum.

———. (1993). Acknowledging the infrasystem: A critical feminist analysis of systems theory. *Public Relations Review, 19*(2), pp. 157–167.

Dow, B. J. (2004). Fixing feminism: Women's liberation and the rhetoric of television documentary. *Quarterly Journal of Speech, 90*(1), pp. 53–80.

Eisenberg, E. M., & Goodall, H. L. (2004). *Organizational communication: Balancing creativity and constraint* (4th ed.). Boston: Bedford/ St. Martin's.

Faludi, S. (1991). *Backlash: The undeclared war against American women.* New York: Anchor.

Friedlin, J. (2002). Second and third wave feminists clash over the future. *Women's e-News.* Run date May 26, 2002. Accessed March 28, 2004, from www.womensenews.org/article.cfm/dyn/aid/920/context/cover.

German, K. (1995). Critical theory in public relations inquiry: Future directions for analysis in a public relations context. In W. N. Elwood (Ed.), *Public relations inquiry as rhetorical criticism: Case studies of corporate discourse and social influence* (pp. 279–294). Westport, CT: Praeger.

Grunig, J. (1992) Excellency in public relations & communication management. NJ: Lawrence Erlbaum.

Grunig, L. A. (1991). Court-ordered relief from sex discrimination in the foreign service: Implications for women working in development communication. In J. E. Grunig and L. A. Grunig (Eds.), *Public relations research annual* (vol. 3, pp. 85–114). Hillsdale, NJ: Lawrence Erlbaum.

Grunig, L. A., Toth, E. L., & Hon, L C. (2000). Feminist values in public relations. *Journal of Public Relations Research, 12*(1), pp. 49–69.

———. (2001). *Women in public relations: How gender influences practice.* New York: Guilford.

Hayden, S. (2003). Family metaphors and the nation: Promoting a politics of care through the Million Mom March. *Quarterly Journal of Speech, 89*(3), pp. 196–215.

Henry, S. (1998). Dissonant notes of a retiring feminist: Doris E. Fleischman's later years. *Journal of Public Relations Research, 10*(1), pp. 1–33.

Holtzhausen, D. R. (2000). Postmodern values in public relations. *Journal of Public Relations Research, 12*(1), pp. 93–114.

Hon, L. C. (1995). Toward a feminist theory of public relations, *Journal of Public Relations Research,* vol. 7, no. 1, 27–88.

Hon, L. C., Grunig, L. A., Dozier, D. (1992). Women in public relations: Problems and opportunities. In J. Grunig (Ed.), *Excellence in public relations and communication management* (pp. 419–438). Hillsdale, NJ: Lawrence Erlbaum.

Kowalski, T. J. (2000). *Public relations in schools* (2nd ed.). Upper Saddle River, NJ: Prentice-Hall.

Lauzen, M. (1992). Effects of gender on professional encroachment in public relations. *Journalism Quarterly, 69*(1), pp. 173–182.

Leyland, A. (2001a). Gender has negligible impact on salary in PR. *PR Week,* May 21.

Leyland, A. (2001b). Sex, lies and multiple regression analysis. *PR Week,* May 21, p. 9.

Martin, J. (2003). Feminist theory and critical theory: Unexplored synergies. In M. Alvesson & H. Willmott (Eds.), *Studying management critically* (pp. 66–91). London: Sage.

McKie, D. (2001). Updating public relations: "New science," research paradigms, and uneven developments. In R. L. Heath (Ed.), *Handbook of public relations* (pp. 75–91). Thousand Oaks, CA: Sage.

Nicotera, A. M. (1999). The woman academic as subject/object/self: Dismantling the illusion of duality. *Communication Theory, 9,* pp. 430–464.

Olasky, M. N. (1989). The aborted debate within public relations: An approach through Kuhn's paradigm. In J. E. Grunig and L. A. Grunig (Eds.), *Public relations research annual* (vol. 1, pp. 87–96). Hillsdale, NJ: Lawrence Erlbaum.

O'Neil, J. (2003). An analysis of the relationship among structure, influence and gender: Helping to build a feminist theory of public relations. *Journal of Public Relations Research 15*(2); pp. 151–179.

Pompper, D. (2004). Linking ethnic diversity and two-way symmetry: Modeling African American practitioner roles. *Journal of Public Relations Research, 16,*(3), pp. 269–299.

Renegar, V. R., and Sowards, St. K. (2003). Liberal irony, rhetoric, and feminist thought. A unifying third wave feminist theory. *Philosophy and Rhetoric, 36*(4), pp. 330–352.

Rice, S. (1999). Feminism and philosophy of education. *Encyclopedia of Philosophy of Education.* Accessed June 6, 2004, from www.vusst.hr/ENCYCLOPAEDIA/feminism.htm.

Riessman, C. K. (1993). *Narrative analysis. Qualitative research methods series, 30.* Newbury Park, CA: Sage.

Roos, P. A., & Jones, K. W. (1993). Shifting gender boundaries: Women's inroads into academic sociology. *Work and Occupations, 20*(4), pp. 395–428.

Ruddick, S. (1995). *Maternal thinking: Toward a politics of peace.* New York: Ballantine.

Sallot, L. M., Lyon, L. J., Acostsa-Alzuru, C., & Jones, K. O. (2003). From aardvark to zebra: A new millennium analysis of theory development in public relations academic journals. *Journal of Public Relations Research, 15*(1), pp. 27–90.

Sha, B. (2001). The feminization of public rela-tions: Contributing to a more ethical practice. In E. L.

Toth & L. Aldoory (Eds.), *The gender challenge to media: Diverse voices from the field* (pp. 153–182). Cresskill, NJ: Hampton.

Straughan, D. (2001). Women's work: Public relations efforts of the U.S. Children's Bureau to reduce infant and maternal mortality, 1912–1921. *Public Relations Review, 27*(3), pp. 337–352.

Stromberg,

Tetreault, M. T. (1985). Feminist phase theory: An experience-derived evaluation model. *Journal of Higher Education, 56,* pp. 363–384.

Tobler, J. (2000). Learning the difference: Religion, education, citizenship, and gendered subjectivity. In R. Jackdon (Ed.), *International perspectives on citizenship, education and religious diversity* (pp. 125–144). New York: Routledge.

Tong, R. (1998). *Feminist thought: A more comprehensive introduction* (2nd ed.). Boulder, CO: Westview.

Tong, Ro. (2003). Feminist ethics. *Stanford encyclopedia of philosophy.* Accessed June 8, 2004, from plato.stanford.edu/entries/feminism-ethics.

Toth, E. L. (1992). The case for pluralistic studies on public relations: Rhetorical, critical, and systems perspectives. In E. L. Toth & R. L. Heath (Eds.), *Rhetorical and critical approaches to public relations* (pp. 3–15). Hillsdale, NJ: Lawrence Erlbaum.

———. (2001). How feminist theory advanced the practice of public relations. In R. L. Heath & G. Vasquez (Eds.), *The handbook of public relations.* (pp. 237–246). Thousand Oaks, CA: Sage.

Toth, E. L., & Cline, C. G. (1991). Public relations practitioner attitudes toward gender issues: A benchmark study. *Public Relations Review, 17,* pp. 161–174.

Toth, E. L., & Grunig, L. A. (1993). The missing story of women in public relations. *Journal of Public Relations Research, 5,* pp. 153–176.

Weaver-Larissy, R. A., Cameron, G. T., & Sweep, D. D. (1994). Women in higher education public relations: An inkling of change? *Journal of Public Relations Research, 6,* pp. 125–140.

Weaver-Larissy, R. A., Sallot, L., & Cameron, G. T. (1996). Justice and gender: An instrumental and symbolic explication. *Journal of Public Relations Research, 8,* pp. 107–121.

Williams, M. E. (Ed.). (1998). *Working women: Opposing viewpoints series.* San Diego, CA: Greenhaven.

Wood, J. T. (1997). *Communication theories in action: An introduction.* Belmont, CA: Wadsworth.

Woyshner, C. (2003). Race, gender, and the early PTA: Civic engagement and public education, 1987–1924. *Teachers College Record, 105*(3), pp. 520–544.

Wrigley, B. J. (2002). Glass ceiling? What glass ceiling? A qualitative study of how women view the glass ceiling in public relations and communications management. *Journal of Public Relations Research, 14*(1), pp. 27–55.

CHAPTER TWENTY

FROM AARDVARK TO ZEBRA REDUX

An Analysis of Theory Development in Public Relations Academic Journals into the Twenty-First Century

LYNNE M. SALLOT

LISA J. LYON

CAROLINA ACOSTA-ALZURU

KARYN OGATA JONES

In a replication and extension of a study by Ferguson (1984) and an extension of research published by Sallot, Lyon, Acosta-Alzuru, and Jones (2003) that reviewed theory development in public relations through 2000, this chapter presents results of an investigation of the status of theory building by public relations scholars from 2001 to 2003. One hundred-thirty abstracts and/or articles published in *Public Relations Review* and *Journal of Public Relations Research* for the first three years of the twenty first century were subjected to content analysis. More than half of the articles analyzed were found to have contributed to theory development in public relations, compared to only 4 percent in Ferguson's (1984) study and 20 percent in Sallot and colleagues' article. Theory was most prevalent in articles about international-global public relations, public relationships, and crisis response topics. Several new categories emerged, including agenda setting/building/ framing, health communication, and postmodernism. These and other influences are expected to contribute to evermore theory building in public relations. Proportionally, *Journal of Public Relations Research* made the greatest contributions to theory development, although *Public Relations Review* published the greatest number of articles contributing to theory development, a growing trend for the journal.

At the start of the new millennium, the most prolific authors contributing to theory development were Maureen Taylor, Derina Holtzhausen, Michael Kent, and Elizabeth Toth.

As the twenty-first century begins, what is the status of theory building by public relations scholars? What themes are strengthening or emerging in theory building in public relations? Are new scholars contributing to theory building in public relations and, if so, who are they? How are the academic journals in public relations serving theory building into the new millennium? How are the journals' theory-building thematic content similar? How is content in the journals different?

M. A. Ferguson (1984), grounding her work in Kuhn (1970), analyzed nearly ten years' worth of abstracts of articles published in public relations' then-sole academic journal, *Public Relations Review*. Ferguson concluded that there had not been much productive theory development at all. She argued that public relationships, in which the unit of study is the relationships between organizations and their publics, offered "the most opportunity for a paradigm focus to speed the development of theory in this field" (p. ii). Ferguson presented her findings to the Public Relations Division of the Association for Education in Journalism and Mass Communication. Although her paper has been widely cited (see, for example, Cancel, Cameron, Sallot, & Mitrook, 1997; J. Grunig, 1993; Heath, 2001), it was never published.

In 2003, L. Sallot, L. Lyon, C. Acosta-Alzuru, and K. Jones published their replication and extension of Ferguson's study to investigate the status of theory building by public relations scholars. Sallot and colleagues conducted a content analysis of 748 abstracts and/or articles published in *Public Relations Review, Journal of Public Relations Research,* and its predecessor, *Public Relations Research Annual,* from their inceptions through 2000. Nearly 20 percent of articles analyzed in the 2003 study were found to have contributed to theory development in public relations, compared to only 4 percent in Ferguson's study. Theory was most prevalent in articles about excellence/symmetry, public relationships, ethics and social responsibility, crisis response, critical-cultural, feminism/diversity, and international topics. Sallot and colleagues (2003) projected that these and interdisciplinary influences would continue to contribute to evermore theory building in public relations. *Public Relations Review* and *Journal of Public Relations Research* published comparable numbers of articles regarding excellence theory, public relationships, and crisis response theory. However, *Public Relations Review* published far more articles on theories about academic versus applied research, ethics/social responsibility, international and role theory than *Journal of Public Relations Research*. Conversely, *Journal of Public Relations Research* published more content about situational theory and gender/diversity theories than *Public Relations Review*. Most prolific authors contributing to theory development were J. E. Grunig, R. L. Heath, L. S. Grunig, W. T. Coombs, and J. A. Ledingham.

The start of a new century and the timely publication of this book present an ideal opportunity to look back, Janus-like, to see where we have been and to look forward to see where we might be heading. Such analysis will provide an advance peek of how theory development in public relations is progressing into the twenty-first century. This chapter briefly reviews theory building in general (from which this chapter draws its odd name), our 2003 study, and Ferguson's 1984 study in more detail, and the status of theory building in public relations to date. It then presents findings and discussion of the present analysis of 130 articles published in *Public Relations Review* and *Journal of Public Relations Research* from 2001–2003, and compares these findings to those of the 2003 work. Similarities and differences in the content of these primary public relations academic journals are investigated, and scholars making the most significant contributions to theory-building research published in these journals are identified.

WHAT IS THEORY?

Volumes discussing theory and theory development fill libraries at countless institutions of learning, and it is well beyond the scope of this chapter to do little more than explain how "theory" as a concept has been used in preceding self-examinations of the public relations academy and how it was operationalized for the purposes of this study.

In reviewing academic literature about theory, it is striking that animal similes are used often to describe theory and development of ways of thinking, or paradigms, and the sets of theoretical and methodological axioms that come to constitute a discipline (hence the "animalistic" title of this chapter and the 2003 article similarly titled). For instance, Causey (1977) likened "a good, general theory" to the torso of an octopus, with "auxiliary hypotheses . . . like tentacles" (p. 398), and suggested that when theory grows more than eight arms and spawns new auxiliary hypotheses, then theory becomes a myriapus. Ferguson (1984) likened the theory of public relations to a unicorn, and playfully characterized it as "a green one at that" (p. 28). Kavoori and Gurevitch (1993) compared the supposed fragmentation of mass communication as a discipline to a platypus, a zoological embarrassment defying classification. Discussing theories and models, Rosengren (1993) employed frog ponds for comparison. Charting problems in histories of communication studies in the United States, Robinson (1988) drew on dragons for analogy. There are so many such animalistic allusions in academic literature about theory, history, and philosophies of science that D. C. Phillips called his guide to fabled threats to—and defenses of—"naturalistic" social science *The Social Scientist's Bestiary* (1992).[*] Given that so many scholars have used animal similes to describe theory, the authors of the *From Aardvark to Zebra* works have come to think of our academic journals as arks, as in Noah's ark, the protective repository for pairs of every living theoretical creature imaginable.

Traditionally, in what Craig (1993) described as the "received view" theory has been thought to comprise a body of scientific generalizations describing functional

---

[*]A bestiary, according to *Webster's Dictionary,* is a work in verse or prose describing with an allegorical moralizing commentary the appearance and habits of real and fabled animals. This animalistic approach pervades science—even Hanson, for example, used drawings of duck-rabbits, antelope-pelicans, and the like, in which an object appears to be one thing sometimes and an entirely different thing other times, to test sensory core theory (Suppe, 1977a).

relationships among empirically measured or inferred variables. The goals of scientific theory traditionally have been description, explanation, understanding, prediction, and control of phenomena. Communication researchers have been encouraged to build "theories of the middle-range," those that would yield hypotheses about a "delimited range of phenomena" that could be rigorously tested (p. 27). These middle-range theories were thought to be superior to speculative "grand theories" and to "isolated empirical generalizations," such as those concerning effects of fear appeals on attitude change. Popper (1959) had taught scholars that *falsifiability* is the sine qua non of scientific theory and that "speculative grand theories inherently lacked this essential quality" (p. 67). Likewise, isolated empirical generalizations or "sets of laws" were inferior to "conceptually integrated" middle-range theories because they lacked "organizing and heuristic advantages" (Craig, 1993, p. 27).

Following Kuhn's (1970) postpositivist history and philosophy of science, communication science was thought to be in a "preparadigmatic state" in search of a paradigm (Craig, 1993, p. 27). Judging by many predominant publications about communication science and current communication theory textbooks, this received view continues to dominate, and communication scholars and students alike continue to define theory largely in the traditional terms, as Craig (1993) discussed them above. However, the assumption implicit in the writings of Kuhn and others that theories are "deep conceptual systems that provide a *Weltanschauung*,* or perspective for viewing the world" (Suppe, 1977a, p. 114), has been called into question. Given that an individual's whole background, including "training, experience, knowledge, beliefs, and intellectual profile," can be relevant in "working with a theory," it becomes "exceedingly doubtful" whether a *Weltanschauung* can be the "joint possession" of a group of scientists, as required by Kuhn, according to Suppe (p. 218). Rather, it is more likely that groups of scientists in a particular community share the same or similar language (p. 220). This seems true of the public relations academy. For example, we presume most of its members, asked to free associate "excellence theory," would think "James Grunig."

Additionally, because of increasing interdisciplinary discourse such as that stimulated by postmodernism, deconstruction, critical/cultural, and other influences, Craig (1993) argues the humanities have "mounted a serious challenge to received notions of scientific theory" (p. 29). In what he attributes to a "rhetorical turn" (Simons, 1990), Craig suggests theory can be conceived as practical, historically situated discourse. Such theory-as-discourse poses a challenge to epistemological criteria, such as falsifiability to the theory-as-knowledge received view. This theory-as-discourse may make the traditional vocabulary of scientific theory construction "irrelevant" to the new forms of theory. Craig further asserts, "However much one may like or dislike this situation, to ignore or deny it can only serve to worsen our present state of confusion about theory" (p. 29).

Certainly the received view—and Kuhn's (1970) history and philosophy— guided Ferguson's (1984) research, which our 2003 work and this present study

---

*This linguistic-conceptual approach to the philosophy of science is thought to be heir to the traditions of Nietzsche, Peirce, Lewis, and Quine in a neo-Kantian pragmatism (Suppe, 1977a, pp. 126–127).

replicates and extends. Ferguson worked from the assumption that theory is "not an explanation based on supposition or conjecture" but that theory is "a way to understand events and to predict research findings supporting the theory" (p. 2). She argued that practitioners who question the value of theory in practice have two choices: make decisions based on intuition or conjecture, or make decisions based on generalizations culled from empirical evidence. Generalizations useful to public relations can come from many different fields and bodies of knowledge, she suggested.

Ferguson (1984) acknowledged that some critics of public relations question whether the field was worthy of scholarship and theory-building efforts, and that other critics charge that public relations merely *applied* theories developed in and by other disciplines. Ferguson, influenced by Kuhn (1970), argued that a paradigm focus in public relations research would "greatly enhance" the probability of productive theory development (Ferguson, 1984, p. 1) and would be "essential" for public relations research (or, for that matter, any other academic discipline) to be called a science (p. 6), and, she argued, without a paradigm focus "there may be such activity we call research in public relations but there will not be much theory development" (p. ii).

Kuhn's (1970) work, including his ideas about paradigms and use of that term, which he clarified somewhat through notions of "exemplars" and "disciplinary matrixes," has been roundly criticized.* However, since arguments about paradigms, how they come to be and their usefulness, are beyond the scope of this chapter, they will be set aside.

ASSUMPTIONS OF THE PRESENT RESEARCH ABOUT THEORY

Drawing from Causey (1977) and as in our 2003 study, the present research assumes: that theory involves generalizations culled from empirical evidence; that these generalizations help us describe, explain, understand, and predict phenomena under study; that hypotheses derived from theories can be tested; that testing of hypotheses may result in the identification of relevant variables or attributes and the development of models of relationships between or among these variables; and that theory may determine its own and new applications.

Our work also assumes, as did Ferguson (1984), that theory can be flexible in terms of potential methodologies and units of analysis used to test it. Following Craig's (1993) ideas, it is assumed new theories do not necessarily have to be bound to the traditions of the received view of science.

As Suppe (1977a) suggested, theories are assumed to be interpreted symbolic generalizations. Different interpretations of these symbolic generalizations

---

*For an excellent review of the history and philosophy of theory in science and the social sciences, including criticisms and defenses of Kuhn, see F. Suppe's (1977b) *The Structure of Scientific Theories* (2nd edition), an outgrowth of the symposium by the same title of 1,200 scholars held at the University of Illinois in 1969.

are likely to stimulate a proliferation of theories, and different members of a scientific community are likely to formulate and employ different but possibly related theories, so that there is no one theory that is the "common possession of the community" (p. 144), nor is there one shared worldview from which theory derives, although similar language pertaining to theory might be shared. Theories are assumed to be dynamic, growing entities that cannot be fully understood if they are divorced from the dynamics of their developments. No distinctions are made here between normative, positive, or other "kinds" of theories, for such contemplations are beyond the focus of this work. (For excellent discussions of normative, positive, and other models of theory in public relations, see, for example, Curtin & Boynton, 2001; Grunig, 2001; Grunig & Grunig, 1990; Heath, 2001; and Leeper, 2001.) And, finally, theories and theory development are assumed in the present work to be desirable in an academic discipline, specifically public relations.

FERGUSON'S RESEARCH FURTHER REVIEWED

There have been a fair number of introspective investigations of the public relations academy ranging from analyses of gaps in the body of knowledge (McElreath & Blamphin, 1994; Synnott & McKie, 1997) and of citations and differences in research agendas between journals (see, for example, Broom, Cox, Krueger, & Liebler, 1989; Pasadeos & Renfro, 1992; and Pasadeos, Renfro, & Hanily, 1999). However, the first scholar to study general theory development in the field was M. A. Ferguson. To investigate the main foci or themes in public relations research, Ferguson (1984) conducted content analysis of 171 abstracts and/or articles published in *Public Relations Review* over a ten-year span. At the time Ferguson conducted her analysis, *Public Relations Review* was the only academic journal being published about public relations; Ferguson's analysis covered articles published from the journal's inception—volume 1, issue 1—in 1975 and into 1984—through volume 10, issue 2. Ferguson concluded from her analysis that there were three overall foci of research conducted in public relations from 1975 to 1984 that lent themselves to productive theory development: social responsibility and ethics, social issues and issues management, and public relationships. She predicted that the area of public relationships offered the best opportunity for theory development in public relations for the following reasons:

1. By putting the research focus on relationships rather than on the organization or on the public, researchers can come to better understandings of what is important about these relationships, both to the public and to the organization. In a relationship-centric model, the relationship is assumed to be the prime issue of concern, not the parties involved.

2. This type of focus at the macrolevel should result in new methodologies with which to study the phenomenon of public relationships. To study relationships rather than organizations or groups, different units of analysis will be needed.

3. Focusing public relations scholars' concerns on public relationships should create a niche or domain for the field's research efforts. Students of public relationships should all come to share similar assumptions and knowledge.

4. Including the organization and the public in new models along with communication variables should allow integration of findings from many fields to aid in understandings of public relationships.

5. Theories that focus on the relationship as the unit of analysis can be as broad or as narrow as the researcher desires.

6. A research paradigm focus that comes to understand the study of public relations as the study of relationships between organizations and publics will do as much to "legitimize" the field of public relations as have past efforts at defining the field in terms of the activities of those who practice it (Ferguson, 1984, pp. 25–26).

In sum, Ferguson's recommendations represented a potential area for theory development in public relations that she predicted would serve to unify a variety of research methods, constructs, and applications under an overall focus of organization-public relationships.

A RELATIONAL THEORY OF PUBLIC RELATIONS

Since Ferguson's recommendations, several researchers have tested and extended concepts associated with adopting a relational theory approach to public relations research; our 2003 study and this present research are tangible results of Ferguson's prediction. For example, in a discussion of the roles of "image" and "substance" in public relations, J. Grunig (1993) cited Ferguson's identification of attributes of relationships that researchers can use to define and measure organization-public relationships: their dynamic nature; the level of openness; the degree of satisfaction for both parties; the power distribution; and the extent of mutuality of understanding, agreement, and consensus. To this list, J. Grunig recommended adding two additional relational concepts: "trust and credibility" and "the concept of reciprocity" (p. 135). J. Grunig distinguished between symbolic relationships, which he described as a focus on image, and behavioral relationships, or "the actual interaction between an organization and its publics" (p. 123). He concluded:

> For public relations to be valued by the organizations it serves, practitioners must be able to demonstrate that their efforts contribute to the goals of these organizations by building long-term behavioral relationships with strategic publics . . . [and] must strive to build linkages between the two sets of relationships [symbolic and behavioral] if their work is to make organizations more effective. (p. 136)

Also building on Ferguson's (1984) assertions regarding the potential for organization-public relationships as a theoretical focus in public relations research, Broom, Casey, and Ritchey (1997) proposed a model for constructing such a theory, including specific variables that may impact these relationships as either antecedent conditions or consequences. Broom, Casey, and Richards (1997) pointed to other research fields, such as interpersonal communication, psychotherapy, organizational communication, and systems theory in developing their conclusions and recommendations. Broom and colleagues proposed a concept of relationships as involving properties of exchanges, transactions, communications, and "other interconnected activities." They identified "antecedent conditions" of organization-public relationships, including social and cultural norms, collective perceptions and expectations, needs for resources, perceptions of an uncertain environment, and legal/ voluntary necessity. Finally, "consequences" of organization-public relationships included goal achievement, dependency/loss of autonomy, and routine and institutionalized behavior. Broom and colleagues called for further explication conceptually of organization-public relationships and development of empirical descriptions and measurements of organization-public relationships.

Several researchers have successfully expanded and tested Broom and colleagues' (1997) recommendations for an organization-public relationship approach to theory-building and research in public relations. Kent and Taylor (1998) studied use of the World Wide Web in public relations practice and proposed dialogic communication as a theoretical framework to guide relationship building between organizations and publics, and they offered several strategies for practitioners to create dialogic relationships via the Internet to build relationships with publics. After publishing several journal articles, Ledingham and Bruning published their book, *Public Relations as Relationship Management* (2000), which included the development and testing of a scale to measure organization-public relationships. Taylor (2000) proposed a public relations approach to nation building based on Broom and colleagues' (1997) relationship-building processes. Taylor found that nation building requires two levels of relationships: those between individuals and those between individuals and government. Such relationships can be fostered through communication and must be negotiated in social contexts.

These are only a few examples of how public relationships became a focus of research in the field through 2000. Several scholars have examined scholarly productivity in public relations to better understand the field.

INTROSPECTIVE INVESTIGATIONS OF PUBLIC RELATIONS ACADEMY REVIEWED

An analysis of publishing activity provides evidence by which disciplines are often judged. Cole and Bowers (1973) contend that published scholarly journal activity exposes ideas to "cleansing" evaluations and criticism by colleagues and provides an objective measurement of research in the field of mass communication. Studies providing a description of article activity measure contributions of certain disciplines to the discovery, dissemination, and verification of knowledge (Soley & Reid, 1983, 1988).

As previously mentioned, there have been a fair number of introspective investigations of the public relations academy. J. Grunig and Hickson (1976) surveyed the literature in several disciplines to identify theoretical concepts useful in research on organizational communication and public relations. They concluded that most research related to public relations was being conducted by scholars in other fields and that little research—much less "theorizing"—was being done by researchers in public relations.

In an update on the status of public relations research at the 1978 Association for Education in Journalism annual conference, J. Grunig acknowledged an increase in research-based articles in *Public Relations Review,* but expressed discouragement with scholarship available to his students. He pronounced the status of public relations research as "not good" (J. Grunig, 1978, p. 22). Several others at that conference debated the differences between academic versus applied research, with J. Grunig and Lindenmann calling for more theory-based research (Broom, Cox, Krueger, & Liebler, 1989). J. Grunig expounded on his frustrations in a an article in *Public Relations Review,* titled "The Two Worlds of PR Research" (J. Grunig, 1979). Several others who spoke at the conference, including J. Tirone and S. Cutlip, voiced their perspectives in the same first issue of volume 5 of *Public Relations Review.*

Broom, Cox, Krueger, and Liebler (1989) compared the content of *Public Relations Review,* volumes 1 through 8, and *Public Relations Journal* during the same period, volumes 31 through 38. They found that the dominant content of *Public Relations Review* concerned analyses of the profession, while *Public Relations Journal* content was more often concerned with the process of how practitioners work day-by-day. Broom and colleagues concluded that in focusing on introspection about the profession, *Public Relations Review* offered "relatively little cross-situational, theory-building research that adds to the systematic body of knowledge on which the practice is based" (p. 154).

Pasadeos and Renfro (1992) conducted a bibliometric citation analysis of articles concerning public relations in *Journalism Quarterly, Public Relations Review, Public Relations Research and Education,* and *Public Relations Research Annual* from 1975 through 1989. After analyzing sources of citations made in the articles, the authors concluded that public relations had matured rapidly. In the early years, most citations were to the social sciences and other fields; later public relations scholars were citing each other, indicating a coalescing around a body of knowledge. There was also a dramatic increase in the number of educator-authors and relative decrease in the number of practitioners contributing to scholarly public relations literature.

Pasadeos, Renfro, and Hanily (1999) updated their earlier study by examining all articles published from 1990 through 1995 in *Public Relations Review, Journal of Public Relations Research,* and *Journalism Quarterly/Journalism and Mass Communication Quarterly.* They found that J. E. Grunig was by far the most-cited scholar, that *Managing Public Relations* (Grunig & Hunt, 1984) was the most-cited work, and public relations roles was the most-cited content category. They concluded that public relations would benefit from "a certain amount of paradigmatic or topical diversity in the future" (Pasadeos, Renfro & Hardy 1999, p. 48).

In the 1980s and 1990s McElreath conducted a series of Delphi studies involving dozens of leading scholars and practitioners to identify contemporary priority research questions in public relations. McElreath and Blamphin (1994) used their Delphi panel to identify gaps in the Public Relations Society of America's (PRSA) Body of knowledge. They concluded that more sophisticated theories are available to understand the managing of public relations and should be used. They called for more development in systems-based contingency and situational theories, symbolic interaction theories, legal and public policy issues, feminist concepts of equity and nurturing, ethics, conflict resolution, and multicultural general systems theories among increasingly differentiated publics.

Morton and Lin (1995) conducted a content and citation analysis of *Public Relations Review* from 1975 through 1993 to investigate if research methods, types of statistical analyses used, and topics affected citation of published research by others. Quantitative research was cited more often than qualitative. Professional topics were most often cited, followed by management topics and technical topics, although "professional topic" research was also the most often published, followed by research with management and technical topics, respectively.

Our study (Sallot, Lyon, Acosta-Alzuru, & Jones, 2003) took the longest overview, analyzing 748 articles published in the three major public relations journals from 1984 through 2000 for thematic content. The details of our findings are reported in our article in *Journal of Public Relations Research* and are recapped in the tables in this chapter's results section and in the discussion. The next section presents some background about the journals under study.

PUBLIC RELATIONS ACADEMIC JOURNALS

Three academic journals with refereed content relevant to public relations have made substantial contributions to the field and were the focus of our 2003 study.[*] *Public Relations Review* published twenty-six volumes of four issues a year from 1975 to 2000, and continued to do so from 2001 to 2003. When it published volume 1, number 1 in summer 1995, *Public Relations Review* stated in an introductory note ("Why a New Journal," 1975) its purpose was "to build a bridge between the worlds of social and behavioral science and communication research and the world of professional public relations" by translating and interpreting the findings of "the scientists" so they can be applied by the practitioner (p. 3). Its notice to contributors called for original research or commentary on existing research or needs for future research, but stressing applied research. Articles were to reflect high standards of scholarship as well as practical applications to public relations. Its inaugural chairman and editor was R. E. Hiebert, then dean of the College of Journalism at the University of Maryland, home to the new journal.

Hiebert has remained editor throughout all of *Public Relations Review*'s volumes; for a few years its associate editor was J. E. Grunig, who would go on to

---

[*]A journal titled *Public Relations Research and Education* (*PRR & E*) was published briefly by the public relations division of the Association for Education in Journalism and Mass Communication in 1984 and 1985. Its editor was James E. Grunig. *PRR & E* was not included in our 2003 study.

be the founding co-editor, along with L. S. Grunig, of the other two journals analyzed in our study. *Public Relations Review* was initially funded by the Foundation
for Public Relations Research and Education, and the University of Maryland was
its publisher. In 1979, Communication Research Associates Inc. became publisher.
In 1990, Hiebert was honored with the National Communication Association's PR
Division's Pride Award for editing *Public Relations Review.* In spring 1991, JAI Press
became publisher. In 1999, Pergamon, a division of Elsevier Science Inc., became
publisher, and *Public Relations Review* began emphasizing international practice.
Since its fourth issue in its first year, *Public Relations Review* has published an
annual bibliography, often as a part of the journal, but for some years and currently it has been and is published separately.* Our present study extends our
analysis from volume 27 to 29.

Public Relations Research Annual published only three volumes in 1989–1991.
The editors noted in their preface to the first volume (J. Grunig & L. Grunig, 1989)
that the purpose of the annual was to publish original academic research on public
relations or in-depth reviews of such research, with a view toward building theory
in the field. Its intended audience was "innovative" teachers, practitioners, and
researchers, and the journal had no intent to "compete" with the "many" trade publications and semischolarly journals already in the field (pp. ix–x). The journal was
sponsored/nominally "published" by the Public Relations Division of the Association
for Education in Journalism and Mass Communication and was published/produced
by Lawrence Erlbaum Associates Inc. of Hillsdale, New Jersey. Our present study
includes brief recaps of our 2003 findings about the journal only for comparison in
tables in this chapter's results section and in the discussion section.

Journal of Public Relations Research, an extension of *Public Relations Research
Annual,* began publishing four issues a year beginning with its first volume, numbered "4" in 1992, and published nine volumes through 2000. The founding edi-
tors, J. and L. Grunig, continued their editorship from the *Annual,* and AEJMC/
Erlbaum continued as sponsor/publisher/producer. In 1995, E. L. Toth of Syra-
cuse University became editor, and in 1999 she expanded the number of pages in
each issue to accommodate more and/or longer articles (Toth, 1999). In 2001,
L. C. Hon of the University of Florida became editor of *Journal of Public Relations
Research.* Our present study extends our analysis to cover volumes 13–15, which
Hon edited.

Research Questions Revisited

Only new analyses of the academic literature can answer with any confidence the
primary research question of the present study, which is "As we enter the twenty-
first century, what is the status of theory building by public relations scholars in
their academic field?" Secondary research questions concern how the journals are
serving theory building and identification of leading theory builders into the new
millennium.

---

*The bibliographies of *Public Relations Review* were not included in data analyzed in this study.

Method

As in our 2003 study, an informal, descriptive method was deemed most appropriate for our research presented in this chapter. Instead of testing preconceived hypotheses, a descriptive approach permitted the researchers to obtain a more comprehensive understanding of the topic at hand (Hon, 1997). Krippendorff (1980) justified the importance of descriptive aims in content analysis studies. While such studies are presented as factual, they are most meaningful when placed in the context of the problem that makes it significant. The primary goal of the present research is to better understand the breadth and scope of public relations scholarship, and the role that theory development plays in that scholarship.

The present study extends our 2003 research and consists of content analysis of all articles published in *Public Relations Review* from volume 27, number 1 (spring 2001) through volume 29, number 4 (November 2003)[*], as well as all articles in *Journal of Public Relations Research* from volume 13, number 1 (2001) through volume 15, number 4 (2003). While these journals are not a complete representation of public relations scholarship, their contents are assumed to be representative of the foci of public relations scholarship, both past and present.

Analysis began by using the same classification system we used in 2003 that had been developed by Ferguson (1984). We read the titles, abstracts, and/or articles, then arranged them into three primary classifications that had emerged in the previous studies: articles that were *introspective*, articles that related to the *practice or application of public relations*, and articles that involved *theory development in public relations*. We further placed the articles into several subcategories. While we used the classes and subcategories from our 2003 work, we also allowed others to emerge.

The unit of analysis was the title and abstract and/or article. In many cases, abstracts include the article's purpose, theoretical stance, method(s), findings, and implications. This information was often adequate to classify the article. In some cases where there was no abstract, or where the abstract was ambiguous or insufficient with regard to the article's relationship with theory, we then analyzed the articles. An article was placed in the *theory development* primary class when it: (a) attempted to conceptualize or reconceptualize public relations; (b) assessed the usefulness of a particular theory; (c) "fine-tuned" a theory through presenting or reviewing empirical evidence; or (d) developed a new perspective that helps describe, explain, understand, or predict the practice of public relations.

There were four coders in all: the authors of the 2003 article and of this chapter. All of us are public relations faculty holding doctoral degrees in mass communication with emphasis in public relations; all are conversant with public relations academic literature. Each title and abstract/article was read and coded as belonging to the most appropriate main class and subcategory, using our 2003 categorization system as a guide but, as coding progressed, letting new categories

---

[*]With volume 28, number 1, *Public Relations Review* changed its titling from seasons to months.

emerge as warranted. Each unit was coded into only one category[*]; side notes were made suggesting possible alternative categories for any units thought by coders to belong to multiple classes or subcategories. Also, when a coder did not see an appropriate existing category, she noted a recommended classification. These notes regarding possible alternative or new categorizations were considered by all fours coders in a group discussion to a check for goodness of fit, with special attention given to suggested alternate or new categories that had emerged; several new categories were adopted.

Coders again reviewed articles for which they disagreed on categorization and tried to resolve their disagreements, each coder noting her justification in writing for discussion purposes. Finally, after discussion, a summary of coding disagreements was created. After this final round of coding had been completed, descriptive results were compiled in a table, Appendix A (see pages 375–386). It is important to reiterate that this exhaustive coding process was created and implemented to obtain a descriptive overview of the scholarship in the field of public relations.

To investigate the secondary research questions about content in the individual journals and authorship, all articles listed in Appendix A were numerically coded by the following criteria: the journal in which they were published; thematic content category to which they were assigned; year, volume, and issue in which they were published; number of pages of the article; number of authors of the article; and who were sole, lead, second, third, and fourth authors of the articles analyzed. The data were then subjected to various statistical analyses.

Results

In total, 130 titles, abstracts, and/or articles were analyzed (see Appendix A for themed categorizations by titles of articles). In all, there was unanimous agreement among the coders on initial categorizations for 120 (92.3 percent) of the articles. After discussion, nine articles (6.9 percent) were agreed on by all four coders or three out of four coders; majority ruled in the few instances that were not unanimous categorizations. Only one article (.8 percent) resulted in split (2 to 2) votes. Therefore, intercoder reliability was .92.[†] Table 20.1 summarizes the subcategories for each of the three primary classes 2001–2003—introspective, practice/application, and theory development—and, for informal comparison, also presents the classifications frequencies of the 748 articles analyzed through 2000.

Introspective Articles.   Of the 130 articles reviewed in the present study, thirty-six (26.4 percent) were placed into the introspective class—the second highest

---

[*]The authors acknowledge that the categories are not mutually exclusive. Articles were classified according to the coders' assessment of the article's predominant aim.

[†]Cohen's kappa, which corrects for the number of categories used and also for the probable frequency of use when there are more than two coders, was used to calculate inter-coder reliability (Wimmer & Dominick, 2003).

TABLE 20.1   Categorization of articles by primary classes and subcategories

	THROUGH 2000		2001–2003	
	N	%	N	%
CLASS I: INTROSPECTIVE				
Introspective: Pedagogy/Education in PR	70		16	
Introspective: Ethics and Social Responsibility	69		1	
Introspective: This History of PR	59		9	
Introspective: The Profession of PR	36		1	
Introspective: Women and Minorities	35		-	
Introspective: International PR Practices	18		5	
Introspective: Scholarly Research	5		1	
Introspective: Image/Reputation/Impression Management	3		2	
Introspective: Professional Development for Educators (New Category)	-		1	
Total	295	40.2	36	26.4
CLASS II: PRACTICE/APPLICATION OF PUBLIC RELATIONS				
Practice/Application of PR: Implementing/Evaluating PR Programs and Campaigns	92		4	
Practice/Application of PR: Ethics and Social Responsibility	51		-	
Practice/Application of PR: Applied Research Issues and Methodologies	32		1	
Practice/Application of PR: Organizational Communication	26		-	
Practice/Application of PR: Management in PR/Decision Making/Problem Solving	23		-	
Practice/Application of PR: Crisis Response/Communication	22		5	
Practice/Application of PR: New Communication Technologies	21		6	
Practice/Application of PR: Legal Issues	16		1	
Practice/Application of PR: Integrated Marketing Communications	6		-	
Practice/Application of PR: Ethics in Practice	1		-	
Practice/Application of PR: Image/Reputation/Impression Management	1		1	
Practice/Application of PR: International PR (New Category)	-		3	
Total	291	39.6	21	15.4
CLASS III: THEORY DEVELOPMENT IN PUBLIC RELATIONS				
Theory Development: Excellence Theory/Symmetrical Communication/Grunig's Model				
Theory Development: Public Relationships/Relational Theory	19		1	

(*Continued*)

Theory Development: Crisis Response Theory	14	9	
Theory Development: Critical/Cultural	14	9	
Theory Development: Ethics/Social Responsibility	11	-	
Theory Development: Academic Versus Applied	11	-	
Research	10	-	
Theory Development: Situational/Publics Theory	9	1	
Theory Development: Women's Studies/Feminist			
School/Gender/Diversity/Minority	9	4	
Theory Development: Organizational Communication	9	1	
Theory Development: International Public Relations	8	11	
Theory Development: Role Theory/Models	7	2	
Theory Development: Rhetorical Underpinnings	6	4	
Theory Development: Public Opinion/Persuasion	5	4	
Theory Development: Fund-Raising	4	1	
Theory Development: Risk Communication	4	3	
Theory Development: Social Issues and Issues			
Management	4	2	
Theory Development: Contingency Theory	2	1	
Theory Development: Complexity Theory	1	-	
Theory Development: General Social Science Theory	1	-	
Theory Development: Agenda Setting/Building/			
Framing (New Category)	-	4	
Theory Development: Reputation Management			
(New Category)	-	2	
Theory Development: Concept of Practice			
(New Category)	-	1	
Theory Development: Health Communication	-	3	
Theory Development: Rumor Theory (New Category)	-	1	
Theory Development: Dialogic Theory (New Category)	-	1	
Theory Development: Post Modernism	-	3	
Theory Development: Cognitive Theory (New Category)	-	1	
Total	148	20.2	69	50.7

number of titles in the three classes. The eight subcategories used in this class in this study, listed here in descending order of frequency counts, were: (a) sixteen titles in pedagogy/education in public relations; (b) nine in history of public relations; (c) five in international public relations; (d) two in image/reputation/impression management; (e) one in ethics and social responsibility; (f) one in the profession of public relations; (g) one in scholarly research about academic research; and (h), one in "professional development for educators," a new subcategory that emerged in the introspection class. There were no titles in the "women and minorities" subcategory.

Practice/Application Articles.   The practice/application of public relations class had twenty-one articles (15.4 percent), the least number of titles in the three classes.

The seven subcategories occurring in this class in this study, listed here in descending order of frequency counts, were: (a) six titles in new communication technologies; (b) five in crisis communication and response; (c) four in implementing/evaluating public relations programs and campaigns; (d) four in applied research issues and methodologies; (e) three in a subcategory new to this study, "international public relations"; (f) one in legal issues; and (g) one in image/reputation/impression management. There were no titles in the following subcategories: social issues/issues management, organizational communication, management in public relations, integrated marketing communications, and ethics in practice.

Theory Development Articles.   A total of sixty-nine titles (50.7 percent) were placed in theory development, the most in any class. The twenty-two subcategories occurring in this study, listed here in descending order of frequency counts, were: (a) eleven titles in international public relations; (b) nine in public relationships; (c) nine in crisis response theory; (d) four in women's studies/feminist school/gender/diversity/minority theories; (e) four in rhetorical underpinnings; (f) four in public opinion/persuasion; (g) four in a new subcategory, agenda setting/ building/framing; (h) three in risk communication; (i) three in a new category, health communication; (j) three in a new category, postmodernism; (k) two in role theory/models; (l) two in social issues and issues management; (m) two in a new category, reputation management; (n) one in excellence theory/symmetrical communication/J. Grunig's models; (o) one in situational theory; (p) one in organizational communication; (q) one in fund-raising; (r) one in contingency theory; and four additional new subcategories with 1 title each: (s) concept of practice, (t) rumor theory, (u) dialogic theory, and, (v) cognitive theory. There were a total of eight new subcategories in the theory development class. However, there were no titles in the following subcategories designated in our previous study: critical/cultural, ethics-social responsibility, academic versus applied research, complexity theory, and general social science theory.

Articles Relating to the Publication Itself.   Three titles were placed into a fourth class of "relating to the publication itself." These titles consisted of editors' notes to readers about the journal or issue, and are listed in Appendix A under the heading "Class IV." Unless otherwise noted, these titles were not included in further analyses.

Summary of Disagreements in Coding.   The one article for which our coding was evenly split is listed in Appendix A under the heading "Class V." We were equally divided across class categorization and subcategory and, unless otherwise noted, this article was not included in further analyses.

Thematic Categorizations by Journal.   Of the remaining 126 titles of articles listed in Appendix A, ninety-one (66.9 percent) were published in *Public Relations Review* and thirty-five (26.4 percent) were published in *Journal of Public Relations Research.* The most articles, forty-three, were published in both journals combined in the year 2001, with forty-two articles published in both journals in each of

2002 and 2003. *Public Relations Review* published thirty-one articles in 2001, and thirty articles in 2002 and 2003. *Journal of Public Relations Research* published twelve articles in 2001 and 2002, and eleven in 2003. The lengthiest article had sixty-four pages, which appeared in *Journal of Public Relations Research,* compared with sixty-two pages in the previous study. The average length of articles published was 17.8 pages, compared with 13.6 pages in the previous study. In a one-way ANOVA, article length between the two journals was significantly different (F = [1, 127] 123.02, p < .0001). Articles in *Public Relations Review* averaged 13.8 pages while articles in *Journal of Public Relations Research* averaged 17.8 pages.

A chi-square test of expected frequencies of the three major thematic classifications—introspective, practical/applied, and theory—by the two journals' content in 2001–2003 was significant (X^2[2, N = 126] = 18.8, p < .0003).[*] Results are summarized in Table 20.2, which also presents the classifications frequencies of the 748 articles analyzed through 2000 for comparison.

Because of sheer volume, more articles in all three classes were published in *Public Relations Review* in 2001–2003, which also published proportionally more articles in the introspective and practical/applied categories. However, proportionally more theory articles were published in *Journal of Public Relations Research* in 2001–2003, which was also the case in our previous study analyzing articles published through 2000. A chi-square analysis of the combined data sets, including all articles published in *Public Relations Review* and *Journal of Public Relations Research* through 2003 (articles published in *Public Relations Research Annual* were omitted from this test of the combined data sets), was significant (X^2[2, N = 830] = 86.1, p < .0001).

Results of cross-tab analyses of the thematic class-subcategory categorizations of the 126 titles in the Appendix A by journal are reported in Tables 20.3–20.5, which also present the classifications frequencies of the 748 articles analyzed through 2000 for comparison (percentages may not sum to 100 because of rounding). Of the thirty-six titles categorized as introspective, thirty-three (91.7 percent) were published in *Public Relations Review* (see Table 20.3).

The most frequent subcategories were sixteen in pedagogy/education in public relations, four in international public relations, two in image/reputation management, and one each in the profession of public relations, ethics/social responsibility, and professional development for educators. Only three articles categorized as introspective appeared in *Journal of Public Relations Research.* They were in the subcategories history of public relations, international public relations, and scholarly research about the profession.

Of the twenty-one articles classified as practice/application of public relations, nineteen (90.5 percent) were published in *Public Relations Review* (see Table 20.4).

The most frequent subcategories were six in new communication technologies, five in crisis response and communication, three each in implementing programs/campaigns and international public relations, and one each in applied

---

[*]The Introspective and the Practical/Applied articles cells for the *Journal of Public Relations Research* 2001–2003 have fewer than five cases, a violation of chi-square assumptions.

TABLE 20.2 Results of chi-square analyses of thematic classes by journal through 2000 compared with 2001–2003

CATEGORY	PR REVIEW THROUGH 2000		PR RESEARCH ANNUAL THROUGH 2000		JOURNAL OF PR RESEARCH THROUGH 2000		TOTAL THROUGH 2000		PR REVIEW 2001–2003		JOURNAL OF PR RESEARCH 2001–2003		TOTAL 2001–2003	
	N	%	N	%	N	%	N	%	N	%	N	%	N	%
Introspective	264		3		28		295	40.2	33		3		36	25.6
Practical/ Applied	243		12		36		291	39.6	19		2		21	16.2
Theory	83		15		50		148	20.2	39		30		69	53.1
Total	590	80.4	30	4.1	114	15.5	734	100.0	91	66.9	35	26.4	126	100.0

*One cell in the "through 2000" analysis has fewer than five cases, a violation of chi-square assumptions. Likewise, two cells in the "2001–2003" analysis have fewer than five cases. Classes IV and V were omitted in each analysis.

*Note: Percentages may not sum to 100 because of rounding.

TABLE 20.3 Introspective class subcategories by journal: Comparing articles published "through 2000" with articles published "2001–2003"

CATEGORY	PR REVIEW THROUGH 2000		PR RESEARCH ANNUAL THROUGH 2000		JOURNAL OF PR RESEARCH THROUGH 2000		PR REVIEW 2001–2003		JOURNAL OF PR RESEARCH 2001–2003	
	N	%	N	%	N	%	N	%	N	%
Pedagogy/Education	67	25.30	-	-	2	.07	16	12.40	-	-
The Profession of PR	60	22.70	3	1.00	7	25.00	1	.08	-	-
History of PR	54	20.50	-	-	-	-	-	-	1	.08
Ethics/ Social Responsibility	33	12.50	-	-	2	.07	1	.08	-	-
International PR	32	12.10	-	-	4	14.30	4	3.20	1	.08
Women/Minorities	14	5.30	-	-	4	14.30	-	-	-	-
Scholarly Research	3	1.10	-	-	2	.07	-	-	1	.08
Image/Reputation Management	1	.04	-	-	2	.07	2	1.60	-	-
Professional Dev't For Educators*	-	-	-	-	-	-	1	.08	-	-
Total	264	89.50	3	1.00	28	9.50	33	91.0	3	8.30

*Denotes new category for "2001–2003"

Note: Percentages may not sum to 100 because of rounding.

TABLE 20.4 Practice/application class subcategories by journal: Comparing articles published "through 2000" with articles published "2001–2003"

CATEGORY	PR REVIEW THROUGH 2000		PR RESEARCH ANNUAL THROUGH 2000		JOURNAL OF PR RESEARCH THROUGH 2000		PR REVIEW 2001–2003		JOURNAL OF PR RESEARCH 2001–2003	
	N	%	N	%	N	%	N	%	N	%
Implementing Programs/Campaigns	75	30.9	2	16.6	15	41.7	3	2.3	1	.8
Social Issues/Issues Management	41	16.9	3	25.0	7	19.4	-	-	-	-
Applied Research Issues/Methodologies	30	12.3	1	8.3	1	2.7	1	.8	-	-
Crisis Response/Communication	22	9.1	-	-	-	-	5	3.9	-	-
New Communication Technologies	19	7.8	-	-	2	5.5	6	4.7	-	-
Management in PR	18	7.4	1	8.3	4	11.1	-	-	-	-
Organizational Comm.	17	7.0	4	33.3	5	13.9	-	-	-	-
Legal Issues	15	6.1	-	-	1	2.7	-	-	1	.8
Integrated Marketing Communications	5	2.1	-	-	1	2.7	-	-	-	-
Image/Reputation/Impression Management	-	-	-	-	1	2.7	1	.8	-	-
Ethics (in practice)	1	.4	-	-	-	-	-	-	-	-
International PR*	-	-	-	-	-	-	3	2.3	-	-
Total	243	83.5	12	4.1	36	12.4	19	90.5	2	9.5

*Denotes new category for "2001–2003"

Note: Percentages may not sum to 100 because of rounding.

research issues/methodologies and in image/reputation/impression management. Two articles, 9.54 percent of all articles categorized as practice/application, appeared in *Journal of Public Relations Research,* one each in implementing programs/campaigns and in legal issues.

Of the sixty-nine articles classified as theory development, eighty-three (56.1 percent) were published in *Public Relations Review* (see Table 20.5).

The most frequent subcategories were seven titles in crisis response theory, five in public relationships, three in agenda setting/building/framing, two each in rhetorical underpinnings, persuasion/public opinion, health communication, and post modernism, and one each in excellence theory, risk communication, social issues/issues management, fund-raising, reputation management, concept of practice, rumor theory, and dialogic theory.

Thirty (43.5 percent) articles classified as theory development were published in *Journal of Public Relations Research.* The most popular subcategories were four each in public relationships, international public relations, and women's-feminist/ gender/diversity theory; two each in crisis response theory, role theory/models, rhetorical underpinnings, risk communication, and persuasion/public opinion; and one each in situational theory, social issues/issues management, contingency theory, agenda setting/building/framing, reputation management, health communication, post modernism and cognitive theory.

Public Relations Review published two special theme issues, listed at the end of Appendix A. Both addressed public relations education and pedagogy, with the first published in 2001 and the other in 2002. Through 2000, *Public Relations Review* had published twenty specially themed issues on a variety of subjects and *Journal of Public Relations Research* had published one; *Journal of Public Relations Research* had not published any in 2001–2003.

Authorship in Public Relations Journals.   Of the 130 articles analyzed, including editors' notes and the one title over which the coders disagreed, seventy-nine were sole-authored, thirty-four had two authors, twelve had three authors, and five had four authors; no article had more than four authors. Thirty-four authors were credited with authorship of two or more articles in any of the three classes; their names are listed in Appendix B with an analysis of number of publications and order of authorship for each of those individuals. A total of ninety-four authors authored one or more articles in the theory development class; their names are listed in Appendix B with an analysis of number of publications and order of authorship for each of those individuals.

Prolific Authors in Public Relations Theory Development.   The most prolific authors of articles classified as theory development in the two public relations journals in 2001–2003 were, with a total of five publications, M. Taylor; with three publications each: D. Holtzhausen, M. Kent, and E. L. Toth; with two publications each: J. O'Neil, J. Park, L. Aldoory, S. Bruning, W. T. Coombs, C. Callison, B. Wrigley, P. Curtin, and R. L. Heath (see Table 20.6). The top thirteen authors of theory development articles through 2000 are also presented in Table 20.6.

TABLE 20.5 Theory development class subcategories by journal: Comparing articles published "through 2000" with articles published "2001–2003"

CATEGORY	PR REVIEW THROUGH 2000		PR RESEARCH ANNUAL THROUGH 2000		JOURNAL OF PR RESEARCH THROUGH 2000		PR REVIEW 2001–2003		JOURNAL OF PR RESEARCH 2001–2003	
	N	%	N	%	N	%	N	%	N	%
Academic vs. Applied Research	9	10.8	-	-	1	2.0	-	-	-	-
Ethics/Social Responsibility	9	10.8	2	13.3	-	-	-	-	-	-
Crisis Response Theory	8	9.6	-	-	6	12.0	7	5.6	2	1.6
Excellence Theory/Symmetrical Comm./Grunig's Models	8	9.6	-	-	8	16.0	1	.8	-	-
Public Relationships	8	9.6	-	-	6	2.0	5	4.0	4	3.2
Critical/Cultural Theory	7	8.4	-	-	4	8.0	-	-	-	-
Organizational Comm.	5	6.0	1	6.6	3	6.0	1	.8	1	.8
Situational Theory	3	3.6	1	6.6	5	10.0	-	-	2	1.6
Role Theory/Models	5	6.0	2	13.3	-	-	-	-	2	1.6
International PR	5	6.0	1	6.6	2	4.0	7	5.6	4	3.2
Women's Studies/Feminist School/Gender/Diversity/Minorities	2	2.4	2	13.3	5	10.0	-	-	4	3.1
Rhetorical Underpinnings	4	4.8	-	-	2	4.0	2	1.6	2	1.6

	N	%	N	%	N	%	N	%	N	%
Risk Communication	-	-	1	6.6	3	6.0	1	.8	2	1.6
Social Issues/Issues Management	3	3.6	-	-	1	2.0	1	.8	1	.8
Fund Raising	2	2.4	-	-	2	4.0	1	.8	-	-
Persuasion/Public Opinion	2	2.4	2	13.3	1	2.0	2	1.6	2	1.6
Complexity Theory	1	1.2	-	-	-	-	-	-	-	-
Contingency Theory	1	1.2	-	-	1	1.2	-	-	1	.8
Social Science Theory	1	1.2	-	-	-	-	-	-	-	-
Agenda Setting/Building/Framing*	-	-	-	-	-	-	3	2.4	1	.8
Health Communication*	-	-	-	-	-	-	2	1.6	1	.8
Post Modernism*	-	-	-	-	-	-	2	1.6	1	.8
Reputation Management*	-	-	-	-	-	-	1	.8	1	.8
Concept of Practice*	-	-	-	-	-	-	1	.8	-	-
Rumor Theory*	-	-	-	-	-	-	1	.8	-	-
Dialogic Theory*	-	-	-	-	-	-	1	.8	-	-
Cognitive Theory*	-	-	-	-	-	-	-	-	1	.8
Total	83	56.1	15	10.1	50	33.8	39	56.5	30	43.5

*Denotes new category for "2001–2003"

Note: Percentages may not sum to 100 because of rounding.

TABLE 20.6 Most-published authors and frequencies of authorship of articles: Categorized as "theory development" published in *Journal of Public Relations Research* and *Public Relations Review:* Comparing "through 2000" with "2001–2003"

AUTHOR'S NAME	"THROUGH 2000" NO. SOLE AUTHORED	NO. LEAD AUTHORED	NO. SECOND AUTHORED	AUTHOR'S NAME	"2001–2003" NO. SOLE AUTHORED	NO. LEAD AUTHORED	NO. SECOND AUTHORED
James E. Grunig	6	4	1	Maureen Taylor*	-	2	3
Robert L. Heath	2	5	1	Derina Holtzhausen*	1	2	-
W. Timothy Coombs	4	2	-	Michael Kent*	-	2	1
Larissa Grunig	3	1	3	Elizabeth Toth	1	1	1
Priscilla Murphy	4	-	-	Julie O'Neil*	2	-	-
Gabriel Vasquez	3	1	-	Jongmin Park*	2	1	-
Glen Broom	2	2	-	Linda Aldoory*	1	1	-
Kathleen Kelly	3	-	1	Stephen Bruning	1	1	-
John Ledingham	1	3	1	W. Timothy Coombs	1	1	-
Elizabeth Toth	2	1	1	Coy Callison*	1	1	-
David Dozier	1	1	2	Brenda J. Wrigley*	1	1	-
Glen T. Cameron	1	-	3	Patricia Curtin*	-	1	1
Stephen Bruning	-	1	3	Robert L. Heath	-	1	1

*Denotes author new to this list "2001–2003" compared with "through 2000"

Discussion

In the past century, public relations was thought to suffer from lack of a unifying theory or even satisfactory theory development (Ferguson, 1984).* Perhaps interpreting too literally Lewin's (1951) oft-quoted observation that there is nothing so practical as a good theory, some argued that effective public relations should draw from both professional practice and theory (IPRA, 1982; Ferguson, 1984). In the 1990s, some suggested that public relations has evolved into two overlapping, sometimes conflicting branches—the applied branch and the theory-based research/scholarship branch—and as a result the field is in a paradigm struggle, perhaps sparked by new models and theories of public relations developed since the 1980s (Botan, 1993).

In Ferguson's 1984 analysis of articles published in one major journal over nearly ten years, only 4 percent contributed to theory development in public relations. In our previous analysis of articles published in the major public relations journals through 2000, we found that nearly 20 percent contributed to theory development. By comparison, our research presented in this chapter, covering articles published in the two major public relations journals in 2001–2003, we found that 51 percent contributed to theory development.

Given this finding, the answer to the primary research question of this study—"As we enter the twenty-first century, what is the status of theory building by public relations scholars?"—is a resounding: "We've more than doubled our scholarship toward building theory in the last century; it is a new millennium, thank you, after all." Happily, public relations scholars have come a *very* long way since 1984 when Ferguson noted that many scholars and professionals alike would react to the term *public relations theory* by saying, "What a quaint notion."†

It is important to note once more that this study was limited to an analysis of theory published in the academic *journals* in the field. If numerous theory-building books about public relations published in 2001–2003 had been taken into account as well, the growth in public relations' theoretical base would be seen to be even

---

*From a fascinating chautauqua in *Communication Monographs* asking, "Why are there so few communication theories?" it might be surmised that public relations' sufferance was in very good company indeed—apparently the company of the entire field of communication. Berger (1991) lamented that the communications field does not foster theory development because of lack of commerce and unity among the subgroups and risk aversions among academics and graduate students. Burleson (1992) suggested scholars need to take the field more seriously and develop a philosophy of communication. Redding (1992), resisting applied-theoretical and practical-pure dichotomies, argued that valuable theories can emerge from the applied and that descriptive quasi-theories might be useful. Likewise, Proctor (1992) noted that ties between the discipline and practical communication activities are an asset instead of a liability. Purcell (1992) noted there are plenty of theories harking back to 2,500 years of rhetorical traditions. Berger (1992) replied to all that communication theory has failed to answer very basic questions about how communication works, but that attacking some of those fundamentals will help motivate the theory development still needed to increase our understanding about communication. In concluding the chautauqua in *Journal of Communication*, Craig (1993) *asked*, "Why are there so *many* communication theories?" But he believes *more* theories are needed, not fewer.

†In the interest of full disclosure, the authors wish to report that we coded our article published in 2003, which is the predecessor of this chapter, as "Introspective: Scholarly Research."

more robust than this study suggests. All one needs to do is thumb through any of the major "mass communication" or "communication" book publishers' catalogs and bask in the rosy glow of certainty that public relations' theory building is a fit fiddle, indeed.[*]

No Dominant Paradigms.   Contrary to Ferguson's (1984) expectations, however, we again argue at the beginning of this century, as we did as the last century ended, that no dominant paradigms per se have emerged. Of articles classified as theory development in our previous work, the largest share—but still only 13 percent—was categorized as concerned with excellence theory, arguably the closest public relations has come to having a paradigm.[†] In our present analysis, of sixty-nine articles classified as contributing to theory, only one article used excellence theory as a theoretic frame.

Ferguson (1984) again proved more prescient when she predicted the potential for developing theory about public relationships. In our earlier research, public relationships accounted for nearly 10 percent of the articles in the theory development class; in this research, public relationships were the focus of nine articles, 13 percent of all theory development articles, surpassed only by international public relations with eleven articles, 16 percent of the class. The only other clear contender for dominance is crisis response theory, also nine articles (13 percent). While ethics and social responsibility accounted for nearly 8 percent of theory development in our previous research, there were no articles in that category this time. It is noteworthy that the proliferation of theory development since our earlier research drove us to add several new subcategories to the theory development class. Newcomers include agenda setting/building/framing, which garnered 5.8 percent of the theory class; health communication and post modernism, which each accounted for 4.3 percent of the theory class, followed by reputation management, concept of practice, cognitive theory, and dialogic theory (in our coding of the dialogic theory article, we thought it required a new category rather than categorizing it as "symmetrical/excellence theory"), and rumor theory. These reflect the published research only three years into the new century (see Appendix A). We expect publishing activity in all these areas, except perhaps for "rumor theory," to flourish. In our present research, several categories of theory building that we used before did not have any articles. Since this research covers only three years, it is probably too early to close the books on those categories, and no doubt new themes will arise since theory building in public relations gives

---

[*]In no particular order, a few recent books that have contributed to public relations theory include *Excellent Public Relations and Effective Organizations* (2002) by L. Grunig, J. Grunig, and D. Dozier; T. Mickey's *Deconstructing Public Relations* (2003); *The Global Public Relations Handbook* (2003), edited by K. Sriramesh and D. Vercic; *A Rhetorical Approach to Crisis Communication* (2004), edited by D. Millar and R. Heath; *Public Relations Theory II* (2006), edited by V. Hazleton and C. Botan; and this book, *Public Relations: From Theory to Practice* (2007), edited by T. L. Hansen-Horn and B. Dostal Neff.

[†]Of course, many might *still* argue that excellence theory is the dominant paradigm in public relations. Certainly, J. Grunig and colleagues have stimulated much reflection, discussion, and research in the field, and are to be commended for their contributions.

every appearance of thriving. In the spirit of Craig (1993), let a thousand flowers bloom, and the more theories, the merrier, for the more theories developed will mean the more thriving, stimulating, and vibrant our discipline will be.

Both Journals Publishing More Theory-Based Content. The secondary research questions in this study concerned more focused analysis about the "ark" repositories for our theory—"creatures"—how are these two public relations journals alike as we start the new century? How are they different? And who are the authors making the most contributions to theory building in public relations as we begin the new millennium?

In our previous research, the content of *Journal of Public Relations Research* proportionally made the greatest contributions to theory development, but *Public Relations Review* is catching up, and again it published the greater number of articles contributing to theory development. It is clear that *Public Relations Review* is publishing more theory-based research contributing to the public relations body of knowledge in recent years than it did in its earlier years. The proliferation of theory-based articles in both journals may well be because more public relations research is theory-based than ever before.

As Pasadeos, Renfro, and Hanily (1999) predicted, public relations scholarship has benefited greatly from paradigmatic, topical diversity. And when the list of research priorities identified by McElreath and Blamphin (1994) is compared with more recent scholarship, it is readily apparent that the gaps in the public relations body of knowledge are being filled with more systems-based and situational theories; more symbolic-interaction theories to explain and predict public and organizational relationships; more research about multicultural-global public relations, and crisis response theories.

Further, it is interesting that *Journal of Public Relations Research* published only three introspective articles and only two practical/application articles, while *Public Relations Review* continues to publish all the articles about new communication technologies and about pedagogy/education in the field, in part because of its two themed issues. Certainly, *Public Relations Review* can be expected to continue its new emphasis on international practice and the globalization of public relations because its editor, R. E. Hiebert, has stated such intentions (Hiebert, 2000), but international/global research also is well represented in *Journal of Public Relations Research*.

What all this theory building means to the practice of public relations falls under the category "to be further investigated." After considering how practitioners interpret, reframe, and adapt theories to practice, Cornelissen (2000) suggested a "translation model" of theory application based on the premise that scientific knowledge is seldom used in unaltered form in practice. The model is worthy of additional research in public relations.

Authors Contributing to Theory Building. For those conversant with public relations research literature over the long-term, the list of most prolific authors contributing to theory building in 2001–2003 may be a bit of a surprise. With nine new names in the baker's dozen of authors listed, compared with most prolific theory-development authors through 2000, there appears to be the beginnings of a "changing of the guard." At the start of the new millennium, authors new to this list are M. Taylor, D. Holtzhausen, M. Kent, J. O'Neil, J. Park, L. Aldoory, C. Callison, B. Wrigley, and P. Curtin. Returning authors are E. Toth, S. Bruning, W. T. Coombs, and R. L. Heath. The public relations academy owes great debts to J. Grunig and L. S. Grunig, as it does to all the distinguished scholars listed in Table 20.6 (p. 366), some of whom are concentrating their efforts on publishing books rather than journal articles at this stage in their careers. While we made no attempt to formally analyze which authors contributed to which thematic content areas, this can readily be discerned by examining the theory development class subcategorizations in Appendix A.

Improved Clarifications of Theory Implications in Publications.   In our 2003 article, we recommended to editors of journals and authors of journal articles that when publication content has a relationship with theory and/or theory development, it would be a great service to readers if the titles and abstracts as well as the articles themselves clearly reflected this. Specifically, we called for clear statements of any relationships to theory, such as: Is a particular theory used as a frame? Is a particular theory being tested? Do findings support or refute a particular theory? We were gratified to find in this analysis that relationships with theory in general were much more clear in articles published in 2001–2003 than previously.

FUTURE RESEARCH

While the present study was limited to analyzing content of *Public Relations Review* and *Journal of Public Relations Research,* it would be useful to extend the analysis to scholarly books as well as other academic journals, such as *Journalism and Mass Communication Quarterly, Journalism Monographs, Communication Yearbook, Management Communication Quarterly,* the British-based *Journal of Communication Management,* and others. We intend to pursue some of this research, and we invite others to replicate and extend our work, as we did with Ferguson's (1984) research.

A network analysis of "schools"—using that term to describe philosophic orientations as well as institutions of higher learning prominent in public relations scholarship—linking scholars and thematic content areas would also be of value. For example, it is clear the influence of the University of Maryland has dominated all journals we have analyzed to date.

And finally, a narrative story or history of the public relations journals begs to be written by some gifted historian. No doubt the stories behind the journals are more colorful than the little bit of background presented here.

CONCLUSION

From this study, it appears our "arks" of theory development in public relations are quite capable of accommodating the ever-larger passenger-cargo manifests filled with so many brilliant, beguiling breeds of theory-beasts. It is quite apparent from this update and extension of our previous research that our growing zoo—all these beguiling theoretic creatures from "aardvarks" to "zebras"—are galloping into the twenty-first century. We are indeed fortunate to have their company as they lead us on our mystical voyages into the magical realm of theory, these daring journeys we undertake to help better describe, explain, understand, and predict the world of public relations.

QUESTIONS FOR APPLICATION

1. Do you see the academic versus applied approach less as separate entities and more merged in the future? How does this merger develop from an academic perspective? How does this merger develop from a practitioner's perspective?

2. What is the usefulness of particular theories? Cite at least three theories and discuss the usefulness of each theory to public relations professionals (academics and practitioners).

3. As you review the top number of categories with articles in public relations theory development (international, public relationships, crisis response diversity, rhetorical, persuasion, and framing), what does this say about the public relations discipline? How does this suggest the strength and weakness in theory development? What suggestions do you have for further theory development?

4. As one reviews these findings covering the most recent focus on theory, what expectations do you have for theory development for the years after 2003?

5. There are many parallels to other disciplines in the development of public relations as a field of study. Reference has been made to the early reputations of medicine and law, for example. Now references relate to the similar infrastructure developed along the lines of zoology (naming of animals). Create your own system for theory development in public relations.

REFERENCES

Berger, C. R. (1991). Communication theories and other curios. *Communication Monographs, 58*(1), pp. 101–113.

———. (1992). Curiouser and curiouser curios. *Communication Monographs, 59*(1), pp. 101–107.

Botan, C. H. (1993). Introduction to the paradigm struggle in public relations. *Public Relations Review, 19*(2), pp. 107–110.

Botan, C. H., & Hazleton, V. (1989). *Public relations theory.* Hillsdale, NJ: Lawrence Erlbaum.

Broom, G. M., Casey, S., & Ritchey, J. (1997). Toward a concept and theory of organization-public relationships. *Journal of Public Relations Research, 9*(2), pp. 83–98.

Broom, G. M., Cox, M. S., Krueger, E. A., & Liebler, C. M. (1989). The gap between professional and research agendas in public relations journals. In

J. Grunig and L. Grunig (Eds.), *Public relations research annual* (Vol. 1, pp. 141–154). Hillsdale, NJ: Lawrence Erlbaum.

Bruning, S. D., & Ledingham, J. A. (1999). Relationships between organizations and publics: Development of a multi-dimensional organization-public relationship scale. *Public Relations Review, 25*(2), pp. 157–170.

Burleson, B. R. (1992). Taking communication seriously. *Communication Monographs, 59*(1), pp. 79–86.

Cancel, A. E., Cameron, G. T., Sallot, L. M., & Mitrook, M. A. (1997). It depends: A contingency theory of accommodation in public relations. *Journal of Public Relations Research, 9*(1), pp. 31–63.

Causey, R. L. (1977). Professor Bohm's view of the structure and development of theories. In F. Suppe (Ed.), *The structure of scientific theories,*

(2nd ed.), (pp. 392–419). Urbana: University of Illinois Press.

Cole, R., & Bowers, T. (1973). Research article productivity of U.S. journalism faculties. *Journalism Quarterly, 50,* pp. 246–254.

Cornelissen, J. P. (2000). Toward an understanding of the use of academic theories in public relations practice. *Public Relations Review, 26*(3), pp. 315–326.

Craig, R. T. (1993). Why are there so many communication theories? *Journal of Communication, 43*(3), pp. 26–33.

Curtin, P., & Boynton, L. (2001). Ethics in public relations: Theory and practice. In R. L. Heath (Ed.), *Handbook of public relations* (pp. 411–421). Thousand Oaks, CA: Sage.

Ferguson, M. A. (1984, August). *Building theory in public relations: Interorganizational relationships as a public relations paradigm.* Paper presented to the Public Relations Division, Association for Education in Journalism and Mass Communication Annual Convention, Gainesville, FL.

Grunig, J. E. (1978, August). *The status of public relations research.* Paper presented to the Public Relations Division, Association for Education in Journalism Annual Convention, Seattle, WA.

———. (1979). Special section: The two worlds of PR research. *Public Relations Review, 5*(1), pp. 11–14.

———. (Ed.). (1992). *Excellence in public relations and communication management.* Hillsdale, NJ: Lawrence Erlbaum.

———. (1993). Image and substance: From symbolic to behavioral relationships. *Public Relations Review, 19*(2), pp. 121–139.

———. (2001). Two-way symmetrical public relations: Past, present, and future. In R. L. Heath (Ed.), *Handbook of public relations* (pp. 11–30). Thousand Oaks, CA: Sage.

Grunig, J. E., & Grunig, L. A. (1989). Preface. In J. Grunig and L. Grunig (Eds.), *Public relations research annual* (Vol. 1, pp. ix–x). Hillsdale, NJ: Lawrence Erlbaum.

———. (1990, August). *Models of public relations: A review and reconceptualization.* Paper presented to the Public Relations Division, Association for Education in Journalism Annual Convention, Minneapolis, MN.

Grunig, J. E., & Hickson, R. H. (1976). An evaluation of academic research in public relations. *Public Relations Review, 2*(1), pp. 31–43.

Grunig, J. E., & Hunt, T. (1984). *Managing public relations.* New York: Holt, Rinehart and Winston.

Heath, R. L. (Ed.). (2001). *Handbook of public relations.* Thousand Oaks, CA: Sage.

Hiebert, R. E. (1990). The next 25 years of publication. *Public Relations Review, 26*(4), pp. 383–385.

———. (2000). *Public Relations Review* gets a new publisher: JAI Press. *Public Relations Review, 16*(4), pp. 3–4.

Hon, L. C. (1995). Toward a feminist theory of public relations. *Journal of Public Relations Research, 7*(1), pp. 27–88.

———. (1997). What have you done for me lately? Exploring effectiveness in public relations. *Journal of Public Relations Research, 9*(1), pp. 1–30.

IPRA Education and Research Committee. (1982, January). *A model for public relations education for professional practice,* Gold Paper No. 4. International Public Relations Association, London.

Kavoori, A. P., and Gurevitch, M. (1993). The purebred and the platypus: Disciplinarity and site in mass communication research. *Journal of Communication, 43*(4), pp. 173–181.

Kelly, K. S. (1991). *Fund raising and public relations: A critical analysis.* Hillsdale, NJ: Lawrence Erlbaum.

———. (1998). *Effective fund-raising management.* Mahwah, NJ: Lawrence Erlbaum.

Kent, M. L., & Taylor, M. (1998). Building dialogic relationships through the World Wide Web. *Public Relations Review, 24*(3), pp. 321–334.

Kuhn, T. S. (1970). *The structure of scientific revolutions* (2nd ed.). Chicago: University of Chicago Press.

Krippendorf, K. (1980). *Content analysis: An introduction to its methodology.* Beverly Hills, CA: Sage.

Kruckeberg, D., & Starck, K. (1988). *Public relations and community: A reconstructed theory.* New York: Praeger.

Ledingham, J. A., & Bruning, S. D. (2000). *Public relationship as management: A relational approach to the study and practice of public relations.* Mahwah, NJ: Lawrence Erlbaum.

Leeper, R. (2001). In search of a metatheory for public relations: An argument for communitarianism. In R. L. Heath (Ed.), *Handbook of public relations* (pp. 93–104). Thousand Oaks, CA: Sage.

Lesly, P. (1992). Coping with opposition groups. *Public Relations Review, 18,* pp. 325–334.

Lewin, K. (1951). *Field theory in social science.* New York: Harper & Row.

McElreath, M., & Blamphin, J. (1994). Partial answers to priority research questions—and gaps—found in PRSA's body of knowledge. *Journal of Public Relations Research, 6*(2), pp. 69–104.

Morton, L., & Lin, L. Y. (1995). Content and citation analyses of *Public Relations Review. Public Relations Review, 21*(4), pp. 337–349.

Pasadeos, Y., & Renfro, B. (1992). A bibliometric analysis of public relations research. *Journal of Public Relations Research, 4*(3), pp. 167–187.

Pasadeos, Y., Renfro, B., & Hanily, M. (1999). Influential authors and works of public relations scholarly literature: A network of recent research. *Journal of Public Relations Research, 11*(1), pp. 29–52.

Phillips, D. C. (1992). *The social scientist's bestiary: A guide to fabled threats to, and defenses of, naturalistic social science.* Oxford, UK: Pergamon.

Popper, K. R. (1959). *The logic of scientific discovery.* New York: Basic Books.

Proctor, R. F. II. (1992). Preserving the tie that binds: A response to Berger's essay. *Communication Monographs, 59*(1), pp. 98–100.

Purcell, W. M. (1992). Are there so few communication theories? *Communication Monographs, 59*(1), pp. 94–97.

Redding, W. C. (1992). Response to Professor Berger's essay: Its meaning for organizational communication. *Communication Monographs, 59*(1), pp. 87–93.

Robinson, G. J. (1988). "Here be dragons": Problems in charting the U.S. history of communication studies. *Communication, 10,* pp. 97–119.

Rosengren, K. E. (1993). From field to frog ponds. *Journal of Communication, 43*(3), pp. 6–17.

Sallot, L., Lyon, L., Acosta-Alzuru, C., & Jones, K. (2003). From aardvark to zebra: A new millennium analysis of theory development in public relations academic journals. *Journal of Public Relations Research, 15*(1), pp. 27–89.

Simons, H. E. (Ed.). (1990). *The rhetorical turn: Invention and persuasion in the conduct of inquiry.* Chicago: University of Chicago Press.

Soley, W. C., & Reid, L. N. (1983). Advertising article productivity of the U.S. academic community. *Journalism Quarterly, 60*(3), pp. 464–469, 542.

———. (1988). Advertising article productivity updated. *Journalism Quarterly, 65*(1), pp. 157–164.

Suppe, F. (1977a). Alternatives to the received view and their critics. In F. Suppe (Ed.), *The structure of scientific theories* (2nd ed.) (pp. 119–232). Urbana: University of Illinois Press.

———. (Ed.). (1977b) *The structure of scientific theories* (2nd ed.). Urbana: University of Illinois Press.

Synnott, G., and McKie, D. (1997). International issues in PR: Researching research and prioritizing priorities. *Journal of Public Relations Research, 9*(4), pp. 259–282.

Taylor, M. (2000). Toward a public relations approach to nation building. *Journal of Public Relations Research, 12*(2), pp. 179–210.

Toth, E. L. (1999). Editor's note. *Journal of Public Relations Research, 11*(1), p. 1.

Toth, E. L., & Heath, R. L. (Eds.). (1992). *Rhetorical and critical approaches to public relations.* Hillsdale, NJ: Lawrence Erlbaum.

Why a new journal? To build a bridge . . . (1975). *Public Relations Review, 1*(1), pp. 3–4.

Wimmer, R. D., & Dominick, J. R. (2003). *Mass media research:* An introduction (7th ed.). Belmont, CA: Wadsworth/Thomson Learning.

APPENDIX A

CLASS I: INTROSPECTIVE

101 Introspective: Pedagogy/Education in PR

Introduction: Resources for Public Relations Teaching: Facilitating the Growth of Public Relations Education (W. Timothy Coombs), 2001, PRR, 27(1), 1–2.

The Client-Centered Approach as a Foundation for Teaching the Introductory Course in Public Relations (Melissa Motschall & Michele A. Najor), 2001, PRR, 27(1), 3–25.

The Write Stuff: Teaching the Introductory Public Relations Writing Course (Cynthia M. King), 2001, PRR, 27(1), 27–46.

Teaching the Public Relations Campaigns Course (Debra A. Worley), 2001, PRR, 27(1), 47–58.

Teaching Mediated Public Relations (Michael L. Kent), 2001, PRR, 27(1), 59–71.

Internationalizing the Public Relations Curriculum (Maureen Taylor), 2001, PRR, 27(1), 73–88.

Teaching the Crisis Management/Communication Course (W. Timothy Coombs), 2001, PRR, 27(1), 89–101.

Integrating Leadership Processes: Redefining the Principles Course (Bonita Dostal Neff), 2002, PRR, 28(2), 137–147.

The Linked Classroom as Studio: Connectivity and the Etymology of Networks (Claire Hoertz Badaracco), 2002, PRR, 28(2), 149–156.

Using Alternative Teaching Techniques to Enhance Student Performance in the Traditional Introductory Public Relations Course (Charles A. Lubbers), 2002, PRR, 28(2), 157–166.

The Socratic Method in the Introductory PR Course: An Alternative Pedagogy (Michael G. Parkinson & Daradirek Ekachai), 2002, PRR, 28(2), 167–174.

Papayas and Pedagogy: Geographically Dispersed Teams and Internet Self-Efficacy (Michelle O'Malley & Tom Kelleher), 2002, PRR, 28(2), 175–184.

Loyalty, Harm and Duty: PBL in a Media Ethics Course (Karen L. Slattery), 2002, PRR, 28(2), 185–190.

Applying Active Learning at the Graduate Level: Merger Issues at Newco (Bruce K. Berger), 2002, PRR, 28(2), 191–200.

Teaching Ethics across the Public Relations Curriculum (Liese L. Hutchison), 2002, PRR, 28(3), 301–309.

"I Thought It Would Be More Glamorous": Preconceptions and Misconceptions among Students in the Public Relations Principles Course (Shannon A. Bowen), 2003, PRR, 29(2), 199–214.

102 Introspective: Ethics and Social Responsibility

Ethical Standards Appear to Change with Age and Ideology: A Survey of Practitioners (Yungwook Kim & Youjin Choi), 2003, PRR, 29(1), 79–89.

103 Introspective: The History of Public Relations

Ivy Lee and the Rockefellers' Response to the 1913–1914 Colorado Coal Strike (Kirk Hallahan), 2002, JPRR, 14(4), 265–315.

Women's Work: Public Relations Efforts of the U.S. Children's Bureau to Reduce Infant and Maternal Mortality, 1912–1921 (Dulcie Straughan), 2001, PRR, 27(3), 337–351.

The 1939 Major League Baseball Centennial Celebration: How Steve Hannagan & Associates Helped Tie Business to Americana (William B. Anderson), 2001, PRR, 27(3), 353–366.

The Federal Public Relations Administration: History's Near Miss (Mordecai Lee), 2002, PRR, 28(1), 87–98.

Greater Dead Heroes Than Live Husbands: Widows as Image-Makers (Marion K. Pinsdorf), 2002, PRR, 28(3), 283–299.

Journalists' Hostility toward Public Relations: An Historical Analysis (Denise E. DeLorme & Fred Fedler), 2003, PRR, 29(2), 99–124.

A Matter of Chance: The Emergence of Probability and the Rise of Public Relations (Robert E. Brown), 2003, PRR, 29(4), 385–399.

W. L. Mackenzie King: Rockefeller's "Other" Public Relations Counselor in Colorado (Kirk Hallahan), 2003, PRR, 29(4), 401–414.

The First Federal Public Information Service, 1920–1933: At the U.S. Bureau of Efficiency! (Mordecai Lee), 2003, PRR, 29(4), 415–425.

104 Introspective: The Profession of Public Relations

Public Relations Is the Architect of Its Future: Counsel or Courtier? Pros Offer Opinions (John F. Budd Jr.), 2003, PRR, 29(4), 375–383.

130 Introspective: Women and Minorities

(No articles 2001–2003)

131 Introspective: International PR Practice

Ascending Cultural Competence Potential: An Assessment and Profile of U.S. Public Relations Practitioners' Preparation for International Assignments (Alan R. Freitag), 2002, JPRR, 14(3), 207–227.

Opinion: Foreign Policy Acumen Needed by Global CEOs (John F. Budd Jr.), 2001, PRR, 27(2), 123–134.

The Genesis of Public Relations in British Colonial Practice (Rosaleen Smyth), 2001, PRR, 27(2), 149–161.

Public Relations and the New Golden Age of Spain: A Confluence of Democracy, Economic Development and the Media (Donn James Tilson & Pilar Saura Perez), 2003, PRR, 29(2), 125–143.

Public Relations Licensing in Brazil: Evolution and the Views of Professionals (Juan-Carlos Molleda & Andreia Athaydes), 2003, PRR, 29(3), 271–279.

132 Introspective: Image/Reputation/Impression Management

The Image of the Government Flack: Movie Depictions of Public Relations in Public Administration (Mordecai Lee), 2001, PRR, 27(3), 297–315.

Public Relations Battles and Wars: Journalistic Cliches and the Potential for Conflict Resolution (Judith Scrimger & Trudie Richards), 2003, PRR, 29(4), 485–492.

150 Introspective: Professional Development for Educators (New Category)

Communication Faculty Internships (Dirk C. Gibson), 2001, PRR, 27(1), 103–117.

199 Introspective: Scholarly Research

From Aardvark to Zebra: A New Millennium Analysis of Theory Development in Public Relations Academic Journals (Lynne M. Sallot, Lisa J. Lyon, Carolina Acosta-Alzuru, & Karyn Ogata Jones), 2003, JPRR, 15(1), 27–90.

CLASS II: PRACTICE/APPLICATION OF PUBLIC RELATIONS

205 Practice/Application of PR: Management in Public Relations/Decision Making/Problem Solving

(No articles 2001–2003)

206 Practice/Application of PR: Implementing/Evaluating Public Relations Programs and Campaigns

Trivial Pursuits: Views of Public Meetings (Katherine A. McComas), 2003, JPRR, 15(2), 91–115.

Posibilidad Y Problema: An Historical/Critical Analysis of Hispanic Public Relations (Dirk C. Gibson), 2002, PRR, 28(1), 63–85.

Intranet Effectiveness: A Public Relations Paper-and-Pencil Checklist (Marie E. Murgolo-Poore, Leyland F. Pitt, & Michael T. Ewing), 2002, PRR, 28(1), 113–123.

British Newspapers Privilege Health and Medicine Topics over Other Science News (Emma Weitkamp), 2003, PRR, 29(3), 321–333.

207 Practice/Application of PR: Applied Research Issues and Methodologies

Improving Public Relations Web Sites through Usability Research (Kirk Hallahan), 2001, PRR, 27(2), 223–239.

208 Practice/Application of PR: Organizational Communication

(No articles 2001–2003)

209 Practice/Application of PR: Social Issues and Issues Management in Public Relations

(No articles 2001–2003)

210 Practice/Application of PR: New Communication Technologies

How Television News Programs Use Video News Releases (Mark D. Harmon & Candace White), 2001, PRR, 27(2), 213–222.

Wired Science: Use of World Wide Web and E-Mail in Science Public Relations (Shearlean Duke), 2002, PRR, 28(3), 311–324.

Media Relations and the Internet: How Fortune 500 Company Web Sites Assist Journalists in News Gathering (Coy Callison), 2003, PRR, 29(1), 29–41.

Perceptions of Public Relations Web Sites by Computer Industry Journalists (David Hachigian & Kirk Hallahan), 2003, PRR, 29(1), 43–62.

Corporate Intelligence Dissemination as a Consequence of Intranet Effectiveness: An Empirical Study (Marie E. Murgolo-Poore, Leyland F. Pitt, Pierre R. Berthon, & Gerard Pendegast), 2003, PRR, 29(2), 171–184.

Public Relations and the Web: Organizational Problems, Gender, and Institution Type (Michael Ryan), 2003, PRR, 29(3), 335–349.

211 Practice/Application of PR: Legal Issues

Mythic Battles: Examining the Lawyer-Public Relations Counselor Dynamic (Bryan H. Reber, Fritz Cropp, & Glen T. Cameron), 2001, JPRR, 13(3), 187–218.

240 Practice/Application of PR: Crisis Response/Communication

A Successful Failure: NASA's Crisis Communications Regarding Apollo 13 (James Kauffman), 2001, PRR, 27(4), 437–448.

The Internet as a Crisis Management Tool: A Critique of Banking Sites during Y2K (Anne Marie DiNardo), 2002, PRR, 28(4), 367–378.

United Airlines' and American Airlines' Online Crisis Communication following the September 11 Terrorist Attacks (Clark F. Greer & Kurt D. Moreland), 2003, PRR, 29(4), 427–441.

How Corporate America Grieves: Responses to September 11 in Public Relations Advertising (Katherine N. Kinnick), 2003, PRR, 29(4), 443–459.

The Oxford Incident: Organizational Culture's Role in an Anthrax Crisis (Kurt Wise), 2003, PRR, 29(4), 461–472.

241 Practice/Application of PR: Integrated Marketing Communications

(No articles 2001–2003)

242 Practice/Application of PR: Image/Reputation/Impression Management

Can Your Institution's Name Influence Constituent Response? An Initial Assessment of Consumer Response to College Names (D. F. Treadwell), 2003, PRR, 29(2), 185–197.

243 Practice/Application of PR: Ethics in Practice

(No articles 2001–2003)

244 Practice/Application of PR: International Public Relations (New Category)

Kisha Kurabu and Koho: Japanese Media Relations and Public Relations (William Kelly, Tomoko Masumoto, & Dirk Gibson), 2002, PRR, 28(3), 265–281.

China's Agenda Building and Image Polishing in the US: Assessing and International Public Relations Campaign (Juyan Zhang & Glen T. Cameron), 2003, PRR, 29(1), 13–28.

Public Relations in Taiwan: Roles, Professionalism, and Relationship to Marketing (Ming-Yi Wu & Maureen Taylor), 2003, PRR, 29(4), 473–483.

CLASS III: THEORY DEVELOPMENT IN PUBLIC RELATIONS

312 Theory Development: Role Theory/Models

Lobbyists and Their Stories: Classic PR Practitioner Role Models as Functions of Burkean Human Motivations (Valerie Terry), 2001, JPRR, 13(3), 235–263.

Public Relations Roles and Media Choice (Tom Kelleher), 2001, JPRR, 13(4), 303–320.

313 Theory Development: Risk Communication

Another Part of the Risk Communication Model Analysis of Communication Processes and Message Content (Michael J. Palenchar & Robert L. Heath), 2002, JPRR, 14(2), 127–158.

Community Relationship Building: Local Leadership in the Risk Communication Infrastructure (Robert L. Heath, Julie Bradshaw, & Jaesub Lee), 2002, JPRR, 14(4), 317–353.

Challenges to the Notion of Publics in Public Relations: Implications of the Risk Society for the Discipline (Richard Jones), 2002, PRR, 28(1), 49–62.

314 Theory Development: Excellence Theory/ Symmetrical Communication/Grunig's Models

St. Paul as a Public Relations Practitioner: A Metatheoretical Speculation on Messianic Communication and Symmetry (R. E. Brown), 2003, PRR, 29(1), 1–12/Erratum version: 2003, PRR, 29(2), 229–240.

315 Theory Development: Rhetorical Underpinnings

Toward an Ethical Framework for Advocacy in Public Relations (Ruth Edgett), 2002, JPRR, 14(1), 1–26.

The Cultural Tribes of Public Relations (Greg Leichty), 2003, JPRR, 15(4), 277–304.

The Rhetoric of Arrogance: The Public Relations Response of the Standard Oil Trust (Josh Boyd), 2001, PRR, 27(2), 163–178.

Antecedents of Two-Way Symmetry in Classical Greek Rhetoric: The Rhetoric of Isocrates (Charles Marsh), 2003, PRR, 29(3), 351–367.

316 Theory Development: Fund-Raising

The Critical Role of Stewardship in Fund Raising: The Coaches vs. Cancer Campaign (Debra A. Worley & Jennifer K. Little), 2002, PRR, 28(1), 99–112.

317 Theory Development: Women's Studies/ Feminist School/Gender/Diversity/Minority

Glass Ceiling? What Glass Ceiling? A Qualitative Study of How Women View the Glass Ceiling in Public Relations and Communications Management (Brenda J. Wrigley), 2002, JPRR, 14(1), 27–55.

Gender Discrepancies in a Gendered Profession: A Developing Theory for Public Relations (Linda Aldoory and Elizabeth Toth), 2002, JPRR, 14(2), 103–126.

The Influence of Gender Composition in Powerful Positions on Public Relations Practitioners' Gender-Related Perceptions (Youjin Choi & Linda Childers Hon), 2002, JPRR, 14(3), 229–263.

An Analysis of the Relationships among Structure, Influence, and Gender: Helping to Build a Feminist Theory of Public Relations (Julie O'Neil), 2003, JPRR, 15(2), 151–179.

318 Theory Development: Academic Versus Applied Research

(No articles 2001–2003)

319 Theory Development: Organizational Communication

An Investigation of the Sources of Influence of Corporate Public Relations Practitioners (Julie O'Neil), 2003, PRR, 29(2), 159–169.

320 Theory Development: Situational/ Publics Theory

Revisiting Publics: A Critical Archaelogy of Publics in the Thai HIV/AIDS Issue (Constance Chay-Nemeth), 2001, JPRR, 13(2), 127–161.

321 Theory Development: Ethics/ Social Responsibility

(No articles 2001–2003)

322 Theory Development: Social Issues and Issues Management

The Dynamics of Issues Activation and Response: An Issues Processes Model (Kirk Hallahan), 2001, JPRR, 13(1), 27–59.

Merck and AIDS Activists: Engagement as a Framework for Extending Issues Management (Maureen Taylor, Gabriel M. Vasquez, & John Doorley), 2003, PRR, 29(3), 257–270.

323 Theory Development: Public Relationships/Relational Theory

OPRA: A Cross-Cultural, Multiple-Item Scale for Measuring Organization-Public Relationships (Yi-Hui Huang), 2001, JPRR, 13(1), 61–90.

Values of Public Relations: Effects on Organization-Public Relationships Mediating Conflict Resolution (Yi-Hui Huang), 2001, JPRR, 13(4), 265–301.

Explicating Relationship Management as a General Theory of Public Relations (John A. Ledingham), 2003, JPRR, 15(2), 181–198.

The Effect of Web Characteristics on Relationship Building (Samsup Jo & Yungwook Kim), 2003, JPRR, 15(3), 199–223.

How Activist Organizations Are Using the Internet to Build Relationships (Maureen Taylor, Michael L. Kent, & William J. White), 2001, PRR, 27(3), 263–284.

Government-Community Relationships: Extending the Relational Theory of Public Relations (John A. Ledingham), 2001, PRR, 27(3), 285–295.

Relationship Building as a Retention Strategy: Linking Relationship Attitudes and Satisfaction Evaluations to Behavioral Outcomes (Stephen D. Bruning), 2002, PRR, 28(1), 39–48.

The Relationship between Web Site Design and Organizational Responsiveness to Stakeholders (Michael L. Kent, Maureen Taylor, & William J. White), 2003, PRR, 29(1), 63–77.

Expanding the Organization-Public Relationship Scale: Exploring the Role That Structural and Personal Commitment Play in Organization-Public Relationships (Stephen D. Bruning & Tara Galloway), 2003, PRR, 29(3), 309–319.

333 Theory Development: International Public Relations

Global Public Relations: A Cross-Cultural Study of the Excellence Theory in South Korea (Yunna Rhee), 2002, JPRR, 14(3), 159–184.

Rupturing Public Relations Narratives: The Example of India (Nilanjana Bardhan), 2003, JPRR, 15(3), 225–248.

Discrepancy between Korean Government and Corporate Practitioners Regarding Professional Standards in Public Relations: A Co-Orientation Approach (Jongmin Park), 2003, JPRR, 15(3), 249–275.

Exploding the Myth of the Symmetrical/Asymmetrical Dichotomy: Public Relations Models in the New South Africa (Derina R. Holtzhausen, Barbara K. Petersen, & Natalie T. J. Tinall), 2003, JPRR, 15(4), 305–341.

"In-Awareness" Approach to International Public Relations (R. S. Zaharna), 2001, PRR, 27(2), 135–148.

Exploring Societal and Cultural Influences on Taiwanese Public Relations (Ming-Yi Wu, Maureen Taylor, & Mong-Ju Chen), 2001, PRR, 27(3), 317–336.

On the Definition of Public Relations: A European View (Dejan Vercic, Betteke van Ruler, Gerhard Butschi, & Bertil Flodin), 2001, PRR, 27(4), 373–387.

Public Relations Practice in Japan: An Exploratory Study (David R. Watson & Lynne M. Sallot), 2001, PRR, 27(4), 389–402.

Images of "Hong Bo (Public Relations)" and PR in Korean Newspapers (Jongmin Park), 2001, PRR, 27(4), 403–420.

Relationship Building as Integral to British Activism: Its Impact on Accountability in Broadcasting (Rachel Kovacs), 2001, PRR, 27(4), 421–436.

Dealing with Activism in Canada: An Ideal Cultural Fit for the Two-Way Symmetrical Public Relations Model (John E. Guiniven), 2002, PRR, 28(4), 393–402.

334 Theory Development: Contingency Theory

Impossible Odds: Contributions of Legal Counsel and Public Relations Practitioners in a Hostile Bid for Conrail Inc. by Norfolk Southern Corporation (Bryan H. Reber, Fritz Cropp, & Glen T. Cameron), 2003, JPRR, 15(1), 1–25.

335 Theory Development: Crisis Response Theory

An Extended Examination of the Crisis Situations: A Fusion of the Relational Management and Symbolic Approaches (W. Timothy Coombs & Sherry J. Holladay), 2001, JPRR, 13(4), 321–340.

Defending the Mercedes A-Class: Combining and Changing Crisis-Response Strategies (Oyvind Ihlen), 2002, JPRR, 14(3), 185–206.

Chaos and Crisis: Propositions for a General Theory of Crisis Communication (Matthew W. Seeger), 2002, PRR, 28(4), 329–337.

Deep and Surface Threats: Conceptual and Practical Implications for "Crisis" vs. "Problem" (W. Timothy Coombs), 2002, PRR, 28(4), 339–345.

The Good Organization Speaking Well: A Paradigm Case for Religious Institutional Crisis Management (Jeffrey L. Courtright & Keith Michael Hearit), 2002, PRR, 28(4), 347–360.

Crisis Management and the Discourse of Renewal: Understanding the Potential for Positive Outcomes of Crisis (Robert R. Ulmer & Timothy L. Sellnow), 2002, PRR, 28(4), 361–365.

Blowout!: Firestone's Image Restoration Campaign (Joseph R. Blaney, William L. Benoit, & LeAnn M. Brazeal), 2002, PRR, 28(4), 379–392.

Crisis Management Planning and the Threat of Bioterrorism (Brenda J. Wrigley, Charles T. Salmon, & Hyun Soon Park), 2003, PRR, 29(3), 281–290.

Stormy Weather: Testing "Stealing Thunder" as a Crisis Communication Strategy to Improve Communication Flow between Organizations and Journalists (Laura M. Arpan & Donnalyn Pompper), 2003, PRR, 29(3), 291–308.

336 Theory Development: Public Opinion/Persuasion

Do PR Practitioners Have a PR Problem? The Effect of Associating a Source with Public Relations and Client-Negative News on Audience Perception of Credibility (Coy Callison), 2001, JPRR, 13(3), 219–234.

Company Affiliation and Communicative Ability: How Perceived Organizational Ties Influence Source Persuasiveness in a Company-Negative News Environment (Coy Callison & Dolf Zillman), 2002, JPRR, 14(2), 85–102.

Targeting the Young, the Poor, the Less Educated: Thinking beyond Traditional Media (Erik L. Collins & Lynn M. Zoch), 2001, PRR, 27(2), 197–212.

Public Relations and Propaganda in Framing the Iraq War: A Preliminary Review (Ray Eldon Hiebert), 2003, PRR, 29(3), 243–255.

337 Theory Development: Critical/Cultural

(No articles 2001–2003)

338 Theory Development: Complexity Theory

(No articles 2001–2003)

339 Theory Development: General Social Science Theory

(No articles 2001–2003)

340 Theory Development: Agenda Setting/ Building/Framing (New Category)

Private Issues and Public Policy: Locating the Corporate Agenda in Agenda-Setting Theory (Bruce K. Berger), 2001, JPRR, 13(2), 91–126.

Building the News Media Agenda on the Environment: A Comparison of Public Relations and Journalistic Sources (Patricia A. Curtin & Eric Rhodenbaugh), 2001, PRR, 27(2), 179–195.

The Media Battle between Celebrex and Vioxx: Influencing Media Coverage but Not Content (William B. Anderson), 2001, PRR, 27(4), 449–460.

The Saga of the Crown Pilot: Framing, Reframing, and Reconsideration (Stuart L. Esrock, Joy L. Hart, Margaret U. D'Silva, & Kathy J. Werking), 2002, PRR, 28(3), 209–227.

341 Theory Development: Reputation Management (New Category)

Measuring the Economic Value of Public Relations (Yungwook Kim), 2001, JPRR, 13(1), 3–26.

Reputation Management: The New Face of Corporate Public Relations? (James G. Hutton, Michael B. Goodman, Jill B. Alexander, & Christina M. Genest), 2001, PRR, 27(3), 247–261.

342 Theory Development: Concept of Practice (New Category)

Public Relations as "Practice": Applying the Theory of Alasdair MacIntyre (Roy V. Leeper & Kathie A. Leeper), 2001, PRR, 27(4), 461–473.

343 Theory Development: Health Communication (New Category)

Making Health Messages Meaningful for Women: Factors That Influence Involvement (Linda Aldoory), 2001, JPRR, 13(2), 163–185.

Opportunities for Public Relations Research in Public Health (Kurt Wise), 2001, PRR, 27(4), 475–487.

Delineating (and Delimiting) the Boundary Spanning Role of the Medical Public Information Officer (Raymond N. Ankney & Patricia A. Curtin), 2002, PRR, 28(3), 229–241.

344 Theory Development: Rumor Theory (New Category)

Corporate Rumor Activity, Belief and Accuracy (Nicholas DiFonzo & Prashant Bordia), 2002, PRR, 28(1), 1–19.

345 Theory Development: Dialogic Theory (New Category)

Toward a Dialogic Theory of Public Relations (Michael L. Kent & Maureen Taylor), 2002, PRR, 28(1), 21–37.

346 Theory Development: Post Modernism (New Category)

Resistance from the Margins: The Postmodern Public Relations Practitioner as Organizational Activist (Derina R. Holtzhausen and Rosina Voto), 2002, JPRR, 14(1), 57–84.

Postmodernism for Modernist Public Relations: The Cash Value and Application of Research in Public Relations (Elizabeth L. Toth), 2002, PRR, 28(3), 243–250.

Towards a Postmodern Research Agenda for Public Relations (Derina R. Holtzhausen), 2002, PRR, 28(3), 251–264.

348 Theory Development: Cognitive Theory (New Category)

Using Cognitive Schema Theory in the Development of Public Relations Strategy: Exploring the Case of Firms and Financial Analysts following Acquisition Announcements (Jerome C. Kuperman), 2003, JPRR, 15(2), 117–150.

CLASS IV: RELATING TO THE PUBLICATION ITSELF

498 Editors' Notes re: Journal

Editor's Note (Linda Childers Hon), 2001, JPRR, 13(1), 1–2.

Editorial: How We Teach: An Introduction to This Special Issue on Innovative Pedagogy (C. H. Badaracco), 2002, PRR, 28(2), 135–136.

Announcements (Ray Hiebert), 2003, PRR, 29(3), 241.

CLASS V: OTHER

500 Coder Disagreements

Barriers to Communication Management in the Executive Suite (Betteke van Ruler & Rob de Lange), 2003, PRR, 29(2), 145–158.

SPECIAL ISSUES

PRR 27(1) 2001: Special Issue on Teaching and Public Relations Education, guest editor W. Timothy Coombs

PRR 28(2) 2002: Special Issue on Innovative Pedagogy, guest editor Claire Badaracco.

MOST-PUBLISHED AUTHORS AND ALL AUTHORS OF ARTICLES CLASSIFIED AS "THEORY DEVELOPMENT" WITH FREQUENCIES OF AUTHORSHIP AS PUBLISHED IN *JOURNAL OF PUBLIC RELATIONS RESEARCH* AND *PUBLIC RELATIONS REVIEW*, 2001–2003

NAME	AUTHORS OF TWO OR MORE ARTICLES IN ANY CATEGORY			AUTHORS OF ONE OR MORE ARTICLES CATEGORIZED AS "THEORY DEVELOPMENT"		
	# SOLE AUTHORED	# LEAD AUTHORED	# SECOND + AUTHORED	# SOLE AUTHORED	# LEAD AUTHORED	# SECOND + AUTHORED
Maureen Taylor	1	2	4	–	2	3
W. Timothy Coombs	3	1	–	1	1	–
Kirk Hallahan	3	–	1	–	–	–
Mordecai Lee	3	–	–	–	–	–
Coy Gallison	2	1	–	1	1	–
Dirk Gibson	2	–	1	–	–	–
Derina Holtzhausen	1	2	–	1	2	–
Michael Kent	1	2	–	–	1	1
Elizabeth Toth	1	1	1	1	1	1
Glen Cameron	–	–	3	–	–	1
Claire Badaracco	2	–	–	–	–	–
Bruce Berger	2	–	–	1	–	–
John F. Budd Jr.	2	–	–	–	–	–
Ray Hiebert	2	–	–	1	–	–
Katherine Kinnick	2	–	–	1	–	–
Yi-Hui Huang	2	–	–	1	–	–
William B. Anderson	2	–	–	1	–	–
Julie O'Neil	2	–	–	2	–	–
Jongmin Park	2	–	–	2	–	–
Kurt Wise	2	–	–	1	–	–
Linda Aldoory	1	1	–	1	1	–
Stephen Bruning	1	1	–	1	1	–

(Continued)

(*Continued*)

NAME	# SOLE AUTHORED	# LEAD AUTHORED	# SECOND + AUTHORED	# SOLE AUTHORED	# LEAD AUTHORED	# SECOND + AUTHORED
Debra Worley	1	1	–	–	1	–
Brenda J. Wrigley	1	1	–	1	1	–
Linda Hon	1	–	1	–	–	1
Marie Murgolo-Poore	–	2	–	–	–	–
Bryan Reber	–	2	–	–	1	–
Ming-Yi Wu	–	2	–	–	1	–
William J. White	–	2	–	–	–	1
Leyland Pitt	–	2	–	–	–	–
Patricia Curtin	–	1	1	–	1	1
Robert L. Heath	–	1	1	–	1	1
Lynne Sallot	–	1	1	–	–	1
Betteke van Ruler*	–	1	1	–	–	1

*Note: An article by Betteke van Ruler and Rob de Lange was coded as "Class V: Coder Disagreements" and it was not categorized further.

Authors of one article that was classified as "Theory Development" also fell under the categories of sole authored, lead authored, and/or second + author. Those with a sole authored article were Nilanjana Bardhan, Josh Boyd, R. E. Brown, Constance Chay-Nemeth, John E. Guiniven, David Hachigian, Richard Jones, Rachel Kovacs, Jerome Kuperman, John Ledigham, Greg Leichty, Charles Marsh, Mark McElreath, Deborah D. Miller, Douglas Ann Newsom, Yunna Rhee, Matthew Seeger, Valerie Terry, and R. S. Zaharna. Those serving as lead author were Raymond D. Ankey, Laura M. Arpan, Joseph R. Blaney, Youjin Choi, Erik Collins, Jeffrey Courtright, Nicholas DiFonzo, Stuart Esrock, Jame Hutton, Samsup Jo, Roy Leeper, Michael Palenchar, Robert Ulmer, Dejan Vercic, and David R. Watson. Those serving as second, plus, author were Jill Alexander, William Benoit, Prashat Bordia, Julie Bradshaw, Leann M. Brazeal, Gerhard Butschi, Mong-Ju Chen, Fritz Cropp, John Doorley, Margaret D'Silva, Bertil Flodin, Christina Genest, Tara Galloway, Michael Goodman, Joy L. Hart, Michael Hearit, Sherry Holladay, Yungwook Kim, Kathie Leeper, Jaesub Lee, Jennifer Little, Hyun Soon Park, Barbara Peterson, Donnalyn Pompper, Eric Rhodenbaugh, Charles Salmon, Timothy Sellnow, Natalie T. Tinall, Gabriel Vasquez, Rosina Voto, Kathy Werking, Dolf Zillman, and Lynn Zoch.

ABOUT THE CONTRIBUTORS

Carolina Acosta-Alzuru (Ph.D. University of Georgia) is an associate professor in the advertising/public relations department of the Grady College of Journalism and Mass Communication at the University of Georgia. Her research examines public relations theory development, and the intersections of media, culture, and society.

William L. Benoit (Ph.D. Wayne State University) is a professor of communication at the University of Missouri; University Fellow at Hong Kong Baptist University Winter 2006. He has published ten books and numerous journal articles/book chapters, mostly on image repair and the functional theory of political campaigns. He edited *Journal of Communication* from 2003 to 2005 and *Communication Studies* from 2007 to 2009.

Shannon Bowen (Ph.D. University of Maryland) is an assistant professor at the University of Maryland. Her research interests include public relations ethics and theory, organizational communication, internal relations, and strategic issues management (she has studied issues in the pharmaceutical industry extensively). She teaches graduate and undergraduate courses in public relations and communication management. Dr. Bowen's research applies moral philosophy, particularly Kantian perspectives, to the communication process. Bowen has authored top faculty papers and her research won the ICA Public Relations Division Outstanding Dissertation Award. Her work applies sociological and mass communication theory to communication involving terrorism. She has authored numerous book chapters and her research is published in such premier journals as *Journal of Business Ethics, Journal of Public Relations Research, Journal of Mass Media Ethics, Journal of Public Affairs,* and *Public Relations Review.* She was editorial adviser to the Sage *Encyclopedia of Public Relations,* coauthor of the ninth edition of the textbook *Effective Public Relations,* and is the principal investigator on a grant sponsored by the International Association of Business Communicators (IABC) Research Foundation to study communication ethics.

Glen Cameron (Ph.D. University of Texas–Austin) is the Maxine Wilson Gregory Chair in Journalism Research for the University of Missouri–Columbia School of Journalism. He has authored more than one hundred books, chapters, articles, and convention papers. He has received numerous national awards for individual research projects as well as the Baskett-Mosse and Pathfinder awards for his entire body of work. Cameron's expert system program, Publics PR Research Software™, is widely used as a targeting research tool in marketing and public relations. He is a coauthor of *Public Relations: Strategies and Tactics,* published by Allyn & Bacon, and he serves on the editorial board of several scholarly journals and book series.

Ann R. Carden (M.S. Buffalo State College) is an assistant professor of communication at the State University of New York at Fredonia. She is the coauthor of the second edition of *Public Relations Worktext: A Writing and Planning Resource* and frequently publishes articles on the use of public relations in the travel and tourism industry.

W. Timothy Coombs (Ph.D. Purdue University) is an associate professor in the department of communication studies at Eastern Illinois University. He is the 2002 recipient of Jackson, Jackson, & Wagner Behavioral Science Prize from PRSA. His research led to the development and testing of the Situational Crisis Communication Theory (SCCT).

Patricia A. Curtin (Ph.D. University of Georgia) is a professor and endowed chair of public relations in the School of Journalism and Communication at the University of Oregon in Eugene, Ore. She also is liaison to IABC (International Association of Business Communicators). She is coauthor of "Public Relations and the Production of News: A Critical Review and a Theoretical Framework" in *Communication Yearbook 20*. Her articles have appeared in *American Journalism, Journalism Quarterly, Journalism Educator, Journal of Mediated Communication,* and *Teaching Public Relations.* Her research interests include agenda building, effects of new technologies, history, and critical and cultural studies.

T. Kenn Gaither (Ph.D. University of North Carolina–Chapel Hill) is an assistant professor at Elon University.

Joye Gordon (Ph.D. Purdue University) is head of the public relations sequence at the A. Q. Miller School of Journalism and Mass Communications at Kansas State University. Her research focuses primarily on risk communication. Her doctorate is in the areas of public affairs and issue management.

Kirk Hallahan (Ph.D. University of Wisconsin–Madison) is an associate professor at Colorado State University–Fort Collins. He is the executive in charge of public affairs for two California banks and a major state trade organization; and account supervisor for a firm serving, among others, the Pasadena Tournament of Roses and the Academy of Motion Picture Arts and Sciences. He is also a Fellow with the Public Relations Society of America.

Tricia L. Hansen-Horn (Ph.D. Purdue University) is an associate professor of public relations at the University of Central Missouri (formerly Central Missouri State University), where she also serves as the coordinator for the public relations program. Hansen-Horn's long-term professional interests lie in image management and theory development. The present book is the result of her theory interests.

Robert L. Heath (Ph.D. University of Illinois) is recently retired as a professor of communication at the University of Houston, has published thirteen books and hundred articles and chapters on key aspects of communication and public relations. His most recent books address terrorism and explain modern principles of public relations, issues management, crisis communication, and risk communication. With Tim Coombs he published *Today's Public Relations* (2006). In 2005, he edited the *Encyclopedia of Public Relations* and in 2004 *Responding to Crisis: A Rhetorical Approach to Crisis Communication.* Heath also recently coedited *Communication and the Media* (Praeger Publications, Westport, CT, 2005) with H. Dan O'Hair, and Gerald Ledlow, which is volume 3 of the series *Community Preparedness and Response to Terrorism* (general editors, James A. Johnson, Gerald Ledlow, and Mark A. Cwiek). He edited the *Handbook of Public Relations* (2001), and wrote *Strategic Issues Management: How Organizations Meet Public Policy Challenges* (1997). He has received many awards, including the Pride Award for his publications and academic accomplishments.

Yan Jin (Ph.D. University of Missouri–Columbia) is an assistant professor of public relations at the School of Mass Communications, Virginia Commonwealth University. As the recipient of several Top Paper awards, Yan has published and presented numerous research papers at leading national and international mass communication and business conferences. She has also authored book chapters and journal articles on public relations theories and online strategic communications. She has worked as research consultant for several national media groups and consumer product brands. While lecturing at the Missouri School of Journalism and serving as faculty adviser, Yan and her student team were awarded first place in the 2005 Case Study Competition in Corporate Communications, sponsored by the Arthur W. Page Society and the Institute for Public Relations.

Karyn Ogata Jones (Ph.D. University of Georgia) has been a member of the Clemson University faculty since 2002. Her primary area of research is health communication. She has also published work in political communication, relational communication, and public relations.

Gary L. Kreps (Ph.D. University of South Carolina) is professor and chair of the department of communication at George Mason University, where he holds the Eileen and Steve Mandell Endowed Chair in Health Communication. His published work includes more than 225 books, articles, and chapters concerning the applications of communication knowledge in society.

María E. Len-Ríos (Ph.D. University of Kansas) is an assistant professor in the University of Missouri–Columbia School of Journalism. Her research interests lie in public perceptions and how they relate to individuals' decision making. Specifically her studies focus on the uses and effects of web site communications, health communication and underrepresented groups. She is published in *Journalism & Mass Communication Quarterly, The Journal of Promotion Management, Public Relations Review,* and *Public Relations Quarterly.*

Thomas Mickey (Ph.D. University of Iowa) is a professor of public relations at Bridgewater State University in Massachusetts. He is the author of two books, *Deconstructing Public Relations: Public Relations Criticism* and *Sociodrama: An Interpre-*

tive Theory for the Practice of Public Relations. He has also had several articles published in *Public Relations Review.* He was a 2005 recipient of the Haupt Fellowship from the Smithsonian Institution in Washington, DC. He will explore the topic, "How Advertising in 19th Century Garden Catalogs Constructed a Middle Class."

Bonita Dostal Neff (Ph.D. University of Michigan) is an associate professor and head of the public relations major at Valparaiso University. As a member of the executive committee on the Commission for Public Relations Education, she is working on a national survey of public relations programs. Neff founded or was one of the founders of the PR divisions for NCA, CSCA, ICA, and the Miami research conference. In the area of research, her work focuses on theory, public relations curriculum, technology, and communication infrastructure. She teaches in Croatia and South Korea.

Aydemir Okay (Ph.D. Marmara University) is an associate professor on the communication faculty at Istanbul University. He was born in Mutlu village, Konya, Turkey, in 1968. He graduated cum laude from School of Journalism, Marmara University, Istanbul, in 1989. He received his master's and doctoral degrees from Marmara University, respectively in 1992 and 1997. Prior to joining Istanbul University in 2001, he worked at Marmara University and Mediterranean University. He is the author or coauthor of five books, and is currently working on a book on corporate communication. His research focuses on public relations theory, corporate communication, and sponsorship. He is a member of European Union Public Relations Education and Research Association (EUPRERA).

Ayla Okay (Ph.D. Istanbul University) is an associate professor on the communication faculty at Istanbul University.

Susan K. Opt (Ph.D. Ohio State University) is chair and associate professor in the communication department at Salem College, Winston-Salem, NC. Her research interests include social/cultural change from a rhetorical perspective, college students' perceptions of HIV/AIDS, and the relationship of Myers-Briggs personality types to communication variables.

Augustine Pang (Ph.D. University of Missouri–Columbia) worked as a newspaper correspondent; magazine chief editor; and journalism lecturer at Nanyang Technological University in Singapore. His research focuses on crisis communication, image repair, and media sociology.

Lisa J. Lyon (Ph.D. University of Georgia) was a faculty member in the department of communication at Kennesaw State University for five years until she moved to Virginia, where she currently teaches at Virginia Wesleyan College. Her teaching and scholarship emphases lie in public relations.

Peter Pellegrin (Ph.D. University of Louisiana–Lafayette) is lead humanities instructor for Cloud County Community College, Geary County Campus, in Junction City, Kansas. His areas of specialty include rhetoric, philosophy, language, and medieval mysticism. His doctorate is in medieval studies.

Terry L. Rentner (Ph.D. Bowling Green State University) is an associate professor of journalism. Areas of research include public relations, health communication, public relations ethics, and women's studies. Her graduate teaching focuses on persuasion and areas of communication pedagogy.

Theresa A. Russell-Loretz (Ph.D. Purdue University) is an assistant professor at Millersville University, teaches public relations, public speaking, and rhetoric courses. She has advised local nonprofit organizations, as well as public and parochial schools. Her scholarship interests include organizational identity for schools and nonprofits, recruitment rhetoric, service-learning pedagogy, and feminist public relations.

Lynne M. Sallot (Ph.D. University of Florida) teaches public relations campaigns, public relations communication, public relations research, and graduate public relations theory. She is a member of the UGA graduate faculty. In 1998, she received one of three UGA Richard B. Russell Awards for excellence in undergraduate teaching and a UGA Lilly Teaching Fellow in 1995–1997. Dr. Sallot has authored or coauthored articles or chapters in *Communication Yearbook, Journalism and Mass Communication Quarterly, Journal of Public Relations Research, Public Relations Review, Journal of Communication Management,* and *Journalism and Mass Communication Educator.* She is the editor of the third edition of *Learning to Teach: What You Need to Know to Develop a Successful Career as a Public Relations Educator;* she also edited the second edition. *Learning to Teach* is published by the Public Relations Society of America's Educators Academy. She was faculty advisor of the UGA Chapter of the Public Relations Student Society of America, named Outstanding National Chapter in 1997 and 1999. She was named Outstanding National Faculty Advisor in 1997. She was faculty coordinator of the annual PR Day at the Grady College from 1994 through 2001. Dr. Sallot served as a director of the Georgia PRSA Chapter; has been elected/appointed to national offices in PRSA, Association for Education in Journalism and National Communication, and National Communication Association. She was elected to PRSA's College of Fellows for her twenty-year distinguished career. She worked in agency PR for fourteen years, specializing in travel/tourism and nonprofit, and owned and operated her own firm. She taught previously at the University of Florida and as an adjunct professor at the University of Miami.

INDEX